Baseball America's

1999

Directory

**Major And Minor League
Names, Addresses, Schedules,
Phone and FAX Numbers**

**Detailed Information
On International, College and
Amateur Baseball**

PUBLISHED BY
BASEBALL AMERICA

Baseball America's

1999 Directory

Published By Baseball America

EDITOR
Allan Simpson

ASSOCIATE EDITOR
James Bailey

ASSISTANT EDITORS
Mark Derewicz
John Royster

PRODUCTION DIRECTOR
Valerie Holbert

PRODUCTION ASSISTANTS
Brandon Donnell
Justin Peaks

BASEBALL AMERICA, INC.

PUBLISHER
Lee Folger

EDITOR
Allan Simpson

MANAGING EDITOR
Will Lingo

PRODUCTION DIRECTOR
Valerie Holbert

TABLE OF CONTENTS

MAJOR LEAGUES

MINOR LEAGUES

MISCELLANEOUS

1999-2000 CALENDAR

March, 1999

Sun	Mon	Tues	Wed	Thur	Fri	Sat
	1	2	3	4	5	6
7	8	9	10	11	12	13
14	15	16	17	18	19	20
21	22	23	24	25	26	27
28	29	30	31			

April, 1999

Sun	Mon	Tues	Wed	Thur	Fri	Sat
				1	2	3
4	5	6	7	8	9	10
11	12	13	14	15	16	17
18	19	20	21	22	23	24
25	26	27	28	29	30	

May, 1999

Sun	Mon	Tues	Wed	Thur	Fri	Sat
						1
2	3	4	5	6	7	8
9	10	11	12	13	14	15
16	17	18	19	20	21	22
23	24	25	26	27	28	29
30	31					

June, 1999

Sun	Mon	Tues	Wed	Thur	Fri	Sat
		1	2	3	4	5
6	7	8	9	10	11	12
13	14	15	16	17	18	19
20	21	22	23	24	25	26
27	28	29	30			

July, 1999

Sun	Mon	Tues	Wed	Thur	Fri	Sat
				1	2	3
4	5	6	7	8	9	10
11	12	13	14	15	16	17
18	19	20	21	22	23	24
25	26	27	28	29	30	31

August, 1999

Sun	Mon	Tues	Wed	Thur	Fri	Sat
1	2	3	4	5	6	7
8	9	10	11	12	13	14
15	16	17	18	19	20	21
22	23	24	25	26	27	28
29	30	31				

September, 1999

Sun	Mon	Tues	Wed	Thur	Fri	Sat
			1	2	3	4
5	6	7	8	9	10	11
12	13	14	15	16	17	18
19	20	21	22	23	24	25
26	27	28	29	30		

October, 1999

Sun	Mon	Tues	Wed	Thur	Fri	Sat
					1	2
3	4	5	6	7	8	9
10	11	12	13	14	15	16
17	18	19	20	21	22	23
24	25	26	27	28	29	30
31						

November, 1999

Sun	Mon	Tues	Wed	Thur	Fri	Sat
	1	2	3	4	5	6
7	8	9	10	11	12	13
14	15	16	17	18	19	20
21	22	23	24	25	26	27
28	29	30				

December, 1999

Sun	Mon	Tues	Wed	Thur	Fri	Sat
			1	2	3	4
5	6	7	8	9	10	11
12	13	14	15	16	17	18
19	20	21	22	23	24	25
26	27	28	29	30	31	

January, 2000

Sun	Mon	Tues	Wed	Thur	Fri	Sat
						1
2	3	4	5	6	7	8
9	10	11	12	13	14	15
16	17	18	19	20	21	22
23	24	25	26	27	28	29
30	31					

February, 2000

Sun	Mon	Tues	Wed	Thur	Fri	Sat
		1	2	3	4	5
6	7	8	9	10	11	12
13	14	15	16	17	18	19
20	21	22	23	24	25	26
27	28	29				

March, 2000

Sun	Mon	Tues	Wed	Thur	Fri	Sat
			1	2	3	4
5	6	7	8	9	10	11
12	13	14	15	16	17	18
19	20	21	22	23	24	25
26	27	28	29	30	31	

April, 2000

Sun	Mon	Tues	Wed	Thur	Fri	Sat
						1
2	3	4	5	6	7	8
9	10	11	12	13	14	15
16	17	18	19	20	21	22
23	24	25	26	27	28	29
30						

DESIGN & PLANNING
INNOVATION
BUILT ON TRADITION

"McKechnie Field,

Bradenton Florida, the
Grapefruit League home of
the Pittsburgh Pirates, is
loaded with old-time ballpark
character, the Fenway of
spring parks. Green fence,
green seats, the definition of
ballpark intimacy."

• USA TODAY
FEBRUARY 3, 1999

Contacts:
Jeffrey P. Slusarick, AIA
Christopher R. Haupt, AIA

Pittsburgh PA, 15222
www.ldastorino.com
412.765.1700

L.D. ASTORINO COMPANIES

Architecture ■   Engineering ■   Environmental ■

EVENTS CALENDAR

March 1999-February 2000

March

17—Opening Day: Mexican League.

April

2—Opening Day: Japan Central League.
3—Opening Day: Japan Pacific League.
4—Opening Day: National League (Colorado vs. San Diego at Monterrey, Mexico).
5—Opening Day: American League (Tampa Bay at Baltimore, Boston at Kansas City, White Sox at Seattle, Yankees at Oakland, Detroit at Texas).
5—Opening Day: National League (Philadelphia at Atlanta, Mets at Florida, Montreal at Pittsburgh, San Francisco at Cincinnati, Milwaukee at St. Louis, Arizona at Los Angeles).
5—National Classic High School Tournament at Orange County, Calif. (thru April 8).
6—Opening Day: American League (Cleveland at Anaheim, Toronto at Minnesota).
6—Opening Day: National League (Cubs at Houston).
8—Opening Day: International League, Pacific Coast League, Southern League, Texas League, California League, Carolina League, Florida State League, Midwest League, South Atlantic League.
9—Opening Day: Eastern League.

May

5—Opening Day: Atlantic League.
15—Junior College Division III World Series at Batavia, N.Y. (thru May 21).
21—Opening Day: Western League.
22—NCAA Division II World Series at Montgomery, Ala. (thru May 29).
24—NAIA World Series at Jupiter, Fla. (thru May 31).
27—Opening Day: Texas-Louisiana League.
28—NCAA Division I Regionals at campus sites (thru May 30).
28—NCAA Division III World Series at Salem, Va. (thru June 1).
28—Opening Day: Northern League.
29—Junior College Division II World Series at Millington, Tenn. (thru June 5).
29—Junior College World Series at Grand Junction, Colo. (thru June 5).
31—Mexican League All-Star Game at Oaxaca, Mexico.

June

1—Opening Day: Dominican Summer League, Venezuelan Summer League.
1—Opening Day: Atlantic Collegiate League.
2—Amateur free agent draft (thru June 3).
2—Opening Day: Frontier League.
4—NCAA Division I Super Regionals at campus sites (thru June 6).
4—Opening Day: Coastal Plain League; Jayhawk League; Northwoods League.
4—First Interleague Games (EAST—Montreal at Toronto, Mets at Yankees, Philadelphia at Baltimore, Atlanta at Boston, Florida at Tampa Bay. CEN-TRAL—Houston at Minnesota, Cincinnati at Kansas City, Cubs at Cleveland, St. Louis at Detroit, Pittsburgh at White Sox. WEST—Anaheim at Los Angeles, Texas at Arizona, Seattle at San Diego, Oakland at San Francisco.
6—Opening Day: New England Collegiate League.
9—Opening Day: Alaska League.
11—53rd College World Series at Omaha (thru June 19).
11—Opening Day: Central Illinois Collegiate League; Northeastern Collegiate League; Great Lakes League; Shenandoah Valley League; Cape Cod League.
16—Opening Day: New York-Penn League; Pioneer League.
18—Opening Day: Northwest League; Appalachian League; Gulf Coast League.
18—Team One National Showcase at St. Petersburg, Fla. (thru June 20).
19—USA Junior Olympic Championship at Tucson (thru June 26).
19—Florida State League all-star game at Lakeland, Fla.
22—California League/Carolina League all-star game at Lake Elsinore, Calif.

22—South Atlantic League all-star game at Salisbury, Md.
22—Midwest League all-star game at Lansing, Mich.
22—Sunbelt Classic Baseball Series at Shawnee/Tecumseh, Okla. (thru June 26)
23—Southern League All-Star Game at Jackson, Tenn.
23—Opening Day: Arizona League.

July

11—1st Major League Futures Game at Fenway Park, Boston.
12—Western League All-Star Game at Chico, Calif.
13—70th Major League All-Star Game at Fenway Park, Boston.
14—Triple-A All-Star Game at New Orleans.
14—Double-A All-Star Game at Mobile, Ala.
14—Atlantic League All-Star Game at Bridgeport, Conn.
14—Frontier League All-Star Game at Huntingburg, Ind.
24—Cape Cod League All-Star Game at Wareham, Mass.
24—Pan American Games at Winnipeg, Manitoba (thru Aug. 2).
24—Japan All-Star Game I at Seibu Dome.
25—Japan All-Star Game II at Koshien Stadium.
25—Hall of Fame induction ceremonies, Cooperstown.
26—Hall of Fame Game, Kansas City vs. Texas at Cooperstown.
27—Japan All-Star Game III at Muscat Stadium, Kurashiki.
27—Texas League All-Star Game at Tulsa.

August

1—End of major league trading period without waivers.
2—Northern League All-Star Game at Fargo, N.D.
3—National Baseball Congress World Series at Wichita (thru Aug. 17).
4—Eastern Professional Baseball Showcase at Wilmington, N.C. (thru Aug. 7).
6—Connie Mack World Series at Farmington, N.M. (thru Aug. 12).
6—IBA World Junior Championship at Kaoshiung, Taiwan (thru Aug. 15).
8—Area Code Games at Long Beach (thru Aug. 14).
14—Pony League World Series at Washington, Pa. (thru Aug. 21).
20—American Legion World Series at Middletown, Conn. (thru Aug. 24).
21—Babe Ruth 13-15 World Series at Abbeville, La. (thru Aug. 28).
21—Babe Ruth 16-18 World Series at Stamford, Conn. (thru Aug. 28).
22—Little League World Series at Williamsport, Pa. (thru Aug. 28).
31—Postseason major league roster eligibility frozen.

September

1—Major league roster limits expanded from 25 to 40.
20—Triple-A World Series at Las Vegas, International League vs. Pacific Coast League (thru Sept. 25).
29—Opening Day: Arizona Fall League.

October

3—Major league season ends.
4—Beginning of major league trading period without waivers.
5—Major league Division Series begin.
12—Major League Championship Series begin.
23—World Series begins at home of National League champion.
23—Japan Series begins at home of Pacific League champion.

November

4—XIV Intercontinental Cup at Sydney, Australia (thru Nov. 14).
20—Forty-man major league winter rosters must be filed.

December

3—National High School Baseball Coaches Association convention at Tucson (thru Dec. 5).
10—97th annual Winter Meetings at Anaheim (thru Dec. 14).
13—Rule 5 major league/minor league drafts.

January 2000

6—American Baseball Coaches Association convention at Chicago (thru Jan. 9)
8—NCAA National Convention at San Diego (thru Jan. 11)

February 2000

2—Caribbean World Series at Santo Domingo, Dominican Republic (thru Feb. 7).

Baseball America Online

······▶ is coming at you like a *95-mph fastball*.

Come visit us at **www.baseballamerica.com** to see the

best baseball site on the Net.

While you're there,

get the latest **prospect information**,

stats, news and coverage

of **special events** like the draft.

www.baseballamerica.com

BASEBALL AMERICA

ESTABLISHED 1981

PUBLISHER: Lee Folger

EDITOR: Allan Simpson

MANAGING EDITOR: Will Lingo

SENIOR EDITOR: John Royster

ASSOCIATE EDITOR: James Bailey

ASSOCIATE EDITOR: Lacy Lusk

ASSOCIATE EDITOR: John Manuel

SENIOR WRITER: Alan Schwarz

NATIONAL CORRESPONDENT: David Rawnsley

EDITORIAL ASSISTANT: Mark Derewicz

PRODUCTION DIRECTOR: Valerie Holbert

PRODUCTION ASSISTANT: Brandon Donnell

CUSTOMER SERVICE: Ronnie McCabe, Maxine Tillman

ADVERTISING SALES
Kris Korteweg, Advertising Manager
P.O. Box 2089, Durham, NC 27702
Phone (800) 845-2726; FAX: 919-682-2880

NATIONAL NEWSSTAND CONSULTANT
John Blassingame, Linden, NJ

BASEBALL AMERICA, Inc.
PRESIDENT: Miles Wolff
P.O. Box 2089, Durham, NC 27702
Street Address: 600 S. Duke St., Durham, NC 27701
Phone: (919) 682-9635 • Toll-Free: (800) 845-2726
FAX: (919) 682-2880
E-Mail Address: ba@interpath.com
Website: www.baseballamerica.com

BASEBALL AMERICA, the nation's most complete all-baseball newspaper, publishes 26 issues a year. Subscription rates are $48.95 for one year, payable in U.S. funds.

BASEBALL AMERICA PUBLICATIONS

1999 Almanac: A comprehensive look at the 1998 season, featuring major and minor league statistics and commentary. **$12.95**

1999 Directory: Names, addresses, phone numbers, major and minor league schedules—vital to baseball insiders and fans. **$12.95**

1999 Super Register: A complete record, with biographical information, of every player who played professional baseball in 1998. **$24.95**

1999 Great Minor League Ballparks Calendar: $10.95

Encyclopedia of Minor League Baseball: The first total compilation of the teams and standings in the 90-year history of minor league baseball. The ultimate research tool. **$48.95 hardcover, $39.95 softcover**

The Minor League Register: An updated compilation of SABR's The Minor League Stars with more than 200 new entries, minor league milestones. **$39.95 softcover**

BASEBALLAMERICA

1998 AWARD WINNERS

MAJOR LEAGUES

Player of the Year
Mark McGwire, 1b, St. Louis

Pitcher of the Year
Roger Clemens, rhp, Toronto

Rookie of the Year
Kerry Wood, rhp, Chicago (NL)

Manager of the Year
Larry Dierker, Houston

Executive of the Year
Doug Melvin, Texas

MINOR LEAGUES

Organization of the Year
New York Yankees

Player of the Year (overall)
Eric Chavez, 3b, Huntsville (Southern)/Edmonton (Pacific Coast)

Manager of the Year
Terry Kennedy, Iowa (Pacific Coast)

Team of the Year
Mobile BayBears (Southern)

Players of the Year
Triple-A: Brian Daubach, of, Charlotte
Double-A: Eric Chavez, 3b, Huntsville
Class A: Brad Penny, rhp, High Desert
Short-Season: Michael Restovich, of, Elizabethton

Freitas Awards
Triple-A: Salt Lake Buzz (Pacific Coast)
Double-A: Trenton Thunder (Eastern)
Class A: West Michigan Whitecaps (Midwest)
Short-Season: Hudson Valley Renegades (New York-Penn)

INDEPENDENT BASEBALL

Player of the Year
Morgan Burkhart, 1b, Richmond (Frontier)

WINTER BASEBALL

Player of the Year
Bob Abreu, of, Caracas (Venezuela)

COLLEGE BASEBALL

Player of the Year
Jeff Austin, rhp, Stanford

Coach of the Year
Pat Murphy, Arizona State

Freshman of the Year
Xavier Nady, 2b, California

AMATEUR BASEBALL

Summer Player of the Year
Bobby Kielty, of, Brewster (Cape Cod)

HIGH SCHOOL BASEBALL

Player of the Year
Drew Henson, ss-rhp, Brighton (Mich.) HS

TOLLFREENUMBERS

Airlines

Aeromexico	800-237-6639
Air Canada	800-776-3000
Alaska Airlines	800-426-0333
Aloha Airlines	800-227-4900
America West	800-235-9292
American Airlines	800-433-7300
Continental Airlines	800-525-0280
Delta Air Lines	800-221-1212
Japan Air Lines	800-525-3663
Korean Air	800-438-5000
Midway Airlines	800-446-4392
Northwest Airlines	800-225-2525
Olympic Airways	800-223-1226
Qantas Airways	800-227-4500
Southwest Airlines	800-435-9792
Trans World Airlines	800-221-2000
United Airlines	800-631-1500
U.S. Airways	800-428-4322

Car Rentals

Alamo (except Florida)	800-327-9633
Alamo (Florida only)	800-732-3232
Avis	800-331-1212
Avis International	800-331-1084
Budget	800-527-0700
Dollar	800-800-4000
Enterprise	800-325-8007
Hertz	800-654-3131
Hertz International	800-654-3001
National	800-227-7368
Thrifty	800-367-2277

Hotels/Motels

Best Western	800-528-1234
Choice Hotels	800-424-6423
Courtyard by Marriott	800-321-2211
Days Inn	800-325-2525
Doubletree Hotels/Guest Suites	800-424-2900
Embassy Suites	800-362-2779
Hampton Inns	800-426-7866
Hilton Hotels	800-445-8667
Holiday Inns	800-465-4329
Howard Johnsons Motor Lodges	800-654-2000
Hyatt Hotels	800-228-9000
La Quinta	800-531-5900
Marriott Hotels	800-228-9290
Omni Hotels	800-843-6664
Radisson Hotels	800-333-3333
Ramada Inns	800-228-2828
Red Roof Inns	800-843-7663
Sheraton Hotels	800-325-3535
Renaissance Hotels/Resorts	800-468-3571
TraveLodge	800-578-7878
Westin Hotels	800-228-3000

Rail

Amtrak	800-872-7245

WHAT'S NEW IN '99

MAJOR LEAGUE BASEBALL

BALLPARKS
- Seattle: Safeco Field (opens July 15)

MINOR LEAGUES

Triple-A

- **AFFILIATION CHANGES:**
  Anaheim from Vancouver to Edmonton
  Chicago (AL) from Calgary to Charlotte
  Florida from Charlotte to Calgary
  Oakland from Edmonton to Vancouver

Double-A

- Expansion franchises granted to Altoona (Eastern) and Erie (Eastern)
- **AFFILIATION CHANGES:**
  Anaheim from Midland to Erie
  Arizona to El Paso
  Colorado from New Haven to Carolina
  Milwaukee from El Paso to Huntsville
  Oakland from Huntsville to Midland
  Pittsburgh from Carolina to Altoona
  Seattle from Orlando to New Haven
  Tampa Bay to Orlando

Class A

- Danville (Carolina) relocated to Myrtle Beach, S.C.
- **AFFILIATION CHANGES:**
  Boston from Michigan to Augusta
  Chicago (AL) from Hickory to Burlington
  Chicago (NL) from Rockford to Lansing
  Cincinnati from Burlington to Clinton; Cincinnati from Charleston, W.Va.,
    to Rockford
  Houston from Quad City to Michigan
  Kansas City from Lansing to Charleston, W.Va.
  Minnesota from Fort Wayne to Quad City
  Pittsburgh from Augusta to Hickory
  San Diego from Clinton to Fort Wayne

Short-Season

- Erie (New York-Penn) relocated to Mahoning Valley
- Lethbridge (Pioneer) relocated to Missoula
- Watertown (New York-Penn) relocated to Staten Island
- **AFFILIATION CHANGES:**
  Atlanta from Eugene to Jamestown
  Chicago (NL) from Williamsport to Eugene
  Cincinnati adds Gulf Coast League team
  Cleveland from Watertown to Mahoning Valley
  Detroit from Jamestown to Oneonta
  Houston from Gulf Coast League to Martinsville
  New York (AL) from Oneonta to Staten Island
  Philadelphia from Martinsville to Gulf Coast League
  Pittsburgh from Erie to Williamsport
  Tampa Bay drops Gulf Coast League team

NICKNAMES

- Louisville from Redbirds to RiverBats
- Midland from Angels to RockHounds
- Omaha from Royals to Golden Spikes
- Oneonta from Yankees to Tigers
- Rockford from Cubbies to Reds
- Williamsport from Cubs to Crosscutters

INDEPENDENT LEAGUES

- Heartland League disbanded
- Northern League adds Northeast League in merger

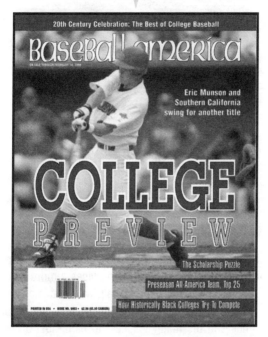

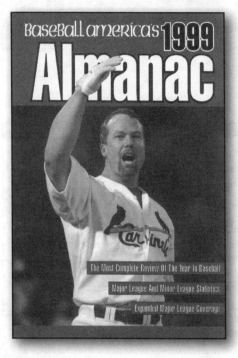

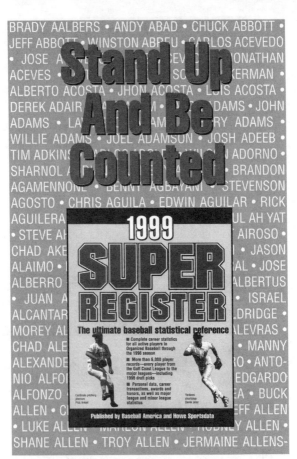

Some Internet providers are like Big Brother.
We're more like the cool cousin with the Harley.®

EASY SET-UP, INCREDIBLY FAST CONNECTIONS,
KILLER 24-HR. SUPPORT AND FLEXIBLE PRICING FROM
$6.95/MO. INCLUDING $19.95/MO. FOR UNLIMITED ACCESS.
WE ALSO OFFER BIG PREPAYMENT DISCOUNTS. OUR
INTERNET SERVICES WERE DESIGNED WITH YOU IN MIND.™

MindSpring®
INTERNET SERVICES   1-888-MSPRING

Major Leagues

MAJORLEAGUEBASEBALL

Mailing Address: 245 Park Ave., New York, NY 10167. **Telephone:** (212) 931-7800. **Website:** www.majorleaguebaseball.com.

Commissioner: Allan H. "Bud" Selig.

Senior Executive Assistant to Commissioner: Lori Keck. **Administrative Assistant to Commissioner:** Sandy Ronback.

Chief Operating Officer: Paul Beeston.

Bud Selig

Baseball Operations

Executive Vice President: Sandy Alderson.

Executive Director: Bill Murray. **Director:** Roy Krasik. **Administrator:** Jeff Pfeifer. **Records Coordinator:** George Moreira.

Executive Director, Minor League Operations: Jimmie Lee Solomon.

General Administration

Executive Vice President: Robert DuPuy.

Executive VP, Labor Relations/Human Resources: Robert Manfred.

General Counsel, Office of the Commissioner: Thomas Ostertag.

General Labor Counsel: Francis Coonelly. **General Counsel, MLB Enterprises:** Ethan Orlinsky.

Vice President, Finance: Thomas Duffy. **Chief Financial Officer:** Jeffrey White.

Executive Director, Security/Facilities Management: Kevin Hallinan.

Senior Vice President, MLB Productions: Stephen Hellmuth.

Vice President, Broadcasting/New Media: Leslie Sullivan.

Vice President, Marketing: Kathy Francis.

Vice President, Team Services: Mark Gorris.

Vice President, Events: Marla Miller.

Vice President, Licensing: Howard Smith.

Executive Director, Human Resources/Office Services: Wendy Lewis.

Paul Beeston

Executive Director, Baseball Assistance Team: James Martin.

Public Relations

Telephone: (212) 931-7878. **FAX:** (212) 949-5654.

Executive Director: Richard Levin.

Managers: Pat Courtney, Carole Coleman.

Manager, Baseball Information System: Rob Doelger. **Supervisor:** Kathleen Fineout. **Administrators:** Matt Gould, Lisa Quinn. **Assistant, Public Relations:** Blakely Blum. **Assistant, Public Relations/Baseball Information System:** John Blundell. **Administrative Assistant:** Heather Flock.

Major League Baseball International

Mailing Address: 245 Park Ave., 30th Floor, New York, NY 10167. **Telephone:** (212) 931-7500. **FAX:** (212) 949-5795.

Sandy Alderson

Senior Vice President, Domestic and International Licensing: Tim Brosnan.

VP, International Licensing: Shawn Lawson Cummings. **International Licensing Manager, Latin America:** Deidra Varona.

VP, International Broadcasting/Sponsorship Sales: Paul Archey. **Manager, Sponsorship/Broadcasting Promotions:** Sara Loarte. **Supervisor, Client Services:** Michael Luscher.

VP, Market Development: Jim Small. **Manager, Business Affairs:** Peter Carton. **Coordinator, Market Development:** Chris Tobias.

VP, International Production/Television Operations: Russell Gabay. **Field Production Supervisor, International Broadcasting:** Margie O'Neill. **Coordinator, Broadcasting/Television:** Marcia Price. **Director, European Operations:** Clive Russell. **Director, Australian Operations:** Simon Gray.

Events

1999 Major League All-Star Game: July 13 at Fenway Park, Boston.

1999 World Series: Begins Oct. 23 at home of National League champion.

American League

AMERICAN LEAGUE

Mailing Address: 245 Park Ave., 28th Floor, New York, NY 10167. **Telephone:** (212) 931-7600. **FAX:** Unavailable.

Years League Active: 1901-.
President: Gene Budig.
Vice President: Carl Pohlad (Minnesota).
Board of Directors: Anaheim, Baltimore, Boston, Chicago, Cleveland, Kansas City.
Executive Director, Umpiring: Marty Springstead. **Coordinator, Umpire Operations:** Philip Janssen. **Administrator, Umpire Travel:** Tess Marino.
Senior Vice President: Phyllis Merhige.
Vice President, Finance: Derek Irwin.
Director, Waiver and Player Records: Brian Small.
Administrative Assistant, Secretary to President: Carolyn Coen. **Administrative Assistant, Secretary to Vice Presidents:** Angelica Cintron.

Gene Budig

Receptionist: Nancy Navarro.
1999 Opening Date: April 5. **Closing Date:** Oct. 3.
Regular Season: 162 games.
Division Structure: East—Baltimore, Boston, New York, Tampa Bay, Toronto. **Central**—Chicago, Cleveland, Detroit, Kansas City, Minnesota. **West**—Anaheim, Oakland, Seattle, Texas.
Playoff Format: Three division champions and second-place team with best record play in best-of-5 Division Series. Winners meet in best-of-7 League Championship Series.
All-Star Game: July 13 at Boston (American League vs. National League).
Roster Limit: 25, through Aug. 31 when rosters expand to 40.
Brand of Baseball: Rawlings.
Statistician: Elias Sports Bureau, 500 Fifth Ave., New York, NY 10110.
Umpires: Larry Barnett (Prospect, OH), Joe Brinkman (Cocoa, FL), Gary Cedarstrom (Minot, ND), Al Clark (Williamsburg, VA), Drew Coble (Graham, NC), Derryl Cousins (Hermosa Beach, CA), Terry Craft (Sarasota, FL), Jim Evans (Castle Rock, CO), Dale Ford (Jonesboro, TN), Rich Garcia (Clearwater, FL), Ted Hendry (Scottsdale, AZ), Ed Hickox (Daytona Beach, FL), John Hirschbeck (Poland, OH), Mark Johnson (Honolulu, HI), Jim Joyce (Beaverton, OR), Ken Kaiser (Pompano Beach, FL), Greg Kosc (Medina, OH), Tim McClelland (West Des Moines, IA), Larry McCoy (Greenway, AR), Jim McKean (St. Petersburg, FL), Chuck Meriwether (Nashville, TN), Durwood Merrill (Hooks, TX), Dan Morrison (Largo, FL), Dave Phillips (Lake St. Louis, MO), Rick Reed (Rochester Hills, MI), Mike Reilly (Battle Creek, MI), Rocky Roe (Milford, MI), Dale Scott (Portland, OR), John Shulock (Vero Beach, FL), Tim Tschida (Turtle Lake, WI), Tim Welke (Kalamazoo, MI), Larry Young (Roscoe, IL).

Stadium Information

City	Stadium	Dimensions			Capacity	'98 Att.
		LF	CF	RF		
Anaheim	Edison International	365	406	365	45,050	2,519,210
Baltimore	Camden Yards	333	410	318	48,876	3,685,194
Boston	Fenway Park	310	390	302	33,871	2,314,721
Chicago	Comiskey Park	347	400	347	44,321	1,391,146
Cleveland	Jacobs Field	325	405	325	43,863	3,467,299
Detroit	Tiger Stadium	340	440	325	46,945	1,409,391
Kansas City	Kauffman Stadium	330	400	330	40,529	1,494,875
Minnesota	Humphrey Metrodome	343	408	327	48,678	1,165,980
New York	Yankee Stadium	318	408	314	57,545	2,949,734
Oakland	Alameda County	330	400	330	43,012	1,232,339
Seattle	Kingdome	331	405	312	59,084	2,644,166
	Safeco Field (July 15)	331	405	326	45,600	—
Tampa Bay	Tropicana Field	315	407	322	45,200	2,506,023
Texas	Ballpark in Arlington	334	400	325	49,166	2,927,409
Toronto	SkyDome	328	400	328	50,516	2,454,303

ANAHEIM

Telephone, Address
Office Address: Edison International Field of Anaheim, 2000 Gene Autry Way, Anaheim, CA 92806. **Mailing Address:** P.O. Box 2000, Anaheim, CA 92803. **Telephone:** (714) 940-2000. **FAX:** (714) 940-2205. **Website:** www.angelsbaseball.com.

Ownership
Operated by: Anaheim Sports, Inc. (A division of the Walt Disney Company).

Chairman/Chief Executive Officer: Michael Eisner. **President:** Tony Tavares.

BUSINESS OPERATIONS

Michael Eisner

Vice President, Finance/Administration: Andy Roundtree. **Administrative Assistant:** Monica Campanis.

Vice President, Business Operations: Spencer Neumann. **Administrative Assistant:** Debbie Tierney.

Vice President, Business/Legal Affairs: Rick Schlesinger. **Administrative Assistant:** Tia Wood.

Manager, Human Resources: Jenny Price. **Administrative Assistant:** Cindy Williams.

Finance
Director, Finance: John Rinehart. **Assistant Controllers:** Cristina Fisher, Melody Martin.

Marketing, Sales
Vice President, Sales/Marketing: Ron Minegar. **Administrative Assistant:** Roberta Maslanka.

Vice President, Advertising Sales/Sponsor Services: Bob Wagner. **Administrative Assistant:** Sonia Salem.

Director, Entertainment: Rod Murray. **Manager, Broadcasting:** Dan Patin. **Manager, Sponsorship Sales:** Sue O'Shea. **Manager, Marketing:** Lisa Manning. **Manager, Group Sales:** Andy Silverman. **Managers, Advertising/Broadcast Sales:** John Covarrubias, Richard McClemmy. **Sponsorship Services Representative:** Jennifer Guran.

Public Relations, Communications
Telephone: (714) 940-2014. **FAX:** (714) 940-2205.

Vice President, Communications: Tim Mead.

Manager, Baseball Information: Larry Babcock. **Manager, Media Services:** Nancy Mazmanian. **Manager, Publications:** Doug Ward. **Media/Travel Representative:** Tom Taylor. **Media Relations Representatives:** Eric Kay, Aaron Tom. **Communications Assistant:** Lisa Parris.

Manager, Community Relations: Dennis Bickmeier.

Stadium Operations
Vice President, Stadium Operations: Kevin Uhlich. **Administrative Assistant:** Leslie Flammini.

Manager, Facility Services: Mike McKay. **Manager, Event Services:** John Drum. **Manager, Field/Ground Services:** Barney Lopas.

PA Announcer: David Courtney. **Official Scorer:** Ed Munson.

Ticketing
Telephone: (714) 634-2000.

Manager, Ticket Operations: Sheila Brazelton. **Assistant Manager, Ticket Operations:** Susan Weiss.

Travel, Clubhouse
Equipment Manager: Ken Higdon. **Assistant Equipment Manager:** Keith Tarter. **Visiting Clubhouse:** Brian Harkins.

Senior Video Coordinator: Diego Lopez.

General Information

Home Dugout: Third Base. **Playing Surface:** Grass.

Stadium Location: Highway 57 (Orange Freeway) to Katella Avenue exit, west on Katella, stadium on west side of Orange Freeway. **Standard Game Times:** 7:05 p.m., Wed. 7:35, Sun. 5:05.

Player Representative: Tim Salmon.

ANGELS

BASEBALL OPERATIONS
Vice President/General Manager: Bill Bavasi.
Assistant General Manager: Ken Forsch.
Administrative Assistant to GM: Cathy Carey.

Major League Staff
Manager: Terry Collins.
Coaches: Pitching—Dick Pole; Batting—Rod Carew; First Base—George Hendrick; Third Base—Larry Bowa; Bullpen—Joe Coleman; Bullpen Coordinator—Mick Billmeyer.

Medical, Training
Trainers: Ned Bergert, Rick Smith. Strength and Conditioning: Brian Grapes.

Bill Bavasi

Player Development
Telephone: (714) 940-2031. FAX: (714) 940-2203.
Director, Player Development: Jeff Parker.
Manager, Baseball Operations: Tony Reagins.
Administrative Assistant: Laura Fazioli. Administration Manager, Mesa Complex: Eric Blum.
Facility Manager: Scott Lingle.
Coordinator, Instruction: Marcel Lachemann.
Roving Instructors: Bob Clear (special assignment), Mike Couchee (pitching), Trent Clark (strength and conditioning), Bruce Hines (defense), John McNamara (catching), Gene Richards (hitting).

Terry Collins

Farm System

Class	Farm Team	Manager	Coach	Pitching Coach
AAA	Edmonton	Carney Lansford	Leon Durham	Rick Wise
AA	Erie	Garry Templeton	Bill Lachemann	Howie Gershberg
A	Lake Elsinore	Mario Mendoza	John Orton	Kernan Ronan
A	Cedar Rapids	Mitch Seoane	Tyrone Boykin	Greg Minton
A	Boise	Tom Kotchman	Todd Claus	Jim Bennett
R	Butte	Joe Urso	Orlando Mercado	Zeke Zimmerman
R	DSL	Charlie Romero	Jose Gomez	Unavailable

Scouting
Telephone: (714) 940-2038. FAX: (714) 940-2203.
Director, Scouting: Bob Fontaine.
Assistant to Director: Janet Mitchell.
Advance Scout: Matt Keough (Coto de Caza, CA).
Special Assignment Scout: Bob Harrison (Long Beach, CA).
Major League Scouts: Dave Garcia (El Cajon, CA), Jay Hankins (Greenwood, MO), Nick Kamzic (Evergreen Park, IL), Joe McDonald (Lakeland, FL), Moose Stubing (Villa Park, CA), Dale Sutherland (La Crescenta, CA), Gary Sutherland (Monrovia, CA).

Bob Fontaine

National Crosscheckers: Rick Ingalls (Belmont Shores, CA), Hal Keller (Issaquah, WA). Free-Agent Supervisors: West—Tom Davis (Ripon, CA), Midwest—Tony LaCava (Oakmont, PA), East—Jon Neiderer (Johnstown, PA), South—Paul Robinson (Fort Worth, TX). Area Scouts: Don Archer (Surrey, British Columbia), John Burden (Fairfield, OH), Tom Burns (Harrisburg, PA), Todd Claus (Tamarac, FL), Pete Coachman (Cottonwood, AL), Red Gaskill (La Marque, TX), Steve Gruwell (West Covina, CA), Tim Kelly (Carlsbad, CA), Kris Kline (Arlington, TX), Tom Kotchman (Seminole, FL), Ron Marigny (Lake Charles, LA), Darrell Miller (Yorba Linda, CA), Steve Oleschuk (Montreal, Quebec), John Orton (Watsonville, CA), Tom Osowski (Milwaukee, WI), Rick Schroeder (San Jose, CA), Jerry Streeter (Modesto, CA), Rip Tutor (Lenoir, NC), Jack Uhey (Vancouver, WA), Dick Wilson (Sun Valley, NV).
Coordinator, Latin America: George Lauzerique (Wellington, FL).
Coordinator, International Scouting: Rich Schlenker (Walnut Creek, CA).
Director, Far East Operations: Ta Honda (Osaka, Japan).

BALTIMORE

Telephone, Address
Office Address: 333 W Camden St., Baltimore, MD 21201. Telephone: (410) 685-9800. FAX: (410) 547-6272. Website: www.theorioles.com.

Ownership
Operated by: The Home Team Limited Partnership.

Chairman, Chief Executive Officer: Peter Angelos. Vice Chairman, Community Projects/ Public Affairs: Tom Clancy. Executive Vice President: John Angelos.

BUSINESS OPERATIONS
Vice Chairman, Chief Operating Officer: Joe Foss. General Counsel: Russell Smouse.

Director, Human Resources: Martena Clinton.

Peter Angelos

Finance
Vice President, Chief Financial Officer: Robert Ames. Controller: Edward Kabernagel.

Marketing, Sales
Vice President, Marketing and Broadcasting: Mike Lehr.

Director, Marketing/Advertising: Scott Nickle. Manager, Advertising/ Promotions: Jim Brylewski.

Director, Sales: Matt Dryer.

Director, Fan Services: Don Grove.

Public Relations, Communications
Telephone: (410) 547-6150. FAX: (410) 547-6272.

Director, Public Relations: John Maroon. Assistant Director, Public Relations: Bill Stetka. Administrative Assistant, Public Relations: Heather Tilles.

Assistant Director, Publications: Jessica Fisher.

Director, Community Relations: Julie Wagner. Manager, Community Relations: Stephani Lewis. Administrative Assistant, Community Relations: Jennifer Steier.

Stadium Operations
Director, Ballpark Operations: Roger Hayden.

Head Groundskeeper: Paul Zwaska.

PA Announcer: Dave McGowan. Official Scorers: Jim Henneman, Dave Hughes, Marc Jacobson.

Ticketing
Telephone: (410) 547-6600. FAX: (410) 547-6270.

Manager, Ticket Office: Audrey Brown.

Travel, Clubhouse
Traveling Secretary: Phil Itzoe.

Equipment Manager, Home: Jim Tyler. Equipment Manager, Visitors: Fred Tyler.

General Information
Home Dugout: First Base. Playing Surface: Grass.

Standard Games Times: 7:05 p.m., (June-Aug.) 7:35; Sat. 1:15, 1:35, 7:05; Sun. 1:35.

Stadium Location: I-95 to exit 395, downtown to Russell Street.

Player Representative: Mike Mussina.

ORIOLES

BASEBALL OPERATIONS
Telephone: (410) 547-6122. **FAX:** (410) 547-6271.
General Manager: Frank Wren.
Assistant General Manager: Bruce Manno.
Special Assistants to General Manager: Syd Thrift, Fred Uhlman Sr.

Major League Staff
Manager: Ray Miller.
Coaches: Bench—Eddie Murray; Pitching—Bruce Kison; Batting—Terry Crowley; First Base—Marv Foley; Third Base—Sam Perlozzo; Bullpen—Elrod Hendricks.

Frank Wren

Medical, Training
Club Physician: Dr. William Goldiner.
Head Trainer: Richie Bancells. **Assistant Trainer:** Brian Ebel. **Strength and Conditioning Coach:** Tim Bishop.

Player Development
Telephone: (410) 547-6112. **FAX:** (410) 547-6298.
Director, Player Development: Tom Trebelhorn. **Assistant Director, Player Development:** Don Buford. **Administrator:** Tripp Norton. **Administrative Assistant, Player Development:** Ann Lange.
Camp Coordinator: Lenny Johnston.
Roving Instructors: Bo McLaughlin (pitching), David Stockstill (hitting), Denny Walling (hitting, defense).
Medical Coordinator: Guido Van Ryssegem.
Strength and Conditioning: Pat Hedge.

Ray Miller

Farm System

Class	Farm Team	Manager	Coach	Pitching Coach
AAA	Rochester	Dave Machemer	Dave Cash	Larry McCall
AA	Bowie	Joe Ferguson	Bien Figueroa	Dave Schmidt
A	Frederick	Andy Etchebarren	Floyd Rayford	Larry Jaster
A	Delmarva	Butch Davis	Bobby Rodriguez	Moe Drabowsky
R	Bluefield	Duffy Dyer	Unavailable	Charlie Puleo
R	Sarasota	Jesus Alfaro	Joe Tanner	John O'Donoghue
R	DSL	Salvador Ramirez	Miguel Jabalara	Euripides Nunez

Scouting
Telephone: (410) 547-6187. **FAX:** (410) 547-6298.
Director, Scouting: Tony DeMacio.
Administrative Assistants: Brian Hopkins, Marcy Zerhusen.
Advance Scouts: Bob Schaefer (Fort Myers, FL), Fred Uhlman Sr. (Baltimore, MD), Don Welke (Louisville, KY).
Special Assignment Scouts: Curt Motton (Woodstock, MD), Deacon Jones (Sugar Land, TX).
National Crosschecker: Mike Ledna (Arlington Heights, IL). **Regional Supervisors:** East—Shawn Pender (Dreyer Hill, PA); West—Logan White (Phoenix, AZ); Midwest—Earl Winn (Bowling Green, KY).

Tony DeMacio

Area Scouts: Dean Decillis (Tamarac, FL), Lane Decker (Piedmont, OK), Gerald Elam (St. Louis, MO), John Gillette (Kirkland, WA), Jim Howard (Clifton Park, NY), Ray Krawczyk (Lake Forest, CA), Gil Kubski (Huntington Beach, CA), Jeff Morris (Tucson, AZ), Lamar North (Rossville, GA), Deron Rombach (Arlington, TX), Harry Shelton (Ocoee, FL), Ed Sprague (Lodi, CA), Marc Tramuta (Germantown, MD), Mike Tullier (New Orleans, LA), Marc Ziegler (Canal Winchester, OH).
Director, International Scouting: Jeff Wren (Ridge Manor, FL).
International Scouts: Jesus Halabi (Aruba), Ubaldo Heredia (Venezuela), Salvador Ramirez (Dominican Republic), Arturo Sanchez (Venezuela).

BOSTON

Telephone, Address
Office Address: Fenway Park, 4 Yawkey Way, Boston, MA 02215. **Telephone:** (617) 267-9440. **FAX:** (617) 375-0944. **Internet Address:** www.red-sox.com.

John Harrington

Ownership
Operated by: Boston Red Sox Baseball Club.

General Partner: Jean R. Yawkey Trust (Trustees: John Harrington, William Gutfarb). **Limited Partners:** ARAMARK Corporation (Chairman: Joseph Neubauer); Dexter Group (Principal: Harold Alfond); Jean R. Yawkey Trust; Dr. Arthur Pappas; Samuel Tamposi Trust; Thomas DiBenedetto; John Harrington; John Kaneb.

Chief Executive Officer: John Harrington.

BUSINESS OPERATIONS
Executive Vice President, Administration: John Buckley. **Executive Administrative Assistant:** Jeanne Bill.

Director, Human Resources/Office Management: Michele Julian.

Finance
Vice President, Chief Financial Officer: Robert Furbush.

Controller: Stanley Tran. **Senior Staff Accountant:** Robin Yeingst. **Staff Accountant:** Catherine Fahy.

Sales, Marketing
Vice President, Sales/Marketing: Larry Cancro.

Marketing Administrator: Deborah McIntyre. **Director, Advertising/Sponsorships:** Jeffrey Goldenberg.

Manager, Promotions: Marcita Davis-Thompson. **Manager, Group Sales:** Corey Bowdre. **Manager, Season Tickets:** Joseph Matthews.

Vice President, Broadcasting/Technology: Jim Healey. **Manager, Broadcasting:** James Shannahan. **Manager, Information Technology:** Clay Rondon.

Public Affairs, Community Relations
Vice President, Public Affairs: Dick Bresciani.

Executive Consultant, Public Affairs: Lou Gorman. **Public Affairs Administrator:** Mary Jane Ryan. **Manager, Publications:** Debra Matson. **Manager, Community Relations:** Ron Burton. **Manager, Customer Relations:** Ann Marie Starzyk. **Public Affairs Assistant:** Roderick Oreste.

Stadium Operations
Vice President, Stadium Operations: Joe McDermott.

Director, Facilities Management: Thomas Queenan Jr. **Manager, Property Maintenance:** John Caron. **Facilities Maintenance:** Donald Gardiner, Glen McGlinchey.

Superintendent, Grounds/Maintenance: Joe Mooney. **Manager, Ground Crew:** Casey Erven.

PA Announcer: Ed Brickley. **Official Scorer:** Charlie Scoggins.

Ticketing
Telephone: (617) 267-1700. **FAX:** (617) 236-6640.

Director, Ticket Operations: Joe Helyar. **Manager, Ticket Office:** Dick Beaton.

Travel, Clubhouse
Traveling Secretary: John McCormick.

Equipment Manager/Clubhouse Operations: Joe Cochran. **Visiting Clubhouse:** Tom McLaughlin.

General Information
Home Dugout: First Base. **Playing Surface:** Grass.

Standard Games Times: 7:05 p.m.; Sat. 1:05, 4:05, Sun. 1:05.

Directions to Stadium: Massachusetts Turnpike (I-90) to Prudential exit (stay left), right at first set of lights, right on Dalton Street, left on Boylston Street, right on Ipswich Street.

Player Representative: Tim Wakefield.

RED SOX

BASEBALL OPERATIONS

Telephone: (617) 267-9440. **FAX:** (617) 236-6649.
Executive Vice President, General Manager: Dan Duquette.
Vice President, Baseball Operations: Mike Port. **Vice President, Assistant GM/Legal Counsel:** Elaine Steward.
Assistant General Manager: Ed Kenney. **Special Assistant to GM:** Lee Thomas. **Executive Administrative Assistant:** Lorraine Leong.
Director, Communications/Baseball Information: Kevin Shea. **Coordinator, Communications Credentials:** Kate Gordon. **Coordinator, Baseball Information:** Glenn Wilburn.

Dan Duquette

Jimy Williams

Major League Staff

Manager: Jimy Williams.
Coaches: Major League—Grady Little; Pitching—Joe Kerrigan; Batting—Jim Rice; First Base—Dave Jauss; Third Base—Wendell Kim; Bullpen—John Cumberland.

Medical, Training

Medical Director: Dr. Arthur Pappas.
Trainer: Jim Rowe. **Coordinator, Strength/Conditioning:** B.J. Baker. **Physical Therapist:** Rich Zawacki.

Player Development

Telephone: (617) 267-9440. **FAX:** (617) 236-6695.
Director, Player Development: Kent Qualls. **Special Assistant, Player Development:** Johnny Pesky. **Administrative Assistant:** Andrae Wyatt.
Field Coordinator: Buddy Bailey. **Assistant Field Coordinator:** Dick Berardino. **Roving Instructors:** Mike Gallego (infield), Bobby Mitchell (outfield/baserunning), Gerald Perry (hitting), Eddie Popowski (general), Herm Starrette (pitching), Ralph Treuel (pitching).
Coordinator, Latin American Instruction: Felix Maldonado.

Farm System

Class	Farm Team	Manager	Coach	Pitching Coach
AAA	Pawtucket	Gary Jones	Gene Tenace	Rich Bombard
AA	Trenton	DeMarlo Hale	Steve Braun	Mike Griffin
A	Sarasota	Butch Hobson	Unavailable	Dave Tomlin
A	Augusta	Billy Gardner	Gomer Hodge	Larry Pierson
A	Lowell	Luis Aguayo	Ino Guerrero	Dennis Rasmussen
R	Fort Myers	John Sanders	Victor Rodriguez	Bob Kipper
R	DSL	Nelson Norman	Guadalupe Jabalera	Milciades Olivo

Scouting

Vice President, Scouting: Wayne Britton. **Assistant Director, Scouting:** Tom Moore.
Major League Scouts: Frank Malzone (Needham, MA), Eddie Robinson (Fort Worth, TX), Jerry Stephenson (Fullerton, CA). **Special Assignment Scout:** Eddie Haas (Paducah, KY).
National Crosscheckers: Kevin Burrell (Sharpsburg, GA), Ray Crone (Cedar Hill, TX).
Area Scouts: Ray Blanco (Miami, FL), Ben Cherington (Myersville, MD), Ray Fagnant (Manchester, CT), Matt Haas (Cincinnati, OH), Ernie Jacobs (Wichita, KS), Steve McAllister (Chillicothe, IL), Gary Rajsich (Lake Oswego, OR), Jim Robinson (Mansfield, TX), Ed Roebuck (Lakewood, CA), Matt Sczesny (Deer Park, NY), Harry Smith (Oceanside, CA), Fay Thompson (Vallejo, CA), Luke Wrenn (Lakeland, FL), Jeff Zona (Mechanicsville, VA).

Wayne Britton

Executive Director, International Operations: Ray Poitevint (Shadow Hills, CA). **Director, Latin America Scouting:** Levy Ochoa (Venezuela).

CHICAGO

Telephone, Address
Office Address: 333 W. 35th St., Chicago, IL 60616. Telephone: (312) 674-1000. FAX: (312) 674-5116. Website: www.chisox.com.

Ownership
Operated by: Chicago White Sox, Ltd.
Chairman: Jerry Reinsdorf. Vice Chairman: Eddie Einhorn.
Board of Directors: Fred Brzozowski, Jack Gould, Robert Judelson, Judd Malkin, Robert Mazer, Allan Muchin, Jay Pinsky, Larry Pogofsky, Lee Stern, Sanford Takiff, Burton Ury, Charles Walsh.
General Counsel: Allan Muchin.

Jerry Reinsdorf

BUSINESS OPERATIONS
Executive Vice President: Howard Pizer.
Director, Information Services: Don Brown. Director, Human Resources: Moira Foy. Assistant to Chairman: Anita Fasano.

Finance
Vice President, Administration/Finance: Tim Buzard.
Controller: Bill Waters. Accounting Manager: Julie O'Shea.

Marketing, Sales
Senior Vice President, Marketing/Broadcasting: Rob Gallas.
Director, Marketing/Broadcasting: Bob Grim. Manager, Promotions/Marketing Services: Sharon Sreniawski.
Manager, Scoreboard Operations/Production: Jeff Szynal. Manager, Broadcasting/Marketing Services: Jo Simmons. Coordinator, Promotions/Marketing Services: David Bender.
Director, Sales: Jim Muno.
Manager, Suiteholder Relations: Martha Black. Manager, Ticket Sales: Carola Ross. Manager, Sponsorship Sales: Dave Eck. Coordinator, Sponsorship Sales: Gail Tucker.
Marketing Account Executives: Jim Biegalski, Pam Walsh.
Director, Advertising/Community Relations: Christine Makowski. Coordinator, Community Relations: Amber Simons. Director, Marketing Communications: Amy Kress. Manager, Design Services: David Ortega. Coordinator, Publications: Kyle White.

Public Relations
Telephone: (312) 674-5300. FAX: (312) 674-5116.
Director, Public Relations: Scott Reifert. Manager, Public Relations: Bob Beghtol. Coordinator, Public Relations: Jennifer Sloan.
Coordinator, Baseball Information: Eric Phillips.

Stadium Operations
Vice President, Stadium Operations: Terry Savarise.
Director, Park Operations: David Schaffer. Director, Guest Services/Diamond Suite Operations: Julie Taylor.
Head Groundskeeper: Roger Bossard.
PA Announcer: Gene Honda. Official Scorer: Bob Rosenberg.

Ticketing
Telephone: (312) 674-1000. FAX: (312) 674-5102.
Director, Ticket Operations: Bob Devoy.
Manager, Ticket Operations: Mike Mazza. Manager, Ticket Accounting Administration: Ken Wisz.

Travel, Clubhouse
Traveling Secretary: Glen Rosenbaum.
Equipment Manager/Clubhouse Operations: Vince Fresso. Visiting Clubhouse: Gabe Morell. Umpires Clubhouse: Joey McNamara.

General Information
Home Dugout: Third Base. Playing Surface: Grass.
Standard Game Times: 7:05 p.m., Sat. 6:05, Sun. 1:05.
Stadium Location: 35th Street exit off Dan Ryan Expressway (I-90/94).
Player Representative: James Baldwin.

WHITE SOX

BASEBALL OPERATIONS

Senior Vice President, Major League Operations: Ron Schueler. Senior Vice President, Baseball: Jack Gould.

Director, Baseball Operations: Dan Evans. Assistant, Baseball Operations: Brian Porter. Computer Scouting Analyst: Mike Gellinger.

Major League Staff

Manager: Jerry Manuel.

Coaches: Dugout—Joe Nossek; Pitching—Nardi Contreras; Batting—Von Joshua; First Base—Bryan Little; Third Base—Wallace Johnson; Bullpen—Art Kusnyer.

Ron Schueler

Medical, Training

Senior Team Physician: Dr. James Boscardin.

Head Trainer: Herm Schneider. Assistant Trainer: Mark Anderson. Director, Conditioning: Steve Odgers.

Player Development

Telephone: (312) 674-1000. FAX: (312) 674-5105.

Vice President, Player Development: Ken Williams.

Assistant Director, Minor League Administration: Grace Zwit.

Coordinator, Instruction: Jim Snyder.

Secretary to Vice President: Julie Osborne.

Minor League Clubhouse/Equipment Manager: Dan Flood. Coordinator, Minor League Trainers: Greg Latta.

Roving Instructors: Trung Cao (conditioning), Don Cooper (pitching), Mike Lum (hitting), Gary Pettis (outfield/baserunning), Rafael Santana (infield), Tommy Thompson (catching).

Jerry Manuel

Farm System

Class	Farm Team	Manager	Coach	Pitching Coach
AAA	Charlotte	Tom Spencer	Gary Ward	Kirk Champion
AA	Birmingham	Chris Cron	Steve Whitaker	Curt Hasler
A	Winston-Salem	Jerry Terrell	Gregg Ritchie	Juan Nieves
A	Burlington	Nick Capra	Daryl Boston	J.R. Perdew
R	Bristol	Mark Haley	Dallas Williams	Sean Snedeker
R	Tucson	Jerry Hairston	Orsino Hill	Chris Sinacori

Scouting

Telephone: (312) 674-1000. FAX: (312) 451-5105.

Vice President, Free Agent and Major League Scouting: Larry Monroe.

Director, Scouting: Duane Shaffer.

Assistant Director, Scouting and Minor League Operations: Dan Fabian.

Special Assignment Scouts: Ed Brinkman (Cincinnati, OH), Mike Pazik (Bethesda, MD), Dave Yoakum (Orlando, FL).

National Crosschecker: Doug Laumann (Florence, KY).

Regional Supervisors: East Coast—George Bradley (Tampa, FL), West Coast—Ed Pebley (Brigham City, UT), Midwest—Ken Stauffer (Katy, TX).

Duane Shaffer

Area Scouts: Joe Butler (Long Beach, CA), Scott Cerny (Rocklin, CA), Rico Cortes (Tampa, FL), Alex Cosmidis (Raleigh, NC), Nathan Durst (Chicago, IL), Larry Grefer (Park Hills, KY), Warren Hughes (Mobile, AL), George Kashigian (Coronado, CA), John Kazanas (Phoenix, AZ), Jose Ortega (Fort Lauderdale, FL), Gary Pellant (Chandler, AZ), Paul Provas (Arlington, TX), John Tumminia (Newburgh, NY).

Latin America Coordinator: Mike Sgobba (Scottsdale, AZ).

International Scouts: Denny Gonzalez (Dominican Republic), Miguel Ibarra (Panama), Hector Rincones (Venezuela).

CLEVELAND

Telephone, Address
Office Address: Jacobs Field, 2401 Ontario St., Cleveland, OH 44115. **Telephone:** (216) 420-4200. **FAX:** (216) 420-4396. **Website:** www.indians.com.

Ownership
Operated by: Richard E. Jacobs Group.

Board of Directors: Robert Brown, Martin Cleary, Raymond Park, Edward Ptaszek, William Summers.

Chairman/Chief Executive Officer: Richard Jacobs. **Vice President:** Martin Cleary.

Richard Jacobs

BUSINESS OPERATIONS
Executive Vice President, Business: Dennis Lehman. **Manager, Human Resources:** Sara Lehrke.

Manager, Spring Training: Jerry Crabb.

Finance
Vice President, Finance: Ken Stefanov.

Director, Corporate Planning/Development: Ron McQuate. **Controller:** Lisa Ostry. **Director, Information Systems:** Dave Powell. **Manager, Accounting:** Karen Menzing. **Network Manager:** Kelly Janda.

Marketing, Sales
Vice President, Marketing/Communications: Jeff Overton.

Senior Director, Corporate Marketing/Broadcasting: Jon Starrett. **Manager, Corporate Marketing:** Chris Previte. **Director, Advertising/Publications:** Valerie Arcuri. **Manager, Advertising/Publications:** Bernadette Repko.

Senior Director, Merchandising/Licensing: Jayne Churchmack. **Manager, Merchandise:** Michael Thom. **Manager, Operations:** Marie Patten.

Manager, Broadcasting/Special Events: Nadine Glinski.

Public Relations, Communications
Telephone: (216) 420-4350. **FAX:** (216) 420-4396.

Vice President, Public Relations: Bob DiBiasio.

Director, Media Relations: Bart Swain. **Manager, Media Relations/Administration:** Susie Giuliano. **Coordinator, Media Relations:** Curtis Danburg. **Press Box Supervisor:** John Krepop.

Coordinator, Public Relations: Angela Brdar.

Director, Community Relations: Allen Davis. **Manager, Community Relations:** Melissa Zapanta.

Stadium Operations
Senior Director, Ballpark Operations: Jim Folk. **Manager, Ballpark Operations:** Mike DeCore. **Manager, Building Maintenance:** Chris Donahoe. **Manager, Field Maintenance:** Brandon Koehnke.

PA Announcer: Mark Tromba. **Official Scorers:** Hank Kosloski, Bill Nichols, Rick Rembielak.

Ticketing
Telephone: (216) 420-4240. **FAX:** (216) 420-4481.

Director, Ticket Services: John Schulze. **Manager, Box Office:** Gail Liebenguth. **Controller, Box Office:** Carolyne Villao. **Director, Ticket Sales:** Scott Sterneckert. **Manager, Ticket Sales:** Larry Abel. **Senior Account Executive:** Dick Sapara.

Travel, Clubhouse
Director, Team Travel: Mike Seghi.

Home Clubhouse/Equipment Manager: Ted Walsh. **Visiting Clubhouse Manager:** Cy Buynak.

General Information
Home Dugout: Third Base. **Playing Surface:** Grass.

Standard Game Times: 7:05 p.m., Sat.-Sun. 1:05.

Stadium Location: From south, I-77 North to East Ninth Street exit, to Ontario Street; From east, I-90/Route 2 west to downtown, remain on Route 2 to East Ninth Street, left to stadium.

Player Representative: Kenny Lofton.

INDIANS

BASEBALL OPERATIONS

Telephone: (216) 420-4305. **FAX:** (216) 420-4321.
Executive Vice President, General Manager: John Hart.

Vice President, Baseball Operations/Assistant General Manager: Mark Shapiro. **Administrator, Player Personnel:** Wendy Hughes. **Executive Administrative Assistant, Baseball Operations:** Ethel LaRue. **Assistant, Baseball Operations:** Chris Antonetti. **Administrative Assistant, Baseball Operations:** Barbara Lessman.

Coordinator, Baseball Systems: Dan Mendlik.

John Hart

Major League Staff

Manager: Mike Hargrove.
Coaches: Pitching—Phil Regan; Batting—Charlie Manuel; Infield—Brian Graham; Outfield—Clarence Jones; Third Base—Jeff Newman; Bullpen—Luis Isaac.

Mike Hargrove

Medical, Training

Medical Director: Dr. William Wilder.
Head Trainer: Paul Spicuzza. **Assistant Trainer:** Jim Warfield. **Strength and Conditioning Coach:** Fernando Montes.

Player Development

Director, Player Development: Neal Huntington. **Assistant Director:** Mike Brown. **Assistant, Player Development:** David Shapiro. **Administrative Assistant:** Joan Pachinger.

Field Coordinator: Boyd Coffie. **Roving Instructors:** Mike Brown (pitching), Al Bumbry (outfield/baserunning), Johnny Goryl (defense), Dave Keller (hitting), Ted Kubiak (infield).

Farm System

Class	Farm Team	Manager	Coach	Pitch Coach
AAA	Buffalo	Jeff Datz	Bill Madlock	Ken Rowe
AA	Akron	Joel Skinner	Eric Fox	Tony Arnold
A	Kinston	Eric Wedge	Mike Sarbaugh	Dave Miller
A	Columbus	Brad Komminsk	Rick Gutierrez	Carl Willis
A	Mahoning Valley	Ted Kubiak	Willie Aviles	Steve Lyons
R	Burlington	Jack Mull	Billy Williams	Sam Militello
R	DSL	Felix Fermin	J. Urena/V. Veras	Juan Jimenez

Scouting

Telephone: (216) 420-4309. **FAX:** (216) 420-4321.
Director, Scouting: Josh Byrnes.
Assistant Director, Scouting: Brad Grant.
Assistant, Scouting Operations: Scott Meaney.

Major League/Special Assignment Scouts: Dan Carnevale (Buffalo, NY), Dom Chiti (Bartlett, TN), Bob Gardner (Oviedo, FL), Tom Giordano (Amityville, NY), Tom McDevitt (Charleston, IL), Jay Robertson (Citrus Heights, CA), Ted Simmons (Chesterfield, MO), Bill Werle (San Mateo, CA).

National Crosschecker: Bill Schmidt (Yorba Linda, CA). **Regional Supervisors:** West—Jesse Flores (Sacramento, CA), East—Jerry Jordan (Wise, VA), Midwest—Bob Mayer (Somerset, PA).

Josh Byrnes

Area Scouts: Steve Abney (Lawrence, KS), Steve Avila (Olympia, WA), Doug Baker (Carlsbad, CA), Keith Boeck (Chandler, AZ), Ted Brzenk (Waukesha, WI), Paul Cogan (Rocklin, CA), Henry Cruz (Fajardo, PR), Jim Gabella (Deltona, FL), Rene Gayo (Galveston, TX), Mark Germann (Chattanooga, TN), Chris Jefts (Redondo Beach, CA), Chad MacDonald (Arlington, TX), Guy Mader (Tewksbury, MA), Chuck Ricci (Germantown, MD), Bill Schudlich (Dearborn, MI), Max Semler (Spanish Fort, AL).

Latin America Supervisors: Luis Aponte (Venezuela), Winston Llenas (Dominican Republic).

DETROIT

Telephone, Address
Office Address: Tiger Stadium, 2121 Trumbull Ave., Detroit, MI 48216. Telephone: (313) 962-4000. FAX: (313) 965-2138. Website: www.detroit-tigers.com.

Ownership
Operated by: Detroit Tigers, Inc.
Principal Owner/Chairman: Mike Ilitch.
President, Chief Executive Officer: John McHale Jr. Assistant to President: Margaret Gramlich.

BUSINESS OPERATIONS
Vice President, Business Operations: David Glazier. Assistant to Vice President: Stephanie Mulrine.
Director, Human Resources: Lara Baremor.

John McHale Jr.

Finance
Senior Director, Finance: Steve Quinn. Controller: Jennifer Marroso. Manager, Payroll Administration: Maureen Kraatz. Corporate Accountant: Steve Dady. Supervisor, Accounts Payable: Christine Edwards.

Marketing, Sales, Merchandising
Manager, Marketing: Howard Krugel. Marketing Coordinator: Holly Moulton.
Manager, Promotions: Joel Scott. Promotions Coordinator: Jodi Kniesteadt.
Director, Season Ticket Sales: Mike Stanfield. Assistant Director, Ticket Sales: Chris Morgan.
Broadcast Coordinator: Kirsten Szlachetka.

Media, Community Relations
Telephone: (313) 965-2114. FAX: (313) 965-2138.
Director, Public Relations: Tyler Barnes. Assistant Director, Public Relations: David Matheson. Coordinator, Public Relations: Giovanni Loria. Administrative Assistant, Public Relations: Christina Branham. Coordinator, Internet: Melanie Waters.
Manager, Community Relations: Celia Bobrowsky. Coordinators, Community Relations: Fred Feliciano, Herman Jenkins.

Stadium Operations
Director, Stadium Operations: Tom Folk.
Supervisor, Stadium Services: Ed Goward. Manager, Guest Services: Jodi Engler. Coordinator, Guest Services: Mary Lehnert.
PA Announcer: Jimmy Barrett. Official Scorer: Unavailable.

Ticketing
Telephone: (313) 963-2050. FAX: (313) 965-2179.
Director, Ticket Services: Ken Marchetti. Assistant Director, Ticket Services: James Cleary.

Travel, Clubhouse
Traveling Secretary: Bill Brown.
Manager, Tiger Clubhouse: Jim Schmakel. Assistant Manager, Visitors Clubhouse: John Nelson. Baseball Video Operations: Tom Progar.

General Information
Home Dugout: Third Base. Playing Surface: Grass.
Standard Game Times: Day—1:05 p.m. Night—7:05, Sat. 5:05.
Stadium Directions: From north, I-75 South to exit 49A, or I-96 East to Lodge Freeway (US 10), to Rosa Parks Boulevard exit; From south, I-75 North to exit 49A; From east, I-94 West to exit 215A, to Lodge Freeway (US 10), to I-75 South, to Trumbull Avenue exit; From west, I-94 East to exit 213B, to Lodge Freeway (US 10), to Rosa Parks Boulevard.
Player Representative: Damion Easley.

TIGERS

BASEBALL OPERATIONS
Telephone: (313) 965-2098. FAX: (313) 965-2099.
Vice President, Baseball Operations/General Manager: Randy Smith.
Special Assistants to General Manager: Al Hargesheimer, Randy Johnson. Assistant to General Manager: Gwen Keating. Assistant, Baseball Operations: Ricky Bennett.

Major League Staff
Manager: Larry Parrish.
Coaches: Defensive Coordinator—Perry Hill; Pitching—Rick Adair; Batting—Alan Trammell; First Base—Juan Samuel; Third Base—Lance Parrish; Bullpen—Jeff Jones.

Randy Smith

Medical, Training
Team Physicians: Dr. David Collon, Dr. Terry Lock, Dr. Michael Workings.
Head Trainer: Russ Miller. Assistant Trainer: Steve Carter. Strength and Conditioning Coach: Brad Andress.

Larry Parrish

Player Development
Telephone, Detroit: (313) 965-2096. FAX: (313) 965-2099. Telephone, Florida Operations: (941) 686-8075. FAX: (941) 688-9589.
Assistant GM/Director, Player Development: Steve Lubratich.
Director, Minor League Operations: Dave Miller. Administrative Assistant, Minor Leagues: Audrey Zielinski.
Coordinator, Instruction: Steve Boros.
Roving Instructors: Glenn Ezell (catching), Mike Humphreys (outfield/baserunning), Marty Martinez (infield), Jon Matlack (pitching), Tom Runnells (hitting).

Farm System

Class	Farm Team	Manager	Coach	Pitching Coach
AAA	Toledo	Gene Roof	Skeeter Barnes	Dan Warthen
AA	Jacksonville	Dave Anderson	Matt Martin	Steve McCatty
A	Lakeland	Mark Meleski	Tim Torricelli	Joe Georger
A	West Michigan	Bruce Fields	Gary Green	Joe Boever
A	Oneonta	Kevin Bradshaw	Unavailable	Unavailable
R	Lakeland	Unavailable	Basilio Cabrera	Greg Sabat
R	DSL	Max Diaz	Felix Nivar	Jose Tapia

Scouting
Telephone: (313) 965-2098. FAX: (313) 965-2099.
Director, Scouting: Greg Smith.
Administrative Assistant, Scouting: Gwen Keating.
Major League Scout: Larry Bearnarth (St. Petersburg, FL).
National Crosschecker: John Mirabelli (Cary, NC). Regional Supervisors: Midwest—Dave Owen (Arlington, TX), Northeast—Rob Guzik (Latrobe, PA), Southeast—Jeff Wetherby (Wesley Chapel, FL), West—Jeff Malinoff (Lopez, WA).
Area Scouts: Bill Buck (Manassas, VA), Tim Grieve (Altamonte Springs, FL), Jack Hays (Lake Oswego, OR), Ray Hayward (Oklahoma City, OK),

Greg Smith

Lou Laslo (Pemberville, OH), Steve Lemke (Lincolnshire, IL), Dennis Lieberthal (Westlake, CA), Mark Monahan (Saline, MI), Pat Murtaugh (Lafayette, IN), Jim Olander (Tucson, AZ), Buddy Paine (Harrison, NY), Rusty Pendergrass (Sugar Land, TX), Derrick Ross (Manchester, CT), Clyde Weir (Allendale, MI), Rob Wilfong (West Covina, CA), Ellis Williams (Colton, CA), Gary York (Rome, GA).
International Scouting: Ramon Pena (Dominican Republic).

KANSAS CITY

Telephone, Address
Office Address: One Royal Way, Kansas City, MO 64129. **Mailing Address:** P.O. Box 419969, Kansas City, MO 64141. **Telephone:** (816) 921-8000. **FAX:** (816) 921-1366. **Website:** www.kcroyals.com.

David Glass

Ownership
Operated by: Kansas City Royals Baseball Club, Inc. **Principal Owner:** Greater Kansas City Community Foundation.

Chairman, Chief Executive Officer: David Glass.

Board of Directors: Richard Green, Michael Herman, Julia Kauffman, Janice Kreamer, Joe McGuff, Louis Smith.

General Counsel/Assistant Secretary: Jay Newcom.

BUSINESS OPERATIONS
Senior Vice President, Business Operations/Administration: Art Chaudry. **VP, Development/Administration:** Lloyd Arnsmeyer.

Senior Director, Stadium Administration: John Johnson. **Director, Human Resources:** Lauris Hawthorne. **Executive Administrative Assistant:** Cindy Hamilton. **Administrator, Human Resouces:** Lynne Elder.

Finance
Vice President, Finance: Dale Rohr.

Senior Director/Controller: John Luther. **Director, Payroll/Benefits Accounting:** Tom Pfannenstiel. **Manager, Accounting:** Scott Stamp. **Senior Administrative Assistant:** Janet Duncan. **Director, Information Systems:** Jim Edwards. **Chief Investment Advisor:** Judith Elsea.

Marketing, Sales
Vice President, Marketing/Communications: Mike Levy.

Director, Marketing: Tonya Mangels. **Coordinator, Marketing:** Kim Hillix. **Administrative Assistant, Marketing:** Patty Bowen.

Director, Corporate Sponsorships: Vernice Givens Monroe. **Manager, Community Relations/Special Markets:** Shani Tate. **Senior Administrative Assistant:** Rachelle Smith. **Administrative Assistant, Communications/Community Relations:** Diana Lehman.

Public Relations, Communications
Telephone: (816) 921-8000. **FAX:** (816) 921-5775.

Senior Director, Communications/Publicity: Jim Lachimia.

Director, Media Relations: Steve Fink. **Coordinator, Media Relations:** Chris Stathos. **Coordinator, Publications/Internet:** Chad Rader.

Stadium Operations
Manager, Stadium Operations: Rodney Lewallen. **Coordinator, Stadium Operations:** Judy VanMeter.

Director, Groundskeeping/Landscaping: Trevor Vance. **Manager, Groundskeeping:** Jonnie Reed.

PA Announcer: Dan Hurst. **Official Scorers:** Del Black, Sid Bordman.

Ticketing
Telephone: (816) 921-8000. **FAX:** (816) 504-4144.

Director, Ticket Operations: Christine Burgeson. **Director, Season Ticket Services:** Joe Grigoli. **Director, Group Sales:** Michelle Kammerer. **Director, Lancer Program:** Larry Sherrard.

Travel, Clubhouse
Director, Team Travel: David Witty.

Equipment Manager: Mike Burkhalter. **Visiting Clubhouse Manager:** Chuck Hawke.

General Information
Home Dugout: First Base. **Playing Surface:** Grass.

Standard Game Times: 7:05 p.m.; Sun. 1:05.

Stadium Location: From north or south, take I-435 to stadium exits. From east or west, take I-70 to stadium exits.

Player Representative: Johnny Damon.

ROYALS

BASEBALL OPERATIONS

Telephone: (816) 921-8000. **FAX:** (816) 924-0347.
Executive Vice President, General Manager: Herk Robinson.
Vice President, Baseball Operations: George Brett. **Vice President/Assistant GM, Baseball Operations:** Allard Baird. **Assistant GM, Baseball Administration:** Jay Hinrichs.
Senior Special Assistant to GM: Art Stewart.
Executive Administrative Assistant: Joanne Snow.

Major League Staff

Manager: Tony Muser.
Coaches: Bench—Jamie Quirk; Pitching—Mark Wiley; Batting—Lamar Johnson; First Base—Frank White; Third Base—Rich Dauer; Bullpen—Tom Burgmeier.

Herk Robinson

Medical, Training

Team Physician: Dr. Steve Joyce.
Head Trainer: Nick Swartz. **Assistant Trainer:** Lee Kuntz. **Coordinator, Strength and Conditioning:** Tim Maxey.

Tony Muser

Player Development

Telephone: (816) 921-8000. **FAX:** (816) 924-0347.
Senior Director, Minor League Operations: Bob Hegman. **Coordinator, Minor League Operations:** Jeff Wood. **Administrative Assistant:** Mindy Walker.
Coordinator, Instruction: Mike Jirschele. **Roving Instructors:** Juan Agosto (pitching), Sixto Lezcano (outfield), Mark Littell (pitching), Brian Poldberg (catching), U.L. Washington (hitting).
Coordinator, Equipment: Mike Crouse. **Coordinator, Rehabilitation:** Frank Kyte. **Assistant Coordinator, Strength/Conditioning:** Chris Sobonya.

Farm System

Class	Farm Team	Manager	Coach	Pitching Coach
AAA	Omaha	Ron Johnson	Bob Herold	Gary Lance
AA	Wichita	John Mizerock	Phil Stephenson	Mike Mason
A	Wilmington	Jeff Garber	Steve Balboni	Steve Crawford
A	Charleston, W.Va.	Tom Poquette	Steve Hosey	Larry Carter
A	Spokane	Kevin Long	Joe Szekely	Randy Smith
R	Baseball City	Andre David	Jose Tartabull	Juan Agosto
R	DSL	Oscar Martinez	Pablo Paredes	Andres Lopez

Scouting

Senior Director, Scouting: Terry Wetzel.
Coordinator, Scouting: Phil Huttmann. **Administrator, Scouting:** Karol Kyte.
Advance Scout: Ron Clark (Largo, FL). **Major League Scout:** Gail Henley (La Verne, CA).
Special Assignment Scouts: Carlos Pascual (Miami, FL), John Wathan (Blue Springs, MO).
Professional Scout: Carl Blando (Lenexa, KS).
National Crosschecker: Steve Flores (Temecula, CA). **Regional Supervisors:** Canada—Jason Bryans (Detroit, MI); East—Pat Jones (Coconut Creek, FL); West—Jeff McKay (Walterville, OR).
Area Scouts: Frank Baez (Los Angeles, CA), Paul Baretta (Kensington, CT), Bob Bishop (San Dimas, CA), Paul Faulk (Raleigh, NC), Albert Gonzalez (Pembroke Pines, FL), Dave Herrera (Danville, CA), Keith Hughes (Berwyn, PA), Gary Johnson (Costa Mesa, CA), Mike Lee (Greenbrier, AR), Cliff Pastornicky (Venice, FL), Bill Price (Austin, TX), Johnny Ramos (Carolina, PR), Wil Rutenschroer (Cincinnati, OH), Chet Sergo (Houston, TX), Greg Smith (Harrington, WA), Craig Struss (Grand Island, NE), Gerald Turner (Euless, TX), Dennis Woody (Pensacola, FL).
Coordinator, Latin America: Luis Silverio (Dominican Republic).

Terry Wetzel

MINNESOTA

Telephone, Address
Office Address: 34 Kirby Puckett Place, Minneapolis, MN 55415. **Telephone:** (612) 375-1366. **Website:** www.twinsbaseball.com.

Ownership
Operated by: The Minnesota Twins.
Owner: Carl Pohlad. **Chairman, Executive Committee:** Howard Fox.
Executive Board: Jerry Bell, Chris Clouser, Carl Pohlad, Eloise Pohlad, James Pohlad, Robert Pohlad, William Pohlad, Kirby Puckett.
President: Jerry Bell.

Carl Pohlad

BUSINESS OPERATIONS
Vice President, Operations: Matt Hoy. **Administrative Assistant to President/Office Manager:** Joan Boeser.

Finance
Chief Financial Officer: Kip Elliott.
Assistant Controller: Angela Meagher. **Payroll Manager:** Lori Beasley. **Accountant:** Jerry McLaughlin. **Accounts Payable:** Marlys Keeney
Vice President, Human Resources/Diversity: Raenell Dorn. **Coordinator, Human Resources:** Leticia Fuentes.
Director, Information Systems: Wade Navratil. **Manager, Network/Baseball Information Systems:** John Avenson.

Marketing, Promotions
Manager, Group Sales: Jon Arends. **Senior Account Sales Executive:** Scott O'Connell. **Account Sales Executives:** Greg Bagan, Jack Blesi, Chris Malek, Wayne Sorensen. **Manager, Sales Administration:** Beth Vail. **Manager, Telemarketing:** Skip Harman. **Assistant Manager, Telemarketing:** Patrick Forsland. **Corporate Sales Executives:** Mike Roslansky, Dick Schultz, George Yunis. **Manager, Advertising:** Wayne Petersen. **Manager, Promotions:** Julie Arndt.

Communications
Telephone: (612) 375-1366. **FAX:** (612) 375-7473.
Vice President, Corporate Communications: Dave St. Peter.
Manager, Media Relations: Sean Harlin. **Assistant Manager, Media Relations:** Brad Smith. **Assistant, Media Relations:** Reed Varner. **Coordinator, Media Relations:** Denise Johnson.
Manager, Community Affairs: Darrell Cunningham. **Coordinators, Community Affairs:** Chad Jackson, Gloria Westerdahl.

Stadium Operations
Manager, Stadium Operations: Ric Johnson. **Assistant Manager, Stadium Operations:** Dave Horsman. **Coordinator, Operations:** Heidi Sammon. **Manager, Security:** Doug Wills. **Managers, Pro Shop:** Mike Pitzen, Dave Strobel.
Head Groundskeeper: Leo Pidde.
PA Announcer: Bob Casey. **Official Scorers:** Tom Mee, Barry Fritz.

Ticketing
Telephone: (612) 338-9467. **FAX:** (612) 375-7464.
Director, Ticket Operations: Paul Froehle. **Assistant Ticket Manager:** Mike Stiles. **Supervisor, Ticket Office:** Karl Dedenbach.

Travel, Clubhouse
Traveling Secretary: Remzi Kiratli.
Equipment Manager: Jim Dunn. **Visitors Clubhouse:** Troy Matchan. **Internal Video Specialist:** Nyal Peterson.

General Information
Home Dugout: Third Base. **Playing Surface:** Artificial turf.
Standard Game Times: 12:15 p.m., 7:05, Sun. 1:05.
Stadium Directions: I-35W south to Washington Avenue exit or I-35W north to Third Street exit. I-94 East to I-35W north to Third Street exit or I-94 West to Fifth Street exit.
Player Representative: Denny Hocking.

TWINS

BASEBALL OPERATIONS
Telephone: (612) 375-1366. **FAX:** (612) 375-7417.
Vice President, General Manager: Terry Ryan.
Executive Vice President, Baseball: Kirby
Puckett. **Vice President, Assistant General
Manager:** Bill Smith. **Assistant General Manager:**
Wayne Krivsky (Arlington, TX). **Special Assistant
to GM:** Joe McIlvaine (Tuckahoe, NY).
Director, Baseball Operations: Rob Antony.
Administrative Assistant, Major League Operations: Juanita Lagos-Benson.

Major League Staff
Manager: Tom Kelly.
Coaches: Pitching—Dick Such; Batting—Scott
Ullger; First Base—Jerry White; Third Base—Ron Gardenhire; Bullpen—
Rick Stelmaszek.

Terry Ryan

Medical, Training
Club Physicians: Dr. Tom Jetzer, Dr. John Steubs.
Head Trainer: Dick Martin. **Assistant Trainer:**
Jim Kahmann. **Strength and Conditioning
Coach:** Randy Popple.

Player Development
Telephone: (612) 375-7488. **FAX:** (612) 375-7417.
Director, Minor Leagues: Jim Rantz. **Administrative Assistant, Minor Leagues:** Colleen
Schroeder.
Field Coordinator: Steve Liddle. **Roving
Instructors:** Jim Dwyer (hitting), Rick Knapp (pitching).

Tom Kelly

Farm System
Class	Farm Team	Manager	Coach	Pitching Coach
AAA	Salt Lake	Phil Roof	Bill Springman	Rick Anderson
AA	New Britain	John Russell	Jeff Carter	Stu Cliburn
A	Fort Myers	Mike Boulanger	Jarvis Brown	Eric Rasmussen
A	Quad City	Jose Marzan	Riccardo Ingram	David Perez
R	Elizabethton	Jon Mathews	Ray Smith	Jim Shellenback
R	Fort Myers	Al Newman	Rob Ellis	Unavailable

Scouting
Telephone: (612) 375-7477. **FAX:** (612) 375-7417.
Director, Scouting: Mike Radcliff.
Administrative Assistant, Scouting: Alison Walk.
Coordinator, Professional Scouting: Vern
Followell (Buena Park, CA).
Special Assignment Scouts: Larry Corrigan
(Fort Myers, FL), Cal Ermer (Chattanooga, TN), Bill
Harford (Chicago, IL).
Scouting Supervisors: East—Earl Frishman
(Tampa, FL); West—Deron Johnson (Antioch, CA);
Midwest—Mike Ruth (Lee's Summit, MO).
Area Scouts: Kevin Bootay (Sacramento, CA),
Ellsworth Brown (Beason, IL), Gene DeBoer
(Brandon, WI), Marty Esposito (Hewitt, TX), John

Mike Radcliff

Leavitt (Garden Grove, CA), Joel Lepel (Plato, MN), Bill Lohr (Centralia,
WA), Lee MacPhail (Tempe, AZ), Gregg Miller (Pratt, KS), Bill Milos (South
Holland, IL), Kevin Murphy (Studio City, CA), Tim O'Neil (Lexington, KY),
Hector Otero (Guaynabo, PR), Mark Quimuyog (Lynn Haven, FL), Ricky
Taylor (Hickory, NC), Brad Weitzel (Haines City, FL), John Wilson (West
Paterson, NJ).
International Scouts: Enrique Brito (Venezuela), Howard Norsetter
(Australia, Canada), Yoshi Okamoto (Japan), Johnny Sierra (Dominican
Republic).

NEW YORK

Telephone, Address
Office Address: Yankee Stadium, 161st Street and River Avenue, Bronx, NY 10451. Telephone: (718) 293-4300. FAX: (718) 293-8431. Website: www.yankees.com.

Ownership
Operated by: New York Yankees.

Principal Owner: George Steinbrenner. General Partners: Stephen Swindal, Harold Steinbrenner.

George Steinbrenner

Limited Partners: Daniel Crown, James Crown, Lester Crown, Michael Friedman, Marvin Goldklang, Barry Halper, John Henry, Daniel McCarthy, Jessica Molloy, Harry Nederlander, James Nederlander, Robert Nederlander, William Rose Jr., Edward Rosenthal, Jack Satter, Henry Steinbrenner, Joan Steinbrenner, Jennifer Swindal, Charlotte Witkind, Richard Witkind.

BUSINESS OPERATIONS
Executive Vice President, General Counsel: Lonn Trost.
Vice President, Business Development: Joseph Perello.
Director, Office Administration: Harvey Winston.

Finance
Vice President, Chief Financial Officer: Marty Greenspan.
Controller: Robert Brown.

Marketing, Public Relations
Director, Marketing: Deborah Tymon.
Director, Community Relations: Brian Smith. Assistant Director, Community Relations: Sean Sullivan. Director, Yankee Alumni Association: Jim Ogle. Director, Entertainment: Stanley Kay. Special Assistant: Joe Pepitone.

Media Relations, Publications
Telephone: (718) 293-4300. FAX: (718) 293-8414.
Special Advisor/Consultant: Arthur Richman.
Director, Media Relations/Publicity: Rick Cerrone. Assistant Director, Media Relations: Jason Zillo.
Director, Publications/Multimedia: Dan Cahalane. Manager, Publications: Kara McGovern.

Stadium Operations
Vice President, Administration: Sonny Hight.
Director, Stadium Operations: Kirk Randazzo. Assistant, Stadium Operations: Bob Pelegrino. Stadium Superintendent: Bob Wilkinson. Head Groundskeeper: Dan Cunningham.
Director, Customer Services: Joel White.
Assistant, Broadcasting/Video Operations: Joe Pullia.
PA Announcer: Bob Sheppard. Official Scorers: Bill Shannon, Red Foley.

Ticketing
Telephone: (718) 293-6000. FAX: (718) 293-4841.
Vice President, Ticket Operations: Frank Swaine. Executive Director, Ticket Operations: Jeff Kline. Ticket Director: Ken Skrypek.

Travel, Clubhouse
Traveling Secretary: David Szen.
Equipment Manager: Rob Cucuzza. Visiting Clubhouse: Lou Cucuzza.

General Information
Home Dugout: First Base. Playing Surface: Grass.
Standard Game Times: 7:35 p.m., Weekends 1:35.
Stadium Directions: From I-95 North, George Washington Bridge to Cross Bronx Expressway to exit 1C, Major Deegan South (I-87) to exit G (161st Street); I-87 North to 149th or 155th Streets; I-87 South to 161st Street.
Player Representative: David Cone.

YANKEES

BASEBALL OPERATIONS

General Manager: Brian Cashman. **Assistant General Manager:** Kim Ng.

Major League Administrator: Tom May. **Special Advisory Group:** Clyde King, Dick Williams.

Major League Staff

Manager: Joe Torre.

Coaches: Dugout—Don Zimmer; Pitching—Mel Stottlemyre; Batting—Chris Chambliss; First Base/Outfield—Jose Cardenal; Third Base/Infield—Willie Randolph; Bullpen—Tony Cloninger.

Medical, Training

Team Physician: Dr. Stuart Hershon. **Head Trainer:** Gene Monahan. **Assistant Trainer:** Steve Donohue. **Strength and Conditioning Coach:** Jeff Mangold.

Brian Cashman

Joe Torre

Player Development

Florida Complex: 3102 N Himes Ave., Tampa, FL 33607. **Telephone:** (813) 875-7569. **FAX:** (813) 873-2302.

Vice President, Player Development/Scouting: Mark Newman.

Director, Player Personnel: Billy Connors. **Special Assistant to GM for Player Development/Scouting:** Stump Merrill.

Director, Baseball Operations: Dan Matheson. **Assistant Director, Baseball Operations/Player Development:** Rigo Garcia. **Administrative Assistant, Baseball Operations:** Mike Walsh.

Coordinator, Instruction: Rob Thomson. **Roving Instructors:** Gary Denbo (hitting), Mick Kelleher (defense), Greg Pavlick (pitching).

Head Trainer: Mark Littlefield. **Strength and Conditioning Coordinator:** Shawn Powell. **Equipment Manager:** Dave Hays. **Clubhouse Manager:** Eric Sims. **Video Coordinator:** Mark Ferrar.

Farm System

Class	Farm Team	Manager	Coach	Pitching Coach
AAA	Columbus	Trey Hillman	Cassady/Robinson	Rick Tomlin
AA	Norwich	Lee Mazzilli	Arnie Beyeler	Tom Filer
A	Tampa	Tom Nieto	Derek Shelton	Rich Monteleone
A	Greensboro	Stan Hough	Tony Perezchica	Steve Webber
A	Staten Island	Joe Arnold	Unavailable	Unavailable
R	Tampa	Ken Dominguez	Hawkins/Lopez	Mark Shiflett
R	DSL	Freddy Tiburcio	Unavailable	Unavailable

Scouting

Telephone: (813) 875-7569. **FAX:** (813) 348-9198.

Director, Scouting: Lin Garrett. **Assistant Director, Scouting:** Tommy Larsen.

Director, International and Professional Scouting: Gordon Blakeley.

Special Assignment Scouts: Ket Barber (Ocala, FL), Mike Naples (Buffalo, NY).

Professional Scouts: Joe Caro (Tampa, FL), Bill Emslie (Safety Harbor, FL), Mick Kelleher (Solvang, CA).

National Crosscheckers: Damon Oppenheimer (Phoenix, AZ), Donny Rowland (Orlando, FL).

Lin Garrett

Area Scouts: Joe Arnold (Lakeland, FL), Mike Baker (Cave Creek, AZ), Mark Batchko (Arlington, TX), Lee Elder (Martinez, GA), Tim Kelly (New Lenox, IL), Greg Orr (Sacramento, CA), Scott Pleis (Lake St. Louis, MO), Cesar Presbott (Bronx, NY), Gus Quattlebaum (Seattle, WA), Joe Robison (Dayton, TX), Phil Rossi (Jessup, PA), Steve Webber (Watkinsville, GA), Leon Wurth (Long Beach, CA), Bill Young (Long Beach, CA).

Coordinator, Pacific Rim Scouting: John Cox (Redlands, CA). **Director, Canadian Scouting:** Dick Groch (Marysville, MI).

OAKLAND

Telephone, Address
Office Address: 7677 Oakport St., Second Floor, Oakland, CA 94621. **Telephone:** (510) 638-4900. **FAX:** (510) 562-1633. **Website:** www.oaklandathletics.com.

Ownership
Operated by: Athletics Investment Group LLC (1996).
Co-Owner/Managing Partner: Steve Schott. **Partner/Owner:** Ken Hofmann.
President: Michael Crowley. **Executive Assistant to President:** Betty Shinoda.

Steve Schott

BUSINESS OPERATIONS
Director, Human Resources: Eleanor Yee.

Finance
Controller: Paul Wong. **Assistant Controller:** Linda Rease.

Marketing, Sales
Senior Director, Sales/Marketing: David Alioto.
Director, Business Services: David Lozow. **Director, Merchandising:** Drew Bruno. **Director, Corporate Advertising Sales:** Franklin Lowe.
Director, Promotions/Special Events: Susan Bress. **Director, Marketing Communications:** Jim Bloom. **Director, Premium Seating/Advertising:** Nancy O'Brien.
Manager, Special Projects/Publications: Audrey Minagawa. **Manager, Spring Training Marketing and Operations:** Travis Dray. **Manager, Multi-cultural Marketing:** Cindy Carrasquilla.

Broadcasting, Communications
Telephone: (510) 563-2207. **FAX:** (510) 562-1633.
Senior Director, Broadcasting/Communications: Ken Pries.
Manager, Baseball Information: Mike Selleck. **Manager, Public Relations:** Eric Carrington. **Manager, Broadcasting:** Robert Buan. **Manager, Community Relations:** Matt Bennett. **Public Relations Assistant:** Debbie Gallas.
Director, Stadium Entertainment: Troy Smith. **Director, Multimedia Services:** David Don. **Diamond Vision Coordinator:** David Martindale.

Stadium Operations
Senior Director, Stadium Operations: David Rinetti.
Director, Game Day Services: Martha Hutchinson. **Manager, Stadium Operations/Facility and Special Events:** Matt Fucile.

Ticketing
Director, Ticket Sales: Dennis Murphy. **Manager, Ticket Sales:** Andy Fiske. **Manager, Box Office/Customer Service:** Steve Fanelli. **Manager, Season Tickets:** Michael Ono. **Manager, Ticket Operations:** Gary Phillips.

Travel, Clubhouse
Director, Team Travel: Mickey Morabito.
Equipment Manager: Steve Vucinich. **Visitors Clubhouse:** Mike Thalblum. **Assistant Equipment Manager:** Brian Davis. **Head Groundskeeper:** Clay Wood.

General Information
Home Dugout: Third Base. **Playing Surface:** Grass.
Standard Game Times: Weekday—1:05 p.m., 7:05, 7:35. Weekend—1:05.
Stadium Location: From San Jose—north on I-880 to Oakland, exit at 66th Avenue; From San Francisco—east on Bay Bridge to I-580 toward Hayward, to downtown Oakland and I-880 south, exit at 66th Avenue; From Sacramento—I-80 west to Oakland, I-580 toward Hayward and I-980 to downtown Oakland, then I-880 South, exit at 66th Avenue.
Player Representative: Matt Stairs.

ATHLETICS

BASEBALL OPERATIONS
General Manager: Billy Beane.
Assistant General Manager: Paul DePodesta. **Assistant to GM:** Dave Seifert. **Special Assistant to General Manager:** Bill Rigney.
Director, Player Personnel: J.P. Ricciardi.
Director, Baseball Administration: Pamela Pitts.

Major League Staff
Manager: Art Howe.
Coaches: Dugout—Ken Macha; Pitching—Rick Peterson; Batting—Dave Hudgens; First Base—Thad Bosley; Third Base—Ron Washington; Bullpen—Brad Fischer.

Billy Beane

Medical, Training
Team Physician: Dr. Allan Pont. **Team Orthopedist:** Dr. Jerrald Goldman.
Head Trainer: Larry Davis. **Assistant Trainer:** Steve Sayles. **Strength and Conditioning Coordinator:** Bob Alejo.

Player Development
Telephone, Oakland: (510) 638-4900. **FAX:** (510) 563-2376.
Arizona Complex: Papago Park Baseball Complex, 1802 N 64th St., Phoenix, AZ 85008. **Telephone:** (602) 949-5951. **FAX:** (602) 945-0557.
Director, Player Development: Keith Lieppman.
Director, Arizona Operations: Ted Polakowski.
Roving Instructors: Orv Franchuk (hitting), Ron Plaza (general), Ron Romanick (pitching).
Minor League Strength and Conditioning Coach: Greg Hauck.

Art Howe

Farm System

Class	Farm Team	Manager	Coach	Pitching Coach
AAA	Vancouver	Mike Quade	Roy White	Pete Richert
AA	Midland	Tony DeFrancesco	Webster Garrison	Glenn Abbott
A	Modesto	Bob Geren	Brian McArn	Rick Rodriguez
A	Visalia	Juan Navarrete	Dave Joppie	Curt Young
A	So. Oregon	Greg Sparks	Billy Owens	Gil Lopez
R	Scottsdale	John Kuehl	Ruben Escalera	Fernando Arroyo
R	DSL I	Evaristo Lantigua	Darwin Hernandez	Leandro Mejia
R	DSL II	Luis Gomez	Tomas Silverio	Nasusel Cabrera

Scouting
Telephone: (510) 638-4900, ext. 2213. **FAX:** (510) 563-2376.
Director, Scouting: Grady Fuson. **Assistant, Scouting:** Danny McCormack.
Special Assignment Scout: Dick Bogard (La Palma, CA). **Advance/Major League Scout:** Bob Johnson (Rockaway, NJ).
National Crosscheckers: Ron Hopkins (Seattle, WA), Chris Pittaro (Hamilton, NJ).
Area Scouts: Steve Bowden (Houston, TX), Tom Clark (Worcester, MA), Ruben Escalera (Villa Carolina, PR), Tim Holt (Dallas, TX), John Kuehl (Fountain Hills, AZ), Rick Magnante (Van Nuys, CA), Gary McGraw (Newberg, OR), Billy Owens

Grady Fuson

(Raleigh, NC), John Poloni (Tarpon Springs, FL), Jim Pransky (Davenport, IA), Will Schock (Oakland, CA), Mike Soper (Tampa, FL), Rich Sparks (Sterling Heights, MI), Ron Vaughn (Corona, CA).
Latin American Supervisor: Karl Kuehl (Fountain Hills, AZ). **Pacific Rim Coordinator:** Eric Kubota (Oakland, CA).
International Scouts: Herberto Andrade (Venezuela), Rafael Espinal (Dominican Republic), Angel Eusebio (Dominican Republic), Julio Franco (Venezuela), Gerardo Santana (Dominican Republic).

Telephone, Address

Office Address: 83 S King St., Seattle, WA 98104. Safeco Field, First and Atlantic, Seattle, WA 98104 (after July 15). **Mailing Address:** P.O. Box 4100, Seattle, WA 98104. **Telephone:** (206) 346-4000. **FAX:** (206) 346-4050.

E-Mail Address: mariners@mariners.org. **Website:** www.mariners.org.

Chuck Armstrong

Ownership

Operated by: Baseball Club of Seattle, LP.

Board of Directors: Minoru Arakawa, John Ellis, Chris Larson, Howard Lincoln, John McCaw, Frank Shrontz, Craig Watjen.

Chairman, Chief Executive Officer: John Ellis. **President, Chief Operating Officer:** Chuck Armstrong.

BUSINESS OPERATIONS

Vice President, Business Development: Paul Isaki. **Vice President, Ballpark Planning and Development:** John Palmer.

Director, Human Resources: Marianne Short.

Finance

Vice President, Finance/Administration: Kevin Mather.

Controller: Tim Kornegay. **Assistant Controller:** Greg Massey. **Systems Director:** Larry Witherspoon.

Director, Merchandising: Todd Vecchio.

Marketing, Sales

Vice President, Business/Sales: Bob Aylward.

Director, Corporate Business: Joe Chard. **Director, Corporate Marketing:** Gail Hunter. **Director, Marketing:** Kevin Martinez. **Manager, Marketing:** Jon Schuller. **Director, Regional Marketing/Community Relations:** David Venneri. **Director, Ticket Sales:** Ron Babes. **New Ballpark Suite Sales:** Moose Clausen.

Public Relations, Communications

Telephone: (206) 346-4000. **FAX:** (206) 346-4400.

Vice President, Communications: Randy Adamack.

Director, Broadcast/Communications: Dave Aust. **Director, Baseball Information:** Tim Hevly. **Director, Public Relations:** Rebecca Hale. **Assistant, Baseball Information:** Brian Tom.

Coordinator, Community Projects: Sean Grindley. **Coordinator, Community Relations:** Gina Hasson.

Ticketing

Telephone: (206) 346-4001. **FAX:** (206) 346-4100.

Director, Ticket Services: Kristin Fortier. **Manager, Ticket Services:** Rob Brautigam. **Manager, Ticket Operations:** Connie McKay. **Coordinator, Group Tickets:** Jennifer Sweigert. **Coordinator, Ticket Sales:** Kasey Marolich. **Coordinator, Suite Sales:** Tristan Baird.

Stadium Operations

Vice President, Ballpark Operations: Neil Campbell. **Director, Ballpark Operations:** Tony Pereira. **Assistant Director, Ballpark Operations:** Kameron Durham. **Manager, Ballpark Engineering/Maintenance:** Mike Allison. **Coordinator, Ballpark Operations:** Sylvia Gonzales.

PA Announcer: Tom Hutyler. **Official Scorer:** Unavailable.

Travel, Clubhouse

Director, Team Travel: Ron Spellecy.

Clubhouse Manager: Scott Gilbert. **Visiting Clubhouse Manager:** Henry Genzale. **Video Coordinator:** Carl Hamilton.

General Information

Home Dugout: Third Base (Kingdome), First Base (Safeco). **Playing Surface:** Artificial turf (Kingdome), Grass (Safeco).

Standard Game Times: 7:05 p.m., Sun. 1:35.

Stadium Location: I-5 or I-90 to Fourth Avenue South exit.

Player Representative: Dan Wilson

MARINERS

BASEBALL OPERATIONS

Vice President, Baseball Operations: Woody Woodward. **Vice President, Scouting/Player Development:** Roger Jongewaard.

Vice President, Baseball Administration: Lee Pelekoudas. **Assistants to Vice President, Baseball Operations:** Larry Beinfest, George Zuraw. **Administrator, Baseball Operations:** Debbie Larsen.

Woody Woodward

Major League Staff

Manager: Lou Piniella.

Coaches: Dugout—Steve Smith; Pitching—Stan Williams; Batting—Jesse Barfield; First Base—Sam Mejias; Third Base—John McLaren; Bullpen—Matt Sinatro.

Lou Piniella

Medical, Training

Medical Director: Dr. Larry Pedegana. **Club Physician:** Dr. Mitch Storey.

Head Trainer: Rick Griffin. **Assistant Trainer:** Tom Newberg. **Strength and Conditioning Coach:** Allen Wirtala.

Player Development

Telephone: (206) 346-4313. **FAX:** (206) 346-4300.

Director, Player Development: Benny Looper. **Assistant Director, Player Development:** Greg Hunter. **Administrator, Player Development:** Jan Plein.

Coordinator, Instruction: Mike Goff. **Roving Instructors:** James Clifford (strength and conditioning), Bryan Price (pitching), Scott Steinmann (catching).

Farm System

Class	Farm Team	Manager	Coach	Pitching Coach
AAA	Tacoma	Dave Myers	Dave Brundage	Jim Slaton
AA	New Haven	Dan Rohn	Henry Cotto	Pat Rice
A	Lancaster	Darrin Garner	Dana Williams	Greg Harris
A	Wisconsin	Steve Roadcap	Omer Munoz	Steve Peck
A	Everett	Terry Pollreisz	Andy Bottin	Rafael Chaves
R	Peoria	Gary Thurman	Tommy Cruz	Gary Wheelock
R	DSL	Ramon de los Santos	Roberto Valdez	Alvarez/Martinez

Scouting

Telephone: (206) 346-4000. **FAX:** (206) 346-4300.

Director, Scouting: Frank Mattox (Long Beach, CA). **Administrator, Scouting:** Hallie Larson.

Advance Scout: John Moses (Issaquah, WA).

Major League Scouts: Brandy Davis (Newark, DE), Bill Kearns (Milton, MA), Steve Pope (Asheville, NC).

Director, Professional Scouting: Ken Compton (Cypress, CA).

National Crosschecker: Steve Jongewaard (Manhattan Beach, CA).

Regional Supervisors: West—Curtis Dishman (San Juan Capistrano, CA); East—John McMichen (Treasure Island, FL); Midwest—Carroll Sembera (Shiner, TX); Canada—Ken Madeja (Novi, MI).

Frank Mattox

Area Scouts: Dave Alexander (Lafayette, IN), Rodney Davis (Glendale, AZ), Phil Geisler (Milwaukie, OR), Des Hamilton (Tulsa, OK), Larry Harper (San Francisco, CA), John Martin (New Port Richey, FL), Tom McNamara (Bronx, NY), Billy Merkel (Columbia, TN), Don Poplin (Norwood, NC), Steve Rath (Newport Beach, CA), Alex Smith (Abingdon, MD), Derek Valenzuela (Lakewood, CA), Kyle Van Hook (Brenham, TX).

Director, Pacific Rim Operations: Jim Colborn (Ventura, CA). **Supervisor, Latin America Scouting:** Fernando Arguelles (Miami, FL).

Telephone, Address

Office Address: Tropicana Field, One Tropicana Dr., St. Petersburg, FL 33705. **Telephone:** (727) 825-3137. **FAX:** (727) 825-3300. **Website:** www.devilray.com.

Ownership

Operated by: Tampa Bay Devil Rays, Ltd. **Principal Owner:** Vincent Naimoli.

BUSINESS OPERATIONS

Senior Vice President, General Counsel: John Higgins.

Manager, Human Resources: Jeep Weber. **Administrator, Human Resources:** Jennifer Thayer.

Vince Naimoli

Finance

Senior VP, Chief Financial Officer: Raymond Naimoli.

Controller: Patrick Smith. **Manager, Accounting:** Sandra Faulkner. **Payroll Supervisor:** Debbie Clement.

Marketing, Sales

Senior VP, Sales/Marketing: Mike Veeck.

Directors, Corporate Marketing: John Browne, Larry McCabe. **Marketing Assistant:** Bina Kumar.

Director, Merchandise: Rob Katz. **Director, Ticket Sales:** Dick Barry. **Director, Sales Operations:** Drew Cloud. **Manager, Suites/Customer Liaison:** Cass Halpin. **Managers, Sponsorship Coordination:** Tammy Atmore, Chris Dean, Kara Emerling.

Public Relations, Communications

Telephone: (727) 825-3242. **FAX:** (727) 825-3111.

Vice President, Public Relations: Rick Vaughn.

Manager, Media Relations: Chris Costello. **Assistant, Media Relations:** Steve Matesich. **Assistant to Vice President, Public Relations:** Carmen Molina.

Director, Publications: Mike Flanagan. **Assistant Director, Publications:** Matt Lorenz.

Director, Community Relations: Julie Williamson. **Assistant Director, Community Relations:** Liz Lauck.

Director, Event Production: John Franzone. **Assistant Event Producer:** Jen Olson. **Team Photographer:** Robert Rogers.

Stadium Operations

VP, Operations/Facilities: Rick Nafe. **Administrative Assistant, Facilities:** Tom Buscemi.

General Manager, Tropicana Field: Bob Leighton. **Building Superintendent:** Robert Gardner. **Event Manager:** Tom Karac. **Event Coordinator:** Scott Kelyman. **Booking Coordinator:** Caren Gramley.

Director, Business Administration: Bill Wiener. **Head Groundskeeper:** Mike Williams. **Director, Audio Visual Services:** Todd Schirmer.

PA Announcer: Bill Couch. **Official Scorers:** Jim Ferguson, Allen Lewis.

Ticketing

Telephone: (727) 825-3250. **FAX:** (727) 825-3294.

Director, Ticket Operations: Robert Bennett. **Assistant Director, Ticket Operations:** Ken Mallory.

Manager, Customer Service: Karen Smith.

Travel, Clubhouse

Traveling Secretary: Jeff Ziegler. **Equipment Manager/Home Clubhouse:** Carlos Ledezma. **Visitors Clubhouse:** Guy Gallagher.

General Information

Home Dugout: First Base. **Playing Surface:** Artificial Turf.

Standard Games Times: 7:05 p.m., Sat. 6:35, Sun. 1:05.

Directions to Stadium: I-275 South to St. Petersburg, exit 11, left onto Fifth Avenue, right onto 16th Street.

Player Representative: Mike Difelice.

DEVIL RAYS

BASEBALL OPERATIONS
Telephone: (727) 825-3170. **FAX:** (727) 825-3365.
Senior Vice President, Baseball Operations/ General Manager: Chuck LaMar.
Assistant GM, Baseball Operations: Bart Braun. **Assistant GM, Administration:** Scott Proefrock.
Special Assistants to General Manager: Eddie Bane (Carlsbad, CA), Bart Johnson (Bridgeview, IL), Bill Livesey (St. Pete Beach, FL). **Executive Assistant to General Manager:** Sandra Dengler.

Chuck LaMar

Major League Staff
Manager: Larry Rothschild.
Coaches: Dugout—Frank Howard; Pitching— Rick Williams; Batting—Leon Roberts; First Base—Billy Hatcher; Third Base—Greg Riddoch; Bullpen—Orlando Gomez.

Medical, Training
Medical Director: Dr. James Andrews. **Club Physicians:** Dr. William Carson, Dr. Koco Eaton, Dr. Michael Reilly.
Head Trainer: Jamie Reed. **Assistant Trainer:** Ken Crenshaw. **Strength and Conditioning Coach:** Kevin Harmon.

Minor Leagues
Telephone: (727) 384-5604. **FAX:** (727) 343-5479.
Director, Minor League Operations: Tom Foley. **Assistant, Player Development:** Mitch Lukevics. **Administrative Assistant, Player Development:** Denise Vega-Smith.

Larry Rothschild

Minor League Coordinators: Buddy Biancalana (infield), Steve Henderson (hitting), Chuck Hernandez (pitching), Tom Mohr (strength/conditioning), Ron Porterfield (medical/rehab).

Farm System
Class	Farm Team	Manager	Coach	Pitching Coach
AAA	Durham	Bill Evers	George Foster	Pete Filson
AA	Orlando	Bill Russell	Steve Livesey	Ray Searage
A	St. Petersburg	Roy Silver	Julio Garcia	Bryan Kelly
A	Charleston, S.C.	Charlie Montoyo	Brad Rippelmeyer	Milt Hill
A	Hudson Valley	Edwin Rodriguez	Unavailable	Unavailable
R	Princeton	Bobby Ramos	Mike Tosar	Steve Mumaw
R	DSL	Manny Castillo	Hector del Pozo	Marcos Matos

Scouting
Telephone: (727) 825-3241. **FAX:** (727) 825-3493.
Director, Scouting: Dan Jennings. **Assistant Director, Scouting:** Mike Hill. **Administrative Assistant, Scouting:** LaRonda Graham.
Major League Scouts: Jerry Gardner (Los Alamitos, CA), Al LaMacchia (San Antonio, TX), Don Lindeberg (Anaheim, CA), Don Williams (Paragould, AR).
National Crosscheckers: Jack Gillis (Sarasota, FL), R.J. Harrison (Phoenix, AZ), Stan Meek (Norman, OK).

Dan Jennings

Area Scouts: Fernando Arango (Oklahoma City, OK), Todd Brown (Mesa, AZ), Skip Bundy (Birmingham, AL), Tim Corcoran (La Verne, CA), Matt Dodd (Boston, MA), Kevin Elfering (Wesley Chapel, FL), Steve Foster (Weston, WI), Doug Gassaway (Blum, TX), Matt Kinzer (Fort Wayne, IN), Paul Kirsch (Tigard, OR), Mark McKnight (Atlanta, GA), Edwin Rodriguez (Mayaguez, PR), Charles Scott (Novato, CA), Craig Weissmann (LaCosta, CA), Doug Witt (St. Petersburg, FL).
Director, International Scouting: Rudy Santin (Miami, FL).

Telephone, Address

Office Address: 1000 Ballpark Way, Arlington, TX 76011. **Mailing Address:** P.O. Box 90111, Arlington, TX 76004. **Telephone:** (817) 273-5222. **FAX:** (817) 273-5206.

Website: www.texasrangers.com.

Ownership

Owner/Chairman: Tom Hicks.

President: Thomas Schieffer. **Assistant to the President:** Nolan Ryan.

BUSINESS OPERATIONS

Vice President, Business Operations/Treasurer: John McMichael.

Tom Schieffer

Vice President, Human Resources: Kimberly Smith. **Vice President, Information Technology:** Steve McNeill. **Assistant Vice President, Controller:** Charles Sawicki. **Assistant Controller:** Susan Capps.

Marketing, Sales

Vice President, Marketing: Charles Seraphin.

Director, Corporate Sales: Mike Phillips. **Director, In-Park Entertainment:** Chuck Morgan. **Director, Merchandising:** Nancy Hill. **Director, Sales:** Ross Scott. **Director, Special Events:** Jennifer Lumley. **Manager, Promotions:** Sherry Flow. **Account Executive:** Jim Cochrane. **Coordinator, Corporate Hospitality:** Melinda Bantz.

Director, Camps and Clinics: Jack Lazorko.

Public Relations, Communications

Telephone: (817) 273-5203. **FAX:** (817) 273-5206.

Vice President, Public Relations: John Blake.

Assistant Director, Public Relations: Brad Horn. **Assistant Director, Public Relations/Community and Ballpark Activities:** Lydia Traina. **Coordinator, Public Relations:** Amy Gunter.

Director, Publications: Michelle Lancaster. **Director, Player Relations:** Taunee Taylor. **Assistant Director, Player Relations:** Dana Wilcox. **Director, Spanish Broadcasting/Latin American Liaison:** Luis Mayoral. **Vice President, Community Development:** Norman Lyons.

Coordinator, Special Projects: Dana Williams. **Coordinator, Community Relations:** Rhonda Houston.

Stadium Operations

Assistant Vice President, Facilities: Billy Ray Johnson.

Director, Ballpark Operations: Kevin Jimison. **Director, Field Operations:** Tom Burns. **Youth Ballpark Groundskeeper:** Andrew Gulley. **Director, Complex Grounds:** Gib Searight. **Director, Security:** John Hardin. **Property Manager:** Anita Handy.

PA Announcer: Chuck Morgan. **Official Scorers:** Kurt Iverson, John Mocek, Steve Weller.

Ticketing

Telephone: (817) 273-5100. **FAX:** (817) 273-5190.

Assistant Director, Ticket Operations: Michael Wood.

Manager, Season/Group Sales: Bob Benson. **Coordinator, Box Office:** David Larson. **Coordinator, Season Sales:** Mike Lentz. **Coordinator, Phone Sales:** Mike Deichert. **Vault Supervisor:** Kelly Livingston. **Customer Service Representative:** Larry Christian.

Travel, Clubhouse

Director, Travel: Chris Lyngos.

Equipment/Home Clubhouse Manager: Zack Minasian. **Visiting Clubhouse Manager:** Joe Macko.

General Information

Home Dugout: First Base. **Playing Surface:** Grass.

Game Times: 7:35 p.m.; Sun. (April-May, Sept.) 2:05, (June-Aug.) 7:05.

Directions to Stadium: From I-30, take Ballpark Way exit, south on Ballpark Way; From Route 360, take Randol Mill exit, west on Randol Mill.

Player Representative: Tim Crabtree.

RANGERS

BASEBALL OPERATIONS
Telephone: (817) 273-5222. FAX: (817) 273-5285.
Executive Vice President, General Manager: Doug Melvin.
Assistant General Manager: Dan O'Brien. Director, Major League Administration: Judy Johns.

Major League Staff
Manager: Johnny Oates.
Coaches: Dugout—Bucky Dent; Pitching—Dick Bosman; Batting—Rudy Jaramillo; First Base—Ed Napoleon; Third Base—Jerry Narron; Bullpen—Larry Hardy.

Doug Melvin

Medical, Training
Medical Director: Dr. John Conway. Team Internist: Dr. Scott Hunter.
Head Trainer: Danny Wheat. Assistant Trainer: Ray Ramirez. Director, Strength and Conditioning: Tim Lang.

Player Development
Telephone: (817) 273-5222. FAX: (817) 273-5285.
Director, Player Development: Reid Nichols.
Assistant Director, Player Development: Alex Smith.
Field Coordinator: Bob Miscik. Roving Instructors: Dick McLaughlin (outfield/baserunning), Al Nipper (pitching), Butch Wynegar (hitting).
Medical Coordinator: Frank Neville.

Johnny Oates

Farm System

Class	Farm Team	Manager	Coach	Pitching Coach
AAA	Oklahoma	Greg Biagini	Bruce Crabbe	Brad Arnsberg
AA	Tulsa	Bobby Jones	None	Lee Tunnell
A	Charlotte	James Byrd	Vince Roman	Eli Grba
A	Savannah	Paul Carey	Jim Murphy	Aris Tirado
R	Pulaski	Bruce Crabbe	Unavailable	Unavailable
R	Port Charlotte	Darryl Kennedy	Carlos Subero	Jaime Garcia

Scouting
Director, Scouting: Chuck McMichael. Assistant to Director, Scouting: Debbie Bent.
Assistant Director, Professional/International Scouting: Monty Clegg.
Advance Scout: Mike Paul (Tucson, AZ).
Professional Scouts: Ray Coley (Gold Canyon, AZ), Toney Howell (Country Club Hills, IL), Bryan Lambe (North Massapequa, NY), Bob Reasonover (Smyrna, TN), Rudy Terrasas (Pasadena, TX).
National Crosscheckers: Tim Hallgren (Chandler, AZ), Dave Klipstein (Eupora, MS), Jeff Taylor (Newark, DE).

Chuck McMichael

Area Scouts: Dave Birecki (Peoria, AZ), Mike Cadahia (Miami, FL), Mike Daughtry (St. Charles, IL), Jay Eddings (Sperry, OK), Kip Fagg (Manteca, CA), Jim Fairey (Clemson, SC), Tim Fortugno (Huntington Beach, CA), Mark Giegler (Fenton, MI), Joel Grampietro (Shrewsbury, MA), Mike Grouse (Independence, MO), Todd Guggiana (Garden Grove, CA), Doug Harris (Carlisle, PA), Bobby Heck (Orlando, FL), Zachary Hoyrst (Tallahassee, FL), Jim Lentine (San Clemente, CA), Randy Taylor (Katy, TX), Greg Whitworth (Dillon, MT).
Latin Coordinator: Manny Batista (Vega Alta, PR).
International Scouts: Hector Acevedo (Dominican Republic), Roney Calderon (Venezuela), Juan Cruz (Colombia), Pedro Gonzalez (Dominican Republic), Court Hall (Germany), Luis Jimenez (Nicaragua), Luis Ortiz (Panama), Graciano Ravelo (Venezuela), Edgar Suarez (Venezuela), Richard Seko (Pacific Rim), Danilo Troncoso (Dominican Republic), Guido Verducci (Southern Europe).

TORONTO

Telephone, Address
Office/Mailing Address: 1 Blue Jays Way, Suite 3200, Toronto, Ontario M5V 1J1. Telephone: (416) 341-1000. FAX: (416) 341-1250. E-Mail Address: bluejay@bluejays.ca. Website: www.bluejays.ca.

Ownership
Operated by: Toronto Blue Jays Baseball Club. Principal Owner: Interbrew SA.
Board of Directors: Allan Chapin, Derek Hayes, Luc Missorten, Hugo Powell, George Taylor.
Chairman/Chief Executive Officer: Sam Pollock.

Sam Pollock

BUSINESS OPERATIONS
Executive Vice President: Bob Nicholson.

Finance
Vice President, Finance and Administration: Susan Quigley.
Controller: Cathy McNamara-MacKay. Manager, Employee Compensation: Perry Nicoletta. Manager, Information Systems: Chris Skyrme.

Sales, Marketing
Director, Corporate Partnerships: Mark Lemmon. Senior Account Executive: Robert MacKay.
General Manager, TBJ Merchandising: Michael Andrejek.

Media Relations, Communications
Telephone: (416) 341-1301/1303. FAX: (416) 341-1250.
Vice President, Media Relations: Howard Starkman.
Assistant Director, Media Relations: Jay Stenhouse. Assistant, Public Relations: Laura Ammendolia.
Director, Communications: Peter Cosentino. Manager, Promotions/Game Entertainment: Janis Davidson Pressick. Manager, Community Relations/Special Events: Laurel Lindsay. Manager, Amateur Baseball/Alumni Affairs: Julian Franklin.

Stadium Operations
Vice President, Sales and Operations: George Holm.
Manager, Game Operations: Mario Coutinho. Manager, Office Services: Anne Fulford. Head Groundskeeper: Tom Farrell.
PA Announcer: Murray Eldon. Official Scorers: Joe Sawchuk, Doug Hobbs, Neil MacCarl, Louis Cauz.

Ticketing
Telephone: (416) 341-1280. FAX: (416) 341-1177.
Assistant Director, Ticket Operations/Box Office Manager: Randy Low. Manager, Group Sales: Maureen Haffey. Manager, Ticket Vault Services: Paul Goodyear. Manager, Subscriber Services: Doug Barr. Manager, Mail Order Services: Sandra Wilbur. Manager, Special Ticket Services: Sheila Cantarutti. Manager, Telephone Order Services: Jan Marshall.

Travel, Clubhouse
Director, Team Travel: John Brioux.
Equipment Manager: Jeff Ross. Clubhouse Operations: Kevin Malloy. Visitors Clubhouse: Len Frejlich.

General Information
Home Dugout: Third Base. Playing Surface: Artificial turf.
Standard Game Times: 7:05 p.m.; Sat. 4:05; Sun. 1:05.
Stadium Location: From west, take QEW/Gardiner Expressway eastbound and exit at Spadina Avenue, go north on Spadina one block, right on Bremner Boulevard. From east, take Gardiner Expressway westbound and exit at Spadina Avenue, north on Spadina one block, right on Bremner Boulevard.
Player Representative: Darrin Fletcher.

BLUE JAYS

BASEBALL OPERATIONS

Telephone: (416) 341-1000. **FAX:** (416) 341-1245.
Executive Vice President, General Manager:
Gord Ash. **Vice President, Baseball:** Bob Mattick.
Senior Advisor, Baseball Operation: Bob Engle.
Assistant General Managers: Tim McCleary, Dave
Stewart. **Director, Baseball Operations:** Bob Nelson.
Director, Employee Assistance Program: Tim
Hewes. **Executive Administrative Assistant:**
Fran Brown.

Gord Ash

Major League Staff

Manager: Tim Johnson.
Coaches: Bench—Jim Lett; Pitching—Mel
Queen; Batting—Gary Matthews; First Base—
Lloyd Moseby; Third Base—Sal Butera; Bullpen—Marty Pevey.

Tim Johnson

Medical, Training

Club Physicians: Dr. Ron Taylor, Dr. Allan
Gross, Dr. Steve Mirabello, Dr. Tony Miniaci.
Head Trainer: Tommy Craig. **Assistant Trainer:**
Scott Shannon. **Strength and Conditioning Coor-
dinator:** Brian McNamee.

Player Development

Telephone: (416) 341-1228. **FAX:** (416) 341-1245.
Director, Player Development: Jim Hoff.
Administrative Assistant: Heather Connolly.
Baseball Assistant: Charlie Wilson.
Roving Instructors: George Bell (hitting), Garth
Iorg (defense), Jeff Krushnell (strength/conditioning),
Rance Mulliniks (hitting), Eddie Rodriguez (infield),
Bruce Walton (pitching), Ernie Whitt (catching).

Farm System

Class	Farm Team	Manager	Coach	Pitching Coach
AAA	Syracuse	Terry Bevington	Hector Torres	Rick Langford
AA	Knoxville	Omar Malave	Randy Phillips	Darren Balsley
A	Dunedin	Rocket Wheeler	Dennis Holmberg	Scott Breeden
A	Hagerstown	Rolando Pino	Ken Landreaux	Hector Berrios
A	St. Catharines	Eddie Rodriguez	Unavailable	Neil Allen
R	Medicine Hat	Paul Elliott	Geovany Miranda	Craig Lefferts
R	DSL	Hilario Soriano	Miguel Rodriguez	Mariano Alcala
R	VSL	Alexis Infante	Hedbertt Hurtado	Lester Straker

Scouting

Telephone: (416) 341-1342. **FAX:** (416) 341-1245.
Director, Scouting: Tim Wilken.
Assistant Director, Scouting: Chris Buckley.
Administrative Assistant, Scouting: Donna Kuzoff.
Advance Scout: Pat Kelly.
Special Assignment Scouts: Chris Bourjos
(Scottsdale, AZ), Duane Larson (Knoxville, TN).
Regional Supervisors: West—Tom Hinkle
(Atascadero, CA); East—Ted Lekas (Worcester,
MA); Central—Mark Snipp (Fort Worth, TX).
Scouting Supervisors: Charles Aliano (West
Hempstead, NY), Tony Arias (Miami Lakes, FL),
Andy Beene (Oak Leaf, TX), David Blume (Elk
Grove, CA), Bus Campbell (Littleton, CO), Rick

Tim Wilken

Cerrone (Boulder City, NV), John Cole (Lake Forest, CA), Jeff Cornell (Lee's
Summit, MO), Ellis Dungan (Pensacola, FL), Joe Ford (Yukon, OK), Tim
Huff (Tulsa, OK), Jim Hughes (Prosper, TX), Ben McLure (Hummelstown,
PA), Marty Miller (Chicago, IL), Bill Moore (Alta Loma, CA), Ty Nichols
(Dodge City, KS), Andy Pienovi (Portland, OR), Jorge Rivera (Puerto
Nuevo, PR), Marteese Robinson (Scottsdale, AZ), Joe Siers (Lexington,
KY), Ron Tostenson (Issaquah, WA), Steve Williams (Raleigh, NC).
Director, International Scouting: Wayne Morgan (Morgan Hill, CA).
Director, Canadian Scouting: Bill Byckowski. **Australian Scouting:** Greg
Wade.

National League

NATIONAL LEAGUE

Mailing Address: 245 Park Ave., New York, NY 10167. Telephone: (212) 339-7700. FAX: Unavailable.

Years League Active: 1876-.

President: Leonard Coleman.

Executive Committee: Claude Brochu (Montreal), Larry Lucchino (San Diego), Peter Magowan (San Francisco).

Senior Vice President, Secretary: Katy Feeney.

Executive Director, Umpires: Paul Runge. Administrator, Umpires: Cathy Davis. Supervisor, Umpires: Tom Lepperd.

Executive Director, Public Relations: Ricky Clemons.

Executive Director, Player Records: Nancy Crofts. Assistant, Media Relations/ Player Records: Moises Rodriguez.

Leonard Coleman

Executive Secretary: Rita Aughavin.

1999 Opening Date: April 4. Closing Date: Oct. 3.

Regular Season: 162 games.

Division Structure: East—Atlanta, Florida, Montreal, New York, Philadelphia. Central—Chicago, Cincinnati, Houston, Milwaukee, Pittsburgh, St. Louis. West—Arizona, Colorado, Los Angeles, San Diego, San Francisco.

Playoff Format: Three division champions and second-place team with best record play in best-of-5 Division Series. Winners meet in best-of-7 League Championship Series.

All-Star Game: July 13 at Boston, MA (American League vs. National League).

Roster Limit: 25, through Aug. 31 when rosters expand to 40.

Brand of Baseball: Rawlings.

Statistician: Elias Sports Bureau, 500 Fifth Ave., New York, NY 10110.

Umpires: Wally Bell (Canfield, OH), Greg Bonin (Broussard, LA), Gerry Crawford (Havertown, PA), Gary Darling (Phoenix, AZ), Bob Davidson (Littleton, CO), Gerry Davis (Appleton, WI), Dana DeMuth (Gilbert, AZ), Bruce Froemming (Vero Beach, FL), Brian Gorman (Camarillo, CA), Eric Gregg (Philadelphia, PA), Tom Hallion (Louisville, KY), Angel Hernandez (Hollywood, FL), Mark Hirschbeck (Stratford, CT), Bill Hohn (Collegeville, PA), Jeff Kellogg (Ypsilanti Township, MI), Jerry Layne (Winter Haven, FL), Randy Marsh (Edgewood, KY), Ed Montague (San Mateo, CA), Larry Poncino (Tucson, AZ), Frank Pulli (Palm Harbor, FL), Ed Rapuano (North Haven, CT), Charlie Reliford (Tampa, FL), Rich Rieker (St. Louis, MO), Steve Rippley (Seminole, FL), Terry Tata (Cheshire, CT), Larry Vanover (Antioch, TN), Joe West (Kitty Hawk, NC), Charlie Williams (Chicago, IL), Mike Winters (Poway, CA).

Stadium Information

City	Stadium	Dimensions			Capacity	'98 Att.
		LF	CF	RF		
Arizona	Bank One Ballpark	330	407	334	48,500	3,600,412
Atlanta	Turner Field	335	401	330	50,528	3,361,350
Chicago	Wrigley Field	355	400	353	38,884	2,623,000
Cincinnati	Cinergy Field	330	404	330	52,953	1,793,679
Colorado	Coors Field	347	415	350	50,200	3,789,347
Florida	Pro Player Stadium	335	410	345	40,585	1,750,395
Houston	Astrodome	325	400	325	54,370	2,450,451
Los Angeles	Dodger Stadium	330	395	330	56,000	3,089,201
Milwaukee	County Stadium	315	402	315	53,192	1,811,548
Montreal	Olympic Stadium	325	404	325	46,500	914,717
New York	Shea Stadium	338	410	338	55,777	2,287,942
Philadelphia	Veterans Stadium	330	408	330	62,363	1,715,702
Pittsburgh	Three Rivers	335	400	335	48,044	1,560,950
St. Louis	Busch Stadium	330	402	330	49,676	3,194,092
San Diego	Qualcomm Stadium	327	405	327	46,510	2,555,901
San Francisco	3Com Park	335	400	328	63,000	1,925,634

ARIZONA

Telephone, Address

Office Address: Bank One Ballpark, 401 E Jefferson St., Phoenix, AZ 85004. **Mailing Address:** P.O. Box 2095, Phoenix, AZ 85001. **Telephone:** (602) 462-6500. **FAX:** (602) 462-6599. **Website:** www.azdiamondbacks.com.

Ownership

Operated by: AZPB Limited Partnership.
Chairman: Jerry Colangelo.
Advisory Committee: George Getz, Dale Jensen, David Moore, Jerry Moyes, Rich Stephan.

BUSINESS OPERATIONS

Jerry Colangelo

President: Richard Dozer. **Assistant to President:** Michelle Avella.
General Counsel: Jane Birge.
Director, Human Resources: Cheryl Naumann.

Finance

Vice President, Finance: Tom Harris.
Controller: Larry White. **Director, Management Information Systems:** Bill Bolt. **Manager, Accounting:** Barbara Ragsdale. **Office Manager:** Pat Perez.

Marketing, Sales

Senior Vice President, Sales and Marketing: Scott Brubaker.
Vice President, Sales: Blake Edwards.
Director, Hispanic Marketing: Richard Saenz. **Director, Tucson Operations:** Mark Fernandez. **Director, Broadcasting:** Scott Geyer. **Manager, Broadcast Services:** Leo Gilmartin. **Manager, Marketing:** Gina Giallonardo. **Assistant, Marketing:** Kelly Wilson.

Public Relations, Communications

Telephone: (602) 462-6519. **FAX:** (602) 462-6527.
Director, Public Relations: Mike Swanson. **Manager, Media Relations:** Bob Crawford. **Media Coordinator:** Brenda Morse. **Assistants, Media Relations:** Chris Haydock, Jeff Munn, David Pape. **Editor, Diamondbacks Magazine:** Joel Horn.
Director, Community Affairs: Craig Pletenik. **Manager, Community Affairs:** Veronica Zendejas. **Manager, Corporate Alliances:** Susan Hirohata.

Stadium Operations

President/General Manager: Bob Machen.
Vice President/Assistant GM: Alvan Adams. **Director, Operations:** Gary Rich. **Director, Engineering:** John Hansen. **Director, Ballpark Services:** Russ Amaral. **Director, Suite Services:** Diney Mahoney. **Director, Ballpark Attractions:** Charlene Vazquez-Inzunza.
Head Groundskeeper: Grant Trenbeath.
PA Announcer: Jeff Munn. **Official Scorers:** Bob Eger, Gary Rausch.

Ticketing

Telephone: (602) 514-8400. **FAX:** (602) 462-4141.
Vice President, Ticket Operations and Special Services: Dianne Aguilar.
Director, Sales: Rob Kiese. **Director, Ticket Operations:** Darrin Mitch.

Travel, Clubhouse

Director, Team Travel: Roger Riley.
Equipment Manager/Home Clubhouse: Chris Guth. **Vistitors Clubhouse:** Bob Doty.

General Information

Home Dugout: Third Base. **Playing Surface:** Grass.
Standard Game Times: 7:05 p.m., Sun. 1:05, 5:05.
Directions to Stadium: Exit at Seventh Street from I-10 and turn south, or I-17 and turn north.
Player Representative: Brian Anderson.

DIAMONDBACKS

BASEBALL OPERATIONS

Telephone: (602) 462-6000. **FAX:** (602) 462-6599.
Vice President, General Manager: Joe Garagiola Jr.

Senior Executive Vice President, Baseball Operations: Roland Hemond. **Assistant General Manager:** Sandy Johnson. **Senior Assistant to General Manager:** Mel Didier. **Director, Baseball Administration:** Ralph Nelson. **Special Assistants to GM:** Shooty Babitt, Ron Hassey, Dick Scott.

Director, Pacific Rim Operations: Jim Marshall. **Business Manager, Baseball Operations:** Craig Bradley.

Joe Garagiola Jr.

Buck Showalter

Major League Staff

Manager: Buck Showalter.

Coaches: Bench—Carlos Tosca; Pitching—Mark Connor; Batting—Jim Presley; First Base—Dwayne Murphy; Third Base—Brian Butterfield; Bullpen—Glenn Sherlock.

Medical, Training

Club Physicians: Dr. David Zeman, Dr. Roger McCoy.

Head Trainer: Paul Lessard. **Assistant Trainer:** Dave Edwards. **Strength and Conditioning Coach:** Jeff Forney.

Minor Leagues

Telephone: (602) 462-6500. **FAX:** (602) 462-6527.
Director, Minor League Operations: Tommy Jones. **Coordinator, Player Records:** Alyssa Johnson.

Field Coordinator: Bobby Dickerson. **Roving Instructors:** Roly de Armas (catching), Rafael Landestoy (outfield/baserunning), Bob Mariano (hitting), Gil Patterson (pitching).

Farm System

Class	Farm Team	Manager	Coach	Pitching Coach
AAA	Tucson	Chris Speier	Mike Barnett	Chuck Kniffin
AA	El Paso	Don Wakamatsu	Ty Van Burkleo	Dennis Lewallyn
A	High Desert	Derek Bryant	Rick Schu	Mike Parrott
A	South Bend	Mike Brumley	Vic Ramirez	Dave Jorn
R	Missoula	Joe Almaraz	Rafael Landestoy	Royal Clayton
R	Tucson	Roly de Armas	Luis Medina	Mark Davis
R	DSL	Andres Thomas	Gregorio Ramirez	Pablo Frias

Scouting

Director, Scouting: Don Mitchell.

Assistant Director, Scouting: Bob Miller. **Administrative Assistant, Scouting:** Lisa Ventresca.

Professional Scouts: Brannon Bonifay (Okeechobee, FL), Ed Durkin (Safety Harbor, FL), Bill Earnhart (Point Clear, AL), Julian Mock (Peachtree City, GA).

National Coordinator: Kendall Carter.

National Supervisors: East—Howard McCullough (Greenville, NC); Central—Mike Rizzo (Rolling Meadows, IL); West—Steve Springer (Huntington Beach, CA).

Area Supervisors: David Cassidy (Torrance, CA), Arnold Cochran (Ponce, PR), Ray Corbett (College Station, TX), Jason Goligoski (Vancouver, WA), Brian Guinn (Richmond, CA), Scott Jaster (Midland, MI), James Keller (Long Beach, CA), Chris Knabenshue (Edmond, OK), Greg Lonigro (Connellsville, PA), David May (Newark, DE), Luis Medina (Phoenix, AZ), Matt Merullo (Madison, CT), Mike Piatnik (Winter Haven, FL), Mac Seibert (Molino, FL), Steve Swail (Macon, GA), Mike Valarezo (Cantonment, FL), Brad Vaughn (Griffithville, AR), Harold Zonder (Louisville, KY).

International Coordinator: Clay Daniel. **Latin American Coordinator:** Junior Noboa.

Don Mitchell

ATLANTA

Telephone, Address
Office Address: 755 Hank Aaron Dr., Atlanta, GA 30315. Mailing Address: P.O. Box 4064, Atlanta, GA 30302. Telephone: (404) 522-7630. FAX: (404) 614-1391. Website: www.atlantabraves.com.

Stan Kasten

Ownership
Operated by: Atlanta National Baseball Club, Inc.

Principal Owner: Ted Turner. Chairman: Bill Bartholomay.

Board of Directors: Henry Aaron, Bill Bartholomay, Bobby Cox, Stan Kasten, Rubye Lucas, Terry McGuirk, John Schuerholz, M.B. Seretean, Ted Turner.

President: Stan Kasten.

Senior Vice President, Assistant to President: Henry Aaron.

BUSINESS OPERATIONS
Senior Vice President, Administration: Bob Wolfe. Team Counsel: David Payne. Director, Human Resources: Michele Thomas.

Finance
Vice President, Controller: Chip Moore.

Marketing, Sales
Vice President, Marketing/Broadcasting: Wayne Long.

Senior Director, Promotions/Civic Affairs: Miles McRea. Director, Ticket Sales: Paul Adams. Director, Community Relations: Cara Maglione. Director, Braves Foundation: Danny Goodwin.

Public Relations, Communications
Telephone: (404) 614-1302. FAX: (404) 614-1391.

Director, Public Relations: Jim Schultz.

Manager, Media Relations: Glen Serra. Assistants, Public Relations: Joan Hicks, Steve Copses, Robert Gahagan, Kim Ziegler.

Stadium Operations
Director, Stadium Operations/Security: Larry Bowman. Field Director: Ed Mangan.

PA Announcer: Bill Bowers. Official Scorer: Mark Frederickson.

Director, Audio-Video Operations: Jennifer Berger.

Ticketing
Telephone: (800) 326-4000. FAX: (404) 614-1391.

Director, Ticket Operations: Ed Newman.

Travel, Clubhouse
Director, Team Travel/Equipment Manager: Bill Acree. Visiting Clubhouse Manager: John Holland.

General Information
Home Dugout: First Base. Playing Surface: Grass.

Standard Game Times: 7:40 p.m.; Sat. 7:10, Sun. 1:10.

Directions to Stadium: I-75/85 northbound/southbound, take exit 91 (Fulton Street); I-20 westbound, take exit 24 (Capitol Avenue); I-20 eastbound, take exit 22 (Windsor Street), right on Windsor Street, left on Fulton Street.

Player Representative: Tom Glavine.

BRAVES

BASEBALL OPERATIONS
Telephone: (404) 522-7630. **FAX:** (404) 523-3962.
Executive Vice President, General Manager: John Schuerholz.

Assistant General Manager: Dean Taylor. **Special Assistant to GM/Player Development:** Jose Martinez. **Executive Assistant:** June Cornillaud. **Administrative Coordinator:** Linda Smith.

Major League Staff
Manager: Bobby Cox.

Coaches: Dugout—Pat Corrales; Pitching—Leo Mazzone; Batting—Don Baylor; First Base—Glenn Hubbard; Third Base—Ned Yost; Bullpen—Bobby Dews.

John Schuerholz

Bobby Cox

Medical, Training
Team Physician: Dr. David Watson. **Trainer:** Dave Pursley. **Assistant Trainer:** Jeff Porter. **Strength and Conditioning Coach:** Frank Fultz.

Player Development
Telephone: (404) 614-1323. **FAX:** (404) 614-1350.
Director, Scouting/Player Development: Paul Snyder.

Director, Minor League Operations: Deric Ladnier. **Special Assistant, Scouting/Player Development:** Guy Hansen. **Assistant, Baseball Operations:** Tyrone Brooks. **Administrative Assistants, Minor Leagues:** Lena Burney, Kathy Miller.

Field Coordinator: Chino Cadahia. **Coordinator, Dominican Republic:** Pedro Gonzalez. **Roving Instructors:** Jim Beauchamp (outfield), Phil Falco (strength and conditioning), Frank Fultz (fitness), Jerry Nyman (pitching), Franklin Stubbs (hitting).

Farm System
Class	Farm Team	Manager	Coach	Pitching Coach
AAA	Richmond	Randy Ingle	Mel Roberts	Bill Fischer
AA	Greenville	Paul Runge	Bobby Moore	Mike Alvarez
A	Myrtle Beach	Brian Snitker	Dan Norman	Bruce Dal Canton
A	Macon	Jeff Treadway	Tommy Gregg	Kent Willis
A	Jamestown	Jim Saul	Manny Jimenez	Mark Ross
R	Danville	J.J. Cannon	Ralph Henriquez	Jerry Nyman
R	Orlando	Rick Albert	Edinson Renteria	Perez/Watt
R	DSL	Dario Paulino	Thomas Vasquez	Andres Mena

Scouting
Director, Scouting: Paul Snyder. **Assistant Director, Scouting:** Dayton Moore.

Advance Scout: Bobby Wine (Norristown, PA).

Special Assignment Scouts: Dick Balderson (Aurora, CO), Bill Lajoie (Osprey, FL), Brian Murphy (Sarasota, FL), Scott Nethery (Houston, TX).

National Crosscheckers: Roy Clark (Martinsville, VA), Bob Wadsworth (Westminster, CA).

Regional Supervisors: East—Hep Cronin (Cincinnati, OH); Midwest—John Flannery (Austin, TX); West—Butch Baccala (Windsor, CA).

Area Scouts: Mike Baker (Santa Ana, CA), Stu Cann (Bradley, IL), Sherard Clinkscales (Indianapolis, IN), Bob Dunning (Phoenix, AZ), Rob English (Duluth, GA), Rene Francisco (Lake Worth, FL), Ralph Garr (Missouri City, TX), Rod Gilbreath (Lilburn, GA), John Hagemann (Staten Island, NY), Dexter Harris (Chambersburg, PA), J. Harrison (Sacramento, CA), Ray Jackson (Hoover, AL), Kurt Kemp (Eugene, OR), Brian Kohlscheen (Norman, OK), Al Kubski (Carlsbad, CA), Robert Lucas (Atlanta, GA), Jim Martz (Lima, OH), Marco Paddy (Palm Coast, FL), John Ramey (Murrieta, CA), Charlie Smith (Austin, TX), Doug Smith (Fairfield, OH), John Stewart (Granville, NY), Junior Vizcaino (Wake Forest, NC).

International Supervisor: Bill Clark (Columbia, MO).

Paul Snyder

Telephone, Address

Office Address: Wrigley Field, 1060 W Addison St., Chicago, IL 60613. **Telephone:** (773) 404-2827. **FAX:** (773) 404-4129. **E-Mail Address:** cubs@cubs.com. **Website:** www.cubs.com.

Ownership

Operated by: Chicago National League Ball Club, Inc. **Owner:** Tribune Company.

Board of Directors: James Dowdle, Andy MacPhail, Andrew McKenna.

President/Chief Executive Officer: Andy MacPhail.

BUSINESS OPERATIONS

Andy MacPhail

Executive Vice President, Business Operations: Mark McGuire.

Manager, Information Systems: Carl Rice.

PC Systems Analyst: Kyle Hoker. **Senior Legal Counsel/Corporate Secretary:** Crane Kenney. **Executive Secretary, Business Operations:** Annette Hannah.

Director, Human Resources: Jenifer Surma.

Finance

Controller: Jodi Norman. **Manager, Accounting:** Terri Lynn. **Payroll Administrator:** Mary Jane Iorio. **Senior Accountant:** Peter Huynh.

Marketing, Broadcasting

Vice President, Marketing/Broadcasting: John McDonough.

Director, Promotions/Advertising: Jay Blunk. **Manager, Cubs Care/Community Relations:** Rebecca Polihronis. **Coordinator, Cubs Care/Community Relations:** Mary Dosek. **Manager, Mezzanine Suites:** Louis Artiaga. **Manager, Sponsorship Sales:** Susan Otolski.

Media Relations, Publications

Telephone: (773) 404-4191. **FAX:** (773) 404-4129.

Director, Media Relations: Sharon Pannozzo. **Coordinator, Media Information:** Chuck Wasserstrom. **Assistant, Media Relations:** Benjamin de la Fuente.

Director, Publications/Special Projects: Ernie Roth. **Editorial Specialists, Publications:** Jim McArdle, Jay Rand. **Graphic Design Specialist:** Joaquin Castillo. **Internet Coordinator:** John Davila. **Photographer:** Stephen Green.

Stadium Operations

Director, Stadium Operations: Paul Rathje.

Manager, Event Operations/Security: Mike Hill. **Coordinator, Event Operations/Security:** Julius Farrell. **Head Groundskeeper:** Roger Baird. **Facility Supervisor:** Bill Scott. **Coordinator, Office Services:** Randy Skocz. **Coordinator, Stadium Operations:** Danielle Alexa. **Switchboard Operator:** Brenda Morgan.

PA Announcer: Paul Friedman. **Official Scorers:** Bob Rosenberg, Don Friske.

Ticketing

Telephone: (773) 404-2827. **FAX:** (773) 404-4014.

Director, Ticket Operations: Frank Maloney. **Assistant Director, Ticket Sales:** Brian Garza. **Assistant Director, Ticket Services:** Joe Kirchen. **Vault Room Supervisor:** Cherie Blake.

Travel, Clubhouse

Traveling Secretary: Jimmy Bank.

Equipment Manager: Yosh Kawano. **Assistant Equipment Manager:** Dana Noeltner. **Visiting Clubhouse Manager:** Tom Hellmann.

General Information

Home Dugout: Third Base. **Playing Surface:** Grass.

Standard Game Times: 1:20 p.m., 7:05; Sat. 12:15, 1:20, 3:05; Sun. 1:20.

Stadium Location: From I-90/94 take Addison Street exit, follow Addison five miles to ballpark. One mile west of Lakeshore Drive—exit at Belmont going northbound; exit at Irving Park going southbound.

Player Representative: Steve Trachsel.

CUBS

BASEBALL OPERATIONS
Telephone: (773) 404-4037. **FAX:** (773) 404-4111.
Vice President, General Manager: Ed Lynch.
Assistant General Manager: David Wilder.
Director, Baseball Operations: Scott Nelson.
Special Assistants to General Manager: Larry Himes (Mesa, AZ), Ken Kravec (Sarasota, FL).

Executive Assistant to President and General Manager: Arlene Gill. **Baseball Operations Assistant:** Michelle Blanco.

Ed Lynch

Major League Staff
Manager: Jim Riggleman.
Coaches: Bench—Billy Williams; Pitching—Marty DeMerritt; Batting—Jeff Pentland; First Base—Dan Radison; Third Base—Tom Gamboa; Bullpen—Dave Bialas.

Medical, Training
Team Physicians: Dr. John Marquardt, Dr. Michael Schafer.

Head Trainer: David Tumbas. **Assistant Trainer:** Steve Melendez. **Physical Development Coordinator:** Bruce Hammel.

Player Development
Telephone: (773) 404-4035. **FAX:** (773) 404-4147.
Director, Player Development and Scouting: Jim Hendry.
Assistant, Minor League Operations: Patti Kargakis.
Coordinator, Instruction: Alan Regier.
Roving Instructors: Sandy Alomar Sr. (infield), Randy Bush (hitting), Jimmy Piersall (outfield), Lester Strode (pitching).
Equipment Manager: Michael Burkhart.

Jim Riggleman

Farm System

Class	Farm Team	Manager	Coach	Pitching Coach
AAA	Iowa	Terry Kennedy	Glenn Adams	Rick Kranitz
AA	West Tenn	Dave Trembley	Tack Wilson	Alan Dunn
A	Daytona	Nate Oliver	Richie Zisk	Rick Tronerud
A	Lansing	Oscar Acosta	Steve McFarland	Stan Kyles
A	Eugene	Bob Ralston	Damon Farmar	Tom Pratt
R	Mesa	Carmelo Martinez	John Pierson	Jose Santiago
R	DSL	Julio Valdez	Unavailable	Leo Hernandez

Scouting
Telephone: (773) 404-4034. **FAX:** (773) 404-4147.
Coordinator, Scouting: John Stockstill.
Secretary, Scouting: Patricia Honzik.
Major League Advance Scout: Keith Champion (Ballwin, MO). **Special Player Consultant:** Hugh Alexander (Brooksville, FL). **Scouting Consultant:** Vedie Himsl. **Major League Scout:** Bill Harford.

Regional Supervisors: East—Joe Housey (Hollywood, FL); Central—Brad Kelley (Glendale, AZ); West—Larry Maxie (Upland, CA).

Area Scouts: Mark Adair (Fairfield, OH), Billy Blitzer (Brooklyn, NY), Jim Crawford (Columbia, TN), Steve Fuller (Brea, CA), Al Geddes (Canby, OR), John Gracio (Chandler, AZ), Gene Handley (Huntington Beach, CA), Steve Hinton (Sacramento, CA), Sam Hughes (Marietta, GA), Spider Jorgensen (Rancho Cucamonga, CA), Buzzy Keller (Seguin, TX), Scott May (Wonder Lake, IL), Brian Milner (Edgecliff Village, TX), Fred Petersen (Glendale, CA), Marc Russo (Mooresville, NC), Mark Servais (La Crosse, WI), Tom Shafer (Hartford, CT), Billy Swoope (Norfolk, VA), Harry Von Suskil (Coral Gables, FL).

Director, International Scouting: Oneri Fleita (Omaha, NE).
Coordinator, Pacific Rim: Leon Lee (Folsom, CA).

Jim Hendry

CINCINNATI

Telephone, Address
Office Address: 100 Cinergy Field, Cincinnati, OH 45202. **Telephone:** (513) 421-4510. **FAX:** (513) 421-7342. **Website:** www.cincinnatireds.com.

Ownership
Operated by: The Cincinnati Reds, Inc.
General Partner: Marge Schott.
Partners: Gannett Co., Inc.; Carl Kroch; Carl Lindner; Mrs. Louis Nippert; William Reik Jr.; George Strike.
Managing Executive: John Allen.

John Allen

BUSINESS OPERATIONS
General Counsel, Treasurer: Robert Martin.
Executive Assistant, Administrative Offices: Joyce Pfarr.

Finance
Controller: Anthony Ward. **Systems Analyst:** Kelly Gronotte. **Payroll Supervisor:** Cathy Secor. **Accounts Payable/Receivable:** Kelly Whitelaw. **Administrative Assistant, Accounting:** Lois Wingo.

Marketing, Sales
Director, Marketing: Cal Levy. **Assistants, Marketing:** Jen Black, Beth Giadura, Molly Mott.
Director, Season Ticket Sales: Pat McCaffrey. **Director, Group Sales:** Barbara McManus. **Assistant, Group Sales:** Brad Callahan. **Sales Representatives, Season Tickets:** Brad Blettner, Shannon Bohman, Chris Herrell.

Public Relations, Communications
Telephone: (513) 421-2990. **FAX:** (513) 421-7342.
Director, Media Relations: Rob Butcher. **Assistant Director, Media Relations:** Mark Walpole. **Assistant, Public Relations:** Larry Herms.
Director, Communications: Mike Ringering.

Stadium Operations
Director, Stadium Operations: Jody Pettyjohn. **Superintendent, Stadium Operations:** Bob Harrison. **Stadium Superintendent:** Jeff Guilkey. **Administrative Assistant, Stadium Operations:** Mitzi Harmeyer. **Switchboard Supervisor:** Lauren Gaghan.
Director, Field Maintenance: Dennis McMullen.
PA Announcer: John Walton. **Official Scorers:** Ron Roth, Glenn Sample.

Ticketing
Telephone: (513) 421-4510. **FAX:** (513) 421-7342.
Director, Ticket Operations: John O'Brien. **Assistant Ticket Director:** Ken Ayer. **Customer Service:** Coleen Brown, Hallie Kinney. **Administrative Assistant, Season Tickets:** Cyndi Strzynski.

Travel, Clubhouse
Traveling Secretary: Gary Wahoff.
Equipment Manager: Bernie Stowe. **Home Clubhouse:** Rick Stowe. **Visitors Clubhouse:** Mark Stowe.

General Information
Home Dugout: First Base. **Playing Surface:** Artificial turf.
Standard Game Times: 7:05 p.m.; Sat. 1:15, 7:05, Sun. 1:15.
Stadium Location: From I-75 South, exit onto I-71 North, exit at Pete Rose Way (exit 1B), left off ramp; From I-71 South, go left at Vine Street/Covington (exit 1C), right off ramp onto Third Street, right on Broadway, right onto Mehring Way. From I-75/I-71 North, cross over Brent Spence Bridge, exit at Pete Rose Way (exit 1B), left off ramp.
Player Representative: Brook Fordyce.

REDS

BASEBALL OPERATIONS
Telephone: (513) 421-4510. FAX: (513) 579-9145.
General Manager: Jim Bowden.
Assistant General Manager: Darrell "Doc" Rodgers. Executive Assistant to General Manager: Lois Schneider.
Director, Baseball Administration: Brad Kullman.

Major League Staff
Manager: Jack McKeon.
Coaches: Dugout—Ken Griffey Sr.; Pitching—Don Gullett; Batting—Denis Menke; First Base—Ron Oester. Third Base—Harry Dunlop; Bullpen—Tom Hume.

Jim Bowden

Medical, Training
Medical Director: Dr. Tim Kremchek.
Head Trainer: Greg Lynn. Assistant Trainer: Mark Mann. Director, Strength and Conditioning: Lance Sewell.

Player Development
Senior Director, Player Development/Scouting: Leland Maddox. Senior Advisor, Player Development: Chief Bender.
Director, Player Development: Muzzy Jackson. Administrative Assistant, Player Development: Lois Hudson.
Field Coordinator: Buddy Bell. Assistant Field Coordinator: Bill Doran (infield). Roving Instructors: Dave Collins (outfield/baserunning), Sammy Ellis (pitching), Toby Harrah (hitting), Jim Hickman (hitting), Jim Thrift (offense).

Jack McKeon

Farm System

Class	Farm Team	Manager	Coach	Pitching Coach
AAA	Indianapolis	Dave Miley	Mark Berry	Grant Jackson
AA	Chattanooga	Phillip Wellman	Unavailable	Mack Jenkins
A	Rockford	Mike Rojas	Unavailable	Derek Botelho
A	Clinton	Freddie Benavides	Unavailable	Andre Rabouin
R	Billings	Russ Nixon	Brian Wilson	Terry Abbott
R	Sarasota	Donnie Scott	L. Diaz/L. Miller	Jeff Gray
R	DSL	Jose Moreno	Roberto Valdez	Jose Duran

Scouting
Telephone: (513) 421-4510. FAX: (513) 579-9145.
Director, Scouting: DeJon Watson.
Director, Scouting Administration: Wilma Mann. Senior Advisor, Scouting: Bob Zuk (Redlands, CA).
Advance Scout: Gene Bennett (Wheelersburg, OH). Special Assignment Scouts: Larry Barton (Leona Valley, CA), Johnny Bench (Cincinnati, OH), Bob Boone (Villa Park, CA), Al Goldis (Sarasota, FL), Kasey McKeon (Burlington, NC).
Regional Crosscheckers: Latin America/Mexico—Johnny Almaraz (Spring Branch, TX); West—Jeff Barton (Gilbert, AZ); Central—Alvin Rittman (Memphis, TN).

DeJon Watson

Scouting Supervisors: Ray Bellino (Freehold, NJ), Howard Bowens (Tacoma, WA), John Brickley (Melrose, MA), Robert Filotei (Wilmer, AL), Jerry Flowers (Dolton, IL), Jimmy Gonzales (San Antonio, TX), Dick Hager (Sunnyvale, CA), David Jennings (St. Charles, MO), Robert Koontz (McConnellsburg, PA), Steve Kring (Charlotte, NC), Mike Mangan (Clermont, FL), Brian Mejia (Miami, FL), Ross Sapp (Cherry Valley, CA), Bill Scherrer (Buffalo, NY), Tom Severtson (Denver, CO), Bob Szymkowski (Dyer, IN), Marion Trumbo (Bluemont, VA), Mike Wallace (Escondido, CA), Brian Wilson (Albany, TX).

COLORADO

Telephone, Address
Office Address: 2001 Blake St., Denver, CO
80205. **Telephone:** (303) 292-0200. **FAX:** (303)
312-2116. **Website:** www.coloradorockies.com.

Ownership
Operated by: Colorado Rockies Baseball Club, Ltd.
Principal Owners: Jerry McMorris, Charles
Monfort, Richard Monfort.
Chairman/Chief Executive Officer: Jerry McMorris.

Jerry McMorris

BUSINESS OPERATIONS
Executive Vice President, Business Operations: Keli McGregor. **Senior Vice President, Corporate Counsel:** Clark Weaver.
Senior Director, Personnel and Administration: Elizabeth Stecklein.

Finance
Senior Vice President, Chief Financial Officer: Hal Roth. **Vice President, Finance:** Michael Kent.
Director, Information Systems: Mary Burns. **Director, Accounting:** Gary Lawrence. **Senior Accountant:** Phil Emerson. **Accountant:** Matt Vinnola.

Marketing, Sales
Vice President, Sales/Marketing: Greg Feasel. **Vice President, Ticket Operations/Sales:** Sue Ann McClaren.
Senior Director, Corporate Sales: Marcy English Glasser. **Assistant Director, Sales/Marketing:** Dave Madsen. **Account Executives:** Carey Brandt, Renata Pollard.
Director, Promotions: Alan Bossart.
Director, Broadcasting: Eric Brummond.
Director, Merchandising: Jim Kellogg. **Assistant to Director, Merchandising:** Kelly Hall.

Public Relations, Communications
Telephone: (303) 312-2325. **FAX:** (303) 312-2319.
Director, Public Relations: Jay Alves. **Assistant to Director, Public Relations:** Zak Gilbert. **Coordinator, Public Relations:** Charity Stowell.
Director, Publications: Jimmy Oldham.
Director, Community Affairs: Roger Kinney. **Coordinators, Community Affairs:** Angela Keenan, Stacy Schafer.

Stadium Operations
Senior Director, Coors Field Operations: Kevin Kahn. **Director, Coors Field Administration/Development:** Dave Moore. **Director, Guest Services:** Mike Rock.
Head Groundskeeper: Mark Razum.
PA Announcer: Kelly Burnham. **Official Scorers:** Dave Einspahr, Jack Rose.

Ticketing
Telephone: (303) ROCKIES, (800) 388-ROCK. **FAX:** (303) 312-2115.
Director, Ticket Operations: Kevin Fenton. **Director, Ticket Sales:** Jill Roberts. **Director, Ticket Services:** Chuck Javernick. **Assistant Director, Group Sales:** Jeff Spector. **Assistant Director, Season Tickets:** Jeff Benner.

Travel, Clubhouse
Director, Team Travel: Brandy Lay. **Assistant to Director, Team Travel/Coordinator, Player Relations:** Adele Armagost.
Clubhouse and Equipment Manager: Dan McGinn. **Visiting Clubhouse Manager:** Keith Schulz.

General Information
Hometown Dugout: First Base. **Playing Surface:** Grass.
Standard Game Times: 7:05 p.m., 1:05, 3:05, 6:05; Sun. 1:05.
Stadium Location: From I-70 to I-25 South to exit 213 (Park Avenue)
or 212C (20th Street); I-25 to 20th Street, east to park.
Player Representative: Todd Helton.

ROCKIES

BASEBALL OPERATIONS

Telephone: (303) 292-0200. **FAX:** (303) 312-2320.

Executive Vice President, General Manager: Bob Gebhard. **Vice President, Player Personnel:** Gary Hughes. **Director, Baseball Administration:** Tony Siegle. **Assistant to Executive VP/GM:** Stacie Flores.

Major League Staff

Manager: Jim Leyland.

Coaches: Bench—Bruce Kimm; Pitching—Milt May; Batting—Clint Hurdle; First Base—Tommy Sandt; Third Base—Rich Donnelly; Bullpen—Lorenzo Bundy.

Bob Gebhard

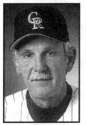

Medical, Training

Club Physicians: Dr. Wayne Gersoff, Dr. Anthony Motz, Dr. Allen Schreiber.

Head Trainer: Tom Probst. **Assistant Trainer:** Keith Dugger. **Strength and Conditioning Coordinator:** Mark Wilbert.

Player Development

Telephone: (303) 292-0200. **FAX:** (303) 312-2320.

Director, Player Development: Paul Egins. **Assistant Director, Player Development:** Marc Gustafson. **Administrative Assistant, Player Development:** Chris Rice.

Jim Leyland

Coordinator, Instruction: Rick Mathews (pitching). **Roving Instructors:** Greg Gross (hitting/outfield), Joe Marchese (infield/baserunning), Rolando Fernandez (Latin coordinator).

Farm System

Class	Farm Team	Manager	Coach	Pitching Coach
AAA	Colo. Springs	Bill Hayes	Tony Torchia	Jim Wright
AA	Carolina	Jay Loviglio	Theron Todd	Jerry Cram
A	Salem	Ron Gideon	Javier Gonzalez	Bob McClure
A	Asheville	Jim Eppard	Billy White	Jack Lamabe
A	Portland	Alan Cockrell	Stu Cole	Tom Edens
R	Tucson	P.J. Carey	Al Bleser/Fred Ocasio	Cam Walker
R	DSL	Dario Arias	Unavailable	Unavailable
R	VSL	Mauro Mendez	Francisco Cartaya	Jesus Rizales

Scouting

Telephone: (303) 292-0200. **FAX:** (303) 312-2320.

Vice President, Scouting: Pat Daugherty.

Assistant Director, Scouting: Coley Brannon. **Assistant to VP, Scouting:** Holly Burkett.

Director, Professional/International Scouting: Jeff Schugel. **Advance Scout:** Elanis Westbrooks.

Major League Scouts: Jim Fanning (St. Lazare, Quebec), Bill Harford (Chicago, IL), Larry High (Mesa, AZ), John Van Ornum (Bass Lake, CA), Bill Wood (Coppell, TX).

National Crosscheckers: Bill Gayton (Houston, TX), Dave Holliday (Coalgate, OK). **Regional Crosscheckers:** West—Danny Montgomery (San Francisco, CA); Midwest—Jay Darnell (Plano, TX); East—Robyn Lynch (Safety Harbor, FL).

Pat Daugherty

Area Scouts: John Cedarburg (Fort Myers, FL), Ty Coslow (Louisville, KY), Dar Cox (Red Oak, TX), Mike Ericson (Glendale, AZ), Abe Flores (Huntington Beach, CA), Mike Garlatti (Edison, NJ), Bert Holt (Visalia, CA), Greg Hopkins (Portland, OR), Bill Hughes (Sherman Oaks, CA), Damon Iannelli (Brandon, MS), Eric Johnson (Stafford, TX), Bill MacKenzie (Ottawa, Ontario), Jay Matthews (Charlotte, NC), Lance Nichols (Dodge City, KS), Art Pontarelli (Cranston, RI), Brooks Roybal, Ed Santa (Columbus, OH), Nick Venuto (Merrillville, IN), Tom Wheeler (Pleasant Hill, CA).

FLORIDA

Telephone, Address
Office Address: Pro Player Stadium, 2267 NW 199th St., Miami, FL 33056. Telephone: (305) 626-7400. FAX: (305) 626-7428. Website: www.flamarlins.com.

Ownership
Operated by: Florida Marlins Baseball Club, Inc.
Chairman: John Henry.
Executive Assistant to Chairman: Patty Sweeney.

BUSINESS OPERATIONS

Finance
Senior Vice President, Finance/Administration: Jonathan Mariner.
Director, Finance/Controller: Susan Jaison. Senior Staff Accountant: Nancy Hernandez. Executive Secretary to Vice President: Ann Saliwanchik. Director, Information Technology: Esther Fleming.

John Henry

Marketing, Sales
Vice President, Sales/Marketing: James Ross. Director, Sales/Marketing: John Pierce.
Director, Communications: Mark Geddis. Director, Creative Services: Leslie Riguero. Director, Community Affairs: Nancy Olson. Manager, Marketing Programs: Stacy Ostrau.
Director, In-Game Entertainment/Marketing: Susan Julian Budd. Director, Marketing Partnerships: Ben Creed.

Media Relations, Communications
Telephone: (305) 626-7429. FAX: (305) 626-7302.
Director, Baseball Information/Publicity: Ron Colangelo. Assistant Director, Baseball Information/Publicity: Julio Sarmiento. Coordinator, Baseball Information/Publicity: Sandra van Meek.

Stadium Operations
President, Stadium Operations: Bob Kramm. Vice President/General Manager, Stadium Operations: Bruce Schulze. Director, Guest Services: Steve Froot. Director, Event Operations/Security: Todd Ellzey. Head Groundskeeper: Alan Sigwardt.
PA Announcer: Tom Cummings. Official Scorers: Sonny Hirsch, Doug Pett.

Ticketing
Telephone: (305) 930-4487. FAX: (305) 626-7432.
Vice President, Ticket Operations: Bill Galante. Director, Season Tickets/Group Sales: Lou DePaoli.

Travel, Clubhouse
Director, Team Travel: Bill Beck.
Equipment Manager/Home Clubhouse: Mike Wallace. Visitors Clubhouse: Matt Rosenthal. Video Coordinator: Cullen McRae.

General Information
Home Dugout: First Base. Playing Surface: Grass.
Standard Game Times: 7:05 p.m.; Sun. 4:05.
Stadium Location: From south, Florida Turnpike extension to stadium exit; From north, I-95 to I-595 West to Florida Turnpike to stadium exit; From west, I-75 to I-595 to Florida Turnpike to stadium exit; From east, Highway 826 West to NW 27th Avenue, north to 199th Street, right to stadium.
Player Representative: Mark Kotsay.

MARLINS

BASEBALL OPERATIONS

Telephone: (305) 626-7400. **FAX:** (305) 626-7433.
Executive Vice President, General Manager: Dave Dombrowski.

Vice President, Assistant General Manager: Dave Littlefield. **Director, Major League Administration:** Dan Lunetta. **Special Assistant to General Manager:** Tony Perez.

Major League Staff

Manager: John Boles.

Coaches: Dugout—Joe Breeden; Pitching—Rich Dubee; Batting—Jack Maloof; First Base—Rusty Kuntz; Third Base—Fredi Gonzalez; Infield—Tony Taylor.

Dave Dombrowski

John Boles

Medical, Training

Club Physician: Dr. Dan Kanell.

Head Trainer: Larry Starr. **Assistant Trainer:** Kevin Rand. **Director, Strength and Conditioning:** Rick Slate.

Player Development

Office Address: 5600 Stadium Parkway, Melbourne, FL 32940. **Telephone:** (407) 633-8119. **FAX:** (407) 633-9216.

Director, Field Operations: Rob Leary. **Manager, Minor League Operations:** Mike Parkinson. **Manager, Minor League Administration:** Kim-Lee Carkeek Luchs. **Administrative Assistant, Minor League Operations:** Robert Perez.

Roving Instructors: Britt Burns (pitching), Manny Crespo (infield), Adrian Garrett (hitting), Bob Natal (catching), Brian Peterson (performance enhancement), Pookie Wilson (outfield/baserunning).

Farm System

Class	Farm Team	Manager	Coach	Pitching Coach
AAA	Calgary	Lynn Jones	Sal Rende	Randy Hennis
AA	Portland	Frank Cacciatore	Jose Castro	Steve Luebber
A	Brevard County	Dave Huppert	Juan Bustabad	Larry Pardo
A	Kane County	Rick Renteria	Matt Winters	Rick Mahler
A	Utica	Ken Joyce	Joe Aversa	Bill Sizemore
R	Melbourne	Jon Deeble	Hayward Cook	Euclides Rojas
R	DSL	Nelson Silverio	Andres Duncan	Pablo Blanco

Scouting

Telephone: (305) 626-7216. **FAX:** (305) 626-7294.
Director, Scouting: Al Avila.

Manager, Scouting Administration: Cheryl Evans. **Assistant, Scouting:** James Orr.

Major League Scouts: Orrin Freeman (Parkland, FL), Scott Reid (Phoeniz, AZ). **Special Assistant:** Whitey Lockman (Scottsdale, AZ).

Professional Scouts: Dick Egan (Phoenix, AZ), Manny Estrada (Brandon, FL), Will George (Merchantville, NJ).

National Crosscheckers: Jax Robertson (Cary, NC), Bill Singer (Decatur, AL). **Regional Crosscheckers:** East—Murray Cook (Washington, DC); Midwest—David Chadd (Wichita, KS); West—Tim Schmidt (San Bernardino, CA).

Al Avila

Area Scouts: Ty Brown (Ruther Glen, VA), John Castleberry (High Point, NC), Brad Del Barba (Taylor Mill, KY), Whitey DeHart (Woodburn, OR), David Finley (San Diego, CA), Bob Laurie (Plano, TX), Steve Minor (Long Beach, CA), Steve Mondile (Wenonah, NJ), Cucho Rodriguez (San Juan, PR), Jim Rough (Wichita, KS), Mike Russell (Gulf Breeze, FL), Dennis Sheehan (Glasco, NY), Dick Smith (Galveston, TX), Keith Snider (Stockton, CA), Wally Walker (Reno, NV), Stan Zielinski (Winfield, IL).

Coordinator, Latin American Scouting: Louie Eljaua (Pembroke Pines, FL). **International Scout:** Jon Deeble (Australia).

HOUSTON

Telephone, Address
Office Address: 8400 Kirby Dr., Houston, TX 77054. Mailing Address: P.O. Box 288, Houston, TX 77001. Telephone: (713) 799-9500. FAX: (713) 799-9794. E-Mail Address: twinspin@astros.com. Website: www.astros.com.

Ownership
Operated by: McLane Group, LP.
Principal Owner, Chairman: Drayton McLane Jr.
Board of Directors: Drayton McLane Jr., Bob McClaren, Sandy Sanford, Webb Stickney.
President: Tal Smith.

Drayton McLane

BUSINESS OPERATIONS
Vice President, Business Operations: Bob McClaren.
Director, Human Resources: Mike Anders.

Finance
Vice President, Finance: Webb Stickney.
Controller: Robert McBurnett. Management Information Systems: Jeff Paschal. Accounts Receivable: Mary Ann Bell. Accounts Payabale: Irene Dumenil. Manager, General Accounting: Mary Duvernay. Manager, Payroll: Ruth Kelly.

Marketing, Sales
Vice President, Marketing: Pam Gardner.
Assistant Director, Advertising Sales/Promotions: Jim Ballweg. Coordinator, Advertising: Duone Byars. Director, Promotions/Broadcast Operations: Jamie Hildreth. Coordinator, Promotions: Greg Grissom. Coordinator, Broadcast Traffic: Rita Suchma.

Public Relations, Communications
Telephone: (713) 799-9600. FAX: (713) 799-9881.
Director, Media Relations: Rob Matwick. Assistant Directors, Media Relations: Alyson Footer, Warren Miller. Administrative Assistant, Media Relations: Desta Kimmel.
Director, Community Relations: Marian Harper. Coordinator, Community Relations: Phoenix Mak.

Stadium Operations
Director, Stadium Operations: Don Collins. Assistant Director: Greg Golightly. Head Groundskeeper: Willie Berry.
PA Announcer: Bob Ford. Official Scorers: Rick Blount, Fred Duckett, Ivy McLemore.

Ticketing
Telephone: (713) 799-9555.
Director, Ticket Operations: Tina Cash. Director, Ticket Services: John Sorrentino. Ticket Manager: Marcia Coronado. Manager, Premium Sales: Shannon Sawyer. Administrative Assistant, Group and Season Sales: Joannie Cobb. Account Representatives: Brent Broussard, Steve Lake, Dave Manning, George Mouton, Matt Rogers, Scott Witherow.

Clubhouse
Equipment Manager/Home Clubhouse: Dennis Liborio. Visiting Clubhouse: Steve Perry.

General Information
Home Dugout: First Base. Playing Surface: Artificial turf.
Standard Game Times: 7:05 p.m., Sun. 1:35.
Stadium Location: From I-10, exit 610 South to Kirby Drive exit, right on Kirby Drive to Murworth Gate, right to stadium. From I-45, exit 288 South to 610 West, take Kirby Drive exit to Murworth Gate.
Player Representative: Shane Reynolds.

```
        BOOKS-A-MILLION #195
        EASTWOODMALL SUITE E-1400
        7703 CRESTWOOD BLVD.
        BIRMINGHAM      AL   35210
STORE #0195    REGISTER #  2
1 04 BASEBALL AMERICA'S 1999    12.95
SUB TOTAL        :      12.95
SALES TAX 8.000%:       1.04
TOTAL            :      13.99
AMOUNT TENDERED :       20.00
CHANGE DUE       :       6.01
  1  CASH              88
  18:01:02      7/16/99  BB
THANKS-A-MILLION FOR SHOPPING AT
BOOKS-A-MILLION. OUR STORE HOURS ARE
9:00AM TO 11:00PM 7 DAYS A WEEK.
PLEASE KEEP RECEIPT FOR RETURNS,
WITHOUT RECEIPT EXCHANGE ONLY.
------------- JOIN OUR CLUB !! ------------
YOU WOULD HAVE SAVED TODAY        $1.41
```

ASTROS

BASEBALL OPERATIONS
Telephone: (713) 799-9500. **FAX:** (713) 799-9562.
General Manager: Gerry Hunsicker.
Special Assistant to General Manager for International Scouting and Development: Andres Reiner. **Director, Baseball Administration:** Barry Waters. **Administrative Assistant:** Beverly Rains.

Major League Staff
Manager: Larry Dierker.
Coaches: Dugout—Matt Galante; Pitching—Vern Ruhle; Batting—Tom McCraw; First Base—Jose Cruz Sr.; Third Base—Mike Cubbage; Bullpen—John Tamargo.

Gerry Hunsicker

Medical, Training
Medical Director: Dr. Bill Bryan.
Head Trainer: Dave Labossiere. **Assistant Trainer:** Rex Jones. **Strength and Conditioning Coach:** Dr. Gene Coleman.

Player Development
Assistant GM/Director, Player Development: Tim Purpura. **Administrator, Minor Leagues:** Jay Edmiston. **Administrative Assistant:** Carol Wogsland.
Field Coordinator: Harry Spilman. **Roving Instructors:** Ivan DeJesus (infield), Johnny Lewis (hitting), Joe Mikulik (outfield/baserunning), Dewey Robinson (pitching).

Larry Dierker

Farm System

Class	Farm Team	Manager	Coach	Pitching Coach
AAA	New Orleans	Tony Pena	Jorge Orta	Jim Hickey
AA	Jackson	Jim Pankovits	Mark Bailey	Charley Taylor
A	Kissimmee	Manny Acta	Scott Makarewicz	Jack Billingham
A	Michigan	Al Pedrique	Unavailable	Bill Ballou
A	Auburn	Lyle Yates	Darwin Pennye	Gregg Langbehn
R	Martinsville	Brad Wellman	Gordy MacKenzie	Stan Boroski
R	DSL	Rafael Ramirez	Miguel de la Cruz	Rick Aponte
R	VSL	Cesar Cedeno	Wolfgang Ramos	Oscar Padron

Scouting
Director, Scouting: David Lakey.
Assistant Director, Scouting: Pat Murphy.
Administrative Assistant, Scouting: Traci Dearing.
Advance Scout: Tom Wiedenbauer (Ormond Beach, FL). **Major League Scouts:** Stan Benjamin (Port Charlotte, FL), Walt Matthews (Texarkana, TX), Tom Mooney (Pittsfield, MA), Bob Skinner (San Diego, CA), Paul Weaver (Phoenix, AZ).
Coordinator, Professional Scouting: Paul Ricciarini (Pittsfield, MA). **Professional Scouts:** Kimball Crossley (Providence, RI), Leo Labossiere (Lincoln, RI), Fred Nelson (Richmond, TX), Joe Pittman (Columbus, GA), Tom Romenesko (Santee, CA), Scipio Spinks (Houston, TX), Lynwood Stallings (Kingsport, TN).

David Lakey

National Supervisor: Bill Kelso (Bedford, TX).
Regional Supervisors: East—Gerry Craft (St. Clairsville, OH); West—Bob King (La Mesa, CA); Central—Tad Slowik (Niles, IL).
Area Scouts: Bob Blair (Commack, NY), Joe Bogar (Carmel, IN), Ralph Bratton (Dripping Springs, TX), Chuck Carlson (Orlando, FL), Doug Deutsch (Costa Mesa, CA), James Farrar (Shreveport, LA), David Henderson (Oklahoma City, OK), Dan Huston (Bellevue, WA), Mark Johnson (Englewood, CO), Brian Keegan (Charlotte, NC), Mike Maggart (Penn Yan, NY), Jerry Marik (Chicago, IL), Mel Nelson (Highland, CA), Bob Poole (Redwood City, CA), Joe Robinson (Burlington, IA), Deron Rombach (Arlington, TX), Steve Smith (Marietta, GA), Frankie Thon (Guaynabo, PR), Tim Tolman (Tucson, AZ), Gene Wellman (Danville, CA).

LOS ANGELES

Telephone, Address
Office Address: 1000 Elysian Park Ave., Los Angeles, CA 90012. **Telephone:** (323) 224-1500. **FAX:** (323) 224-1269. **Website:** www.dodgers.com.

Ownership
Operated by: Los Angeles Dodgers, Inc. **Principal Owner:** News Corp.

President/Chief Executive Officer: Bob Graziano.

Bob Graziano

Board of Directors: Chase Carey, Peter Chernin, Sam Fernandez, Bob Graziano, Peter O'Malley.

Senior Vice President: Tommy Lasorda.

Vice President, Campo las Palmas complex (Dominican Republic): Ralph Avila.

BUSINESS OPERATIONS
Director, Human Resources/Administration: Gina Galasso. **Administrator, Human Resources:** Leonor Romero. **Assistant, Human Resources:** Silvia Camacho. **Manager, Administrative Services:** Linda Cohen. **Assistant, Administrative Services:** George Barajas.

Managing Director, Dodgertown: Craig Callan.

Finance
Director, Accounting/Finance: Cristine Hurley. **Director, Management Information Services:** Mike Mularky.

Marketing, Sales
Vice President, Marketing: Barry Stockhamer.

Director, Ticket Marketing: Bob Wymbs. **Manager, Group Sales:** Lisa Johnson. **Manager, Youth Marketing:** Steve Everett. **Senior Manager, Marketing Services:** Monique LaVeau-Brennan.

Media Relations, Public Affairs
Telephone: (323) 224-1301. **FAX:** (323) 224-1459.

Vice President, Communications: Tommy Hawkins.

Director, Community Relations: Don Newcombe. **Director, Public Affairs:** Monique Brandon.

Director, Media Relations/Broadcasting: Brent Shyer. **Assistant Director, Publicity, Baseball Information:** Shaun Rachau. **Assistant Director, Publicity, Media Relations:** John Olguin. **Office Coordinator:** Barbara Conway. **Assistant, Baseball Information:** David Tuttle. **Supervisor, Media Relations/Publicity:** Paul Gomez.

Stadium Operations
Director, Stadium Operations: Doug Duennes. **Assistant Director, Stadium Operations:** Chris Fighera. **Manager, Stadium Operations:** David Born. **Superintendent, Turf and Grounds:** Eric Hansen.

PA Announcer: Mike Carlucci. **Official Scorers:** Don Hartack, Larry Kahn, Irv Kaze.

Ticketing
Telephone: (323) 224-1471. **FAX:** (323) 224-2609.

Director, Ticket Operations: Debra Kay Duncan. **Assistant Director, Ticket Operations:** Billy Hunter.

Travel, Clubhouse
Traveling Secretary: Billy DeLury.

Equipment Manager/Dodger Clubhouse Manager: David Wright. **Visiting Clubhouse Manager:** Jerry Turner.

General Information
Home Dugout: Third Base. **Playing Surface:** Grass.

Stadium Location: I-5 to Stadium Way exit, left on Stadium Way, right on Academy Road, left to Stadium Way to Elysian Park Avenue, left to stadium; I-110 to Dodger Stadium exit, left on Stadium Way, right on Elysian Park Avenue; US 101 to Alvarado exit, right on Sunset, left on Elysian Park Avenue.

Standard Game Times: 7:10 p.m., Wed. 7:35, Sun. 1:05.

Player Representative: Devon White.

DODGERS

BASEBALL OPERATIONS

Telephone: (323) 224-1306. **FAX:** (323) 224-1269.
Executive Vice President, General Manager: Kevin Malone. **Administrator, Baseball Operations:** Robert Schweppe.

Major League Staff

Manager: Davey Johnson.
Coaches: Bench—Jim Tracy; Pitching—Charlie Hough; Batting—Rick Down; First Base—John Shelby; Third Base—Rick Dempsey; Bullpen—Glenn Hoffman.

Kevin Malone

Medical, Training

Team Physicians: Dr. Herndon Harding, Dr. Frank Jobe, Dr. Michael Mellman.
Head Trainer: Charlie Strasser. **Assistant Trainer:** Stan Johnston. **Strength and Conditioning:** Todd Claussen.

Player Development

Assistant to General Manager, Minor Leagues: Bill Geivett. **Administrator, Minor Leagues:** Luchy Guerra. **Project Coordinator:** Joe Bohringer. **Administrative Assistant:** Jeff Antoon.

Davey Johnson

Special Advisor, Player Development: Del Crandall. **Field Coordinator:** Rick Sofield.
Roving Instructors: Jim Benedict (pitching), Tom Beyers (hitting), Chico Fernandez (infield), Jerry Weinstein (catching), Joe Vavra (baserunning).

Farm System

Class	Farm Team	Manager	Coach	Pitching Coach
AAA	Albuquerque	Mike Scioscia	Mickey Hatcher	Claude Osteen
AA	San Antonio	Jimmy Johnson	John Shoemaker	Dean Treanor
A	Vero Beach	Alvaro Espinoza	Jon Debus	Jim Stoeckel
A	San Bernardino	Rick Burleson	Steve Yeager	Mark Brewer
A	Yakima	Dino Ebel	Mitch Webster	Max Leon
R	Great Falls	Tony Harris	Quinn Mack	Greg Gohr
R	DSL I	Pedro Mega	Algona Read	Silvano Quezada
R	DSL II	Teddy Martinez	Ramon Valdez	Luis Barreiro

Scouting

Assistant to General Manager/Scouting: Ed Creech. **Assistant Director, Scouting:** Matt Slater. **Project Coordinator, Scouting:** Tasha Noriega.
Advance Scout: Mark Weidemaier (Tierre Verde, FL). **Major League Scouts:** Phil Favia (Apache Junction, AZ); Carl Loewenstine (Hamilton, OH).
Coordinator, Minor League Scouting: Terry Reynolds (Altadena, CA). **Professional Scouts:** Marty Maier (Piedmont, CA), Tommy Mixon (Macon, GA), Jim Stoeckel (Vero Beach, FL), Timmy Thompson (Lewistown, PA).
National Crosscheckers: Gib Bodet (San Clemente, CA), Jimmy Lester (Columbus, GA).

Ed Creech

Regional Supervisors: East—John Barr (Palm City, FL); West Coast—Joe Ferrone (Valencia, CA); Midwest—Mike Hankins (Lee's Summit, MO).
Area Scouts: Jim Chapman (Delta, British Columbia), Edwin Correa (Carolina, PR), Bobby Darwin (Cerritos, CA), Scott Groot (Mission Viejo, CA), Hank Jones (Vancouver, WA), Lon Joyce (Spartanburg, SC), John Kosciak (Milford, MA), Marty Lamb (Lexington, KY), Mike Leuzinger (Grand Prairie, TX), Dale McReynolds (Walworth, WI), Bump Merriweather (Los Angeles, CA), Bill Pleis (Parrish, FL), Willie Powell (Pensacola, FL), Eddie Rodriguez (Anasco, PR), Scott Sharp (Sykesville, MD), Mark Sheehy (Sacramento, CA), Chris Smith (Montgomery, TX), Tom Thomas (Phoenix, AZ), Glen Van Proyen (West Chicago, IL).
Director, International Operations: Jack Zduriencik.

MILWAUKEE

Telephone, Address

Office Address: County Stadium, 201 S 46th St., Milwaukee, WI 53214. **Mailing Address:** P.O. Box 3099, Milwaukee, WI 53201. **Telephone:** (414) 933-4114. **FAX:** (414) 933-3251. **Website:** www.milwaukeebrewers.com.

Ownership

Operated by: Milwaukee Brewers Baseball Club.

Board of Directors: John Canning Jr., Mitchell Fromstein, Michael Grebe, Charles Krause, Jack MacDonough, Wendy Selig-Prieb.

President, Chief Executive Officer: Wendy Selig-Prieb.

Wendy Selig-Prieb

Vice President, General Counsel: Tom Gausden. **Assistant General Counsel:** Eugene Randolph. **Executive Assistant to President:** Mary Burns.

BUSINESS OPERATIONS

Vice President, New Ballpark Development: Michael Bucek. **Director, Suite Sales/Advertising:** Geoff Campion.

Finance

Vice President, Finance: Paul Baniel. **Director, Management Information Systems:** Dan Krautkramer.

Corporate Affairs, Marketing

Vice President, Corporate Affairs: Laurel Prieb.

Director, Corporate Sales: Dean Rennicke. **Managers, Corporate Sales:** Matt Groniger, Amy Welch. **Coordinator, Corporate Sales:** Cathy Bradley. **Associate, Corporate Sales:** Nicole Clark.

Public Relations, Communications

Telephone: (414) 933-6975. **FAX:** (414) 933-3251.

Director, Media Relations: Jon Greenberg. **Associates, Media Relations:** Amy Abramczyk, Jason Parry.

Director, Publications: Mario Ziino.

Director, Community Relations: Mike Downs. **Manager, Community Relations:** Marquette Baylor.

Director, Broadcasting: Tim Van Wagoner. **Manager, Broadcasting:** Aleta Mercer.

Stadium Operations

Vice President, Stadium Operations: Scott Jenkins.

Director, Event Services: Steve Ethier. **Director, Grounds:** Gary Vanden Berg. **Assistant Director, Grounds:** David Mellor.

PA Announcer: Unavailable. **Official Scorers:** Tim O'Driscoll, Wayne Franke.

Ticketing

Telephone: (414) 933-9000. **FAX:** (414) 933-3547.

Vice President, Ticket Sales: Bob Voight.

Director, Ticket Operations: John Barnes. **Assistant Director, Ticket Operations:** Nancy Jorgensen. **Operations Manager, Ticketing:** Scott Parsons.

Director, Season Tickets/Group Sales: Jim Bathey.

Travel, Clubhouse

Traveling Secretary: Dan Larrea.

Director, Clubhouse Operations: Tony Migliaccio. **Coordinator, Visiting Clubhouse:** Phil Rozewicz. **Assistant, Home Clubhouse:** Meshach Belle. **Assistant, Visiting Clubhouse:** Darnell Bowden. **Coordinator, Umpires Room:** Duane Lewis.

General Information

Home Dugout: First Base. **Playing Surface:** Grass.

Standard Game Times: 7:05 p.m., (April) 6:05; Day, Sun. 1:05.

Stadium Location: From airport/south, I-94 West to Madison exit, to stadium.

Player Representative: Scott Karl.

BREWERS

BASEBALL OPERATIONS
Senior Vice President, Baseball Operations: Sal Bando. **Assistant General Manager/Director, Baseball Operations:** Fred Stanley.

Baseball Administrator: Barbara Stark. **Administrative Assistant, Baseball Operations:** Kate Geenen. **Coordinator, Baseball Information:** Tom Flanagan.

Major League Staff
Manager: Phil Garner.
Coaches: Bench—Bob Melvin. Pitching—Bill Campbell; Batting—Jim Lefebvre; First Base—Ron Jackson; Third Base—Doug Mansolino; Bullpen—Bill Castro.

Sal Bando

Phil Garner

Medical, Training
Senior Medial Advisor: Dr. Richard Franklin. **Team Physician:** Dr. Angelo Mattalino.
Head Trainer: John Adam. **Assistant Trainer:** Roger Caplinger. **Strength and Conditioning Coach:** John Rewolinski.

Player Development
Telephone: (414) 933-4114. **FAX:** (414) 933-4655.
Director, Player Development: Cecil Cooper. **Assistant Director:** Scott Martens.
Field Coordinator: Ralph Dickenson. **Roving Instructors:** Tim Blackwell (catching), Mike Caldwell (pitching), Ed Romero (infield), Ed Sedar (outfield).

Farm System
Class	Farm Team	Manager	Coach	Pitching Coach
AAA	Louisville	Gary Allenson	Luis Salazar	Dwight Bernard
AA	Huntsville	Darrell Evans	Herm Winningham	Steve Renko
A	Stockton	Bernie Moncallo	Carlos Ponce	Randy Kramer
A	Beloit	Don Money	John Mallee	Todd Frohwirth
R	Helena	Carlos Lezcano	Unavailable	R.C. Lichtenstein
R	Ogden	Jon Pont	Tom Houk	Steve Cline

Scouting
Director, Scouting: Ken Califano.
Administrative Assistant: Adela Martinez.
Special Assignment Scouts—Professional Coverage: Chris Bando (Cedarburg, WI), Larry Haney (Orange, VA), Al Monchak (Bradenton, FL), Chuck Tanner (New Castle, PA).
Special Assignment Scouts—Amateur Coverage: Felix Delgado (Rio Piedras, PR), Walter Youse (Sykesville, MD).
National Crosscheckers: Midwest—Fred Beene (Oakhurst, TX); Southeast—Russ Bove (Apopka, FL); West—Kevin Christman (Elk Grove, CA); East—Ron Rizzi (Joppa, MD); Southwest—Ric Wilson (Chandler, AZ).

Ken Califano

Scouts: Walt Boggan (Fairfield, CA), Jeff Brookens (Chambersburg, PA), Rich Chiles (Davis, CA), Steve Connelly (Durham, NC), Dick Fanning (Colorado Springs, CO), Mike Farrell (Indianapolis, IN), Dick Foster (Otis, OR), Danny Garcia (Jericho, NY), Mike Gibbons (West Chester, OH), Brian Johnson (Phoenix, AZ), Harvey Kuenn Jr. (New Berlin, WI), Johnny Logan (Milwaukee, WI), Demie Mainieri (Tamarac, FL), Alex Morales (Lake Worth, FL), Doug Reynolds (Tallahassee, FL), Corey Rodriguez (Hermosa Beach, CA), Bruce Seid (Hermosa Beach, CA), Bob Sloan (Amarillo, TX), Jonathan Story (Gulfport, MS), Tom Tanous (Swansea, MA), Red Whitsett (Villa Rica, GA), David Young (Kountze, TX).
Director, International Scouting: Epy Guerrero (Santo Domingo, DR).
International Scouts: Domingo Carrasquel (Venezuela), Manolo Hernandez (Puerto Rico), Elvio Jimenez (Dominican Republic), John Viney (Australia).

MONTREAL

Telephone, Address
Office Address: 4549 Pierre-de-Coubertin Ave., Montreal, Quebec H1V 3N7. **Mailing Address:** P.O. Box 500, Station M, Montreal, Quebec H1V 3P2. **Telephone:** (514) 253-3434. **FAX:** (514) 253-8282. **Website:** www.montrealexpos.com.

Ownership
Operated by: Montreal Baseball Club, Inc. **President/General Partner:** Claude Brochu.

Chairman, Partnership Committee: Jacques Menard. **Vice Chairmen, Partnership Committee:** Raymond Bachand, Guy Marier, Jocelyn Proteau. **Executive Assistant:** Monique Chibok.

Claude Brochu

BUSINESS OPERATIONS

Finance
Executive Vice President, Development: Laurier Carpentier. **Vice President, Finance/Treasurer:** Michel Bussiere.

Accounting Manager: Martin Gilbert. **Financial Analyst:** Paolo Schiavoni. **Risk Manager:** Marlene Auclair.

Sales, Marketing
Vice President, Sales/Marketing: Richard Morency.

Directors, Advertising Sales: Luigi Carola, John Di Terlizzi, Danielle La Roche. **Director, Promotions/Special Events:** Gina Hackl. **Director, Adminstration, Sales/Marketing:** Stephany Peschlow.

Director, Business Development: Real Sureau.

Coordinator, Broadcast Services: Marc Griffin. **Producer, Scoreboard Operations:** Louis Simard.

Media Relations, Communications
Vice President, Communications: Johanne Heroux.

Director, Media Relations: P.J. Loyello. **Director, Media Services:** Monique Giroux. **Coordinator, Media Relations:** Francois Boutin. **Secretary:** Sina Gabrielli.

Stadium Operations
Vice President, Stadium Operations: Claude Delorme. **Director, Stadium Operations:** Denis Pare. **Director, Management Information System:** Yves Poulin. **Manager, Souvenirs:** Peggy O'Leary.

Ticketing
Director, Season Ticket Sales: Gilles Beauregard.

Sales Representatives: Gary Connelly, Michael D'Aliesio, Catherine Filion, Marlene Yelle.

Director, Stadium Ticket Office: Hubert Richard. **Director, Downtown Ticket Office:** Chantal Dalpe. **Account Executive, Season Ticket Sales:** Jean-Sebastien Brault. **Account Executive, Group Sales:** Suzanne LeMoignan.

Travel, Clubhouse
Coordinator, Team Travel/Conditioning: Sean Cunningham.

Equipment Manager: John Silverman. **Visiting Clubhouse:** Bryan Greenberg.

General Information
Home Dugout: First Base. **Playing Surface:** Artificial turf.

Standard Game Times: Day 1:35 p.m.; Night 7:35.

Stadium Location: From New England, take I-87 North from Vermont to Quebec Highway 15 to the Jacques Cartier Bridge, exit left, right on Sherbrooke. From upstate New York, take I-81 North to Trans Canada Highway 401, east to Quebec Highway 20, north to Highway 40 to Boulevard Pie IX exit south to stadium. Access by subway from downtown Montreal to Pie IX Metro station.

Player Representative: Anthony Telford.

EXPOS

BASEBALL OPERATIONS
Vice President/General Manager: Jim Beattie.
Vice President, Baseball Operations: Bill Stoneman.
Administrative Assistant: Marcia Schnaar.

Major League Staff
Manager: Felipe Alou.
Coaches: Dugout—Luis Pujols; Pitching—Bobby Cuellar; Batting—Tommy Harper; First Base—Gene Glynn; Third Base—Pete Mackanin; Bullpen—Pierre Arsenault.

Medical, Training
Team Physician: Dr. Michael Thomassin. Team Orthopedist: Dr. Larry Coughlin.
Head Trainer: Ron McClain. Assistant Trainer: Mike Kozak. Coordinator, Conditioning: Sean Cunningham.

Jim Beattie

Felipe Alou

Player Development
Office Address: Roger Dean Stadium, 4657 Main St., Jupiter, FL 33458. Mailing Address: P.O. Box 8978, Jupiter, FL 33468. Telephone: (561) 775-1818. FAX: (561) 775-9935.
Director, Player Development: Don Reynolds. Administrative Assistants, Player Development: Maria Arellano, Mike Fiol, Adam Wogan.
Field Coordinator: Rick Sweet. Minor League Coordinators: Paul Fournier (conditioning/rehabilitation), Jeffrey Leonard (hitting), Jerry Royster (infield/baserunning), Brent Strom (pitching).
Clubhouse Manager/Equipment Supervisor: Sean Wilson.

Farm System

Class	Farm Team	Manager	Coach	Pitching Coach
AAA	Ottawa	Jeff Cox	Tim Leiper	Randy St. Claire
AA	Harrisburg	Doug Sisson	Steve Phillips	Wayne Rosenthal
A	Jupiter	Luis Dorante	Bert Heffernan	Ace Adams
A	Cape Fear	Frank Kremblas	Gary Robinson	Tom Signore
A	Vermont	Tony Barbone	Rich Morales	Craig Bjornson
R	Jupiter	Bill Masse	Bob Fiori	Fred Corral
R	DSL	Arturo DeFreites	Jose Zapata	Salomon Torres
R	VSL	Carlos Moreno	Unavailable	Unavailable

Scouting
Telephone: (561) 775-1818. FAX: (561) 775-9935.
Director, Scouting: Jim Fleming (Purcell, OK).
Assistant Director, Scouting: Gregg Leonard.
Major League Scout: Bob Cluck (La Mesa, CA).
National Crosschecker: Len Strelitz (Temple City, CA).
Regional Supervisors: East—Mike Berger (Pittsburgh, PA); West—Dave Malpass (Huntington Beach, CA).
Area Scouts: Alex Agostino (St. Bruno, Quebec), Matt Anderson (Montoursville, PA), Mark Baca (Tustin Ranch, CA), Dennis Cardoza (Denton, TX), Robby Corsaro (Adelanto, CA), Dave Dangler (Birmingham, AL), Marc DelPiano (Auburn, NY), Dan Freed (Bloomington, IL), Scott Goldby (Vancouver, WA), John Hughes (Walnut Creek, CA), Joe Jordan (Blanchard, OK), Mark Leavitt (Orlando, FL), Darryl Monroe (Marietta, GA), Bob Oldis (Iowa City, IA) Scott Stanley (Peoria, AZ), Tommy Thompson (Durham, NC).
Vice President/Director, International Operations: Fred Ferreira (Fort Lauderdale, FL). Assistant Director, International Scouting: Randy Kierce.
International Scouts: Carlos Acosta (Venezuela), Arturo DeFreites (Dominican Republic), Juan Loyola (Puerto Rico), Carlos Moreno (Venezuela), German Obando (Panama), Rene Picota (Panama).

NEW YORK

Telephone, Address
Office Address: 123-01 Roosevelt Ave., Flushing, NY 11368. **Telephone:** (718) 507-6387. **FAX:** (718) 507-6395. **Website:** www.mets.com.

Ownership
Operated by: Sterling Doubleday Enterprises, LP. **Chairman:** Nelson Doubleday. **President, Chief Executive Officer:** Fred Wilpon.
Vice President/Consultant: Frank Cashen.

Fred Wilpon

BUSINESS OPERATIONS
Senior Vice President, Business/Legal Affairs: David Howard.
General Counsel: David Cohen. **Director, Human Resources:** Ray Scott. **Director, Administration/Data Processing:** Russ Richardson.

Finance
Senior VP, Treasurer: Harry O'Shaughnessy.
Controller: Lenny Labita. **Chief Accountant:** Alon Kindler.

Marketing, Sales
Senior Vice President, Marketing/Broadcasting: Mark Bingham.
Director, Marketing: Kit Geis. **Administrative Assistant, Marketing:** Lorraine Hamilton. **Director, Marketing Productions:** Tim Gunkel.
Director, Promotions: Jim Plummer. **Director, Corporate Sales:** Paul Danforth. **Diamond View Suites:** Kevin Riley.

Media Relations, Community Relations
Telephone: (718) 565-4330. **FAX:** (718) 639-3619.
Director, Media Relations: Jay Horwitz. **Assistant Director, Media Relations:** Rafael Morffi. **Media Relations Specialists:** Shannon Dalton, Stella Fiore, Chris Lieble.
Manager, Publications: Jill Grabill. **Team Photographer:** Mark Levine.
Director, Community Outreach: Jill Knee. **Coordinator, Community Outreach:** Jonathan Rosenberg.

Stadium Operations
Vice President, Stadium Operations: Bob Mandt.
Stadium Manager: Kevin McCarthy. **Administrative Assistant:** Rose Lynch. **Head Groundskeeper:** Pete Flynn.
PA Announcer: Del DeMontreux. **Official Scorers:** Joe Donnelly, Red Foley, Bill Shannon.

Ticketing
Telephone: (718) 507-8499. **FAX:** (718) 507-6396.
Vice President, Ticket Sales/Services: Bill Ianniciello.
Director, Group/Ticket Sales Services: Thomas Fersch. **Director, Ticket Operations:** Dan DeMato. **Manager, Ticket Sales Development:** Robert Livingston.

Travel, Clubhouse
Equipment Manager/Associate Travel Director: Charlie Samuels.
Assistant Equipment Manager: Vinny Greco. **Visiting Clubhouse Manager:** Tony Carullo. **Video Editor:** Joe Scarola.

General Information

Home Dugout: First Base. **Playing Surface:** Grass.
Standard Game Times: 7:10 p.m., (June-Aug.) 7:40; Sat. 1:40, 7:10; Sun. 1:40.
Stadium Location: From Bronx and Westchester, take Cross Bronx Expressway to Bronx-Whitestone Bridge, then take bridge to Whitestone Expressway to Northern Boulevard/Shea Stadium exit. From Brooklyn, take Eastbound BQE to Eastbound Grand Central Parkway. From Long Island, take either Northern State Parkway or LIE to Westbound Grand Central Parkway. From northern New Jersey, take George Washington Bridge to Cross Bronx Expressway. From Southern New Jersey, take any of bridge crossings to Verazzano Bridge, and then take either Belt Parkway or BQE to Grand Central Parkway.
Player Representative: John Franco.

METS

BASEBALL OPERATIONS

Telephone: (718) 565-4315. FAX: (718) 507-6391.
Senior VP, General Manager: Steve Phillips.
Senior Assistant General Manager/International Scouting: Omar Minaya. Senior Executive Advisor, Player Personnel: Dave Wallace.
Special Assistants to General Manager: Larry Doughty, Darrell Johnson, Harry Minor.

Major League Staff
Manager: Bobby Valentine.
Coaches: Batting—Tim Robson; Pitching—Bob Apodaca; First Base/Outfield—Mookie Wilson; Third Base—Cookie Rojas; Bullpen—Randy Niemann; Catching—Bruce Benedict.

Steve Phillips

Medical, Training
Team Physicians: Dr. David Altchek, Dr. John Olichney.
Head Trainer: Fred Hina. Assistant Trainer: Scott Lawrenson. Fitness Coach: Barry Heyden.

Player Development
Telephone: (718) 507-6387. FAX: (718) 205-7920.
Assistant GM, Player Personnel: Jim Duquette. Assistant to Director/Player Personnel: Kevin Morgan. Coordinator, Minor League Administration: Maureen Cooke.
Latin American Coordinator: Juan Lopez.

Bobby Valentine

Minor League Advisor: Chuck Hiller.
Coordinator, Instruction: Bob Floyd. Roving Instructors: Mickey Brantley (hitting), Tim Foli (infield/baserunning), Al Jackson (pitching), Rich Miller (outfield/baserunning), Ray Rippelmeyer (pitching).

Farm System

Class	Farm Team	Manager	Coach	Pitching Coach
AAA	Norfolk	John Gibbons	Tom Lawless	Rick Waits
AA	Binghamton	Doug Davis	Roger LaFrancois	Bob Stanley
A	St. Lucie	Howie Freiling	E. Alfonzo, G. Ward	Buzz Capra
A	Capital City	Dave Engle	Lee May Jr.	Mickey Weston
A	Pittsfield	Tony Tijerina	Ken Berry	Doug Simons
R	Kingsport	Guy Conti	Juan Lopez	Bill Champion
R	Port St. Lucie	John Stephenson	Luis Natera	Ray Rippelmeyer
R	DSL	Miguel Dilone	J. Guillen, H. Sierra	Jesus Hernaiz

Scouting
Assistant GM/Professional Scouting: Carmen Fusco. Assistant GM/Amateur Scouting: Gary LaRocque. Assistant Director, Amateur Scouting: Fred Wright.
Advance Scout: John Stearns (Denver, CO).
Professional Scouts: Erwin Bryant (Lexington, KY), Howard Johnson (Lake Arrowhead, CA), Roland Johnson (Newington, CT), Bill Latham (Trussville, AL), Harry Minor (Long Beach, CA), Tim Teufel (Poway, CA), Mike Toomey (Washington, DC).
National Crosschecker: Jack Bowen (Bethel Park, PA). Regional Supervisors: West—Paul Fryer (Calabasas, CA), East—Gene Kerns (Hagerstown, MD), Midwest—Terry Tripp (Harrisburg, IL).

Gary LaRocque

Area Supervisors: Tom Allison (Scottsdale, AZ), Kevin Blankenship (Rocklin, CA), Quincy Boyd (Naperville, IL), Larry Chase (Pearcy, AR), Joe Delli Carri (Longwood, FL), Chuck Hensley (Oxnard, CA), Bob Lavallee (Plaistow, NH), Dave Lottsfeldt (Richardson, TX), Fred Mazuca (Tustin, CA), Marlin McPhail (Irmo, SC), Randy Milligan (Owings Mills, MD), Bob Minor (Garden Grove, CA), Joe Morlan (New Albany, OH), Joe Nigro (Staten Island, NY), Jim Reeves (Camas, WA), Junior Roman (San Sebastian, PR), Bob Rossi (Baton Rouge, LA), Joe Salerno (Miami Lakes, FL), Greg Tubbs (Cookeville, TN).

PHILADELPHIA

Telephone, Address
Office Address: Veterans Stadium, 3501 S Broad St., Philadelphia, PA 19148. Mailing Address: P.O. Box 7575, Philadelphia, PA 19101. Telephone: (215) 463-6000. FAX: (215) 389-3050. Website: www.phillies.com.

Ownership
Operated by: The Phillies.

Managing General Partner: David Montgomery. General Partner: Bill Giles.

Partners: Claire Betz, Fitz Eugene Dixon, Double Play Inc. (John Middleton), Tri-Play Associates (Alexander Buck, Mahlon Buck, William Buck).

David Montgomery

BUSINESS OPERATIONS
President/Chief Executive Officer: David Montgomery. Chairman: Bill Giles.

Secretary/General Counsel: Bill Webb. Special Assistant to President: Sharon Swainson. Director, Business Development: Joe Giles. Executive Administrator: Nancy Nolan. Administrator: Bettyanne Robb.

Finance
Senior Vice President: Jerry Clothier.

Executive Secretary/Benefits Administrator: JoAnn Marano. Controller: John Fusco.

Marketing, Promotions
Vice President, Advertising Sales: Dave Buck.

Manager, Client Services: Debbie Nocito. Manager, Radio Sales: Rob MacPherson. Manager, Advertising Sales: Casey Murray. Director, Events: Kurt Funk. Manager, Entertainment: Chrissy Legault Long. Manager, Promotions: John Brazer. Director, Broadcasting/Video Services: Rory McNeil.

Public Relations, Communications
Telephone: (215) 463-6000. FAX: (215) 389-3050.

Vice President, Public Relations: Larry Shenk.

Manager, Print/Creative Services: Tina Urban. Manager, Publicity: Leigh Tobin. Manager, Media Relations: Gene Dias. Administrator, Public Relations: Christine Negley.

Director, Community Relations: Regina Castellani. Speakers' Bureau Representative: Maje McDonnell.

Director, Information Systems: Brian Lamoreaux.

Stadium Operations
Director, Stadium Operations: Mike DiMuzio. Assistant Director, Stadium Operations: Eric Tobin. Secretary, Stadium Operations: Bernie Mansi. Operations Assistant, Concessionaire Liaison: Bruce Leith.

Supervisor, Field/Maintenance Operations: Ralph Frangipani.

PA Announcer: Dan Baker. Official Scorers: Jay Dunn, Bob Kenney, John McAdams.

Ticketing
Telephone: (215) 463-1000. FAX: (215) 463-9878.

Vice President, Ticket Operations: Richard Deats.

Director, Ticket Department: Dan Goroff. Director, Sales: John Weber. Director, Group Sales: Kathy Killian. Manager, Premium Seating: Tom Mashek. Manager, Phone Center: Phil Feather.

Travel, Clubhouse
Traveling Secretary: Eddie Ferenz.

Equipment Manager/Home Clubhouse: Frank Coppenbarger. Assistant Equipment Manager: Joe Dunn. Manager, Visiting Clubhouse: Kevin Steinhour. Assistant, Home Clubhouse: Pete Cera.

General Information
Home Dugout: First Base. Playing Surface: Artificial turf.
Game Times: 7:05 p.m.; (June-Aug.) 7:35; Sat. 7:05; Sun. 1:35.
Stadium Location: I-95 or I-76 to Broad Street exit.
Player Representative: Curt Schilling.

PHILLIES

BASEBALL OPERATIONS

Vice President, General Manager: Ed Wade.
Assistant General Manager: Ruben Amaro Jr.
Senior Advisors to GM: Dallas Green, Paul Owens. **Executive Assistant to GM:** Susan Ingersoll. **Computer Analysis:** Jay McLaughlin.

Major League Staff

Manager: Terry Francona.
Coaches: Dugout—Chuck Cottier; Pitching—Galen Cisco; Batting—Hal McRae; First Base—Brad Mills; Third Base—John Vukovich; Bullpen—Ramon Henderson.

Ed Wade

Medical, Training

Team Physician: Dr. Phillip Marone.
Head Trainer: Jeff Cooper. **Assistant Trainer:** Mark Andersen. **Conditioning Coordinator:** Scott Hoffman.

Player Development

Director, Minor League Operations: Steve Noworyta. **Director, Minor League Personnel/ Field Coordinator:** Lee Elia.
Director, Latin America Operations: Sal Artiaga. **Director, Florida Operations:** John Timberlake.
Assistant to Director, Minor Leagues: Rob Holiday. **Secretary, Minor Leagues/Scouting:** Karen Nocella. **Administrative Assistant, Minor Leagues/Scouting:** Mike Ondo.
Assistant Field Coordinator: Ruben Amaro Sr. **Coordinator, Pitching:** Gary Ruby. **Special Assistants to Field Coordinator:** Billy DeMars, Johnny Podres. **Roving Instructors:** Steve Lake (catching), Don Long (hitting).

Terry Francona

Farm System

Class	Farm Team	Manager	Coach	Pitching Coach
AAA	Scranton/W-B	Marc Bombard	Al LeBoeuf	Glenn Gregson
AA	Reading	Gary Varsho	Milt Thompson	Gorman Heimueller
A	Clearwater	Bill Dancy	Tony Scott	Darold Knowles
A	Piedmont	Ken Oberkfell	Jerry Martin	Carlos Arroyo
A	Batavia	Greg Legg	Frank Klebe	Ken Westray
R	Clearwater	Ramon Aviles	Alberto Fana	Warren Brusstar
R	DSL	Alex Taveras	Domingo Brito	Cesar Mejia

Scouting

Telephone: (215) 952-8228. **FAX:** (215) 755-9324.
Director, Scouting: Mike Arbuckle (Liberty, MO).
National Supervisor: Marti Wolever (Papillion, NE).
Director, Major League Scouts: Gordon Lakey (Barker, TX). **Major League Scout:** Jimmy Stewart (Odessa, FL).
Coordinator, Professional Coverage: Dick Lawlor (Windsor, CT). **Professional Scouts:** Hank King (Limerick, PA), Larry Rojas (Clearwater, FL), Del Unser (Dove Canyon, CA). **Special Assignment Scout:** Jim Fregosi Jr. (Murrieta, CA).

Mike Arbuckle

Regional Supervisors: Central—Sonny Bowers (Waco, TX); West—Dean Jongewaard (Fountain Valley, CA); East—Scott Trcka (Hobart, IN).
Area Scouts: Emil Belich (West Allis, WI), Steve Gillispie (Birmingham, AL), Bill Harper (Corvallis, OR), Ken Hultzapple (Newport, PA), Jerry Lafferty (Trenton, MO), Terry Logan (Brenham, TX), Miguel Machado (Miami, FL), Lloyd Merritt (Franklin, TN), Willie Montanez (Caguas, PR), Venice Murray (Merrillville, IN), Art Parrack (Oklahoma City, OK), Mark Ralston (Chatsworth, CA), Scott Ramsay (Nampa, ID), Mitch Sokol (Phoenix, AZ), Roy Tanner (Charleston, SC).
International Supervisor: Sal Agostinelli (Deer Park, NY). **Pacific Rim Supervisor:** Doug Takaragawa (Walnut Creek, CA).

PITTSBURGH

Telephone, Address
Office Address: 600 Stadium Circle, Pittsburgh, PA 15212. **Mailing Address:** P.O. Box 7000, Pittsburgh, PA 15212. **Telephone:** (412) 323-5000. **FAX:** (412) 323-5024. **Website:** www.pirateball.com.

Ownership
Operated by: Pittsburgh Pirates Acquisition, Inc. **Principal Owner:** Kevin McClatchy.

Board of Directors: William Allen, Don Beaver, Frank Brenner, Chip Ganassi, Kevin McClatchy, Thomas Murphy Jr., Ogden Nutting, William Springer.

Kevin McClatchy

BUSINESS OPERATIONS
Executive Vice President, Chief Operating Officer: Dick Freeman. **Director, Human Resources:** Sarah Tarosky.

Finance
Vice President, Finance: Jim Plake.

Controller: David Bowman. **Director, Finance:** Patti Mistick. **Director, Information Systems:** Terry Zeigler.

Marketing, Sales
Vice President, Marketing/Sales: Vic Gregovits.

Director, Marketing/Sales: Mike Harmon. **Senior Account Executives:** Jim Alexander, Chris Cronin.

Director, Promotions: Rick Orienza. **Director, Broadcast Operations:** Mark Ferraco. **Coordinator, Broadcasting:** Marc Garda.

Public Relations, Communications
Telephone: (412) 323-5031. **FAX:** (412) 323-5009.

Vice President, Communications/Ballpark Development: Steven Greenberg.

Director, Media Relations: Jim Trdinich. **Assistant Director, Media Relations:** Ben Bouma. **Assistant, Media Relations:** Mike Kennedy. **Assistants, Public Relations:** Sherry Rusiski, Chris Serkoch.

Director, Player Relations: Kathy Guy.

Director, Marketing Communications: Michael Gordon. **Director, Corporate Affairs:** Nelson Briles. **Director, Community Sales:** Al Gordon.

Stadium Operations
Vice President, Stadium Operations: Dennis DaPra.

Assistant Director, Stadium Operations: Chris Hunter.

Manager, In-Game Operations: Eric Wolff.

Head Groundskeeper: Tony LaPia.

PA Announcer: Tim DeBacco. **Official Scorers:** Tony Krizmanich, Evan Pattak, Bob Webb.

Ticketing
Telephone: (412) 321-2827. **FAX:** (412) 323-9133.

Director, Ticket Operations: Gary Remlinger. **Manager, Ticket Sales:** David Wysocki. **Assistant Director, Ticket Sales:** Jeff Smith.

Travel, Clubhouse
Traveling Secretary: Greg Johnson.

Equipment Manager/Home Clubhouse Operations: Roger Wilson. **Visitors Clubhouse Operations:** Kevin Conrad.

General Information
Home Dugout: First Base. **Playing Surface:** Artificial turf.

Standard Game Times: 7:05 p.m., Sun. 1:35.

Stadium Directions: From south, I-279 through Fort Pitt Tunnel, make left off bridge to Fort Duquesne Bridge, cross Fort Duquesne Bridge, follow signs to Three Rivers Stadium, make left to stadium parking at light. From north, I-279 to Three Rivers Stadium exit (exit 12, left lane), follow directions to parking.

Player Representative: Al Martin.

PIRATES

BASEBALL OPERATIONS

Telephone: (412) 323-5012. **FAX:** (412) 323-5024.

Senior Vice President, General Manager: Cam Bonifay.

Assistant General Managers: John Sirignano, Roy Smith. **Special Assistants to General Manager:** Chet Montgomery, Kenny Parker, Willie Stargell, Lenny Yochim. **Administrative Assistant, Baseball Operations:** Jeannie Donatelli.

Major League Staff

Manager: Gene Lamont.

Coaches: Bench—Rick Renick; Pitching—Pete Vuckovich; Batting—Lloyd McClendon; First Base—Joe Jones; Third Base—Jack Lind; Bullpen—Spin Williams.

Cam Bonifay

Medical, Training

Team Physicians: Dr. Joe Coroso, Dr. Jack Failla.

Head Trainer: Kent Biggerstaff. **Assistant Trainer:** Bill Henry. **Strength and Conditioning Coach:** Dr. Warren Sipp.

Minor Leagues

Telephone: (412) 323-5033. **FAX:** (412) 323-5024.

Director, Player Development: Paul Tinnell. **Assistant Director, Player Development:** Bill Bryk. **Administrator, Minor Leagues:** Diane Grimaldi.

Gene Lamont

Coordinator, Instruction: Steve Demeter.

Roving Instructors: Bill Bryk (pitching), Marc Hill (catching), Bobby Meacham (infield/baserunning), Pat Roessler (hitting).

Farm System

Class	Farm Team	Manager	Coach	Pitching Coach
AAA	Nashville	Trent Jewett	Richie Hebner	Bruce Tanner
AA	Altoona	Marty Brown	Jeff Livesey	Scott Lovekamp
A	Lynchburg	Scott Little	Greg Briley	Jim Bibby
A	Hickory	Tracy Woodson	Ben Oglivie	Steve Watson
A	Williamsport	Curtis Wilkerson	Ramon Sambo	Blaine Beatty
R	Bradenton	Woody Huyke	Tony Beasley	Dave Rajsich
R	DSL	Ramon Zapata	Unavailable	Miguel Bonilla

Scouting

Telephone: (412) 323-5035. **FAX:** (412) 323-5024.

Director, Scouting: Mickey White.

Assistant to Director, Scouting: Ron King (Sacramento, CA). **Assistant to Scouting/ Director, Amateur Development:** Jon Mercurio. **Coordinator, Scouting Systems:** Sandy Deutsch.

Advance Scout: Chris Lein (Boca Raton, FL).

Special Assignment Scouts: Jack Bloomfield, John Green (Phoenix, AZ).

National Crosschecker: Jim Guinn (Fairfield, CA). **Regional Coordinators:** Midwest—Tom Barnard (Houston, TX); East—Steve Fleming (Matoaca, VA); West—Scott Littlefield (Long Beach, CA).

Mickey White

Area Supervisors: Jason Angel (Glen Allen, VA), Russell Bowen (Charlotte, NC), Grant Brittain (Oklahoma City, OK), Dana Brown (Somerset, NJ), Dan Durst (Rockford, IL), Duane Gustavson (Columbus, OH), James House (Seattle, WA), Mike Kendall (Walnut Creek, CA), Craig Kornfeld (Los Angeles, CA), Greg McClain (Chandler, AZ), Jack Powell (Sweetwater, TN), Steve Riha (Houston, TX), Delvy Santiago (Vega Alta, PR), Rob Sidwell (Windermere, FL), George Swain (Raleigh, NC), Mike Williams (Oakland, CA).

Latin America Coordinators: Pablo Cruz (Dominican Republic), Jose Luna (Miami, FL).

ST. LOUIS

Telephone, Address
Office Address: 250 Stadium Plaza, St. Louis, MO 63102. Telephone: (314) 421-3060. FAX: (314) 425-0640. Website: www.stlcardinals.com.

Ownership
Operated by: St. Louis Cardinals, LP.

General Partner/Chairman of the Board: William DeWitt Jr. Chairman: Fred Hanser. Secretary/Treasurer: Andrew Baur.

President: Mark Lamping.

Mark Lamping

BUSINESS OPERATIONS
Director, Human Resources: Marian Rhodes. Senior Administrative Assistants: Grace Hale, Julie Laningham. Contract Coordinator/Office Services Assistant: Karen Brown.

Finance
Vice President, Controller: Brad Wood.

Director, Information Systems: Sally Lemons. Director, Accounting: Deborah Pfaff. Administrative Assistant: Beverly Finger. Senior Accountant: Michelle Flach.

Marketing, Sales
Vice President, Corporate Sales: Dan Farrell. Vice President, Business Development: Bill DeWitt III.

Administrative Assistant, Corporate Sales: Gail Ruhling. Corporate Sales Assistants: Matt Gifford, Theron Morgan, Tony Simokaitis, Kevin Stretch.

Director, Promotions: Thane van Brueusegen.

Director, Group Sales: Joe Strohm. Account Executives, Group Sales: Mary Clare Bena, Linda Burnside, Mike Hall.

Public Relations, Communications
Telephone: (314) 421-3060. FAX: (314) 982-7399.

Director, Media Relations: Brian Bartow. Assistant Director, Media Relations: Brad Hainje. Administrative Assistant, Media Relations: Melody Yount.

Manager, Publications/Media Relations: Steve Zesch.

Vice President, Community Relations: Marty Hendin. Administrative Assistant, Community Relations: Mary Ellen Edmiston.

Director, Speakers Bureau: Shawn Bertani. Director, Target Marketing: Ted Savage.

Stadium Operations
Vice President, Stadium Operations: Joe Abernathy.

Director, Stadium Operations: Mike Bertani. Director, Food/Beverage: Vicki Bryant. Director, Security/Special Services: Joe Walsh.

Head Groundskeeper: Bill Findley.

Ticketing
Telephone: (314) 421-2400. FAX: (314) 425-0649.

Director, Ticket Operations: Josie Arnold. Manager, Customer Service/Telephone Operations: Patti McCormick.

Group Director, Sales: Kevin Wade. Manager, Season Sales: Mark Murray. Deluxe Suite Services: Dennis Dolan.

Travel, Clubhouse
Traveling Secretary: C.J. Cherre.

Equipment Manager: Buddy Bates. Assistant Equipment Manager: Rip Rowan. Visiting Clubhouse Manager: Jerry Risch. Video Coordinator: Chad Blair.

General Information
Home Dugout: First Base. Playing Surface: Grass.

Standard Game Times: Weekdays 7:10 p.m.; Sat. 12:15, 1:10; Sun. 1:10.

Stadium Directions: From Illinois, take I-55 South, I-64 West, I-70 West or US 40 West across the Mississippi River (Poplar Street Bridge) to Busch Stadium exit. In Missouri, take I-55 North, I-64 East, I-70 East, I-44 East or US 40 East to downtown St. Louis and Busch Stadium exit.

Player Representative: John Frascatore.

CARDINALS

BASEBALL OPERATIONS
Telephone: (314) 425-0687. **FAX:** (314) 425-0648.
Vice President, General Manager: Walt Jocketty.
Vice President, Player Personnel: Jerry Walker. **Senior Executive Assistant to General Manager:** Judy Carpenter-Barada.

Major League Staff
Manager: Tony La Russa.
Coaches: Dugout—Jose Oquendo; Pitching—Dave Duncan; Batting—Mike Easler; First Base—Dave McKay; Third Base—Rene Lachemann; Bullpen—Mark DeJohn.

Walt Jocketty

Medical, Training
Club Physician: Dr. George Paletta.
Head Trainer: Barry Weinberg. **Assistant Trainer:** Brad Henderson.
Coordinator, Medical/Rehabilitation: Mark O'Neal.

Player Development
Telephone: (314) 421-3060. **FAX:** (314) 425-0638.
Director, Player Development: Mike Jorgensen.
Director, Minor League Operations: Scott Smulczenski. **Manager, Baseball Information/Assistant, Player Development:** John Vuch. **Administrative Assistant:** Judy Francis.
Senior Field Coordinator: George Kissell. **Field Coordinator:** Joe Pettini. **Pitching Coordinator:** Mark Riggins. **Hitting Coordinator:** Mitchell Page.

Tony La Russa

Roving Instructors: Luis Melendez (hitting), Dyar Miller (pitching), Pete Prinzi (strength/conditioning), Dave Ricketts (catching).

Farm System
Class	Farm Team	Manager	Coach	Pitching Coach
AAA	Memphis	Gaylen Pitts	Boots Day	Marty Mason
AA	Arkansas	Chris Maloney	Glen Brummer	Rich Folkers
A	Potomac	Joe Cunningham	Todd Steverson	Mark Grater
A	Peoria	Brian Rupp	Tony Diggs	Mike Snyder
A	New Jersey	Jeff Shireman	None	Gary Buckels
R	Johnson City	Steve Turco	None	Elias Sosa

Scouting
Telephone: (314) 516-0152. **FAX:** (314) 425-0638.
Director, Scouting: John Mozeliak. **Director, Player Procurement:** Jeff Scott. **Administrative Assistant, Scouting:** Linda Brauer.
Advance Scout: Joe Sparks (Phoenix, AZ).
Special Assignment Scouts: Marty Keough (Scottsdale, AZ), Fred McAlister (Katy, TX), Mike Squires (Kalamazoo, MI).
National Crosschecker: Mike Roberts (Kansas City, MO). **Regional Crosscheckers:** East—Tim Conroy (Monroeville, PA); West—Clark Crist (Tucson, AZ).
Professional Scouts: Chuck Fick (Newbury Park, CA), Joe Rigoli (Parsippany, NJ).

John Mozeliak

Area Scouts: Randy Benson (Salisbury, NC), Doug Carpenter (Boca Raton, FL), Chuck Fick (Newbury Park, CA), Ben Galante (Houston, TX), Steve Grilli (Baldwinsville, NY), Manny Guerra (Las Vegas, NV), Tim Hanser (St. Louis, MO), Dave Karaff (Lee's Summit, MO), Scott Melvin (Quincy, IL), Scott Nichols (Richland, MS), Jay North (Vacaville, CA), Dan Ontiveros (Santa Clara, CA), Tommy Shields (Lititz, PA), Roger Smith (Eastman, GA), Dane Walker (Canby, OR).
Coordinator, International Scouting: Tim Hanser.

SAN DIEGO

Telephone, Address
Office Address: 8880 Rio San Diego Dr., Suite 400, San Diego, CA 92108. **Mailing Address:** P.O. Box 122000, San Diego, CA 92112. **Telephone:** (619) 881-6500. **FAX:** (619) 497-5454. **Website:** www.padres.com.

Ownership
Operated by: Padres, LP.
Principal Owners: John Moores, Larry Lucchino.
Chairman: John Moores. **President, Chief Executive Officer:** Larry Lucchino.
Board of Directors: Calvin Hill, William Jones, Jeremy Kapstein, Larry Lucchino, John Moores, Charles Noell, Dan Okimoto, John Watson, Tom Werner, George Will.

John Moores

BUSINESS OPERATIONS
Executive Vice President, Business Operations: Bill Adams.
Vice President, General Counsel: Alan Ostfield.
Director, Administrative Services: Lucy Freeman.

Finance
Vice President, Finance: Bob Wells.
Controller: Steve Fitch. **Secretary to VP, Finance:** Melissa Garcia. **Manager, Accounting:** Duane Wright.

Marketing, Sales
Vice President, Corporate Development: Mike Dee.
Director, Sponsorship Services: Cheryl Smith. **Director, Multi-cultural Marketing:** Enrique Morones. **Manager, Compadres Club:** Brook Govan.

Public Relations, Community Relations
Telephone: (619) 881-6510. **FAX:** (619) 497-5454.
Senior Vice President, Public Affairs: Dr. Charles Steinberg. **Assistant to Senior VP, Public Affairs:** Dayle Boyd.
Director, Public Relations: Glenn Geffner. **Director, Publications:** John Schlegel. **Assistant, Media Relations:** John Dever.
Director, Community Relations: Michele Anderson. **Director, Entertainment:** Tim Young. **Assistant Director, Entertainment/Special Events:** Kate Rummer. **Manager, Advertising:** Darbi Booher. **Director, Fan Services:** Tim Katzman.

Stadium Operations
Director, Stadium Operations: Mark Guglielmo. **Project Manager:** Jack Autry. **Assistant, Stadium Operations:** Ken Kawachi.

Ticketing
Telephone: (619) 283-4494.
Director, Sales: Louie Ruvane. **Assistant Director, Sales:** Ron Bumgarner. **Manager, Sales Operations:** Mark Tilson.
Director, Ticket Operations: Dave Gilmore. **Assistant Director, Ticket Operations:** Jim Kiersnowski. **Assistant Director, Ticket Services:** Bill Risser. **Manager, Ticket Operations:** George Stieren. **Manager, Ticket Services:** Chandra George.

Travel, Clubhouse
Director, Team Travel/Equipment Manager: Brian Prilaman. **Visitors Clubhouse Operations:** David Bacharach.

General Information
Home Dugout: First Base. **Playing Surface:** Grass.
Standard Game Times: 7:05 p.m.; Wed. 7:35; Thurs. 2:05; Sun. 1:05.
Stadium Location: From downtown, Route 163 North to Friars Road, east to stadium. From north, I-15 South to Friars Road, west to stadium, or I-805 South to Route 163 South to Friars Road, west to stadium. From east, I-8 West to I-15 North to Friars Road, west to stadium. From west, I-8 East to Route 163 North to Friars Road, east to stadium.
Player Representative: Brian Boehringer.

PADRES

BASEBALL OPERATIONS
Telephone: (619) 881-6526. **FAX:** (619) 497-5338.
Senior Vice President/General Manager: Kevin Towers.

Assistant General Manager: Fred Uhlman Jr. **Special Assistant to General Manager:** Ken Bracey. **Director, Baseball Operations:** Eddie Epstein. **Assistant, Baseball Operations:** Theo Epstein.

Major League Staff
Manager: Bruce Bochy.
Coaches: Bench—Rob Picciolo; Pitching— Dave Smith; Batting—Merv Rettenmund; First Base—Davey Lopes; Third Base—Tim Flannery; Bullpen—Greg Booker.

Kevin Towers

Medical, Training
Club Physician: Scripps Clinic medical staff.
Head Trainer: Todd Hutcheson. **Assistant Trainer:** Jim Daniel. **Strength and Conditioning Coach:** Sam Gannelli.

Player Development
Telephone: (619) 881-6525. **FAX:** (619) 497-5338.
Director, Player Development: Jim Skaalen.
Assistant Director, Player Development: Jason McLeod. **Director, Minor League Operations:** Priscilla Oppenheimer. **Administrative Assistant, Minor Leagues:** Earleen Bender.
Coordinator of Instruction: Tye Waller. **Roving Instructors:** Jeff Andrews (pitching), Ben Bethea (strength/conditioning), Doug Dascenzo (outfield/baserunning), Duane Espy (hitting), Tony Franklin (infield), Don Werner (catching).

Bruce Bochy

Farm System

Class	Farm Team	Manager	Coach	Pitching Coach
AAA	Las Vegas	Mike Ramsey	Craig Colbert	Tom Brown
AA	Mobile	Mike Basso	Jim Bowie	Don Alexander
A	R. Cucamonga	Tom LeVasseur	Unavailable	Darrel Akerfelds
A	Fort Wayne	Dan Simonds	Eric Bullock	Tony Phillips
R	Idaho Falls	Don Werner	Gary Kendall	Darryl Milne
R	Peoria	Randy Whisler	Angel Morris	Sid Monge
R	DSL	Roberto Perez	Coronado/Melo	Roberto Sanchez

Scouting
Director, Scouting: Brad Sloan (Brimfield, IL).
Administrative Assistant, Scouting: Herta Bingham.

Major League Scouts: Ken Bracey (Lincoln, IL), Ray Crone (Waxahachie, TX), Moose Johnson (Arvada, CO). **Advance Scout:** Jeff Gardner (Newport Beach, CA).

National Supervisor: Bob Cummings (Oak Lawn, IL). **Regional Supervisors:** East—Andy Hancock (Tryon, NC); West—Jim Woodward (La Mirada, CA).

Professional Scouts: Charles Bolton (San Diego, CA), Gary Roenicke (Nevada City, CA), Gene Watson (Temple, TX).

Brad Sloan

Area Scouts: Joe Bochy (Plant City, FL), Rich Bordi (Rohnert Park, CA), Jimmy Dreyer (Euless, TX), Chris Gwynn (Alta Loma, CA), Rich Hacker (Belleville, IL), Mike Keenan (Chicago, IL), Gary Kendall (Baltimore, MD), Don Lyle (Sacramento, CA), Tim McWilliam (San Diego, CA), Bill Mele (El Segundo, CA), Darryl Milne (Denver, CO), Rene Mons (Manchester, NH), Steve Nichols (Mount Dora, FL), Jack Pierce (Laredo, TX), Van Smith (Belleville, IL), Mark Wasinger (El Paso, TX).

Director, International Scouting: Gary Nickels (Naperville, IL).

International Scouts: Ronquito Garcia (Puerto Rico), Juan Melo (Dominican Republic).

SAN FRANCISCO

Telephone, Address
Office Address: 3Com Park at Candlestick Point, San Francisco, CA 94124. Telephone: (415) 468-3700. FAX: (415) 467-0485. Website: www.sf giants.com.

Ownership
Operated by: San Francisco Baseball Associates, LP.

President, Managing General Partner: Peter Magowan. Senior General Partner: Harmon Burns.

Special Assistant to President: Willie Mays.

Peter Magowan

BUSINESS OPERATIONS
Executive Vice President, Chief Operating Officer: Larry Baer. Senior Vice President, Business Operations: Pat Gallagher.

Vice President, General Counsel: Jack Bair. Vice President, Public Affairs: Staci Slaughter.

Director, Human Resources: Joyce Thomas.

Finance
Senior Vice President, Chief Financial Officer: John Yee.

Director, Finance: Robert Quinn. Director, Information Systems: Jerry Drobny.

Marketing, Sales
Vice President, Marketing and Sales: Mario Alioto.

Director, Corporate Sponsorship: Jason Pearl. Promotions Manager: Valerie McGuire.

General Manager, Retail/Internet: Connie Kullberg. Director, Retail Operations: Derik Landry.

Public Relations, Communications
Telephone: (415) 330-2448. FAX: (415) 467-0485.

Vice President, Communications: Bob Rose.

Manager, Media Relations: Jim Moorehead. Coordinator, Media Services/Broadcast: Maria Jacinto. Coordinator, Media and Player Relations: Blake Rhodes. Assistant, Media Relations: Dan Martinez. Director, Publications: Nancy Donati.

Stadium Operations
Vice President, Stadium Operations/Security: Jorge Costa.

Director, Stadium Operations: Gene Telucci. Director, Maintenance: Willie Guzman.

PA Announcer: Sherry Davis. Official Scorers: Chuck Dybdal, Dick O'Connor, Art Santo Domingo, Bob Stevens.

Ticketing
Telephone: (415) 467-8000. FAX: (415) 330-2572.

Vice President, Ticket Services: Russ Stanley. Manager, Ticket Services: Bob Bisio. Manager, Ticket Accounting: Kem Easley. Manager, Customer Service: Craig Hedrick. Manager, Ticket Operations: Anita Sprinkles.

Vice President, Ticket Sales: Mark Norelli.

Director, Group Sales: Jeff Tucker. Manager, Special Accounts: Jane Rand Kaplan. Coordinator, Community Sales: Claire Matthew. Manager, Inside Sales: Chris Schwarze.

Travel, Clubhouse
Director, Travel: Reggie Younger Jr.

Equipment Manager: Mike Murphy. Visitors Clubhouse: Harvey Hodgerney. Assistant Equipment Manager: Richard Cacace.

General Information
Home Dugout: First Base. Playing Surface: Grass.

Standard Game Times: 12:35 p.m., 1:05, 7:05, 7:35; Sat.-Sun. 1:05.

Stadium Location: Highway 101 to 3Com Park exit.

Player Representative: Jeff Kent.

GIANTS

BASEBALL OPERATIONS

Telephone: (415) 468-3700. **FAX:** (415) 330-2691.

Senior Vice President, General Manager: Brian Sabean.

Vice President, Assistant General Manager: Ned Colletti. **Special Assistant to General Manager:** Jim Fregosi.

Executive Assistant, Baseball Administration: Jamie Gaines. **Executive Assistant, Baseball Operations:** Karen Sweeney. **Assistant, Baseball Operations:** Jeremy Shelley.

Brian Sabean

Major League Staff

Manager: Dusty Baker.

Coaches: Bench—Ron Wotus; Pitching—Ron Perranoski; Batting—Gene Clines; First Base—Carlos Alfonso; Third Base—Sonny Jackson; Bullpen—Juan Lopez.

Medical, Training

Team Physicians: Dr. William Montgomery, Dr. Robert Murray.

Head Trainer: Mark Letendre. **Assistant Trainer:** Stan Conte.

Player Development

Vice President, Player Personnel: Dick Tidrow. **Director, Player Development:** Jack Hiatt. **Special Assistant, Player Development:** Joe Amalfitano. **Director, Minor League Administration:** Bobby Evans. **Special Assistant, Player Personnel:** Bobby Bonds.

Coordinator, Instruction: Keith Bodie. **Coordinator, Hitting:** Joe Lefebvre. **Roving Instructors:** Jim Davenport, Dan Gladden, Robby Thompson, Dave Righetti.

Dusty Baker

Farm System

Class	Farm Team	Manager	Coach	Pitching Coach
AAA	Fresno	Ron Roenicke	Mike Hart	Joel Horlen
AA	Shreveport	Shane Turner	Unavailable	Ross Grimsley
A	San Jose	Lenn Sakata	Unavailable	Shawn Barton
A	Bakersfield	Keith Comstock	Mike Felder	Bert Bradley
A	Salem-Keizer	Frank Reberger	Bert Hunter	Gabriel Luckert
R	DSL	Fausto Sosa	Osvaldo Oliva	Jesus Lazos

Scouting

Telephone: (415) 330-2538. **FAX:** (415) 330-2691.

Coordinator, Scouting: Matt Nerland.

Special Assistant, Player Personnel: Ted Uhlaender (McGregor, TX). **Special Assignment Scout:** Joe DiCarlo (Ringwood, NJ).

Advance Scout: Pat Dobson (Key West, FL). **Major League Scouts:** Cal Emery (Lake Forest, CA), Randy Waddill (Valrico, FL).

Regional Crosscheckers: West—Doug Mapson (Phoenix, AZ); North—Stan Saleski (Dayton, OH); South—Paul Turco (Sarasota, FL).

Area Scouts: Steve Arnieri (Palatine, IL), Dick Cole (Costa Mesa, CA), Tom Korenek (Houston, TX), Alan Marr (Bellmore, NY), Doug McMillan

Dick Tidrow

(Shingle Springs, CA), Bobby Myrick (Colonial Heights, VA), Larry Osborne (Woodstock, GA), John Shafer (Portland, OR), Joe Strain (Englewood, CO), Todd Thomas (Dallas, TX), Glenn Tufts (Bridgewater, MA), Darren Wittcke (Laguna Niguel, CA), Tom Zimmer (St. Petersburg, FL).

Coordinator, International Operations: Rick Ragazzo. **Assistant Coordinator, International Operations:** John Dipuglia (Pembroke Pines, FL). **Special Assignment Scouts:** Matty Alou (Dominican Republic), Ozzie Virgil (Glendale, AZ).

Major League Schedules

1998 Standings • Spring Training

AMERICAN LEAGUE

1998 STANDINGS

EAST	W	L	PCT	GB	Manager
New York Yankees	114	48	.704	—	Joe Torre
Boston Red Sox*	92	70	.568	22	Jimy Williams
Toronto Blue Jays	88	74	.543	26	Tim Johnson
Baltimore Orioles	79	83	.488	35	Ray Miller
Tampa Bay Devil Rays	63	99	.389	51	Larry Rothschild

CENTRAL	W	L	PCT	GB	Manager(s)
Cleveland Indians	89	73	.549	—	Mike Hargrove
Chicago White Sox	80	82	.494	9	Jerry Manuel
Kansas City Royals	72	89	.447	16½	Tony Muser
Minnesota Twins	70	92	.432	19	Tom Kelly
Detroit Tigers	65	97	.401	24	Buddy Bell/Larry Parrish

WEST	W	L	PCT	GB	Manager
Texas Rangers	88	74	.543	—	Johnny Oates
Anaheim Angels	85	77	.525	3	Terry Collins
Seattle Mariners	76	85	.472	11½	Lou Piniella
Oakland Athletics	74	88	.457	14	Art Howe

PLAYOFFS: Division Series (best-of-5)—New York defeated Texas 3-0; Cleveland defeated Boston 3-1. **League Championship Series** (best-of-7)—New York defeated Cleveland 4-2.

NATIONAL LEAGUE

1998 STANDINGS

EAST	W	L	PCT	GB	Manager
Atlanta Braves	106	56	.654	—	Bobby Cox
New York Mets	88	74	.543	18	Bobby Valentine
Philadelphia Phillies	75	87	.463	31	Terry Francona
Montreal Expos	65	97	.401	41	Felipe Alou
Florida Marlins	54	108	.333	52	Jim Leyland

CENTRAL	W	L	PCT	GB	Manager
Houston Astros	102	60	.630	—	Larry Dierker
Chicago Cubs*	90	73	.552	12½	Jim Riggleman
St. Louis Cardinals	83	79	.512	19	Tony La Russa
Cincinnati Reds	77	85	.475	25	Jack McKeon
Milwaukee Brewers	74	88	.457	28	Phil Garner
Pittsburgh Pirates	69	93	.426	33	Gene Lamont

WEST	W	L	PCT	GB	Manager(s)
San Diego Padres	98	64	.605	—	Bruce Bochy
San Francisco Giants	89	74	.546	9½	Dusty Baker
Los Angeles Dodgers	83	79	.512	15	B. Russell/G. Hoffman
Colorado Rockies	77	85	.475	21	Don Baylor
Arizona Diamondbacks	65	97	.401	33	Buck Showalter

PLAYOFFS: Division Series (best-of-5)—Atlanta defeated Chicago 3-0; San Diego defeated Houston 3-1. **League Championship Series** (best-of-7)—San Diego defeated Atlanta 4-2.

*Won wild-card playoff berth

WORLD SERIES
(Best-of-7)
New York defeated San Diego 4-0

AMERICANLEAGUE

AMERICAN LEAGUE 1999 SCHEDULE

ANAHEIM ANGELS
Edison International Field

APRIL
6-7-8 .... Cleveland
9-10-**11-12** .... at Texas
13-14-**15** ...... at Oakland
16-17-**18** .... Seattle
20-21-22 ...... at Toronto
23-**24-25** .... at K.C.
26-27-28-29 ..... Toronto
30 .... White Sox
MAY
1-**2-3** .... White Sox
4-5-6 .... at Detroit
7-**8-9** .... at Boston
11-12-13 ...... at Yankees
14-15-16 ..... Tampa Bay
18-19-20 .... at Baltimore
21-22-**23** . at Tampa Bay
25-26-27 ...... Baltimore
28-29-**30** .... K.C.
31 .... Minnesota
JUNE
1-2 .... Minnesota

4-5-6 .... at Los Angeles*
7-**8-9** .... at San Fran.*
11-12-**13** .... Arizona*
15-16-17 .... at Toronto
18-**19-20** ...... at Yankees
22-23-24 ..... at Seattle
25-26-27 .... Oakland
28-29-30 .... Texas
JULY
2-3-**4** .... at Oakland
5-6-7 .... Seattle
9-10-**11** .... at Colo.*
15-16-17 .... L.A.*
18-19-20 ..... San Diego*
21-22 .... at Texas
23-**24-25** .... at Balt.
26-27-28 . at Tampa Bay
30-31 .... Minnesota
AUGUST
1 .... Minnesota
2-3-4 .... K.C.
5-6-7-**8** .... Boston

9-10-11 .... Cleveland
13-**14-15** .... at Detroit
16-17-18-**19** ... at W. Sox
20-21-**22**-23 .... Detroit
24-25 .... Toronto
27-**28-29** ...... at Boston
30-31 .... at Cleveland
SEPTEMBER
1-2 .... at Cleveland
3-**4-5-6** .... Yankees
7-8 .... White Sox
10-**11-12**-13 ...... at K.C.
14-15-16 .... at K.C.
17-18-19 .... Baltimore
20-21-22 ..... Tampa Bay
24-25-**26** ..... at Seattle
28-29-30 .... Oakland
OCTOBER
1-2-**3** .... Texas

BALTIMORE ORIOLES
Oriole Park at Camden Yards

APRIL
5-7-8 .... Tampa Bay
9-**10-11** .... Toronto
13-14-15 ..... at Yankees
16-**17-18** .... at Toronto
20-21-22 . at Tampa Bay
23-**24-25** .... Oakland
27-28-29 ... Kansas City
30 .... Minnesota
MAY
1-**2** .... Minnesota
4-5-6 .... White Sox
7-**8-9** .... at Detroit
10-11-12 ... at Cleveland
13-14-15-**16** ..... at Texas
18-19-20 .... Anaheim
21-**22-23** .... Texas
25-26-27 ..... at Anaheim
28-29-**30** ..... at Oakland
31 .... at Seattle
JUNE
1-2 .... at Seattle

4-5-**6** .... Philadelphia*
7-8-9 .... at Florida*
11-**12**-13 .... at Atlanta*
14-15-**16** ... Kansas City
17-**18**-19-**20** ... at W. Sox
22-23-24 .... Boston
25-**26-27** .... Yankees
29-30 .... at Toronto
JULY
1 .... at Toronto
2-**3-4-5** ...... at Yankees
6-**7-8** .... Toronto
9-10-**11** .... at Phila.*
15-16-17 ...... Montreal*
18-19-20 .... Mets*
21-22 .... at Boston
23-**24-25** .... Anaheim
27-28-**29** .... Texas
30-**31** .... at Seattle
AUGUST
1 .... at Seattle
2-3-**4** .... at Oakland

5-6-7-**8** .... Detroit
9-10-11 .... at Tampa Bay
13-**14-15** ... at Cleveland
17-18-19 .... Minnesota
20-21-**22** ...... White Sox
23-24-25-26 .... at K.C.
27-**28-29** .... at Detroit
31 .... Tampa Bay
SEPTEMBER
1-2 .... Tampa Bay
3-**4-5-6** .... Cleveland
7-8-9 ...... at Minnesota
10-**11-12**-13 ...... Seattle
14-15-**16** .... Oakland
17-18-**19** ..... at Anaheim
21-22 .... at Texas
24-**25-26**-27 ... at Boston
28-29-30 .... Yankees
OCTOBER
1-2-3 .... Boston

NOTE: Dates in **bold** indicate afternoon games.
* Interleague Series

BOSTON RED SOX
Fenway Park

APRIL
5-7-8 .... at K.C.
9-10-**11**.... at Tampa Bay
13-15 .... White Sox
16-**17-18-19** Tampa Bay
20-21-**22**........ at Detroit
23-**24-25**...... Cleveland
26-27-**28**....... at Minn.
30 .... at Oakland

MAY
1-2-3 .... at Oakland
5-6 .... Texas
7-**8-9**............... Anaheim
10-11-12............. Seattle
14-**15-16-17** .. at Toronto
18-19-20........... Yankees
21-**22-23**........... Toronto
24-25-26...... at Cleveland
28-**29-30** .. at Cleveland
31 .... Detroit

JUNE
1-2 .... Detroit

4-**5-6** .... Atlanta*
7-8-9 .... at Montreal*
11-**12-13**.......... at Mets*
14-15-16-17......... Minn.
18-19-20-21 .... Texas
22-23-24 .... at Baltimore
25-**26-27-28**...... W. Sox
30 .... Tampa Bay

JULY
1 .... Tampa Bay
2-3-**4** .... at White Sox
5-6-7-8 ... at Tampa Bay
9-10-11 .... at Atlanta*
15-16-**17**... Philadelphia*
18-19-20 .... Florida*
21-22.............. Baltimore
23-**24-25** .... at Detroit
27-28............. at Toronto
30-**31** .... Yankees

AUGUST
1 .... Yankees
2-3-**4**.............. Cleveland

5-6-7-**8** .... at Anaheim
9-10-**11**........ at K.C.
13-**14-15** .... Seattle
16-17-18-19.... Oakland
20-21-22 ...... at Texas
23-24-25 ..... at Minn.
27-**28-29**...... Anaheim
30-31 ...... Kansas City

SEPTEMBER
1-2 .... Kansas City
3-4-**5-6** .... at Seattle
7-**8** .... at Oakland
10-**11-12** ..... at Yankees
13-14-15 ... at Cleveland
17-**18-19** .... Detroit
21-22-23............. Toronto
24-**25-26**-27 .... Balt.
28-29-30 ...... at W. Sox

OCTOBER
1-2-3 .... at Baltimore

CHICAGO WHITE SOX
Comiskey Park

APRIL
5-6-7 .... at Seattle
9-10-11 ...... Kansas City
13-15 .... at Boston
16-**17-18** .... at K.C.
20-21-**22** .... Seattle
23-**24-25** .... Detroit
27-28-29...... Tampa Bay
30 .... at Anaheim

MAY
1-2-3 .... at Anaheim
4-5-**6** .... at Baltimore
7-8-**9** .... Oakland
10-11-12............... Texas
14-**15-16**...... at Yankees
17-18-19......... Cleveland
21-22-**23**........... Yankees
24-25-26 .. at Cleveland
27-28-**29-30**.... at Detroit

JUNE
1-2-**3**............ at Toronto

4-**5-6** .... Pittsburgh*
7-8-9............... Houston*
11-12-13 .... at Cubs*
14-15-16..... Tampa Bay
17-**18**-19-**20** .. Baltimore
22-23-24........... Minnesota
25-**26-27-28**.... at Boston
29-30 ..... at Kansas City

JULY
1 .... at Kansas City
2-3-4 .... Boston
6-7-**8** .... Kansas City
9-10-11 .... Cubs*
15-16-17... at St. Louis*
18-19-20 . at Milwaukee*
21-22 .... at Minnesota
23-24-25-26 ...... Toronto
27-28-**29** .... Yankees
30-**31**......... at Cleveland

AUGUST
1 .... at Cleveland

2-3 .... at Detroit
5-6-**7-8**........ at Oakland
9-10-11........ at Seattle
13-**14-15** .... Texas
16-17-18-**19** .... Anaheim
20-21-22 ..... at Oakland
23-24-25-**26**. at Tampa Bay
27-28-**29** .... Oakland
30-31.................. Seattle

SEPTEMBER
1................................ Seattle
3-4-**5-6**............... at Texas
7-8.................. at Anaheim
10-11-**12**........ Cleveland
13-14-15 .... Detroit
17-**18-19**........ at Toronto
21-22-**23**......... at Yankees
24-25-**26**-27 ..... at Minn.
28-29-30 .... Boston

OCTOBER
1-2-3 .... Minnesota

CLEVELAND INDIANS
Jacobs Field

APRIL
6-7-8 .... at Anaheim
9-10-11.... at Minnesota
12-14-15 ... Kansas City
16-**17-18**....... Minnesota
20-21-22 .... Oakland
23-**24-25** .... at Boston
26-27-**28-29**. at Oakland
30.................... at Texas

MAY
1-2-3 .... at Texas
5-6..................... Seattle
7-**8-9**........... Tampa Bay
10-11-12......... Baltimore
14-**15-16**....... at Detroit
17-18-19 .. at White Sox
21-**22-23**............ Detroit
24-25-26 ...... White Sox
28-**29-30**.......... Boston
31 .... at Yankees

JUNE
1-2 .... at Yankees

4-**5-6**..................... Cubs*
8-9-10 ....Milwaukee*
11-**12-13**... at Cincinnati*
15-16-17 .... Oakland
18-**19-20**-21 .... Seattle
22-23-24....... at Toronto
25-26-**27-28** ..... at K.C.
29-30 .... Minnesota

JULY
1 .... Minnesota
2-3-**4** .... Kansas City
6-7-**8** .... at Minnesota
9-10-11........ Cincinnati*
15-16-**17**.. at Pittsburgh*
18-19-20... at Houston*
21-22............... Toronto
23-**24-25**....... at Yankees
26-27-28 .... Detroit
30-**31** .... White Sox

AUGUST
1 .... White Sox
2-3-**4** .... at Boston

6-7-**8** ...... at Tampa Bay
9-10-**11**....... at Anaheim
13-**14-15** .... Baltimore
16-17-18-19 .... Texas
20-**21-22-23** ... at Seattle
24-25 .... at Oakland
27-**28-29**...... Tampa Bay
30-31 .... Anaheim

SEPTEMBER
1-2........................ Anaheim
3-4-**5-6** .... at Baltimore
7-**8** .... at Texas
10-11-**12** ... at White Sox
13-14-15 .... Boston
16-17-**18-19**...... Yankees
20-21-22-23... at Detroit
24-**25-26**....... at Toronto
28-29 ..... at Kansas City
30 .... Toronto

OCTOBER
1-2-**3**.................. Toronto

DETROIT TIGERS
Tiger Stadium

APRIL
5-6-7 .... at Texas
9-10-11 .... at Yankees
12-14-15 ...... Minnesota
16-**17-18** .... Yankees
20-21-**22** .... Boston
23-**24-25** .... at W. Sox
26-27-28-**29** ... at Seattle
30 .... at Tampa Bay

MAY
1-2-3 ...... at Tampa Bay
4-5-6 .... Anaheim
7-8-9 .... Baltimore
11-12 .... Oakland
14-**15-16** .... Cleveland
18-19-20 .... at Toronto
21-**22-23** ... at Cleveland
24-25-26 .... Toronto
27-28-**29-30** ..... W. Sox
31 .... at Boston

JUNE
1-2 .... at Boston

4-**5-6** .... St. Louis*
7-8-9 .... Pittsburgh*
11-12-**13** ... at St. Louis*
14-15-16-17 ...... Seattle
18-**19-20-21** ..... Oakland
22-23-24 .... at K.C.
25-**26-27** .... Minnesota
29-**30** .... at Yankees

JULY
1 .... at Yankees
2-**3-4** .... at Minnesota
6-7-8 .... Yankees
9-**10-11** .... Milwaukee*
15-16-17 ... at Houston*
18-19-20 .. at Cincinnati*
21-**22** .... Kansas City
23-**24-25** .... Boston
26-27-28 ... at Cleveland
30-**31** .... at Toronto

AUGUST
1 .... at Toronto
2-3 .... White Sox

5-6-7-**8** ...... at Baltimore
10-11-**12** .... at Texas
13-**14-15** .... Anaheim
16-17-18 ... Tampa Bay
20-21-**22**-23 .. at Anaheim
24-25 .... at Seattle
27-28-**29** .... Baltimore
30-31 .... Texas

SEPTEMBER
1-2 .... Texas
3-**4-5-6** .... at Oakland
8-9 ...... at Tampa Bay
10-11-**12** .... Toronto
13-14-15 ... at White Sox
17-**18-19** .... at Boston
20-21-22-23 .. Cleveland
24-**25-26-27** .... K.C.
28-29-30 ...... at Minn.

OCTOBER
1-2-3 ... at Kansas City

KANSAS CITY ROYALS
Kauffman Stadium

APRIL
5-7-8 .... Boston
9-10-11 ...... at White Sox
12-14-15 ... at Cleveland
16-**17-18** ..... White Sox
19-20-21 ...... Minnesota
23-**24-25** .... Anaheim
27-28-29 ... at Baltimore
30 .... Yankees

MAY
1-2-3 .... Yankees
4-**5-6** .... at Tampa Bay
7-8-**9-10** ... at Minnesota
11-12-**13** .... Toronto
14-**15-16** .... at Seattle
18-19-20 .... Oakland
21-22-**23** .... Seattle
25-**26-27** ...... at Oakland
28-29-**30** ...... at Anaheim
31 .... at Texas

JUNE
1-2 .... at Texas

4-5-**6** .... Cincinnati*
7-8-9 .... St. Louis*
11-12-**13** ... at Pittsburgh*
14-15-16-17 ... at Baltimore
18-**19-20-21** .. at Toronto
22-23-**24** .... Detroit
25-26-27-**28** .. Cleveland
29-30 .... White Sox

JULY
1 .... White Sox
2-**3-4** .... at Cleveland
6-7-8 .... at White Sox
9-10-11 .... Houston*
15-16-17 ... at Milwaukee*
18-19-20 .... at Cubs*
21-**22** .... at Detroit
23-24-25 .... Oakland
27-28-**29** .... Seattle
30-31 .... at Texas

AUGUST
1 .... at Texas
2-3-4 .... at Anaheim

6-7-8 .... Minnesota
9-10-11 .... Boston
12-13-14-**15** Tampa Bay
17-18-**19** ..... at Yankees
20-21-**22** . at Tampa Bay
23-24-25-26 ... Baltimore
27-28-**29** .... at Minn.
30-31 .... at Boston

SEPTEMBER
1-2 .... at Boston
3-**4-5** .... Toronto
7-8 .... Yankees
10-11-**12**-13 .... Texas
14-**15-16** .... Anaheim
17-**18-19** .... at Oakland
20-21-22 .... at Seattle
24-**25-26-27** ..... at Detroit
28-29 .... Cleveland

OCTOBER
1-2-3 .... Detroit

MINNESOTA TWINS
Hubert H. Humphrey Metrodome

APRIL
6-7-8 .... Toronto
9-10-**11** .... Cleveland
12-14-15 ...... at Detroit
16-**17-18** ... at Cleveland
19-20-21 .... at K.C.
22-23-**24-25** .... Texas
26-27-**28** .... Boston
30 .... at Baltimore

MAY
1-2 .... at Baltimore
4-**5-6** .... Yankees
7-8-**9**-10 ... Kansas City
11-**12** .... at Tampa Bay
14-**15-16** .... at Oakland
17-18-19 .... at Seattle
21-22-**23** .... Oakland
24-25-26 .... Seattle
28-29-**30** .... at Texas
31 .... at Anaheim

JUNE
1-2 .... at Anaheim

4-5-**6** .... Houston*
7-8-9 .... Cincinnati*
11-12-**13** . at Milwaukee*
14-15-16-17 ...... at Boston
18-**19-20-21** Tampa Bay
22-23-**24** ... at White Sox
25-**26-27** .... at Detroit
29-30 .... at Cleveland

JULY
1 .... at Cleveland
2-**3-4** .... Detroit
6-7-8 .... Cleveland
9-10-**11** .... Pittsburgh*
15-**16-17** .... at Cubs*
18-19-20 ... at St. Louis*
21-22 .... White Sox
23-24-25 .... Seattle
26-27-**28** .... Oakland
30-31 .... at Anaheim

AUGUST
1 .... at Anaheim
2-3-4 .... at Texas

6-7-8 ...... at Kansas City
10-11-**12** .... Toronto
13-**14-15**-16. at Yankees
17-18-19 ... at Baltimore
20-21-**22** .... Yankees
23-24-25 .... Boston
27-28-**29** ... Kansas City
30-31 .... at Toronto

SEPTEMBER
1-2 .... at Toronto
3-4-**5-6** .... at Tampa Bay
7-8-9 .... Baltimore
10-11-**12**-13..... Anaheim
14-15 .... Texas
17-18-**19** .... at Seattle
20-**21-22** .... at Oakland
24-25-26-**27** .. White Sox
28-29-30 .... Detroit

OCTOBER
1-2-**3** ...... at White Sox

NEW YORK YANKEES
Yankee Stadium

APRIL
5-6-**7** .... at Oakland
9-10-11 .... Detroit
13-14-15 .... Baltimore
16-**17-18** .... at Detroit
20-21 .... Texas
23-**24-25** .... Toronto
27-28-29 .... at Texas
30 .... at Kansas City
MAY
1-2-3 .... at Kansas City
4-5-**6** .... at Minnesota
7-**8-9** .... Seattle
11-12-13 .... Anaheim
14-**15-16** .... White Sox
18-19-20 .... at Boston
21-22-**23** .... at W. Sox
24-25-26 .... Boston
28-**29-30** ...... at Toronto
31 .... Cleveland
JUNE
1-2 .... Cleveland

4-5-6 .... Mets*
7-8-9 ... at Philadelphia*
11-12-**13** .... at Florida*
14-15-16-17 .... Texas
18-**19**-20 .... Anaheim
22-23-24 . at Tampa Bay
25-**26-27** ...... at Baltimore
29-**30** .... Detroit
JULY
1 .... Detroit
2-3-**4**-5 .... Baltimore
6-7-8 .... at Detroit
9-10-**11** .... at Mets*
15-16-**17** .... Atlanta*
18-19-20 .... Montreal*
21-22 .... Tampa Bay
23-**24-25** .... Cleveland
27-**28-29** .... at W. Sox
30-**31** .... at Boston
AUGUST
1 .... at Boston
2-3-**4** .... Toronto

5-6-7-**8** .... at Seattle
9-10-11 .... at Oakland
13-**14-15**-16 .... Minn.
17-18-**19** .... Kansas City
20-21-**22** .... at Minn.
23-24-25 .... at Texas
27-**28-29** .... Seattle
30-31 .... at Oakland
SEPTEMBER
1-2 .... Oakland
3-4-**5-6** .... at Anaheim
7-8 .... at Kansas City
10-**11-12** .... Boston
13-14-15 .... at Toronto
16-17-**18-19** at Cleveland
21-22-23 ...... White Sox
24-**25-26-27** Tampa Bay
28-29-30 ... at Baltimore
OCTOBER
1-2-**3** .... at Tampa Bay

OAKLAND ATHLETICS
Oakland-Alameda County Coliseum

APRIL
5-6-**7** .... Yankees
9-10-**11**-12 ..... at Seattle
13-14-15 ....Anaheim
16-**17-18** .... Texas
20-21-22 ... at Cleveland
23-**24-25** .... at Baltimore
26-27-28-**29** . Cleveland
30 .... Boston
MAY
1-2-3 .... Boston
4-5-6 .... at Toronto
7-**8-9** .... at White Sox
11-12 .... at Detroit
14-**15-16** .... Minnesota
18-19-20 .... at K.C
21-22-**23** .... at Minn.
25-**26-27** .... Kansas City
28-**29-30** .... Baltimore
31 .... Tampa Bay
JUNE
1-**2** .... Tampa Bay

4-5-**6** .... at San Fran.*
8-9-**10** ... at San Diego*
11-12-13... Los Angeles*
15-16-17 ... at Cleveland
18-**19**-20-21 ... at Detroit
22-23-24 ...... at Texas
25-26-**27** ..... at Anaheim
29-30 .... Seattle
JULY
1 .... Seattle
2-3-4 .... Anaheim
5-6-**7** .... Texas
9-10-**11** .... at Arizona*
15-16-**17** ... San Fran.*
18-**19-20** .... Colorado*
21-22 .... at Seattle
23-24-25 .... at K.C.
26-27-**28** .... at Minn.
30-**31** .... Tampa Bay
AUGUST
1 .... Tampa Bay
2-3-**4** .... Baltimore

5-6-**7-8** .... White Sox
9-10-11 .... Yankees
13-**14-15** .... at Toronto
16-17-18-19 .. at Boston
20-21-**22-23** ...... Toronto
24-**25** .... Cleveland
27-28-**29** ...... at W. Sox
30-31 .... at Yankees
SEPTEMBER
1-2 .... at Yankees
3-4-5-6 .... Detroit
7-**8** .... Boston
10-11-**12-13** ...... at T.B.
14-15-**16** ... at Baltimore
17-**18-19** ... Kansas City
20-21-**22** ..... Minnesota
24-**25-26** ...... at Texas
28-29-30 ..... at Anaheim
OCTOBER
1-**2-3** .... Seattle

SEATTLE MARINERS
Kingdome/Safeco Field

APRIL
5-6-7 .... White Sox
9-10-**11**-12 .... Oakland
13-14-**15** .... Texas
16-17-**18** ...... at Anaheim
20-21-**22** .... at W. Sox
23-24-**25** . at Tampa Bay
26-27-28-**29** .... Detroit
30 .... Toronto
MAY
1-2-3 .... Toronto
5-**6** .... at Cleveland
7-**8-9** .... at Yankees
10-11-12 .... at Boston
14-**15-16** ...... Kansas City
17-18-19 ...... Minnesota
21-22-**23** .... at K.C.
24-25-**26** .... at Minn.
28-**29-30** ...... Tampa Bay
31 .... Baltimore
JUNE
1-2 .... Baltimore

4-5-**6** .... at San Diego*
7-8-9 ...... at Colorado*
11-12-13...... San Fran.*
14-15-16-17.... at Detroit
18-**19**-20-21 ... at Cleve.
22-23-24 .... Anaheim
25-**26-27** .... Texas
29-30 .... at Oakland
JULY
1 .... at Oakland
2-3-4 .... at Texas
5-6-**7** .... at Anaheim
9-10-**11** .... at L.A.*
15-16-17 ..... San Diego*
18-19-20 ...... Arizona*
21-**22** .... Oakland
23-24-**25** .... at Minn.
27-28-**29** .... at K.C.
30-**31** .... Baltimore
AUGUST
1 .... Baltimore
2-3-4 .... Tampa Bay

5-6-**7-8** .... Yankees
9-10-11 .... White Sox
13-**14-15** .... at Boston
16-17-**18** .... at Toronto
20-21-22-**23** .. Cleveland
24-25 .... Detroit
27-**28-29** ...... at Yankees
30-31 .... at W. Sox
SEPTEMBER
1 .... at W. Sox
3-4-**5-6** .... Boston
7-**8** .... Toronto
10-**11-12-13** . at Baltimore
14-15-16 . at Tampa Bay
17-**18-19** .... Minnesota
20-21-22 ... Kansas City
24-25-**26** .... Anaheim
27-28-29-30.... at Texas
OCTOBER
1-**2-3** .... at Oakland

TAMPA BAY DEVIL RAYS
Tropicana Field

APRIL
5-7-8 .... at Baltimore
9-10-**11**.............. Boston
12-13-14-15 .. at Toronto
16-**17-18-19** .. at Boston
20-21-22 .... Baltimore
23-24-**25** .... Seattle
27-28-**29** .... at W. Sox
30 .... Detroit

MAY
1-2-3 .... Detroit
4-5-6 .... Kansas City
7-**8-9** ..... at Cleveland
11-12 .... Minnesota
14-15-**16** ..... at Anaheim
17-18-**19** ...... at Texas
21-22-23......... Anaheim
24-25-26 .... Texas
28-29-**30** .... at Seattle
31 .... at Oakland

JUNE
1-**2** .... at Oakland

4-5-**6** .... Florida*
7-8-9 .... at Atlanta*
11-12-**13** .... at Montreal*
14-15-16 ..... at W. Sox
18-19-**20-21** .... at Minn.
22-23-24 .... Yankees
25-26-**27**-28 ...... Toronto
30.................. at Boston

JULY
1 .... at Boston
2-3-4............ at Toronto
5-6-7-8 .... Boston
9-10-11 ...... at Florida*
15-16-**17** .... Mets*
18-19-**20**... Philadelphia*
21-22 .... at Yankees
23-24-**25** .... Texas
26-27-28........ Anaheim
30-**31** .... at Oakland

AUGUST
1 .... at Oakland
2-3-4 .... at Seattle

6-7-**8**............. Cleveland
9-10-11.......... Baltimore
12-13-14-**15** .... at K.C.
16-17-18......... at Detroit
20-21-**22** .... Kansas City
23-24-25-**26**.. White Sox
27-**28-29** ... at Cleveland
31............. at Baltimore

SEPTEMBER
1-2 .... at Baltimore
3-4-**5-6**................. Minn.
8-9 .... Detroit
10-11-**12**-13 .... Oakland
14-15-16 .... Seattle
17-18-**19** ...... at Texas
20-21-22 ..... at Anaheim
24-**25-26**-27.. at Yankees
28-29 .... Toronto

OCTOBER
1-2-3 .... Yankees

TEXAS RANGERS
Ballpark in Arlington

APRIL
5-6-7 .... Detroit
9-10-**11-12**...... Anaheim
13-14-**15** .... at Seattle
16-**17-18** ...... at Oakland
20-21 .... at Yankees
22-23-24-**25** ..... at Minn.
27-28-29 .... Yankees
30 .... Cleveland

MAY
1-2-3............... Cleveland
5-6 .... at Boston
7-**8-9**............ at Toronto
10-11-12 ..... at W. Sox
13-14-15-**16** ... Baltimore
17-18-**19**...... Tampa Bay
21-**22-23** .... at Toronto
24-25-26 . at Tampa Bay
28-29-**30** .... Minnesota
31............. Kansas City

JUNE
1-**2** .... Kansas City

4-5-**6** .... at Arizona*
7-8-9 .... at Los Angeles*
11-12-**13**........ Colorado*
14-15-16-17. at Yankees
18-19-**20**-21 .. at Boston
22-23-24 .... Oakland
25-**26-27** .... at Seattle
28-29-30 .... at Anaheim

JULY
2-3-4 .... Seattle
5-6-**7** .... at Oakland
9-**10-11** .. at San Diego*
15-16-17 .... Arizona*
18-19-20 . San Francisco*
21-22 .... Anaheim
23-24-**25** . at Tampa Bay
27-28-**29** ... at Baltimore
30-31 .... Kansas City

AUGUST
1 .... Kansas City
2-3-4 .... Minnesota
6-7-8-9 .... Toronto

10-11-**12** .... Detroit
13-14-**15**........ at W. Sox
16-17-18-19 ... at Cleve.
20-21-22 .... Boston
23-24-25 .... Yankees
27-**28-29**....... at Toronto
30-31 .... at Detroit

SEPTEMBER
1-**2** .... at Detroit
3-**4**-5-6 .... White Sox
7-8 .... Cleveland
10-11-**12**-13...... at K.C.
14-15 .... at Minnesota
17-18-**19**...... Tampa Bay
21-22 .... Baltimore
24-25-**26** .... Oakland
27-28-29-30 .... Seattle

OCTOBER
1-2-3 .... at Anaheim

TORONTO BLUE JAYS
SkyDome

APRIL
6-7-8......... at Minnesota
9-**10-11** ...... at Baltimore
12-13-14-15 Tampa Bay
16-**17-18** ...... Baltimore
20-21-22.......... Anaheim
23-**24-25**..... at Yankees
26-27-28-29 at Anaheim
30.................. at Seattle

MAY
1-2-3 .... at Seattle
4-5-6 .... Oakland
7-**8-9** .... Texas
11-12-**13**............ at K.C.
14-**15-16-17** ...... Boston
18-19-20 .... Detroit
21-**22-23** ...... at Detroit
24-25-26 .... at Detroit
28-**29-30** .... Yankees

JUNE
1-2-3 .... White Sox
4-**5-6** .... Montreal*

7-8-9 .... at Mets*
11-12-**13** .... at Phil.*
15-16-17.......... Anaheim
18-19-**20**-21 . Kansas City
22-23-24.......... Cleveland
25-26-**27**-28. at Tampa Bay
29-30............. Baltimore

JULY
1 .... Baltimore
2-3-4.......... Tampa Bay
6-7-8 .... at Baltimore
9-10-**11** ...... at Montreal*
15-16-**17** .... Florida*
18-19-20 .... Atlanta*
21-22 .... at Cleveland
23-24-**25-26**... at W. Sox
27-28.............. Boston
30-**31** .... Detroit

AUGUST
1 .... Detroit
2-3-**4**............ at Yankees
6-7-8-9 .... at Texas

10-11-**12** .... at Minn.
13-**14-15** .... Oakland
16-17-**18** .... Seattle
20-21-**22-23** .. at Anaheim
24-25............ at Anaheim
27-**28-29** .... Texas
30-31 .... Minnesota

SEPTEMBER
1-2 .... Minnesota
3-4-**5** ...... at Kansas City
7-8 .... at Seattle
10-**11-12** ...... at Detroit
13-14-15........ Yankees
17-**18-19**...... White Sox
21-22-23 .... at Boston
24-**25-26**....... Cleveland
28-29....... at Tampa Bay
30 .... at Cleveland

OCTOBER
1-2-3 .... at Cleveland

NATIONALLEAGUE

ATLANTA BRAVES
Turner Field

APRIL
5-6-7-8....... Philadelphia
9-10-**11**............. Arizona
12-14-15 at Philadelphia
16-**17-18**.... at Colorado
19-20-21 .... at L.A.
23-24-**25**-26 ... at Florida
27-28-29 .... Pittsburgh
30 .... Cincinnati

MAY
1-**2**................. Cincinnati
3-4-**5** .... St. Louis
7-8-**9**...... at San Fran.
10-11-**12**.... at San Fran.
14-**15**-**16** .... at Cubs
17-18-**19** ...... Pittsburgh
20-21-22-**23** .... Cubs
24-25-26-**27**..... at Mil.
28-29-30.... Los Angeles
31 .... Colorado

JUNE
1-2 .... Colorado

4-5-**6**............ at Boston*
7-8-9 .... Tampa Bay*
11-**12**-13 ...... Baltimore*
14-15-16-17. at Houston
18-19-20 ..... at Arizona
22-23-**24**......... Montreal
25-26-**27**............. Mets
28-29-30 .... at Montreal

JULY
1 .... at Montreal
2-3-4................ at Mets
5-6-7-8 .... Florida
9-**10**-**11** .... Boston*
15-16-**17** .... at Yankees*
18-19-20 .... at Toronto*
21-22............ at Florida
23-24-**25** at Philadelphia
26-27-28..... Milwaukee
30-31 .... Philadelphia

AUGUST
1 .... Philadelphia
3-4-5 ..... at Pittsburgh

6-7-**8** ...... San Francisco
9-10-11 .... Houston
13-14-15 .... at L.A.
16-17-**18**..... at Colorado
20-**21-22**..... San Diego
23-24-**25**...... Cincinnati
27-**28-29** .... at St. Louis
30-31 ...... at Cincinnati

SEPTEMBER
1 .... at Cincinnati
3-4-**5**............... Arizona
6-7-8 .... St. Louis
10-**11**-**12** .... at S.F.
13-14-15.. at San Diego
17-18-**19**......... Montreal
21-22-**23**.............. Mets
24-25-26 .... at Montreal
28-29-30.......... at Mets

OCTOBER
1-2-**3**.................. Florida

ARIZONA DIAMONDBACKS
Bank One Ballpark

APRIL
5-6-7..... at Los Angeles
9-10-11.......... at Atlanta
12-13-14-15. Los Angeles
16-**17-18** San Francisco
19-20-21 ... Philadelphia
23-24-**25**... at San Diego
26-27-28-29. at Houston
30 .... at Milwaukee

MAY
1-**2**........... at Milwaukee
3-4-5........ at Cincinnati
7-**8**-**9**..................... Mets
10-11-12.......... Montreal
14-**15**-16 .... Colorado
17-18-**19**. at San Francisco
20-21-**22**-23 at Colorado
24-25-26....... San Diego
28-**29-30**........... at Mets
31 .... at Montreal

JUNE
1-2............... at Montreal

4-5-**6** .... Texas*
7-8-9 .... Cubs
11-12-13 ... at Anaheim*
14-15-16............ Florida
18-19-20............ Atlanta
21-22-23.......... Cincinnati
24-25-26-27 .... St. Louis
29-30......... at Cincinnati

JULY
1 .... at Cincinnati
2-**3**-4-**5**........ at St. Louis
6-7-8 .... Houston
9-10-**11** .... Oakland*
15-16-17......... at Texas*
18-19-20 ..... at Seattle*
21-22 .... at Houston
23-24-25..... Los Angeles
27-28-**29**... at San Diego
30-31 ..... at Los Angeles

AUGUST
1 .... at Los Angeles
2-3-4 ...... San Francisco

6-7-**8**...... at Philadelphia
9-10-11 .... at Cubs
13-14-15......... Milwaukee
16-17-18 .... Cubs
20-21-**22**-23 at Pittsburgh
24-25-**26** ...... at Florida
27-28-29................ Mets
30-31 .... Montreal

SEPTEMBER
1 .... Montreal
3-4-**5** .... at Atlanta
7-8-**9** ...... at Milwaukee
10-11-12 .... Philadelphia
13-14-15 .... Pittsburgh
17-**18-19**............. Florida
20-21-**22**..... at Colorado
24-**25-26**. at San Francisco
27-28-29 .... Colorado
30 .... San Diego

OCTOBER
1-2-**3**............. San Diego

NOTE: Dates in **bold** indicate afternoon games.
* Interleague Series

CHICAGO CUBS
Wrigley Field

APRIL
6-7-8 .... at Houston
9-**10-11** ..... at Pittsburgh
12-14-15 .... Cincinnati
16-17-18 .. at Milwaukee
20-**21-22** .... Houston
23-24-25 .... Mets
27-**28-29** .... at Florida
30 .... San Diego

MAY
1-2 .... San Diego
3-**4-5** .... Colorado
7-**8-9** .... at Cincinnati
10-11-12 at Los Angeles
14-15-16 .... Atlanta
17-18-19 .... at Florida
20-21-**22-23** .... at Atlanta
24-25-26 .... Florida
28-29-30 .... St. Louis

JUNE
1-2-3 .... San Diego

4-5-6 .... at Cleveland*
7-8-9 .... at Arizona
11-12-13 ...... White Sox*
14-15-16 .. at Milwaukee
17-18-19-**20** at San Fran.
22-23-24 ...... at Colorado
25-26-27 ...... Philadelphia
29-**30** .... Milwaukee

JULY
1 .... Milwaukee
2-3-4 ...... at Philadelphia
5-6-7-8 ..... at Pittsburgh
9-**10-11** .... at White Sox*
15-**16-17** ...... Minnesota*
18-19-20 ...... Kansas City*
21-22 .... Pittsburgh
23-**24-25** .... at Mets
26-27-28 .... at Montreal
30-31 .... Mets

AUGUST
1 .... Mets

2-3-**4-5** .... Montreal
6-7-8 .... Houston
9-10-**11** .... Arizona
13-**14-15** ...... at St. Louis
16-17-18 ...... at Arizona
20-21-22 .... Colorado
23-**24-25-26** .. San Fran.
27-**28-29** at Los Angeles
30-31 ...... at San Diego

SEPTEMBER
1 .... at San Diego
3-4-5 .... Los Angeles
6-7-8-9 .... Cincinnati
10-**11-12** .... at Houston
14-15-16 .... at Cincinnati
17-18-19 .... Milwaukee
20-21-**22** .... St. Louis
23-**24-25-26** .. Pittsburgh
28-29-30 at Philadelphia

OCTOBER
1-2-3 .... at St. Louis

CINCINNATI REDS
Cinergy Field

APRIL
5-6-7 ...... San Francisco
9-**10-11** .... at St. Louis
12-14-15 .... at Cubs
16-**17-18** ...... Pittsburgh
20-21-**22** .... Mets
23-**24-25** .... Houston
27-28-29 at Philadelphia
30 .... at Atlanta

MAY
1-2 .... at Atlanta
3-**4-5** .... Arizona
7-**8-9** .... Cubs
11-12 .... Milwaukee
14-15-16 .... San Diego
17-**18-19** .... at Colorado
21-22-**23** .... at San Diego
25-26-**27** .. Los Angeles
28-29-30 .... at Florida
31 .... at Mets

JUNE
1-2 .... at Mets

4-5-**6** ..... at Kansas City*
7-8-9 ..... at Minnesota*
11-12-**13** ...... Cleveland*
14-15-16 .... Mets
17-18-19-**20** . Milwaukee
21-22-23 .... at Arizona
24-25-**26-27**. at Houston
29-30 .... Arizona

JULY
1 .... Arizona
2-3-**4-5** .... Houston
6-7-8 .... at St. Louis
9-**10-11** .... at Cleveland*
15-**16-17** .... Colorado
18-19-20 .... Detroit*
21-22 .... St. Louis
23-**24-25** ..... at San Fran.
26-27-**28-29** .... at L.A.
30-31 .... San Francisco

AUGUST
1 .... San Francisco
3-**4-5** .... Colorado

6-7-8 .... at Milwaukee
9-10-11 ..... at Pittsburgh
13-14-**15** ...... Philadelphia
16-17-18-19 .. Pittsburgh
20-21-**22** .... Montreal
23-24-25 ...... at Atlanta
26-27-28-**29** at Montreal
30-31 .... Atlanta

SEPTEMBER
1 .... Atlanta
3-**4-5** ...... at Philadelphia
6-7-8-9 .... at Cubs
10-11-**12-13** ...... Florida
14-15-16 .... Cubs
17-18-**19** .... at Pittsburgh
20-21-22 .... at S.D.
24-**25-26-27** .... St. Louis
28-29 .... at Houston

OCTOBER
1-2-3 ...... at Milwaukee

COLORADO ROCKIES
Coors Field

APRIL
4-6-**7** .... at San Diego
8-9-**10-11** .... at L.A.
12-14-15 .... San Diego
16-**17-18** .... Atlanta
19-20-**21** .... Montreal
22-23-24-25 at San Fran.
27-**28-29** ..... at St. Louis
30 .... at Pittsburgh

MAY
1-2 .... at Pittsburgh
3-4-5 .... at Cubs
7-**8-9** .... Philadelphia
10-11-**12** .... Mets
14-15-16 ...... at Arizona
17-18-19 .... Cincinnati
20-21-**22-23** ...... Arizona
24-25-26-**27** .. at Houston
28-29-30 .... at Phil.
31 .... at Atlanta

JUNE
1-2 .... at Atlanta

4-5-**6** .... Milwaukee
7-8-9 .... Seattle*
11-12-**13** .... at Texas*
14-15-16 ...... San Fran.
18-19-**20** .... Florida
22-23-24 .... Cubs
25-26-**27-28** .... at S.D.
29-**30** .... at San Fran.

JULY
1 .... at San Fran.
2-3-**4** .... San Diego
5-6-**7-8** ...... Los Angeles
9-**10-11** .... Anaheim*
15-16-17 .... at Cincinnati
18-19-20 ...... at Oakland*
21-22 .... at L.A.
23-**24-25** .... St. Louis
26-27-**28-29** ..... Houston
30-31 .... at St. Louis

AUGUST
1 .... at St. Louis
3-**4-5** .... at Cincinnati

6-7-8 .... at Florida
9-10-**11** ..... at Milwaukee
13-14-**15** .... Montreal
16-17-**18** .... Atlanta
20-21-22 .... at Cubs
24-25-26 .... at Pittsburgh
27-28-29 .. Philadelphia
30-31 .... Pittsburgh

SEPTEMBER
1 .... Pittsburgh
3-**4-5** .... at Mets
6-7-8 .... at Montreal
10-11-12 ..... Milwaukee
13-14-**15** .... Mets
17-**18-19** .... Los Angeles
20-21-**22** .... Arizona
24-25-**26** .... at Florida
27-28-29 ...... at Arizona

OCTOBER
1-2-3 ...... San Francisco

FLORIDA MARLINS
Pro Player Stadium

APRIL
5-6-7.....................Mets
9-10-**11**.......... Philadelphia
12-14-15............ at Mets
16-17-**18**............ at Phil.
19-20-**21**..... at San Fran.
23-24-**25**-26 ...... Atlanta
27-28-**29**.............. Cubs
30.................... Houston

MAY
1-2 .... Houston
3-4-**5**.......... Milwaukee
7-8-**9**................. at L.A.
10-11-12 .. at San Diego
14-15-**16** .. at Milwaukee
17-18-19................ Cubs
20-21-22-23 .. Pittsburgh
24-25-**26** .... at Cubs
28-29-**30**.......... Cincinnati
31 .... St. Louis

JUNE
1-2-3 .... St. Louis

4-5-**6** ...... at Tampa Bay*
7-8-9 .... Baltimore*
11-12-**13**.......... Yankees*
14-15-16 .... at Arizona
18-19-**20**..... at Colorado
22-23-**24**.......... at Mets
25-26-27 ...... at Montreal
28-29-30.................. Mets

JULY
1 .... Mets
2-3-**4**.............. Montreal
5-6-7-8 .... at Atlanta
9-10-**11** ..... Tampa Bay*
15-16-**17**..... at Toronto*
18-19-20 ...... at Boston*
21-22................ Atlanta
23-24-**25**....... Milwaukee
26-27-28-**29** ...... at Phil.
30-31 .... at Pittsburgh

AUGUST
1 .... at Pittsburgh
3-4-5 .... Philadelphia

6-7-8................. Colorado
9-10-**11**... San Francisco
13-14-**15**... at San Diego
16-17-18............ at L.A.
20-21-**22**.......... Houston
24-25-**26**.......... Arizona
27-28-**29** ..... at Houston
30-31........... at St. Louis

SEPTEMBER
1 .... at St. Louis
3-4-**5**........... San Diego
6-7-8........... Los Angeles
10-11-**12**-**13** ...... at Cinc.
14-15-16..... at San Fran.
17-**18**-19 .... at Arizona
21-22-**23**.......... Montreal
24-25-**26** .... Colorado
27-28-29 ..... at Montreal

OCTOBER
1-2-3 .... at Atlanta

HOUSTON ASTROS
Astrodome

APRIL
6-7-8 .... Cubs
9-10-**11** .... Milwaukee
13-14-**15**... at San Fran.
16-17-**18**........ St. Louis
20-**21**-22........... Cubs
23-**24**-25..... at Cincinnati
26-27-28-**29** ...... Arizona
30.................. at Florida

MAY
1-**2**.............. at Florida
3-4-5................ at Mets
7-8-**9**.............. Montreal
10-11-12........... at L.A.
14-15-16 San Francisco
18-19-20 .... at L.A.
21-**22**-23 ... at San Fran.
24-25-26-**27**.... Colorado
28-29-**30** ... at Pittsburgh

JUNE
1-2-3 .... at Milwaukee

4-5-**6** ...... at Minnesota*
7-8-9..... at White Sox*
11-12-**13**......... San Diego
14-15-16-17 .... Atlanta
18-19-**20**.......... Montreal
21-22-23 ... at St. Louis
24-25-**26**-**27**... Cincinnati
29-30........... St. Louis

JULY
1 .... St. Louis
2-3-**4**-**5** .... at Cincinnati
6-7-8 .... at Arizona
9-10-**11**.. at Kansas City*
15-16-**17**.......... Detroit*
18-19-20 ...... Cleveland*
21-22................ Arizona
23-**24**-**25**........ San Diego
26-27-28-**29** at Colorado
30-**31**........ at San Diego

AUGUST
1 .... at San Diego

3-4-**5**.......... Los Angeles
6-**7**-**8**............... at Cubs
9-10-11........ at Atlanta
13-14-**15** .... Pittsburgh
16-17-18-**19** . Milwaukee
20-21-**22** ..... at Florida
23-24-25......... at Mets
27-28-**29**.......... Florida
30-31................. Mets

SEPTEMBER
1 .... Mets
3-4-**5** .... at Montreal
6-7-8-9... at Philadelphia
10-11-**12** .... Cubs
13-14-15...... Philadelphia
17-**18**-19 .... at St. Louis
20-21-22 .. at Pittsburgh
24-25-**26** .. at Milwaukee
28-29 .... Cincinnati

OCTOBER
1-2-**3**.......... Los Angeles

LOS ANGELES DODGERS
Dodger Stadium

APRIL
5-6-7................... Arizona
8-9-**10**-**11** .... Colorado
12-13-14-15 .. at Arizona
16-17-**18**... at San Diego
19-20-21............. Atlanta
23-24-25 .... St. Louis
27-28-**29** .. at Milwaukee
30 .... at Philadelphia

MAY
1-2 .... at Philadelphia
3-4-5 .... at Montreal
7-8-**9** .... Florida
10-11-12 .... Cubs
14-15-16 ..... at St. Louis
18-19-20 .... Houston
21-22-**23** .... St. Louis
25-26-27.... at Cincinnati
28-29-**30** .... at Atlanta
31............. at Pittsburgh

JUNE
1-2 .... at Pittsburgh

4-5-**6** .... Anaheim*
7-8-9................... Texas*
11-**12**-**13** .... at Oakland*
15-16-17 ...... Pittsburgh
18-**19**-**20** .... Philadelphia
22-23-24......... San Diego
25-**26**-27.... at San Fran.
29-30........ at San Diego

JULY
1 .... at San Diego
2-3-4 ...... San Francisco
5-6-7-**8**........... at Colorado
9-10-**11** .... Seattle*
15-16-**17** .... at Anaheim*
18-19-20 .... at Pittsburgh
21-**22**............ Colorado
23-24-25 ...... at Arizona
26-27-28-**29** .... Cinc.
30-31............... Arizona

AUGUST
1 .... Arizona
3-4-**5** .... at Houston

6-7-**8**-9 .... at Mets
10-11-**12**..... at Montreal
13-14-15............ Atlanta
16-17-18.............. Florida
20-21-**22** .... at Phil.
23-24-**25** .. at Milwaukee
27-**28**-29 .... Cubs
30-31........... Milwaukee

SEPTEMBER
1 .... Milwaukee
3-4-**5** .... at Cubs
6-7-8 .... at Florida
9-10-11-12........ Mets
13-14-15.......... Montreal
17-**18**-19 .... at Colorado
20-21-22-23.......... S.F.
24-**25**-26....... San Diego
28-29-**30**... at San Fran.

OCTOBER
1-2-3 .... at Houston

MILWAUKEE BREWERS
County Stadium

APRIL
5-7-**8**	at St. Louis
9-10-**11**	at Houston
13-14-**15**	at Montreal
16-17-18	Cubs
19-20-**21**	St. Louis
23-**24-25**	at Houston
27-28-**29**	Los Angeles
30	Arizona

MAY
1-2	Arizona
3-4-5	at Florida
7-**8-9**	at San Fran.
11-12	at Cincinnati
14-15-**16**	Florida
17-18-19-20	at Mets
21-22-**23**	at Montreal
24-25-26-**27**	Atlanta
28-29-**30-31**	San Diego

JUNE
1-2-**3**	Houston

JULY
1	at Cubs
2-3-**4**	at Pittsburgh
5-6-7	at Philadelphia
9-10-11	at Detroit*
15-16-17	Kansas City*
18-19-20	White Sox*
21-22	Philadelphia
23-24-**25**	at Florida
26-27-28	at Atlanta
30-31	Montreal

AUGUST
1	Montreal

(2nd column)
4-5-**6**	at Colorado
8-9-10	at Cleveland*
11-12-**13**	Minnesota*
14-15-**16**	Cubs
17-18-19-**20**	at Cinc.
21-**22-23**	at San Fran.
25-26-**27**	Pittsburgh
29-30	at Cubs

(3rd column)
2-3-**4**	Mets
6-7-**8**	Cincinnati
9-10-**11**	Colorado
13-14-15	at Arizona
16-17-18-**19**	at Houston
20-**21-22**	San Fran.
23-24-**25**	Los Angeles
26-27-28-**29**	at S.D.
30-31	at Los Angeles

SEPTEMBER
1	at Los Angeles
2-3-**4-5**	St. Louis
7-**8-9**	Arizona
10-11-12	at Colorado
13-14-15	at St. Louis
17-18-19	at Cubs
20-21-22-**23**	Philadelphia
24-25-**26**	Houston
28-29-30	Pittsburgh

OCTOBER
1-**2-3**	Cincinnati

MONTREAL EXPOS
Olympic Stadium

APRIL
5-6-7	at Pittsburgh
8-9-**10-11**	Mets
13-14-**15**	Milwaukee
16-**17-18**	at Mets
19-20-21	at Colorado
23-**24-25**	Philadelphia
27-28-29	San Francisco
30	St. Louis

MAY
1-2	St. Louis
3-4-5	Los Angeles
7-**8-9**	at Houston
10-11-12	at Arizona
14-15-16	at Pittsburgh
17-18-19	Philadelphia
21-22-**23**	Milwaukee
24-25-26	at Philadelphia
28-29-**30**	San Francisco
31	Arizona

JUNE
1-2	Arizona

(2nd column)
4-**5-6**	at Toronto*
7-8-9	Boston*
11-12-**13**	Tampa Bay*
14-15-16	at St. Louis
18-19-**20**	at Houston
22-23-**24**	at Atlanta
25-26-27	Florida
28-29-30	Atlanta

JULY
1	Atlanta
2-3-**4**	at Florida
5-6-**7-8**	at Mets
9-10-11	Toronto*
15-16-17	at Baltimore*
18-19-**20**	at Yankees*
21-22	Mets
23-24-**25**	Pittsburgh
26-27-28	Cubs
30-31	at Milwaukee

AUGUST
1	at Milwaukee
2-3-**4-5**	at Cubs

(3rd column)
6-7-**8-9**	San Diego
10-11-**12**	Los Angeles
13-14-15	at Colorado
16-**17-18**	at San Fran.
20-21-**22**	at Cincinnati
23-24-25	St. Louis
26-27-28-**29**	Cincinnati
30-31	at Arizona

SEPTEMBER
1	at Arizona
3-4-**5**	Houston
6-**7-8**	Colorado
9-10-11-**12**	at San Diego
13-14-15	at Los Angeles
17-18-**19**	at Atlanta
21-22-**23**	at Florida
24-25-**26**	Atlanta
27-28-29	Florida

OCTOBER
1-2-**3**	at Philadelphia

NEW YORK METS
Shea Stadium

APRIL
5-6-7	at Florida
8-9-**10-11**	at Montreal
12-14-15	Florida
16-**17-18**	Montreal
20-21-22	at Cincinnati
23-24-25	at Cubs
27-28-**29**	San Diego
30	San Francisco

MAY
1-2	San Francisco
3-4-5	Houston
7-**8-9**	at Arizona
10-11-**12**	at Colorado
14-15-16	at Philadelphia
17-18-19-20	Milwaukee
21-**22-23**	Philadelphia
24-25-26	at Pittsburgh
28-**29-30**	Arizona
31	Cincinnati

JUNE
1-2	Cincinnati

(2nd column)
4-**5-6**	at Yankees*
7-8-9	Toronto*
11-**12-13**	Boston*
14-15-**16**	at Cincinnati
17-18-**19-20**	at St. Louis
22-23-**24**	Florida
25-26-**27**	at Atlanta
28-29-30	at Florida

JULY
1	at Florida
2-3-**4**	Atlanta
5-6-**7-8**	Montreal
9-**10-11**	Yankees*
15-16-**17**	Tampa Bay*
18-19-20	at Baltimore*
21-22	at Montreal
23-**24-25**	Cubs
26-27-**28**	Pittsburgh
30-31	at Cubs

AUGUST
1	at Cubs
2-3-4	at Milwaukee

(3rd column)
6-7-**8-9**	Los Angeles
10-11-**12**	San Diego
13-14-15	at San Fran.
16-17-18	at San Diego
20-**21-22**	St. Louis
23-24-25	Houston
27-28-29	at Arizona
30-31	at Houston

SEPTEMBER
1	at Houston
3-4-5	Colorado
6-7-8	San Francisco
9-10-**11-12**	at Los Angeles
13-14-**15**	at Colorado
17-18-**19**	Philadelphia
21-22-**23**	at Atlanta
24-25-**26**	at Philadelphia
28-29-30	Atlanta

OCTOBER
1-2-3	Pittsburgh

PHILADELPHIA PHILLIES
Veterans Stadium

APRIL
5-6-7-8 .... at Atlanta
9-10-**11** ...... at Florida
12-14-15........ Atlanta
16-17-**18**.......... Florida
19-20-21 ...... at Arizona
23-24-**25** ...... at Atlanta
27-28-29 .... Cincinnati
30 .... Los Angeles

MAY
1-2 .... Los Angeles
3-4-**5**........... San Diego
7-8-**9**.......... at Colorado
10-11-**12**...... at St. Louis
14-15-**16** .... Mets
17-18-19 ...... at Montreal
21-**22-23** .... at Mets
24-25-26.......... Montreal
28-29-**30** .... Colorado
31 .... San Francisco

JUNE
1-2-**3** ...... San Francisco

4-5-**6** .... at Baltimore*
7-8-9 .... Yankees*
11-12-**13** .... Toronto*
15-16-**17**... at San Diego
18-**19**-20 at Los Angeles
22-23-**24** .... Pittsburgh
25-26-27 .... at Cubs
28-29-30 .. at Pittsburgh

JULY
1 .... at Pittsburgh
2-3-**4** .... Cubs
5-6-7 .... Milwaukee
9-10-**11** .... Baltimore*
15-16-**17** ...... at Boston*
18-19-**20** at Tampa Bay*
21-**22** .... at Milwaukee
23-24-**25**.......... Atlanta
26-27-28-**29** ...... Florida
30-31 .... at Atlanta

AUGUST
1 .... at Atlanta
3-4-5 .... at Florida

6-7-**8**.................. Arizona
9-10-11 .... St. Louis
13-14-**15**.... at Cincinnati
16-17-18 ..... at St. Louis
20-21-**22** .... Los Angeles
23-24-**25**....... San Diego
27-28-**29** .... at Colorado
30-31.. at San Francisco

SEPTEMBER
1-**2**.... at San Francisco
3-4-**5**........... Cincinnati
6-7-8-9 .... Houston
10-11-12....... at Arizona
13-14-15 ..... at Houston
17-18-**19** .... at Mets
20-21-22-**23**.. at Milwaukee
24-25-**26** .... Mets
28-29-30 .... Cubs

OCTOBER
1-2-**3**................ Montreal

PITTSBURGH PIRATES
Three Rivers Stadium

APRIL
5-6-7 .... Montreal
9-10-**11** .... Cubs
13-14-15 .... St. Louis
16-**17**-**18**... at Cincinnati
19-20-21... at San Diego
23-24-**25** ...... Milwaukee
27-28-29 ...... at Atlanta
30 .... Colorado

MAY
1-2 .... Colorado
3-4-5 ...... San Francisco
6-7-**8-9** .... at St. Louis
10-11-12 ...... at Houston
14-**15-16**......... Montreal
17-18-19 ...... at Atlanta
20-21-22-**23** .. at Florida
24-25-26............... Mets
28-29-**30** .... Houston
31 .... Los Angeles

JUNE
1-2 .... Los Angeles

4-5-**6**........ at White Sox*
7-8-9 .... at Detroit*
11-12-**13** ... Kansas City*
15-16-17 at Los Angeles
18-19-**20**.... at San Diego
22-23-**24** .. at Philadelphia
25-26-**27** .. at Milwaukee
28-29-30 ...... Philadelphia

JULY
1 .... Philadelphia
2-3-**4**............ Milwaukee
5-6-7-**8** .... Cubs
9-10-**11**.... at Minnesota*
15-16-**17** .... Cleveland*
18-19-**20** .... Los Angeles
21-22 .... at Cubs
23-24-25 ...... at Montreal
26-27-**28** .... at Mets
30-31 .... Florida

AUGUST
1 .... Florida
3-4-5.................... Atlanta

6-7-**8** .... St. Louis
9-10-11 .... Cincinnati
13-14-**15** ...... at Houston
16-17-18-19.. at Cincinnati
20-21-**22**-23 ...... Arizona
24-25-**26** .... Colorado
27-**28-29**.... at San Fran.
30-31 .... at Colorado

SEPTEMBER
1 .... at Colorado
3-4-5 ...... San Francisco
6-7-8.............. San Diego
10-11-**12**.... at St. Louis
13-14-15 ...... at Arizona
17-18-**19** .... Cincinnati
20-21-22 .... Houston
23-**24-25-26** ....at Cubs
28-29-30 .. at Milwaukee

OCTOBER
1-2-**3**.............. at Mets

ST. LOUIS CARDINALS
Busch Stadium

APRIL
5-7-**8**............. Milwaukee
9-10-11 .... Cincinnati
13-14-**15** ... at Pittsburgh
16-17-**18** ...... at Houston
19-20-21 .. at Milwaukee
23-24-**25** .... at L.A.
27-28-**29** .... Colorado
30 .... at Montreal

MAY
1-**2** .... at Montreal
3-4-**5** .... at Atlanta
6-7-8-**9** .... Pittsburgh
10-11-**12** .... Philadelphia
14-15-**16** .... Los Angeles
18-19-**20**... at San Diego
21-22-**23** .... at L.A.
25-26-**27** .. San Franciso
28-29-30 .... at Cubs
31 .... at Florida

JUNE
1-2-3 .... at Florida

4-5-6 .... at Detroit*
7-8-9 .... at K.C.*
11-12-**13** .... Detroit*
14-15-16 .... Montreal
17-18-**19-20**.......... Mets
21-22-23 .... Houston
24-25-26-27 .. at Arizona
29-30 ...... at Houston

JULY
1 .... at Houston
2-3-**4-5** .... Arizona
6-7-8 .... Cincinnati
9-10-**11** ...... at San Fran.
15-16-17 ...... White Sox*
18-19-**20**....... Minnesota*
21-**22** .... at Cincinnati
23-**24-25** ...... at Colorado
26-27-**28**.... at San Fran.
30-31 .... Colorado

AUGUST
1 .... Colorado
2-3-4-5 .... San Diego

6-7-**8** .... at Pittsburgh
9-10-11 .. at Philadelphia
13-14-15 .... Cubs
16-17-18 .... Philadelphia
20-**21-22** .... at Mets
23-24-25 ...... at Montreal
27-**28**-29....... Atlanta
30-31 .... Florida

SEPTEMBER
1 .... Florida
2-3-**4-5** ..... at Milwaukee
6-7-8 .... at Atlanta
10-11-**12** ...... Pittsburgh
13-14-15 .... Milwaukee
17-18-**19** .... Houston
20-21-**22** .... at Cubs
24-**25-26-27**. at Cincinnati
28-29 .... San Diego

OCTOBER
1-**2**-**3** .... Cubs

SAN DIEGO PADRES
Jack Murphy Stadium

APRIL
4-6-**7** .... Colorado
8-9-**10-11**.. at San Fran.
12-14-**15** ..... at Colorado
16-17-**18** .... Los Angeles
19-20-21 .... Pittsburgh
23-24-**25** .... Arizona
27-28-**29** .... at Mets
30 .... at Cubs

MAY
1-2 .... at Cubs
3-4-**5** ...... at Philadelphia
7-8-**9** .... Atlanta
10-11-12 .... Florida
14-15-16... at Cincinnati
18-19-**20** .... St. Louis
21-22-**23** .... Cincinnati
24-25-26 .... at Arizona
28-29-**30-31** .... at Mil.

JUNE
1-2-3 .... at Cubs
4-5-**6** .... Seattle*

8-9-**10** .... Oakland*
11-12-**13** ...... at Houston
15-16-17 .... Philadelphia
18-19-**20** ...... Pittsburgh
22-23-24 .... at L.A.
25-26-**27**-28 .... Colorado
29-30 ...... Los Angeles

JULY
1 .... Los Angeles
2-3-**4** .... at Colorado
5-6-7 ...... San Francisco
9-**10-11** .... Texas*
15-16-**17** ...... at Seattle*
18-19-**20** ... at Anaheim*
21-**22** .... at San Fran.
23-**24-25** ...... at Houston
27-28-**29** .... Arizona
30-31 .... Houston

AUGUST
1 .... Houston
2-3-4-5 ...... at St. Louis
6-7-**8**-9 ..... at Montreal

10-11-**12** .... at Mets
13-14-**15**.......... Florida
16-17-18................ Mets
20-**21**-22 .... at Atlanta
23-24-**25** .... at Phil.
26-27-28-**29** .... Mil.
30-31 .... Cubs

SEPTEMBER
1............................ Cubs
3-4-**5** .... at Florida
6-7-8 .... at Pittsburgh
9-10-11-**12**....... Montreal
17-**18**-19..... San. Fran.
20-21-22........ Cincinnati
24-**25**-26 .... at L.A.
28-29 .... at St. Louis
30................... at Arizona

OCTOBER
1-2-3 .... at Arizona

SAN FRANCISCO GIANTS
3Com Park at Candlestick Point

APRIL
5-6-**7** .... at Cincinnati
8-9-**10-11** ..... San Diego
13-14-**15** .... Houston
16-**17-18** .... at Arizona
19-20-**21** .... Florida
22-23-**24-25**.... Colorado
27-28-29 .... at Montreal
30 .... at Mets

MAY
1-2 .... at Mets
3-4-5 .... at Pittsburgh
7-**8-9**............ Milwaukee
10-**11-12**...... at Houston
14-15-16 ...... at Houston
17-18-**19**........... Arizona
21-**22**-23 .... Houston
25-26-**27** ..... at St. Louis
28-29-**30** ..... at Montreal
31 .... at Philadelphia

JUNE
1-2-**3**.... at Philadelphia

4-5-6 .... Oakland*
7-8-9 .... Anaheim*
11-12-**13** ..... at Seattle*
14-15-**16**...... at Colorado
17-18-**19-20** .... Cubs
21-**22-23**...... Milwaukee
25-**26**-27 .... Los Angeles
29-**30** .... Colorado

JULY
1 .... Colorado
2-3-**4** ..... at Los Angeles
5-6-7........ at San Diego
9-**10-11**........ St. Louis
15-16-**17**.... at Oakland*
18-19-20.... at Texas*
21-**22** .... San Diego
23-**24-25**........ Cincinnati
26-**27-28** .... St. Louis
30-31 .... at Cincinnati

AUGUST
1 .... at Cincinnati
2-3-4 .... at Arizona

6-7-8 .... at Atlanta
9-**10-11** .... at Florida
13-**14-15**............. Mets
16-**17-18**....... Montreal
20-**21**-22 .... at Mil.
23-**24-25-26**..... at Cubs
27-**28-29** .... Pittsburgh
30-31 .... Philadelphia

SEPTEMBER
1-2 .... Philadelphia
3-4-**5** .... at Pittsburgh
6-7-8.............. at Mets
10-**11-12**........... Atlanta
14-15-16............. Florida
17-**18**-19 .... at S.D.
20-21-22-23........ at L.A.
24-**25-26**............ Arizona
28-29-**30**.... Los Angeles

OCTOBER
1-2-3........... at Colorado

INTERLEAGUE SCHEDULE

JUNE 4

Texas at Arizona
Anaheim at Los Angeles
Seattle at San Diego
Oakland at San Francisco
Montreal at Toronto
Mets at Yankees
Philadelphia at Baltimore

Atlanta at Boston
Florida at Tampa Bay
Pittsburgh at White Sox
Cincinnati at Kansas City
Cubs at Cleveland
St. Louis at Detroit
Houston at Minnesota

JUNE 5

Texas at Arizona
Anaheim at Los Angeles
Seattle at San Diego
Oakland at San Francisco
Montreal at Toronto
Mets at Yankees
Philadelphia at Baltimore

Atlanta at Boston
Florida at Tampa Bay
Pittsburgh at White Sox
Cincinnati at Kansas City
Cubs at Cleveland
St. Louis at Detroit
Houston at Minnesota

JUNE 6

Texas at Arizona
Anaheim at Los Angeles
Seattle at San Diego
Oakland at San Francisco
Montreal at Toronto
Mets at Yankees
Philadelphia at Baltimore

Atlanta at Boston
Florida at Tampa Bay
Pittsburgh at White Sox
Cincinnati at Kansas City
Cubs at Cleveland
St. Louis at Detroit
Houston at Minnesota

JUNE 7

Boston at Montreal
Toronto at Mets
Yankees at Philadelphia
Tampa Bay at Atlanta
Baltimore at Florida
Pittsburgh at Detroit

Cincinnati at Minnesota
St. Louis at Kansas City
Houston at White Sox
Seattle at Colorado
Texas at Los Angeles
Anaheim at San Francisco

JUNE 8

Boston at Montreal
Toronto at Mets
Yankees at Philadelphia
Tampa Bay at Atlanta
Baltimore at Florida
Pittsburgh at Detroit
Cincinnati at Minnesota

Milwaukee at Cleveland
St. Louis at Kansas City
Houston at White Sox
Seattle at Colorado
Texas at Los Angeles
Oakland at San Diego
Anaheim at San Francisco

JUNE 9

Boston at Montreal
Toronto at Mets
Yankees at Philadelphia
Tampa Bay at Atlanta
Baltimore at Florida
Pittsburgh at Detroit
Cincinnati at Minnesota

Milwaukee at Cleveland
St. Louis at Kansas City
Houston at White Sox
Seattle at Colorado
Texas at Los Angeles
Oakland at San Diego
Anaheim at San Francisco

JUNE 10

Milwaukee at Cleveland

Oakland at San Diego

JUNE 11

Toronto at Philadelphia
Tampa Bay at Montreal
Baltimore at Atlanta
Yankees at Florida
Boston at Mets
Kansas City at Pittsburgh
Minnesota at Milwaukee

White Sox at Cubs
Detroit at St. Louis
Cleveland at Cincinnati
San Francisco at Seattle
Los Angeles at Oakland
Arizona at Anaheim
Colorado at Texas

JUNE 12

Toronto at Philadelphia
Tampa Bay at Montreal
Baltimore at Atlanta
Yankees at Florida
Boston at Mets
Kansas City at Pittsburgh
Minnesota at Milwaukee

White Sox at Cubs
Detroit at St. Louis
Cleveland at Cincinnati
San Francisco at Seattle
Los Angeles at Oakland
Arizona at Anaheim
Colorado at Texas

JUNE 13

Toronto at Philadelphia
Tampa Bay at Montreal

White Sox at Cubs
Detroit at St. Louis

Baltimore at Atlanta	Cleveland at Cincinnati
Yankees at Florida	San Francisco at Seattle
Boston at Mets	Los Angeles at Oakland
Kansas City at Pittsburgh	Arizona at Anaheim
Minnesota at Milwaukee	Colorado at Texas

JULY 9

Toronto at Montreal	Cubs at White Sox
Tampa Bay at Florida	Milwaukee at Detroit
Baltimore at Philadelphia	Cincinnati at Cleveland
Yankees at Mets	Seattle at Los Angeles
Boston at Atlanta	Oakland at Arizona
Houston at Kansas City	Anaheim at Colorado
Pittsburgh at Minnesota	Texas at San Diego

JULY 10

Toronto at Montreal	Cubs at White Sox
Tampa Bay at Florida	Milwaukee at Detroit
Baltimore at Philadelphia	Cincinnati at Cleveland
Yankees at Mets	Seattle at Los Angeles
Boston at Atlanta	Oakland at Arizona
Houston at Kansas City	Anaheim at Colorado
Pittsburgh at Minnesota	Texas at San Diego

JULY 11

Toronto at Montreal	Cubs at White Sox
Tampa Bay at Florida	Milwaukee at Detroit
Baltimore at Philadelphia	Cincinnati at Cleveland
Yankees at Mets	Seattle at Los Angeles
Boston at Atlanta	Oakland at Arizona
Houston at Kansas City	Anaheim at Colorado
Pittsburgh at Minnesota	Texas at San Diego

JULY 15

Florida at Toronto	White Sox at St. Louis
Mets at Tampa Bay	Detroit at Houston
Montreal at Baltimore	Cleveland at Pittsburgh
Atlanta at Yankees	San Diego at Seattle
Philadelphia at Boston	San Francisco at Oakland
Kansas City at Milwaukee	Los Angeles at Anaheim
Minnesota at Cubs	Arizona at Texas

JULY 16

Florida at Toronto	White Sox at St. Louis
Mets at Tampa Bay	Detroit at Houston
Montreal at Baltimore	Cleveland at Pittsburgh
Atlanta at Yankees	San Diego at Seattle
Philadelphia at Boston	San Francisco at Oakland
Kansas City at Milwaukee	Los Angeles at Anaheim
Minnesota at Cubs	Arizona at Texas

JULY 17

Florida at Toronto	White Sox at St. Louis
Mets at Tampa Bay	Detroit at Houston
Montreal at Baltimore	Cleveland at Pittsburgh
Atlanta at Yankees	San Diego at Seattle
Philadelphia at Boston	San Francisco at Oakland
Kansas City at Milwaukee	Los Angeles at Anaheim
Minnesota at Cubs	Arizona at Texas

JULY 18

Atlanta at Toronto	White Sox at Milwaukee
Philadelphia at Tampa Bay	Detroit at Cincinnati
Mets at Baltimore	Cleveland at Houston
Montreal at Yankees	Arizona at Seattle
Florida at Boston	Colorado at Oakland
Kansas City at Cubs	San Diego at Anaheim
Minnesota at St. Louis	San Francisco at Texas

JULY 19

Atlanta at Toronto	White Sox at Milwaukee
Philadelphia at Tampa Bay	Detroit at Cincinnati
Mets at Baltimore	Cleveland at Houston
Montreal at Yankees	Arizona at Seattle
Florida at Boston	Colorado at Oakland
Kansas City at Cubs	San Diego at Anaheim
Minnesota at St. Louis	San Francisco at Texas

JULY 20

Atlanta at Toronto	White Sox at Milwaukee
Philadelphia at Tampa Bay	Detroit at Cincinnati
Mets at Baltimore	Cleveland at Houston
Montreal at Yankees	Arizona at Seattle
Florida at Boston	Colorado at Oakland
Kansas City at Cubs	San Diego at Anaheim
Minnesota at St. Louis	San Francisco at Texas

SPRINGTRAINING

ANAHEIM ANGELS
Major League Club

Complex Address (first year): Diablo Stadium (1993), 2200 W Alameda, Tempe, AZ 85282. Telephone: (602) 438-4300. FAX: (602) 438-7950. **Seating Capacity:** 9,785.

Hotel Address: Fiesta Inn, 2100 S Priest Dr., Tempe, AZ 85282. Telephone: (602) 967-1441. FAX: (602) 967-0224.

Minor League Clubs

Complex Address: Gene Autry Park, 4125 E McKellips, Mesa, AZ 85205. Telephone: (602) 830-4137. FAX: (602) 438-7950. **Hotel Address:** Lindsay Palms, 2855 E Broadway, Mesa, AZ 85204.

ARIZONA DIAMONDBACKS
Major League Club

Complex Address (first year): Tucson Electric Park (1998), 2500 Ajo Way, Tucson, AZ 85713. Telephone: (520) 434-1400. FAX: (520) 434-1443. **Seating Capacity:** 11,000.

Hotel Address: Doubletree Suites, 6555 E Speedway, Tucson, AZ 85710. Telephone: (520) 721-7100. FAX: (520) 721-1991.

Minor League Clubs

Complex Address: Kino Veterans Memorial Sportspark, 3600 S Country Club, Tucson, AZ 85713. Telephone: (520) 434-1400. FAX: (520) 434-1443. **Hotel Address:** Holiday Inn, 181 W Broadway, Tucson, AZ 85701. Telephone: (520) 624-8711. FAX: (520) 623-8121.

CHICAGO CUBS
Major League Club

Complex Address (first year): HoHoKam Park (1979), 1235 N Center St., Mesa, AZ 85201. Telephone: (602) 668-0500. FAX: (602) 668-4541. **Seating Capacity:** 8,963.

Hotel Address: Best Western Dobson Ranch Inn, 1666 S Dobson Rd., Mesa, AZ 85202. Telephone: (602) 831-7000.

Minor League Clubs

Complex Address: Fitch Park, 160 C Sixth Pl., Mesa, AZ 85201. Telephone: (602) 668-0500. FAX: (602) 668-4501. **Hotel Address:** Best Western Mezona, 250 W Main St., Mesa, AZ 85201. Telephone: (602) 834-9233.

CHICAGO WHITE SOX
Major League Club

Complex Address (first year): Tucson Electric Park (1998), 2500 E Ajo Way, Tucson, AZ 85713. Telephone: (520) 434-1300. **Seating Capacity:** 11,000.

Hotel Address: Best Western Inn-Airport, 7060 S Tucson Blvd., Tucson, AZ 85706 Telephone: (520) 746-0271, (800) 772-3847.

Minor League Clubs

Complex Address: Same as major league club. **Hotel Address:** Ramada Palo Verde, 5251 S Julian Dr., Tucson, AZ 85706. Telephone: (520) 294-5250.

COLORADO ROCKIES
Major League Club
Complex Address (first year): U.S. West Sports Complex at Hi Corbett Field (1993), 3400 E Camino Campestre, Tucson, AZ 85716. Telephone: (520) 322-4500. FAX: (520) 322-4545. **Seating Capacity:** 9,500.

Hotel Address: Tucson Hilton East, 7600 E Broadway, Tucson, AZ 85710. Telephone: (520) 721-5600.

Minor League Clubs
Complex Address: Same as major league club. **Hotel Address:** Holiday Inn-Palo Verde, 4550 S Palo Verde Blvd., Tucson, AZ 85714. Telephone: (520) 746-1161.

MILWAUKEE BREWERS
Major League Club
Complex Address (first year): Maryvale Baseball Park (1998), 3600 N 51st Ave., Phoeniz, AZ 85031. Telephone: (602) 245-5555. FAX: (602) 247-7404.

Hotel Address: Holiday Inn, 1500 N 51st Ave., Phoenix, AZ 85043 Telephone: (602) 484-9009.

Minor League Clubs
Complex Address: Maryvale Baseball Complex, 3805 N 53rd Ave., Phoenix, AZ 85031. Telephone: (602) 245-5600. FAX: (602) 849-8941. **Hotel Address:** Red Roof Inn, 17222 N Black Canyon Fwy., Phoenix, AZ 85023. Telephone: (602) 866-1049.

OAKLAND ATHLETICS
Major League Club
Complex Address (first year): Phoenix Municipal Stadium (1982), 5999 E Van Buren, Phoenix, AZ 85008. Telephone: (602) 225-9400. FAX: (602) 225-9473. **Seating Capacity:** 8,500.

Hotel Address: Doubletree Suites Hotel, 320 N 44th St., Phoenix, AZ 85008. Telephone: (602) 225-0500.

Minor League Clubs
Complex Address: Papago Park Baseball Complex, 1802 N 64th St., Phoenix, AZ 85008. Telephone: (602) 949-5951. FAX: (602) 945-0557. **Hotel Address:** Fairfield Inn, 5101 N Scottsdale Rd., Scottsdale, AZ 85251. Telephone: (602) 945-4392.

SAN DIEGO PADRES
Major League Club
Complex Address (first year): Peoria Sports Complex (1994), 8131 W Paradise Ln., Peoria, AZ 85382. Telephone: (602) 486-7000. FAX: (602) 486-9341. **Seating Capacity:** 10,000.

Hotel Address: Comfort Suites, 8473 W Paradise Ln., Peoria, AZ 85382. Telephone: (602) 334-3993.

Minor League Clubs
Complex/Hotel Address: Same as major league club.

SAN FRANCISCO GIANTS
Major League Club
Complex Address (first year): Scottsdale Stadium (1981), 7408 E Osborn Rd., Scottsdale, AZ 85251. Telephone: (602) 990-7972. FAX: (602) 990-2643. **Seating Capacity:** 10,500.

Hotel Address: Mountain Shadows Marriott Resort and Golf Club, 5641 E Lincoln Dr., Scottsdale, AZ 85253. Telephone: (602) 948-7111.

Minor League Clubs
Complex Address: Indian School Park, 4289 N Hayden Road at Camelback Road, Scottsdale, AZ 85251. Telephone: (602) 990-0052. **Hotel Address:** Days Inn, 4710 N Scottsdale Rd., Scottsdale, AZ 85351. Telephone: (602) 947-5411.

SEATTLE MARINERS
Major League Club
Complex Address (first year): Peoria Sports Complex (1993), 15707 N 83rd Ave., Peoria, AZ 85382. Telephone: (602) 412-9000. FAX: (602) 412-9382. **Seating Capacity:** 10,000.

Hotel Address: Wyndham Metrocenter, 10220 N Metro Parkway, Phoenix, AZ 85051. Telephone: (602) 997-5900.

Minor League Clubs
Complex Address: Same as major league club. **Hotel Address:** Comfort Inn, 1711 W Bell Rd., Phoenix, AZ 85023. Telephone: (602) 866-2089.

ATLANTA BRAVES
Major League Club
Stadium Address (first year): Disney's Wide World of Sports Complex (1998), 700 S Victory Way, Kissimmee, FL 34747. Telephone: (407) 939-2200. **Seating Capacity:** 9,100.

Hotel Address: Coronado Springs Resort, 1000 W Buena Vista Dr., Lake Buena Vista, FL 32830. Telephone: (407) 939-1000.

Minor League Clubs
Complex Address: Same as major league club. Telephone: (407) 939-8630. FAX: (407) 939-1001. **Hotel Address:** Days Inn Suites, 5820 W Irlo Bronson Memorial Hwy., Kissimmee, FL 34746. Telephone: (407) 396-7900.

BALTIMORE ORIOLES
Major League Club
Complex Address (first year): Fort Lauderdale Stadium (1996), 5301 NW 12th Ave., Fort Lauderdale, FL 33309. Telephone: (954) 776-1921. FAX: (954) 938-9798. **Seating Capacity:** 8,340.

Hotel Address: Sheraton Suites, 555 NW 62nd St., Fort Lauderdale, FL 33309. Telephone: (954) 772-5400. FAX: (954) 772-5490.

Minor League Clubs
Complex Address: Twin Lakes Park, 6700 Clark Rd., Sarasota, FL 34241. Telephone: (941) 923-1996. **Hotel Address:** Ramada Inn Osprey, 1660 S Tamiami Trail, Osprey, FL 34229. Telephone: (941) 966-2121.

BOSTON RED SOX
Major League Club
Complex Address (first year): City of Palms Park (1993), 2201 Edison Ave., Fort Myers, FL 33901. Telephone: (941) 334-4799. FAX: (941) 334-6060. **Seating Capacity:** 6,850.

Hotel Address: Amtel Marina Hotel, 2500 Edwards Dr., Fort Myers, FL 33901. Telephone: (941) 337-0300.

Minor League Clubs
Complex Address: Red Sox Minor League Complex, 4301 Edison Ave., Fort Myers, FL 33916. Telephone: (941) 332-8106. FAX: (941) 332-8107. **Hotel Address:** La Quinta Inn, 4850 Cleveland Ave., Fort Myers, FL 33901. Telephone: (941) 275-3300.

CINCINNATI REDS
Major League Club
Complex Address (first year): Ed Smith Stadium (1998), 12th St. and Tuttle Ave., Sarasota, FL 34237. Telephone: (941) 955-6501. FAX: (941) 955-6365. **Seating Capacity:** 7,500.

Hotel Address: Marriott Residence Inn, 1040 University Pkwy., Sarasota, FL 34234. Telephone: (941) 358-1468.

Minor League Clubs
Complex Address: Same as major league club. **Hotel Address:** Quality Inn, 2303 First St. E, Bradenton, FL 34208. Telephone: (941) 747-6465.

CLEVELAND INDIANS
Major League Club
Complex Address (first year): Chain O' Lakes Park (1993), Cypress Gardens Blvd. at US 17, Winter Haven, FL 33880. Telephone: (941) 293-5405. FAX: (941) 291-5772. **Seating Capacity:** 7,000.

Hotel Address: Holiday Inn, 1150 Third St. SW, Winter Haven, FL 33880. Telephone: (941) 294-4451.
Minor League Clubs
Complex/Hotel Address: Same as major league club.

DETROIT TIGERS
Major League Club
Complex Address (first year): Joker Marchant Stadium (1946), 2301 Lakeland Hills Blvd., Lakeland, FL 33805. Telephone: (941) 686-8075. FAX: (941) 988-9589. **Seating Capacity:** 7,027.

Hotel Address: Hoilday Inn South, 3405 S Florida Ave., Lakeland, FL 33803. Telephone: (941) 646-5731. FAX: (941) 646-5215.
Minor League Clubs
Complex/Hotel Address: Tigertown, 2125 N Lake Ave., Lakeland, FL 33805. Telephone: (941) 686-8075. FAX: (941) 688-9589).

FLORIDA MARLINS
Major League Club
Complex Address (first year): Space Coast Stadium (1993), 5800 Stadium Pkwy., Viera, FL 32940. Telephone: (407) 633-9200. FAX: (407) 633-9210. **Seating Capacity:** 7,200.

Hotel Address: Melbourne Airport Hilton, 200 Rialto Pl., Melbourne, FL 32901. Telephone: (407) 768-0200.
Minor League Clubs
Complex Address: Carl Barger Baseball Complex, 5600 Stadium Pkwy., Viera, FL 32940. Telephone: (407) 633-8119. FAX: (407) 633-9216. **Hotel Address:** Holiday Inn Cocoa Beach Resort, 1300 N Atlantic Ave., Cocoa Beach, FL 32931. Telephone: (407) 783-2271.

HOUSTON ASTROS
Major League Club
Complex Address (first year): Osceola County Stadium (1985), 1000 Bill Beck Blvd., Kissimmee, FL 34744. Telephone: (407) 933-6500. FAX: (407) 847-6237. **Seating Capacity:** 5,130.
Minor League Clubs
Complex Address: Same as major league club. Telephone: (407) 933-5500. FAX: (407) 847-6237. **Hotel Address:** Holiday Inn-Kissimmee, 2009 West Vine St. (US 192), Kissimmee, FL 34741. Telephone: (407) 846-2713.

KANSAS CITY ROYALS
Major League Club
Complex Address (first year): Baseball City Sports Complex (1988), 300 Stadium Way, Davenport, FL 33837. Telephone: (941) 424-7211. FAX: (941) 424-5611. **Seating Capacity:** 8,000.

Hotel Address: Holiday Inn Express, 5225 U.S. Hwy. 27 N, Davenport, FL 33837. Telephone: (941) 424-2120.
Minor League Clubs
Complex/Hotel Address: Same as major league club.

LOS ANGELES DODGERS
Major League Club
Complex Address (first year): Holman Stadium (1948). **Seating Capacity:** 6,500.

Hotel Address: Dodgertown, 4001 26th St., Vero Beach, FL 32960. Telephone: (561) 569-4900. FAX: (561) 567-0819.
Minor League Clubs
Complex/Hotel Address: Same as major league club.

MINNESOTA TWINS
Major League Club
Complex Address (first year): Lee County Sports Complex/Hammond Stadium (1991), 14100 Six Mile Cypress Pkwy., Fort Myers, FL 33912. Telephone: (941) 768-4200. FAX: (941) 768-4207. **Seating Capacity:** 7,500.

Hotel Address: Radisson Inn, 12635 Cleveland Ave., Fort Myers, FL 33907. Telephone: (941) 936-4300. FAX: (941) 936-2058.
Minor League Clubs
Complex Address: Lee County Sports Complex, 14200 Six Mile Cypress Pkwy., Fort Myers, FL 33912. Telephone: (941) 768-4282. FAX: (941) 768-4211. **Hotel Address:** Same as major league club.

MONTREAL EXPOS
Major League Club

Complex Address (first year): Roger Dean Stadium (1998), 4657 Main St., Jupiter, FL 33458. Telephone: (561) 775-1818. **Seating Capacity:** 7,000.

Hotel Address: Doubletree Hotel, 4431 PGA Blvd. at I-95, Palm Beach Gardens, FL 33403. **Telephone:** (561) 622-2260.

Minor League Clubs

Complex Address: Same as major league club. **Hotel Address:** Holiday Inn Express, 13950 U.S. Hwy. 1, Juno Beach, FL 33409. Telephone: (561) 622-4366.

NEW YORK METS
Major League Club

Complex Address (first year): St. Lucie County Sports Complex (1987), 525 NW Peacock Blvd., Port St. Lucie, FL 34986. Telephone: (561) 871-2100. FAX: (561) 878-9802. **Seating Capacity:** 7,347.

Hotel Address: Holiday Inn, 10120 South Federal Hwy., Port St. Lucie, FL 34952. Telephone: (561) 337-2200. FAX: (561) 335-7872.

Minor League Clubs

Complex/Hotel Address: Same as major league club. Telephone: (561) 871-2132. FAX: (561) 871-2181.

NEW YORK YANKEES
Major League Club

Complex Address (first year): Legends Field (1996), One Stein-brenner Drive, Tampa, FL 33614. Telephone: (813) 875-7753. FAX: (813) 673-3176. **Seating Capacity:** 10,000.

Hotel Address: Radisson Bay Harbor Inn, 770 Courtney Campbell Causeway, Tampa, FL 33607. Telephone: (813) 281-8900.

Minor League Clubs

Complex Address: Yankees Minor League Complex, 3102 N Himes Ave., Tampa, FL 33607. Telephone: (813) 875-7769. FAX: (813) 873-2302. **Hotel Address:** Holiday Inn Express, 4732 N Dale Mabry, Tampa, FL 33614.

PHILADELPHIA PHILLIES
Major League Club

Complex Address (first year): Jack Russell Memorial Stadium (1947), 800 Phillies Dr., Clearwater, FL 33755. Telephone: (727) 441-9941. FAX: (727) 461-7768. **Seating Capacity:** 6,882.

Hotel: None.

Minor League Clubs

Complex Address: Carpenter Complex, 651 Old Coachman Rd., Clearwater, FL 33765. Telephone: (727) 799-0503. FAX: (727) 726-1793. **Hotel Addresses:** Hampton Inn, 21030 U.S. Highway 19 North, Clearwater, FL 34625. Telephone: (727) 797-8173; Econolodge, 21252 U.S. Highway 19, Clearwater, FL 34625. Telephone: (727) 799-1569.

PITTSBURGH PIRATES
Major League Club

Stadium Address (first year): McKechnie Field (1969), 17th Ave. W and Ninth St. W, Bradenton, FL 34205. **Seating Capacity:** 6,562.

Complex/Hotel Address: Pirate City, Roberto Clemente Memorial Drive, 1701 27th St. E, Bradenton, FL 34208. Telephone: (941) 747-3031. FAX: (941) 747-9549.

Minor League Clubs

Complex/Hotel Address: Same as major league club.

ST. LOUIS CARDINALS
Major League Club

Stadium Address (first year): Roger Dean Stadium (1998), 4751 Main St., Jupiter, FL 33458. **Seating Capacity:** 6,871. **Complex Address:** Cardinals Complex, 4795 Main St., Jupiter, FL 33458. Telephone: (561) 775-1818. FAX: (561) 630-1831.

Hotel Address: Palm Beach Gardens Marriott, 4000 RCA Blvd., Palm Beach Gardens, FL 33410. Telephone: (561) 622-8888. FAX: (561) 622-0052.

Minor League Clubs

Complex: Same as major league club. **Hotel:** Doubletree Hotel, 4431 PGA Blvd., Palm Beach Gardens, FL 33410. Telephone: (561) 622-2260. FAX: (561) 624-1043.

TAMPA BAY DEVIL RAYS
Major League Club

Stadium Address (first year): Florida Power Park, Al Lang Field (1998), 180 Second Ave. SE, St. Petersburg, FL 33701. Telephone: (727)

344-1306. FAX: (813) 334-1905. **Seating Capacity:** 6,438. **Complex Address:** Devil Rays Spring Training Complex, 7901 30th Ave. N, St. Petersburg, FL 33710. Telephone: (727) 344-1803. FAX: (727) 344-1905.

Hotel Address: St. Petersburg Bayfront Hilton, 333 First St. S, St. Petersburg, FL 33705. Telephone: (727) 894-5000.

Minor Legue Clubs

Complex/Hotel: Same as major league club.

TEXAS RANGERS
Major League Club

Complex Address (first year): Charlotte County Stadium (1987), 2300 El Jobean Rd., Port Charlotte, FL 33948. Telephone: (941) 625-9500. FAX: (941) 624-5168. **Seating Capacity:** 6,026.

Hotel Address: Days Inn, 1941 Tamiami Trail, Murdock, FL 33938. Telephone: (941) 627-8900.

Minor League Clubs

Complex/Hotel Address: Same as major league club.

TORONTO BLUE JAYS
Major League Club

Stadium Address (first year): Dunedin Stadium (1977), 373 Douglas Ave., Dunedin, FL 34697. Telephone: (727) 933-9302. **Seating Capacity:** 6,106. **Complex Address:** Englebert Complex, 1700 Solon Ave., Dunedin, FL 34697. Telephone: (727) 733-3339. FAX: (727) 733-9389.

Hotel: None.

Minor League Clubs

Complex Address: Same as major league club. **Hotel Address:** Red Roof Inn, 3200 U.S. 19 N, Clearwater, FL 34684. Telephone: (727) 786-2529.

MEDIA INFORMATION

American League

ANAHEIM ANGELS
Radio Announcers: Brian Barnhart, Mario Impemba. **Flagship Station:** KLAC 570-AM.

TV Announcers: Rex Hudler, Steve Physioc. **Flagship Stations:** KCAL Channel 9, Fox Sports West (regional cable).

NEWSPAPERS, Daily Coverage (beat writers): Long Beach Press Telegram, Los Angeles Times (Mike DiGiovanna, Ross Newhan, Bill Shaikin), Orange County Register (Kevin Acee, Earl Bloom), Riverside Press Enterprise, San Gabriel Valley Tribune (Joe Haakenson), Inland Valley Daily Bulletin (Lance Pugmire).

BALTIMORE ORIOLES
Radio Announcers: Jim Hunter, Fred Manfra, Chuck Thompson. **Flagship Station:** WBAL 1090-AM.

TV Announcer: Michael Reghi. **Flagship Station:** WJZ-TV, WNUV-TV, Home Team Sports (regional cable).

NEWSPAPERS, Daily Coverage (beat writers): Baltimore Sun (Roch Kubatko, Peter Schmuck, Joe Strauss), Washington Post (Richard Justice), Washington Times (Kevin Seifert), York (Pa.) Daily Record (Dave Buscema).

BOSTON RED SOX
Radio Announcers: Joe Castiglione, Jerry Trupiano. **Flagship Station:** WEEI 850-AM.

TV Announcers: WLVI—Unavailable; WB—Unavailable; NESN—Bob Kurtz, Jerry Remy. **Flagship Stations:** WLVI, WB, New England Sports Network (regional cable).

NEWSPAPERS, Daily Coverage (beat writers): Boston Globe (Gordon Edes), Boston Herald (Tony Massarotti), Quincy Patriot Ledger (Seth Livingstone), Providence Journal (Steve Krasner, Sean McAdam), Worcester Telegram (Bill Ballou, Phil O'Neill), Hartford Courant (Paul Doyle).

CHICAGO WHITE SOX
Radio Announcers: John Rooney, Ed Farmer. **Flagship Station:** ESPN Radio 1000-AM.

TV Announcers: Ken Harrelson, Tom Paciorek. **Flagship Stations:** WGN TV-9, FOX Sports Chicago (regional cable).

NEWSPAPERS, Daily Coverage (beat writers): Chicago Sun-Times (Joe Goddard, Dave Van Dyck), Chicago Tribune (Teddy Greenstein, Jerome Holtzman, Phil Rogers), Arlington Heights Daily Herald (Scot Gregor), Daily Southtown (Joe Cowley).

CLEVELAND INDIANS
Radio Announcers: Tom Hamilton, Mike Hegan, Dave Nelson. **Flagship Station:** WTAM 1100-AM.

TV Announcers: WUAB—Jack Corrigan, Mike Hegan. FOX—Rick Manning, John Sanders. **Flagship Stations:** WUAB-TV 43, Fox Sports Ohio.

NEWSPAPERS, Daily Coverage (beat writers): Cleveland Plain Dealer (Paul Hoynes), Lake County News-Herald (Jim Ingraham), Akron Beacon-Journal (Sheldon Ocker).

DETROIT TIGERS
Radio Announcers: Ernie Harwell, Jim Price. **Flagship Station:** WJR 760-AM.

TV Announcers: Unavailable. **Flagship Stations:** WKBD 50, FOX Sports Detroit (regional cable).

NEWSPAPERS, Daily Coverage (beat writers): Detroit Free Press (John Lowe, Gene Guidi), Detroit News (Tom Gage), Oakland Press (Pat Caputo), Booth Newspaper Group (Danny Knobler).

KANSAS CITY ROYALS
Radio Announcers: Ryan Lefebvre, Denny Matthews. **Flagship Station:** KMBZ 980-AM.

TV Announcers: Bob Davis, Paul Splittorff. **Flagship Stations:** KMBC-9, KCWE-29, Fox Sports Midwest (regional cable).

NEWSPAPERS, Daily Coverage (beat writers): Kansas City Star (Dick Kaegel), Topeka Capital Journal (Alan Eskew).

MINNESOTA TWINS
Radio Announcers: Herb Carneal, John Gordon. **Flagship Station:** WCCO 830-AM.

TV Announcers: Bert Blyleven, Dick Bremer. **Flagship Stations:** KMSP-TV, Midwest Sports Channel (regional cable).

NEWSPAPERS, Daily Coverage (beat writers): St. Paul Pioneer Press (Scott Miller), Star Tribune (La Velle Neal).

NEW YORK YANKEES
Radio Announcers: Michael Kay, John Sterling. **Flagship Station:** WABC 770-AM.

TV Announcers: Unavailable. **Flagship Stations:** Madison Square Garden Network (regional cable), Fox Channel 5.

NEWSPAPERS, Daily Coverage (beat writers): New York Daily News, New York Post (George King), New York Times (Murray Chass, Jack Curry, Buster Olney), Newark Star-Ledger, The Bergen Record, Newsday, Hartford Courant.

OAKLAND ATHLETICS
Radio Announcers: Bill King, Ray Fosse, Ken Korach. **Flagship Station:** KNEW 910-AM.

TV Announcers: Ray Fosse, Greg Papa. **Flagship Stations:** KICU, FOX Sports Bay Area (regional cable).

NEWSPAPERS, Daily Coverage: San Francisco Chronicle, Oakland Tribune, Contra Costa Times, Sacramento Bee, San Francisco Examiner, San Jose Mercury-News, Hayward Daily Review.

SEATTLE MARINERS
Radio Announcers: Dave Niehaus, Ron Fairly, Rick Rizzs. **Flagship Station:** KIRO 710-AM.

TV Announcers: Dave Niehaus, Ron Fairly, Rick Rizzs. **Flagship Station:** KIRO Channel 7, Fox Sports Northwest (regional cable).

NEWSPAPERS, Daily Coverage (beat writers): Seattle Times (Bob Finnigan, Bob Sherwin), Seattle Post-Intelligencer (Jim Street), Tacoma News Tribune (Larry LaRue).

TAMPA BAY DEVIL RAYS
Radio Announcers: Paul Olden, Charlie Slowes. **Flagship Station:** WFLA 970-AM.

TV Announcers: DeWayne Staats, Joe Magrane. **Flagship Stations:** WWWB-TV 32, WTSP-TV 10, SportsChannel Florida (regional cable).

NEWSPAPERS, Daily Coverage (beat writers): St. Petersburg Times (Roger Mills, John Romano, Marc Topkin), Tampa Tribune (Bill Chastain, Joe Henderson), Bradenton Herald (Roger Mooney), Lakeland Ledger (Pat Zier), Sarasota Herald Tribune (Chris Anderson), Orlando Sentinel (Dave Cunningham).

TEXAS RANGERS
Radio Announcers: Eric Nadel, Vince Cotroneo, Luis Mayoral (Spanish), Josue Perez (Spanish). **Flagship Station:** KRLD 1080-AM. **TV Announcers:** Bill Jones, Tom Grieve. **Flagship Stations:** KXAS, KXTX, Fox Sports Southwest (regional cable)

NEWSPAPERS, Daily Coverage (beat writers): Dallas Morning News (Ken Daley, Gerry Fraley, Evan Grant), Fort Worth Star-Telegram (Johnny Paul), Arlington Morning News (Kevin Lonnquist).

TORONTO BLUE JAYS
Radio Announcers: Tom Cheek, Jerry Howarth. **Flagship Station:** CHUM 1050-AM.

TV Announcers: CBC—Brian Williams, John Cerutti; TSN—Buck Martinez, Dan Shulman; CTV—Unavailable. **Flagship Stations:** CBC, The Sports Network (cable), CTV Sports Net (cable).

NEWSPAPERS, Daily Coverage (beat writers): Toronto Sun (Mike Rutsey, Bob Elliott, Mike Ganter), Toronto Star (Jim Byers, Richard Griffin, Alan Ryan), Globe and Mail (Larry Millson), Southam News (Tom Maloney).

National League

ARIZONA DIAMONDBACKS
Radio Announcers: Thom Brennaman, Greg Schulte, Rod Allen, Miguel Quintana (Spanish). **Flagship Stations:** KTAR 620-AM, KPHX 1480-AM (Spanish).

TV Announcers: Thom Brennaman, Greg Schulte, Bob Brenly. **Flagship Stations:** KTVK-TV 3, FOX Sports Arizona (regional cable). **Spanish TV Announcer:** Miguel Quintana. **Spanish Flagship Station:** KDR-TV 64.

NEWSPAPERS, Daily Coverage (beat writers): Arizona Republic (Don

Ketchum), Tribune Newspapers (Ed Price), Arizona Star (Jack Magruder), Tucson Citizen (Chris Walsh).

ATLANTA BRAVES

Radio Announcers: Skip Caray, Don Sutton, Joe Simpson, Pete Van Wieren. **Flagship Station:** WSB 750-AM.

TV Announcers: TBS—Skip Caray, Pete Van Wieren, Don Sutton, Joe Simpson. SportSouth—Ernie Johnson, Bob Rathbun. **Flagship Stations:** TBS Channel 17 (national cable), Fox SportSouth (regional cable).

NEWSPAPERS, Daily Coverage (beat writers): Atlanta Journal-Constitution (Carroll Rogers, I.J. Rosenberg), Morris News Service (Bill Zack).

CHICAGO CUBS

Radio Announcers: Pat Hughes, Ron Santo. **Flagship Station:** WGN 720-AM.

TV Announcers: Chip Caray, Steve Stone. **Flagship Stations:** WGN Channel 9 (national cable), Chicagoland-TV (regional cable).

NEWSPAPERS, Daily Coverage (beat writers): Chicago Tribune (Jerome Holtzman, Phil Rogers, Paul Sullivan), Chicago Sun-Times (Mike Kiley, Dave Van Dyck), Arlington Daily Herald (Bruce Miles).

CINCINNATI REDS

Radio Announcers: Marty Brennaman, Joe Nuxhall. **Flagship Station:** WLW 700-AM.

TV Announcers: George Grande, Chris Welsh. **Flagship Station:** FOX Sports Ohio (regional cable).

NEWSPAPERS, Daily Coverage (beat writers): Cincinnati Enquirer (Chris Haft), Cincinnati Post (Jeff Horrigan), Dayton Daily News (Hal McCoy), Columbus Dispatch (Jim Massie).

COLORADO ROCKIES

Radio Announcers: Wayne Hagin, Jeff Kingery. **Flagship Station:** KOA 850-AM.

TV Announcers: Dave Armstrong, George Frazier. **Flagship Station:** KWGN-TV Channel 2, Fox Sports Rocky Mountain (regional cable).

NEWSPAPERS, Daily Coverage (beat writers): Rocky Mountain News (Tracy Ringolsby, Jack Etkin), Denver Post (Mike Klis, John Henderson), Boulder Daily Camera (Barney Hutchinson), Colorado Springs Gazette-Telegraph (Ray McNulty).

FLORIDA MARLINS

Radio Announcers: Joe Angel, Dave O'Brien, Jon Sciambi, Manolo Alvarez (Spanish), Felo Ramirez (Spanish). **Flagship Stations:** WQAM 560-AM, WQBA 1140-AM (Spanish).

TV Announcers: Joe Angel, Dave O'Brien, Tommy Hutton. **Flagship Stations:** WAMI Channel 69, Sports Channel Florida (regional cable).

NEWSPAPERS, Daily Coverage (beat writers): Miami Herald (Mike Phillips, Dave Sheinin), Fort Lauderdale Sun-Sentinel (Mike Berardino, David O'Brien), Palm Beach Post (Dan Graziano), Florida Today (Juan Rodriguez). Spanish—El Nuevo Herald (Aurelio Moreno).

HOUSTON ASTROS

Radio Announcers: Alan Ashby, Bill Brown, Jim Deshaies, Milo Hamilton. **Flagship Station:** KTRH 740-AM.

TV Announcers: Bill Brown, Jim Deshaies, Milo Hamilton, Bill Worrell. **Flagship Stations:** KNWS, Fox Sports Southwest (regional cable).

NEWSPAPERS, Daily Coverage (beat writers): Houston Chronicle (Joseph Duarte, Carlton Thompson), Houston Today (Jim Molony), Beaumont Enterprise (Kenton Brooks, Joe Heiling).

LOS ANGELES DODGERS

Radio Announcers: Vin Scully, Rick Monday, Ross Porter, Jaime Jarrin (Spanish), Pepe Yniguez (Spanish). **Flagship Stations:** KXTA 1150-AM, KWKW 1330-AM (Spanish).

TV Announcers: Vin Scully, Rick Monday, Ross Porter. **Flagship Station:** KTLA Channel 5, Fox Sports West 2 (regional cable).

NEWSPAPERS, Daily Coverage (beat writers): Los Angeles Times (Ross Newhan, Jason Reid), South Bay Daily Breeze (Bill Cizek), Los Angeles Daily News (Matt McHale), Riverside Press Enterprise (Jorge Valencia), Orange County Register (Robert Kuwada), San Bernardino Sun (Steve Dilbeck).

MILWAUKEE BREWERS

Radio Announcers: Bob Uecker, Jim Powell. **Flagship Station:** WTMJ 620-AM.

TV Announcers: Bill Schroeder, Matt Vasgersian. **Flagship Station:** Midwest Sports Channel, WCGV Channel 24.

NEWSPAPERS, Daily Coverage (beat writers): Milwaukee Journal Sentinel (Tom Haudricourt, Drew Olson).

MONTREAL EXPOS

Radio Announcers: Dave Van Horne, Elliott Price, Joe Cannon, Jacques Doucet (French), Rodger Brulotte (French), Alain Chantelois (French). **Flagship Stations:** CIQC 600-AM, CKAC 730-AM (French).

TV Announcers: Dave Van Horne, Gary Carter; SRC/French—Rene Pothier, Claude Raymond; RDS/French—Denis Casavant, Rodger Brulotte. **Flagship Stations:** The Sports Network (national cable); French—Societe Radio Canada.

NEWSPAPERS, Daily Coverage (beat writers): English—Montreal Gazette (Stephanie Myles). French—La Presse Canadienne (Michel Lajeunesse, Richard Milo), La Presse (Ronald King, Pierre Ladouceur), Le Journal de Montreal (Serge Touchette).

NEW YORK METS

Radio Announcers: Gary Cohen, Ed Coleman, Bob Murphy. **Flagship Stations:** WFAN 660-AM.

TV Announcers: Fran Healy, Ralph Kiner, Matt Loughlin, Howie Rose, Tom Seaver. **Flagship Station:** Fox Sports New York (regional cable).

NEWSPAPERS, Daily Coverage (beat writers): New York Times (Jason Diamos), New York Daily News (Thomas Hill), New York Post (Dave Waldstein), Newsday (Marty Noble), Newark Star-Ledger (Rafael Hermoso), The Record (T.J. Quinn), Gannett Suburban (Kit Stier).

PHILADELPHIA PHILLIES

Radio Announcers: Larry Andersen, Scott Graham, Harry Kalas, Andy Musser, Chris Wheeler. **Flagship Station:** WPHT 1210-AM.

Television Announcers: Larry Andersen, Scott Graham, Harry Kalas, Andy Musser, Chris Wheeler. **Flagship Stations:** WPSG UPN Channel 57, Comcast SportsNet (regional cable).

NEWSPAPERS, Daily Coverage (beat writers): Philadelphia Inquirer (Jim Salisbury, Jayson Stark), Philadelphia Daily News (Paul Hagen), Bucks County Courier-Times (Randy Miller), Camden Courier Post (Kevin Roberts), Delaware County Times (Bob Brookover), Wilmington News-Journal (Doug Lesmerises), Trenton Times (Chris Edwards).

PITTSBURGH PIRATES

Radio Announcers: Steve Blass, Greg Brown, Lanny Frattare, Bob Walk. **Flagship Station:** KDKA 1020-AM.

TV Announcers: Steve Blass, Greg Brown, Lanny Frattare, Bob Walk. **Flagship Station:** Fox Sports Pittsburgh (regional cable).

NEWSPAPERS, Daily Coverage (beat writers): Pittsburgh Post-Gazette (Paul Meyer), Pittsburgh Tribune-Review (Joe Rutter), Beaver County Times (John Perrotto).

ST. LOUIS CARDINALS

Radio Announcers: Jack Buck, Joe Buck, Mike Shannon. **Flagship Station:** KMOX 1120-AM.

TV Announcers: Bob Carpenter, Al Hrabosky, Bob Ramsey. **Flagship Stations:** KPLR Channel 11, Fox Sports Midwest (regional cable).

NEWSPAPERS, Daily Coverage (beat writers): St. Louis Post-Dispatch (Mike Eisenbath, Rick Hummel), Belleville News Democrat (Joe Ostermaier).

SAN DIEGO PADRES

Radio Announcers: Jerry Coleman, Ted Leitner, Bob Chandler, Juan Avila (Spanish), Eduardo Ortega (Spanish). **Flagship Stations:** KFMB 760-AM, KURS 1040-AM (Spanish).

TV Announcers: Mel Proctor, Rick Sutcliffe, Mark Grant. **Flagship Stations:** KUSI TV-51, Channel 4 Padres (regional cable).

NEWSPAPERS, Daily Coverage (beat writers): San Diego Union-Tribune (Bill Center, Tom Krasovic), North County Times (Joe Christensen, John Maffei).

SAN FRANCISCO GIANTS

Radio Announcers: Jon Miller, Mike Krukow, Ted Robinson, Duane Kuiper, Lon Simmons, Erwin Higueros (Spanish), Amaury Pi-Gonzalez (Spanish). **Flagship Station:** KNBR 680-AM.

TV Announcers: FOX—Jon Miller, Duane Kuiper. KTVU—Mike Krukow, Ted Robinson, Lon Simmons, Jon Miller. **Flagship Stations:** KTVU-TV 2, FOX Sports Bay Area (regional cable).

NEWSPAPERS, Daily Coverage (beat writers): San Francisco Chronicle (Henry Schulman), San Francisco Examiner (John Shea), San Jose Mercury News (Mark Gonzales), Contra Costa Times (Joe Roderick), Sacramento Bee (Nick Peters), Oakland Tribune (Mark Saxon), Santa Rosa Press Democrat (Jeff Fletcher).

GENERAL INFORMATION

BASEBALL STATISTICS

ELIAS SPORTS BUREAU, INC.
Official Major League Statistician
Mailing Address: 500 Fifth Ave., New York, NY 10110. **Telephone:** (212) 869-1530. **FAX:** (212) 354-0980.
President/General Manager: Seymour Siwoff.
Executive Vice President: Steve Hirdt. **Data Processing Manager:** Chris Thorn.

HOWE SPORTSDATA
(A service of SportsTicker, LP)
Official Minor League Statistician
Mailing Address: Boston Fish Pier, West Bldg. #1, Suite 302, Boston, MA 02210. **Telephone:** (617) 951-0070. **Stats Service:** (617) 951-1379. **FAX:** (617) 737-9960.
President/General Manager: Jay Virshbo.
Assistant General Manager: Jim Keller. **Programmer/Analysts:** John Foley, Walter Kent, Chris Pollari. **Senior Editor:** Vin Vitro. **Senior Bureau Managers:** Brian Joura, Paul LaRocca. **Bureau Managers:** Bob Chaban, Tom Graham, Mike Walczak. **Associate Bureau Managers:** Joe Barbieri, David Rourke, Matt Santillo, Marshall Wright.
Historical Consultant: Bill Weiss.

STATS, INC.
Mailing Address: 8130 Lehigh Ave., Morton Grove, IL 60053. **Telephone:** (847) 677-3322. **FAX:** (847) 470-9160. **Website:** www.stats.com.
President/Chief Executive Officer: John Dewan.
President: Alan Leib. **Vice President, Research/Development:** Susan Dewan. **Vice President, Commercial Products:** Robert Meyerhoff. **Vice President, Publishing Products:** Don Zminda. **Vice President, Interactive Products:** Jim Capuano. **Vice President, Fantasy Products:** Steve Byrd. **Vice President, Sports Operations:** Doug Abel. **Director, Major League Operations:** Craig Wright.

TELEVISION NETWORKS

ESPN/ESPN2
- *Sunday Night Baseball, 1999*
- *Wednesday Night Doubleheaders, 1999*
- *Division Series, 1999*

Mailing Address, Connecticut Office: ESPN Plaza, Bristol, CT 06010. **Telephone:** (860) 766-2000. **FAX:** (860) 766-2213.
Mailing Address, New York Office: 605 Third Ave., New York, NY 10152. **Telephone:** (212) 916-9200. **FAX:** (212) 916-9312.
Website: www.espn.com.
Chairman, Chief Executive Officer: Steve Bornstein. **President:** George Bodenheimer.
Executive Vice President, Administration: Ed Durso. **Executive Vice President, Programming:** Dick Glover. **Executive Vice President, Production:** Howard Katz.
Senior Vice President, Production: Steve Anderson. **Senior Vice President, Executive Editor:** John Walsh. **Senior Vice President, Programming:** John Wildhack.
Vice President, Remote Production: Jed Drake. **Vice President, Managing Editor/Studio Programs:** Bob Eaton. **Vice President, Programming:** Steve Risser.
Assistant Managing Editor/News Director, Studio Programs: Vince Doria. **Senior Coordinating Producer, Baseball Tonight/Studio:** Norby Williamson. **Coordinating Producer, Baseball Tonight/Studio:** Jeff Schneider. **Coordinating Producer:** Tim Scanlan.
General Manager, ESPN Radio: Eric Schoenfeld.
Executive Producer, ESPN.com: Jim Jenks.
Manager, Communications: Diane Lamb. **Coordinator, Communications:** Josh Krulewitz.
Sunday Night Telecasts: Play-by-play—Jon Miller. Analyst—Joe Morgan.
Studio Hosts: Chris Berman, Karl Ravech. **Studio Analysts:** Peter Gammons, Ray Knight, Harold Reynolds.
Play-by-Play Announcers: Dave Barnett, Bob Carpenter, Dave Ryan,

Dan Shulman, Charley Steiner, Gary Thorne. **Analysts:** Dave Campbell, Kevin Kennedy.

FOX SPORTS

- *Saturday Afternoon Game of the Week, 1999*
- *All-Star Game,1999*
- *Division Series, 1999*
- *American League Championship Series, 1999*

Mailing Address, Los Angeles: FOX Nework Center, Building 101, 10201 W Pico Blvd., Los Angeles, CA 90035. **Telephone:** (310) 369-6000. **FAX:** (310) 969-6192.

Mailing Address, New York: 1211 Avenue of the Americas, 2nd Floor, New York, NY 10036. **Telephone:** (212) 556-2500. **FAX:** (212) 354-6902.

President: David Hill. **Executive Producer:** Ed Goren. **Senior Coordinating Producer, Major League Baseball on FOX:** John Filippelli. **Senior Producer:** Bill Brown. **Vice President, Media Relations:** Lou D'Ermilio. **Manager, Media Relations:** Dan Bell.

Play-by-Play Announcers (Analysts): Thom Brennaman (Bob Brenly), Joe Buck (Tim McCarver), Kenny Albert (Jeff Torborg), Josh Lewin (George Brett/Frank Robinson).

FOX SPORTS NET

- *Baseball Thursday (Game of the Week), 1999*

Mailing Address: 1440 S Sepulveda Blvd., Suite 286, Los Angeles, CA 90025. **Telephone:** (310) 444-8123. **FAX:** (310) 479-8856.

President/Chief Executive Officer (FOX/Liberty Network): Tony Ball. **Chief Operating Officer:** Tracy Dolgin. **Executive Vice President, Programming/Production:** Arthur Smith. **Executive Vice President/ Rights Acquisitions and Regional Network Operations:** Bob Thompson. **Manager, Media Relations:** Dennis Johnson.

FX

- *Saturday Night Game of the Week, 1999*

Mailing Address, Los Angeles: 1440 S Sepulveda Blvd., Suite 286, Los Angeles, CA 90025. **Telephone:** (310) 444-8281. **FAX:** (310) 479-8856. **President:** Peter Liquori.

NBC SPORTS

- *Division Series, 1999*
- *National League Championship Series, 1999*
- *World Series, 1999*

Mailing Address: 30 Rockefeller Plaza, Suite 1558, New York, NY 10112. **Telephone:** (212) 664-4444. **FAX:** (212) 664-3602.

Chairman, NBC Sports: Dick Ebersol. **President, NBC Sports:** Ken Schanzer.

Vice President, Sports Information/Special Projects: Ed Markey. **Play-by-Play Announcer:** Bob Costas. **Analyst:** Joe Morgan.

Other Television Networks

ABC SPORTS

Mailing Address: 47 West 66th St., New York, NY 10023. **Telephone:** (212) 456-7777. **FAX:** (212) 456-2877.

President, ABC Sports: Steve Bornstein. **Executive Vice President/ General Manager:** Brian McAndrews. **Director, Public Relations:** Mark Mandel.

CBS SPORTS

Mailing Address: 51 W 52nd St., New York, NY 10019. **Telephone:** (212) 975-5230. **FAX:** (212) 975-4063.

President, CBS Sports: Sean McManus. **Executive Producer, CBS Sports:** Terry Ewart. **Director, Communications:** Leslie Ann Wade.

CNN/SI

Mailing Address: One CNN Center, Atlanta, GA 30303. **Telephone:** (404) 878-1600. **FAX:** (404) 588-2057.

President: Jim Walton.

Managing Editor: Steve Robinson. **Coordinating Producers:** Greg Agvent, Tony Florkowski, Bill Galvin, Gus Lalone, Sandy Malcolm, Howard Sappington. **Assignment Manager:** Tony Lamb. **Publicist:** Jane Tronnier.

CTV AND CTV SPORTSNET (CANADA)

Mailing Address: Box 9, Station O, Toronto, Ontario M4A 2M9. **Telephone:** (416) 299-2000. **FAX:** (416) 299-2076.

Senior Vice President/General Manager: Suzanne Steeves. **Vice President/Managing Director:** Doug Beeforth. **Vice President, Production:** Scott Moore. **Manager, Communications:** David Rashford.

Play-by-Play Announcers: Rod Black, Rob Faulds.

THE SPORTS NETWORK (CANADA)

Mailing Address: 2225 Sheppard Ave. E, Suite 100, North York, Ontario M2J 5C2. **Telephone:** (416) 494-1212. **FAX:** (416) 490-7010.

President/General Manager: Rick Brace. **Senior Vice President, Programming/Production:** Keith Pelley. **Executive Producer, Baseball:** Rick Briggs-Jude. **Executive Producer, News/Information:** Mike Day.

Commentators: Dan Shulman (Blue Jays), Dave Van Horne (Expos). **Analysts:** Buck Martinez (Blue Jays), Gary Carter (Expos).

Baseball Today/Tonight: Rod Smith (host), Pat Tabler (analyst).

Super Stations

TBS, Atlanta
(Atlanta Braves)
Mailing Address: One CNN Center, P.O. Box 105366, Atlanta, GA 30348. **Telephone:** (404) 827-1700. **FAX:** (404) 827-1593.

Executive Producer: Glenn Diamond.

WGN, Chicago
(Chicago Cubs, Chicago White Sox)
Mailing Address: 2501 W Bradley Pl., Chicago, IL 60618. **Telephone:** (773) 528-2311. **FAX:** (773) 528-6050. **Website:** www.wgntv.com.

RADIO NETWORKS

ESPN RADIO

■ *All-Star Game, 1999*
■ *All postseason games, 1999*
■ *Sunday Night Game of the Week, 1999*

Mailing Address: ESPN Plaza, Bristol, CT 06010. **Telephone:** (860) 766-2661. **FAX:** (860) 766-5523.

General Manager: Eric Schoenfeld. **Assistant General Manager/Program Director:** Len Weiner. **Executive Producer:** John Martin.

ABC RADIO NETWORK SPORTS

Mailing Address: 125 West End Ave., 6th floor, New York, NY 10023. **Telephone:** (212) 456-5185. **FAX:** (212) 456-5405.

Vice President: Bernard Gershon. **General Manager:** Chris Berry. **Director, Sports/Executive Producer:** Mike Rizzo.

Fabulous Sports Babe Show
Coordinating Producer: Steve Barenfeld.

ONE-ON-ONE SPORTS RADIO NETWORK

Mailing Address: 1935 Techny Rd., Suite 18, Northbrook, IL 60062. **Telephone:** (847) 509-1661. **Guest Line:** (800) 224-2004. **FAX:** (847) 509-8149.

President: Chris Brennan. **Vice President, Programming:** Richard Bonn. **Sports Director:** Bob Berger. **Executive Producer:** Tim Parker.

SPORTS BYLINE USA

Mailing Address: 300 Broadway, Suite 8, San Francisco, CA 94133. **Telephone:** (415) 434-8300. **Guest Line:** (800) 878-7529. **FAX:** (415) 391-2569. **Website:** www.sportsbyline.com.

General Manager: Darren Peck.

SPORTSFAN RADIO NETWORK

Mailing Address: 1455 E Tropicana Ave., Suite 250, Las Vegas, NV 89119. **Telephone:** (800) 895-1022, (702) 740-4240. **FAX:** (702) 740-4171.

Executive Producer: Jay Sherman.

NEWS ORGANIZATIONS

ASSOCIATED PRESS

Mailing Address: 50 Rockefeller Plaza, New York, NY 10020. **Telephone:** (212) 621-1630. **FAX:** (212) 621-1639.

Sports Editor: Terry Taylor. **Deputy Sports Editor:** Brian Friedman. **Assistant Sports Editor:** Aaron Watson. **Agate Editor:** Paul Montella. **Sports Photo Editor:** Brian Horton. **Baseball Writers:** Ron Blum, Josh Dubow, Ben Walker.

BLOOMBERG SPORTS NEWS

Mailing Address: P.O. Box 888, Princeton, NJ 08542. **Telephone:** (609) 279-4061. **FAX:** (609) 279-5878.

Sports Editor: Jay Beberman. **National Baseball Writer:** Jerry Crasnick.

ESPN/SPORTSTICKER

Mailing Address: Harborside Financial Center, 600 Plaza Two, 8th Floor, Jersey City, NJ 07311. **Telephone:** (201) 309-1200. **FAX:** (800) 336-

0383, (201) 860-9742. **E-Mail Address:** sportstick@aol.com.

Vice President, General Manager: Rick Alessandri. **Executive Director, News:** Jim Morganthaler. **General Manager, News:** John Mastroberardino. **Senior Editor, Major League Baseball:** Doug Mittler. **Director, Marketing/Newsroom Services:** Lou Monaco.

CANADIAN PRESS

Mailing Address: 36 King St. East, Toronto, Ontario M5C 2L9. **Telephone:** (416) 507-2154. **E-Mail Address:** sports@cp.org.

General Sports Editor: Neil Davidson. **Baseball Writer:** Glen Colbourn.

PRESS ASSOCIATIONS

BASEBALL WRITERS ASSOCIATION OF AMERICA

Mailing Address: 78 Olive St., Lake Grove, NY 11755. **Telephone:** (516) 981-7938. **FAX:** (516) 585-4669. **E-Mail Address:** bbwaa@aol.com.

President: Bob Elliott (Toronto Sun). **Vice President:** Charles Scoggins (Lowell, Mass., Sun).

Board of Directors: Gerry Fraley (Dallas Morning News), Tom Keegan (New York Post), Patrick Reusse (Minneapolis Star Tribune), Jim Street (Seattle Post-Intelligencer).

Secretary-Treasurer: Jack O'Connell (Hartford Courant). **Assistant Secretary:** Jack Lang (SportsTicker).

NATIONAL ASSOCIATION OF BASEBALL WRITERS AND BROADCASTERS

Mailing Address: P.O. Box A, St. Petersburg, FL 33731. **Telephone:** (727) 822-6937. **FAX:** (727) 821-5819.

Secretary-Treasurer: Jim Ferguson (National Association).

NATIONAL COLLEGIATE BASEBALL WRITERS ASSOCIATION

Mailing Address: 35 E. Wacker Dr., Suite 650, Chicago, IL 60601. **Telephone:** (312) 553-0483. **FAX:** (312) 553-0495.

Board of Directors: Bo Carter (Big 12 Conference), Bob Bradley (Clemson), Tom Price (South Carolina).

President: Ken Krisolovic (St. Joseph's). **First Vice President:** Charles Bloom (Southeastern Conference) **Secretary-Treasurer:** Russ Anderson (Conference USA).

Newsletter Editor: John Askins, Sports Media Group. Telephone: (713) 686-0201. E-Mail Address: jaskins@sprynet.com.

NEWSPAPERS/PERIODICALS

USA TODAY

Mailing Address: 1000 Wilson Blvd., Arlington, VA 22229. **Telephone/Baseball Desk:** (703) 276-3731, 276-3744, 276-3725. **FAX:** (703) 558-3988.

Publishing Frequency: Daily (Monday-Friday).

Baseball Editors: John Porter, Denise Tom, John Tkach. **Baseball Columnist:** Hal Bodley. **Major League Beat Writers:** Chuck Johnson (National Leage), Mel Antonen (American League). **Baseball Reporters:** Rod Beaton, Mike Dodd. **Agate Editor:** Matt Seaman.

THE SPORTING NEWS

Mailing Address: 10176 Corporate Square Dr., Suite 200, St. Louis, MO 63132. **Telephone:** (314) 997-7111. **FAX:** (314) 997-0765.

Publishing Frequency: Weekly.

Editor: John Rawlings. **Executive Editor:** Steve Meyerhoff. **Managing Editor:** Bob Hille. **Managing Editor/Online:** Barry Reeves. **Senior Writer:** Michael Knisley. **Photo Editor:** Paul Nisely.

SPORTS ILLUSTRATED

Mailing Address: Time & Life Building, 1271 Avenue of the Americas, New York, NY 10020. **Telephone:** (212) 522-1212. **FAX, Editorial:** (212) 522-4543. **FAX, Public Relations:** (212) 522-4832.

Publishing Frequency: Weekly.

Managing Editor: Bill Colson. **Senior Editors:** Dick Friedman, Richard O'Brien. **Senior Writers:** Gerry Callahan, Tim Crothers, Tom Verducci.

Director, Communications: Art Berke. **Director, Publicity:** Joe Assad.

USA TODAY BASEBALL WEEKLY

Mailing Address: 1000 Wilson Blvd., 21st Floor, Arlington, VA 22229. **Telephone:** (703) 558-5630. **FAX:** (703) 558-4678.

Publishing Frequency: Weekly.

Publisher: Keith Cutler. **Executive Editor:** Lee Ivory. **Deputy Editor:**

Tim McQuay. **Deputy Editor/Operations:** Gary Kicinski. **Assignment Editor:** Margaret McCahill. **Editor:** Paul White.

Ad Services: Gloria Ryan. **Manager, Classified Advertising:** Lynn Busby.

STREET AND SMITH'S
SPORTS BUSINESS JOURNAL

Mailing Address: 120 W Morehead St., Suite 310, Charlotte, NC 28202. **Telephone:** (704) 973-1400.

Publishing Frequency: Weekly.

ESPN THE MAGAZINE

Mailing Address: 19 E 34th St., 7th Floor, New York, NY 10016. **Telephone:** (212) 515-1000. **FAX:** (212) 515-1290.

Publishing Frequency: Bi-weekly.

Publisher: Michael Rooney. **Editor:** John Papanek. **Executive Editor:** Steve Wulf. **Senior Editor, Baseball**: Glen Waggoner. **Associate Editor, Baseball:** Jeff Bradley. **Senior Writer:** Tim Kurkjian. **Writer/Reporter:** Brendan O'Connor.

SPORT MAGAZINE

Mailing Address: 110 Fifth Ave., New York, NY 10011. **Telephone:** (212) 880-3600. **FAX:** (212) 229-4838.

Publishing Frequency: Monthly.

Editor: Norb Garrett. **Managing Editor:** Steve Gordon.

BASEBALL DIGEST

Mailing Address: 990 Grove St., Evanston, IL 60201. **Telephone:** (847) 491-6440. **FAX:** (847) 491-6203. **E-Mail Address:** century@wwa.com.

Publishing Frequency: Monthly.

Publisher: Norman Jacobs. **Editor:** John Kuenster. **Managing Editor:** Bob Kuenster.

COLLEGIATE BASEBALL

Mailing Address: P.O. Box 50566, Tucson, AZ 85703. **Telephone:** (520) 623-4530. **FAX:** (520) 624-5501. **E-Mail Address:** editor@baseballnews.com. Website: www.baseballnews.com.

Publishing Frequency: Bi-weekly (Jan.-June)

Publisher: Lou Pavlovich. **Editor:** Lou Pavlovich Jr.

JUNIOR BASEBALL MAGAZINE

Mailing Address: P.O. Box 9099, Canoga Park, CA 91309. **Telephone:** (818) 710-1234. **FAX:** (818) 710-1877. **Website:** www.juniorbaseball.com.

Publishing Frequency: Bi-Monthly.

Publisher/Editor: Dave Destler.

INTERNATIONAL BASEBALL RUNDOWN

Mailing Address: P.O. Box 608, Glen Ellyn, IL 60138. **Telephone:** (630) 790-3087. **FAX:** (630) 790-3182. **E-Mail Address:** ibrundown@aol.com.

Publishing Frequency: Monthly.

Editor: Jeff Elijah.

SPORTS ILLUSTRATED FOR KIDS

Mailing Address: Time & Life Building, Rockefeller Center, New York, NY 10020. **Telephone:** (212) 522-4876. **FAX:** (212) 522-0120. **Website:** www.sikids.com.

Publishing Frequency: Monthly.

Managing Editor: Neil Cohen. **Deputy Managing Editor:** Stephen Malley.

BASEBALL PARENT

Mailing Address: 4437 Kingston Pike, Suite 2204, Knoxville, TN 37919. **Telephone:** (423) 523-1274. **FAX:** (423) 673-8926. **Website:** www.members.aol.com/baseparent.

Publishing Frequency: Quarterly.

Publisher/Editor: Wayne Christensen.

Baseball Annuals

ATHLON'S BASEBALL

Mailing Address: 220 25th Ave. N, Suite 200, Nashville, TN 37203. **Telephone:** (615) 327-0747. **FAX:** (615) 327-1149. **E-Mail Address:** athlon@nashville.net.

Chief Executive Officer: Chuck Allen. **Managing Editor:** Charlie Miller. **Senior Editor:** Rob Doster.

STREET AND SMITH'S BASEBALL

Mailing Address: 342 Madison Ave., New York, NY 10017. **Telephone:** (212) 880-8698. **FAX:** (212) 880-4347.

Publisher: Sal Schiliro. **Editor:** Gerard Kavanagh.

THE SPORTING NEWS BASEBALL YEARBOOK

Mailing Address: 10176 Corporate Square Dr., Suite 200, St. Louis, MO 63132. **Telephone:** (314) 997-7111. **FAX:** (314) 997-0705.

Editor: John Rawlings. **Executive Editor:** Steve Meyerhoff. **Managing Editor:** Bob Hille.

SPRING TRAINING BASEBALL YEARBOOK

Mailing Address: Vanguard Sports Publications, P.O. Box 667, Chapel Hill, NC 27514. **Telephone:** (919) 967-2420. **FAX:** (919) 967-6294. **E-Mail Address:** vanguard@interpath.com. **Website:** www.springtrainingmagazine.com.

Publisher: Merle Thorpe. **Editor:** Myles Friedman.

ULTIMATE SPORTS BASEBALL

Mailing Address: Ultimate Sports Publishing, P.O. Box 75299, Seattle, WA 98125. **Editorial Telephone:** (206) 301-9466. **FAX:** (206) 301-9420. **Business Telephone:** (319) 322-8110. **Website:** www.ultsports.com.

Publisher: Shane O'Neill. **Editor:** Nick Rousso.

Baseball Encyclopedias

TOTAL BASEBALL
The Official Encyclopedia of Major League Baseball

Mailing Address: 445 Park Ave., 19th Floor, New York, NY 10022. **Telephone:** (212) 319-6611. **FAX:** (212) 319-3820. **E-Mail Address:** info@totalsports.net. **Website:** www.totalbaseball.com.

Co-Editors: Mike Gershman, John Thorn. **Statistician:** Pete Palmer.

BASEBALL WEBSITES

GENERAL SPORTS

CBS Sportsline	www.sportsline.com
CNNSI	www.cnnsi.com
ESPN	www.espn.go.com
NANDO Sports	www.sportserver.com
USA Today	www.usatoday.com

BASEBALL ONLY

Fanlink	www.fanlink.com
Fastball	www.fastball.com
John Skilton's Baseball Links	www.baseball-links.com
Major League Baseball	www.majorleaguebaseball.com
National Association	www.minorleaguebaseball.com
Players Association	www.bigleaguers.com

HOBBY PUBLICATIONS

BECKETT PUBLICATIONS
Beckett Baseball Card Monthly

Mailing Address: 15850 Dallas Pkwy., Dallas, TX 75248. **Telephone:** (972) 991-6657. **FAX:** (972) 991-8930.

KRAUSE PUBLICATIONS

Mailing Address: 700 E State St., Iola, WI 54990. **Telephone:** (715) 445-2214. **FAX:** (715) 445-4087.

Publisher: Hugh McAloon.

Editor, Fantasy Sports/Sports Cards Magazine: Greg Ambrosius. **Editor, Sports Collectors Digest:** Tom Mortenson.

TEAM PUBLICATIONS

COMAN PUBLISHING, INC.
(Boston Red Sox, New York Mets)

Mailing Address: P.O. Box 2331, Durham, NC 27702. **Telephone:** (800) 421-7751; (919) 688-0218. **FAX:** (919) 682-1532.

Publisher: Stuart Coman.

Diehard (Boston Red Sox)—**Editor:** George Whitney. **Managing Editor:** Todd McGee.

New York Mets Inside Pitch—Managing Editor: Chris Riffer.

PHILLIES REPORT
(Philadelphia Phillies)

Mailing Address: P.O. Box 306, Whitehall, PA 18052. **Telephone:** (888) 409-2200. **Website:** www.philliesreport.com. **Editor:** Jeff Moeller.

VINE LINE
(Chicago Cubs)

Mailing Address: Chicago Cubs Publications, 1060 W. Addison St.,

Chicago, IL 60613. **Telephone:** (773) 404-2827. **FAX:** (773) 404-4129. **Managing Editor:** Lena McDonagh. **Editor:** Jay Rand.

YANKEES MAGAZINE
(New York Yankees)

Mailing Address: Yankee Stadium, Bronx, NY 10451. **Telephone:** (718) 579-4495. **Publisher:** Dan Cahalane. **Editor:** Stephanie Geosits.

JET MEDIA/INDIANS INK
(Cleveland Indians)

Mailing Address: P.O. Box 539, Mentor, OH 44061. **Telephone:** (440) 953-2200. **FAX:** (440) 953-2202. **Editor:** Frank Derry.

OUTSIDE PITCH
(Baltimore Orioles)

Mailing Address: P.O. Box 27143, Baltimore, MD 21230. **Telephone:** (410) 234-8888. **FAX:** (410) 234-1029. **Publisher:** David Simone. **Editor:** David Hill.

REDS REPORT
(Cincinnati Reds)

Mailing Address: Columbus Sports Publications, P.O. Box 12453, Columbus, OH 43212. **Telephone:** (614) 486-2202. **FAX:** (614) 486-3650. **Publisher:** Frank Moskowitz. **Editor:** Steve Helwagen.

FANTASY BASEBALL

THE SPORTING NEWS
FANTASY BASEBALL YEARBOOK

Mailing Address: 10176 Corporate Square Dr., Suite 200, St. Louis, MO 63132. **Telephone:** (314) 997-7111. **FAX:** (314) 993-7726. **Managing Editor:** Mike Nahrstedt.

HAWES FANTASY BASEBALL GUIDE

Mailing Address: Ultimate Sports Publishing, P.O. Box 75299, Seattle, WA 98125. **Editorial Telephone:** (206) 301-9466. **FAX:** (206) 301-9420. **Business Telephone:** (319) 322-8110. **Website:** www.ultsports.com. **Publisher:** Shane O'Neill. **Editor:** Nick Rousso.

JOHN BENSON'S
FANTASY BASEBALL

Mailing Address: 15 Cannon Rd., Wilton, CT 06897. **Telephone:** (203) 834-1231. **Website:** www.johnbenson,com. **Editor:** John Benson.

Majors-Other Information

GENERALINFORMATION

MAJOR LEAGUE BASEBALL
PLAYERS ASSOCIATION

Mailing Address: 12 E 49th St., 24th Floor, New York, NY 10017. **Telephone:** (212) 826-0808. **FAX:** (212) 752-4378. **Website:** www.big leaguers.com.

Year Founded: 1966.

Executive Director, General Counsel: Donald Fehr.

Special Assistants: Tony Bernazard, Phil Bradley, Steve Rogers.

Associate General Counsel: Gene Orza. **Assistant General Counsel:** Robert Lenaghan, Doyle Pryor, Michael Weiner.

Director, Licensing: Judy Heeter. **General Manager:** Richard White. **Manager, Marketing Services:** Allyne Price. **Category Director, Publishing and New Products:** Scott Barrett. **Category Manager, Apparel:** Richard Fullerton. **Category Manager, Novelties:** Evan Kaplan. **Category Director, Interactive Games:** John Olshan. **Administrative Manager:** Tina Morris. **Editor, Website:** Chris Dahl. **Licensing Assistant:** Heather Saks.

Executive Board: Player representatives of the 30 major league clubs.

League Representatives: American League—David Cone; **National League**—Tom Glavine.

MAJOR LEAGUE
BASEBALL PRODUCTIONS

Mailing Address: 245 Park Ave., New York, NY 10167. **Telephone:** (212) 931-7900. **FAX:** (212) 949-5795, 949-5692.

Senior Vice President, General Manager: Steve Hellmuth. **Executive Producer:** David Gavant. **Vice President, Programming/Sales:** James Scott. **Director, Home Videos/Marketing:** Chris Brande. **Director, Operations:** Michael Kusama.

SCOUTING

MAJOR LEAGUE
SCOUTING BUREAU

Mailing Address: 3500 Porsche Way, Suite 100, Ontario, CA 91764. **Telephone:** (909) 980-1881. **FAX:** (909) 980-7794.

Year Founded: 1974.

Director: Frank Marcos. **Assistant Director:** Rick Oliver.

Administrator: RoseMary Durgin. **Administrative Assistant:** Joanne Costanzo. **Secretary:** Rease Leverenz.

Board of Directors: Bill Murray, chairman; Bill Bavasi (Angels), Dave Dombrowski (Marlins), Dan Duquette (Red Sox), Bob Gebhard (Rockies), Roland Hemond (Diamondbacks), Frank Marcos, Randy Smith (Tigers), Art Stewart (Royals).

Scouts: Rick Arnold (Northridge, CA), Mike Childers (Lexington, KY), Dick Colpaert (Utica, MI), Dan Dixon (Temecula, CA), J.D. Elliby (Richmond, VA), Jim Elliott (Mission, KS), Art Gardner (Walnut Grove, MS), Rusty Gerhardt (New London, TX), Mike Hamilton (Arlington, TX), Doug Horning (Schererville, IN), Don Jacoby (Winter Haven, FL), Brad Kohler (Bethlehem, PA), Don Kohler (Asbury Park, NJ), Mike Larson (Waseca, MN), Jethro McIntyre (Pittsburg, CA), Bob Meisner (Golden, CO), Lenny Merullo (Reading, MA), Paul Mirocke (Lutz, FL), Carl Moesche (Gresham, OR), Tim Osborne (Woodstock, GA), Buddy Pritchard (Fullerton, CA), Gary Randall (Rock Hill, SC), Willie Romay (Miami, FL), Al Ronning (Sunnyvale, CA), Kevin Saucier (Pensacola, FL), Kirk Shrider (Long Beach, CA), Pat Shortt (South Hempstead, NY), Craig Smajstrla (Pearland, TX), Ed Sukla (Irvine, CA), Marv Thompson (Glendale, AZ), Tom Valcke (Fresno, CA), Jim Walton (Shattuck, OK).

Canadian Scouts: Walt Burrows (Brentwood Bay, B.C.), supervisor; Jim Baba (Saskatoon, Saskatchewan), Curtis Bailey (Red Deer, Alberta), Kevin Bly (North York, Ontario), Robert Davidson (Peterborough, Ontario), Gerry Falk (Carman, Manitoba), Bill Green (Vancouver, B.C.), Sean Gulliver (St. John's, Newfoundland), Lowell Hodges (North Saanich, B.C.), Ian Jordan (Pointe-Claire, Quebec), Jay Lapp (London, Ontario), Ken Lenihan (Bedford, N.S.), Dave McConnell (Kelowna, B.C.), Jean Marc Mercier (Charlesbourg, Quebec).

Puerto Rican Scout: Pepito Centeno (Bayamon), supervisor.

MAJOR LEAGUE
UMPIRES ASSOCIATION

Mailing Address: 1735 Market St., Suite 3420, Philadelphia, PA 19103.
Telephone: (215) 979-3200. **FAX:** (215) 979-3201.

Year Founded: 1967.

General Counsel: Richie Phillips. **Associate General Counsel:** Pat Campbell.

PROFESSIONAL BASEBALL
UMPIRE CORPORATION

Office Address: 201 Bayshore Dr. SE, St. Petersburg, FL 33701.
Mailing Address: P.O. Box A, St. Petersburg, FL 33731. **Telephone:** (727) 822-6937. **FAX:** (727) 821-5819.

President: Mike Moore.

Treasurer/Vice President, Administration: Pat O'Conner. **Secretary/ General Counsel:** Ben Hayes.

Administrator: Eric Krupa. **Assistant to Administrator:** Lillian Patterson.

Director, PBUC: Mike Fitzpatrick (Kalamazoo, MI).

Field Evaluators/Instructors: Dennis Cregg (Webster, MA), Mike Felt (Lansing, MI), Cris Jones (Wheat Ridge, CO).

UMPIRE DEVELOPMENT SCHOOLS
Harry Wendelstedt Umpire School

Mailing Address: 88 S St. Andrews Dr., Ormond Beach, FL 32174.
Telephone: (904) 672-4879. **FAX:** (904) 672-3212. **Website:** www.um-pireschool.com.

Operator: Harry Wendelstedt.

Jim Evans Academy of Professional Umpiring

Mailing Address: 12741 Research Blvd., Suite 401, Austin, TX 78759.
Telephone: (512) 335-5959. **FAX:** (512) 335-5411. **E-Mail Address:** jim-sacademy@earthlink.net. **Website:** www.umpireacademy.com.

Operator: Jim Evans.

PROFESSIONAL BASEBALL
ATHLETIC TRAINERS SOCIETY

Mailing Address: 400 Colony Square, Suite 1750, 1201 Peachtree St., Atlanta, GA 30361. **Telephone:** (404) 875-4000. **FAX:** (404) 892-8560.

Year Founded: 1983.

President: Kent Biggerstaff (Pittsburgh Pirates). **American League Representative:** Paul Spicuzza (Cleveland Indians). **National League Representative:** Charlie Strasser (Los Angeles Dodgers) **Secretary:** Dave Labossiere (Houston Astros).

General Counsel: Rollin Mallernee.

BABE RUTH BIRTHPLACE
and OFFICIAL ORIOLES MUSEUM

Office Address: 216 Emory St., Baltimore, MD 21230. **Telephone:** (410) 727-1539. **FAX:** (410) 727-1652. **Website:** www.baberuthmuseum.com.

Year Founded: 1973.

Executive Director: Mike Gibbons. **Curator:** Greg Schwalenberg.

Museum Hours: April-October, 10 a.m.-5 p.m. (10 a.m.-7 p.m. for Baltimore Orioles home games); November-March, 10 a.m.-4 p.m..

CANADIAN BASEBALL
HALL OF FAME and MUSEUM

Office Address: 386 Church St., St. Marys, Ontario N4X 1C2. **Mailing Address:** P.O. Box 1838, St. Marys, Ontario N4X 1C2. **Telephone:** (519) 284-1838. **FAX:** (519) 284-1234. **Website:** www.baseballhof.ca.

Year Founded: 1983.

Executive Director: John Harlton. **Curator:** Carl McCoomb.

Museum Hours: May 1-October 10, 10:30 a.m.-4:30 p.m. Closed Wednesday.

FIELD OF DREAMS
MOVIE SITE

Site Address: 28963 Lansing Rd., Dyersville, IA 52040. **Telephone:** (319) 875-8404. **FAX:** (319) 875-7253. **Website:** www.fieldofdreamsmoviesite.com.

Year Founded: 1989.

Manager, Business/Marketing: Betty Boeckenstedt.
Museum Hours: April-November, 9 a.m.-6 p.m.

LITTLE LEAGUE
BASEBALL MUSEUM

Office Address: Rte. 15 S, Williamsport, PA 17701. **Mailing Address:** P.O. Box 3485, Williamsport, PA 17701. **Telephone:** (570) 326-3607. **FAX:** (570) 326-2267. **Website:** www.littleleague.org/museum.

Year Founded: 1982.

Director: Cynthia Stearns. **Curator:** Michael Miller.

Museum Hours: Memorial Day-Labor Day, 9 a.m.-7 p.m., Sun. 12-7; September-May, 9 a.m.-5 p.m., Sun. 12-5. Open every day except Thanksgiving, Christmas Day, New Year's Day.

LOUISVILLE SLUGGER MUSEUM

Office Address: 800 W Main St., Louisville, KY 40202. **Telephone:** (502) 588-7228. **FAX:** (502) 585-1179. **Website:** www.slugger.com/museum.

Year Founded: 1996.

Museum Hours: Jan. 2-Dec. 23, 9 a.m.-5 p.m. Closed Sunday.

NATIONAL BASEBALL
HALL OF FAME AND MUSEUM

Office Address: 25 Main St., Cooperstown, NY 13326. **Mailing Address:** P.O. Box 590, Cooperstown, NY 13326. **Telephone:** (607) 547-7200. **FAX:** (607) 547-2044. **Website:** www.baseballhalloffame.org.

Year Founded: 1939.

Chairman: Ed Stack. **Vice President:** Frank Simio. **Controller:** Fran Althiser. **Curator of Collections:** Peter Clark. **Executive Director, Communications:** Jeff Idelson. **Director, Communications:** John Ralph. **Executive Director, Retail Marketing:** Barbara Shinn. **Curator:** Ted Spencer. **Librarian:** Jim Gates.

Museum Hours: Oct. 1-April 30—9 a.m.-5 p.m.; May 1-Sept. 30—9 a.m.-9 p.m. Open every day except Thanksgiving, Christmas Day, New Year's Day.

1999 Hall of Fame Induction Ceremonies: July 25, 2:30 p.m., Cooperstown, NY. **Hall of Fame Game:** July 26, 2 p.m., Kansas City vs. Texas.

NEGRO LEAGUES
BASEBALL MUSEUM

Office Address: 1616 E 18th St., Kansas City, MO 64108. **Mailing Address:** P.O. Box 414897, Kansas City, MO 64141. **Telephone:** (816) 221-1920. **FAX:** (816) 221-8424. **Website:** www.nlbm.com.

Year Founded: 1990.

Chairman: Buck O'Neil. **President:** Randall Ferguson.

Executive Director: Don Motley.

Museum Hours: Tues.-Sat. 9 a.m.-6 p.m., Sun. 12 p.m.-6 p.m. Closed Monday.

RESEARCH

SOCIETY FOR
AMERICAN BASEBALL RESEARCH

Mailing Address: 812 Huron Rd. E, Suite 719, Cleveland, OH 44115. **Telephone:** (216) 575-0500. **FAX:** (216) 575-0502. **Website:** www.sabr.org.

Year Founded: 1971.

President: Larry Gerlach (Salt Lake City, UT). **Vice President:** Frederick Ivor-Campbell (Warren, RI). **Secretary:** Dick Beverage (Placentia, CA). **Treasurer:** Paul Andresen (Corvallis, OR). **Directors:** Steve Gietschier, Lois Nicholson, Jim Riley, Tom Shieber.

Executive Director: Morris Eckhouse. **Manager, Membership Services:** John Zajc. **Director, Publications:** Mark Alvarez.

ALUMNI ASSOCIATIONS

MLB PLAYERS ALUMNI ASSOCIATION

Mailing Address, National Headquarters: 1631 Mesa Ave., Suite C, Colorado Springs, CO 80906. **Telephone:** (719) 477-1870. **FAX:** (719) 477-1875.

Mailing Address, Florida Operations Center: 33 Sixth St. S, St. Petersburg, FL 33701. **Telephone:** (727) 892-6744. **FAX:** (727) 892-6771.

Year Founded: 1982.

President: Brooks Robinson.

Vice Presidents: Bob Boone, George Brett, Carl Erskine, Mike Hegan,

Chuck Hinton, Al Kaline, Rusty Staub, Robin Yount.

Board of Directors: Paul Beeston, Nellie Briles, Darrel Chaney, Denny Doyle, Don Fehr, Jim "Mudcat" Grant, Rich Hand, Jim Hannan (chairman), Jerry Moses, Ken Sanders, Jose Valdivielso, Fred Valentine.

Legal Counsel: Sam Moore. **Executive Vice President:** Dan Foster. **Director, Special Events:** Chris Torgusen. **Coordinators, Special Events:** Geoff Hixson, Mike Morey. **Coordinator, Youth Baseball:** Lance James. **Office Manager/Membership Coordinator:** Chandra Von Nostrand.

ASSOCIATION OF PROFESSIONAL BASEBALL PLAYERS OF AMERICA

Mailing Address: 12062 Valley View St., Suite 211, Garden Grove, CA 92845. **Telephone:** (714) 892-9900. **FAX:** (714) 897-0233.

Year Founded: 1924.

President: John McHale.

1st Vice President: Joe DiMaggio. **2nd Vice President:** Arthur Richman. **3rd Vice President:** Bob Kennedy.

Advisory Council: Calvin Griffith, Eddie Sawyer.

Secretary-Treasurer: Dick Beverage.

BASEBALL ASSISTANCE TEAM (BAT)

Mailing Address: 245 Park Ave., 31st Floor, New York, NY 10167. **Telephone:** (212) 931-7822. **FAX:** (212) 949-5652.

Year Founded: 1986.

Chairman: Ralph Branca. **President:** Joe Garagiola. **Vice Presidents:** Joe Black, Earl Wilson.

Executive Director: James Martin. **Secretary:** Thomas Ostertag. **Treasurer:** Jeff White. **Administrator:** Meredith Firmani. **Consultant:** Sam McDowell.

DEVOTION

BASEBALL CHAPEL

Mailing Address: 1315 Main St., Darby, PA 19023. **Telephone:** (610) 586-4537. **FAX:** (610) 586-4538. **E-Mail Address:** baseballchapel@juno.com.

Year Founded: 1972.

President: Gary Carter. **Vice President:** Tim Burke.

Executive Director: Vince Nauss.

BASEBALL FAMILY
(Minor Leagues)

Mailing Address: 8744 Warm Springs Way, Knoxville, TN 37923. **Telephone:** (423) 692-9291. **FAX:** (423) 769-4386. **E-Mail Address:** donnakirby@juno.com.

Year Founded: 1991.

Coordinator: Donna Kirby.

TRADE, EMPLOYMENT

THE BASEBALL TRADE SHOW

Mailing Address: P.O. Box A, St. Petersburg, FL 33731. **Telephone:** (727) 822-6937. **FAX:** (727) 821-5819.

Manager, Trade Show: Reghan Guptill.

1999 Convention: Dec. 10-14 at Anaheim, CA.

PROFESSIONAL BASEBALL EMPLOYMENT OPPORTUNITIES

Mailing Address: P.O. Box 310, Old Fort, NC 28762. **Telephone:** (800) 842-5618. **FAX:** (828) 668-4762.

Director: Ann Perkins.

SENIOR LEAGUES

MEN'S SENIOR BASEBALL LEAGUE
(30 and Over, 40 and Over)

Mailing Address: One Huntington Quadrangle, Suite 3N07, Mellville, NY 11747. **Telephone:** (516) 753-6725. **FAX:** (516) 753-4031.

President: Steve Sigler. **Vice President:** Gary D'Ambrisi.

1999 World Series: Oct. 25-Nov. 6, Phoenix, AZ; Nov. 1-6, St. Petersburg, FL.

MEN'S ADULT BASEBALL LEAGUE
(18 and Over)

Mailing Address: One Huntington Quadrangle, Suite 3N07, Mellville, NY 11747. **Telephone:** (516) 753-6725. **FAX:** (516) 753-4031.

President: Steve Sigler. **Vice President:** Gary D'Ambrisi.

1999 World Series: Oct. 21-24, Phoenix, AZ; Oct. 29-Nov. 1, St. Petersburg, FL.

NATIONAL ADULT BASEBALL ASSOCIATION
(18-65)

Mailing Address: 3900 E Mexico Ave., Suite GL8, Denver, CO 80210.
Telephone: (303) 639-9955. **FAX:** (303) 639-6605. **E-Mail Address:** nabanatl@aol.com. **Website:** www.dugout.org.

President/National Director: Shane Fugita.

1999 National Championship: 18 and Over—Oct. 7-10, Phoenix, AZ. **Senior** (30 and over, 40 and over, 50 and over)—Oct. 9-14, Phoenix, AZ.

ROY HOBBS BASEBALL
(Open, 30-Over, 40-Over, 48-Over, 58-Over, Women's open)

Mailing Address: 2224 Akron Peninsula Rd., Akron, OH 44313.
Telephone: (888) 484-7422. **FAX:** (330) 923-1967. **E-Mail Address:** tom@royhobbs.com. **Website:** www.royhobbs.com.

President: Tom Giffen. **Vice President:** Ellen Giffen. **Director, Operations:** Todd Windhorst.

1999 World Series: 30s (30 and over; AAAA, AAA, AA and A divisions)—Oct. 30-Nov. 6, Fort Myers, FL; **40s** (40 and over; AAAA, AAA, AA and A divisions)—Nov. 7-13, Fort Myers, FL; **Masters** (48 and over; AAAA, AAA and AA divisions)—Nov. 14-21, Fort Myers, FL; **Classics** (58 and over; AA division)—Nov. 14-21, Fort Myers, FL; **Women's Division** (AWBL; open division)—Nov. 14-21, Fort Myers, FL.

1999 Millenium Games: 30 and over, Dec. 27, 1999-Jan. 1, 2000, Fort Myers, FL.

FANTASY CAMPS

LOS ANGELES DODGERS
ADULT BASEBALL CAMP

Mailing Address: Dodgertown, P.O. Box 2887, Vero Beach, FL 32961.
Telephone: (407) 569-4900. **FAX:** (407) 770-2424.

RANDY HUNDLEY'S
FANTASY BASEBALL CAMPS

Mailing Address: 128 S Northwest Hwy., Palatine, IL 60067.
Telephone/FAX: (847) 991-9595.

BASEBALL CARD MANUFACTURERS

FLEER/SKYBOX INTERNATIONAL

Mailing Address: Executive Plaza, 1120 Route 73, Suite 300, Mount Laurel, NJ 08054. **Telephone:** (609) 231-6200. **FAX:** (609) 727-9460.

GRANDSTAND CARDS

Mailing Address: 22647 Ventura Blvd., #192, Woodland Hills, CA 91364. **Telephone:** (818) 992-5642. **FAX:** (818) 348-9122.

PACIFIC TRADING CARDS

Mailing Address: 18424 Hwy. 99, Lynnwood, WA 98037. **Telephone:** (800) 551-2002. **Website:** www.pacifictradingcards.com.

PLAYOFF

Mailing Address: 1517 W North Carrier Pkwy., Suite 155, Grand Prairie, TX 75050. **Telephone:** (972) 595-1180. **FAX:** (972) 595-1190.

TEAM BEST

Mailing Address: 7115 Oak Ridge Pkwy., Suite 180, Austell, GA 30168.
Telephone: (770) 745-3434. **FAX:** (770) 745-3433.

TOPPS

Mailing Address: One Whitehall St., New York, NY 10004. **Telephone:** (212) 376-0300. **FAX:** (212) 376-0573.

UPPER DECK

Mailing Address: 5909 Sea Otter Place, Carlsbad, CA 92008.
Telephone: (760) 929-6500. **FAX:** (760) 929-6556.

ALL-STAR PROMOTIONS MAKE WINNING ATTRACTIONS

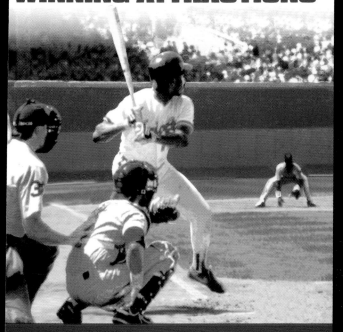

eams that take advantage of our prize coverage and services are promotional winners. They increase attendance, enhance media interest and sponsorship participation while greatly extending their budget.

Through SCA you can offer prizes up to $1,000,000 for only a fraction of their value. SCA takes the risk and covers the cost of the prize.

Here are a few of the ways SCA can help you establish your promotional mix:

- Pre-game and 7th inning Contests – Baseball Toss, Three Strikes You Win, Blooper, Play At The Plate

- Outstanding Plays – Grand Slams, No-Hitters, Triple Plays, Knothole Homeruns.

- Sponsor, Player and Broadcaster Tie-ins

For more information on how to turn your current game plan into an ongoing promotional bonanza, play it safe, call us today and get the best in sports marketing promotions.

Minor Leagues

NATIONALASSOCIATION

NATIONAL ASSOCIATION OF PROFESSIONAL BASEBALL LEAGUES

Office Address: 201 Bayshore Dr. SE, St. Petersburg, FL 33701. **Mailing Address:** P.O. Box A, St. Petersburg, FL 33731. **Telephone:** (727) 822-6937. **FAX:** (727) 821-5819.

Year Founded: 1901.

President/Chief Executive Officer: Mike Moore.

Assistant to President: Carolyn Ashe.

Vice President: Stan Brand (Washington, DC).

Treasurer/Chief Operating Officer and VP, Administration: Pat O'Conner. **Assistant to VP, Administration:** Mary Wooters.

Secretary/General Counsel: Ben Hayes. **Assistant to General Counsel:** Debbie Carlisle.

Mike Moore

Executive Director, Development: Rob Dlugozima. **Executive Director, Special Operations:** Misann Ellmaker.

Director, Baseball Operations: Tim Brunswick.

Director, Media Relations: Jim Ferguson. **Assistant Director, Media Relations:** Steve Densa.

Director, Business and Finance: Eric Krupa. **Assistant to Director, Business and Finance:** Lillian Patterson. **Manager, Information Services:** Corey Leong.

Official Statistician: Howe Sportsdata, Boston Fish Pier, West Bldg. #1, Suite 302, Boston, MA 02210. Telephone: (617) 951-0070.

1999 WINTER MEETINGS: Dec. 10-14, Anaheim, CA.

Affiliated Members/Council of League Presidents

Class AAA

League	President	Telephone	FAX Number
International	Randy Mobley	(614) 791-9300	(614) 791-9009
Mexican	Pedro Treto Cisneros	(525) 557-1007	(525) 395-2454
Pacific Coast	Branch Rickey	(719) 636-3399	(719) 636-1199

Class AA

League	President	Telephone	FAX Number
Eastern	Bill Troubh	(207) 761-2700	(207) 761-7064
Southern	Arnold Fielkow	(770) 428-4749	(770) 428-4849
Texas	Tom Kayser	(210) 545-5297	(210) 545-5298

Class A Advanced

League	President	Telephone	FAX Number
California	Joe Gagliardi	(408) 369-8038	(408) 369-1409
Carolina	John Hopkins	(336) 691-9030	(336) 691-9070
Florida State	Chuck Murphy	(904) 252-7479	(904) 252-7495

Class A

League	President	Telephone	FAX Number
Midwest	George Spelius	(608) 364-1188	(608) 364-1913
South Atlantic	John Moss	(704) 739-3466	(704) 739-1974

Short-Season Class A

League	President	Telephone	FAX Number
New York-Penn	Bob Julian	(315) 733-8036	(315) 797-7403
Northwest	Bob Richmond	(602) 483-8224	(602) 443-3450

Rookie Advanced

League	President	Telephone	FAX Number
Appalachian	Lee Landers	(704) 873-5300	(704) 873-4333
Pioneer	Jim McCurdy	(509) 456-7615	(509) 456-0136

Rookie

League	President	Telephone	FAX Number
Arizona	Bob Richmond	(602) 483-8224	(602) 443-3450
Dominican Summer	Freddy Jana	(809) 563-3233	(809) 563-2455
Gulf Coast	Tom Saffell	(941) 966-6407	(941) 966-6872
Venez. Summer	Saul Gonzalez	(584) 354-4632	(584) 354-4134

PROFESSIONAL BASEBALL
PROMOTION CORPORATION

Office Address: 201 Bayshore Dr. SE, St. Petersburg, FL 33701. **Mailing Address:** P.O. Box A, St. Petersburg, FL 33731. **Telephone:** (727) 822-6937. **FAX/Marketing:** (727) 894-4227. **FAX/Licensing:** (727) 825-3785.

President/Chief Executive Officer: Mike Moore.

Treasurer/Chief Operating Officer and VP, Administration: Pat O'Conner. **Assistant to Chief Operating Officer:** Mary Wooters.

Executive Director, Development: Rob Dlugozima. **Executive Director, Special Operations:** Misann Ellmaker. **Assistant Director, Special Operations:** Kelly Butler.

Director, Licensing: Brian Earle. **Assistant Director, Licensing:** Tina Gust.

Director, Marketing: Rod Meadows. **Assistant Directors, Marketing:** Sandi Dean, Dale Stickney.

Director, Professional Baseball Employment Opportunities: Ann Perkins (Old Fort, NC). **Manager, Trade Show:** Reghan Guptill. **Manager, Trademarks and Contracts:** Derek Johnson.

PROFESSIONAL BASEBALL
UMPIRE CORPORATION

Office Address: 201 Bayshore Dr. SE, St. Petersburg, FL 33701. **Mailing Address:** P.O. Box A, St. Petersburg, FL 33731. **Telephone:** (727) 822-6937. **FAX:** (727) 821-5819.

President: Mike Moore.

Treasurer/Vice President, Administration: Pat O'Conner. **Secretary/General Counsel:** Ben Hayes.

Administrator: Eric Krupa. **Assistant to Administrator:** Lillian Patterson.

Director, PBUC: Mike Fitzpatrick (Kalamazoo, MI).

Field Evaluators/Instructors: Dennis Cregg (Webster, MA), Mike Felt (Lansing, MI), Cris Jones (Wheat Ridge, CO).

MINORLEAGUES

1998 STANDINGS

Parent club in parentheses. *Split-season champion.

INTERNATIONAL LEAGUE   AAA

EAST	W	L	PCT	GB	Manager
Buffalo (Indians)	81	62	.566	—	Jeff Datz
Syracuse (Blue Jays)	80	62	.563	½	Terry Bevington
Pawtucket (Red Sox)	77	64	.546	3	Ken Macha
Rochester (Orioles)	70	74	.486	11½	Marv Foley
Ottawa (Expos)	69	74	.483	12	Pat Kelly
Scranton/W-B (Phillies)	67	75	.472	13½	Marc Bombard
WEST	**W**	**L**	**PCT**	**GB**	**Manager**
Louisville (Brewers)	77	67	.535	—	Gary Allenson
Indianapolis (Reds)	76	67	.531	½	Dave Miley
Columbus (Yankees)	67	77	.465	10	Stump Merrill
Toledo (Tigers)	52	89	.369	23½	Gene Roof
SOUTH	**W**	**L**	**PCT**	**GB**	**Manager**
Durham (Devil Rays)	80	64	.556	—	Bill Evers
Norfolk (Mets)	70	72	.493	9	Rick Dempsey
Charlotte (Marlins)	70	73	.490	9½	Fredi Gonzalez
Richmond (Braves)	64	80	.444	16	Jeff Cox

PLAYOFFS: Semifinals (best-of-5)—Durham defeated Louisville 3-0; Buffalo defeated Syracuse 3-0. **Finals** (best-of-5)—Buffalo defeated Durham 3-2.

PACIFIC COAST LEAGUE   AAA

AMERICAN/EAST	W	L	PCT	GB	Manager
New Orleans (Astros)	76	66	.535	—	John Tamargo
Memphis (Cardinals)	74	70	.514	3	Gaylen Pitts
Oklahoma (Rangers)	74	70	.514	3	Greg Biagini
Nashville (Pirates)	67	76	.469	9½	Trent Jewett
AMERICAN/CENTRAL	**W**	**L**	**PCT**	**GB**	**Managers**
Iowa (Cubs)	85	59	.590	—	Terry Kennedy
Omaha (Royals)	79	64	.552	5½	Ron Johnson
Albuquerque (Dodgers)	61	82	.427	23½	Glenn Hoffman/Ron Roenicke
Colorado Springs (Rockies)	55	89	.382	30	Paul Zuvella
PACIFIC/SOUTH	**W**	**L**	**PCT**	**GB**	**Manager**
Fresno (Giants)	81	62	.566	—	Jim Davenport
Salt Lake (Twins)	79	64	.552	2	Phil Roof
Las Vegas (Padres)	70	72	.493	10½	Jerry Royster
Tucson (Diamondbacks)	57	85	.401	23½	Chris Speier
PACIFIC/WEST	**W**	**L**	**PCT**	**GB**	**Manager**
Calgary (White Sox)	81	62	.566	—	Tom Spencer
Tacoma (Mariners)	77	67	.535	4½	Dave Myers
Edmonton (Athletics)	76	67	.531	5	Mike Quade
Vancouver (Angels)	53	90	.371	28	Mitch Seoane

PLAYOFFS: Semifinals (best-of-5)—Calgary defeated Fresno 3-2; New Orleans defeated Iowa 2-1 (rain-shortened; reduced to best-of-3). **Finals** (best-of-5)—New Orleans defeated Calgary 3-2.

EASTERN LEAGUE   AA

NORTH	W	L	PCT	GB	Manager
New Britain (Twins)	83	59	.585	—	John Russell
Binghamton (Mets)	82	60	.577	1	John Gibbons
Portland (Marlins)	66	75	.468	16½	Lynn Jones
Norwich (Yankees)	66	76	.465	17	Trey Hillman
New Haven (Rockies)	59	83	.415	24	Tim Blackwell
SOUTH	**W**	**L**	**PCT**	**GB**	**Manager**
Akron (Indians)	81	60	.574	—	Joel Skinner
Harrisburg (Expos)	73	69	.514	8½	Rick Sweet
Trenton (Red Sox)	71	70	.504	10	DeMarlo Hale
Bowie (Orioles)	71	71	.500	10½	Joe Ferguson
Reading (Phillies)	56	85	.397	25	Al LeBoeuf

PLAYOFFS: Semifinals (best-of-5)—Harrisburg defeated Akron 3-1; New Britain defeated Binghamton 3-1. **Finals** (best-of-5)—Harrisburg defeated New Britain 3-1.

SOUTHERN LEAGUE   AA

EAST	W	L	PCT	GB	Manager
*Jacksonville (Tigers)	86	54	.614	—	Dave Anderson

	W	L	PCT	GB	Manager
*Knoxville (Blue Jays)	71	69	.507	15	Omar Malave
Orlando (Mariners)	67	71	.486	18	Dan Rohn
Greenville (Braves)	67	72	.482	18½	Randy Ingle
Carolina (Pirates)	59	80	.424	26½	Jeff Banister
WEST	**W**	**L**	**PCT**	**GB**	**Manager**
**Mobile (Padres)	86	54	.614	—	Mike Ramsey
Huntsville (Athletics)	72	68	.514	14	Jeffrey Leonard
Chattanooga (Reds)	65	73	.471	20	Mark Berry
West Tenn (Cubs)	66	74	.471	20	Dave Trembley
Birmingham (White Sox)	58	82	.414	28	Dave Huppert

PLAYOFFS: Semifinals (best-of-5)—Jacksonville defeated Knoxville 3-0; Mobile defeated Huntsville 3-0. **Finals** (best-of-5)—Mobile defeated Jacksonville 3-1.

TEXAS LEAGUE   AA

EAST	W	L	PCT	GB	Manager
*Arkansas (Cardinals)	80	60	.571	—	Chris Maloney
*Tulsa (Rangers)	78	62	.557	2	Bobby Jones
Jackson (Astros)	70	70	.500	10	Jim Pankovits
Shreveport (Giants)	57	83	.407	23	Mike Hart
WEST	**W**	**L**	**PCT**	**GB**	**Manager(s)**
*Wichita (Royals)	75	65	.536	—	John Mizerock
El Paso (Brewers)	69	71	.493	6	Ed Romero
*San Antonio (Dodgers)	67	73	.479	8	Ron Roenicke/Lance Parrish
Midland (Angels)	64	76	.457	11	Don Long

PLAYOFFS: Semifinals (best-of-5)—Tulsa defeated Arkansas 3-0; Wichita defeated San Antonio 3-2. **Finals** (best-of-7)—Tulsa defeated Wichita 4-3.

CALIFORNIA LEAGUE   A

VALLEY	W	L	PCT	GB	Manager
*San Jose (Giants)	83	57	.593	—	Shane Turner
*High Desert (Diamondbacks)	82	58	.586	1	Don Wakamatsu
Lancaster (Mariners)	78	62	.557	5	Rick Burleson
Modesto (Athletics)	77	63	.550	6	Juan Navarrete
Stockton (Brewers)	66	74	.471	17	Bernie Moncallo
FREEWAY	**W**	**L**	**PCT**	**GB**	**Manager(s)**
**Rancho Cuca. (Padres)	77	63	.550	—	Mike Basso
Visalia (Athletics)	67	73	.479	10	Tony DeFrancesco
Lake Elsinore (Angels)	66	74	.471	11	Mario Mendoza
San Bernardino (Dodgers)	55	85	.393	22	Mickey Hatcher/Tim Wallach
Bakersfield (Giants)	49	91	.350	28	Frank Reberger

PLAYOFFS: First Round (best-of-3)—Lake Elsinore defeated Visalia 2-0; High Desert defeated Lancaster 2-0. **Semifinals** (best-of-5)—Rancho Cucamonga defeated Lake Elsinore 3-0; San Jose defeated High Desert 3-2. **Finals** (best-of-5)—San Jose defeated Rancho Cucamonga 3-1.

CAROLINA LEAGUE   A

NORTH	W	L	PCT	GB	Manager(s)
**Wilmington (Royals)	86	54	.614	—	Darrell Evans/Brian Poldberg
Prince William (Cardinals)	72	67	.518	13½	Joe Cunningham
Lynchburg (Pirates)	69	71	.493	17	Jeff Richardson/Jeff Livesey
Frederick (Orioles)	64	76	.457	22	Tommy Shields
SOUTH	**W**	**L**	**PCT**	**GB**	**Manager**
**Winston-Salem (Wh. Sox)	79	60	.568	—	Chris Cron
Kinston (Indians)	69	71	.493	10½	Max Olivares
Salem (Rockies)	62	78	.443	17½	Jay Loviglio
Danville (Braves)	58	82	.414	21½	Paul Runge

PLAYOFFS: Finals (best-of-5)—Wilmington defeated Winston-Salem 3-1.

FLORIDA STATE LEAGUE   A

EAST	W	L	PCT	GB	Manager
**Jupiter (Expos)	80	60	.571	—	Doug Sisson
St. Lucie (Mets)	70	66	.515	8	Howie Freiling
Daytona (Cubs)	67	73	.479	13	Steve Roadcap
Kissimmee (Astros)	64	75	.460	15½	Manny Acta
Vero Beach (Dodgers)	58	81	.417	21½	John Shoemaker
Brevard County (Marlins)	43	97	.307	37	Rick Renteria
WEST	**W**	**L**	**PCT**	**GB**	**Manager**
*Charlotte (Rangers)	82	56	.594	—	James Byrd
Clearwater (Phillies)	82	58	.586	1	Bill Dancy
Dunedin (Blue Jays)	82	58	.586	1	Rocket Wheeler
Sarasota (Red Sox)	76	61	.555	5½	Bob Geren
*Tampa (Yankees)	72	67	.518	10½	Lee Mazzilli

Lakeland (Tigers)	67	72	.482	15½	Mark Meleski
Fort Myers (Twins)	65	73	.471	17	Mike Boulanger
St. Petersburg (Devil Rays)	64	75	.460	18½	Ron Silver

PLAYOFFS: Semifinals (best-of-3)—St. Lucie defeated Jupiter 2-0; Tampa defeated Charlotte 2-0. **Finals** (best-of-5)—St. Lucie defeated Tampa 3-2.

MIDWEST LEAGUE   A

EAST	W	L	PCT	GB	Manager
*West Michigan (Tigers)	83	57	.593	—	Bruce Fields
Fort Wayne (Twins)	79	61	.564	4	Jose Marzan
*Michigan (Red Sox)	79	61	.564	4	Billy Gardner
Lansing (Royals)	71	69	.507	12	Bob Herold
South Bend (Diamondbacks)	40	100	.286	43	Roly de Armas
CENTRAL	**W**	**L**	**PCT**	**GB**	**Manager**
*Wisconsin (Mariners)	72	65	.526	—	Gary Varsho
Peoria (Cardinals)	72	68	.514	1½	Jeff Shireman
*Rockford (Cubs)	71	68	.511	2	Ruben Amaro
Kane County (Marlins)	69	71	.493	4½	Juan Bustabad
Beloit (Brewers)	64	75	.460	9	Don Money
WEST	**W**	**L**	**PCT**	**GB**	**Manager**
**Quad City (Astros)	77	62	.554	—	Mike Rojas
Cedar Rapids (Angels)	71	69	.507	6½	Garry Templeton
Clinton (Padres)	65	73	.471	11½	Tom LeVasseur
Burlington (Reds)	63	77	.450	14½	Phillip Wellman

PLAYOFFS: First Round (best-of-3)—Clinton defeated Quad City 2-1; West Michigan defeated Michigan 2-1; Fort Wayne defeated Peoria 2-1; Rockford defeated Wisconsin 2-1. **Semifinals** (best-of-3)—West Michigan defeated Clinton 2-0; Rockford defeated Fort Wayne 2-0. **Finals** (best-of-5)—West Michigan defeated Rockford 3-1.

SOUTH ATLANTIC LEAGUE   A

NORTH	W	L	PCT	GB	Manager
*Hagerstown (Blue Jays)	81	60	.574	—	Marty Pevey
*Delmarva (Orioles)	81	61	.570	½	Dave Machemer
Cape Fear (Expos)	80	61	.567	1	Luis Dorante
Charleson, W.Va. (Reds)	44	96	.314	36½	Barry Lyons
CENTRAL	**W**	**L**	**PCT**	**GB**	**Manager**
**Capital City (Mets)	90	51	.638	—	Doug Davis
Greensboro (Yankees)	79	63	.556	11½	Tom Nieto
Piedmont (Phillies)	76	65	.539	14	Ken Oberkfell
Asheville (Rockies)	71	69	.507	18½	Ron Gideon
Charleston, S.C. (D. Rays)	67	74	.475	23	Greg Mahlberg
Hickory (White Sox)	56	84	.400	33½	Mark Haley
SOUTH	**W**	**L**	**PCT**	**GB**	**Manager**
*Macon (Braves)	69	72	.489	—	Brian Snitker
Augusta (Pirates)	68	74	.479	1½	Marty Brown
*Savannah (Rangers)	66	76	.465	3½	Paul Carey
Columbus (Indians)	59	81	.421	9½	Eric Wedge

PLAYOFFS: First Round (best-of-3)—Augusta defeated Macon 2-0; Hagerstown defeated Delmarva 2-0; Capital City defeated Piedmont 2-0; Greensboro defeated Cape Fear 2-0. **Semifinals** (best-of-3)—Greensboro defeated Augusta 2-0; Capital City defeated Hagerstown 2-1. **Finals** (best-of-3)—Capital City defeated Greensboro 2-1.

NEW YORK-PENN LEAGUE   SHORT-SEASON A

McNAMARA	W	L	PCT	GB	Manager
Hudson Valley (Devil Rays)	50	26	.658	—	Charlie Montoyo
Vermont (Expos)	36	40	.474	14	Tony Barbone
Pittsfield (Mets)	35	41	.461	15	Roger LaFrancois
New Jersey (Cardinals)	34	41	.453	15½	Jose Oquendo
Lowell (Red Sox)	32	44	.421	18	Dick Berardino
PINCKNEY	**W**	**L**	**PCT**	**GB**	**Manager**
Oneonta (Yankees)	45	31	.592	—	Joe Arnold
Auburn (Astros)	43	32	.573	1½	Lyle Yates
Watertown (Indians)	42	34	.553	3	Ted Kubiak
Williamsport (Cubs)	39	36	.520	5½	Bob Ralston
Utica (Marlins)	35	41	.461	10	Ken Joyce
STEDLER	**W**	**L**	**PCT**	**GB**	**Manager**
Batavia (Phillies)	43	33	.566	—	Frank Klebe
St. Catharines (Blue Jays)	38	38	.500	5	Duane Larson
Jamestown (Tigers)	32	43	.427	10½	Tom Torricelli
Erie (Pirates)	26	50	.342	17	Tracy Woodson

PLAYOFFS: Semifinals (best-of-3)—Oneonta defeated Hudson Valley 2-0; Auburn defeated Batavia 2-1. **Finals**—Series canceled due to rain; Auburn and Oneonta declared co-champions.

NORTHWEST LEAGUE — SHORT-SEASON A

NORTH

	W	L	PCT	GB	Manager
Boise (Angels)	47	29	.618	—	Tom Kotchman
Spokane (Royals)	47	29	.618	—	Jeff Garber
Everett (Mariners)	34	42	.447	13	Terry Pollreisz
Yakima (Dodgers)	32	44	.421	15	Tony Harris

SOUTH

	W	L	PCT	GB	Manager
Salem-Keizer (Giants)	43	33	.566	—	Keith Comstock
Southern Oregon (Athletics)	43	33	.566	—	Greg Sparks
Portland (Rockies)	34	42	.447	9	Jim Eppard
Eugene (Braves)	24	52	.316	19	Jim Saul

PLAYOFFS: Finals (best-of-3)—Salem-Keizer defeated Boise 2-0.

APPALACHIAN LEAGUE — ROOKIE

EAST

	W	L	PCT	GB	Manager
Princeton (Devil Rays)	38	30	.559	—	David Howard
Bluefield (Orioles)	33	34	.493	4½	Andy Etchebarren
Martinsville (Phillies)	32	36	.471	6	Greg Legg
Burlington (Indians)	31	36	.463	6½	Joe Mikulik
Danville (Braves)	30	38	.441	8	Franklin Stubbs

WEST

	W	L	PCT	GB	Manager
Bristol (White Sox)	42	24	.636	—	Nick Capra
Elizabethton (Twins)	38	29	.567	4½	Jon Mathews
Kingsport (Mets)	38	30	.559	5	Tim Foli
Pulaski (Rangers)	29	37	.439	13	Bruce Crabbe
Johnson City (Cardinals)	25	42	.373	17½	Steve Turco

PLAYOFFS: Finals (best-of-3)—Bristol defeated Princeton 2-0.

PIONEER LEAGUE — ROOKIE

NORTH

	W	L	PCT	GB	Manager
Medicine Hat (Blue Jays)	46	28	.622	—	Rolando Pino
*Lethbridge (D'backs)	43	32	.573	3½	Joe Almaraz
*Great Falls (Dodgers)	40	35	.533	6½	Dino Ebel
Helena (Brewers)	21	55	.276	26	Tom Houk

SOUTH

	W	L	PCT	GB	Manager
*Idaho Falls (Padres)	47	29	.618	—	Don Werner
Billings (Reds)	40	34	.541	6	Russ Nixon
*Ogden (Brewers)	38	38	.500	9	Ed Sedar
Butte (Angels)	26	50	.342	21	Bill Lachemann

PLAYOFFS: Semifinals (best-of-3)—Lethbridge defeated Great Falls 2-1; Idaho Falls defeated Ogden 2-0. **Finals** (best-of-3)—Idaho Falls defeated Lethbridge 2-1.

GULF COAST LEAGUE — ROOKIE

EAST

	W	L	PCT	GB	Manager
Melbourne Marlins	38	22	.633	—	Jon Deeble
Jupiter Expos	32	27	.542	5½	Frank Kremblas
Orlando Braves	25	35	.417	13	Rick Albert
Port St. Lucie Mets	24	35	.407	13½	John Stephenson

NORTH

	W	L	PCT	GB	Manager
St. Petersburg Devil Rays	36	24	.600	—	Bobby Ramos
Tampa Yankees	34	26	.567	2	Ken Dominguez
Lakeland Tigers	28	32	.467	8	Kevin Bradshaw
Kissimmee Astros	22	38	.367	14	Julio Linares

WEST

	W	L	PCT	GB	Manager
Fort Myers Twins	34	26	.567	—	Steve Liddle
Port Charlotte Rangers	34	26	.567	—	Darryl Kennedy
Fort Myers Royals	32	28	.533	2	Andre David
Sarasota Orioles	28	32	.467	6	Butch Davis
Fort Myers Red Sox	27	33	.450	7	Luis Aguayo
Bradenton Pirates	25	35	.417	9	Woody Huyke

PLAYOFFS: Semifinals (one-game)—Rangers defeated Twins; Devil Rays defeated Marlins. **Finals** (best-of-3)—Rangers defeated Devil Rays 2-0.

ARIZONA LEAGUE — ROOKIE

	W	L	PCT	GB	Manager
Tucson Rockies	42	14	.750	—	P.J. Carey
Peoria Mariners	31	24	.564	10½	Darrin Garner
Mesa Cubs	29	26	.527	12½	Nate Oliver
Phoenix Athletics	29	27	.518	13	John Kuehl
Tucson Diamondbacks	24	31	.436	17½	Mike Brumley
Peoria Padres	23	31	.426	18	Randy Whisler
Mexican All-Stars	23	33	.400	19½	Abelardo Vega
Tucson White Sox	20	34	.370	21	Tony Pena

PLAYOFFS: None.

INTERNATIONAL LEAGUE

Class AAA

Office Address: 55 S High St., Suite 202, Dublin, OH 43017. **Telephone:** (614) 791-9300. **FAX:** (614) 791-9009. **E-Mail Address:** office@ilbaseball.com. **Website:** www.ilbaseball.com.

Years League Active: 1884-.

President/Treasurer: Randy Mobley.

Vice Presidents: Harold Cooper, Dave Rosenfield (Norfolk), Tex Simone (Syracuse), George Sisler Jr. **Corporate Secretary:** Richard Davis.

Directors: Peter Anlyan (Durham), Bruce Baldwin (Richmond), Don Beaver (Charlotte), Gene Cook (Toledo), Howard Darwin (Ottawa), Rick Muntean (Scranton/Wilkes-Barre), Bob Rich Jr. (Buffalo), Dave Rosenfield (Norfolk), Ken Schnacke (Columbus), Max Schumacher (Indianapolis), Naomi Silver (Rochester), John Simone (Syracuse), Mike Tamburro (Pawtucket), Dan Ulmer (Louisville).

Randy Mobley

Office Manager: Linda Miller. **Assistant to the President:** Nathan Blackmon.

1999 Opening Date: April 8. **Closing Date:** Sept. 6.

Regular Season: 144 games.

Division Structure: North—Buffalo, Ottawa, Pawtucket, Rochester, Scranton/Wilkes-Barre, Syracuse. **West**—Columbus, Indianapolis, Louisville, Toledo. **South**—Charlotte, Durham, Norfolk, Richmond.

Playoff Format: West champion plays South champion in best-of-5 series; wild-card club (non-division winner with best record) plays North champion in best-of-5 series. Winners meet in best-of-5 series for Governors' Cup championship. **Triple-A World Series:** Best-of-5 series vs. Pacific Coast League champion, Sept. 20-25 at Las Vegas.

All-Star Game: July 14 at New Orleans (IL vs. Pacific Coast League).

Roster Limit: 23 active, until midnight Aug. 10 when roster can expand to 25. **Player Eligibility Rule:** No restrictions.

Brand of Baseball: Rawlings ROM-INT.

Statistician: Howe Sportsdata, Boston Fish Pier, West Bldg. #1, Suite 302, Boston MA 02210.

Umpires: Jorge Bauza (San Juan, PR), Mike Billings (Pembroke Pines, FL), David Brandt (Mission, KS), C.B. Bucknor (Brooklyn, NY), Mark Carlson (Joliet, IL), Robert Cook (Blacklick, OH), John Creek (Kalamazoo, MI), Field Culbreth (Inman, SC), Philip Cuzzi (Nutley, NJ), Lazaro Diaz (Miami, FL), Paul Emmel (Sanford, MI), Cory Erickson (St. Petersburg, FL), Mark Facto (Ellicott City, MD), Marty Foster (Beloit, WI), Brian Gibbons (South Bend, IN), Greg Gibson (Catlettsburg, KY), Marvin Hudson (Washington, GA), Matt Hughes (Louisville, KY), Dan Iassogna (Smyrna, GA), Jeff Kowalczyk (Bloomington, IL), Paul Nauert (Lawrenceville, GA), Brian O'Nora (Youngstown, OH), Jim Reynolds (Rocky Hill, CT), Stuart Robertson (Gretna, VA), Juan Rodriguez (Bayamon, PR), Jeff Spedoske (Lansing, MI), Tim Timmons (Columbus, OH), Mike VanVleet (Battle Creek, MI), Bill Welke (Coldwater, MI).

Stadium Information

Club	Stadium	Dimensions			Capacity	'98 Att.
		LF	CF	RF		
Buffalo	North AmeriCare	325	404	325	21,050	743,463
Charlotte	Knights	325	400	325	10,000	299,664
Columbus	Cooper	355	400	330	15,000	488,674
Durham	Durham Bulls Athletic	305	400	327	10,000	477,709
Indianapolis	Victory Field	320	402	320	15,500	659,237
Louisville	Cardinal	360	405	312	33,500	409,853
Norfolk	Harbor Park	333	410	338	12,069	479,222
Ottawa	JetForm Park	325	404	325	10,332	224,351
Pawtucket	McCoy	325	400	325	10,000	475,659
Richmond	The Diamond	330	402	330	12,156	528,230
Rochester	Frontier Field	335	402	325	10,868	515,436
Scranton	Lackawanna County	330	408	330	10,982	406,735
Syracuse	P&C	328	404	328	11,602	420,488
Toledo	Ned Skeldon	325	410	325	10,197	311,652

Buffalo
BISONS

Office Address: 275 Washington St., Buffalo, NY 14203. Mailing Address: P.O. Box 450, Buffalo, NY 14205. Telephone: (716) 846-2000. FAX: (716) 852-6530. E-Mail Address: bisons@buffnet.net. Website: www.bisons.com.

Affiliation (first year): Cleveland Indians (1995). Years in League: 1886-90, 1912-70, 1998-.

Ownership, Management

Operated by: Rich Products Corp.

Principal Owner/President: Robert E. Rich Jr. Chairman: Robert E. Rich Sr. President, Rich Entertainment Group: Melinda Rich. Executive Vice President, Rich Entertainment Group: Jon Dandes. Vice President/Treasurer: David Rich. Vice President/Secretary: William Gisel Jr. Vice President/Sales and Marketing: Marta Hiczewski.

General Manager: Mike Buczkowski. Controller: Joe Segarra. Senior Account Representatives: Kathleen Ascioti, Leigh Balcom, Jim Bower, Jim Mack. Stadium Operations Manager: John Wiedeman. Director, Public Relations/Marketing: Tom Burns. Assistant, Public Relations: Matt Herring. Game Day Coordinator/CSP Assistant: Alex Moser. Coordinator, Community Relations: Don Feldmann. Director, Merchandising: Nancy Martin. Director, Food Services: Eric Nelson. Restaurant Manager: David Pruett. Suite Manager: Judith McQueeney. Office Manager: Margaret Russo. Head Groundskeeper: Jim Hornung. Director, Clubhouse Operations: Ron Krauza.

Field Staff

Manager: Jeff Datz. Coach: Bill Madlock. Pitching Coach: Ken Rowe. Trainer: Rick Jameyson.

Game Information

Radio Announcer: Jim Rosenhaus. No. of Games Broadcast: Home-72, Away-72. Flagship Station: WWKB 1520-AM.

PA Announcer: John Summers. Official Scorers: Kevin Lester, Duke McGuire.

Stadium Name (year opened): North AmeriCare Park (1988). Location: From north, take I-190 to Elm Street exit, left onto Swan Street. From east, take I-90 West to exit 51 (Route 33) to end, exit at Oak Street, right onto Swan Street. From west, take I-90 East, exit 53 to I-190 North, exit at Elm Street, left onto Swan Street. Standard Game Times: 7:05 p.m.; Wed 1:05; Sat. 2:05, 7:05; Sun 2:05.

Visiting Club Hotel: Holiday Inn Downtown, 620 Delaware Ave., Buffalo, NY 14202. Telephone: (716) 886-2121.

Charlotte
KNIGHTS

Office Address: 2280 Deerfield Dr., Fort Mill, SC 29715. Mailing Address: P.O. Box 1207, Fort Mill, SC 29716. Telephone: (704) 357-8071, (803) 548-8050. FAX: (704) 329-2155, (803) 548-8055. E-Mail Address: knights@aaaknights.com. Website: www.aaaknights.com.

Affiliation (first year): Chicago White Sox (1999). Years in League: 1993-.

Ownership, Management

Operated by: Knights Baseball, LLC.

Principal Owners: Bill Allen, Don Beaver, Derick Close.

President: Don Beaver. Vice President: Tim Newman.

Vice President/General Manager: Marty Steele. Assistant GM, Sales/Marketing: Derrick Grubbs. Assistant GM, Stadium Operations: Jon Percival. Director, Ticket Operations: Melissa Dudek. Director, Media/Community Relations: Shannon Motley. Director, Group Sales: Randy Habluetzel. Director, Community Relations: Tommy John. Director, Broadcasting: Matt Swierad. Stadium Operations Manager: Brandon Witherspoon. Business Manager/Team Travel Coordinator: Keta Stogner. Director, Advertising Sales: Julie Sigmon. Advertising Sales Representative: Anthony DeNino. Mascot Coordinator: Billy Yandle. Head Groundskeeper: Joey Simmons. Facility Maintenance Supervisor: Joe Sistare. Ticket Sales Representatives: Adam

Deschenes, Erica Poag, Michael Schline, Chris Semmens. **Office Manager:** Ronda Lessmeister.

Field Staff
Manager: Tom Spencer. **Coach:** Gary Ward. **Pitching Coach:** Kirk Champion. **Trainer:** Scott Johnson.

Game Information
Radio Announcers: Matt Swierad, Tommy John. **No. of Games Broadcast:** Home-72, Away-72. **Flagship Station:** Unavailable.

PA Announcer: Derrick Grubbs. **Official Scorers:** Brent Stastny, Ed Walton.

Stadium Name (year opened): Knights Stadium (1990). **Location:** Exit 88 off I-77, east on Gold Hill Road. **Standard Game Times:** 7:15 p.m., Sun. 2.

Visiting Club Hotel: Charlotte Hilton Executive Park, 5624 W Park Dr., Charlotte, NC 28217. Telephone: (704) 527-8000.

Columbus
CLIPPERS

Office Address: 1155 W Mound St., Columbus, OH 43223. **Telephone:** (614) 462-5250. **FAX:** (614) 462-3271. **E-Mail Address:** colsclippers@earthlink.net. **Website:** www.clippersbaseball.com.

Affiliation (first year): New York Yankees (1979). **Years in League:** 1955-70, 1977-.

Ownership, Management
Operated by: Columbus Baseball Team, Inc.
Principal Owner: Franklin County, Ohio.
Chairman: Donald Borror. **President:** Richard Smith.
General Manager: Ken Schnacke. **Assistant General Manager:** Mark Warren. **Assistant GM/Park Supervisor:** Dick Fitzpatrick. **Director, Stadium Operations:** Steve Dalin. **Director, Ticket Sales:** Scott Ziegler. **Director, Media Relations:** Chris Daugherty. **Director, Sales:** Mark Galuska. **Director, Marketing:** Shawne Beck. **Director, Merchandising:** Jacque Brown. **Director, Advertising:** Todd Pfeil. **Director, Finance:** Chris Burleson. **Assistant Director, Marketing:** Richard Groat. **Assistant Director, Advertising:** Steve Thomas. **Assistant Director, Sales:** Jason Harris. **Assistant to General Manager:** Judi Timmons. **Secretary:** Kelly Ryther.

Field Staff
Manager: Trey Hillman. **Coaches:** Hop Cassady, Bill Robinson. **Pitching Coach:** Rick Tomlin. **Trainer:** Darren London.

Game Information
Radio Announcers: Gary Richards, Terry Smith. **No. of Games Broadcast:** Home-72, Away-72. **Flagship Station:** WSMZ 103.1-FM.

PA Announcers: Bob Lewis, Eric Mauk, John Ross. **Official Scorers:** Chuck Emmerling, Frank Fraas, Kris Hutchins, Joe Santry.

Stadium Name (year opened): Cooper Stadium (1977). **Location:** From north/south, I-71 to I-70 West, exit at Mound Street. From west, I-70 East, exit at Broad Street, east to Glenwood, south to Mound Street. From east, I-70 West, exit at Mound Street. **Standard Game Times:** 7:15 p.m.; Sat. 6:15, 7:15, 7:35; Sun. 2:15, 6:15.

Visiting Club Hotels: Best Western-Columbus North, 888 E Dublin-Granville Rd., Columbus, OH 43229. Telephone: (614) 888-8230; Clarion Hotel, 7007 N High St., Columbus, OH 43085. Telephone: (614) 436-0700.

Durham
BULLS

Office Address: 409 Blackwell St., Durham, NC 27701. **Mailing Address:** P.O. Box 507, Durham, NC 27702. **Telephone:** (919) 687-6500. **FAX:** (919) 687-6560. **Website:** www.dbulls.com.

Affiliation (first year): Tampa Bay Devil Rays (1998). **Years in League:** 1998-.

Ownership, Management
Operated by: Capitol Broadcasting Co., Inc.
President/Chief Executive Officer: Jim Goodmon.
Division Vice President: George Habel. **Vice President/Legal**

Counsel: Mike Hill.

Vice President/General Manager: Peter Anlyan. Assistant General Manager: Mike Birling. Manager, Sales: Matt West. Manager, Accounting: Jerry Riggsbee. Manager, Office Systems: Andrea Harris. Manager, Merchandise: Allan Long. Manager, Concessions: Jamie Jenkins. Manager, Promotions/Marketing: Brian Crichton. Coordinator, Media/Public Relations: Jessica Wucki. Facility Superintendent: Steve Banos. Director, Group Sales: Tammie Weis. Coordinators, Group Outings: Ryan Berry, Cheri Lisko. Coordinator, Box Office: Chrystal Rowe. Representative, Ticket Sales: Jon Bishop. Account Executives, Sponsorship: Mike Davis, Chip Hutchinson. Advertising Sales Administrator: Janel Doyle. Supervisor, Operations: Tim Neubauer. Head Groundskeeper: Kevin Robinson. Assistant Head Groundskeeper: Ed Kovalesky. Director, Security: Ed Sarvis. Executive Secretary: Libby Hamilton. Accouting Clerk: Anna Maynard. Assistant, Accounting/Ballpark: Jewell White. Receptionist/Secretary: Barbara Goss. Assistant, Office/Ballpark: Gennell Curry.

Field Staff

Manager: Bill Evers. Coach: George Foster. Pitching Coach: Pete Filson. Trainer: Paul Harker.

Game Information

Radio Announcer: Steve Barnes. No. of Games Broadcast: Home-72, Away-72. Flagship Station: WDNC 620-AM.

PA Announcer: Bill Law. Official Scorer: Brent Belvin.

Stadium Name (year opened): Durham Bulls Athletic Park (1995). Location: From Raleigh, I-40 West to Highway 147 North, exit 12B to Willard, two blocks on Willard to stadium. From I-85, Gregson Street exit to downtown, left on Chapel Hill Street, right on Mangum Street. Standard Game Times: 7 p.m.; Sun. 5.

Visiting Club Hotel: Durham Marriott at the Civic Center, 201 Foster St., Durham, NC 27701. Telephone: (919) 768-6000.

Office Address: 501 W Maryland St., Indianapolis, IN 46225. Telephone: (317) 269-3542. FAX: (317) 269-3541. E-Mail Address: indians@indyindians.com. Website: www.indyindians.com.

Affiliation (first year): Cincinnati Reds (1993). Years in League: 1963, 1998-.

Ownership, Management

Operated by: Indians, Inc.

Chairman/President: Max Schumacher.

General Manager: Cal Burleson. Director, Business Operations: Brad Morris. Director, Stadium Operations: Randy Lewandowski. Head Groundskeeper: Mike Boekholder. Director, Media/Public Relations: Tim Harms. Director, Sales/Marketing: Daryle Keith. Director, Community Relations: Chris Herndon. Director, Ticket Sales: Mike Schneider. Director, Group Sales: Suzy Pavone. Assistant Manager, Box Office: Robin Ellet. Director, Merchandising: Mark Schumacher. Director, Food Services: Mike Moos. Director, Special Projects: Bruce Schumacher. Clubhouse Operations: John Rinaldi. Facility Director: Bill Sampson. Director, Maintenance: Tim Hughes. Director, Suiteholder Services: Dave McGhee. Office Manager: Scott Rubin.

Field Staff

Manager: Dave Miley. Coach: Mark Berry. Pitching Coach: Grant Jackson. Trainer: John Young.

Game Information

Radio Announcers: Brian Giffin, Howard Kellman. No. of Games Broadcast: Home-72, Away-72. Flagship Stations: WGOM 860-AM, WNDE 1260-AM.

PA Announcer: Bruce Schumacher. Official Scorers: Bill MacAfee, Kim Rogers.

Stadium Name (year opened): Victory Field (1996). Location: I-70 to West Street exit, north on West Street to ballpark; I-65 to Martin Luther King and West Street exit, south on West Street to ballpark. Standard Game Times: 7 p.m.; Sun. 2.

Visiting Club Hotels: Courtyard by Marriott, 501 W Washington St., Indianapolis, IN 46204. Telephone: (317) 635-4443; Comfort Inn, 530 S Capitol, Indianapolis, IN 46204. Telephone: (317) 631-9000.

Louisville
RIVERBATS

Office Address: Cardinal Stadium, Phillips Lane at Freedom Way, Louisville, KY 40213. Mailing Address: P.O. Box 36407, Louisville, KY 40233. Telephone: (502) 367-9121. FAX: (502) 368-5120. E-Mail Address: info@batsbaseball.com.

Affiliation (first year): Milwaukee Brewers (1998). Years in League: 1998-.

Ownership, Management
Operated by: Louisville Baseball Club, Inc.

Board of Directors: Dan Ulmer, Jack Hillerich, Dale Owens, Ed Glasscock, Kenny Huber, Jim Morrissey, Tom Musselman, Bob Stallings, Gary Ulmer.

Chairman: Dan Ulmer. President: Gary Ulmer.

Vice President/General Manager: Dale Owens. Assistant General Manager/Director, Marketing: Greg Galiette. Director, Baseball Operations: Mary Barney. Director, Sales: David Gardner. Director, Broadcasting: Jim Kelch. Director, Stadium Operations: Scott Shoemaker. Accounting Manager: Michele Anderson. Public Relations Coordinator: Matt Gorsky. Group Sales Manager: James Breeding. Ticket Manager: George Veith. Account Executives: Chris Sobczyk, Colgan Tyler. Sales Representatives: Jamee Green, Jeff Hollis, Chris Parker. Head Groundskeeper: Mark Whitworth. Clubhouse Manager: Trey Hyberger.

Field Staff
Manager: Gary Allenson. Coach: Luis Salazar. Pitching Coach: Dwight Bernard. Trainer: Richard Stark.

Game Information
Radio Announcers: Mark Gorsky, Jim Kelch. No. of Games Broadcast: Home-72, Away-72. Flagship Station: WLKY 970-AM.

PA Announcer: Charles Gazaway. Official Scorer: Unavailable.

Stadium Name (year opened): Cardinal Stadium (1956). Location: Intersection of I-65 and I-264 at Kentucky Fair and Expo Center. Standard Game Times: 7:15 p.m.; Tue. 12:05; Sun. 2.

Visiting Club Hotel: Executive Inn, 978 Phillips Ln., Louisville, KY 40209. Telephone: (502) 367-6161.

Norfolk
TIDES

Office Address: 150 Park Ave., Norfolk, VA 23510. Telephone: (757) 622-2222. FAX: (757) 624-9090. E-Mail Address: info@norfolktides.com. Website: www.norfolktides.com.

Affiliation (first year): New York Mets (1969). Years in League: 1969-.

Ownership, Management
Operated by: Tides Baseball Club, LP.

President: Ken Young.

General Manager: Dave Rosenfield. Assistant General Manager: Joe Gorza. Director, Sales/Marketing: Jay Richardson. Director, Media Relations: Shon Sbarra. Director, Community Relations: Susan Pinckney. Director, Ticket Operations: Glenn Riggs. Ticket Manager: Linda Waisanen. Accounting Manager: Lew Schwartz. Director, Group Sales: Dave Harrah. Assistant, Group Sales: Heather Harkins. Director, Merchandising: Mike Giedlin. Manager, Operations: Chris Vtipil. Manager, Equipment/Clubhouse: Kevin Kierst. Head Groundskeeper: Ken Magner. Assistant Groundskeeper: Keith Collins.

Field Staff
Manager: John Gibbons. Coach: Tom Lawless. Pitching Coach: Rick Waits. Trainer: Joe Hawkins.

Game Information
Radio Announcers: John Castleberry, Rob Evans. No. of Games Broadcast: Home-72, Away-72. Flagship Station: Unavailable.

PA Announcer: Unavailable. Official Scorers: Bob Moskowitz, Charlie Denn.

Stadium Name (year opened): Harbor Park (1993). Location: Exit 9, 11A or 11B off I-264, adjacent to the Elizabeth River in downtown Norfolk. Standard Game Times: 7:15 p.m.; Sun. (April-June) 1:15, (July-Sept.) 6:15.

Visiting Club Hotels: Sheraton Waterside, 777 Waterside Dr., Norfolk, VA 23510. Telephone: (757) 622-6664; Doubletree Club Hotel, 880 N Military Hwy., Norfolk, VA 23502. Telephone: (757) 461-9192.

Ottawa
LYNX

Office Address: 300 Coventry Rd., Ottawa, Ontario K1K 4P5. Telephone: (613) 747-5969. FAX: (613) 747-0003. E-Mail Address: lynx@ottawalynx.com. Website: www.ottawalynx.com.

Affiliation (first year): Montreal Expos (1993). Years in League: 1993-.

Ownership, Management
Operated By: Ottawa Triple-A Baseball, Inc.
Principal Owner/President: Howard Darwin.
Director, Baseball Operations: Kevin Whalen. Controller: Richard Paulin. Director, Stadium Operations: Jack Darwin. Head Groundskeepers: Brad Keith, Pete Webb. Director, Media/Public Relations: Ian Mendes. Director, Sales/Marketing: Liz Haines. Senior Account Representative: Peter Leyser. Director, Promotions: Mark Sluban. Director, Ticket Sales: Joe Fagan. Director, Merchandising: Nancy Darwin. Clubhouse Operations: John Bryk. Administrative Assistant: Lorraine Charrette.

Field Staff
Manager: Jeff Cox. Coach: Tim Leiper. Pitching Coach: Randy St. Claire. Trainer: Sean Bearer.

Game Information
Radio: Unavailable.
PA Announcer: Unavailable. Official Scorer: Unavailable.
Stadium Name (year opened): JetForm Park (1993). Location: Highway 417 to Riverside Drive/Vanier Parkway exit, Vanier Parkway north to Coventry Road, right on Coventry to stadium. Standard Game Times: 7:05 p.m.; Sat. 2:05, 7:05; Sun. 2:05.

Visiting Club Hotel: Chimo Inn, 1199 Joseph Cyr St., Gloucester, Ontario K1J 7T4. Telephone: (613) 744-1060.

Pawtucket
RED SOX

Office Address: One Columbus Ave., Pawtucket, RI 02860. Mailing Address: P.O. Box 2365, Pawtucket, RI 02861. Telephone: (401) 724-7300. FAX: (401) 724-2140. E-Mail Address: pawsox@worldnet.att.net. Website: www.pawsox.com.

Affiliation (first year): Boston Red Sox (1973). Years in League: 1973-.

Ownership, Management
Operated by: Pawtucket Red Sox Baseball Club, Inc.
Chairman: Bernard Mondor. President: Mike Tamburro.
Vice President/General Manager: Ludwig Schwechheimer. Vice President, Treasurer: Kathy Crowley. Vice President, Sales/Marketing: Michael Gwynn. Vice President, Stadium Operations: Mick Tedesco. Vice President, Public Relations: Bill Wanless. Office Manager: Kathy Davenport. Ticket Manager: Keith Kuceris. Ticket Operations: Jeff Bradley. Director, Community Relations: Don Orsillo. Director, Sales: Daryl Jasper. Account Executives: Steve Napolillo, Gordon Smith. Secretary: Sandi Browne. Clubhouse Manager: Chris Parent. Head Groundskeeper: Larry DeVito. Director, Stadium Services: Derek Molhan. Director, Concession Services: Dave Johnson. Director, Hospitality: Kathy Walsh. Media Services: Jill Murphy. Game Day Operations: Dave Lancaster.

Field Staff
Manager: Gary Jones. Coach: Gene Tenace. Pitching Coach: Rich Bombard. Trainer: Jim Young.

Game Information
Radio Announcers: Don Orsillo, Mike Logan. **No. of Games Broadcast:** Home-72, Away-72. **Flagship Station:** WSKO 790-AM
PA Announcer: Jim Martin. **Official Scorer:** Bruce Guindon.
Stadium Name (year opened): McCoy Stadium (1999). **Location:** I-95 North to exit 2B (School Street); I-95 South to exit 2A (Newport Avenue).
Standard Game Times: 7 p.m.; Sat. 6; Sun. 1.
Visiting Club Hotel: Comfort Inn, 2 George St., Pawtucket, RI 02860. Telephone: (401) 723-6700.

Richmond
BRAVES

Office Address: 3001 N Boulevard, Richmond, VA 23230. **Mailing Address:** P.O. Box 6667, Richmond, VA 23230. **Telephone:** (804) 359-4444. **FAX:** (804) 359-0731. **E-Mail Address:** rbraves@bznet.com. **Website:** www.rbraves.com.
Affiliation (first year): Atlanta Braves (1966). **Years in League:** 1884, 1915-17, 1954-64, 1966-.

Ownership, Management
Operated by: Atlanta National League Baseball, Inc.
Principal Owner: Ted Turner. **President:** Stan Kasten.
General Manager: Bruce Baldwin. **Assistant General Manager:** Ken Clary. **Manager, Ticket Operations:** Kelly Harris. **Manager, Public Relations:** Todd Feagans. **Manager, Promotions:** Townley Goldsmith. **Manager, Stadium Operations:** Nate Doughty. **Manager, Group Sales:** Jin Wong. **Assistant Ticket Manager:** Todd Justice. **Assistant, Marketing/Group Sales Manager:** Katie McFadden. **Manager, Field Maintenance:** Chad Mulholland. **Office Manager:** Joanne Cornutt. **Receptionist:** Janet Zimmerman. **Intern, Ticket Operations:** Kevin Haury. **Intern, Public Relations:** Brad Guyton. **Interns, Group Sales:** Damon Swenson, Jess Wentworth.

Field Staff
Manager: Randy Ingle. **Coach:** Mel Roberts. **Pitching Coach:** Bill Fischer. **Trainer:** Jim Lovell.

Game Information
Radio Announcer: Robert Fish. **No. of Games Broadcast:** Home-72, Away-72. **Flagship Station:** WRNL 910-AM.
PA Announcer: Mike Blacker. **Official Scorer:** Leonard Alley.
Stadium Name (year opened): The Diamond (1985). **Location:** Exit 78 (Boulevard) at junction of I-64 and I-95, follow signs to park. **Standard Game Times:** 7 p.m., Sun. 2.
Visiting Club Hotel: Quality Inn, 8008 W Broad St., Richmond, VA 23230. Telephone: (804) 346-0000.

Rochester
RED WINGS

Office Address: One Morrie Silver Way, Rochester, NY 14608. **Telephone:** (716) 454-1001. **FAX:** (716) 454-1056. **Website:** www.red-wingsbaseball.com.
Affiliation (first year): Baltimore Orioles (1961). **Years in League:** 1885-89, 1891-92, 1895-.

Ownership, Management
Operated by: Rochester Community Baseball, Inc.
Chairman: Fred Strauss. **President:** Elliot Curwin. **Chief Operating Officer:** Naomi Silver.
General Manager: Dan Mason. **Assistant General Manager:** Will Rumbold. **Director, Business Operations:** Darlene Giardina. **Director, Stadium Operations:** Gene Buonomo. **Director, Media/Public Relations:** Chuck Hinkel. **Director, Sales/Marketing:** Steve Salluzzo. **Account Representatives:** Mike Ciavarri, Ryan Ginsberg. **Director, Community Relations:** Wendy Rose. **Director, Promotions:** Mike Lipani. **Director, Ticket Sales:** Joe Ferrigno. **Director, Group Sales:** Russ Ruter. **Assistant Director, Group Sales:** John Caricati. **Director, Merchandising:** Josh Harris. **Director, Food Services:** Jeff Dodge. **Director, Administration:** Jen Waldow. **Manager, Payroll:** Paula LoVerde. **Clubhouse Operations:**

Paul Dondorfer, Terry Costello. **Assistant Director, Food Services:** Gina Gulino. **Manager, Suites/Catering:** Tracy DonVito. **Business Manager, Concessions:** David Bills. **Executive Secretary:** Ginny Colbert.

Field Staff

Manager: Dave Machemer. **Coach:** Dave Cash. **Pitching Coach:** Larry McCall. **Trainer:** Al Price.

Game Information

Radio Announcer: Joe Castellano. **No. of Games Broadcast:** Home-72, Away-72. **Flagship Station:** WHTK 1280-AM.

PA Announcer: Kevin Spears. **Official Scorer:** Len Lustik.

Stadium Name (year opened): Frontier Field (1997). **Location:** I-490 East to exit 12 (Allen Street), cross Broad Street, follow signs to stadium; I-490 West to exit 14, two intersections to Main Street, turn on Plymouth Avenue, follow signs. **Standard Game Times:** 7:15 p.m., Sun. 2:15.

Visiting Club Hotel: Unavailable.

Scranton/Wilkes-Barre
RED BARONS

Office Address: 235 Montage Mountain Rd., Moosic, PA 18507. **Mailing Address:** P.O. Box 3449, Scranton, PA 18505. **Telephone:** (570) 969-2255. **FAX:** (570) 963-6564. **E-Mail Address:** barons@epix.net. **Website:** www.redbarons.com.

Affiliation (first year): Philadelphia Phillies (1989). **Years in League:** 1989-.

Ownership, Management

Operated by: Lackawanna County Stadium Authority.

Chairman: Bill Jenkins.

General Manager: Rick Muntean. **Director, Media/Public Relations:** Mike Cummings. **Director, Business Operations:** Donna McDonald. **Controller:** Tom Durkin. **Director, Stadium Operations:** Jeremy Ruby. **Head Groundskeeper:** Bill Casterline. **Director, Sales/Marketing:** Ron Prislupski. **Account Representatives:** Jack Gowran, Julie Martin, Joe McConnon, Travis Spencer. **Director, Ticket Sales:** Ann Marie Nocera. **Director, Merchandising:** Ray Midura. **Director, Food Services:** Rich Sweeney. **Director, Special Projects:** Karen Healy. **Director, Telecommunications:** Kelly Byron.

Field Staff

Manager: Marc Bombard. **Coach:** Al LeBoeuf. **Pitching Coach:** Goose Gregson. **Trainer:** Craig Strobel.

Game Information

Radio Announcer: Kent Westling. **No. of Games Broadcast:** Home-72; Away-72. **Flagship Station:** WICK 1400-AM.

PA Announcer: John Davies. **Official Scorer:** Bob McGoff.

Stadium Name (year opened): Lackawanna County Stadium (1989). **Location:** I-81 to exit 51 (Davis Street). **Standard Game Times:** 7:30 p.m.; Sun. 6.

Visiting Club Hotel: Radisson Lackawanna Station Hotel, 700 Lackawanna Ave., Scranton, PA 18503. Telephone: (570) 342-8300.

Syracuse
SKYCHIEFS

Office Address: P&C Stadium, One Tex Simone Dr., Syracuse, NY 13208. **Telephone:** (315) 474-7833. **FAX:** (315) 474-2658. **E-Mail Address:** baseball@skychiefs.com. **Website:** www.skychiefs.com.

Affiliation (first year): Toronto Blue Jays (1978). **Years in League:** 1885-89, 1891-92, 1894-1901, 1918, 1920-27, 1934-55, 1961-.

Ownership, Management

Operated by: Community Owned Baseball Club of Central New York, Inc.

Chairman: Richard Ryan. **President:** Donald Waful. **Executive Vice President/Chief Operating Officer:** Anthony "Tex" Simone.

General Manager: John Simone. **Assistant General Manager:** Tom Van Schaack. **Director, Community Relations/Personnel:** Andy Gee. **Director, Group Sales:** Vic Gallucci. **Director, Ticket Sales:** H.J. Refici.

Assistant Ticket Manager: Ed Holmes. **Business Manager:** Don Lehtonen. **Assistant Bussiness Manager/Sales Associate:** Brian McManus. **Director, Merchandising:** Wendy Schoen. **Director, Food Services:** Kyle Rogers. **Director, Stadium Operations:** John Walters. **Clubhouse Operations:** Ryan Abbott, Mike Maser, Jody Puccello. **Receptionist:** Priscilla Venditti.

Field Staff
Manager: Terry Bevington. **Coach:** Hector Torres. **Pitching Coach:** Rick Langford. **Trainer:** Jon Woodworth.

Game Information
Radio Announcers: Ted DeLuca, Steve Hyder. **No. of Games Broadcast:** Home-72, Away-72. **Flagship Station:** WHEN 620-AM.

PA Announcer: Dave Perkins. **Official Scorers:** Joel Marieniss, Tom Leo.

Stadium Name (year opened): P&C Stadium (1997). **Location:** New York State Thruway to exit 36 (I-81 South), to 7th North Street exit, left on 7th North, right on Hiawatha Boulevard. **Standard Game Times:** 7 p.m.; Sun. 6.

Visiting Club Hotel: Ramada Inn, 1305 Buckley Rd., Syracuse, NY 13212. Telephone: (315) 457-8670.

Toledo
MUD HENS

Office Address: 2901 Key St., Maumee, OH 43537. **Mailing Address:** P.O. Box 6212, Toledo, OH 43614. **Telephone:** (419) 893-9483. **FAX:** (419) 893-5847. **E-Mail Address:** mudhens@mudhens.com. **Website:** www.mudhens.com.

Affiliation (first year): Detroit Tigers (1987). **Years in League:** 1889, 1965-.

Ownership, Management
Operated by: Toledo Mud Hens Baseball Club, Inc.
President: Edwin Bergsmark. **Secretary-Treasurer:** Charles Bracken. **Vice Presidents:** David Huey, Michael Miller.
Executive Vice President/Chief Executive Officer: Gene Cook.
Executive Director: Joe Napoli. **Director, Corporate Sales:** Scott Jeffer. **Director, Marketing and Promotions:** Neil Neukam. **Manager, Promotions:** Kerri White. **Manager, Public Relations:** Brian Britten. **Director, Ticket Sales/Operations:** Bob Palmisano. **Manager, Group Sales:** Erik Ibsen. **Associates, Season Ticket/Group Sales:** Joe Barbarito, Tom Townley. **Manager, Merchandising:** Lori Goon. **Associate, Merchandising:** Greg Setola. **Manager, Stadium Operations:** Greg Elliott. **Business Manager:** Dorothy Welniak. **Controller:** Bob Eldridge. **Office Manager:** Carol Hamilton.

Field Staff
Manager: Gene Roof. **Coach:** Skeeter Barnes. **Pitching Coach:** Dan Warthen. **Trainer:** Lon Pinhey.

Game Information
Radio Announcers: Frank Gilhooley, Jim Weber. **No. of Games Broadcast:** Home-72, Away-72. **Flagship Station:** WMTR 96.1-FM, WFRO 900-AM/99.1-FM.

PA Announcer: John Keller. **Official Scorers:** Guy Lammers, John Wagner.

Stadium Name (year opened): Ned Skeldon Stadium (1965). **Location:** From Ohio Turnpike, exit 4, north to Toledo on Reynolds, right onto Heatherdowns, right onto Key Street; From Detroit, I-75 South to exit 201A (Route 25), right onto Key Street; From Ann Arbor, Route 23 South to Route 475 South, exit 6, left at stoplight, follow Dussel Drive to stadium; From Dayton, I-75 via Route 475 to Maumee exit (Route 24), left onto Key Street. **Standard Game Times:** 7 p.m., Sun. 2.

Visiting Club Hotel: Holiday Inn West, 2340 S Reynolds Rd., Toledo, OH 43614. Telephone: (419) 865-1361.

PACIFIC COAST LEAGUE

Class AAA

Mailing Address: 1631 Mesa Ave., Colorado Springs, CO 80906. **Telephone:** (719) 636-3399. **FAX:** (719) 636-1199. **E-Mail Address:** pcloffice@earthlink.net. **Website:** www.pacificcoastleague.com.

Years League Active: 1903-.

President/Secretary-Treasurer: Branch B. Rickey.

Vice President: Russ Parker (Calgary).

Directors: Gary Arthur (Vancouver), Joe Buzas (Salt Lake), John Carbray (Fresno), Rob Couhig (New Orleans), George Foster (Tacoma), Bob Goughan (Colorado Springs), Ken Grandquist (Iowa), Rick Holtzman (Tucson), Dean Jernigan (Memphis), Rob Knight (Omaha), Mel Kowalchuk (Edmonton), Pat McKernan (Albuquerque), Tim O'Toole (Oklahoma), Russ Parker (Calgary), Hank Stickney (Las Vegas), Mike Woleben (Nashville).

Branch Rickey

Director, Operations: David Sheriff. **Secretary:** Christine Mazzei.

1999 Opening Date: April 8. **Closing Date:** Sept. 6.

Regular Season: 142 games.

Division Structure: American Conference—Central: Albuquerque, Colorado Springs, Iowa, Omaha. **East:** Memphis, Nashville, New Orleans, Oklahoma. **Pacific Conference—South:** Fresno, Las Vegas, Salt Lake, Tucson. **West:** Calgary, Edmonton, Tacoma, Vancouver.

Playoff Format: West champion plays South champion, and Midwest champion plays East champion in best-of-5 semifinal series. Winners meet in best-of-5 series for league championship. **Triple-A World Series:** Best-of-5 series vs. International League champion, Sept. 20-25 at Las Vegas.

All-Star Game: July 14 at New Orleans (International League vs. PCL).

Roster Limit: Unavailable. **Player Eligibility Rule:** No restrictions.

Brand of Baseball: Rawlings ROM.

Umpires: David Aschwege (Lincoln, NE), Lance Barksdale (Jackson, MS), Ted Barrett (Mesa, AZ), Fred Cannon (Brookhaven, MS), Pat Connors (Berlin, WI), Eric Cooper (Des Moines, IA), Mike DiMuro (Chandler, AZ), Robert Drake (Mesa, AZ), Doug Eddings (Las Cruces, NM), Mike Everitt (Chandler, AZ), Joel Fincher (Arlington, TX), Andy Fletcher (Memphis, TN), Dan Gnadt (Moorhead, MN), Morris Hodges (Helena, AL), Heath Jones (Glendale, AZ), Travis Katzenmeier (Liberal, KS), Ron Kulpa (Florissant, MO), Ian Lamplugh (Victoria, British Columbia), Alfonso Marquez (Anaheim, CA), Bill Miller (Aptos, CA), Scott Nance (Castle Rock, CO), Jeff Nelson (Cottage Grove, MN), Ken Page (Phoenix, AZ), Jeff Patterson (Imperial Beach, CA), Anthony Randazzo (Las Cruces, NM), Don Rea (Chandler, AZ), Brian Runge (El Cajon, CA), Jack Samuels (Orange, CA), Kraig Sanders (Little Rock, AR), Chris Taylor (Kansas City, MO), Mark Wegner (Birchwood, MN), Hunter Wendelstedt (Ormond Beach, FL), Jim Wolf (West Hills, CA).

Stadium Information

Club	Stadium	LF	CF	RF	Capacity	'98 Att.
		Dimensions				
Albuquerque	Albuquerque Sports	360	410	340	10,510	308,993
Calgary	Burns	345	400	345	8,000	296,047
Colo. Springs	Sky Sox	350	400	350	9,000	220,281
Edmonton	TELUS	340	420	320	9,200	410,414
Fresno	Beiden Field	331	410	330	6,575	359,076
Iowa	Sec Taylor	335	400	335	10,800	420,713
Las Vegas	Cashman Field	328	433	323	9,334	336,005
Memphis	Tim McCarver	323	398	325	8,800	395,592
Nashville	Herschel Greer	327	400	327	10,700	323,068
New Orleans	Zephyr Field	333	405	332	11,000	519,584
Oklahoma	Southwestern Bell	325	400	325	13,066	491,036
Omaha	Rosenblatt	332	408	332	24,000	401,264
Salt Lake	Franklin Covey	345	420	315	15,500	554,719
Tacoma	Cheney	325	425	325	9,600	337,623
Tucson	Tucson Electric	340	405	340	11,000	300,460
Vancouver	Nat Bailey	335	395	335	6,500	284,935

Albuquerque
DUKES

Office Address: 1601 Avenida Cesar Chavez, Albuquerque, NM 87106. **Telephone:** (505) 243-1791. **FAX:** (505) 842-0561. **E-Mail Address:** coastdukes@aol.com. **Website:** www.dukes.fanlink.com.

Affiliation (first year): Los Angeles Dodgers (1972). **Years in League:** 1972-.

Ownership, Management

Operated by: Albuquerque Professional Baseball, Inc.

Principal Owner/Chairman: Bob Lozinak. **President/General Manager:** P. Patrick McKernan.

Assistant GM/Director, Merchandising: Patrick J. McKernan. **Director, Business Operations/Accounting:** Dawene Shoup. **Director, Stadium Operations:** Mick Byers. **Director, Food Services:** Matthew McKernan. **Director, Media Relations:** Daniel Davidson. **Director, Sales:** Jim Guscott. **Director, Community Relations/Mascot:** Tim Smith. **Director, Ticket Sales:** Sam Roybal. **Director, Facilities:** Fred Chesser. **Director, Group Sales:** Alexander Hamilton. **Home Clubhouse Operations:** Rich Harbin. **Visiting Clubhouse Operations:** Jason Sierra. **Head Groundskeeper:** Louie Garcia.

Field Staff

Manager: Mike Scioscia. **Coach:** Mickey Hatcher. **Pitching Coach:** Claude Osteen. **Trainer:** Matt Wilson.

Game Information

Radio Announcers: Russ Langer, Jim Lawwill. **No. of Games Broadcast:** Home-71, Away-71. **Flagship Station:** Unavailable.

PA Announcer: Alexander Hamilton. **Official Scorer:** Gary Herron.

Stadium Name (year opened): Albuquerque Sports Stadium (1969). **Location:** I-25 to Avenida Cesar Chavez exit, east to stadium. **Standard Game Times:** 7 p.m., Sun. 1.

Visiting Club Hotel: Plaza Inn Albuquerque, 900 Medical Arts NE, Albuquerque, NM 87102. Telephone: (505) 243-5693.

Calgary
CANNONS

Office Address: 2255 Crowchild Trail NW, Calgary, Alberta T2M 4S7. **Telephone:** (403) 284-1111. **FAX:** (403) 284-4343. **E-Mail Address:** cannons@telusplanet.net. **Website:** www.cannons.fanlink.com.

Affiliation (first year): Florida Marlins (1999). **Years in League:** 1985-.

Ownership, Management

Operated by: Braken Holdings Ltd.

Principal Owners: Diane Parker, Russ Parker.

President: Russ Parker. **Secretary/Treasurer:** Diane Parker.

Vice President, Baseball Operations: John Traub. **VP, Marketing:** Bill Cragg. **VP, Finance:** Chris Poffenroth.

Coordinator, Public Relations: Craig Burak. **Director, Ticketing:** Greg Winthers. **Coordinator, Group Sales:** Jason MacAskill. **Sales/Promotions:** Dan Forigo, Johnny Hribar. **Head Groundskeeper/Sales:** Chris Howell. **Groundskeeper:** Dean Dunsby. **Managers, Food Service:** Pat Fehr, Murray Drope. **Administrative Assistant:** Dalyce Binette. **Receptionist:** Roberta Siegel. **Clubhouse Manager:** Blair McAusland. **Clubhouse Operations:** Billy McLeod, Brian Miettinen.

Field Staff

Manager: Lynn Jones. **Coach:** Sal Rende. **Pitching Coach:** Randy Hennis. **Trainer:** Tim Abraham.

Game Information

Radio: Unavailable.

PA Announcer: Bill Clapham. **Official Scorer:** Fred Collins.

Stadium Name (year opened): Burns Stadium (1966). **Location:** Crowchild Trail NW to 24th Avenue, adjacent to McMahon Stadium. **Standard Game Times:** 7:05 p.m., (April) 6:05; Sat. (April-May) 1:35; Sun. 1:35.

Visiting Club Hotel: Unavailable.

Colorado Springs
SKY SOX

Office Address: 4385 Tutt Blvd., Colorado Springs, CO 80922.
Telephone: (719) 597-1449. **FAX:** (719) 597-2491. **E-Mail Address:**
info@skysox.com. **Website:** www.skysox.com.

Affiliation (first year): Colorado Rockies (1993). **Years in League:**
1988-.

Ownership, Management

Operated by: Colorado Springs Sky Sox, Inc.
Principal Owner: David G. Elmore.
President/General Manager: Bob Goughan. **Senior Vice President,**
Administration: Sam Polizzi. **Senior VP, Operations:** Dwight Hall. **Senior**
VP, Marketing: Rai Henniger. **Senior VP, Stadium Operations:** Mark
Leasure. **VP, Advertising:** Nick Sciarratta. **Assistant GM/Group Sales:**
Brien Smith. **Assistant GM, Merchandising:** Robert Stein. **Assistant GM,**
Public Relations: Michael Hirsch. **Director, Finance:** Craig Levin.
Director, Broadcast Operations: Dan Karcher. **Director, Community**
Relations: Jake Pierson. **Home Clubhouse Manager/Marketing**
Representative: Murlin Whitten. **Group Sales/Ticket Operations:** Chip
Dreamer, Mike Humphreys. **Visiting Clubhouse Manager:** Greg Grimaldo.
Marketing Representatives: Charlie Miller, Michael Nemec, Gabriel Ross,
Jeremy Tonniges, Corey Wynn.

Field Staff

Manager: Bill Hayes. **Coach:** Tony Torchia. **Pitching Coach:** Jim
Wright. **Trainer:** Dan DeVoe.

Game Information

Radio Announcers: Dick Chase, Norm Jones, Dan Karcher. **No. of**
Games Broadcast: Home-71, Away-71. **Flagship Station:** KRDO 1240-
AM.

PA Announcer: Nick Sciarratta. **Official Scorer:** Marty Grantz.
Stadium Name (year opened): Sky Sox Stadium (1988). **Location:** I-25
South to Woodmen Road exit, east on Woodmen to Powers Boulevard,
right on Powers to Barnes Road. **Standard Game Times:** 7:05 p.m.; Sat.
(April-May) 1:35; Sun. 3:05.

Visiting Club Hotel: Ramada Inn North, 3125 Sinton Rd., Colorado
Springs, CO 80907. Telephone: (719) 633-5541.

Edmonton
TRAPPERS

Office Address: 10233 96th Ave., Edmonton, Alberta T5K 0A5.
Telephone: (780) 414-4450. **FAX:** (780) 414-4475. **E-Mail Address:** trap-
pers@planet.eon.net. **Website:** www.trappersbaseball.com.

Affiliation (first year): Anaheim Angels (1999). **Years in League:** 1981-.

Ownership, Management

Operated by: Trappers Baseball Corp.
Principal Owner: Peter Pocklington.
President/General Manager: Mel Kowalchuk. **Assistant General**
Manager: Dennis Henke. **Accountant:** Gabrielle Hampel. **Stadium**
Manager: Don Benson. **Head Groundskeeper:** Luke Syme. **Manager,**
Baseball Information: Gary Tater. **Manager, Sales:** Ken Charuk. **Account**
Executives: Craig Leibel, Del Schjefte. **Manager, Marketing:** Trent Houg.
Manager, Tickets: Victor Liew. **Manager, Group Sales:** Jeff Ivanochko.
Manager, Merchandise: Darin Kowalchuk. **Manager, Special**
Events/Assistant to President: Lauri Holomis. **Office Manager:** Debbie
Zaychuk. **Home Clubhouse Manager:** James Rosnau. **Visiting**
Clubhouse Manager: Ian Rose.

Field Staff

Manager: Carney Lansford. **Coach:** Leon Durham. **Pitching Coach:**
Rick Wise. **Trainer:** Alan Russell.

Game Information

Radio Announcer: Al Coates. **No. of Games Broadcast:** Unavailable.
Flagship Station: CHED 630-AM.

PA Announcer: Dean Parthenis. **Official Scorer:** Gary Tater.
Stadium Name (year opened): TELUS Field (1995). **Location:** From

north, 101st Street to 96th Avenue, left on 96th, one block east; From south, Calgary Trail North to Queen Elizabeth Hill, right across Walterdale Bridge, right on 96th Avenue. **Standard Game Times:** 7:05 p.m.; Sun. 2:05.

Visiting Club Hotel: Sheraton Grande, 10235 101st St., Edmonton, Alberta P5J 3E9. Telephone: (780) 428-7111.

Fresno
GRIZZLIES

Office Address: 700 Van Ness Ave., Fresno, CA 93721. **Telephone:** (559) 442-1994. **FAX:** (559) 264-0795. **E-Mail Address:** info@fresnogrizzlies.com. **Website:** www.fresnogrizzlies.com.

Affiliation (first year): San Francisco Giants (1998). **Years in League:** 1998-.

Ownership, Management
Operated by: Fresno Diamond Group.

Principal Owners: John Carbray, Dave Cates, Diane Engelken, Rick Roush. **Chairman:** William Connolly. **President:** John Carbray. **Vice President, Chief Operating Officer:** Diane Engelken. **VP, Chief Financial Officer:** Rick Roush. **VP, Special Projects:** Tim Cullen.

VP/General Manager: Derek Leistra. **Director, Food and Beverage:** Joe Hart. **Director, Sales and Promotions:** David Martin. **Director, Public Relations:** Chris Metz. **Director, Human Resources/Merchandise:** Debbie Scott-Leistra. **Director, Stadium Operations:** Glenn Wolff. **Director, Community Development:** Gus Zernial. **Ticket Manager:** Theresa Graham. **Director, Broadcasting:** Johnny Doskow. **Director, Spanish Broadcasting:** Jess Gonzalez. **Marketing Associates:** Jeff Colville, Ron Thomas. **Accounting Clerk:** Josh Phanco. **Executive Assistants:** Sarrah Soza, Leticia Vazquez. **Ticket Assistant:** Erin Hart. **Merchandise Assistant:** Mike Maiorana. **Receptionist:** Stephanie Calderon.

Field Staff
Manager: Ron Roenicke. **Coach:** Mike Hart. **Pitching Coach:** Joel Horlen. **Trainer:** Dave Groeschner.

Game Information
Radio Announcers: John Doskow, Jess Gonzalez. **No. of Games Broadcast:** Home-71, Away-71. **Flagship Stations:** KYNO 1300-AM, KGST 1600-AM.

PA Announcer: Brian Anthony. **Official Scorer:** Unavailable.

Stadium Name (year opened): Beiden Field (1987). **Location:** Highway 41 to Shaw Avenue, east to Cedar, left to stadium. **Standard Game Times:** 7:05 p.m., 7:35; Sun. 2:05.

Visiting Club Hotel: Doubletree Inn-Fresno, 1055 Van Ness Ave., Fresno, CA 93721. Telephone: (559) 485-9000.

Iowa
CUBS

Office Address: 350 SW 1st St., Des Moines, IA 50309. **Telephone:** (515) 243-6111. **FAX:** (515) 243-5152. **E-Mail:** sbernabe@iowacubs.com. **Website:** www.iowacubs.com.

Affiliation (first year): Chicago Cubs (1981). **Years in League:** 1998-.

Ownership, Management
Operated by: Greater Des Moines Baseball Co., Inc.

Principal Owner/President: Ken Grandquist.

General Manager: Sam Bernabe. **Assistant General Manager:** Jim Nahas. **Director, Media Relations:** Brett Dolan. **Controller:** Sue Tollefson. **Director, Stadium Operations:** Steve Miller. **Director, Group Sales:** Unavailable. **Senior Account Executives:** Scott Fuller, Red Hollis, Jeff Lantz, Jeff Tilley. **Director, Merchandising:** Amy Hansen. **Office Manager:** Peggy Ramsey. **Head Groundskeeper:** Luke Yoder.

Field Staff
Manager: Terry Kennedy. **Coach:** Glenn Adams. **Pitching Coach:** Rick Kranitz. **Trainer:** Bob Grimes.

Game Information
Radio Announcers: Brett Dolan, Deene Ehlis. **No. of Games**

Broadcast: Home-71, Away-71. **Flagship Station:** KXTK 940-AM.

PA Announcers: Mark Hendricks, Chuck Shockley. **Official Scorer:** Dirk Brinkmeyer.

Stadium Name (year opened): Sec Taylor Stadium (1992). **Location:** I-80 or I-35 to I-235, to Third Street exit, south on Third Street, left on Tuttle Street. **Standard Game Times:** 7:15 p.m.; Tues. (April-May) 12:15, (June-Aug.) 3:30; Sun. 6:05.

Visiting Club Hotel: Des Moines Marriott, 700 Grand Ave., Des Moines, IA 50309. Telephone: (515) 245-5500.

Las Vegas
STARS

Office Address: 850 Las Vegas Blvd. N, Las Vegas, NV 89101. **Telephone:** (702) 386-7200. **FAX:** (702) 386-7214. **E-Mail Address:** lvstars@earthlink.net. **Website:** www.lasvegasstars.com.

Affiliation (first year): San Diego Padres (1982). **Years in League:** 1982-.

Ownership, Management

Operated by: Mandalay Sports Entertainment.

Principal Owners: Peter Guber, Paul Schaeffer, Hank Stickney, Ken Stickney.

Chairman: Hank Stickney.

General Manager: Don Logan. **Assistant General Manager:** Mark Grenier. **Controller:** Allen Taylor. **Director, Stadium Operations:** Nick Fitzenreider. **Director, Media/Public Relations:** Jon Sandler. **Manager, Public Relations:** Brad Hickey. **Director, Ticket Sales:** Jeff Eiseman. **Director, Merchandising:** Laurie Wanser. **Office Manager:** Mary McConnell.

Field Staff

Manager: Mike Ramsey. **Coach:** Craig Colbert. **Pitching Coach:** Tom Brown. **Trainer:** George Poulis.

Game Information

Radio Announcers: Tim Neverett, Jon Sandler. **No. of Games Broadcast:** Home-71, Away-71. **Flagship Station:** KBAD 920-AM.

PA Announcer: Dan Bickmore. **Official Scorer:** Jim Gemma.

Stadium Name (year opened): Cashman Field (1983). **Location:** I-15 to U.S. 95 exit (Fremont Street), east on 95 to Las Vegas Boulevard North exit, north on Las Vegas Boulevard. **Standard Game Times:** 7:05 p.m., Sun. 1:05.

Visiting Club Hotel: Main Street Station, 200 N Main St., Las Vegas, NV 89101. Telephone: (800) 713-8933.

Memphis
REDBIRDS

Office Address: 800 Home Run Ln., Memphis, TN 38104. **Telephone:** (901) 721-6050. **FAX:** (901) 721-6017. **Website:** www.memphisredbirds.com.

Affiliation (first year): St. Louis Cardinals (1998). **Years in League:** 1998-.

Ownership, Management

Operated By: Blues City Baseball, Inc.

Principal Owners: Dean Jernigan, Kristi Jernigan.

Chairman: Jim Thomas.

President/General Manager: Allie Prescott. **Assistant General Manager:** Dan Madden. **Assistant to President/Office Manager:** Kipp Williams. **Vice President, Finance:** Chris Jernigan. **Controller:** Don Heitner. **Director, Marketing:** Kim Gaskill. **Director, Promotions/Media Relations:** Richard Flight. **Director, Broadcasting:** Tom Stocker. **Director, Development:** Gwen Driscoll. **Director, Sales:** Pete Rizzo. **Sales Executives:** Reginald Glaspie, Don Rovak, Jeff Seagraves. **Director, Community Relations:** Reggie Williams. **Director, Retail Operations:** Kerry Sewell. **Director, Field Operations:** Steve Horne. **Operations Manager:** Steele Ford. **Ticket Manager:** Phil McKay. **Facilities Managers:** Cecil Jernigan, Jimmy Williams. **Director, Project Development:** Ray Brown. **Administrative Assistants:** Pam Abney, Cathy Allen, Trina Armstrong.

Field Staff
Manager: Gaylen Pitts. **Coach:** Boots Day. **Pitching Coach:** Marty Mason. **Trainer:** Pete Fagan.

Game Information
Radio Announcer: Tom Stocker. **No. of Games Broadcast:** Home-71, Away-71. **Flagship Station:** WHBQ 560-AM.

PA Announcer: Bob Brame. **Official Scorer:** J.J. Guinozzo.

Stadium Name (year opened): Tim McCarver Stadium (1963). **Location:** I-40 West (Sam Cooper Boulevard) to Broad Street, left onto East Parkway, left onto Central Avenue, right onto Early Maxwell Boulevard. **Standard Game Times:** 7:05 p.m., Sat. 6:05, Sun. 2:05.

Visiting Club Hotel: Unavailable.

Nashville
SOUNDS

Office Address: 534 Chestnut St., Nashville, TN 37203. **Telephone:** (615) 242-4371. **FAX:** (615) 256-5684. **E-Mail Address:** soundsemploy@mindspring.com. **Website:** www.nashvillesounds.com.

Affiliation (first year): Pittsburgh Pirates (1998). **Years in League:** 1998-.

Ownership, Management
Operated by: Nashville Sounds Baseball Club, Inc./American Sports Enterprises, Inc.

President: Al Gordon. **Vice Presidents:** Mike Murtaugh, Mike Woleben. **Chief Financial Officer:** Glenn Yaeger.

General Manager: Jeff Sedivy. **Director, Sales/Marketing:** R.J. Martino. **Director, Baseball Operations:** Mike Nutter. **Director, Business Operations:** Chris Snyder. **Director, Group Sales:** Tim Sexton. **Director, Ticket Operations:** David Lorenz. **Director, Merchandise:** Lisa Lorenz. **Director, Stadium Operations:** Brian Harper. **Director, Media Relations:** Steve Selby. **Assistant Manager, Media Relations:** Crystal Richardson. **Personnel Manager:** Jody Whitmore. **Ticket Office:** Ricki Schlabach. **Business Manager:** Judy Franke. **Office Manager:** Sharon Carson. **Assistant Business Manager:** Matt Fisher. **Account Executives:** Brent Bartemeyer, Brian Krueger, Rod Lawless, Phil Laws, Woody McClendon, Greg Milo, Rob Roberts, John Swandal, Gary Shephard, Chuck Valenches. **Clubhouse Manager:** Kevin Bryant. **Head Groundskeeper:** Tom McAfee.

Field Staff
Manager: Trent Jewett. **Coach:** Richie Hebner. **Pitching Coach:** Bruce Tanner. **Trainer:** Sandy Crum.

Game Information
Radio Announcers: Steve Selby, Chuck Valenches. **No. of Games Broadcast:** Home-71, Away-71. **Flagship Station:** Unavailable.

PA Announcer: Chris Champion. **Official Scorer:** Unavailable.

Stadium Name (year opened): Herschel Greer Stadium (1978). **Location:** I-65 to Wedgewood exit, west to Eighth Avenue, right on Eighth to Chestnut Street, right on Chestnut. **Standard Game Times:** 7 p.m., (April) 6; Wed. 12; Sat. 6; Sun. 4.

Visiting Club Hotel: Super 8 Motel, 350 Harding Pl., Nashville, TN 37211. Telephone: (615) 834-0620.

New Orleans
ZEPHYRS

Office Address: 6000 Airline Dr., Metairie, LA 70003. **Telephone:** (504) 734-5155. **FAX:** (504) 734-5118. **E-Mail Address:** zephyrs@zephyrsbaseball.com. **Website:** www.zephyrsbaseball.com.

Affiliation (first year): Houston Astros (1997). **Years in League:** 1998-.

Ownership, Management
Operated by: Airline Place Management.

Principal Owner/President: Rob Couhig.

Vice President/General Manager: Dan Hanrahan. **Assistant VP, Media/Public Relations:** Les East. **Assistant VP, Sales/Marketing:** Dawn Mentel. **Director, Business Operations:** Shawn Kelly. **Director, Stadium Operations:** Steven O'Connor. **Director, Community Relations:** Aaron

Lombard. **Director, Ticket Sales:** David McDonough. **Senior Account Representative:** Rene Nadeau. **Director, Merchandising:** Heather Woods-Menendez. **Director, Food Services:** George Messina. **Head Groundskeeper:** Russell Brown. **Clubhouse Operations:** Richie Runnels. **Office Manager:** Angie Green.

Field Staff
Manager: Tony Pena. **Coach:** Jorge Orta. **Pitching Coach:** Jim Hickey. **Trainer:** Mike Freer.

Game Information
Radio Announcers: Ron Swoboda, Ken Trahan. **No. of Games Broadcast:** Home-71, Away-71. **Flagship Stations:** WWL 870-AM, WSMB 1350-AM.

PA Announcer: Rene Nadeau. **Official Scorer:** J.L. Vangilder.

Stadium Name (year opened): Zephyr Field (1997). **Location:** I-10 to Clearview Parkway South exit, right on Airline Drive (Route 61) for 1 mile. **Standard Game Times:** 7:05 p.m.; Sun. (April-May) 2:05, (June-Sept.) 6:05.

Visiting Club Hotel: Best Western Landmark, 2601 Severn Ave., Metairie, LA 70002. Telephone: (504) 888-9500.

Oklahoma
REDHAWKS

Mailing Address: Southwestern Bell Bricktown Ballpark, 2 S Mickey Mantle Dr., Oklahoma City, OK 73104. **Telephone:** (405) 218-1000. **FAX:** (405) 218-1001. **E-Mail Address:** info@redhawksbaseball.com. **Website:** www.redhawksbaseball.com.

Affiliation (first year): Texas Rangers (1983). **Years in League:** 1963-1968, 1998-.

Ownership, Management
Operated by: OKC Athletic Club, LP.

Principal Owner: Gaylord Entertainment Co.

President/General Manager: Tim O'Toole. **Controller:** Steve McEwen. **Director, Sales/Marketing:** Dianna Bonfiglio. **Director, Baseball Operations:** John Allgood. **Director, Facility Operations:** Harlan Budde. **Director, Promotions:** Brad Tammen. **Ticket Manager:** Sarah Miller. **Manager, Concourse Services:** Mike Prange. **Senior Accountant:** Kristi Bennett. **Senior Account Manager:** Skip Wallace. **Manager, Group Sales:** Johnny Walker. **Account Managers/Special Projects:** Sherie Pierce, Amy Shreck. **Head Groundskeeper:** Monte McCoy. **Clubhouse Manager:** Mike Moulder. **Operations Supervisor:** Beth Stone. **Administrative Assistants:** Amy Farnsworth, Missy Mitchell.

Field Staff
Manager: Greg Biagini. **Coach:** Bruce Crabbe. **Pitching Coach:** Brad Arnsberg. **Trainer:** Greg Harrel.

Game Information
Radio Announcer: Jack Damrill. **No. of Games Broadcast:** Home-71, Away-71. **Flagship Stations:** WWLS 104.9-FM/640-AM.

PA Announcer: Randy Kemp. **Official Scorers:** Bob Colon, Max Nichols, Pat Petree.

Stadium Name (year opened): Southwestern Bell Bricktown Ballpark (1998). **Location:** At interchange of I-235 and I-40, take Reno exit, east on Reno. **Standard Game Times:** 7:05 p.m.; Sun. (April-June) 2:05.

Visiting Club Hotel: Westin Hotel, One N Broadway, Oklahoma City, OK 73102. Telephone: (405) 235-2780.

Omaha
GOLDENSPIKES

Office Address: Rosenblatt Stadium, 1202 Bert Murphy Dr., Omaha, NE 68107. **Telephone:** (402) 734-2550. **FAX:** (402) 734-7166. **E-Mail Address:** omahabaseball@goldenspikes.com. **Website:** www.golden-spikes.com.

Affiliation (first year): Kansas City Royals (1969). **Years in League:** 1998-.

Ownership, Management
Operated by: Omaha Royals, LP.

Principal Owners: Union Pacific Railroad, Warren Buffett, Walter Scott. **President:** Rob Knight.

General Manager: Bill Gorman. **Assistant General Manager:** Terry Wendlandt. **Controller:** Jessica Graner. **Comptroller:** Sue Nicholson. **Director, Media Relations:** Mike Mashanic. **Director, Marketing:** Mike Stephens. **Account Representatives:** Tony Duffek, Andy Lewis, Kevin McNabb, Eric Tomb. **Manager, Ticket Office:** Joe Volquartsen. **Assistant to Ticket Manager:** Marlene Lee. **Assistant, Ticket Office:** Bob Brown. **Head Groundskeeper:** Jesse Cuevas. **General Manager, Concessions:** Chris Benevento. **Administrative Assistants:** Kay Besta, Lois Biggs.

Field Staff

Manager: Ron Johnson. **Coach:** Bob Herold. **Pitching Coach:** Gary Lance. **Trainer:** Jeff Stevenson.

Game Information

Radio Announcer: Kevin McNabb. **No. of Games Broadcast:** Home-71, Away-71. **Flagship Station:** KOSR 1490-AM.

PA Announcers: Walt Gibbs, Bill Jensen, Steve Roberts. **Official Scorers:** Frank Adkisson, Steve Pivovar, Rob White.

Stadium Name (year opened): Rosenblatt Stadium (1948). **Location:** I-80 to 13th Street South exit, south one block. **Standard Game Times:** 7:05 p.m.; Sun. 1:35.

Visiting Club Hotel: Ramada Hotel Central, 7007 Grover St., Omaha, NE 68106. Telephone: (402) 397-7030.

Salt Lake
BUZZ

Office Address: 77 West 1300 S, Salt Lake City, UT 84115. **Mailing Address:** P.O. Box 4108, Salt Lake City, UT 84110. **Telephone:** (801) 485-3800. **FAX:** (801) 485-6017. **E-Mail Address:** slbuzz@earthlink.net. **Website:** www.fanlink.com.

Affiliation (first year): Minnesota Twins (1994). **Years in League:** 1915-25, 1958-65, 1970-84, 1994-.

Ownership, Management

Operated by: Buzas Baseball, Inc.

Principal Owner: Joe Buzas.

President/General Manager: Joe Buzas. **Vice President:** Hilary Buzas-Drammis. **VP/Assistant GM:** Dorsena Picknell. **Director, Media/Public Relations:** Tony Reyna. **Director, Ticket Sales:** Michael O'Conor. **Sales Manager:** Michael Begley. **Director, Sales:** Jim Hochstrasser. **Director, Group Sales:** Paul Hirst. **Director, Stadium Operations:** Mark Hildebrand. **Receptionist:** Mary Sawaya.

Field Staff

Manager: Phil Roof. **Coach:** Bill Springman. **Pitching Coach:** Rick Anderson. **Trainer:** Rick McWane.

Game Information

Radio Announcer: Steve Klauke. **No. of Games Broadcast:** Home-71, Away-71. **Flagship Station:** KFNZ 1320-AM.

PA Announcer: Jeff Reeves. **Official Scorers:** Bruce Hilton, Howard Nakagama.

Stadium Name (year opened): Franklin Covey Field (1994). **Location:** From I-15 North, take 2100 South exit, east at West Temple, north to 1300 South; from I-15 South, take the Beck Street exit, which becomes 300 West, continue south to 1300 South. **Standard Game Times:** 7 p.m., 6:15 (April-May); Sun. (April-June) 2, (July-Aug.) 5.

Visiting Club Hotel: Quality Inn City Center, 154 West 600 S, Salt Lake City, UT 84101. Telephone: (801) 521-2930.

Tacoma
RAINIERS

Office Address: 2502 S Tyler, Tacoma, WA 98405. **Mailing Address:** P.O. Box 11087, Tacoma, WA 98411. **Telephone:** (253) 752-7707. **FAX:** (253) 752-7135. **E-Mail Address:** tacomapcl@aol.com. **Website:** www.fanlink.rainiers.com.

Affiliation (first year): Seattle Mariners (1995). **Years in League:** 1904-05, 1960-.

Ownership, Management

Operated by: George's Pastime, Inc.
Principal Owners: George Foster, Sue Foster.
President: George Foster.
Executive Vice President: Mel Taylor. Assistant General Manager: Colleen Sullivan. Director, Finance: Laurie Yarbrough. Staff Accountant: Saundra Field. Director, Baseball Operations: Kevin Kalal. Director, Broadcasting/Media Relations: Mike Curto. Director, Media Sales/Special Events: Renee Waltz. Director, Sales: Dave Lewis. Account Representatives: Travis Ellingson, Connie Littlejohn-Rivers. Director, Stadium Operations: Twila Elrod. Head Groundskeeper: Bob Christofferson. Director, Ticketing: Phil Cowan. Assistant Ticket Manager: Susie O'Donnell. Director, Merchandising: Jeanette Collett. Director, Food Services: Frank Maryott. Director, Clubhouse Operations: Rob Reagle. Office Manager: Mary Lanier.

Field Staff

Manager: Dave Myers. Coach: Dave Brundage. Pitching Coach: Jim Slaton. Trainer: Randy Roetter.

Game Information

Radio Announcer: Mike Curto. No. of Games Broadcast: Home-71, Away-71. Flagship Station: KHH0 850-AM.
PA Announcer: Jeff Randall. Official Scorers: Mark Johnston, Darin Padur.
Stadium Name (year opened): Cheney Stadium (1960). Location: From I-5, take exit 132 (Highway 16 West) for 1.2 miles to 19th Street East exit, right on Tyler Street for ⅛ mile. Standard Game Times: 7:05 p.m., Sun. 1:35.
Visiting Club Hotel: La Quinta Inn, 1425 E 27th St., Tacoma, WA 98421. Telephone: (253) 383-0146.

Tucson
SIDEWINDERS

Office Address: 2500 E Ajo Way, Tucson, AZ 85713. Mailing Address: P.O. Box 27045, Tucson, AZ 85726. Telephone: (520) 434-1021. FAX: (520) 889-9477. E-Mail Address: tuffy@azstarnet.com. Website: www.tucsonsidewinders.com.
Affiliation (first year): Arizona Diamondbacks (1998). Years in League: 1969-.

Ownership, Management

Operated by: Professional Sports, Inc.
Principal Owner: Martin Stone.
Vice President/General Manager: Mike Feder. Assistant General Manager: Todd Woodford. Director, Operations: Doug Leary. Director, Sales/Marketing: Kristin Taylor. Director, Broadcasting: David Brady. Director, Hispanic Marketing: Francisco Romero. Director, Group Sales: Eric May. Director, Ticket Sales: Louis Butash. Director, Food Services: Jeff Greenleaf. Office Manager: Pattie Feder. Account Executives: Sam Stone, Patrick Ware. Head Groundskeeper: Jamie Ruffle. Clubhouse Operations: Chad Chiffin, Dan Wallin.

Field Staff

Manager: Chris Speier. Coach: Mike Barnett. Pitching Coach: Chuck Kniffin. Trainer: Peter Kolb.

Game Information

Radio Announcer: Dave Brady. No. of Games Broadcast: Home-71, Away-71. Flagship Station: KTKT 990-AM.
PA Announcer: Anthony DeFazio. Official Scorer: Unavailable.
Stadium Name (year opened): Tucson Electric Park (1998). Location: From southeast, I-10 to Palo Verde exit, north to Ajo, west to stadium; From northwest, I-10 to Ajo exit, east on Ajo to stadium. Standard Games Times: 7 p.m., Fri.-Sat. 7:30.
Visiting Club Hotel: Ramada Inn-Foothills, 6944 Tanque Verde Rd., Tucson, AZ 85715. Telephone: (520) 886-9595.

Vancouver
CANADIANS

Office Address: 4601 Ontario St., Vancouver, British Columbia V5V 3H4. **Telephone:** (604) 872-5232. **FAX:** (604) 872-1714. **E-Mail Address:** canadians@ultranet.com. **Website:** www.canadians.fanlink.com.

Affiliation (first year): Oakland Athletics (1999). **Years in League:** 1956-62, 1965-69, 1978-.

Ownership, Management

Operated by: Japan Sports Systems, Inc.

President: John McHale.

Vice President/General Manager: Gary Arthur. **Manager, Accounting/Administration:** Harry Chan. **Manager, Stadium/Field Operations:** Bill Posthumus. **Manager, Media/Public Relations:** Steve Hoem. **Manager, Sales/Marketing:** Ken Cooper. **Manager, Souvenir Operations:** Torchy Pechet. **Corporate Sales:** Rob Evans. **Administrative Assistant:** Simi Uppal.

Field Staff

Manager: Mike Quade. **Coach:** Roy White. **Pitching Coach:** Pete Richert. **Trainer:** Walt Horn.

Game Information

Radio: None.

PA Announcer: Brook Ward. **Official Scorer:** Pat Karl.

Stadium Name (year opened): Nat Bailey Stadium (1952). **Location:** From downtown: Cambie Street Bridge, left on East 33rd Street, left on Clancy Loringer Way, right to stadium; From south: Highway 99 to Oak Street, right on 41st Avenue, left on Ontario. **Standard Game Times:** 7:05 p.m.; Wed. 12:15, Sun. 1:30.

Visiting Club Hotel: Delta Pacific Resort Hotel, 10251 St. Edwards Dr., Richmond, B.C. V6X 2M9. Telephone: (604) 278-9611.

EASTERNLEAGUE

Class AA

Office Address: 511 Congress St., 7th Floor, Portland, ME 04104. **Mailing Address:** P.O. Box 9711, Portland, ME 04104. **Telephone:** (207) 761-2700. **FAX:** (207) 761-7064. **E-Mail Address:** elpb@easternleague.com. **Website:** www.easternleague.com.

Years League Active: 1923-.

President/Treasurer: Bill Troubh.

Vice Presidents: Greg Agganis (Akron), Joe Buzas (New Britain). **Assistant to President:** Joe McEacharn. **Administrative Assistant:** Chris McKibben. **Corporate Secretary:** Gerry Berthiaume (New Britain).

Directors: Greg Agganis (Akron), Joe Buzas (New Britain), Charles Eshbach (Portland), Barry Gordon (Norwich), Peter Kirk (Bowie), Alan Levin (Erie), Bob Lozinak (Altoona), Ed Massey (New Haven), Steve

Bill Troubh

Resnick (Harrisburg), Dick Stanley (Trenton), Craig Stein (Reading), Mike Urda (Binghamton).

1999 Opening Date: April 9. **Closing Date:** Sept. 6.

Regular Season: 142 games.

Division Structure: North—Binghamton, New Britain, New Haven, Norwich, Portland, Trenton. South—Akron, Altoona, Bowie, Erie, Harrisburg, Reading.

Playoff Format: Top two teams in each division play best-of-5 series. Winners meet in best-of-5 series for league championship.

All-Star Game: July 14 at Mobile, AL (joint Double-A game).

Roster Limit: 23 active, until midnight Aug. 10 when roster can be expanded to 24. **Player Eligibility Rule:** No restrictions.

Brand of Baseball: Rawlings ROM-EL.

Statistician: Howe Sportsdata, Boston Fish Pier, West Bldg. #1, Suite 302, Boston MA 02210.

Umpires: Greg Ayers (Boulder, CO), John Bennett (Shelbyville, KY), Troy Blades (Dartmouth, Nova Scotia), Adam Dowdy (Pontiac, IL), Robert Driskell (Panama City, FL), Michael Fichter (Lansing, IL), Don Goller (East Aurora, NY), Matthew Hollowell (Whitehouse Station, NJ), James Hoye (North Olmsted, OH), Justin Klemm (Cataumet, MA), Patrick McGinnis (Joliet, IL), Scott Packard (Horseheads, NY), Timothy Pasch (Plant City, FL), Alexander Rea (Miami, FL), Andrew Shultz (Millersville, PA), Patrick Spieler (Omaha, NE), Neil Taylor (St. Petersburg, FL), Mark Winters (Pleasant Plains, IL).

Stadium Information

Club	Stadium	Dimensions LF	CF	RF	Capacity	'98 Att.
Akron	Canal Park	331	400	337	9,097	521,122
Altoona*	Altoona Ballpark	325	400	325	6,120	—
Binghamton	Binghamton Municipal	330	400	330	6,012	216,191
Bowie	Prince Georges	309	405	309	10,000	400,058
Erie*	Jerry Uht	312	400	328	6,000	—
Harrisburg	RiverSide	335	400	335	6,200	259,381
New Britain	New Britain	330	400	330	6,146	181,643
New Haven	Yale Field	340	405	315	6,200	197,342
Norwich	Thomas J. Dodd	309	401	309	6,275	243,817
Portland	Hadlock Field	315	400	330	6,860	398,800
Reading	Municipal Memorial	330	400	330	8,500	414,658
Trenton	Waterfront Park	330	407	330	6,606	457,344

*Expansion team

Akron
AEROS

Office Address: 300 S Main St., Akron, OH 44308. **Telephone:** (330) 253-5151. **FAX:** (330) 253-3300. **E-Mail Adress:** aaeros@neo.lrun.com. **Website:** www.akronaeros.com.
Affiliation (first year): Cleveland Indians (1989). **Years in League:** 1989-.

Ownership, Management
Operated by: Akron Professional Baseball, Inc.
Principal Owners: Mike Agganis, Greg Agganis.
Chief Executive Officer: Greg Agganis. **Vice President:** Drew Cooke. **Chief Financial Officer:** Bob Larkins.
Executive Vice President/General Manager: Jeff Auman. **Director, Ticket Operations:** Kurt Landes. **Manager, Group Sales:** Kim Usselman. **Assistant Manager, Group Sales:** Matt Ippolito. **Director, Season Ticket/Stadium Club Marketing:** Ben Tolchinsky. **Director, Season Ticket/Suite Services:** Matt Carr. **Senior Account Representative, Group Sales:** Thomas Craven. **Director, Corporate Marketing/Communications:** Erin Wander. **Director, Sponsorship Sales/Video Operations:** Mike Sudduth. **Director, Media Relations:** James Carpenter. **Director, Community Relations:** Katie Dannemiller. **Director, Merchandising:** Kris Roukey. **Director, Field Maintenance:** Rick Izzo. **Director, Stadium Operations:** Dave Darkey. **Receptionist:** Jean Dockus. **Clubhouse Operations:** Fletcher Wilkes, Tom Kackley.

Field Staff
Manager: Joel Skinner. **Coach:** Eric Fox. **Pitching Coach:** Tony Arnold. **Trainer:** Dan DeVoe.

Game Information
Radio Announcers: Todd Bell, Jim Clark. **No. of Games Broadcast:** Home-71, Away-71. **Flagship Station:** WTOU 1350-AM.
PA Announcer: Joe Dunn. **Official Scorers:** Tom Liggett, Will Roleson. **Stadium Name (year opened):** Canal Park (1997). **Location:** From I-76 East or I-77 South, exit onto Route 59 East, exit at Exchange/Cedar and turn right onto Cedar, go left at Main Street. From I-76 West or I-77 North, exit at Main Street/Downtown, follow exit onto Broadway Street, left onto Exchange Street, right at Main Street. **Standard Game Times:** 7:05 p.m.; Sun. 2:05.
Visiting Club Hotel: Radisson Hotel Akron City Centre, 20 W Mill St., Akron, OH 44308. Telephone: (330) 384-1500.

Altoona
CURVE

Office Address: 1000 Park Ave., Altoona, PA 16602. **Mailing Address:** P.O. Box 1029, Altoona, PA 16603. **Telephone:** (814) 943-5400. **FAX:** (814) 943-9050. **E-Mail Address:** curvekid@penn.com. **Website:** www.altoonacurve.com.
Affiliation (first year): Pittsburgh Pirates (1999). **Years in League:** 1999-.

Ownership, Management
Operated by: Altoona Baseball Properties, LLC.
Principal Owner: Bob Lozinak.
General Manager: Sal Baglieri. **Assistant General Manager:** Steve Lozinak. **Director, Sales/Marketing:** Jim Gregory. **Director, Media/Public Relations:** Robin Wentz. **Head Groundskeeper:** Justin Spillman. **Account Representative:** Matt Fiochetta. **Director, Ticket Sales:** Robert Greene. **Director, Group Sales:** Shawn Hicks. **Assistant Ticket Manager:** Shawn Reimer. **Director, Merchandising:** Rich McKeon. **Clubhouse Operations:** Jake Hundt.

Field Staff
Manager: Marty Brown. **Coach:** Jeff Livesey. **Pitching Coach:** Scott Lovekamp. **Trainer:** Mike Sandoval.

Game Information
Radio Announcer: Rob Egan. **No. of Games Broadcast:** Home-71, Away-71. **Flagship Station:** Unavailable.

PA Announcer: Unavailable. Official Scorer: Unavailable.

Stadium Name (year opened): Altoona Ballpark (1999). Location: I-99 to Frankstown Road exit. Standard Game Times: 7:05 p.m., (April-May) 6:05, Sun. 1:05.

Visiting Club Hotel: Days Inn, 3306 Pleasant Valley Blvd., Altoona, PA 16602. Telephone: (814) 944-9661.

Binghamton
METS

Office Address: 211 Henry St., Binghamton, NY 13902. Mailing Address: P.O. Box 598, Binghamton, NY 13902. Telephone: (607) 723-6387. FAX: (607) 723-7779. E-Mail Address: bmets@bmets.com. Website: www.bmets.com.

Affiliation (first year): New York Mets (1992). Years in League: 1923-37, 1940-63, 1966-68, 1992-.

Ownership, Management

Operated by: Binghamton Mets Baseball Club, Inc.

Principal Owners: David Maines, William Maines, R.C. Reuteman, George Scherer, Christopher Urda, Michael Urda.

President: Michael Urda.

Vice President/General Manager: R.C. Reuteman. Assistant General Manager: Scott Brown. Director, Business Operations: Jim Weed. Director, Stadium Operations: Richard Tylicki. Head Groundskeeper: Scott Dobbins. Marketing Representative: Mitch Gorton. Director, Community Relations: Melinda Mayne. Group Sales Manager: Kevin Mahoney. Director, Merchanding: John Willi. Director, Food and Beverage: Pete Brotherton. Clubhouse Operations: Tony Cleary. Office Manager: Sally Hanifin. Bookkeeper: Karen Micalizzi.

Field Staff

Manager: Doug Davis. Coach: Roger LaFrancois. Pitching Coach: Bob Stanley. Trainer: Brandon Sheppard.

Game Information

Radio Announcer: Dave Schultz. No. of Games Broadcast: Home-71, Away-71. Flagship Station: WNBF 1290-AM.

PA Announcer: Roger Neel. Official Scorer: Steve Kraly.

Stadium Name (year opened): Binghamton Municipal (1992). Location: I-81 to exit 4S (Binghamton), Route 11 exit to Henry Street. Standard Game Times: 7 p.m., (April-June 20) 6; Sat. (April-June 25) 1:30; Sun. 1:30.

Visiting Club Hotel: Holiday Inn Arena, Vestal Parkway East, Vestal, NY 13850. Telephone: (607) 729-6371.

Bowie
BAYSOX

Office Address: 4101 NE Crain Hwy., Bowie, MD 20716. Mailing Address: P.O. Box 1661, Bowie, MD 20717. Telephone: (301) 805-6000. FAX: (301) 805-6008. E-Mail Address: marcar@baysox.com. Website: www.baysox.com.

Affiliation (first year): Baltimore Orioles (1993). Years In League: 1993-.

Ownership

Operated by: Maryland Baseball, LLC.

Principal Owners: John Daskalakis, Peter Kirk, Frank Perdue, Hugh Schindel, Pete Simmons.

Chief Executive Officer: Peter Kirk. President: Pete Simmons. Vice Chairman: Hugh Schindel. Senior Vice President, Club Operations: Keith Lupton. Executive Secretary: Jan Varney. Controller: Bob Gast. Director, Public Relations: Charlie Vascellaro.

General Manager: Jon Danos. Assistant GM, Tickets: Mike Munter. Director, Stadium/Clubhouse Operations: Dave Dolney. Head Groundskeeper: Al Capitos. Director, Broadcasting/Media Relations: Dave Collins. Director, Community Relations: Cheryl Legohn-Tubbs. Ticket Operations: Kiyomi Endo, Bill Galletta, Doug George, Ann Hinsberg, Brad Sims, Becci Velasco, Phillip Wrye. Account Managers: Tom DeGroff, Gary Groll, Kelly Weis. Office Manager: Margo Carpenter.

Receptionist: Lynn Cloutier.

Field Staff
Manager: Joe Ferguson. **Coach:** Bien Figueroa. **Pitching Coach:** Dave Schmidt. **Trainer:** Mitch Bibb.

Game Information
Radio Announcer: Dave Collins. **No. of Games Broadcast:** Home-71, Away-71 **Flagship Station:** WNAV 1430-AM.

PA Announcer: Tom DeGroff. **Official Scorer:** Jeff Hertz.

Stadium Name (year opened): Prince Georges Stadium (1994). **Location:** U.S. 50 to U.S. 301 South, left at second light. **Standard Game Times:** 7:05 p.m., Sun. 1:05.

Visiting Club Hotel: Days Inn-Historic Annapolis, 2520 Riva Rd., Annapolis, MD 21401. Telephone: (410) 224-2800.

Erie
SEAWOLVES

Office Address: 110 E 10th St., Erie, PA 16501. **Mailing Address:** P.O. Box 1776, Erie, PA 16507. **Telephone:** (814) 456-1300. **FAX:** (814) 456-7520. **E-Mail Address:** seawolves@seawolves.com. **Website:** www.sea-wolves.com.

Affiliation (first year): Anaheim Angels (1999). **Years in League:** 1893-94, 1999-.

Ownership, Management
Operated by: Palisades Baseball Ltd.

Principal Owner: Alan Levin. **Vice President:** Eric Haig.

General Manager: Keith Hallal. **Assistant General Manager:** Dave Smith. **Director, Finance:** Andy Zmudzinski. **Director, Ticket Operations:** Shawn Carty. **Director, Group Sales:** Shawn Waskiewicz. **Director, Sales/Promotions:** Ryan Gates. **Director, Concessions:** Matt Bresee. **Director, Community Relations:** Steve Glenn. **Director, Media Relations:** Kale Beers. **Accountant:** Bernadette Mulvihill.

Field Staff
Manager: Garry Templeton. **Coach:** Bill Lachemann. **Pitching Coach:** Howie Gershberg. **Trainer:** Doug Baker.

Game Information
Radio: Unavailable.

PA Announcer: Rick Shigo. **Official Scorers** Les Caldwell, Steve Metzler.

Stadium Name (year opened): Jerry Uht Park (1995). **Location:** US 79 North to East 12th Street exit, left on State Street, right on 10th Street. **Standard Game Times:** 7 p.m.; Sun. 2.

Visiting Club Hotel: Avalon Hotel, 16 W 10th St., Erie, PA 16501. Telephone: (814) 459-2220.

Harrisburg
SENATORS

Office Address: RiverSide Stadium, City Island, Harrisburg, PA 17101. **Mailing Address:** P.O. Box 15757, Harrisburg, PA 17105. **Telephone:** (717) 231-4444. **FAX:** (717) 231-4445. **E-Mail Address:** hbgsenator@aol.com. **Website:** www.senatorsbaseball.com.

Affiliation (first year): Montreal Expos (1991). **Years in League:** 1924-35, 1987-.

Ownership, Management
Operated by: Harrisburg Senators Baseball Club, Inc.

Chairman: Greg Martini.

General Manager: Todd Vander Woude. **Business Manager:** Steve Resnick. **Assistant GM, Baseball Operations:** Mark Mattern. **Assistant GM, Business Operations:** Mark Clarke. **Director, Broadcasting/Media Relations:** Brad Sparesus. **Facilities Manager:** Tim Foreman. **Concessions Manager:** Steve Leininger. **Ticket Manager:** Paul Seeley. **Groundskeeper:** Joe Bialek. **Group Sales:** Brian Egli, Mickey Graham. **Picnic Operations:** Carol Baker. **Human Resources:** Sean Carroll. **Community Relations:** Jocelyn Johnson. **Ticket Sales:** Tom Wess. **Clubhouse Operations:** Michael Diehl.

Field Staff

Manager: Doug Sisson. **Coach:** Steve Phillips. **Pitching Coach:** Wayne Rosenthal. **Trainer:** Brian Eggleston.

Game Information

Radio Announcers: Brad Sparesus, Mark Mattern. **No. of Games Broadcast:** Home-71, Away-71. **Flagship Station:** WKBO 1230-AM, WIOO 1000-AM.

PA Announcer: Chris Andre. **Official Scorer:** Gary Ritter.

Stadium Name (year opened): RiverSide Stadium (1987). **Location:** I-83, exit 23 (Second Street) to Market Street, bridge to City Island. **Standard Game Times:** 7:05 p.m.; Sun. 1:05.

Visiting Club Hotel: Hilton Hotel, One N Second St., Harrisburg, PA 17101. **Telephone:** (717) 233-6000.

New Britain
ROCK CATS

Office Address: Willow Brook Park, South Main Street, New Britain, CT 06051. **Mailing Address:** P.O. Box 1718, New Britain, CT 06050. **Telephone:** (860) 224-8383. **FAX:** (860) 225-6267. **E-Mail Address:** buzas.assoc@snet.net. **Website:** www.rockcats.fanlink.com.

Affiliation (first year): Minnesota Twins (1995). **Years in League:** 1983-.

Ownership, Management

Operated by: Buzas Enterprises, Inc.

Chairman: Joe Buzas. **President:** Hilary Buzas-Drammis. **Vice President:** George Burkert.

Executive Vice President/General Manager: Gerry Berthiaume. **Assistant General Manager:** Mark Mogul. **Director, Ticket Operations:** Sebastian Thomas. **Director, Food Operations:** Donna Mogul. **Stadium Operations:** Ryan Donahue. **Director, Public Relations:** Jeff Dooley. **Director, Group Sales:** Chris Faris. **Account Executive:** Evan Levy.

Field Staff

Manager: John Russell. **Coach:** Jeff Carter. **Pitching Coach:** Stu Cliburn. **Trainer:** Dave Pruemer.

Game Information

Radio Announcer: Jeff Dooley. **No. of Games Broadcast:** Home-71, Away-71. **Flagship Station:** WPRX 1120-AM.

PA Announcer: Roy Zurril. **Official Scorer:** Bob Kirschner.

Stadium Name (year opened): New Britain Stadium (1996). **Location:** From I-84, take Route 72 East (exit 35) or Route 9 South (exit 39A), left at Ellis Street (exit 25), left at South Main Street, stadium one mile on right; From Route 91 or Route 5, take Route 9 North to Route 71 (exit 24), first exit. **Standard Game Times:** April-May 6:35 p.m., June-Sept. 7; Sun. 2.

Visiting Club Hotel: Super 8, 1 Industrial Park Rd., Cromwell, CT 06416. **Telephone:** (860) 632-8888.

New Haven
RAVENS

Office Address: 252 Derby Ave., West Haven, CT 06516. **Telephone:** (203) 782-1666, (800) 728-3671. **FAX:** (203) 782-3150. **E-Mail Address:** ravens@connix.com. **Website:** www.ravens.com.

Affiliation (first year): Seattle Mariners (1999). **Years in League:** 1916-32, 1994-.

Ownership, Management

Operated By: New Haven Baseball, LP.

Principal Owner: Edward Massey.

General Manager: Chris Canetti. **Assistant General Manager, Operations:** Roy Kirchner. **Director, Ticket Sales:** Randy Shamber. **Manager, Ticket Operations:** Jay Eylward. **Director, Operations:** Bill Brown. **Director, Public Relations/Marketing:** Bill Berger. **Controller:** Tamara Nolin. **Assistant, Accounting:** Barbara Prato. **Director, Special Services:** Greg Schmidt. **Senior Account Executive:** Lori McCarthy. **Director, Group Sales:** Demetrius Beam. **Account Executive:** Rich Hannan. **Director, Broadcasting:** Bill Schweizer. **Internet Coordinator:** Sam Rubin.

Field Staff
Manager: Dan Rohn. **Coach:** Henry Cotto. **Pitching Coach:** Pat Rice. **Trainer:** Rob Nodine.

Game Information
Radio Announcer: Bill Schweizer. **No. of Games Broadcast:** Home-71, Away-71. **Flagship Station:** WAVZ 1300-AM.

PA Announcer: Unavailable. **Official Scorer:** Tim Bennett.

Stadium Name (year opened): Yale Field (1927). **Location:** From I-95, take eastbound exit 44 or westbound exit 45 to Route 10 and follow the Yale Bowl signs. From Merritt Parkway, take exit 57, follow to 34 East. **Standard Game Times:** 7:05 p.m., Sun. 2:05.

Visiting Club Hotel: Days Hotel, 490 Saw Mill Rd., West Haven, CT 06516. Telephone: (203) 933-0344.

Norwich
NAVIGATORS

Office Address: 14 Stott Ave., Norwich, CT 06360. **Mailing Address:** P.O. Box 6003, Yantic, CT 06389. **Telephone:** (860) 887-7962. **FAX:** (860) 886-5996. **E-Mail Address:** gators@connix.com. **Website:** www.gators.com.

Affiliation (first year): New York Yankees (1995). **Years in League:** 1995-.

Ownership, Management
Operated by: Minor League Sports Enterprises, LP.

Principal Owners: Bob Friedman, Neil Goldman, Barry Gordon, Marc Klee, Hank Smith.

Chairman: Barry Gordon. **President:** Hank Smith.

Vice President/General Manager: Brian Mahoney. **Assistant GM, Operations:** Geoff Brown. **Assistant GM, Marketing:** Tom Hinsch. **Director, Finance:** Richard Darling. **Director, Media/Broadcasting:** Shawn Holliday. **Assistant Director, Broadcasting:** Mark Leinweaver. **Director, Ticket Sales:** Chris Fritz. **Ticket Manager:** Adam Dolliver. **Director, Group Sales:** John Clark. **Group Sales Managers:** John Gilbert, Rosemary Smith. **Merchandise Manager:** Kara Infante. **Director, Food Services:** Richard Heimberg. **Office Manager:** Michelle Sadowski. **Head Groundskeepers:** Kevin Johns, Chris Langley.

Field Staff
Manager: Lee Mazzilli. **Coach:** Arnie Beyeler. **Pitching Coach:** Tom Filer. **Trainer:** Carl Randolph.

Game Information
Radio Announcers: Shawn Holliday, Mark Leinweaver. **No. of Games Broadcast:** Home-71, Away-71. **Flagship Station:** WSUB 980-AM.

PA Announcer: John Tuite. **Official Scorer:** Gene Gumbs.

Stadium Name (year opened): Senator Thomas J. Dodd Memorial Stadium (1995). **Location:** I-395 to exit 82, follow signs to Norwich Industrial Park, stadium is in back of industrial park. **Standard Game Times:** Mon.-Thur. (April-May) 6:35 p.m., (June-Sept.) 7:05; Fri. 7:05; Sat. (April-May) 1:05, (June-Sept.) 7:05; Sun. (April-May) 1:05, (June-Sept.) 4:05.

Visiting Club Hotel: Days Inn-Niantic, 265 Flanders Rd., Niantic, CT 06357. Telephone: (860) 739-6921.

Portland
SEA DOGS

Office Address: 271 Park Ave., Portland, ME 04102. **Mailing Address:** P.O. Box 636, Portland, ME 04104. **Telephone:** (207) 874-9300. **FAX:** (207) 780-0317. **E-Mail Address:** seadogs@portlandseadogs.com. **Website:** www.portlandseadogs.com.

Affiliation (first year): Florida Marlins (1994). **Years in League:** 1994-.

Ownership, Management
Operated By: Portland, Maine, Baseball, Inc.

Principal Owner/Chairman: Daniel Burke.

President/General Manager: Charles Eshbach. **Assistant General Manager:** John Kameisha. **Director, Sales/Marketing:** Mike Gillogly. **Business Manager:** Jim Heffley. **Director, Business Development:** Elliott Barry. **Director, Group Sales:** James Beaudoin. **Director, Ticketing:** Kelli

Hoschtetler. **Box Office Manager:** Chris Cameron. **Associate Director, Food Services/Merchandising:** Katie Harris. **Director, Broadcasting:** Andy Young. **Administrative Assistants:** Mark Christie, Jason LaBossiere, Jennifer Ryder, Shawn Willey. **Office Manager:** Judy Bray. **Clubhouse Managers:** Nancy Goslin, Richard Goslin.

Field Staff
Manager: Frank Cacciatore. **Coach:** Jose Castro. **Pitching Coach:** Steve Luebber. **Trainer:** Harold Williams.

Game Information
Radio Announcers: Steve Pratt, Andy Young. **No. of Games Broadcast:** Home-71, Away-71. **Flagship Station:** WZAN 970-AM.
PA Announcer: Dean Rogers. **Official Scorer:** Leroy Rand.
Stadium Name (year opened): Hadlock Field (1994). **Location:** From south, I-295 to exit 5, merge onto Congress Street, left at St. John Street, merge right onto Park Avenue; From north, I-295 to exit 6A, right on Park Avenue. **Standard Game Times:** (First half) 6 p.m., (second half) 7; Sat. (first half) 1, (second half) 7; Sun. (first half) 1, (second half) 4.
Visiting Club Hotel: Radisson-Eastland, 157 High St., Portland, ME 04101. Telephone: (207) 775-5411.

Reading
PHILLIES

Office Address: Rt. 61 South/1900 Centre Ave., Reading, PA 19601. **Mailing Address:** P.O. Box 15050, Reading, PA 19612. **Telephone:** (610) 375-8469. **FAX:** (610) 373-5868. **E-Mail address:** rphils@voicenet.com. **Website:** www.readingphillies.com.
Affiliation (first year): Philadelphia Phillies (1967). **Years in League:** 1933-35, 1952-61, 1963-65, 1967-.

Ownership, Management
Operated By: E&J Baseball Club, Inc.
Principal Owner/President: Craig Stein.
General Manager: Chuck Domino. **Assistant General Manager:** Scott Hunsicker. **Director, Operations:** Andy Bortz. **Director, Communications/Community Development:** Mark Wallace. **Director, Tickets:** Zach Conen. **Director, Group Sales:** Jeff Tagliaferro. **Director, New Business Development/Game Operations:** Troy Pothoff. **Director, Stadium Grounds:** Dan Douglas. **Director, Office Management:** Denise Haage. **Assistant Director, Operations:** Jamie Keitsock. **Assistant Director, Group Sales:** Joe Pew. **Merchandise Manager/Group Sales Associate:** Kevin Sklenarick. **Assistant Director, Communications/Community Development:** Rob Hackash. **Assistant Director, Tickets:** Mike Becker.

Field Staff
Manager: Gary Varsho. **Coach:** Milt Thompson. **Pitching Coach:** Gorman Heimueller. **Trainer:** Troy Hoffert.

Game Information
Radio Announcer: Steve Degler. **No. of Games Broadcast:** Home-71, Away-71. **Flagship Station:** WRAW 1340-AM.
PA Announcer: Dave Bauman. **Official Scorer:** John Lemke.
Stadium Name (year opened): Reading Municipal Memorial Stadium (1950). **Location:** From east, take Pennsylvania Turnpike West to Morgantown exit, to 176 North, to 422 West, to Route 12 East, to Route 61 South exit. From west, take 422 East to Route 12 East, to Route 61 South exit. From north, take 222 South to Route 12 exit, to Route 61 South exit. From south, take 222 North to 422 West, to Route 12 East exit at Route 61 South. **Standard Game Times:** Mon.-Thurs. (April-May) 6:35, (June-Sept.) 7:05; Fri. 7:05; Sat. (April) 2:05, (May-Sept.) 7:05; Sun. 1:05.
Visiting Club Hotel: Wellesley Inn, 910 Woodland Ave., Wyomissing, PA 19610. Telephone: (610) 374-1500.

Trenton
THUNDER

Office Address: One Thunder Rd., Trenton, NJ 08611. **Telephone:** (609) 394-3300. **FAX:** (609) 394-9666. **E-Mail Address:** office@trenton-thunder.com. **Website:** www.trentonthunder.com.
Affiliation (first year): Boston Red Sox (1995). **Years in League:** 1994-.

Ownership, Management

Operated by: Garden State Baseball, LP.

General Manager/Chief Operating Officer: Wayne Hodes. Assistant General Manager: Tom McCarthy. Director, Marketing/Merchandising: Eric Lipsman. Director, Operations: Rick Brenner. Director, Stadium Operations: Adam Palant. Director, Ticket Operations: Scott Gross. Director, Media/Public Relations: Andy Freed. Controller: John Coletta. Assistant Controller: Kelly Beach. Office Manager: Sue Chassen. Ticket Manager: Kerry Meeres. Group Sales Manager: Jeremy Fishman. Ticket Assistant: Matt Armentano. Community/Stadium Operations: Chris Tobin, Josh Watson. Clubhouse Manager: Donnie Phippen. Head Groundskeeper: Jeff Migliaccio.

Field Staff

Manager: DeMarlo Hale. Coach: Steve Braun. Pitching Coach: Mike Griffin. Trainer: Bryan Jaquette.

Game Information

Radio Announcers: Andy Freed, Tom McCarthy. No. of Games Broadcast: Home-71, Away-71. Flagship Station: WTTM 1680-AM.

PA Announcer: Bill Bromberg. Official Scorers: Jay Dunn, Mike Maconi.

Stadium Name (year opened): Mercer County Waterfront Park (1994). Location: Route 129 North, left at Cass Street; From I-95 take Route 29 South. Standard Game Times: 7:05 p.m.; Sat. (April-June) 1:05, (July-Sept.) 7:05; Sun. 1:05.

Visiting Club Hotel: MacIntosh Inn, 3270 Brunswick Pike, Lawrenceville, NJ 08648. Telephone: (609) 896-3700.

SOUTHERNLEAGUE

Class AA

Mailing Address: One Depot St., Suite 300, Marietta, GA 30060. **Telephone:** (770) 428-4749. **FAX:** (770) 428-4849. **E-Mail Address:** soleague@bellsouth.net. **Website:** www.southernleague.fanlink.com.

Years League Active: 1964-.

President/Secretary-Treasurer: Arnold Fielkow.

Vice President: Don Mincher (Huntsville).

Directors: Don Beaver (Knoxville), Peter Bragan Sr. (Jacksonville), Steve Bryant (Carolina), Frank Burke (Chattanooga), Steve DeSalvo (Greenville), Tony Ensor (Birmingham), David Hersh (West Tenn), Chuck LaMar (Orlando), Eric Margenau (Mobile), Don Mincher (Huntsville).

Arnold Fielkow

Executive Assistant: Lori Webb.

1999 Opening Date: April 8. **Closing Date:** Sept. 6.

Regular Season: 140 games (split schedule).

Division Structure: East—Carolina, Greenville, Jacksonville, Knoxville, Orlando. **West**—Birmingham, Chattanooga, Huntsville, Mobile, West Tenn.

Playoff Format: First-half division champions play second-half division champions in best-of-5 series. Winners meet in best-of-5 series for league championship.

All-Star Games: June 23 at West Tenn; July 14 at Mobile (joint Double-A game).

Roster Limit: 23 active, until midnight Aug. 10 when roster can be expanded to 24. **Player Eligibility Rule:** No restrictions.

Brand of Baseball: Rawlings.

Statistician: Howe Sportsdata, Boston Fish Pier, West Bldg. #1, Suite 302, Boston MA 02210.

Umpires: Mike Alvarado (Moses Lake, WA), Chris Boberg (Charlotte, NC), Robert Daly (Winter Springs, FL), David Dunlevy (Tempe, AZ), William Haze (Gilbert, AZ), Jeff Head (Jasper, AL), Jimmy Horton (Louisville, MS), Jack Kennedy (Frankfort, KY), Brian Knight (Helena, MT), Brian McCraw (Nashville, TN), Scott Nelson (Coshocton, OH), James Thomas (Marietta, GA), Webb Turner (Hope Mills, NC), Roger Walling (Placentia, CA), Greg Williams (Fort Lauderdale, FL).

Stadium Information

Club	Stadium	Dimensions			Capacity	'98 Att.
		LF	CF	RF		
Birmingham	Hoover Metropolitan	340	405	340	10,800	298,054
Carolina	Five County	330	400	330	6,000	230,768
Chattanooga	Engel	325	471	318	7,500	230,475
Greenville	Greenville Municipal	345	400	345	7,048	269,525
Huntsville	Davis Municipal	345	405	330	10,200	257,915
Jacksonville	Wolfson Park	320	390	320	8,200	254,882
Knoxville	Bill Meyer	330	400	330	6,412	123,686
Mobile	Hank Aaron	325	400	310	6,000	271,002
Orlando	Tinker Field	340	425	320	5,104	144,126
West Tenn	Pringles Park	310	395	320	6,000	313,775

Birmingham BARONS

Office Address: 100 Ben Chapman Dr., Birmingham, AL 35244. **Mailing Address:** P.O. Box 360007, Birmingham, AL 35236. **Telephone:** (205) 988-3200. **FAX:** (205) 988-9698. **E-Mail Address:** barons@barons.com. **Website:** www.barons.com.

Affiliation (first year): Chicago White Sox (1986). **Years in League:** 1964-65, 1967-75, 1981-.

Ownership, Management

Operated by: Elmore Sports Group, Ltd.

Principal Owner: Dave Elmore.

Vice President/General Manager: Tony Ensor. **Assistant General Manager:** Jonathan Nelson. **Director, Operations/Merchandising:** Chris Jenkins. **Director, Media Relations:** David Lee. **Director, Sales/Marketing:** George Dennis. **Director, Ticket Sales:** Joe Drake. **Group Sales Associates:** Eric Crook, Ryan Ellis, Ashley Farrar. **Director, Catering:** Jennifer Sicola. **Office Manager:** Norma Rosebrough. **Accounting Clerk:** Kecia Arnold. **Clubhouse Operations:** Ken Dunlap. **Administrative Assistants:** Tate Elder, John Hayden, Luke Larkin, Jeff McKeon, April Phillips.

Field Staff

Manager: Chris Cron. **Coach:** Steve Whitaker. **Pitching Coach:** Curt Hasler. **Trainer:** Scott Takao.

Game Information

Radio Announcer: Curt Bloom. **No. of Games Broadcast:** Home-70, Away-70. **Flagship Station:** WAPI 1070-AM.

PA Announcer: Derek Scudder. **Official Scorer:** Bill Graham.

Stadium Name (year opened): Hoover Metropolitan Stadium (1988). **Location:** I-459 to Highway 150 (exit 10) in Hoover. **Standard Game Times:** 7 p.m.; Sun. (April-June) 2, (July-Sept.) 6.

Visiting Club Hotel: Riverchase Inn, 1800 Riverchase Dr., Birmingham, AL 35244. Telephone: (205) 985-7500.

Carolina MUDCATS

Office Address: 1501 N.C. Hwy. 39, Zebulon, NC 27597. **Mailing Address:** P.O. Drawer 1218, Zebulon, NC 27597. **Telephone:** (919) 269-2287. **FAX:** (919) 269-4910. **E-Mail Address:** mudcats@bellsouth.com. **Website:** www.carolinamudcats.com.

Affiliation (first year): Colorado Rockies (1999). **Years in League:** 1991-.

Ownership, Management

Operated by: Carolina Professional Baseball Club, Inc.

Principal Owner/President: Steve Bryant.

General Manager: Joe Kremer. **Assistant General Manager:** Brian Becknell. **Director, Stadium Operations:** Aaron Banker. **Assistant Director, Operations:** Jeff Curtis. **Head Groundskeeper:** Bill Riggan. **Director, Media Relations:** Nathan Waters. **Director, Sales/Marketing:** Duke Sanders. **Director, Ticket Operations:** Eric Gardner. **Director, Corporate Sales:** Bill Gunger. **Director, Merchandising:** Holly Myers. **Director, Concessions/Operations:** Christopher Kay. **Director, Special Events:** Jim Tennison. **Office Manager:** Jackie DiPrimo. **Group Sales:** Will Barfield, Bob Lord, Beth Reib. **Community Relations:** Allison Lent, Thomas Phelps.

Field Staff

Manager: Jay Loviglio. **Coach:** Theron Todd. **Pitching Coach:** Jerry Cram. **Trainer:** Unavailable.

Game Information

Radio Announcer: Pat Kinas. **No. of Games Broadcast:** Home-70, Away-70. **Flagship Station:** WSAY 98.5-FM.

PA Announcer: Duke Sanders. **Official Scorer:** John Hobgood.

Stadium Name (year opened): Five County Stadium (1991). **Location:** From Raleigh, U.S. 64 East to 264 East, exit at Highway 39 in Zebulon. **Standard Game Times:** 7:05 p.m.; Sun. (April-May) 2:05, (June-Sept.)

5:05.

Visiting Club Hotel: Plantation Inn-Raleigh, 6401 Capital Blvd., Raleigh, NC 27616. Telephone: (919) 876-1411.

Chattanooga
LOOKOUTS

Office Address: 1130 East Third St., Chattanooga, TN 37403. Mailing Address: P.O. Box 11002, Chattanooga, TN 37401. Telephone: (423) 267-2208. FAX: (423) 267-4258.

Affiliation (first year): Cincinnati Reds (1988). Years in League: 1964-65, 1976-.

Ownership, Management
Operated by: Engel Stadium Corporation.
Principal Owners: Daniel Burke, Frank Burke, Charles Eshbach.
President: Frank Burke.
General Manager: Rich Mozingo. Director, Public Relations: Brad Smith. Head Groundskeeper: Tom Nielsen. Director, Promotions/Ticket Sales: Mark Heiser. Director, Food Services: Tim Schuster. Director, Telemarketing: Bill Wheeler. Office Manager: Stephanie Dawn.

Field Staff
Manager: Phillip Wellman. Coach: Unavailable. Pitching Coach: Mack Jenkins. Trainer: Tom Spencer.

Game Information
Radio Announcers: Larry Ward, Todd Agne. No. of Games Broadcast: Home-70, Away-70. Flagship Station: WQMT 98.9-FM.
PA Announcer: Chris Goforth. Official Scorer: Wirt Gammon.
Stadium Name (year opened): Engel Stadium (1930). Location: I-24 to U.S. 27 North to Fourth St. exit, 1¾ miles to O'Neal Street, right on O'Neal.
Standard Game Times: 7 p.m.; Mon. 12:30; Sun. 2.
Visiting Club Hotel: Holiday Inn Southeast, 6700 Ringgold Rd., Chattanooga, TN 37412. Telephone: (800) 722-2332.

Greenville
BRAVES

Office Address: One Braves Ave., Greenville, SC 29607. Mailing Address: P.O. Box 16683, Greenville, SC 29606. Telephone: (864) 299-3456. FAX: (864) 277-7369. Website: www.gbraves.com.

Affiliation (first year): Atlanta Braves (1984). Years in League: 1984-.

Ownership, Management
Operated by: Atlanta National League Baseball Club, Inc.
Principal Owner: Ted Turner. President: Stan Kasten.
General Manager: Steve DeSalvo. Assistant General Manager: Jim Bishop. Ticket Manager: Jimmy Moore. Director, Broadcasting/Public Relations: Mark Hauser. Director, Field Operations: Matt Taylor. Promotions Manager: Hollye Edwards. Administrative Coordinator: Brenda Yoder. Concessions Manager: Jed Anthony.

Field Staff
Manager: Paul Runge. Coach: Bobby Moore. Pitching Coach: Mike Alvarez. Trainer: Jay Williams.

Game Information
Radio Announcers: Stephen Grubba, Mark Hauser. No. of Games Broadcast: Home-70, Away-70. Flagship Station: WCCP 104.9-FM.
PA Announcer: Unavailable. Official Scorer: Jimmy Moore.
Stadium Name (year opened): Greenville Municipal Stadium (1984). Location: I-85 to exit 46 (Mauldin Road), east two miles. Standard Game Times: 7:15 p.m.; Sun. (April-May) 2:15, (June-Aug.) 6:15.
Visiting Club Hotel: Quality Inn, 50 Orchard Park Dr., Greenville, SC 29615. Telephone: (864) 297-9000.

Huntsville
STARS

Office Address: 3125 Leeman Ferry Rd., Huntsville, AL 35801. Mailing Address: P.O. Box 2769, Huntsville, AL 35804. Telephone: (256) 882-2562. FAX: (256) 880-0801. E-Mail Address: stars@traveller.com. Website: www.huntsvillestars.com.

Affiliation (first year): Milwaukee Brewers (1999). Years In League: 1985-.

Ownership, Management
Operated by: Huntsville Stars Baseball, LLC.

President/General Manager: Don Mincher. Vice President/Executive Director: Patrick Nichol.

Assistant General Manager: Bryan Dingo. Director, Business Operations: Pat Mincher. Director, Public Relations/Promotions: Jim Riley. Group Sales Representatives: Shawn Bulman, Mark Gorenc. Director, Merchandising/Office Manager: Devin Rose. Director, Ticket Sales: Cynthia Giles. Head Groundskeeper: Craig Shaw. Director, Broadcasting: Steve Kornya.

Field Staff
Manager: Darrell Evans. Coach: Herm Winningham. Pitching Coach: Steve Renko. Trainer: Bryan Butz.

Game Information
Radio Announcer: Steve Kornya. No. of Games Broadcast: Home-70, Away-70. Flagship Station: WTKI 1450-AM.

PA Announcer: Tommy Hayes. Official Scorer: Larry Smith.

Stadium Name (year opened): Joe W. Davis Municipal Stadium (1985). Location: I-65 to I-565 East, south on Memorial Parkway to Drake Avenue exit. Standard Game Times: 7:05 p.m.; Sun. (April-June) 2:05, (July-Sept.) 7:05.

Visiting Club Hotel: La Quinta Inn, 3141 University Dr., Huntsville, AL 35816. Telephone: (256) 533-0756.

Jacksonville
SUNS

Office Address: 1201 East Duval St., Jacksonville, FL 32202. Mailing Address: P.O. Box 4756, Jacksonville, FL 32201. Telephone: (904) 358-2846. FAX: (904) 358-2845. E-Mail Address: jaxsuns@bellsouth.net. Website: www.jaxsuns.com.

Affiliation (first year): Detroit Tigers (1995). Years in League: 1970-.

Ownership, Management
Operated by: Baseball Jax, Inc.

Principal Owner/President: Peter Bragan Sr. Assistant to President: Jerry LeMoine.

Vice President/General Manager: Peter Bragan Jr. Assistant General Manager: Todd Budnick. Head Groundskeeper: Mark Clay. Director, Marketing: Kirk Goodman. Director, Community Affairs: Shannon Sharp. Director, Ticket Sales: Jamie Smith. Director, Group Sales: Bryan Franker. Director, Food Services: David Leathers. Clubhouse Operations: Ray Sterling. Office Manager: Cathy Wiggins. Administrative Assistant: Jen Adkison.

Field Staff
Manager: Dave Anderson. Coach: Matt Martin. Pitching Coach: Steve McCatty. Trainer: Matt Lewis.

Game Information
Radio Announcer: Dave Schultz. No. of Games Broadcast: Home-70, Away-70. Flagship Station: Unavailable.

PA Announcer: John Leard. Official Scorer: Paul Ivice.

Stadium Name (year opened): Wolfson Park (1955). Location: From I-95 North to 20th Street East exit, take to end, turn right before Jacksonville Municipal Stadium; From I-95 South to Emerson Street exit, take right to Hart Bridge, take Sports Complex exit, left at light to stop sign, take right and quick left; From Mathews Bridge, take A. Phillip Randolph exit, right off ramp, right at stop sign, left at second light to stadium. Standard Game Times: 7:35 p.m; Wed. (April-June) 12:35; Sun. (April-June) 2:35, (July-Sept.) 5:35.

Visiting Club Hotel: La Quinta-Orange Park, 8555 Blanding Blvd., Jacksonville, FL 32244. Telephone: (904) 778-9539.

Knoxville
SMOKIES

Office Address: 633 Jessamine St., Knoxville, TN 37917. Telephone: (423) 637-9494. FAX: (423) 523-9913. E-Mail Address: info@smokies-baseball.com. Website: www.smokiesbaseball.com.

Affiliation (first year): Toronto Blue Jays (1980). Years in League: 1964-67, 1972-.

Ownership, Management

Operated by: Knoxville Smokies Baseball, Inc.
Principal Owner/President: Don Beaver.
Vice President/General Manager: Dan Rajkowski. Assistant General Manager: Brian Cox. Director, Broadcasting/Media Relations: Tim Grubbs. Executive Director, Sales/Marketing: Mark Seaman. Director, Group Sales/Marketing: Jeff Shoaf. Assistant Director, Promotions: Penelope Keller. Director, Ticket Sales: Brandt Tillotson. Director, Stadium Operations: Justin Ewart. Head Groundskeeper: Bob Shoemaker. Administrative Assistant: Heather Sharpe.

Field Staff

Manager: Omar Malave. Coach: Randy Phillips. Pitching Coach: Darren Balsley. Trainer: Mike Wirsta.

Game Information

Radio Announcer: Tim Grubbs. No. of Games Broadcast: Home-70, Away-70. Flagship Station: WQLA 104.9-FM.
PA Announcer: Unavailable. Official Scorer: Unavailable.
Stadium Name (year opened): Bill Meyer Stadium (1955). Location: I-40 to James White Parkway, right on Summit Hill Drive, right on Central Avenue, right on Willow Avenue to park. Standard Game Times: 7:15 p.m., Wed. 12, Sun. 5.
Visiting Club Hotel: Best Western North, 118 Merchants Dr., Knoxville, TN 37912. Telephone: (423) 688-3141.

Mobile
BAYBEARS

Office Address: 755 Bolling Bros. Blvd., Mobile, AL 36606. Mailing Address: P.O. Box 161663, Mobile, AL 36616. Telephone: (334) 479-2327. FAX: (334) 476-1147. E-Mail Address: baybears@mobilebaybears.com. Website: www.mobilebaybears.com.

Affiliation (first year): San Diego Padres (1997). Years in League: 1997-.

Ownership, Management

Operated by: United Sports Ventures.
President: Eric Margenau. Vice President: Bill Shanahan.
General Manager: Tom Simmons. Director, Sales: Travis Toth. Director, Broadcasting/Media Relations: Tom Nichols. Director, Group Sales: Dan Zusman. Director, Regional Sales: Angelo Mazzella. Director, Facility Operations: Patrick White. Director, Merchandising: Betty Adams. Director, Special Events: Allen Jernigan. Director, Ticket Operations: Doug Stephens. Administrator, Financial Services: Amy Haas. Customer Service/Sales Representative: Deneen Owen. Assistant Director, Facility Operations: Scott Balzer. Executive Secretary/Office Manager: Karen Kinsey. Telemarketing: Heather Quinn, Jennifer Risner, La Loni Taylor. Administrative Assistants: Grant Barnet, Drew DeVun, Mike Herret.

Field Staff

Manager: Mike Basso. Coach: Jim Bowie. Pitching Coach: Don Alexander. Trainer: Jason Haeussinger.

Game Information

Radio Announcer: Tom Nichols. No. of Games Broadcast: Home-70, Away-70. Flagship Station: WNSP 105.5-FM.
PA Announcer: Unavailable. Official Scorer: Unavailable.
Stadium Name (year opened): Hank Aaron Stadium (1997). Location:

I-65 to exit 1A (Government Street), right at McVay, right at Bolling Bros. Boulevard.. **Standard Game Times:** 7:05 p.m.; Sun. 2:05, 6:05.

Visiting Club Hotel: Unavailable.

Orlando
RAYS

Office Address: 287 Tampa Ave. South, Orlando, FL 32805. **Telephone:** (407) 649-7297. **FAX:** (407) 649-1637. **E-Mail Address:** orays@aol.com.

Affiliation (first year): Tampa Bay Devil Rays (1999). **Years in League:** 1973-.

Ownership, Management
Operated by: Orlando Rays Baseball, Inc.
Principal Owner: Naimoli Baseball Enterprises, Inc.
Chairman/President: Vincent Naimoli. **Director:** Chuck LaMar.
General Manager: Thomas Ramsberger. **Assistant General Manager:** John Cody. **Director, Sales/Marketing:** Greg Coleman. **Director, Ticket Sales:** Scott Freiberger. **Director, Group Sales:** James Giberson. **Director, Merchandising:** Mack Powell.

Field Staff
Manager: Bill Russell. **Coach:** Steve Livesey. **Pitching Coach:** Ray Searage. **Trainer:** Tom Tisdale.

Game Information
Radio: None.
PA Announcer: Kevin Baldinger. **Official Scorer:** Unavailable.
Stadium Name (year opened): Tinker Field (1923). **Location:** From north: I-4 West to Colonial Drive (Highway 50), west to Tampa Avenue, left on Tampa for 1½ miles; from south: north on Highway 17-92/441, left on Long Street, right on Tampa Avenue; from east or west: East-West Expressway west to Orange Blossom Trail (exit empties onto Long Street), follow Long two blocks to Tampa Avenue, right on Tampa. **Standard Game Times:** 7 p.m.; Sun. (April-May) 2, (June-Sept.) 6.

Visiting Club Hotel: Comfort Inn North, 830 Lee Rd., Orlando, FL 32810. Telephone: (407) 629-4000.

West Tenn
DIAMOND JAXX

Office Address: 4 Fun Pl., Jackson, TN 38305. **Telephone:** (901) 664-2020. **FAX:** (901) 988-5246. **E-Mail Address:** baseball@diamondjaxx.com. **Website:** www.diamondjaxx.com.

Affiliation (first year): Chicago Cubs (1998). **Years In League:** 1998-.

Ownership, Management
Operated by: Professional Sports and Entertainment Associates of Tennessee, LP.
President/General Manager: David Hersh.
Assistant General Manager: Brian Cheever. **Director, Stadium Operations:** Matt Erwin. **Director, Broadcasting/Media Relations:** Matt Park. **Director, Sales:** Russ McBryde. **Director, Marketing:** Jarrod Coates. **Director, Promotions:** Kelly Long. **Director, Group Sales:** Amy Ormes. **Merchandising Manager:** Nicole Piersiak. **Director, Food Services:** Robert Garcia. **Customer Service Specialist:** Patty Haynes. **Accounting Manager:** Terrie Hopper. **Regional Sales Managers:** Martie Cordaro, Catherine Dickey, Kelley Dunn.

Field Staff
Manager: Dave Trembley. **Coach:** Tack Wilson. **Pitching Coach:** Alan Dunn. **Trainer:** Jim O'Reilly.

Game Information
Radio Announcer: Matt Park. **No. of Games Broadcast:** Home-70, Away-70. **Flagship Station:** WNWS 101.5-FM.
PA Announcer: Brad McCoy. **Official Scorers:** Ron Barry, Julie Powell.
Stadium Name (year opened): Pringles Park (1998). **Location:** From I-40, take exit 85 South to F.E. Wright Drive, left on Ridgecrest Extended. **Standard Game Times:** 7:05 p.m.; Sun. (April-May) 2:05, (June-Sept.) 6:05.

Visiting Club Hotel: Garden Plaza Hotel, 1770 Hwy. 45 Bypass, Jackson, TN 38305. Telephone: (901) 664-6900.

TEXAS LEAGUE

Class AA

Mailing Address: 2442 Facet Oak, San Antonio, TX 78232. **Telephone:** (210) 545-5297. **FAX:** (210) 545-5298. **E-Mail Address:** tkayser@iamerica.net.

Years League Active: 1888-1890, 1892, 1895-1899, 1902-1942, 1946-.

President/Treasurer: Tom Kayser.

Vice President: Rick Parr (El Paso). **Corporate Secretary:** Monty Hoppel (Midland).

Directors: Bill Blackwell (Jackson), Chuck Lamson (Tulsa), Taylor Moore (Shreveport), Rick Parr (El Paso), Miles Prentice (Midland), Steve Shaad (Wichita), Bill Valentine (Arkansas), Burl Yarbrough (San Antonio).

Administrative Assistant: Bill Arrowood.

Tom Kayser

1999 Opening Date: April 8. **Closing Date:** Sept. 4.

Regular Season: 140 games (split schedule).

Division Structure: East—Arkansas, Jackson, Shreveport, Tulsa. **West**—El Paso, Midland, San Antonio, Wichita.

Playoff Format: First-half division champions play second-half division champions in best-of-5 series. Winners meet in best-of-7 series for league championship.

1999 All-Star Games: July 27 at Tulsa; July 14 at Mobile, AL (joint Double-A game).

Roster Limit: 23 active, until midnight Aug. 10 when roster can be expanded to 24. **Player Eligibility Rule:** No restrictions.

Brand of Baseball: Rawlings.

Statistician: Howe Sportsdata, Boston Fish Pier, West Bldg. #1, Suite 302, Boston, MA 02210.

Umpires: Ramon Armendariz (Oceanside, CA), Geoff Burr (San Diego, CA), Albert Guarnieri (Spring, TX), Chris Guccione (Salida, CO), Wes Hamilton (Edmond, OK), Scott Higgins (Keizer, OR), Michael Jost (Modesto, CA), Kevin Kelley (Huntington Beach, CA), Steve Mattingly (Phoenix, AZ), Jason Moore (San Bernardino, CA), Pat Riley (Gilbert, AZ), Matt Schaeffer (Clearwater, FL).

Stadium Information

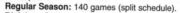
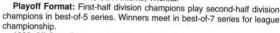

Club	Stadium	Dimensions LF	CF	RF	Capacity	'98 Att.
Arkansas	Ray Winder Field	330	390	345	6,083	190,987
El Paso	Cohen	340	410	340	9,700	296,609
Jackson	Smith-Wills	330	400	330	5,200	110,595
Midland	Christensen	333	398	333	5,000	190,076
San Antonio	Wolff Municipal	310	402	340	6,300	387,715
Shreveport	Fair Grounds Field	330	400	330	6,400	161,940
Tulsa	Drillers	335	390	340	10,955	345,097
Wichita	Lawrence-Dumont	344	401	312	6,109	155,353

Arkansas
TRAVELERS

Office Address: Ray Winder Field at War Memorial Park, Little Rock, AR 72205. Mailing Address: P.O. Box 55066, Little Rock, AR 72215. Telephone: (501) 664-1555. FAX: (501) 664-1834. E-Mail Address: travs@aristotle.net. Website: www.travs.com; www.travsfan.com.

Affiliation (first year): St. Louis Cardinals (1966). Years in League: 1966-.

Ownership, Management

Operated by: Arkansas Travelers Baseball, Inc.

President: Bert Parke.

Executive Vice President/General Manager: Bill Valentine. Assistant GM/Sales, Promotions: Hap Seliga. Assistant GM/Concessions, Merchandising: John Evans. Director, Stadium Operations: Brian Sands. Park Superintendent: Greg Johnston. Assistant Park Superintendent: Reggie Temple. Bookkeeper: Nena Valentine.

Field Staff

Manager: Chris Maloney. Coach: Glenn Brummer. Pitching Coach: Rich Folkers. Trainer: B.J. Maack.

Game Information

Radio Announcer: Bob Harrison. No. of Games Broadcast: Home-70. Flagship Station: KARN 920-AM.

PA Announcer: Bill Downs. Official Scorer: Mike Garrity.

Stadium Name (year opened): Ray Winder Field (1932). Location: I-630 to Fair Park Boulevard exit, go north from exit, turn right after zoo. Standard Game Time: 7:30 p.m., Sun 2.

Visiting Club Hotel: Little Rock Hilton, 925 South University, Little Rock, AR 72204. Telephone: (501) 664-5020.

El Paso
DIABLOS

Office Address: 9700 Gateway North Blvd., El Paso, TX 79924. Mailing Address: P.O. Drawer 4797, El Paso, TX 79914. Telephone: (915) 755-2000. FAX: (915) 757-0671. E-Mail Address: awheeler@elp.rr.com. Website: www.diablos.com.

Affiliation (first year): Arizona Diamondbacks (1999). Years in League: 1962-70, 1972-.

Ownership, Management

Operated by: Diamond Sports, Inc.

Principal Owners: Peter Gray, Bill Pereira.

President: Rick Parr. Vice President, General Manager: Andrew Wheeler. Vice President, Sales/Marketing: Ken Schrom. Controllers: Lee Ryan, Melissa Wachter. Director, Hispanic Marketing: Larry Romero. Director, Media/Community Relations: Rose Lucero. Account Representatives: Matt Hicks, Burke McKinney, Brett Pollock, Bernie Ricono, Kyle Smith. Ticket Manager: Mary Hill. Director, Group Sales: Cori Vasquez. Head Groundskeeper: Sergio Lopez. Office Manager: Heather Smith. Clubhouse Operations: Scott Donovan.

Field Staff

Manager: Don Wakamatsu. Coach: Ty Van Burkleo. Pitching Coach: Dennis Lewallyn. Trainer: Greg Barber.

Game Information

Radio Announcers: Matt Hicks, Brett Pollack (English); Miguel Flores, Juan Gonzalez (Spanish). No. of Games Broadcast: Home-70, Away-70. Flagship Station: KROD 600-AM (English), Radio Unica 1150-AM (Spanish).

PA Announcer: Unavailable. Official Scorer: Bernie Olivas.

Stadium Name (year opened): Cohen Stadium (1990). Location: I-10 to U.S. 54 (Patriot Freeway), east to Diana exit to Gateway North Boulevard. Standard Game Times: April-May 6:30 p.m., June-Aug. 7; Sun. 6:30.

Visiting Club Hotel: Quality Inn, 6201 Gateway Blvd. West, El Paso, TX 79925. Telephone: (915) 778-6611.

Jackson
GENERALS

Office Address: 1200 Lakeland Dr., Jackson, MS 39216. **Mailing Address:** P.O. Box 4209, Jackson, MS 39296. **Telephone:** (601) 981-4664. **FAX:** (601) 981-4669. **E-Mail Address:** generals@jacksongenerals.com. **Website:** www.jacksongenerals.com.

Affiliation (first year): Houston Astros (1991). **Years in League:** 1975-.

Ownership, Management

Operated by: Round Rock Baseball, Inc.

Principal Owners: Rich Hollander, Eddie Maloney, J. Con Maloney, Nolan Ryan, Reid Ryan, Don Sanders.

Chairman: Nolan Ryan. **President:** Reid Ryan. **Vice President/General Manager** (Round Rock, Texas): Jay Miller.

Vice President/General Manager (Jackson): Bill Blackwell. **Assistant GM:** Frank Buccieri. **Head Groundskeeper:** Joe Whipps. **Director, Media/Public Relations:** Ron Bartlett. **Director, Broadcasting/Sales:** Bill Walberg. **Director, Community Relations:** Rick Deaton. **Director, Group Sales/Operations:** Tim Attel. **Clubhouse Operations:** Hugh Staples, Pete Phillips. **Office Manager:** Judy Blackwell.

Field Staff

Manager: Jim Pankovits. **Coach:** Mark Bailey. **Pitching Coach:** Charley Taylor. **Trainer:** Nathan Lucero.

Game Information

Radio Announcer: Bill Walberg. **No. of Games Broadcast:** Home-70, Away-70. **Flagship Station:** WJDX 620-AM.

PA Announcer: Glen Waddle. **Official Scorer:** Unavailable.

Stadium Name (year opened): Smith-Wills Stadium (1975). **Location:** I-55 to Lakeland Drive East exit, ¼ mile on left at Cool Papa Bell Drive. **Standard Game Times:** 7 p.m.; Sun. (April-May) 2:30, (June-Sept.) 6.

Visiting Club Hotel: Red Roof Inn-Coliseum, 700 Larson St., Jackson, MS 39202. Telephone: (601) 969-5006.

Midland
ROCKHOUNDS

Office Address: 4300 N Lamesa Rd., Midland, TX 79705. **Mailing Address:** P.O. Box 51187, Midland, TX 79710. **Telephone:** (915) 683-4251. **FAX:** (915) 683-0994. **Website:** www.midlandrockhounds.org.

Affiliation (first year): Oakland Athletics (1999). **Years in League:** 1972-.

Ownership, Management

Operated by: Midland Sports, Inc.

Principal Owners: Miles Prentice, Bob Richmond.

President: Miles Prentice. **Executive Vice President:** Bob Richmond.

General Manager: Monty Hoppel. **Assistant General Manager:** Rick Carden. **Director, Broadcasting/Publications:** Bob Hards. **Director, Sales/Corporate Development:** Harold Fuller. **Director, Operations:** Jeff Von Holle. **Director, Business Operations:** Eloisa Robledo. **Director, Merchandising:** Ray Fieldhouse. **Director, Customer Service/Group Sales:** Ryan Haskell. **Director, Concessions:** Pat Kerin. **Sales/Marketing Representative:** Bill Levy. **Director, Community/Media Relations:** Jamie Richardson. **Assistant Director, Group Sales:** Scott Stringfield. **Administrative Assistant:** Ryan Lovell. **Clubhouse Attendant:** Joe Harrell. **Head Groundskeeper:** Lee Velarde.

Field Staff

Manager: Tony DeFrancesco. **Coach:** Webster Garrison. **Pitching Coach:** Glenn Abbott. **Trainer:** Brian Thorson.

Game Information

Radio Announcer: Bob Hards. **No. of Games Broadcast:** Home-70, Away-70. **Flagship Station:** KCRS 550-AM.

PA Announcer: Unavailable. **Official Scorer:** Bobby Dunn.

Stadium Name (year opened): Christensen Stadium (1952). **Location:** From I-20, north on Rankin Highway/Big Spring exit to Loop 250, exit right on Lamesa Road. **Standard Game Times:** 7:11 p.m.; Sun. 6.

Visiting Club Hotel: Holiday Inn Hotel and Suites, 4300 Hwy. 80, Midland, TX 79703. Telephone: (915) 697-3181.

San Antonio
MISSIONS

Office Address: 5757 Hwy. 90 W, San Antonio, TX 78227. **Telephone:** (210) 675-7275. **FAX:** (210) 670-0001. **E-Mail Address:** sainfo@21stcenturyacess.com. **Website:** www.samissions.com.

Affiliation (first year): Los Angeles Dodgers (1977). **Years In League:** 1888, 1892, 1895-99, 1907-42, 1946-64, 1967-.

Ownership, Management
Operated by: Elmore Sports Group.
Principal Owner: Dave Elmore. **President:** Burl Yarbrough.
General Manager: David Oldham. **Assistant General Manager:** Jimi Olsen. **Director, Business Operations:** Marc Frey. **Director, Stadium Operations:** Jeff Long. **Head Groundskeeper:** Mike Pankey. **Director, Public Relations:** Jim White. **Director, Sales/Marketing:** Tom Davis. **Account Representatives:** Mac Brown, Jason Davis, Albert Motz. **Director, Community Relations:** Eric VonLehmden. **Director, Ticket Sales:** Ben Rivers. **Director, Group Sales:** Jeff Windle. **Director, Merchandising:** Bill Gerlt. **Office Manager:** Delia Rodriguez.

Field Staff
Manager: Jimmy Johnson. **Coach:** John Shoemaker. **Pitching Coach:** Dean Treanor. **Trainer:** Jim Cranmer.

Game Information
Radio Announcer: Roy Acuff. **No. of Games Broadcast:** Home-70, Away-70. **Flagship Station:** KKYX 680-AM.
PA Announcer: Stan Kelly. **Official Scorer:** David Humphrey.
Stadium Name (year opened): Nelson W. Wolff Stadium (1994). **Location:** From I-10, I-35 or I-37, take U.S. 90 West to Callaghan Road exit, stadium is on right. **Standard Game Times:** 7:05 p.m., Sun. 6:05.
Visiting Club Hotel: Thrifty Inn, 9806 I-10 W, San Antonio, TX 78230. Telephone: (210) 696-0810.

Shreveport
CAPTAINS

Office Address: 2901 Pershing Blvd., Shreveport, LA 71109. **Mailing Address:** P.O. Box 3448, Shreveport, LA 71133. **Telephone:** (318) 636-5555. **FAX:** (318) 636-5670. **E-Mail Address:** shvcaps@iamerica.net. **Website:** www.shreveportcaptains.com.

Affiliation (first year): San Francisco Giants (1979). **Years in League:** 1895, 1908-10, 1915-32, 1938-42, 1946-57, 1968-.

Ownership, Management
Operated by: Shreveport Baseball, Inc.
Principal Owner/President: Taylor Moore.
General Manager: Daniel Robinson. **Assistant GM/Office Manager:** Terri Sipes. **Assistant GM/Sales, Marketing and Promotions:** Michael Beasley. **Director, Stadium Operations:** Steve Bange. **Head Groundskeeper:** Kenny Parr. **Director, Media/Public Relations:** Charlie Cavell. **Director, Merchandising/Ticket Sales:** Sheila Martin. **Director, Food Services:** Leroy Beasley. **Senior Account Representatives:** Roxy Dancy, Brian Dulin, Lisa Porter. **Clubhouse Operations:** J.J. Lewis.

Field Staff
Manager: Shane Turner. **Pitching Coach:** Ross Grimsley. **Trainer:** Donna Papangellin.

Game Information
Radio Announcer: Dave Nitz. **No. of Games Broadcast:** Home-70, Away-70. **Flagship Station:** KWKH 1130-AM.
PA Announcer: Charlie Cavell. **Official Scorer:** Jim Dawson.
Stadium Name (year opened): Fair Grounds Field (1986). **Location:** Hearne Avenue exit off I-20, turn left into Louisiana State Fairgrounds. **Standard Game Times:** April-May 7:05 p.m., June-Sept. 7:35; Sat. 7:35; Sun. 6:05.
Visiting Club Hotel: Shoney's Inn-Bossier City, 1836 Old Minden Rd., Bossier City, LA 71111. Telephone (318) 747-7700.

Tulsa
DRILLERS

Office Address: 4802 E 15th St., Tulsa, OK 74112. Mailing Address: P.O. Box 4448, Tulsa, OK 74159. Telephone: (918) 744-5998. FAX: (918) 747-3267. Website: www.tulsadrillers.com.

Affiliation (first year): Texas Rangers (1977). Years in League: 1933-42, 1946-65, 1977-.

Ownership, Management

Operated by: Tulsa Baseball, Inc.

Principal Owner/President: Went Hubbard.

Executive Vice President/General Manager: Chuck Lamson. Director, Sales/Marketing: Mike Melega. Bookkeeper: Cheryll Moore. Director, Public Relations: Brian Carroll. Director, Stadium Operations: Mark Hilliard. Head Groundskeeper: Gary Shepherd. Promotions Manager: Pam Mowery. Director, Ticket Sales: Debbie Jones. Group Sales Manager: Jeff Gladu. Assistant, Ticket Operations: Charles Bell. Merchandising Manager: Joe Benbow. Office Manager: Reba Bray.

Field Staff

Manager: Bobby Jones. Pitching Coach: Lee Tunnell. Trainer: Mike Quinn.

Game Information

Radio Announcer: Mark Neely. No. of Games Broadcast: Home-70, Away-70. Flagship Station: KQLL 1430-AM.

PA Announcer: Kirk McAnany. Official Scorers: Jeff Brucculeri, Bruce Howard.

Stadium Name (year opened): Drillers Stadium (1981). Location: Three miles north of I-44 and 1½ miles south of I-244 at 15th Street and Yale Avenue. Standard Game Times: 7:35 p.m.; Sun. (April-May) 2:05, (June-Aug.) 6:05.

Visiting Club Hotel: Best Western Tradewinds Central, 3141 E Skelly Dr., Tulsa, OK 74105. Telephone: (918) 749-5561.

Wichita
WRANGLERS

Office Address: 300 S Sycamore, Wichita, KS 67213. Mailing Address: P.O. Box 1420, Wichita, KS 67201. Telephone: (316) 267-3372. FAX: (316) 267-3382. E-Mail Address: wranglers@wichitawranglers.com. Website: www.wichitawranglers.com.

Affiliation (first year): Kansas City Royals (1995). Years in League: 1987-.

Ownership, Management

Operated by: Wichita Baseball, Inc. Principal Owner: Rich Products Corp.

Vice President: Steve Shaad. General Manager: Trevor Hinz. Assistant GM/Business: Chris Taylor. Assistant GM/Sales: Tim Lyons. Manager, Marketing: Kyle Richardson. Sales Coordinator: Angela Haar. Account Executive: Harry Centa. Director, Community Relations: Kristin Lynch. Business Manager: Chris Kloepping. Director, Operations: Shelly Robbins. Office Manager: Mary Luce. Director, Stadium Operations: Lance Deckinger. Coordinator, Stadium/Baseball Operations: Kevin Grimsley. Head Groundskeeper: Randy Welch.

Field Staff

Manager: John Mizerock. Coach: Phil Stephenson. Pitching Coach: Mike Mason. Trainer: John Finley.

Game Information

Radio Announcer: Dennis Higgins. No. of Games Broadcast: Home-70, Away-70. Flagship Station: KQAM 1480-AM.

PA Announcer: Unavailable. Official Scorer: Ted Woodward.

Stadium Name (year opened): Lawrence-Dumont Stadium (1934). Location: I-135 to Kellogg Avenue West, north on Broadway, west on Lewis. Standard Game Times: 7:15 p.m.; Tues. (May-August) 6:15; Sun. (April) 2:15, (May-August) 6:15.

Visiting Club Hotel: The Broadview, 400 W Douglas Ave., Wichita, KS 67201. Telephone: (316) 262-5000.

CALIFORNIALEAGUE

Class A Advanced

Office Address: 2380 S Bascom Ave., Suite 200, Campbell, CA 95008. **Telephone:** (408) 369-8038. **FAX:** (408) 369-1409. **E-Mail Address:** cabaseball@aol.com. **Website:** www.californialeague.com.

Years League Active: 1941-1942, 1946-.
President/Treasurer: Joe Gagliardi.
Vice President: Harry Stavrenos (San Jose). **Corporate Secretary:** Bill Weiss.
Directors: Bobby Brett (High Desert), Chris Chen (Modesto), Mike Ellis (Lancaster), Pat Patton (Bakersfield), Tom Seidler (Stockton), Harry Stavrenos (San Jose), Hank Stickney (Rancho Cucamonga), Ken Stickney (Lake Elsinore), Donna Tuttle (San Bernardino), Jim Wadley (Visalia).

Joe Gagliardi

League Administrator: Kathleen Kelly.
1999 Opening Date: April 8. **Closing Date:** Sept. 5.
Regular Season: 140 games (split schedule).
Division Structure: North—Bakersfield, Modesto, San Jose, Stockton, Visalia. **South**—High Desert, Lake Elsinore, Lancaster, Rancho Cucamonga, San Bernardino.
Playoff Format: Six teams. First-half champions in each division earn first-round bye; second-half champions meet wild card with next best overall record in best-of-3 quarterfinals. Winners meet first-half champions in best-of-5 semifinals. Winners meet in best-of-5 series for league championship.
All-Star Game: June 22 at Lake Elsinore (California League vs. Carolina League).
Roster Limit: 25 active. **Player Eligibility Rule:** No more than two players and one player-coach on active list may have more than six years experience.
Brand of Baseball: Rawlings ROM.
Statistician: Howe Sportsdata, Boston Fish Pier, West Bldg. #1, Suite 302, Boston MA 02210; P.O. Box 5061, San Mateo, CA 94402.
Umpires: Ryan Bleiberg (Simi Valley, CA), John Bullock (North Hollywood, CA), Steven Corvi (Peoria, AZ), Tyler Hoffman (Qualicum Beach, British Columbia), Alan Hoover (Tempe, AZ), Toby Hoy (Lomita, CA), Scott Letendre (Tempe, AZ), Ricardo Losoya (Salinas, CA), Cale Smith (Kirkland, WA), Ray Villeneuve (El Paso, TX).

Stadium Information

Club	Stadium	Dimensions LF	CF	RF	Capacity	'98 Att.
Bakersfield	Sam Lynn Ballpark	328	354	328	4,200	78,027
High Desert	Mavericks	340	401	340	3,808	151,245
Lake Elsinore	Lake Elsinore Diamond	330	400	310	7,866	287,005
Lancaster	Lancaster Municipal	350	410	350	4,500	238,173
Modesto	Thurman Field	312	400	319	4,000	135,620
R. Cucamonga	Epicenter	330	400	330	6,615	338,145
San Bernardino	The Ranch	330	410	330	5,000	223,219
San Jose	Municipal	320	400	320	4,200	141,180
Stockton	Billy Hebert Field	325	392	335	3,500	80,589
Visalia	Recreation Park	320	405	320	1,800	60,154

Bakersfield
BLAZE

Office Address: 4009 Chester Ave., Bakersfield, CA 93301. Mailing Address: P.O. Box 10031, Bakersfield, CA 93389. Telephone: (661) 322-1363. FAX: (661) 322-6199. E-Mail Address: blaze1@bakersfieldblaze.com. Website: www.bakersfieldblaze.com.

Affiliation: San Francisco Giants (1997). Years In League: 1941-42, 1946-75, 1978-79, 1982-.

Ownership, Management

Principal Owner/President: Pat Patton.

Vice President/General Manager: Jack Patton. Assistant General Managers: Dan Shanyfelt, Susan Wells. Director, Baseball Operations: Joe Foye. Director, Stadium Operations: Craig Noren. Head Groundskeeper: Leon Williams. Director, Community Relations: Paul Sheldon. Director, Promotions/Media Relations: Doug Brackett. Director, Special Projects: Cricket Whitaker. Clubhouse Operations: Mike Taylor. Office Manager: Seve Niron.

Field Staff

Manager: Keith Comstock. Coach: Mike Felder. Pitching Coach: Bert Bradley. Trainer: Mark Gruesbeck.

Game Information

Radio Announcers: Dale Parsons, Mark Roberts. No. of Games Broadcast: Home-70, Away-70. Flagship Station: KGEO 1230-AM.

PA Announcer: J.C. Meyerholz. Official Scorer: Tim Wheeler.

Stadium Name (year opened): Sam Lynn Ballpark (1941). Location: Highway 99 to California Avenue, east three miles to Chester Avenue, north two miles to stadium. Standard Game Time: 7:30 p.m.

Visiting Club Hotel: Travelodge Hotel, 818 Real Rd., Bakersfield, CA 93309. Telephone: (661) 324-6666.

High Desert
MAVERICKS

Office Address: 12000 Stadium Way, Adelanto, CA 92301. Telephone: (760) 246-6287. FAX: (760) 246-3197. E-Mail Address: mavsinfo@hdmavs.com. Website: www.hdmavs.com.

Affiliation (first year): Arizona Diamondbacks (1997). Years in League: 1991-.

Ownership, Management

Operated by: High Desert Mavericks, Inc.

Principal Owner: Bobby Brett.

Vice Presidents/General Managers: Mike Guarini, Pete Thuresson. Assistant GM, Operations: Mike Fleming. Assistant GM, Tickets: Rick Janac. Director, Broadcasting: Bryan Goldwater. Director, Public Relations: Jim Thornby. Director, Food Services: Chris Jones. Account Executive: Michael Pope. Ticket Sales Assistant: Doug Aiken. Office Manager: Kaye Allen. Head Groundskeeper: Tino Gonzales. Clubhouse Manager: Mike Weil.

Field Staff

Manager: Derek Bryant. Coach: Rick Schu. Pitching Coach: Mike Parrott. Trainer: Dale Gilbert.

Game Information

Radio Announcer: Bryan Goldwater. No. of Games Broadcast: Home-70, Away-70. Flagship Station: KROY 1590-AM.

PA Announcer: Art Hernandez. Official Scorer: Jim Erwin.

Stadium Name (year opened): Mavericks Stadium (1991). Location: I-15 North to Highway 395 to Adelanto Road. Standard Game Times: 7:05 p.m.; Sun. (April-May) 2:05, (June-Aug.) 5:05.

Visiting Club Hotel: Ramada Inn-Victorville, 15494 Palmdale Rd., Victorville, CA 92392 Telephone: (760) 245-6565.

Lake Elsinore
STORM

Office Address: 500 Diamond Dr., Lake Elsinore, CA 92530. **Mailing Address:** P.O. Box 535, Lake Elsinore, CA 92531. **Telephone:** (909) 245-4487. **FAX:** (909) 245-0305. **E-Mail Address:** lestorm@pe.net. **Website:** www.pe.net/storm.

Affiliation (first year): Anaheim Angels (1994). **Years in League:** 1994-.

Ownership, Management

Operated by: Mandalay Sports Entertainment.

Principal Owner: Ken Stickney. **Chairman:** Peter Guber.

President/General Manager: Kevin Haughian. **Vice President/Assistant General Manager:** Brent Boznanski. **VP, Sales/Marketing:** Darrin Gross. **Director, Ticket Operations:** Kristie Schmitt. **Director, Broadcasting:** Sean McCall. **Director, Business Administration:** Yvonne Hunneman. **Director, Community Relations:** Molly Stockwell. **Director, Media/Public Relations:** Mike Gazda. **Director, Merchandising:** Jennifer Bock. **Director, Operations/Special Events:** Matt DeMargel. **Corporate Marketing Manager:** Matt Allen. **Senior Accounts Manager:** David Jojola. **Accounts Managers:** Jon Brackett, Arin McCarthy. **Ticket Office Manager:** Brian Monsen. **Assistant Ticket Office Manager:** Tom Bougher. **Group Sales:** Trey Magnuson, Mary Stanley. **Office Administrator:** Jo Equila. **Head Groundskeeper:** Francisco Castaneda.

Field Staff

Manager: Mario Mendoza. **Coach:** John Orton. **Pitching Coach:** Kernan Ronan. **Trainer:** Geoff Hostetter.

Game Information

Radio Announcer: Sean McCall. **No. of Games Broadcast:** Home-70, Away-70. **Flagship Station:** KFRG 92.9-FM.

PA Announcer: Joe Martinez. **Official Scorers:** Dennis Bricker, Nelda Bricker.

Stadium Name (year opened): Lake Elsinore Diamond (1994). **Location:** From I-15, exit at Diamond Drive, west for one mile to stadium. **Standard Game Times:** 7:05 p.m.; Sun. 2:05.

Visiting Club Hotel: Lake Elsinore Resort and Casino, 20930 Malaga St., Lake Elsinore, CA 92530. Telephone: (909) 674-3101.

Lancaster
JETHAWKS

Office Address: 45116 Valley Central Way, Lancaster, CA 93536. **Telephone:** (661) 726-5400. **FAX:** (661) 726-5406. **E-Mail Address:** ljethawk@qnet.com. **Website:** www.jethawk.com.

Affiliation (first year): Seattle Mariners (1996). **Years in League:** 1996-.

Ownership, Management

Operated by: Clutch Play Baseball, LLC.

Chairman: Horn Chen. **President:** Mike Ellis.

Vice President/General Manager: Matt Ellis. **Assistant General Managers:** Shelly Poitras, Kevin Younkin. **Director, Finance:** Michele Ellis. **Director, Stadium Operations:** John Laferney. **Director, Ticket Sales:** Chris Hale. **Director, Merchandising:** Lori Mayle. **Director, Food Services:** Andrew Abaya. **Office Manager:** Angela Samuelson. **Head Groundskeeper:** Dave Pfatenhauer.

Field Staff

Manager: Darrin Garner. **Coach:** Dana Williams. **Pitching Coach:** Greg Harris. **Trainer:** Troy McIntosh.

Game Information

Radio Announcer: Dan Hubbard. **No. of Games Broadcast:** Home-70, Away-70. **Flagship Stations:** KUTY 1470-AM, KHJ 1380-AM.

PA Announcer: Larry Thornhill. **Official Scorer:** David Guenther.

Stadium Name (year opened): Lancaster Municipal Stadium (1996). **Location:** Highway 14 in Lancaster to Avenue I exit, west on Avenue I to Valley Central Way. **Standard Game Times:** 7:11 p.m.; Sun. (first half) 2, (second half) 5.

Visiting Club Hotel: Desert Inn, 44219 N Sierra Hwy., Lancaster, CA 93534. Telephone: (805) 942-0376.

Modesto
A's

Office Address: 601 Neece Dr., Modesto, CA 95351. **Mailing Address:** P.O. Box 883, Modesto, CA 95353. **Telephone:** (209) 572-4487. **FAX:** (209) 572-4490. **E-Mail Address:** modestoa@aol.com. **Website:** www.athletics.fanlink.com.

Affiliation (first year): Oakland Athletics (1975). **Years in League:** 1946-64, 1966-.

Ownership, Management
Operated by: Modesto A's Professional Baseball Club, Inc.
Principal Owner/President: Chris Chen.
Vice President, Business Development: Tim Marting.
Interim General Manager: John Katz. **Director, Food Services:** Alan Day. **Director, Broadcasting/Media Relations:** Adam Fox. **Director, Tickets/Group Sales:** Ryan Jamrog. **Administrative Assistant:** Sara Scheffler. **Head Groundskeeper:** Walter Woodley.

Field Staff
Manager: Bob Geren. **Coach:** Brian McArn. **Pitching Coach:** Rick Rodriguez. **Trainer:** Blake Bowers.

Game Information
Radio Announcer: Adam Fox. **No. of Games Broadcast:** Home-50, Away-50. **Flagship Station:** KANM 970-AM.
PA Announcer: Unavailable. **Official Scorer:** Unavailable.
Stadium Name (year opened): John Thurman Field (1952). **Location:** Highway 99 in Southwest Modesto to Tuolomne Boulevard exit, west on Tuolomne for one block to Neece Drive, left for ¼ mile to stadium. **Standard Game Times:** 7:05 p.m.; Sun. (April-June) 1:05, (July-Sept.) 5:05.
Visiting Club Hotel: Vagabond Inn, 1525 McHenry Ave., Modesto, CA 95350. Telephone: (209) 521-6340.

Rancho Cucamonga
QUAKES

Office Address: 8408 Rochester Ave., Rancho Cucamonga, CA 91730. **Mailing Address:** P.O. Box 4139, Rancho Cucamonga, CA 91729. **Telephone:** (909) 481-5000. **FAX:** (909) 481-5005. **E-Mail Address:** rcquakes@aol.com. **Website:** www.rcquakes.com.

Affiliation (first year): San Diego Padres (1993). **Years In League:** 1993-.

Ownership, Management
Operated by: Valley Baseball Inc.
President: Hank Stickney.
General Manager: Pat Filippone. **Assistant General Manager:** Gerry McKearney. **Vice President, Finance:** Jay Middleton. **Director, Broadcasting/Media Relations:** Rob Buska. **Director, Sales/Marketing:** Marlene Merrill. **Account Executive:** James Keyston. **Director, Community Relations:** Heather Williams. **Manager, Community Relations/Marketing:** Cindy Eritano. **Director, Ticket Sales:** Kelli Pickwith. **Director, Group Sales:** Rob Arnold. **Director, Ticket Office:** Andy Molina. **Head Groundskeeper:** Rex Whitney.

Field Staff
Manager: Tom LeVasseur. **Coach:** Unavailable. **Pitching Coach:** Darrel Akerfelds. **Trainer:** Lance Cacanindin.

Game Information
Radio Announcer: Rob Buska. **No. of Games Broadcast:** Home-70, Away-70. **Flagship Station:** KMSL 1510-AM.
PA Announcer: Unavailable. **Official Scorer:** Larry Kavanaugh.
Stadium Name (year opened): The Epicenter (1993). **Location:** I-10 to I-15 North, exit at Foothill Boulevard, left on Foothill, left on Rochester. **Standard Game Times:** 7:15 p.m.; Sun. (first half) 2:15, (second half) 6:15.
Visiting Club Hotel: Best Western-Heritage Inn, 8179 Spruce Ave., Rancho Cucamonga, CA 91730. Telephone: (909) 466-1111.

San Bernardino
STAMPEDE

Office Address: 280 South E St., San Bernardino, CA 92401. **Telephone:** (909) 888-9922. **FAX:** (909) 888-5251. **Website:** www.stampedebaseball.com.

Affiliation (first year): Los Angeles Dodgers (1995). **Years in League:** 1941, 1987-.

Ownership, Management
Operated by: Elmore Sports Group.
Principal Owners: David Elmore, Donna Tuttle.
President: Donna Tuttle.
General Manager: Todd Rahr. **Director, Sales/Marketing:** Paul Stiritz. **Controller:** Gayla Anhaeuser. **Director, Ticket Sales:** Matt Gorman. **Director, Group Sales:** Mike Brown. **Director, Food Services:** Ray Radeka. **Director, Stadium Operations:** Greg Cozzo. **Director, Media/Public Relations:** Jason Ratliff. **Director, Broadcasting:** Mike Saeger. **Director, Community Relations:** Eric Perez. **Director, Promotions:** Brian Rogers. **Director, Group Services:** Leslie Madril. **Director, Guest Services:** Dave Batyi. **Director, Special Projects:** Andy Chidester. **Concessions Manager:** Sherrye Ryan. **Head Groundskeeper:** Al Meyers.

Field Staff
Manager: Rick Burleson. **Coach:** Steve Yeager. **Pitching Coach:** Mark Brewer. **Trainer:** Jason Mahnke.

Game Information
Radio Announcer: Mike Saeger. **No. of Games Broadcast:** Home-70, Away-70. **Flagship Station:** Unavailable.
PA Announcer: J.J. Gould. **Official Scorer:** Unavailable.
Stadium Name (year opened): The Ranch (1996). **Location:** I-215 to San Bernardino, exit at Inland Center Drive, east to E Street. **Standard Game Times:** 7:05 p.m.; Sun. 2:05, 5:05.
Visiting Club Hotel: Radisson Hotel, 295 North E St., San Bernardino, CA 92401. Telephone: (909) 381-6181.

San Jose
GIANTS

Office Address: 588 E Alma Ave., San Jose, CA 95112. **Mailing Address:** P.O. Box 21727, San Jose, CA 95151. **Telephone:** (408) 297-1435. **FAX:** (408) 297-1453. **E-Mail Address:** sanjose_giants@mindspring.com. **Website:** www.sjgiants.com.

Affiliation (first year): San Francisco Giants (1988). **Years in League:** 1942, 1947-58, 1962-76, 1979-.

Ownership, Management
Operated by: Progress Sports Management.
Chairman: Richard Beahrs. **President:** Harry Stavrenos.
General Manager: Mark Wilson. **Assistant General Manager:** Steve Fields. **Director, Sales:** Linda Pereira. **Director, Public Relations:** Dave Moudry. **Stadium Operations:** Rick Tracy. **Clubhouse Operations:** Justin Weaver.

Field Staff
Manager: Lenn Sakata. **Pitching Coach:** Shawn Barton. **Trainer:** Richard Lembo.

Game Information
Radio Announcer: Unavailable. **No. of Games Broadcast:** Unavailable. **Flagship Station:** KSJS 90.5-FM.
PA Announcer: Jim Chapman. **Official Scorers:** John Pletsch, Brian Burkett.
Stadium Name (year opened): Municipal Stadium (1942). **Location:** From I-280, 10th Street exit to Alma, left on Alma, stadium on right. From US 101, Tully Road exit to Senter, right on Senter, left on Alma, stadium on left. **Standard Game Times:** 7 p.m.; Sat. 5; Sun. (April-June) 1, (July-Aug.) 5.
Visiting Club Hotel: Unavailable.

Stockton
PORTS

Office Address: Billy Hebert Field, Alpine and Sutter Streets, Stockton, CA 95204. **Mailing Address:** P.O. Box 8550, Stockton, CA 95208. **Telephone:** (209) 944-5943. **FAX:** (209) 463-4937. **E-Mail Address:** fans@stocktonports.com. **Website:** www.stocktonports.com.

Affiliation (first year): Milwaukee Brewers (1979). **Years in League:** 1941, 1946-72, 1978-.

Ownership, Management

Operated by: Top of the Third, Inc.
Principal Owners: Kevin O'Malley, Tom Seidler.
President: Tom Seidler.
General Manager: Dan Chapman. **Assistant General Manager:** Kevin O'Malley. **Director, Finance:** Jennifer Whiteley. **Director, Media/Public Relations:** Doug Greenwald. **Director, Community Relations/Group Sales:** Lena Urrutia. **Director, Food Services:** Mark Brilton. **Head Groundskeeper:** Joe Moreno. **Clubhouse Operations:** Greg Carpenter. **Office Manager:** Molly Rogers.

Field Staff

Manager: Bernie Moncallo. **Coach:** Carlos Ponce. **Pitching Coach:** Randy Kramer. **Trainer:** Jeff Paxson.

Game Information

Radio Announcer: Doug Greenwald. **No. of Games Broadcast:** Home-70, Away-70. **Flagship Station:** KWG 1230-AM.
PA Announcer: Unavailable. **Official Scorer:** Tim Ankorn.
Stadium Name (year opened): Billy Hebert Field (1927). **Location:** From I-5 North, take Pershing Street exit, right on Harding Way, left on California Street, right on Alpine Street, left on Alvarado into Oak Park, take first left, stadium on right. **Standard Game Times:** 7:05 p.m.; Sun. (first half) 2:05, (second half) 6:05.
Visiting Club Hotel: Best Western Stockton Inn, 4219 E Waterloo Rd., Stockton, CA 95215. Telephone: (209) 931-3131.

Visalia
OAKS

Office Address: 440 N Giddings Ave., Visalia, CA 93291. **Mailing Address:** P.O. Box 48, Visalia, CA 93279. **Telephone:** (559) 625-0480. **FAX:** (559) 739-7732. **E-Mail Address:** visoak@aol.com.

Affiliation: Oakland Athletics (1997). **Years in League:** 1946-62, 1968-75, 1977-.

Ownership, Management

Operated by: Home Run, LLC.
Principal Owner/President: Jim Wadley.
General Manager: Andrew Bettencourt. **Assistant General Manager:** Todd Doten. **Director, Media/Public Relations:** Harry Kargenian. **Director, Ticket Sales:** Kathy Elick. **Head Groundskeeper:** Darren Holt. **Clubhouse Operations:** Peter Thompson.

Field Staff

Manager: Juan Navarrete. **Coach:** Dave Joppie. **Pitching Coach:** Curt Young. **Trainer:** Jeremy Loew.

Game Information

Radio: None.
PA Announcer/Official Scorer: Harry Kargenian.
Stadium Name (year opened): Recreation Park (1946). **Location:** From Highway 99, take 198 East to Mooney Boulevard exit, left on Giddings Avenue. **Standard Game Times:** 7:05 p.m.; Sun. (April) 2:05, (May-Sept.) 6:05.
Visiting Club Hotel: Lamp Liter Inn, 3300 W Mineral King, Visalia, CA 93291. Telephone: (559) 732-4611.

CAROLINA LEAGUE

Class A Advanced

Office Address: 1806 Pembroke Rd., Greensboro, NC 27408. **Mailing Address:** P.O. Box 9503, Greensboro, NC 27429. **Telephone:** (336) 691-9030. **FAX:** (336) 691-9070. **E-Mail Address:** office@carolinaleague.com. **Website:** www.carolinaleague.com.

Years League Active: 1945-.

President/Treasurer: John Hopkins.

Vice Presidents: Kelvin Bowles (Salem), Calvin Falwell (Lynchburg). **Corporate Secretary:** Matt Minker (Wilmington).

Directors: Don Beaver (Winston-Salem), Kelvin Bowles (Salem), Calvin Falwell (Lynchburg), George Habel (Myrtle Beach), North Johnson (Kinston), Peter Kirk (Frederick), Matt Minker (Wilmington), Art Silber (Potomac).

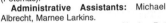

John Hopkins

Administrative Assistants: Michael Albrecht, Marnee Larkins.

1999 Opening Date: April 8. **Closing Date:** Sept. 5.

Regular Season: 140 games (split schedule).

Division Structure: Northern—Frederick, Lynchburg, Potomac, Wilmington. **Southern**—Kinston, Myrtle Beach, Salem, Winston-Salem.

Playoff Format: First-half division champions play second-half division champions in best-of-3 series. Winners meet in best-of-5 series for Mills Cup.

All-Star Game: June 22 at Lake Elsinore, CA (Carolina League vs. California League).

Roster Limit: 25 active. **Player Eligibility Rule:** No age limit. No more than two players and one player-coach on active list may have six or more years of prior minor league service.

Brand of Baseball: Rawlings.

Statistician: Howe Sportsdata, Boston Fish Pier, West Bldg. #1, Suite 302, Boston MA 02210.

Umpires: Damien Beal (Stone Mountain, GA), Peter Cicarelli (East Rutherford, NJ), Duston Dellinger (Mooresville, NC), Troy Fullwood (Hampton, VA), Jared Heeter (Blandford, MA), Adonis Hill (Newberry, SC), Eric MacMillan (Chester, NJ), Darren Spagnardi (Lexington, NC).

Stadium Information

Club	Stadium	Dimensions			Capacity	'98 Att.
		LF	CF	RF		
Frederick	Harry Grove	325	400	325	5,300	301,760
Kinston	Grainger	335	390	335	4,100	143,309
Lynchburg	City	325	390	325	4,000	113,145
Myrtle Beach#	Coastal Federal	325	405	325	5,000	—
Potomac*	Pfitzner	315	400	315	6,000	220,145
Salem	Salem Memorial	325	401	325	6,300	189,069
Wilmington	Frawley	325	400	325	5,900	320,540
Winston-Salem	Ernie Shore	325	400	325	6,280	159,460

Franchise operated in Danville, Va., in 1998
* Franchise known as Prince William in 1998

Frederick
KEYS

Office Address: 6201 New Design Rd., Frederick, MD 21703. Mailing Address: P.O. Box 3169, Frederick, MD 21705. Telephone: (301) 662-0013. FAX: (301) 662-0018. E-Mail Address: frekeys@aol.com. Website: www.frederickkeys.com.

Affiliation (first year): Baltimore Orioles (1989). Years In League: 1989-.

Ownership, Management
Operated by: Maryland Baseball, LP.

Principal Owners: John Daskalakis, Peter Kirk, Frank Perdue, Hugh Schindel, Pete Simmons.

Chairman: Peter Kirk. President: Pete Simmons.

General Manager: Joe Preseren. Assistant General Manager: Joe Pinto. Director, Stadium Operations: Dave Wisner. Director, Public Relations: Heather Clabaugh. Assistant Director, Public Relations: Hannah Brook. Director, Food Services: Mike Brulatour. Director, Marketing: Mark Zeigler. Account Executives: Shaun O'Neal, Warren Orey, Ernie Stepoulos, James Sweet. Director, Ticket Operations/Group Sales: Gina Stepoulos. Head Groundskeeper: Tommy Long.

Field Staff
Manager: Andy Etchebarren. Coach: Floyd Rayford. Pitching Coach: Larry Jaster. Trainer: Dave Walker.

Game Information
Radio Announcer: Bob Socci. No. of Games Broadcast: Home-70, Away-70. Flagship Station: WXTR 820-AM.

PA Announcer: Rick McCauslin. Official Scorers: Bryan Hissey, George Richardson.

Stadium Name (year opened): Harry Grove Stadium (1990). Location: From I-70, take exit 54 (Market Street), left at light. From I-270, take exit 31A for two miles, stadium on left. Standard Game Times: 7:05 p.m.; Sun. 1:05.

Visiting Club Hotel: Comfort Inn, 420 Prospect Blvd., Frederick, MD 21701. Telephone: (301) 695-6200.

Kinston
INDIANS

Office Address: 400 E Grainger Ave., Kinston, NC 28501. Mailing Address: P.O. Box 3542, Kinston, NC 28502. Telephone: (252) 527-9111. FAX: (252) 527-0498. E-mail Address: info@kinstonindians.com. Website: www.kinstonindians.com.

Affiliation (first year): Cleveland Indians (1987). Years in League: 1956-57, 1962-74, 1978-.

Ownership, Management
Operated by: Slugger Partners, LP.

Principal Owners: Cam McRae, North Johnson.

Chairman: Cam McRae. President/General Manager: North Johnson.

Assistant General Manager: John Purvis. Director, Group Sales: Joe Welch. Director, Food Services: Rita Spence. Head Groundskeeper: Tommy Walston. Clubhouse Operations: Robert Smeraldo. Office Manager: Shari Massengill.

Field Staff
Manager: Eric Wedge. Coach: Mike Sarbaugh. Pitching Coach: Dave Miller. Trainer: Teddy Blackwell.

Game Information
Radio Announcer: Josh Whetzel. No. of Games Broadcast: Home-70, Away-70. Flagship Station: WRNS 960-AM.

PA Announcer: Jeff Diamond. Official Scorers: Karl Grant, Keith Spence.

Stadium Name (year opened): Grainger Stadium (1949). Location: From west, take US 70 Business (Vernon Avenue), left on East Street; from east take US 70 W, right on Highway 58, right on Vernon Avenue, right on East Street. Standard Game Times: 7 p.m.; Sun. 2.

Visiting Club Hotel: Best Western, 208 E New Bern Rd., Kinston, NC 28501. Telephone: (252) 527-4155.

Lynchburg
HILLCATS

Office Address: City Stadium, 3180 Fort Ave., Lynchburg, VA 24501. **Mailing Address:** P.O. Box 10213, Lynchburg, VA 24506. **Telephone:** (804) 528-1144. **FAX:** (804) 846-0768. **E-Mail Address:** hillcatsbb@aol.com. **Website:** www.lynchburg-hillcats.com.

Affiliation (first year): Pittsburgh Pirates (1995). **Years in League:** 1966-.

Ownership, Management
Operated by: Lynchburg Baseball Corp.
President: Calvin Falwell.
General Manager: Paul Sunwall. **Assistant General Manager:** Ronnie Roberts. **Director, Sales/Field Supervisor:** Darren Johnson. **Director, Broadcasting:** Matt Provence. **Director, Group Sales:** Bill Papierniak. **Clubhouse Operations:** Chuck Watson, Lou Watson. **Office Manager:** Karen East.

Field Staff
Manager: Scott Little. **Coach:** Greg Briley. **Pitching Coach:** Jim Bibby. **Trainer:** Mark Schoen.

Game Information
Radio Announcer: Matt Provence. **No. of Games Broadcast:** Home-70, Away-70. **Flagship Station:** WBRG 1050-AM.
PA Announcers: David Glass, Chuck Young. **Official Scorers:** Malcolm Haley, Chuck Young.
Stadium Name (year opened): City Stadium (1940). **Location:** U.S. 29 South to City Stadium (exit 6); U.S. 29 North to Lynchburg College/City Stadium (exit 4). **Standard Game Times:** 7:05 p.m.; Sun. (April-May) 2:05, (June-Sept.) 6:05.
Visiting Club Hotel: Best Western, 2815 Candlers Mountain Rd., Lynchburg, VA 24502. Telephone: (804) 237-2986.

Myrtle Beach
PELICANS

Office Address: 1251 21st Ave. N, Myrtle Beach, SC 29577. **Telephone:** (843) 918-6000. **FAX:** (843) 946-6273. **Website:** www.myrtle-beachpelicans.com.

Affiliation (first year): Atlanta Braves (1999). **Years in League:** 1999-.

Ownership, Management
Operated by: Capitol Broadcasting, Inc.
Principal Owner: Jim Goodmon.
Vice President: George Habel.
General Manager: Steve Malliet. **Director, Business Operations:** Anne Frishmuth. **Controller:** Whit Neville. **Director, Media/Public Relations:** Bryan Dolgin. **Director, Sales/Marketing:** Matt Harris. **Account Representative:** Leann Rothrock. **Director, Client Relations:** Melissa McGrath. **Director, Promotions/Merchandising:** Dave Frost. **Director, Ticket Sales:** Gary Saunders. **Director, Group Sales:** Jennifer Violand. **Director, Food Services:** Peter Orth. **Box Office Manager:** Kyle Haden. **Head Groundskeeper:** Bill Butler. **Office Manager:** Ody Perez.

Field Staff
Manager: Brian Snitker. **Coach:** Dan Norman. **Pitching Coach:** Bruce Dal Canton. **Trainer:** Mike Graus.

Game Information
Radio Announcer: Garry Griffith. **No. of Games Broadcast:** Home-70; Away-70. **Flagship Station:** WRNN 94.5-FM.
PA Announcer: Unavailable. **Official Scorer:** Unavailable.
Stadium Name (year opened): Coastal Federal Field (1999). **Location:** Highway 17 bypass to 21st Avenue North, ½ mile to stadium.
Standard Game Times: 7 p.m.
Visiting Club Hotel: Hampton Inn, 4709 N Kings Hwy., Myrtle Beach, SC 29577. Telephone: (843) 449-5231.

Potomac
CANNONS

Office Address: 7 County Complex Ct., Woodbridge, VA 22192. **Mailing Address:** P.O. Box 2148, Woodbridge, VA 22193. **Telephone:** (703) 590-2311. **FAX:** (703) 590-5716. **E-Mail Address:** pwcannons@aol.com. **Website:** www.potomaccannons.com.

Affiliation (first year): St. Louis Cardinals (1997). **Years in League:** 1978-.

Ownership, Management

Operated by: Prince William Professional Baseball Club, Inc.

Principal Owner/President: Art Silber. **Chairman:** John Allen.

General Manager: Dean Sisco. **Assistant General Manager:** Max Baker. **Director, Business Operations:** Lani Silber. **Director, Media/ Public Relations:** Mike Antonellis. **Director, Sales:** Tron Kohlhagen. **Director, Public Affairs:** Rich Arnold. **Director, Marketing:** Rich Girardo. **Director, Ticket Sales:** Tim Phillips. **Director, Group Sales:** Andrew Stuebner. **Director, Food Services:** Brian Gordon. **Clubhouse Operations:** Billy Wardlow. **Head Groundskeeper:** Mike Lundy.

Field Staff

Manager: Joe Cunningham. **Coach:** Todd Steverson. **Pitching Coach:** Mark Grater. **Trainer:** Aaron Bruns.

Game Information

Radio Announcer: Unavailable. **No. of Games Broadcast:** Home-70; Away-70. **Flagship Station:** WAGE 1200-AM.

PA Announcer: Unavailable. **Official Scorers:** John Oravec, Dave Vincent.

Stadium Name (year opened): G. Richard Pfitzner Stadium (1984). **Location:** From I-95, take exit 158B and continue on Prince William Parkway for 5 miles, right into County Complex Court.

Standard Game Times: 7:30 p.m.; Sat. 7; Sun. (April-June) 1:30, (July-Sept.) 6.

Visiting Club Hotel: Days Inn Potomac Mills, 14619 Potomac Mills Rd., Woodbridge, VA 22192. Telephone: (703) 494-4433.

Salem
AVALANCHE

Office Address: 1004 Texas St., Salem, VA 24153. **Mailing Address:** P.O. Box 842, Salem, VA 24153. **Telephone:** (540) 389-3333. **FAX:** (540) 389-9710. **E-Mail Address:** info@salemavalanche.com. **Website:** www.salemavalanche.com.

Affiliation (first year): Colorado Rockies (1995). **Years In League:** 1968-.

Ownership, Management

Operated by: Salem Professional Baseball Club, Inc.

Principal Owner/President: Kelvin Bowles.

General Manager: Dave Oster. **Assistant GM, Sales and Marketing:** Christian Carlson. **Assistant GM, Stadium Operations:** Stan Macko. **Director, Finance:** Brian Bowles. **Director, Community Relations:** Tracy Beskid. **Director, Ticket Sales:** Mike Ranelli. **Director, Group Sales:** Kathy Mair. **Director, Merchandising:** Page Griffin. **Head Groundskeeper:** Mark Bragunier. **Clubhouse Operations:** Robbie Smith.

Field Staff

Manager: Ron Gideon. **Coaches:** Stu Cole, Javier Gonzalez. **Pitching Coach:** Bob McClure. **Trainer:** Travis Anderson.

Game Information

Radio Announcer: Bob McElligott. **No. of Games Broadcast:** Home-70, Away-70. **Flagship Station:** WGMN 1240-AM.

PA Announcer: Bruce Reynolds. **Official Scorer:** Brian Hoffman.

Stadium Name (year opened): Salem Memorial Baseball Stadium (1995). **Location:** I-81 to exit 141 (Route 419), follow signs to Salem Civic Center Complex. **Standard Game Times:** 7 p.m.; Sun. (April-June) 2, (July-Aug.) 6.

Visiting Club Hotel: Days Inn-Airport, 8118 Plantation Rd., Roanoke, VA 24019. Telephone: (540) 366-0341.

Wilmington
BLUE ROCKS

Office Address: 801 S Madison St., Wilmington, DE 19801. **Telephone:** (302) 888-2015. **FAX:** (302) 888-2032. **E-Mail Address:** bluerocks.com. **Website:** www.bluerocks.com.

Affiliation (first year): Kansas City Royals (1993). **Years in League:** 1993-.

Ownership, Management

Operated by: Wilmington Blue Rocks, LP.

President: Matt Minker.

General Manager: Chris Kemple. **Director, Finance:** Craig Bailey. **Director, Stadium Operations:** Andrew Layman. **Head Groundskeeper:** Steve Gold. **Director, Media Relations/Broadcasting:** Mark Nasser. **Director, Sales/Marketing:** Doug Stewart. **Assistant Director, Marketing:** Graham Munda. **Director, Community Relations:** Chris Parise. **Director, Publications/Promotions:** Jim Beck. **Director, Ticket Sales:** Marla Chalfie. **Director, Merchandising:** Paul Siegwarth. **Office Manager:** Michelle Hampson. **Ticket Office Manager:** Kevin Reiter. **Ticket Manager:** Jared Forma.

Field Staff

Manager: Jeff Garber. **Coach:** Steve Balboni. **Pitching Coach:** Steve Crawford. **Trainer:** Chad Spaulding.

Game Information

Radio Announcers: Steve Lenox, Mark Nasser. **No. of Games Broadcast:** Home-70, Away-70. **Flagship Station:** WJBR 1290-AM.

PA Announcer: John McAdams. **Official Scorers:** Mike Brint, E.J. Casey, Dick Shute.

Stadium Name (year opened): Judy Johnson Field at Daniel S. Frawley Stadium (1993). **Location:** I-95 North to Maryland Ave. (exit 6), right onto Maryland Ave., right on Read Street, right on South Madison Street to ballpark; I-95 South to Maryland Ave. (exit 6), left at Martin Luther King Blvd., right on South Madison Street. **Game Times:** 7:05 p.m.; Sat. (April-May) 2:05; Sun. 2:05.

Visiting Club Hotel: Quality Inn-Skyways, 147 N DuPont Hwy., New Castle, DE 19720. Telephone: (302) 328-6666.

Winston-Salem
WARTHOGS

Office Address: 401 Deacon Blvd., Winston-Salem, NC 27105. **Mailing Address:** P.O. Box 4488, Winston-Salem, NC 27115. **Telephone:** (336) 759-2233. **FAX:** (336) 759-2042. **E-Mail Address:** warthogs@warthogs.com. **Website:** www.warthogs.com.

Affiliation (first year): Chicago White Sox (1997). **Years in League:** 1945-.

Ownership, Management

Operated by: Beaver Sports, Inc.

Principal Owner/President: Don Beaver.

General Manager: Peter Fisch. **Assistant General Manager:** Mark Viniard. **Special Assistant to GM:** David Beal. **Director, Community Relations:** Melissa Copeland. **Director, Group Sales:** David Cross. **Head Groundskeeper:** Eddie Busque. **Office Manager:** Pamela Naylor.

Field Staff

Manager: Jerry Terrell. **Coach:** Gregg Ritchie. **Pitching Coach:** Juan Nieves. **Trainer:** Joe Geck.

Game Information

Radio Announcer: Unavailable. **No. of Games Broadcast:** Home-70, Away-70. **Flagship Station:** WIFM 100.9-FM.

PA Announcer: Unavailable. **Official Scorers:** Rodney Cline, Bobby Wood.

Stadium Name (year opened): Ernie Shore Field (1956). **Location:** I-40 Business to Cherry Street exit, north through downtown, right on Deacon Boulevard, park is on left. **Standard Game Times:** 7:15 p.m.; Sun. (April-May) 2:05 (June-Aug.) 6:05.

Visiting Club Hotel: Hawthorne Inn, 420 High St., Winston-Salem, NC 27101. Telephone: (336) 777-3000.

FLORIDA STATE LEAGUE

Class A Advanced

Street Address: 103 E Orange Ave., Daytona Beach, FL 32114. **Mailing Address:** P.O. Box 349, Daytona Beach, FL 32115. **Telephone:** (904) 252-7479. **FAX:** (904) 252-7495. **E-Mail Address:** bballleague@mindspring.com.

Years League Active: 1919-1927, 1936-1941, 1946-.

President/Treasurer: Chuck Murphy.

Vice Presidents: Ken Carson (Dunedin), Jordan Kobritz (Daytona).

Corporate Secretary: David Hood.

Directors: Sammy Arena (Tampa), Ken Carson (Dunedin), Andy Dunn (Brevard County), Tony Flores (St. Petersburg), Marvin Goldklang (Fort Myers), Grant Griesser (Vero Beach), Jim Herlihy (Charlotte), Ed Kenney (Sarasota), Jordan Kobritz (Daytona), Kurt Luttermoser

Chuck Murphy

(Lakeland), Jeff Maultsby (St. Lucie), Tim Purpura (Kissimmee), Rob Rabenecker (Jupiter), John Timberlake (Clearwater).

Office Secretary: Peggy Catigano.

1999 Opening Date: April 8. **Closing Date:** Sept. 5.

Regular Season: 140 games (split schedule).

Division Structure: East—Brevard County, Daytona, Jupiter, Kissimmee, St. Lucie, Vero Beach. **West**—Charlotte, Clearwater, Dunedin, Fort Myers, Lakeland, St. Petersburg, Sarasota, Tampa.

Playoff Format: First-half division champions play second-half champions in best-of-3 series. Winners meet in best-of-5 series for league championship.

All-Star Game: June 19 at Lakeland.

Roster Limit: 25. **Player Eligibility Rule:** No age limit. No more than two players and one player-coach on active list may have six or more years of prior minor league service.

Brand of Baseball: Rawlings.

Statistician: Howe Sportsdata, Boston Fish Pier, West Bldg. #1, Suite 302, Boston, MA 02210.

Umpires: Robert Bainter (Galesburg, IL), Frank Coffland (San Antonio, TX), Bradley Cole (Sioux City, IA), Dan Cricks (Casselberry, FL), David Glass (Atlanta, GA), William Jeffries (Queens Village, NY), Olindo Mattia (Port St. Lucie, FL), Stephen Metheny (Birmingham, AL), Scott Morgan (Rockledge, FL), Casey Moser (Iowa Park, TX), Brian Rayder (Morristown, NJ), David Riley (Indianapolis, IN), Chad Sexton (Mount Pleasant, MI), Scott Walendowski (East China, MI).

Stadium Information

Club	Stadium	Dimensions			Capacity	'98 Att.
		LF	CF	RF		
Brevard Cty.	Space Coast	340	404	340	8,100	107,546
Charlotte	Charlotte County	340	410	340	5,424	43,659
Clearwater	Jack Russell Memorial	340	400	340	6,917	73,300
Daytona	Jackie Robinson Ballpark	317	400	325	4,200	74,082
Dunedin	Dunedin	335	400	315	6,106	60,485
Fort Myers	Hammond	330	405	330	7,500	107,110
Jupiter	Roger Dean	335	400	325	6,871	94,155
Kissimmee	Osceola County	330	410	330	5,200	41,941
Lakeland	Joker Marchant	340	420	340	7,100	35,693
St. Lucie	Thomas J. White	338	410	336	7,500	37,189
St. Petersburg	Al Lang	330	410	330	7,004	87,181
Sarasota	Ed Smith	340	400	340	7,500	43,219
Tampa	Legends Field	318	408	314	10,386	110,341
Vero Beach	Holman	340	400	340	6,500	50,094

Brevard County
MANATEES

Office Address: 5800 Stadium Pkwy., Melbourne, FL 32940. Telephone: (407) 633-9200. FAX: (407) 633-9210. E-Mail Address: marlins@metrolink.net. Website: bcmanatees.com.

Affiliation (first year): Florida Marlins (1994). Years in League: 1994-.

Ownership, Management
Operated by: Florida Marlins, Brevard Operations.
Principal Owner: John Henry.
General Manager: Andy Dunn. Facility Engineer: Jack Haberthier. Head Groundskeeper: Doug Lopas. Coordinator, Media/Public Relations: Kristin Vandeventer. Coordinator, Sales/Marketing: Kim Hill. Ticket Manager: Trey Fraser. Office Manager: Lilya McAtee.

Field Staff
Manager: Dave Huppert. Coach: Juan Bustabad. Pitching Coach: Larry Pardo. Trainer: Mike McGowan.

Game Information
Radio: None.
PA Announcer: Unavailable. Official Scorer: Ron Jernick.
Stadium Name (year opened): Space Coast Stadium (1994). Location: I-95 North to Wickham Road (exit 73), left on Wickham, right on Lake Andrew Drive, right on Stadium Parkway; I-95 South to Fiske Boulevard (exit 74), left on Fiske, follow Fiske/Stadium Parkway. Standard Game Times: 7:05 p.m., Sun. 1:35.
Visiting Club Hotel: Melbourne Airport Hilton, 200 Rialto Pl., Melbourne, FL 32901. Telephone: (407) 768-0200.

Charlotte
RANGERS

Office Address: 2300 El Jobean Rd., Port Charlotte, FL 33948. Telephone: (941) 625-9500. FAX: (941) 624-5158. E-Mail Address: rangers@charlotterangers.com. Website: www.charlotterangers.com.

Affiliation (first year): Texas Rangers (1987). Years in League: 1987-.

Ownership, Management
Operated by: Texas Rangers Baseball Club, Ltd.
Principal Owner: Thomas Hicks. President: John McMichael.
General Manager: Jim Herlihy. Director, Sales/Marketing: Matt LaBranche. Director, Stadium Operations: Matt Becker. Director, Home Run Food Services: Jason Hise. Manager, Customer Service: Tina Buonaiuto. Director, Media Relations: Biff Hodgson. Director, Ticket Sales: Luke Nelson.

Field Staff
Manager: James Byrd. Coach: Vince Roman. Pitching Coach: Eli Grba. Trainer: Frank Velasquez.

Game Information
Radio: None.
PA Announcer: Unavailable. Official Scorer: Dave Tollett.
Stadium Name (year opened): Charlotte County Stadium (1987). Location: I-75 South to exit 32, follow Toledo Blade Blvd. west for seven miles to stop sign at SR 776, right on 776 for one mile. Standard Game Times: 6 p.m., Fri.-Sat. 7, Sun. 2.
Visiting Club Hotel: Days Inn-Murdock, 1941 Tamiami Trail, Murdock, FL 33948. Telephone: (941) 627-8900.

Clearwater
PHILLIES

Office Address: 800 Phillies Dr., Clearwater, FL 33755. Mailing Address: P.O. Box 10336, Clearwater, FL 33757. Telephone: (727) 441-8638. FAX: (727) 447-3924. Website: www.clearwaterphillies.com.

Affiliation (first year): Philadelphia Phillies (1985). Years in League: 1985-.

Ownership, Management

Operated by: The Philadelphia Phillies.

President: David Montgomery.

Director, Florida Operations: John Timberlake. Business Manager, Florida Operations: Dianne Gonzalez. Director, Merchandising: Kerri Leeman. General Manager: Lee McDaniel. Director, Sales: Dan McDonough. Director, Public Relations/Marketing: Andy Shenk. Stadium Operations Manager: Joe Cynar. Account Executive: Jason Adams. Office Manager: Dede Angelillis. Head Groundskeeper: Opie Cheek. Clubhouse Operations: Cliff Armbruster.

Field Staff

Manager: Bill Dancy. Coach: Tony Scott. Pitching Coach: Darold Knowles. Trainer: Clete Sigwart.

Game Information

Radio: None.

PA Announcer: Don Guckian. Official Scorer: Unavailable.

Stadium Name (year opened): Jack Russell Memorial Stadium (1955). Location: US 19 North to Drew Street, west to Greenwood Avenue, north to Seminole Street, right to park. Standard Game Times: 7 p.m., Sun. 5.

Visiting Club Hotel: Econo Lodge, 21252 US 19 North, Clearwater, FL 33765. Telephone: (727) 796-3165.

Daytona
CUBS

Office Address: 105 E Orange Ave., Daytona Beach, FL 32114. Mailing Address: P.O. Box 15080, Daytona Beach, FL 32115. Telephone: (904) 257-3172. FAX: (904) 257-3382.

Affiliation (first year): Chicago Cubs (1993). Years in League: 1920-24, 1928, 1936-41, 1946-73, 1977-87, 1993-.

Ownership, Management

Operated by: Florida Professional Sports, Inc.

Principal Owner/President: Jordan Kobritz.

General Manager: Debbie Berg. Administrative Assistant: Kim Davis.

Field Staff

Manager: Nate Oliver. Coach: Richie Zisk. Pitching Coach: Rick Tronerud. Trainer: Alan Morales.

Game Information

Radio: None.

PA Announcer: Unavailable. Official Scorer: Lyle Fox.

Stadium Name (year opened): Jackie Robinson Ballpark (1930). Location: From I-95, take International Speedway Boulevard exit (Route 92), east to Beach Street, south to Orange Avenue, east to ballpark; From A1A North/South, take Orange Avenue west to ballpark. Standard Game Times: 7 p.m.; Sun. 1.

Visiting Club Hotel: Howard Johnson Plaza/Harbour Beach Resort, 701 S Atlantic Ave., Daytona Beach, FL 32118. Telephone: (904) 258-8522.

Dunedin
BLUE JAYS

Office Address: Dunedin Stadium, 311 Douglas Ave., Dunedin, FL 34698. Mailing Address: P.O. Box 957, Dunedin, FL 34697. Telephone: (727) 733-9302. FAX: (727) 734-7661. Website: www.bluejays.ca/dunedin.com.

Affiliation (first year): Toronto Blue Jays (1987). Years in League: 1978-79, 1987-.

Ownership, Management

Operated by: Toronto Blue Jays.

Director, Florida Operations/General Manager: Ken Carson.

Assistant General Manager: Ed Vonnes. Head Groundskeeper: Steve Perry. Clubhouse Operations: Mickey McGee.

Field Staff

Manager: Rocket Wheeler. Coach: Dennis Holmberg. Pitching Coach: Scott Breeden. Trainer: Jay Inoy.

Game Information

Radio: None.
PA Announcer: Unavailable. **Official Scorer:** Larry Weiderecht.
Stadium Name (year opened): Dunedin Stadium (1990). **Location:** From I-275, north on Highway 19, left on Sunset Point Road for 4½ miles, right on Douglas Avenue, stadium is ½ mile on right. **Standard Game Times:** 7 p.m.; Sun. 5.
Visiting Club Hotel: Red Roof Inn, 32000 US Hwy. 19 N, Palm Harbor, FL 34684. Telephone: (727) 786-2529.

Fort Myers
MIRACLE

Office Address: 14400 Six Mile Cypress Pkwy., Fort Myers, FL 33912. **Telephone:** (941) 768-4210. **FAX:** (941) 768-4211. **E-Mail Address:** miracle@miraclebaseball.com. **Website:** www.miraclebaseball.com.
Affiliation: Minnesota Twins (1993). **Years in League:** 1978-87, 1992-.

Ownership, Management

Operated by: Greater Miami Baseball Club, LP.
Principal Owner: Marvin Goldklang. **President:** Mike Veeck.
General Manager: Derek Sharrer. **Assistant General Manager:** Dave Burke. **Director, Business Operations:** Suzanne Reaves. **Director, Sales/Marketing:** Linda McNabb. **Director, Media/Public Relations:** Rob Malec. **Director, Community Relations:** Lou Slack. **Director, Promotions/Group Sales:** Andrew Seymour. **Account Representatives:** Jody Clarke, Mike Combs, Kurt Schweizer. **Groundskeepers:** Terry Slausen, Scott Swenson, Chad Yoder.

Field Staff

Manager: Mike Boulanger. **Coach:** Jarvis Brown. **Pitching Coach:** Eric Rasmussen. **Trainer:** Larry Benesse.

Game Information

Radio Announcer: Rob Malec. **No. of Games Broadcast:** Home-70, Away-70. **Flagship Station:** WWCN 770-AM.
PA Announcer: Ted Fitzgeorge. **Official Scorer:** Benn Norton.
Stadium Name (year opened): William Hammond Stadium (1991). **Location:** Exit 21 off I-75, west on Daniels Parkway, left on Six Mile Cypress Parkway. **Standard Game Times:** 7:05 p.m.
Visiting Club Hotel: Wellesley Inn Suites, 4400 Ford St. Extension, Fort Myers, FL 33909. Telephone: (941) 278-3949.

Jupiter
HAMMERHEADS

Office Address: 4751 Main St., Jupiter, FL 33458. **Mailing Address:** P.O. Box 8929, Jupiter, FL 33468. **Telephone:** (561) 775-1818. **FAX:** (561) 691-6886. **Website:** www.rogerdeanstadium.com
Affiliation (first year): Montreal Expos (1969). **Years in League:** 1998-.

Ownership, Management

Operated by: Montreal Expos.
Chairman: Jacques Menard. **President:** Claude Brochu.
General Manager: Rob Rabenecker. **Executive Assistant to GM:** Carole Ray Dixon. **Director, Operations:** Todd Pund. **Director, Sales/Marketing:** Jennifer Chalhub. **Director, Ticket Sales:** Brian Barnes. **Director, Merchandising:** Ashley Brown. **Director, Food Services:** Mary Ann Sobota. **Office Manager:** Amie Helm.

Field Staff

Manager: Luis Dorante. **Coach:** Bert Heffernan. **Pitching Coach:** Ace Adams. **Trainer:** David Cohen.

Game Information

Radio: None.
PA Announcer: Dick Sanford. **Official Scorer:** Unavailable.
Stadium Name (year opened): Roger Dean Stadium (1998). **Location:** Exit 58 on I-95, east on Donald Ross Road for ¼ mile. **Standard Game Times:** 7:05 p.m., Sun. 2:05.
Visiting Club Hotel: Wellesley Inn, 34 Fisherman's Wharf, Jupiter, FL 33477. Telephone: (561) 575-7201.

Kissimmee
COBRAS

Office Address: 1000 Bill Beck Blvd., Kissimmee, FL 34744. Mailing Address: P.O. Box 422229, Kissimmee, FL 34742. Telephone: (407) 933-5500. FAX: (407) 847-6237.

Affiliation (first year): Houston Astros (1985). Years In League: 1985-.

Ownership, Management
Operated by: Houston Astros.
Chairman: Drayton McLane. President: Tal Smith.
General Manager: Jeff Kuenzli. Assistant General Manager: David Barnes. Head Groundskeeper: Rick Raasch. Director, Food Services: Jason Marsh. Office Manager: Olga Torres.

Field Staff
Manager: Manny Acta. Coach: Scott Makarewicz. Pitching Coach: Jack Billingham. Trainer: Terry Shoemaker.

Game Information
Radio: None.
PA Announcer: Norm Allen. Official Scorer: Greg Kaye.
Stadium Name (year opened): Osceola County Stadium (1985). Location: Florida Turnpike exit 244, west on US 192, right on Bill Beck Boulevard.; I-4 exit onto 192 East for 12 miles, stadium on left; 17-92 South to US 192, left for three miles. Standard Game Times: 7:05 p.m.; Sun. 2:05.
Visiting Club Hotel: Stadium Inn and Suites, 2039 E Irlo Bronson Hwy., Kissimmee, FL 34744. Telephone: (407) 846-7814.

Lakeland
TIGERS

Office Address: 2125 N Lake Ave., Lakeland, FL 33805. Mailing Address: P.O. Box 90187, Lakeland, FL 33804. Telephone: (941) 688-7911. FAX: (941) 688-9589. Website: www.lakeland-tigers.com.

Affiliation (first year): Detroit Tigers (1967). Years in League: 1919-26, 1953-55, 1960, 1962-64, 1967-.

Ownership, Management
Operated by: Detroit Tigers.
Principal Owner: Mike Ilitch. President: John McHale Jr.
General Manager: Kurt Luttermoser. Director, Sales/Media Relations: Zach Burek. Director, Marketing/Community Relations: Patti Sarano. Director, Group Sales: Rob Fredericks. Director, Merchandising/Concessions: Kay LaLonde. Clubhouse Operations: Dan Price. Director, Tiger Town Cafeteria: Roosevelt Clay.

Field Staff
Manager: Mark Meleski. Coach: Tim Torricelli. Pitching Coach: Joe Georger. Trainer: Matt Rankin.

Game Information
Radio: None.
PA Announcer: Wayne Koehler. Official Scorer: Sandy Shaw.
Stadium Name (year opened): Joker Marchant Stadium (1966). Location: Exit 19 on I-4 to Lakeland Hills Blvd., left 1½ miles. Standard Game Times: 7 p.m.; Sun. 1.
Visiting Club Hotel: Wellesley Inn, 3520 U.S. Hwy. 98 N, Lakeland, FL 33805. Telephone: (941) 859-3399.

St. Lucie
METS

Office Address: 525 NW Peacock Blvd., Port St. Lucie, FL 34986. Telephone: (561) 871-2100. FAX: (561) 878-9802. E-Mail Address: slmets@gate.net.

Affiliation (first year): New York Mets (1988). Years in League: 1988-.

Ownership, Management
Operated by: Sterling/Doubleday Enterprises, LP.
Chairman: Nelson Doubleday. **President:** Fred Wilpon.
General Manager: Jeff Maultsby. **Assistant General Manager:** Rob Croll. **Director, Media/Public Relations:** George McClelland. **Director, Ticket Sales:** Grace Benway. **Office Manager:** JoAnne Colenzo. **Administrative Assistants:** Ben Eversole, Ari Skalet.

Field Staff
Manager: Howie Freiling. **Coaches:** Edgar Alfonzo, Gary Ward. **Pitching Coach:** Buzz Capra. **Trainer:** Billy Wagner.

Game Information
Radio Announcer: Paul DeCastro. **No. of Games Broadcast:** Unavailable. **Flagship Station:** WPSL 1590-AM.
PA Announcer: Mike James. **Official Scorer:** George McClelland.
Stadium Name (year opened): Thomas J. White Stadium (1988). **Location:** Exit 63C (St. Lucie West Boulevard) off I-95, east ½ mile, left on NW Peacock Boulevard. **Standard Game Times:** 7 p.m., Sun. 2.
Visiting Club Hotels: Holiday Inn, 10120 S Federal Hwy., Port St. Lucie, FL 34952. Telephone: (561) 337-2200; Springhill Suites, 2000 NW Courtyard Cir., Port St. Lucie, FL 34986. Telephone: (561) 871-2929.

St. Petersburg
DEVIL RAYS

Office Address: 180 Second Ave. SE, St. Petersburg, FL 33701. **Mailing Address:** P.O. Box 12557, St. Petersburg, FL 33733. **Telephone:** (727) 822-3384. **FAX:** (727) 895-1556. **E-Mail Address:** rays@stpetedevilrays.com. **Website:** stpetedevilrays.com.
Affiliation (first year): Tampa Bay Devil Rays (1997). **Years In League:** 1920-27, 1955-.

Ownership, Management
Operated by: Tampa Bay Devil Rays.
President: Vince Naimoli.
General Manager: Tony Flores. **Assistant General Manager:** Steve Cohen. **Director, Stadium Operations:** Adrian Moore. **Director, Sales/Marketing:** Matt Wolcott. **Director, Community Relations:** Jake Birch. **Head Groundskeeper:** Rand Stollmack.

Field Staff
Manager: Roy Silver. **Coach:** Julio Garcia. **Pitching Coach:** Bryan Kelly. **Trainer:** Mike Libby.

Game Information
Radio: None.
PA Announcer: Jarrod Wronski. **Official Scorer:** Geoffrey Vandal.
Stadium Name (year opened): Florida Power Park/Al Lang Field (1977). **Location:** I-275 to exit 9, left on First Street South to Second Avenue South, stadium is on right. **Standard Game Times:** 7:05 p.m., Sun. 5.
Visiting Club Hotel: Best Western Mirage, 5005 34th St. N, St. Petersburg, FL 33701. Telephone: (727) 525-1181.

Sarasota
RED SOX

Office Address: 2700 12th St., Sarasota, FL 34237. **Mailing Address:** P.O. Box 2816, Sarasota, FL 34230. **Telephone:** (941) 365-4460 ext. 230. **FAX:** (941) 365-4217.
Affiliation (first year): Boston Red Sox (1994). **Years in League:** 1927, 1961-65, 1989-.

Ownership, Management
Operated by: Red Sox of Florida, Inc.
Principal Owner: Boston Red Sox.
General Manager: Fred Seymour Jr.

Field Staff
Manager: Butch Hobson. **Coach:** Unavailable. **Pitching Coach:** Dave Tomlin. **Trainer:** Scott Haglund.

Game Information
Radio: None.

PA Announcer: Unavailable. **Official Scorer:** Walter Jacobus.

Stadium Name (year opened): Ed Smith Stadium (1989). **Location:** I-75 to exit 39, three miles west to Tuttle Avenue, right on Tuttle ½ mile to 12th Street, stadium on left. **Standard Game Times:** 7 p.m., Sun. 5.

Visiting Club Hotel: Wellesley Inn, 1803 N. Tamiami Trail, Sarasota, FL 34234. Telephone: (941) 366-5128.

Tampa
YANKEES

Office Address: One Steinbrenner Dr., Tampa, FL 33614. **Telephone:** (813) 875-7753. **FAX:** (813) 673-3174. **E-Mail Address:** tyank1@aol.com.

Affiliation (first year): New York Yankees (1994). **Years in League:** 1919-27, 1957-1988, 1994-.

Ownership, Management
Operated by: New York Yankees, LP.

Principal Owner: George Steinbrenner.

General Manager: Sam Arena. **Assistant General Manager:** Eddie Robinson III. **Director, Sales/Marketing:** Heath Hardin. **Director, Ticket Sales:** Vance Smith. **Head Groundskeeper:** Gary Lackey.

Field Staff
Manager: Tom Nieto. **Coach:** Derek Shelton. **Pitching Coach:** Rich Monteleone. **Trainer:** Russell Orr.

Game Information
Radio: None.

PA Announcer: Unavailable. **Official Scorer:** J.J. Pizzio.

Stadium Name (year opened): Legends Field (1996). **Location:** I-275 to Martin Luther King, west on Martin Luther King to Dale Mabry. **Standard Game Times:** 7 p.m., Sun. 1.

Visiting Club Hotel: Holiday Inn Express, 4732 N Dale Mabry, Tampa, FL 33614. Telephone: (813) 877-6061.

Vero Beach
DODGERS

Office Address: 4101 26th St., Vero Beach, FL 32960. **Mailing Address:** P.O. Box 2887, Vero Beach, FL 32961. **Telephone:** (561) 569-4900, ext. 305. **FAX:** (561) 567-0819. **Website:** www.vero.com/dodgers.

Affiliation (first year): Los Angeles Dodgers (1980). **Years in League:** 1980-.

Ownership, Management
Operated by: Los Angeles Dodgers, Inc.

President: Bob Graziano.

General Manager: Grant Griesser. **Assistant General Manager:** Nicole Turner. **Head Groundskeeper:** John Yencho. **Director, Ticket Sales:** Louise Boissy. **Director, Merchandising:** Cathy Bond. **Director, Food Services:** Bruce Callahan. **Clubhouse Operations:** Mike Parrish. **Secretary:** Joann Lane.

Field Staff
Manager: Alvaro Espinoza. **Coach:** Jon Debus. **Pitching Coach:** Jim Stoeckel. **Trainer:** Homer Zulaica.

Game Information
Radio Announcer: Unavailable. **No. of Games Broadcast:** Home-70, Away-70. **Flagship Station:** WAXE 1370-AM.

PA Announcer: Unavailable. **Official Scorer:** Randy Phillips.

Stadium Name (year opened): Holman Stadium (1953). **Location:** Exit I-95 to Route 60 East, left on 43rd Avenue, right on Aviation Boulevard. **Standard Game Times:** 7 p.m.; Sun. 2.

Visiting Club Hotel: Vero Beach Inn, 4700 North A1A, Vero Beach, FL 32963. Telephone: (561) 231-1600.

MIDWESTLEAGUE

Class A

Office Address: 1118 Cranston Rd., Beloit, WI 53511. **Mailing Address:** P.O. Box 936, Beloit, WI 53512. **Telephone:** (608) 364-1188. **FAX:** (608) 364-1913. **E-Mail Address:** midwest@inwave.com. **Website:** www.minorleaguebaseball.com/leagues/midwest.

Years League Active: 1947-.
President/Treasurer: George Spelius.
Vice President: Ed Larson. **Legal Counsel/Secretary:** Richard Nussbaum.

Directors: Lew Chamberlin (West Michigan), George Chaney (Clinton), William Collins III (Michigan), Dennis Conerton (Beloit), Tom Dickson (Lansing), Kevin Doyle (Wisconsin), Kevin Krause (Quad City), Wally Krouse (Cedar Rapids), Alan Levin (South Bend), Eric Margenau (Fort Wayne), Mark McGuire (Rockford), Rocky Vonachen (Peoria), Dave Walker (Burlington), Mike Woleben (Kane County).

George Spelius

League Administrator: Stephanie Gray.
1999 Opening Date: April 8. **Closing Date:** Sept. 6.
Regular Season: 140 games (split schedule).
Division Structure: Eastern—Fort Wayne, Lansing, Michigan, South Bend, West Michigan. **Central**—Beloit, Kane County, Peoria, Rockford, Wisconsin. **Western**—Burlington, Cedar Rapids, Clinton, Quad City.
Playoff Format: Eight teams qualify. First-half and second-half division champions, and two wild-card teams, meet in best-of-3 quarterfinal series. Winners advance to best-of-3 semifinals. Winners advance to best-of-5 final for league championship.
All-Star Game: June 22 at Lansing.
Roster Limit: 25 active. **Player Eligibility Rule:** No age limit. No more than two players and one player-coach on active list may have more than five years experience.
Brand of Baseball: Rawlings ROM-MID.
Statistician: Howe Sportsdata, Boston Fish Pier, West Bldg. #1, Suite 302, Boston MA 02210.
Umpires: Paul Chandler (Silverdale, WA), Stephen Cox (Tulsa, OK), Atsushi Daito (Osaka, Japan), Brock Davidson (Great Bend, KS), David Falkavage (Stevens Point, WI), Bryce Fielder (Swisher, IA), Chris Hubler (Dysart, IA), Mark Mauro (San Mateo, CA), Trey Nelson (Lincoln, NE), Daniel Payne (San Jose, CA), Anthony Prater (Portland, OR), Travis Reininger (Brighton, CO), Bill Van Raaphorst (El Cajon, CA), Ryan West (Arvada, CO).

Stadium Information

Club	Stadium	Dimensions			Capacity	'98 Att.
		LF	CF	RF		
Beloit	Pohlman Field	325	380	325	3,501	61,108
Burlington	Community Field	338	403	315	3,502	60,492
Cedar Rapids	Veterans Memorial	325	385	325	6,000	128,742
Clinton	Riverview	335	390	325	2,500	44,401
Fort Wayne	Memorial	330	400	330	6,516	214,702
Kane County	Philip B. Elfstrom	335	400	335	5,900	481,352
Lansing	Oldsmobile Park	305	412	305	11,000	485,815
Michigan	C.O. Brown	323	401	336	6,600	107,137
Peoria	Pete Vonachen	335	383	335	5,200	154,910
Quad City	John O'Donnell	340	390	340	5,200	153,886
Rockford	Marinelli Field	335	405	335	4,500	75,600
South Bend	Coveleski Regional	336	410	336	5,000	196,793
West Michigan	Old Kent Park	327	402	327	10,900	500,083
Wisconsin	Fox Cities	325	405	325	5,500	227,306

Beloit
SNAPPERS

Office Address: 2301 Skyline Dr., Beloit, WI 53511. **Mailing Address:** P.O. Box 855, Beloit, WI 53512. **Telephone:** (608) 362-2272. **FAX:** (608) 362-0418. **Website:** www.snappersbaseball.com.

Affiliation (first year): Milwaukee Brewers (1982). **Years in League:** 1982-.

Ownership, Management
Operated by: Beloit Professional Baseball Association, Inc.
Chairman: Dennis Conerton. **President:** Marcy Olsen.
General Manager: Dave Endress. **Director, Merchandising:** Paul Arens. **Account Executives:** Jared Parcell, Bob Preston, Brian Wright. **Head Groundskeeper:** Jim Haun.

Field Staff
Manager: Don Money. **Coach:** John Mallee. **Pitching Coach:** Todd Frohwirth. **Trainer:** Keith Sayers.

Game Information
Radio: Unavailable.
PA Announcer: Al Fagerli. **Official Scorer:** Steve Clark.
Stadium Name (year opened): Pohlman Field (1982). **Location:** I-90 to exit 185-A, right at Cranston Road for 1½ miles. **Standard Game Times:** 7 p.m.; Sat. 6; Sun. 2.
Visiting Club Hotel: Unavailable.

Burlington
BEES

Office Address: 2712 Mt. Pleasant St., Burlington, IA 52601. **Mailing Address:** P.O. Box 824, Burlington, IA 52601. **Telephone:** (319) 754-5705. **FAX:** (319) 754-5882. **E-Mail Address:** burlbees@lisco.net. **Website:** www.burlbees.com.

Affiliation (first year): Chicago White Sox (1999). **Years In League:** 1962-.

Ownership, Management
Operated by: Burlington Baseball Association, Inc.
President: David Walker.
General Manager: Dan Vaughan. **Assistant General Manager:** Cliff Wiley. **Director, Business Operations:** Bryan Goodall. **Director, Stadium Operations:** Chuck Cannon. **Director, Media/Public Relations:** Randy Wehofer. **Director, Sales/Marketing:** Brenna Goetz.

Field Staff
Manager: Nick Capra. **Coach:** Daryl Boston. **Pitching Coach:** J.R. Perdew. **Trainer:** Unavailable.

Game Information
Radio Announcers: Dan Vaughn, Randy Wehofer. **No. of Games Broadcast:** Home-70, Away-70. **Flagship Station:** KBUR 1490-AM.
PA Announcer: Unavailable. **Official Scorer:** Scott Logas.
Stadium Name (year opened): Community Field (1973). **Location:** From US 34, take US 61 North to Mt. Pleasant Street, east ⅛ mile. **Standard Game Times:** 7:05 p.m.; Sat. (April-May) 6:05; Sun. (April-May) 2:05, (June-Sept.) 6:05.
Visiting Club Hotel: Best Western-Pzazz, 3001 Winegard Dr., Burlington, IA 52601. Telephone: (319) 753-2223.

Cedar Rapids
KERNELS

Office Address: 950 Rockford Rd. SW, Cedar Rapids, IA 52404. **Mailing Address:** P.O. Box 2001, Cedar Rapids, IA 52406. **Telephone:** (319) 363-3887. **FAX:** (319) 363-5631. **E-Mail Address:** kernels@kernels.com. **Website:** www.kernels.com.

Affiliation (first year): Anaheim Angels (1993). **Years in League:** 1962-.

Ownership, Management

Operated by: Cedar Rapids Baseball Club, Inc.
President: Wally Krouse.
General Manager: Jack Roeder. **Assistant General Manager:** Blake Porter. **Director, Community Relations/Gameday Operations:** Kelly Davis. **Director, Broadcasting:** John Rodgers. **Head Groundskeeper:** Bud Curran. **Office Manager:** Nancy Cram. **Clubhouse Operations:** Ron Plein. **Director, Food Services:** John Bateman. **Administrative Assistants:** Al Stacy, Kyle Tadman.

Field Staff

Manager: Mitch Seoane. **Coach:** Tyrone Boykin. **Pitching Coach:** Greg Minton. **Trainer:** Adam Nevela.

Game Information

Radio Announcer: John Rodgers. **No. of Games Broadcast:** Home-70, Away-70. **Flagship Station:** KCRG 1600-AM.
PA Announcer: Dale Brodt. **Official Scorer:** Andy Pantini.
Stadium Name (year opened): Veterans Memorial Stadium (1949). **Location:** I-380 to Wilson Ave. exit, west to Rockford Road, right one mile to corner of 8th Ave. and 15th Street SW. **Standard Game Times:** 7 p.m.; Sun. 2.
Visiting Club Hotels: Best Western Village Inn, 100 F Ave. NW, Cedar Rapids, IA 52405. Telephone (319) 366-5323.

Clinton
LUMBERKINGS

Office Address: Riverview Stadium, Sixth Avenue N and First Avenue, Clinton, IA 52732. **Mailing Address:** P.O. Box 1295, Clinton, IA 52733. **Telephone:** (319) 242-0727. **FAX:** (319) 242-1433. **E-Mail:** lkings@clinton.net. **Website:** www.clinton.net/~lkings.
Affiliation (first year): Cincinnati Reds (1999). **Years in League:** 1956-.

Ownership, Management

Operated by: Clinton Baseball Club, Inc.
Chairman: Don Roode. **President:** George Chaney.
General Manager: Ted Tornow. **Assistant General Manager:** Ben Giancola. **Administrative Assistant:** Leigh Shebeck.

Field Staff

Manager: Freddie Benavides. **Pitching Coach:** Andre Rabouin. **Trainer:** Unavailable.

Game Information

Radio Announcer: Mark Weaver. **No. of Games Broadcast:** Home-70, Away-70. **Flagship Station:** KROS 1340-AM.
PA Announcer: Unavailable. **Official Scorer:** Unavailable.
Stadium Name (year opened): Riverview Stadium (1937). **Location:** Highway 30 East to Sixth Avenue North, right on Sixth, cross railroad tracks, stadium on right. **Standard Game Times:** 6:30 p.m.; Sat. 7; Sun. 2.
Visiting Club Hotel: Ramada Inn, 1522 Lincoln Way, Clinton, IA 52732. Telephone: (319) 243-8841.

Fort Wayne
WIZARDS

Office Address: 4000 Parnell Ave., Fort Wayne, IN 46805. **Telephone:** (219) 482-6400. **FAX:** (219) 471-4678. **E-Mail Address:** info@wizards-baseball.com. **Website:** www.wizardsbaseball.com.
Affiliation (first year): San Diego Padres (1999). **Years in League:** 1993-.

Ownership, Management

Operated by: United Sports Ventures, Inc.
President: Eric Margenau.
General Manager: Bret Staehling. **Assistant General Manager:** Vince Saul. **Director, Business Operations:** Jeff Hyde. **Director, Merchandising:** Vince Slack. **Director, Broadcasting/Media Relations:** Alan Garrett. **Director, Group Sales:** Scott Brumfiel. **Assistant, Marketing:** Ryan Schoener. **Office Manager:** Nancy Murphy. **Assistants, Ticket Sales:** Daniel Hynes, Kyle Musser, Chris Watson, Daniel Wright.

Assistants, Media Relations: Justin Luna, Doug Milliken. **Clubhouse Operations:** Eli Rice.

Field Staff

Manager: Dan Simonds. **Coach:** Eric Bullock. **Pitching Coach:** Tony Phillips. **Trainer:** Brian Komprood.

Game Information

Radio Announcers: Alan Garrett, Kent Hormann. **No. of Games Broadcast:** Home-70, Away-70. **Flagship Station:** WHWD 1380-AM.

PA Announcer: Unavailable. **Official Scorers:** Mark Lazzer, Rich Tavierne.

Stadium Name (year opened): Memorial Stadium (1993). **Location:** Exit 112A (Coldwater Road) off I-69 to Coliseum Boulevard, left on Coliseum to stadium. **Standard Game Times:** 7 p.m., (April-May) 6:30; Sun. 2.

Visiting Club Hotel: Unavailable.

Kane County
COUGARS

Office Address: 34W002 Cherry Ln., Geneva, IL 60134. **Telephone:** (630) 232-8811. **FAX:** (630) 232-8815. **E-Mail Address:** kcougars@aol.com. **Website:** www.kccougars.com.

Affiliation (first year): Florida Marlins (1993). **Years In League:** 1991-.

Ownership, Management

Operated by: Cougars Baseball Partners/American Sports Enterprises, Inc.

President: Al Gordon. **Vice Presidents:** Mike Murtaugh, Mike Woleben. **Chief Financial Officer:** Glenn Yeager.

General Manager: Jeff Sedivy. **Assistant General Manager:** Curtis Haug. **Business Manager:** Mary Almlie. **Director, Media Relations/ Advertising:** Marty Cusack. **Director, Promotions:** Jeff Ney. **Personnel Manager:** Patti Savage. **Coordinators, Group Sales:** Amy Mason, Sue Schlinger. **Coordinator, Season Tickets:** Jennifer Plesa. **Ticket Office/Donations:** Lara Wroblewski. **Assistant Business Manager:** Doug Czurylo. **Account Executives:** Bill Baker, Brad Bober, Greg Heinrichs, John Knechtges, Ed Morgan, Kevin Sullivan, Mike Thibodeau, George Wendel. **Facilities Management:** Mike Fik, Mike Kurns. **Director, Concessions:** Rich Essegian. **Head Groundskeeper:** Pat Skunda.

Field Staff

Manager: Rick Renteria. **Coach:** Matt Winters. **Pitching Coach:** Rick Mahler. **Trainer:** Mike Leon.

Game Information

Radio Announcer: Scott Franzke. **No. of Games Broadcast:** Home-70, Away-70. **Flagship Station:** WKKD 95.9-FM.

PA Announcer: Kevin Sullivan. **Official Scorer:** Marty Cusack.

Stadium Name (year opened): Philip B. Elfstrom Stadium (1991). **Location:** From east or west, I-88 (East-West Tollway) to Farnsworth Road North exit, 5 miles north to Cherry Lane; from north, Route 59 South to Route 64 (North Avenue), west to Kirk Road, south past Route 38 to Cherry Lane; from northwest, I-90 to Randall Road South exit, south to Fabyan Parkway, east to Kirk Road, north to Cherry Lane. **Standard Game Times:** 7 p.m., Sat. 6, Sun. 2.

Visiting Club Hotel: Travelodge, 1617 Naperville Rd., Naperville, IL 60563. Telephone: (630) 505-0200.

Lansing
LUGNUTS

Office Address: 505 E Michigan Ave., Lansing MI 48912. **Telephone:** (517) 485-4500. **FAX:** (517) 485-4518. **E-Mail Address:** lugnuts@tcimet.net. **Web-site:** www.lansinglugnuts.com.

Affiliation (first year): Chicago Cubs (1999). **Years In League:** 1996-.

Ownership, Management

Operated by: Take Me Out to the Ballgame, LLC.

Principal Owner/President: Tom Dickson.

General Manager: Tom Glick. **Assistant GM, Operations:** Greg Rauch. **Director, Operations:** Rich Zizek. **Head Groundskeeper:** Tom Preslar.

Director, Season Ticket Sales/Service: Tom Murphy. Corporate Sales Manager: Kim Chilingirian-Glenn. Director, Marketing: Linda Frederickson. Director, Customer Service/Public Relations: Darla Bowen. Director, Finance/Human Resources: Kimberly Hengesbach. Front Office Administrator: Jennifer Burigana. Sponsorship Account Executive: Elizabeth Panich. Ticket Manager: Jenny Frasco. Group Sales Representatives: Eric Millett, Charles Pattison, Joe Pfeiffer. Assistant Stadium Manager: Jeremy Knuckman. Sponsorship Service Manager: Megan Frazer. Assistant Retail Manager: Melissa VanBuren. Box Office Supervisor: Christopher Troub. Marketing Coordinator: David Prout. Marketing Assistant: Michael Batka.

Field Staff

Manager: Oscar Acosta. Coach: Steve MacFarland. Pitching Coach: Stan Kyles. Trainer: Chris Heitz.

Game Information

Radio Announcer: Jeff Walker. No. of Games Broadcast: Home-70, Away-70. Flagship Station: WJIM 1240-AM.

PA Announcer: Unavailable. Official Scorer: Mike Clark.

Stadium Name (year opened): Oldsmobile Park (1996). Location: I-96 East/West to US 496, exit at Larch Street. Standard Game Times: 7:05 p.m.; April 6:05; Sun. (May-July) 2:05, (August-Sept.) 6:05.

Visiting Club Hotel: Holiday Inn South, 6820 S Cedar St., Lansing, MI 48911. Telephone: (517) 694-8123.

Michigan
BATTLE CATS

Office Address: 1392 Capital Ave. NE, Battle Creek, MI 49017. Telephone: (616) 660-2287. FAX: (616) 660-2288. E-Mail Address: battlecats@juno.com.

Affiliation (first year): Houston Astros (1999). Years in League: 1995-.

Ownership, Management

Operated by: American Baseball Capital II, Inc.

Principal Owner/Chairman: William Collins III. President: William Collins Jr.

General Manager: Jerry Burkot. Assistant General Manager: Kim Godek. Controller: T.J. Egan. Director, Stadium Operations/Head Groundskeeper: Len Matthews. Assistant Head Groundskeeper: Willis Vaughn. Director, Corporate Sales: Neil Himelhoch. Director, Ticket/Group Sales: Barney Storrs. Director, Merchandising/Office Manager: Missy VandenHeuvel. Clubhouse Operations: Kyle Lewis.

Field Staff

Manager: Al Pedrique. Coach: Sid Holland. Pitching Coach: Bill Ballou. Trainer: Ted Robbins.

Game Information

Radio Announcers: Ken Ervin, Terry Newton. No. of Games Broadcast: Home-70; Away-70. Flagship Station: WBCK 930-AM.

PA Announcer: Roy LaFountain. Official Scorer: Robin Hartman.

Stadium Name (year opened): C.O. Brown Stadium (1990). Location: I-94 to exit 98B (downtown), to Capital Avenue and continue five miles east to stadium. Standard Game Times: 7 p.m., (April-May) 6:30; Sat (April-May) 2; Sun. 2.

Visiting Club Hotel: Battle Creek Inn, 5050 Beckley Rd., Battle Creek, MI 49015. Telephone: (616) 979-1100.

Peoria
CHIEFS

Office Address: 1524 W Nebraska Ave., Peoria, IL 61604. Telephone: (309) 688-1622. FAX: (309) 686-4516. E-Mail Address: peochfs@aol.com. Website: www.chiefsnet.com.

Affiliation (first year): St. Louis Cardinals (1995). Years in League: 1983-.

Ownership, Management

Operated by: Peoria Chiefs Community Baseball Club, LLC.

Chairman: Pete Vonachen.

President/General Manager: Rocky Vonachen. **Vice President/Senior Account Executive:** Ralph Rashid. **Assistant GM, Marketing/Promotions:** Michael Baird. **Assistant GM, Operations:** Mark Vonachen. **Director, Broadcasting/Media Relations:** Ed Beach. **Director, Ticket Sales:** John Beintema. **Manager, Group Sales:** Jennifer Blackorby. **Group Sales Representatives:** Kevin Dietz, Greg Gormong. **Head Groundskeeper:** Ryan Middleton. **Office Manager:** Barbara Lindberg. **Receptionist:** Karen Patterson. **Game Day Ticket Operations:** Jay McCormick.

Field Staff
Manager: Brian Rupp. **Coach:** Tony Diggs. **Pitching Coach:** Mike Snyder. **Trainer:** Drew McCarthy.

Game Information
Radio Announcer: Ed Beach. **No. of Games Broadcast:** Home-70, Away-70. **Flagship Station:** WBGE 92.3-FM.

PA Announcer: Unavailable. **Official Scorer:** Kevin Capie.

Stadium Name (year opened): Pete Vonachen Stadium (1984). **Location:** I-74 to exit 91B (University Street North), left on Nebraska Avenue, left to ballpark. **Standard Game Times:** 7 p.m., (April-May) 6:30; Sun. 2.

Visiting Club Hotel: Holiday Inn City Centre, 500 Hamilton Blvd., Peoria, IL 61602. Telephone: (309) 674-2500.

Quad City
RIVER BANDITS

Office Address: 209 S Gaines St., Davenport, IA 52802. **Mailing Address:** P.O. Box 3496, Davenport, IA 52808. **Telephone:** (319) 324-2032. **FAX:** (319) 324-3109. **Website:** www.riverbandits.com.

Affiliation (first year): Minnesota Twins (1999). **Years in League:** 1960-.

Ownership, Management
Operated by: Seventh Inning Stretch, LLC.

Principal Owner/President: Kevin Krause.

General Manager: Tim Bawmann. **Assistant GM, Sales:** Heath Brown. **Assistant GM, Marketing:** Nick Willey. **Director, Media/Public Relations:** Sara Veldhuizen. **Director, Broadcasting:** Cory Dann. **Director, Group Sales:** Grant Dunmire. **Group Sales Assistant:** Brad Lott. **Director, Concessions:** Brian Eggers. **Office Manager:** Shelley Wheeler.

Field Staff
Manager: Jose Marzan. **Coach:** Riccardo Ingram. **Pitching Coach:** David Perez. **Trainer:** Chad Floyd.

Game Information
Radio Announcer: Cory Dann. **No. of Games Broadcast:** Home-70, Away-70. **Flagship Station:** Unavailable.

PA Announcer: Unavailable. **Official Scorer:** Unavailable.

Stadium Name (year opened): John O'Donnell Stadium (1939). **Location:** From I-74, south on SR 61 to corner of South Gaines Street and River Drive; From I-80, take Brady exit to River Drive, right on South Gaines. **Standard Game Times:** 7 p.m., (April) 6; Sun. (April-May) 2, (June-Sept.) 5.

Visiting Club Hotel: Plaza One, Third Ave. and 17th St., Rock Island, IL 61201. Telephone: (309) 794-1212.

Rockford
REDS

Office Address: 101 15th Ave., Rockford, IL 61104. **Telephone:** (815) 962-2827. **FAX:** (815) 961-2002.

Affiliation (first year): Cincinnati Reds (1999). **Years in League:** 1988-.

Ownership, Management
Operated by: Chicago National League Ball Club, Inc.

President: Mark McGuire.

General Manager: Bruce Keiter. **Director, Stadium Operations:** Craig Girling. **Director, Ticket Sales:** David Costello. **Director, Concessions/Retail:** Sarah Skridla. **Director, Game Day Operations:** Brent Wheeler. **Director, Corporate Sales:** Rob Bolton.

Field Staff

Manager: Mike Rojas. **Pitching Coach:** Derek Botelho. **Trainer:** Unavailable.

Game Information

Radio: None.

PA Announcer: Rob Bolton. **Official Scorer:** Dave Shultz.

Stadium Name (year opened): Marinelli Field (1988). **Location:** I-90 West to US 20 West to Main Street (Highway 2), north on Main Street to 15th Avenue. **Standard Game Times:** 7 p.m., (April-May) 6; Sat. (April-May) 2, (June-Sept.) 6; Sun. 2.

Visiting Club Hotel: Howard Johnson, 3909 11th St., Rockford, IL 61109. Telephone: (815) 397-9000.

South Bend
SILVER HAWKS

Office Address: 501 W South St., South Bend, IN 46601. **Mailing Address:** P.O. Box 4218, South Bend, IN 46634. **Telephone:** (219) 235-9988. **FAX:** (219) 235-9950. **E-Mail Address:** hawks@silverhawks.com. **Website:** www.silverhawks.com.

Affiliation (first year): Arizona Diamondbacks (1997). **Years in League:** 1988-.

Ownership, Management

Operated by: Palisades Baseball, Ltd.

Principal Owner: Alan Levin. **Vice President:** Erik Haag.

General Manager: Mike Foss. **Assistant General Manager:** Jon Zeitz. **Director, Finance:** Andy Zmudzinski. **Assistant Director, Finance:** Rene Mitzelfelt. **Director, Broadcasting/Media Relations:** Mike Carver. **Director, Stadium Operations:** Matt Adamsky. **Director, Promotions:** Paul Flindall. **Director, Group Sales:** Mark Gordon. **Group Sales Associate:** Deb Petersen. **Director, Concessions:** Craig Hyatt. **Community Relations Assistant:** Andrea Chlebek. **Office Manager:** Eric Kazmierzak. **Head Groundskeeper:** Joel Reinebold.

Field Staff

Manager: Mike Brumley. **Coaches:** Vic Ramirez, Jim Reinebold. **Pitching Coach:** Dave Jorn. **Trainer:** Colin Foye.

Game Information

Radio: Unavailable.

PA Announcer: Unavailable. **Official Scorer:** Unavailable.

Stadium Name (year opened): Stanley Coveleski Regional Stadium (1988). **Location:** I-80/90 toll road to exit 77, take US 31/33 south to South Bend, to downtown (Main Street), to Western Avenue, right on Western, left on Taylor. **Standard Game Times:** 7 p.m.; Sat. (April-May) 2; Sun. 2.

Visiting Club Hotel: Ramada Inn, 52890 US 31/33 N, South Bend, IN 46637. Telephone: (219) 272-5220.

West Michigan
WHITECAPS

Office Address: 4500 W River Dr., Comstock Park, MI 49321. **Mailing Address:** P.O. Box 428, Comstock Park, MI 49321. **Telephone:** (616) 784-4131. **FAX:** (616) 784-4911. **E-Mail Address:** playball@whitecaps-baseball.com. **Website:** www.whitecaps-baseball.com.

Affiliation (first year): Detroit Tigers (1997). **Years in League:** 1994-.

Ownership, Management

Operated by: Whitecaps Professional Baseball Corp.

Principal Owners: Dennis Baxter, Lew Chamberlin.

President: Dennis Baxter. **Vice President, Managing Partner:** Lew Chamberlin.

General Manager: Scott Lane. **Director, Baseball Operations:** Jim Jarecki. **Director, Sales:** John Guthrie. **Director, Group Sales:** Greg Hill. **Manager, Media Relations/Merchandising:** Lori Clark. **Manager, Gameday Operations:** Matt Costello. **Ticket Manager:** Bruce Radley. **Ticket Office Assistant:** Diana Marker. **Manager, Concessions:** Eddie Sypniewski. **Account Executive/Operations Assistant:** Dan Morrison. **Manager, Facility Maintenance:** Joe Eimer. **Promotions/Sales Assis-**

tant: Kari Rinkeviczie. **Coordinator, Human Resources:** Ellen Chamberlin. **Corporate Accountant:** Dean Haverdink. **Receptionist:** Trina Sicard.

Field Staff
Manager: Bruce Fields. **Coach:** Gary Green. **Pitching Coach:** Joe Boever. **Trainer:** Bryan Goike.

Game Information
Radio Announcers: Rick Berkey, Rob Sanford. **No. of Games Broadcast:** Home-70, Away-70. **Flagship Station:** WOOD 1300-AM.

PA Announcer: Bob Wells. **Official Scorers:** Mike Dean, Don Thomas.

Stadium Name (year opened): Old Kent Park (1994). **Location:** US 131 North from Grand Rapids to exit 91 (West River Drive). **Standard Game Times:** 7 p.m., (April-May) 6:35; Sat. (April-May) 2; Sun. 2.

Visiting Club Hotel: Days Inn-Downtown, 310 Pearl St. NW, Grand Rapids, MI 49504. Telephone: (616) 235-7611.

Wisconsin
TIMBER RATTLERS
TIMBER Rattlers

Office Address: 2400 N Casaloma Dr., Appleton, WI 54915. **Mailing Address:** P.O. Box 464, Appleton, WI 54912. **Telephone:** (920) 733-4152. **FAX:** (920) 733-8032. **E-Mail Address:** rattlers@dataex.com. **Website:** www.timberrattlers.com.

Affiliation (first year): Seattle Mariners (1993). **Years in League:** 1962-.

Ownership, Management
Operated by: Appleton Baseball Club, Inc.

President: Kevin Doyle.

Executive Vice President/Chief Executive Officer: Larry Trucco. **Assistant General Manager:** Gary Mayse. **Director, Business Operations:** Cathy Spanbauer. **Director, Marketing:** Gary Radke. **Account Representative:** Ryan Mangan. **Director, Ticket Sales:** Tim Okonek. **Director, Group Sales:** Kevin Hill. **Assistants, Group Sales:** Aaron Osborne, Rob Zerjau. **Director, Merchandising:** Keith Michlig. **Office Manager:** Mary Robinson. **Groundskeepers:** Josh Hagman, Greg Hofer.

Field Staff
Manager: Steve Roadcap. **Coach:** Omer Munoz. **Pitching Coach:** Steve Peck. **Trainer:** Jeff Carr.

Game Information
Radio Announcers: Unavailable. **No. of Games Broadcast:** Home-70, Away-70. **Flagship Station:** Unavailable.

PA Announcer: Unavailable. **Official Scorer:** Unavailable.

Stadium Name (year opened): Fox Cities Stadium (1995). **Location:** Highway 41 to Wisconsin Avenue exit, west to Casaloma Drive, right on Casaloma, stadium ½ mile on right. **Standard Game Times:** 7 p.m., (April-May) 6:30; Sun. 1, 7.

Visiting Club Hotel: Unavailable.

SOUTH**ATLANTIC**LEAGUE

Class A

Office Address: 504 Crescent Hill, Kings Mountain, NC 28086. **Mailing Address:** P.O. Box 38, Kings Mountain, NC 28086. **Telephone:** (704) 739-3466. **FAX:** (704) 739-1974. **E-Mail Address:** sal@shelby.net. **Website:** www.southatlanticleague.com.

Years League Active: 1948-1952, 1960-.

President/Secretary-Treasurer: John Moss.

Vice Presidents: Winston Blenckstone (Hagerstown), Ron McKee (Asheville).

Directors: Don Beaver (Hickory), Winston Blenckstone (Hagerstown), Chuck Boggs (Charleston, W.Va.), Rob Cohen (Capital City), William Collins III (Greensboro), Marv Goldklang (Charleston, S.C.), Larry Hedrick (Piedmont), Ron McKee (Asheville), Chip Moore (Macon), Martha Morrow (Columbus),

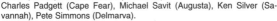

John Moss

Charles Padgett (Cape Fear), Michael Savit (Augusta), Ken Silver (Savannah), Pete Simmons (Delmarva).

Administrative Assistant: Elaine Moss. **Assistant to the President:** Bryan Olson.

1999 Opening Date: April 8. **Closing Date:** Sept. 6.

Regular Season: 142 games (split schedule).

Division Structure: Central—Asheville, Capital City, Charleston, SC, Greensboro, Hickory, Piedmont. **Northern**—Cape Fear, Charleston, WV, Delmarva, Hagerstown. **Southern**—Augusta, Columbus, Macon, Savannah.

Playoff Format: Eight teams qualify. First-half and second-half division champions, and two wild-card teams, meet in best-of-3 quarterfinal series. Winners advance to best-of-3 semifinal series. Winners advance to best-of-3 series for league championship.

All-Star Game: June 22 at Salisbury, MD.

Roster Limit: 25 active. **Player Eligibility Rule:** No age limit. No more than two players and one player-coach on active list may have more than five years of experience.

Brand of Baseball: Rawlings.

Statistician: Howe Sportsdata, Boston Fish Pier, West Bldg. #1, Suite 302, Boston, MA 02210.

Umpires: Michael Cheek (Columbus, GA), Greg Chittenden (Springfield, MO), Chad Fairchild (Bradenton, FL), Craig Funaro (East Haven, CT), Kris Green (York, PA), Brian Hale (Trussville, AL), Scott Kennedy (Frankfort, KY), Bryon Martin (Henderson, KY), Todd Parker (Hugo, OK), Brian Phillips (West Palm Beach, FL), Troy Penrod (Salem, OR), Ed Rogers (Thomson, GA), Butch Trent (Frederick, MD), Darin Williams (Beebe, AR).

Stadium Information

Club	Stadium	LF	CF	RF	Capacity	'98 Att.
Asheville	McCormick Field	328	402	300	4,000	148,638
Augusta	Lake Olmstead	330	400	330	4,322	162,509
Cape Fear	J.P. Riddle	330	405	330	4,000	75,799
Capital City	Capital City	330	395	320	6,000	141,138
Charleston, SC	Riley Ballpark	306	386	336	5,800	234,840
Charleston, WV	Watt Powell Park	340	406	330	5,400	91,219
Columbus	Golden Park	330	415	330	5,000	94,241
Delmarva	Perdue	309	402	309	5,200	295,938
Greensboro	War Memorial	327	401	327	7,500	160,465
Hagerstown	Municipal	335	400	330	4,600	109,932
Hickory	L.P. Frans	330	401	330	5,062	193,258
Macon	Luther Williams	338	402	338	4,000	120,009
Piedmont	Fieldcrest Cannon	330	400	310	4,700	125,653
Savannah	Grayson	290	400	310	8,000	130,509

Dimensions

Asheville
TOURISTS

Office Address: McCormick Field, 30 Buchanan Pl., Asheville, NC 28801. Mailing Address: P.O. Box 1556, Asheville, NC 28802. Telephone: (828) 258-0428. FAX: (828) 258-0320. E-Mail Address: touristsbb@mind spring.com.

Affiliation (first year): Colorado Rockies (1994). Years in League: 1976-.

Ownership, Management
Operated by: Tourists Baseball, Inc.
Principal Owners: Peter Kern, Ron McKee.
President: Peter Kern.
General Manager: Ron McKee. Assistant General Managers: Dave Meyer, Chris Smith. Director, Business Operations: Carolyn McKee. Director, Tickets/Merchandising: Margarita Turner. Director, Stadium Operations: Larry Hawkins. Head Groundskeeper: Grady Gardner.

Field Staff
Manager: Jim Eppard. Coach: Billy White. Pitching Coach: Jack Lamabe. Trainer: Paul Evans.

Game Information
Radio: None.
PA Announcer: Sam Zurich. Official Scorers: Wilt Browning, Mike Gore.
Stadium Name (year opened): McCormick Field (1992). Location: I-240 to Charlotte Street South exit, south one mile on Charlotte, left on McCormick Place. Standard Game Times: 7 p.m., Sun. 2.
Visiting Club Hotel: Days Inn, 199 Tunnel Rd., Asheville, NC 28805. Telephone: (828) 254-4311.

Augusta
GREENJACKETS

Office Address: 78 Milledge Rd., Augusta, GA 30904. Mailing Address: P.O. Box 3746, Augusta, GA 30904. Telephone: (706) 736-7889. FAX: (706) 736-1122. Website: www.greenjackets.com.

Affiliation (first year): Boston Red Sox (1999). Years in League: 1988-.

Ownership, Management
Operated by: H.W.S. Baseball, LLC.
Principal Owners: Michael Savit, Jeffrey Savit.
President: Michael Savit.
General Manager: Chris Scheuer. Assistant General Manager: Scott Skadan. Director, Business Operations: Nancy Crowe. Director, Stadium Operations: Tony DaSilveira. Head Groundskeeper: John Packer. Director, Ticket Sales: David Van Lenten.

Field Staff
Manager: Billy Gardner Jr. Coach: Gomer Hodge. Pitching Coach: Larry Pierson. Trainer: Unavailable.

Game Information
Radio: None.
PA Announcer: Torye Hurst. Official Scorers: Lindy Brown, Steve Cain.
Stadium Name (year opened): Lake Olmstead Stadium (1995). Location: I-20 to exit 65 (Washington Road), east to Broad Street exit, left on Milledge Road, stadium on right. Standard Game Times: 7:05 p.m; Sun. (April-June) 2:30, (July-Aug.) 6:05.
Visiting Club Hotel: The Partridge Inn, 2110 Walton Way, Augusta, GA 30904. Telephone: (800) 476-6888.

Cape Fear
CROCS

Office Address: 2823 Legion Rd., Fayetteville, NC 28306. Mailing Address: P.O Box 64939, Fayetteville, NC 28306. Telephone: (910) 424-6500. FAX: (910) 424-4325. E-Mail Address: salcrocs@aol.com. Website: www.thecapefearcrocs.com.

Affiliation (first year): Montreal Expos (1997). Years in League: 1987-.

Ownership, Management

Operated by: Fayetteville Baseball Club, Inc.

Principal Owner: Charles G. Padgett. Chairman: Charles E. Padgett.

General Manager: Brad Taylor. Director, Stadium Operations: Scott Zapko. Director, Media/Public Relations: Buck Rogers. Director, Sales/Marketing: Yvette Taylor. Director, Ticket Sales/Merchandising: Tim Mueller. Office Manager: Mary Mercer. Head Groundskeeper: Houston Reece.

Field Staff

Manager: Frank Kremblas. Coach: Rich Morales. Pitching Coach: Tom Signore. Trainer: Carl Scheiner.

Game Information

Radio: None.

PA Announcer: Unavailable. Official Scorer: Tom Siter.

Stadium Name (year opened): J.P. Riddle Stadium (1987). Location: From Route 301 (Business 95), west on Owen Drive, left on Southern Avenue/Legion Road. Standard Game Times: 7:05 p.m.; Sun. (April-May) 2:05, (June-Aug.) 5:05.

Visiting Club Hotel: Econo Lodge, 1952 Cedar Creek Rd., Fayetteville, NC 28306. Telephone: (910) 433-2100.

Capital City
BOMBERS

Office Address: 301 S Assembly St., Columbia, SC 29201. Mailing Address: P.O. Box 7845, Columbia, SC 29202. Telephone: (803) 256-4110. FAX: (803) 256-4338. Website: www.bomberball.com.

Affiliation (first year): New York Mets (1983). Years in League: 1960-61, 1983-.

Ownership, Management

Operated by: Capital City Professional Baseball, LLC.

Principal Owner/President: Rob Cohen. Executive Vice President: Marsha Colten.

General Manager: Tim Swain. Director, Stadium Operations: Bob Hook. Director, Media Relations: Mark Bryant. Director, Group Sales/Community Relations: Shirley Broughton. Group Sales Executive: Brian Kenna. Corporate Sales Manager: Flynn Bowie. Director, Ticket Sales: Doug Gehlken. Director, Merchandising: Brian Spencer. Director, Telemarketing Sales: Jesse Reese. Clubhouse Operations: Carl Davis. Grounds Assistant: Mark Brinkley.

Field Staff

Manager: Dave Engle. Coach: Lee May Jr. Pitching Coach: Mickey Weston. Trainer: Eric Montague.

Game Information

Radio Announcer: Mark Bryant. No. of Games Broadcast: Unavailable. Flagship Station: Unavailable.

PA Announcer: Unavailable. Official Scorer: Julian Gibbons.

Stadium Name (year opened): Capital City Stadium (1991). Location: I-26 East to Columbia, Elmwood Avenue to Assembly Street, right on Assembly for four miles; I-77 South to Columbia, exit at State Road 277 (Bull Street), right on Elmwood, left on Assembly. Standard Game Times: 7:05 p.m., Sun. (April-June) 2:05, (July-Sept.) 6:05.

Visiting Club Hotel: Travelodge, 2210 Bush River Rd., Columbia, SC 29210. Telephone: (803) 798-9665.

Charleston, S.C.
RIVERDOGS

Office Address: 360 Fishburne Ave., Charleston, SC 29403. Mailing Address: P.O. Box 20849, Charleston, SC 29413. Telephone: (843) 723-7241. FAX: (843) 723-2641. E-Mail Address: dogsrus@awod.com. Website: www.riverdogs.com.

Affiliation (first year): Tampa Bay Devil Rays (1997). Years in League: 1973-78, 1980-.

Ownership, Management

Operated by: South Carolina Baseball Club, LP.

Principal Owner: Marv Goldklang. Chairman: Bill Murray. President: Mike Veeck.

Vice President/General Manager: Mark Schuster. Assistant General Manager: Dave Echols. Business Manager: Sharon Evans. Director, Broadcast Sales: Jim Lucas. Senior Account Representatives: Jason Bauer, Nancy Bishop, Samantha Startt. Director, Community Relations: Alison O'Connell. Director, Promotions: Rebecca King. Director, Ticket Sales: David Sacchetti. Ticket Manager: Steve Jette. Group Sales Manager: Scott Hannion. Director, Food Services: John Marso. Media Relations: David Raymond. Assistant, Media Relations: Jim Tocco. Office Manager: Mary Jane MacInnes.

Field Staff

Manager: Charlie Montoyo. Coach: Brad Rippelmeyer. Pitching Coach: Milt Hill. Trainer: Unavailable.

Game Information

Radio Announcers: David Raymond, Jim Tocco. No. of Games Broadcast: Home-71, Away-71. Flagship Station: WQNT 1450-AM.

PA Announcer: Unavailable. Official Scorer: Tony Ciuffo.

Stadium Name (year opened): Joseph P. Riley Jr. Ballpark (1997). Location: From U.S. 17, take Lockwood Drive North, right on Fishburne Street. Standard Game Times: 7:05 p.m.; Sun. (April-May) 2:05, (June-Aug.) 5:05.

Visiting Club Hotel: Howard Johnson River Front, Highway 17, Charleston, SC 29403. Telephone: (843) 722-4000.

Charleston, W.Va.
ALLEY CATS

Office Address: 3403 MacCorkle Ave. SE, Charleston, WV 25304. Mailing Address: P.O. Box 4669, Charleston, WV 25304. Telephone: (304) 344-2287. FAX: (304) 344-0083. E-Mail Address: team@charleston-alleycats.com. Website: www.charlestonalleycats.com.

Affiliation (first year): Kansas City Royals (1999). Years in League: 1987-.

Ownership, Management

Operated by: Wheelers Baseball, LP.

Principal Owner: Andy Paterno.

General Manager: Tim Bordner. Assistant General Manager: Pat Twohig. Director, Stadium Operations: Mike Spencer. Director, Media Relations/Broadcasting: Dan Loney. Assistant Director, Media Relations: Pat Day. Director, Merchandising/Concessions: Joe Adkinson. Assistant Director, Merchandising: Jamie Ball. Director, Promotions: Stephanie Renica. Office Manager: Lisa Spoor. Head Groundskeeper: Bob Hartman.

Field Staff

Manager: Tom Poquette. Coach: Steve Hosey. Pitching Coach: Larry Carter. Trainer: Jeff Stevenson.

Game Information

Radio Announcer: Dan Loney. No. of Games Broadcast: Home-71, Away-71. Flagship Station: WQBE 950-AM.

PA Announcer: Tracy Abdalla. Official Scorer: Lee France.

Stadium Name (year opened): Watt Powell Park (1949). Location: From north/west: I-64/77 to exit 98 (35th Street Bridge), cross bridge, ballpark is at MacCorkle; From south/east: I-64/77 to exit 95 (MacCorkle Avenue), take MacCorkle Avenue West ramp (Route 61 North), stadium is 2½ miles on left. Standard Game Times: 7:15 p.m.; Sun. 2:15.

Visiting Club Hotel: TraveLodge of Dunbar, 1007 Dunbar Ave., Dunbar, WV 25064. Telephone: (304) 768-1000.

Columbus
REDSTIXX

Office Address: 100 Fourth St., Columbus, GA 31901. **Mailing Address:** P.O. Box 1886, Columbus, GA 31902. **Telephone:** (706) 571-8866. **FAX:** (706) 571-9107. **Website:** www.redstixx.com.

Affiliation (first year): Cleveland Indians (1991). **Years in League:** 1991-.

Ownership, Management

Operated by: Columbus RedStixx and Professional Baseball, Inc.

Principal Owner/President: Martha Morrow.

General Manager: Bob Flannery. **Director, Business Operations:** Jim White. **Director, Media/Community Relations:** Mark Janow. **Director, Sales/Marketing:** Michael Weisbart. **Senior Account Representative:** Tommy Fountain. **Director, Group Sales/Food Services:** Craig Couture. **Office Manager:** Rosemary Johnson.

Field Staff

Manager: Brad Komminsk. **Coach:** Rick Gutierrez. **Pitching Coach:** Carl Willis. **Trainer:** Unavailable.

Game Information

Radio: None.

PA Announcer: Steve Thiele. **Official Scorer:** Kathy Gierer.

Stadium Name (year opened): Golden Park (1951). **Location:** I-185 South to exit 1 (Victory Drive), west to Fourth Street (Veterans Parkway), in South Commons Complex on left. **Standard Game Times:** 7:15 p.m.; Sun. 2:15.

Visiting Club Hotel: Holiday Inn-Airport North, 2800 Manchester Expy., Columbus, GA 31904. Telephone: (706) 324-0231.

Delmarva
SHOREBIRDS

Office Address: 6400 Hobbs Rd., Salisbury, MD 21804. **Mailing Address:** P.O. Box 1557, Salisbury, MD 21802. **Telephone:** (410) 219-3112. **FAX:** (410) 219-9164. **Website:** www.theshorebirds.com.

Affiliation (first year): Baltimore Orioles (1997). **Years in League:** 1996-.

Ownership, Management

Operated by: Maryland Baseball, LLC.

Principal Owners: John Daskalakis, Peter Kirk, Frank Perdue, Hugh Schindel, Pete Simmons.

Chairman: Peter Kirk. **President:** Pete Simmons.

General Manager: Jim Terrill. **Assistant GM/Sales, Promotions:** Martin Ward. **Assistant GM/Special Projects:** Kathy Clemmer. **Assistant GM/Ticket Sales:** Renee Kulp. **Controller:** Bob Gast. **Director, Stadium Operations:** Charles Shahan. **Director, Media/Public Relations:** Chad Prior. **Director, Community Relations:** Ralph Murray. **Senior Account Representatives:** Kevin Kulp, Chris Ouellet. **Director, Merchandising/Food Services:** Amy Geppi. **Head Groundskeeper:** Ed Attalla. **Office Manager:** Joyce Young. **Ticket Manager:** Jeff Tierney. **Accounting Manager:** Gail Potts. **Game Operations Manager:** Amy Howard. **Interns, Sales:** Chris Fielding, Jon Stafford.

Field Staff

Manager: Butch Davis. **Coach:** Bobby Rodriguez. **Pitching Coach:** Moe Drabowsky. **Trainer:** Mike Myers.

Game Information

Radio Announcer: Shane Griffin. **No. of Games Broadcast:** Home-71, Away-71. **Flagship Station:** WICO 1320-AM.

PA Announcer: C.R. Hook. **Official Scorer:** Barry Grim.

Stadium Name (year opened): Arthur W. Perdue Stadium (1996). **Location:** From U.S. 50 East, right on Hobbs Road; From U.S. 50 West, left on Hobbs Road. **Standard Game Times:** 7:05 p.m., Sun. (April-May) 2:05, (June-Sept.) 6:05.

Visiting Club Hotel: Ramada Inn and Convention Center, 300 S Salisbury Blvd., Salisbury, MD 21801. Telephone: (410) 546-4400.

Greensboro
BATS

Office Address: 510 Yanceyville St., Greensboro, NC 27405.
Telephone: (336) 333-2287. **FAX:** (336) 273-7350. **E-Mail Address:**
thebats@bellsouth.net. **Website:** www.greensborobats.com.
Affiliation (first year): New York Yankees (1990). **Years in League:**
1979-.

Ownership, Management
Operated by: Carolina Diamond Baseball Club, LP.
Principal Owners: William Collins Jr., William Collins III, Tim Cullen,
John Horshok, Bill Lee, George Nethercutt, Harry Rhodes.
Chairman: William Collins III. **President:** William Collins Jr. **Chief
Operating Officer:** John Horshok.
General Manager: John Frey. **Vice President, Sales:** David Mulholland.
Director, Stadium Operations: Mel Lanford. **Director, Corporate Sales:**
Shelton Grant. **Director, Promotions/Media Relations:** Tim Clever.
Director, Business Administration: Jennifer Leung. **Director, Group
Sales:** Chris Bates. **Director, Operations:** Jason Turner. **Director, Mer-
chandising/Grand Stand:** Will Dvoranchik. **Director, Field Operations:**
Jake Holloway.

Field Staff
Manager: Stan Hough. **Coach:** Tony Perezchica. **Pitching Coach:**
Steve Webber. **Trainer:** Dave Wyly.

Game Information
Radio Announcer: Jeff Daniels. **No. of Games Broadcast:** Home-71,
Away-71. **Flagship Station:** WPET 950-AM.
PA Announcer: Jim Scott. **Official Scorer:** Joe Cristy.
Stadium Name (year opened): War Memorial Stadium (1926).
Location: I-40/I-85 to Highway 29, north to Lee Street, west to Bennett
Avenue, right on Bennett. **Standard Game Times:** 7 p.m., Sun. 2.
Visiting Club Hotel: TraveLodge, 2112 W Meadowview Rd.,
Greensboro, NC 27403. Telephone: (336) 292-2020.

Hagerstown
SUNS

Office Address: 274 E Memorial Blvd., Hagerstown, MD 21740. **Mailing
Address:** P.O. Box 230, Hagerstown, MD 21741. **Telephone:** (301) 791-
6266. **FAX:** (301) 791-6066. **E-Mail Address:** hagsuns@intrepid.net.
Website: www.hagerstownsuns.com.
Affiliation (first year): Toronto Blue Jays (1993). **Years in League:**
1993-.

Ownership, Management
Operated by: Norwin Corporation.
Principal Owner/President: Winston Blenckstone.
General Manager: David Blenckstone. **Director, Business Operations:**
Carol Gehr. **Director, Stadium Operations:** Henry Porter. **Director, Media
Relations:** Michael Heckman. **Director, Broadcasting:** Karl Schalk.
Director, Food Services: Morris Anderson.

Field Staff
Manager: Rolando Pino. **Coach:** Ken Landreaux. **Pitching Coach:**
Hector Berrios. **Trainer:** Mike Frostad.

Game Information
Radio Announcer: Karl Schalk. **No. of Games Broadcast:** Home-71,
Away-71. **Flagship Station:** WHAG 1410-AM.
PA Announcer: Unavailable. **Official Scorer:** Jan Marcus.
Stadium Name (year opened): Municipal Stadium (1931). **Location:**
Exit 32B (U.S. 40 West) on I-70 West, left at Eastern Blvd.; Exit 6A (U.S. 40
East) on I-81 South, right at Cleveland Ave. **Standard Game Times:** 7:05
p.m.; Mon. 6:05; Sun. (first half) 2:05; (second half) 5:05.
Visiting Club Hotel: Ramada Inn and Convention Center, 901 Dual
Hwy., Hagerstown, MD 21740. Telephone: (301) 733-5100.

Hickory
CRAWDADS

Office Address: 2500 Clement Blvd. NW, Hickory, NC 28601. Mailing Address: P.O. Box 1268, Hickory, NC 28603. Telephone: (828) 322-3000. FAX: (828) 322-6137. E-Mail Address: crawdad@abts.net. Website: www.hickorycrawdads.com.

Affiliation (first year): Pittsburgh Pirates (1999). Years in League: 1952, 1960, 1993-.

Ownership, Management
Operated by: Hickory Baseball, Inc.
Principal Owners: Don Beaver, Luther Beaver, Charles Young.
President: Don Beaver. Vice President: Tim Newman.
General Manager: David Haas. Assistant General Manager: Nick Reese. Director, Ticket Sales: Mike Congro. Director, Merchandising: Heidi Kemery. Director, Media Relations/Broadcasting: Evan Malter. Ticket Office Manager: Vance Spinks. Office Manager: Jeanna Homesley. Account Representatives: Jason Lamb, Will Moss, Daniel Smith, Chuck Willis.

Field Staff
Manager: Tracy Woodson. Coach: Ben Oglivie. Pitching Coach: Doc Watson. Trainer: David Sentfen.

Game Information
Radio Announcer: Evan Malter. No. of Games Broadcast: Home-71, Away-71. Flagship Station: WMNC 92.1-FM.
PA Announcers: JuJu Phillips, Steve Fisher. Official Scorer: Gary Olinger.
Stadium Name (year opened): L.P. Frans Stadium (1993). Location: I-40 to exit 123 (Lenoir North), 321 North to Clement Blvd., left for ½ mile. Standard Game Times: 7 p.m.; Sun. (April-May) 2, (June-Sept.) 6.
Visiting Club Hotel: Red Roof Inn, 1184 Lenoir Rhyne Blvd., Hickory, NC 28602. Telephone: (828) 323-1500.

Macon
BRAVES

Office Address: Luther Williams Field, Seventh Street, Macon, GA 31201. Mailing Address: P.O. Box 4525, Macon, GA 31208. Telephone: (912) 745-8943. FAX: (912) 743-5559. E-Mail Address: maconbraves@mindspring.com. Website: www.maconbraves.com.

Affiliation (first year): Atlanta Braves (1991). Years in League: 1962-63, 1980-87, 1991-.

Ownership, Management
Operated by: Atlanta National League Baseball Club, Inc.
Principal Owner: Ted Turner. President: Stan Kasten.
General Manager: Michael Dunn. Director, Stadium Operations: Terry Morgan. Head Groundskeeper: George Stephens. Director, Sales/Marketing: Jim Tessmer. Director, Ticket Sales: Kristie Berkley. Director, Special Projects: Mike Miskavech.

Field Staff
Manager: Jeff Treadway. Coach: Tommy Gregg. Pitching Coach: Kent Willis. Trainer: Justin Sharpe.

Game Information
Radio: None.
PA Announcer: Jimmy Jones. Official Scorer: Kevin Coulombe.
Stadium Name (year opened): Luther Williams Field (1926). Location: Exit 4 off I-16, across Otis Redding Bridge to Riverside Drive, follow signs to Central City Park. Standard Game Times: 7 p.m., Sun. 2.
Visiting Club Hotel: Comfort Inn North, 2690 Riverside Dr., Macon, GA 31208. Telephone: (912) 746-8855.

Piedmont
BOLL WEEVILS

Office Address: 2888 Moose Rd., Kannapolis, NC 28083. **Mailing Address:** P.O. Box 64, Kannapolis, NC 28082. **Telephone:** (704) 932-3267. **FAX:** (704) 938-7040. **E-Mail Address:** bollweevils@ctc.net. **Website:** www.bollweevils.com.

Affiliation (first year): Philadelphia Phillies (1995). **Years in League:** 1995-.

Ownership, Management
Operated by: Iredell Trading Co.
Principal Owners: Larry Hedrick, Sue Hedrick.
President: Larry Hedrick.
Vice President/General Manager: Todd Parnell. **Assistant General Manager:** Eric Allman. **Director, Public Relations/Group Sales:** Randy Long. **Director, Tickets Sales:** Chris Zervanos. **Assistant Director, Stadium Operations:** Jaime Pruitt. **Director, Business Development/Manager, Concessions:** Patrick Coakley. **Assistant Director, Group Sales:** Jeremy Hart. **Bookkeeper:** Deb Hall.

Field Staff
Manager: Ken Oberkfell. **Coach:** Jerry Martin. **Pitching Coach:** Carlos Arroyo. **Trainer:** Paul Gabrielson.

Game Information
Radio: None.
PA Announcer: Unavailable. **Official Scorer:** Unavailable.
Stadium Name (year opened): Fieldcrest Cannon Stadium (1995). **Location:** Exit 63 on I-85, west on Lane Street to Stadium Drive. **Standard Game Times:** 7:05 p.m.; Mon.-Thur. (April) 6:35, (May-Sept.) 7:05; Sun. 2:05.
Visiting Club Hotel: Sleep Inn, 321 Bendix Dr., Salisbury, NC 28146. Telephone: (704) 633-5961.

Savannah
SAND GNATS

Office Address: 1401 E Victory Dr., Savannah, GA 31404. **Mailing Address:** P.O. Box 3783, Savannah, GA 31414. **Telephone:** (912) 351-9150. **FAX:** (912) 352-9722. **E-Mail Address:** savgnats@aol.com.

Affiliation (first year): Texas Rangers (1998). **Years in League:** 1962, 1984-.

Ownership, Management
Operated by: Savannah Professional Baseball Club, Inc.
Principal Owner/President: Ken Silver.
General Manager: Nick Brown. **Assistant General Manager:** Brad Haynes. **Director, Media Relations/Merchandise Sales:** Todd Antonopoulos. **Director, Merchandise:** Aaron Fox. **Director, Sales/ Marketing:** Mitch Mann. **Director, Ticket Sales:** Lyle Abbott. **Office Manager:** Delean Garcia. **Head Groundskeeper:** Bob Neikirk.

Field Staff
Manager: Paul Carey. **Coach:** Jim Murphy. **Pitching Coach:** Aris Tirado. **Trainer:** Gene Basham.

Game Information
Radio Announcer: Unavailable. **No. of Games Broadcast:** Unavailable. **Flagship Station:** WSGA 1400-AM.
PA Announcer: Joel Rosen. **Official Scorer:** Marcus Holland.
Stadium Name (year opened): Grayson Stadium (1941). **Location:** I-16 to 37th Street exit, left on 37th, right on Abercorn Street, left on Victory Drive; I-95 to exit 16 (Savannah/Pembroke), east on 204, right on Victory Drive, stadium is on right in Daffin Park. **Standard Game Times:** 7:15 p.m; Sun. 2.
Visiting Club Hotel: Econo Lodge Midtown, 7500 Abercorn St., Savannah, GA 31406. Telephone: (912) 352-1657.

NEW YORK-PENN LEAGUE

Short-Season Class A

Mailing Address: 1629 Oneida St., Utica, NY 13501. **Telephone:** (315) 733-8036. **FAX:** (315) 797-7403. **E-Mail Address:** nypenn@dreamscape.com.

Years League Active: 1939-.
President: Bob Julian.
Vice President: Sam Nader (Oneonta).
Treasurer: Bill Gladstone (Pittsfield). **Corporate Secretary:** Tony Torre (New Jersey).
Directors: Jeff Dumas (Staten Island), Rob Fowler (Utica), Bill Gladstone (Pittsfield), Barry Gordon (New Jersey), Alan Levin (Mahoning Valley), Paul Marriott (Batavia), Sam Nader (Oneonta), Ray Pecor (Vermont), Leo Pinckney (Auburn), Shawn Smith (Lowell), Greg Sorbara (St. Catharines), Paul Velte (Williamsport), Skip Weisman (Hudson Valley), David Wellenzohn (Jamestown).

Bob Julian

Executive Assistant: Pamela Stagliano.
1999 Opening Date: June 16. **Closing Date:** Sept. 2.
Regular Season: 76 games.
Division Structure: McNamara—Hudson Valley, Lowell, New Jersey, Oneonta, Pittsfield, Staten Island, Utica, Vermont. **Pinckney-Stedler**—Auburn, Batavia, Jamestown, Mahoning Valley, St. Catharines, Williamsport.

Playoff Format: Division champions and two wild-card teams meet in best-of-3 semifinals. Winners meet in best-of-3 series for league championship.

All-Star Game: None.

Roster Limit: 30 active, but only 25 may be in uniform and eligible to play in any given game. **Player Eligibility Rule:** No more than four players who are 23 or older. No more than three players on active list may have four or more years of prior service.

Brand of Baseball: Rawlings.

Statistician: Howe Sportsdata, Boston Fish Pier, West Bldg. #1, Suite 302, Boston MA 02210.

Umpires: Chris Bowen (West Burlington, IA), Scott Charlton (Guelph, Ontario), Bill Davis (Marion, OH), Kirk Hutchinson (Odenton, MD), Tony Inzero (Hamden, CT), Joe Johnson (Pennsville, NJ), Cameron Keller (Hastings, NE), Tony Klubertanz (Sun Prairie, WI), Scott McClellan (Fort Wayne, IN), Peter Masterson (Middleburg, FL), Karreem Mebane (Hamden, CT), Joshua Rees (Sheboygan, WI), Nick Siciliano (Youngstown, OH), David Webb (Kitts Hill, OH).

Stadium Information

Club	Stadium	Dimensions			Capacity	'98 Att.
		LF	CF	RF		
Auburn	Falcon Park	330	400	330	2,800	52,597
Batavia	Dwyer	325	400	325	2,600	42,908
Hudson Valley	Dutchess	325	400	325	4,320	158,202
Jamestown	Diethrick Park	335	410	353	4,200	60,481
Lowell	Lelacheur Park	337	400	302	4,863	174,020
Mahoning Valley*	Cafaro Field	335	405	335	6,000	—
New Jersey	Skylands Park	330	392	330	4,336	153,445
Oneonta	Damaschke Field	352	406	350	4,200	57,200
Pittsfield	Wahconah Park	334	374	333	4,500	84,323
St. Catharines	Community Park	320	400	320	2,500	55,787
Staten Island#	Staten Island	325	400	325	4,500	—
Utica	Donovan	324	400	324	4,000	58,902
Vermont	Centennial Field	330	405	323	4,000	105,064
Williamsport	Bowman Field	345	405	350	4,200	60,718

* Club operated in Erie in 1998
\# Club operated in Watertown in 1998

Auburn
DOUBLEDAYS

Office Address: 108 N Division St., Auburn, NY 13021. **Telephone:** (315) 255-2489. **FAX:** (315) 255-2675. **E-Mail Address:** auburndd@relex.com. **Website:** www.doubledays.com.

Affiliation (first year): Houston Astros (1982). **Years in League:** 1958-80, 1982-.

Ownership, Management
Operated by: Auburn Community Baseball, Inc.
Chairman: Thomas Ganey. **President:** Leo Pinckney.
General Manager: Paul Taglieri. **Head Groundskeeper:** Rich Wild. **Director, Ticket Operations/Public Relations:** Kelle Renninger. **Director, Stadium Operations/Merchandising:** Traer Van Allen.

Field Staff
Manager: Lyle Yates. **Coach:** Darwin Pennye. **Pitching Coach:** Gregg Langbehn. **Trainer:** Shawn Moffitt.

Game Information
Radio Announcer: Kevin Nicholson. **No of Games Broadcast:** Away-38. **Flagship Station:** WIN 89.1-FM.
PA Announcer: Kevin Nicholson. **Official Scorer:** Unavailable.
Stadium Name (year opened): Falcon Park (1995). **Location:** I-90 to exit 40, right on Route 34 for 8 miles to York Street, right on York, left on North Division Street. **Standard Game Times:** 7:05 p.m., Sun. 4:05.
Visiting Club Hotel: Unavailable.

Batavia
MUCKDOGS

Office Address: Dwyer Stadium, 299 Bank St., Batavia, NY 14020. **Telephone:** (716) 343-5454. **FAX:** (716) 343-5620. **E-Mail Address:** brrc@hfent.com. **Website:** www.muckdogs.com.

Affiliation (first year): Philadelphia Phillies (1988). **Years in League:** 1939-53, 1957-59, 1961-.

Ownership, Management
Operated by: Genesee County Professional Baseball, Inc.
President: Larry Roth.
General Manager: Paul Marriott. **Assistant General Manager:** Nathan Kelley. **Special Assistant to GM:** Linda Crook. **Office Manager:** Melissa Meeder. **Clubhouse Operations:** Tony Pecora.

Field Staff
Manager: Greg Legg. **Coach:** Frank Klebe. **Pitching Coach:** Ken Westray. **Trainer:** Carl Heldman.

Game Information
Radio Announcer: Unavailable. **No. of Games Broadcast:** Away-38. **Flagship Station:** WBSU 89.1-FM.
PA Announcer/Official Scorer: Wayne Fuller.
Stadium Name (year opened): Dwyer Stadium (1996). **Location:** I-90 to exit 48, left on Route 98 South, left on Richmond Avenue, left on Bank Street. **Standard Game Times:** 7:05 p.m.; Sun. 2:05.
Visiting Club Hotel: Days Inn of Batavia, 200 Oak St., Batavia, NY 14020. Telephone: (716) 343-1440.

Hudson Valley
RENEGADES

Office Address: Dutchess Stadium, Route 9D, Wappingers Falls, NY 12590. **Mailing Address:** P.O. Box 661, Fishkill, NY 12524. **Telephone:** (914) 838-0094. **FAX:** (914) 838-0014. **E-Mail Address:** info@hvrenegades.com. **Website:** www.hvrenegades.com.

Affiliation (first year): Tampa Bay Devil Rays (1996). **Years in League:** 1994-.

Ownership, Management

Operated by: Keystone Professional Baseball Club, Inc.
Principal Owner: Marv Goldklang. **President:** Skip Weisman.
Vice President/General Manager: Steve Gliner. **Assistant General Manager:** Kathy Butsko. **Director, Stadium Operations/Promotions:** Elmer LeSuer. **Director, Ticket Operations:** Sally Berry. **Director, Business Operations:** Jennifer Vitale. **Coordinator, Customer Service:** Kristina Desiderio. **Head Groundskeeper:** Tom Hubmaster. **Assistant Ticket Manager:** Bonnie Johnson. **Administrative Assistants:** Ryan Leone, Owen Duffy.

Field Staff

Manager: Edwin Rodriguez. **Coach:** Unavailable. **Pitching Coach:** Unavailable. **Trainer:** Unavailable.

Game Information

Radio Announcer: Rick Schultz. **No. of Games Broadcast:** Home-38, Away-38. **Flagship Stations:** WBNR 1260-AM, WLNA 1420-AM, WALL 1340-AM.
PA Announcer: Rick Zolzer. **Official Scorer:** Bob Beretta.
Stadium Name (year opened): Dutchess Stadium (1994). **Location:** I-84 to exit 11 (Route 9D North), north 1 mile to stadium. **Standard Game Times:** 7:15 p.m., Sun. 5:15.
Visiting Club Hotel: Unavailable.

Jamestown
JAMMERS

Office Address: 485 Falconer St., Jamestown, NY 14702. **Mailing Address:** P.O. Box 638, Jamestown, NY 14702. **Telephone:** (716) 664-0915. **FAX:** (716) 664-4175. **E-Mail Address:** jjammers@alltel.net.
Affiliation (first year): Atlanta Braves (1999). **Years in League:** 1939-57, 1961-73, 1977-.

Ownership, Management

Operated by: Rich Entertainment Group.
Chairman: Robert Rich Sr. **President:** Robert Rich Jr.
General Manager: David Wellenzohn. **Assistant General Manager:** Norma Marvell. **Director, Stadium Operations:** James Comerford. **Head Groundskeeper:** Tom Casler. **Director, Sales/Marketing:** Gary Kifer. **Director, Food Services:** Rich Ruggerio.

Field Staff

Manager: Jim Saul. **Coach:** Manny Jimenez. **Pitching Coach:** Mark Ross. **Trainer:** Justin Sharpe.

Game Information

Radio Announcer: Unavailable. **No. of Games Broadcast:** Home-38, Away-20. **Flagship Station:** Unavailable.
PA Announcer: Todd Peterson. **Official Scorer:** Jim Riggs.
Stadium Name (year opened): Russell Diethrick Park (1941). **Location:** From I-90, south on Route 60, left on Buffalo Street, left on Falconer Street. **Standard Game Times:** 7:05 p.m.; Sun. 2:05.
Visiting Club Hotel: Unavailable.

Lowell
SPINNERS

Office Address: 450 Aiken St., Lowell, MA 01854. **Telephone:** (978) 459-2255. **FAX:** (978) 459-1674. **E-Mail Address:** generalinfo@lowell spinners.com. **Website:** www.lowellspinners.com.
Affiliation (first year): Boston Red Sox (1996). **Years in League:** 1996-.

Ownership, Management

Operated by: Diamond Action, Inc.
Principal Owners: Drew Weber, Joann Weber.
President: Drew Weber.
General Manager: Shawn Smith. **Assistant General Manager:** Brian Lindsay. **Director, Stadium Operations:** Dan Beaulieu. **Director, Media/Community Relations:** Dan Hoffman. **Controller:** Layla Hey. **Director, Ticket Sales:** Tami Reynolds. **Director, Group Sales:** Chris

Roman. **Director, Merchandising:** Joann Weber. **Business Operations:** Darren Garrity. **Head Groundskeeper:** Greg Arrington.

Field Staff
Manager: Luis Aguayo. **Coach:** Ino Guerrero. **Pitching Coach:** Dennis Rasmussen. **Trainer:** Stan Skolfield.

Game Information
Radio: Unavailable.

PA Announcer: George Brown. **Official Scorer:** Unavailable.

Stadium Name (year opened): Edward LeLacheur Park (1998). **Location:** From Routes 495 and 3, take exit 35C (Lowell Connector), follow connector to exit 5B, Thorndike Street onto Dutton Street, past city hall, left onto Father Morrissette Boulevard, right on Aiken Street. **Standard Game Times:** 7 p.m., Sun. 5.

Visiting Club Hotel: Doubletree Inn, 50 Warren St., Lowell, MA 01852. Telephone: (978) 452-1200.

Mahoning Valley
SCRAPPERS

Office Address: 111 Eastwood Mall Blvd., Niles, OH 44446. **Mailing Address:** P.O. Box 1357, Niles, OH 44446. **Telephone:** (330) 505-0000. **FAX:** (330) 505-9696. **E-Mail Address:** mvscrappers@cboss.com. **Website:** www.mvscrappers.com.

Affiliation (first year): Cleveland Indians (1999). **Years in League:** 1999.

Ownership, Management
Operated by: Palisades Baseball.

Principal Owner: Alan Levin. **Vice President:** Erik Haag. **Director, Finance:** Andy Zmudzinski.

General Manager: Andy Milovich. **Assistant General Manager:** Ken Fogel. **Director, Corporate Relations:** Matt Leider. **Director, Marketing/Promotions:** Andrew Minister. **Director, Ticket Operations:** Rich Leopold. **Accountant:** Mary Crites. **Director, Group Sales:** Brian Heller. **Assistant Director, Group Sales:** Joe Fanto. **Director, Stadium Operations:** Matt Duncan. **Administrative Assistant:** George Gentithes.

Field Staff
Manager: Ted Kubiak. **Coach:** Willie Aviles. **Pitching Coach:** Steve Lyons. **Trainer:** Unavailable.

Game Information
Radio Announcer: Unavailable. **No. of Games Broadcasts:** Home-38, Away-38. **Flagship Station:** Unavailable.

PA Announcer: Unavailable. **Official Scorer:** Unavailable.

Stadium Name (year opened): Cafaro Field (1999). **Location:** I-80 to 11 North to 82 West to 46 South. Stadium located behind Eastwood Mall. **Standard Game Times:** 7 p.m., Sun. 2.

Visiting Club Hotel: Days Inn, 1300 Youngstown-Warren Rd., Niles, OH 44446. Telephone: (330) 544-1301.

New Jersey
CARDINALS

Office Address: 94 Championship Pl., Suite 2, Augusta, NJ 07822. **Telephone:** (973) 579-7500. **FAX:** (973) 579-7502. **E-Mail Address:** office@njcards.com. **Website:** www.njcards.com.

Affiliation (first year): St. Louis Cardinals (1994). **Years in League:** 1994-.

Ownership, Management
Operated by: Minor League Heroes, LP.

Chairman: Barry Gordon. **President:** Marc Klee.

Vice President/General Manager: Tony Torre. **Assistant General Manager:** Herm Sorchar. **Head Groundskeeper:** Ralph Naife. **Director, Promotions:** Bob Commentucci. **Director, Group Sales:** Kecia Tillman. **Group Sales Manager:** Christine Goeti. **Director, Merchandising:** Sweets Wilson. **Director, Special Projects:** John Martin.

Field Staff
Manager: Jeff Shireman. **Pitching Coach:** Gary Buckels. **Trainer:** Ryan Fagan.

Game Information

Radio Announcers: Paul Mirabella, Phil Pepe. **No. of Games Broadcast:** Home-38. **Flagship Stations:** WNNJ 1360-AM, WHCY 106.3-FM.

PA Announcer: Unavailable. **Official Scorer:** Ken Hand.

Stadium Name (year opened): Skylands Park (1994). **Location:** I-80 to exit 34B (Route 15 North) to Route 565 East; I-84 to Route 6 (Matamoras) to Route 206 North to Route 565 East. **Standard Game Times:** 7:15 p.m.; Sat. 5; Sun. 1.

Visiting Club Hotel: Best Western at Hunt's Landing, 120 Routes 6 and 209, Matamoras, PA 18336. Telephone: (800) 308-2378.

Oneonta
TIGERS

Office Address: 95 River St., Oneonta, NY 13820. **Telephone:** (607) 432-6326. **FAX:** (607) 432-1965. **E-Mail Address:** naderas@telenet.net.

Affiliation (first year): Detroit Tigers (1999). **Years in League:** 1966-.

Ownership, Management

Operated by: Oneonta Athletic Corp., Inc.

President/General Manager: Sam Nader. **Director, Business/Stadium Operations:** John Nader. **Controller:** Sidney Levine. **Head Groundskeeper:** Ted Christman. **Director, Media/Public Relations:** Alice O'Conner. **Director, Marketing/Merchandising:** Suzanne Longo. **Director, Special Projects:** Mark Nader. **Director, Ticket Sales:** Bob Zeh. **Director, Food Services:** Brad Zeh.

Field Staff

Manager: Kevin Bradshaw. **Coach:** Unavailable. **Pitching Coach:** Unavailable. **Trainer:** Unavailable.

Game Information

Radio: None.

PA Announcer: Doug Decker. **Official Scorer:** David Bishop.

Stadium Name (year opened): Damaschke Field (1940). **Location:** Exit 15 off I-88. **Standard Game Times:** 7 p.m., Sun. 6.

Visiting Club Hotels: Town House Motor Inn, 318 Main St., Oneonta, NY 13820. Telephone: (607) 432-1313; Oasis Motor Inn, 366 Chestnut St., Oneonta, NY 13820. Telephone: (607) 432-6041.

Pittsfield
METS

Office Address: 136 South St., Pittsfield, MA 01201. **Mailing Address:** P.O. Box 328, Pittsfield, MA 01202. **Telephone:** (413) 499-6387. **FAX:** (413) 443-7144. **E-Mail Address:** pittmets@berkshire.net. **Website:** www.pitts-fieldmets.com.

Affiliation (first year): New York Mets (1989). **Years in League:** 1989-.

Ownership, Management

Operated by: National Pastime Corporation.

Principal Owners: Martin Barr, John Burton, William Gladstone, Richard Murphy, Alfred Roberts, Stephen Siegel.

President: William Gladstone.

General Manager: Richard Murphy. **Assistant General Manager:** Richard Lenfest. **Director, Media/Public Relations:** Ethan Wilson. **Director, Stadium Operations:** Jason Mancivalano. **Director, Ticket Sales:** Bob Gibson. **Director, Special Projects:** Ed Wojtowicz.

Field Staff

Manager: Tony Tijerina. **Coach:** Ken Berry. **Pitching Coach:** Doug Simons. **Trainer:** Brian Chicklo.

Game Information

Radio Announcer: Robert Shade. **No. of Games Broadcast:** Home-38, Away-38. **Flagship Station:** WBRK 101.7-FM.

PA Announcer: Unavailable. **Official Scorer:** Ethan Wilson.

Stadium Name (year opened): Wahconah Park (1919). **Location:** From east: Mass Pike exit 2 to Route 7 North to Pittsfield, right on North Street, left on Wahconah Street; From west: Route 295E to 41 North to 20E into Pittsfield, left on Route 7, right on North Street, left on Wahconah. **Standard Game Times:** 7 p.m.; Sun. 6.

Visiting Club Hotel: Holiday Inn of the Berkshires, 40 Main St., North Adams, MA 01247. Telephone: (413) 663-6500.

St. Catharines
STOMPERS

Office Address: 174 St. Paul St., St. Catharines, Ontario L2R 3M2. **Telephone:** (905) 641-5297. **FAX:** (905) 641-3007. **E-Mail Address:** stompers@vaxxine.com. **Website:** www.stompers.fanlink.com.

Affiliation (first year): Toronto Blue Jays (1986). **Years in League:** 1986-.

Ownership, Management

Operated by: St. Catharines Baseball Club, Ltd.

Principal Owners: Home Innings, Inc.; Leadoff Investments, Ltd.; Ernie Whitt.

President: Greg Sorbara.

General Manager: David Shaw. **Office Manager:** Eleanor Bowman.

Field Staff

Manager: Eddie Rodriguez. **Coach:** Unavailable. **Pitching Coach:** Neil Allen. **Trainer:** Kevin Elliott.

Game Information

Radio: Unavailable.

PA Announcer: Unavailable. **Official Scorer:** Ann Rudge.

Stadium Name (year opened): Community Park (1987). **Location:** From east, Queen Elizabeth Expressway to Glendale exit, turn left then right on Merritt Street, right on Seymour Avenue; From west, Queen Elizabeth Expressway to 406 South, left at Glendale Avenue exit, left on Merritt Street, right on Seymour Avenue. **Standard Game Times:** 7:05 p.m., Sun: 6:05.

Visiting Club Hotel: Ramada Parkway, 327 Ontario St., St. Catharines, Ontario L2R 5L3. Telephone: (905) 688-2324.

Staten Island
YANKEES

Office Address: 2025 Richmond Ave., Suite 212, Staten Island, NY 10314. **Telephone:** (718) 698-9265. **FAX:** (718) 698-9291.

Affiliation (first year): New York Yankees (1999). **Years in League:** 1999.

Ownership, Management

Operated by: Unavailable.

General Manager: Jeff Dumas. **Assistant General Manager:** Jason Smorol. **Director, Ticket Operations:** John Davison.

Field Staff

Manager: Joe Arnold. **Coach:** Unavailable. **Pitching Coach:** Unavailable. **Trainer:** Unavailable.

Game Information

Radio: Unavailable.

PA Announcer: Unavailable. **Official Scorer:** Unavailable.

Stadium Name: College of Staten Island field. **Location:** I-278 to Victory Boulevard exit. **Standard Game Times:** 7 p.m, Sun. 6.

Visiting Club Hotel: Unavailable.

Utica
BLUE SOX

Office Address: 1700 Sunset Ave., Utica, NY 13502. **Mailing Address:** P.O. Box 751, Utica, NY 13503. **Telephone:** (315) 738-0999. **FAX:** (315) 738-0992.

Affiliation (first year): Florida Marlins (1996). **Years in League:** 1977-.

Ownership, Management

Operated by: Utica Baseball Club, Ltd.

Principal Owner/President: Bob Fowler.

General Manager: Rob Fowler. **Assistant General Manager:** Jim

Griffiths. **Head Groundskeeper:** Carmen Russo. **Clubhouse Operations:** Bob Perry.

Field Staff
Manager: Ken Joyce. **Coach:** Joe Aversa. **Pitching Coach:** Bill Sizemore. **Trainer:** Shane Kennedy.

Game Information
Radio: None.
PA Announcer: Dominick Ciccone. **Official Scorer:** Unavailable.
Stadium Name (year opened): Donovan Stadium (1976).
Location: New York State Thruway to exit 31 (Genesee Street), south to Burrstone Road, right to stadium. **Standard Game Times:** 7 p.m.
Visiting Club Hotel: Unavailable.

Vermont
EXPOS

Office Address: 1 Main St., Box 4, Winooski, VT 05404. **Telephone:** (802) 655-4200. **FAX:** (802) 655-5660. **E-Mail Address:** vtexpos@together.net. **Website:** www.vermontexpos.com.
Affiliation (first year): Montreal Expos (1994). **Years in League:** 1994-.

Ownership, Management
Operated by: Vermont Expos, Inc.
Principal Owner/President: Ray Pecor.
General Manager: Kyle Bostwick. **Assistant General Manager:** C.J Knudsen. **Director, Business Operations:** Monica LaLime. **Controller:** Mia Ouellette. **Head Groundskeeper:** Lee Keller. **Director, Public Relations:** Marie Heikkinen. **Director, Media Relations:** Paul Stanfield. **Director, Sales/Marketing:** Chris Corley. **Director, Ticket Sales:** Mike Simpson. **Director, Food Services:** Steve Bernard. **Director, Special Projects:** Onnie Mathews. **Clubhouse Operations:** Phil Schelzo.

Field Staff
Manager: Tony Barbone. **Coach:** Kiki Ayo. **Pitching Coach:** Craig Bjornson. **Trainer:** Liam Frawley.

Game Information
Radio: Unavailable.
PA Announcer: Rich Haskell. **Official Scorer:** Ev Smith.
Stadium Name (year opened): Centennial Field (1922). **Location:** I-89 to exit 14W, right on East Avenue for one mile, right at Colchester Avenue. **Standard Game Times:** 7:05 p.m., Sun. 2:05.
Visiting Club Hotel: Best Western Inn and Conference Center, 1076 Williston Rd., South Burlington, VT 05404. Telephone: (802) 863-1125.

Williamsport
CROSSCUTTERS

Office Address: Bowman Field, 1700 W Fourth St., Williamsport, PA 17701. **Mailing Address:** P.O. Box 3173, Williamsport, PA 17701. **Telephone:** (570) 326-3389. **FAX:** (570) 326-3494. **E-Mail Address:** xcutters@aol.com. **Website:** www.xcutters.fanlink.com.
Affiliation (first year): Pittsburgh Pirates (1999). **Years in League:** 1923-37, 1968-72, 1994-.

Ownership, Management
Operated by: Geneva Cubs Baseball, Inc.
Principal Owner/President: Paul Velte.
General Manager: Doug Estes. **Director, Marketing/Public Relations:** Gabe Sinicropi. **Director, Stadium Operations:** Bob Mungo. **Head Groundskeeper:** Matt Sungerland.

Field Staff
Manager: Curtis Wilkerson. **Coach:** Ramon Sambo. **Pitching Coach:** Blaine Beatty. **Trainer:** Jason Jadgchew.

Game Information
Radio Announcer: Tim Williamson. **No. of Games Broadcast:** Away-30. **Flagship Station:** WMYL 95.5-FM.
PA Announcer: Tom Scott. **Official Scorer:** Ken Myers.
Stadium Name (year opened): Bowman Field (1923). **Location:** From

south, Route 15 to Maynard Street, right on Maynard, left on Fourth Street for one mile; From north, Route 15 to Fourth Street, left on Fourth. **Standard Game Times:** 7:05 p.m.

Visiting Club Hotel: Holiday Inn, 1840 E Third St., Williamsport, PA 17701. Telephone: (570) 326-1981.

NORTHWEST LEAGUE

Short-Season Class A

Office Address: 5900 N Granite Reef Rd., Suite 105, Scottsdale, AZ 85250. **Mailing Address:** P.O. Box 4941, Scottsdale, AZ 85261. **Telephone:** (602) 483-8224. **FAX:** (602) 443-3450.

Years League Active: 1901-1922, 1937-1942, 1946-.

President/Treasurer: Bob Richmond.

Vice President: Bill Pereira (Boise).

Corporate Secretary: Jerry Walker (Salem-Keizer).

Directors: Bob Beban (Eugene), Bobby Brett (Spokane), Jack Cain (Portland), Dave Connell (Yakima), Fred Herrmann (Southern Oregon), Bill Pereira (Boise), Mark Sperandio (Everett), Jerry Walker (Salem-Keizer).

Bob Richmond

Administrative Assistant: Rob Richmond.

1999 Opening Date: June 18. **Closing Date:** Sept. 5.

Regular Season: 76 games.

Division Structure: North—Boise, Everett, Spokane, Yakima. **South**—Eugene, Portland, Salem-Keizer, Southern Oregon.

Playoff Format: Division winners play best-of-5 series for league championship.

All-Star Game: None.

Roster Limit: 30 active, 35 under control. **Player Eligibility Rule:** No more than four players 23 or older. No more than three players on active list may have four or more years of prior service.

Brand of Baseball: Rawlings.

Statistician: Howe Sportsdata, Boston Fish Pier, West Bldg. #1, Suite 302, Boston MA 02210.

Umpires: Andy Hergesheimer (Seattle, WA), Ryan Houchen (Canyon Country, CA), John McMasters (Tacoma, WA), Shawn Rakos (Pacific, WA), Tim Strike (Anchorage, AK), Kevin Sweeney (Rio Rancho, NM), Kevin Walker (Walla Walla, WA), John Woods (Phoenix, AZ).

Stadium Information

Club	Stadium	Dimensions			Capacity	'98 Att.
		LF	CF	RF		
Boise	Memorial	335	400	335	4,000	152,496
Eugene	Civic	335	400	328	6,800	136,310
Everett	Everett Memorial	330	395	330	3,682	119,396
Portland	Civic	308	407	348	23,150	184,172
Salem-Keizer	Volcanoes	325	400	325	4,100	133,980
Southern Oregon	Miles Field	332	384	344	2,900	71,822
Spokane	Seafirst	335	398	335	7,100	186,362
Yakima	Yakima County	295	406	295	3,000	76,049

Boise
HAWKS

Office Address: 5600 Glenwood Dr., Boise, ID 83714. Telephone: (208) 322-5000. FAX: (208) 322-7432. E-Mail Address: gmbhawks@aol.com. Website: www.diamondsportsworld.com/hawks.

Affiliation (first year): Anaheim Angels (1989). Years in League: 1975-76, 1978, 1985-.

Ownership, Management

Operated by: Boise Hawks Baseball Club.

Principal Owner: Bill Pereira.

Chairman: Peter Gray. President: Cord Pereira.

General Manager: Denise Jones. Director, Business Operations: Lee Ryan. Manager, Facility/Grounds: Joe Kelly. Director, Public Relations: Jack Carnefix. Director, Sales/Marketing: Eric Trapp. Director, Promotions: Matt Gentil. Director, Ticket Sales: Carrie Clemens. Director, Group Sales: Kevin Whitworth. Director, Special Projects: Bryan Newton. Director, Food Services: Sodexho Marriott. Clubhouse Operations: Eddy Bush.

Field Staff

Manager: Tom Kotchman. Coach: Todd Claus. Pitching Coach: Jim Bennett. Trainer: Unavailable.

Game Information

Radio Announcers: Rob Simpson, Mark Willard. No. of Games Broadcast: Home-38, Away-38. Flagship Stations: KTIK 1340-AM.

PA Announcer: Greg Culver. Official Scorer: Danny Ward.

Stadium Name (year opened): Memorial Stadium (1989). Location: I-84 to Cole Road, north to Western Idaho Fairgrounds. Standard Game Times: 7:05 p.m.; Sun. 6:05.

Visiting Club Hotel: Holiday Inn, 3300 Vista Ave., Boise, ID 83705. Telephone: (208) 344-8365.

Eugene
EMERALDS

Office Address: 2077 Willamette St., Eugene, OR 97405. Mailing Address: P.O. Box 5566, Eugene, OR 97405. Telephone: (541) 342-5367. FAX: (541) 342-6089. E-Mail Address: ems@go-ems.com. Website: www.go-ems.com.

Affiliation (first year): Chicago Cubs (1999). Years in League: 1955-68, 1974-.

Ownership, Management

Operated by: Elmore Sports Group, Ltd.

Principal Owner: David Elmore.

President/General Manager: Bob Beban. Assistant General Manager: Mark Ruckwardt. Business Manager: Eileen Beban. Director, Marketing/Media Relations: Bryan Beban. Director, Tickets: Ann Brennan. Director, Special Events: Jeff Benjamin. Assistant, Media Relations: Brian Williford. Facilities Director: David Puente. Grounds Superintendent: Jake Witherspoon.

Field Staff

Manager: Bob Ralston. Coach: Damon Farmar. Pitching Coach: Tom Pratt. Trainer: Taleen Noradoukian.

Game Information

Radio Announcer: Unavailable. No. of Games Broadcast: Home-38, Away-38. Flagship Station: KUGN 590-AM.

PA Announcer: Unavailable. Official Scorer: Unavailable.

Stadium Name (year opened): Civic Stadium (1938). Location: From I-5, take I-105 to Exit 2, stay left and follow to downtown, cross over Ferry Street Bridge to Eighth Avenue, left on Pearl Street, south to 20th Avenue. Standard Game Times: 7:05 p.m; Sun. 6:05.

Visiting Club Hotel: Doubletree Inn, 3280 Gateway Rd., Springfield, OR 97477. Telephone: (541) 726-8181.

Everett
AQUASOX

Office Address: 3802 Broadway, Everett, WA 98201. Telephone: (425) 258-3673. FAX: (425) 258-3675. E-Mail Address: aquasox@aquasox.com. Website: www.aquasox.com.

Affiliation (first year): Seattle Mariners (1995). Years in League: 1984-.

Ownership, Management
Operated by: Farm Club Sports, Inc.

President: Bob Bavasi. Vice President: Margaret Bavasi. Ticket Consultant: Mark Sperandio.

General Manager: Robb Stanton. Director, Sales/Marketing: Brian Sloan. Director, Ballpark Operations: Gary Farwell. Director, Ticket Services: Kim Echols. Director, Ticket Sales: Pat Dillon. Director, Group Sales/Community Relations: Mark Baxter. Director, Food Services: Gregg Corbin. Group Sales Assistant: Cris Torres.

Field Staff
Manager: Terry Pollreisz. Coaches: Andy Bottin, Scott Steinmann. Pitching Coach: Rafael Chaves. Trainer: Spyder Webb.

Game Information
Radio Announcer: Pat Dillon. No. of Games Broadcast: Home-38, Away-38. Flagship Station: KSER 90.7-FM.

PA Announcer: Tom Lafferty. Official Scorers: Pat Castro, John VanSandt.

Stadium Name (year opened): Everett Memorial Stadium (1984). Location: I-5, exit 192. Standard Game Times: 7:05 p.m.; Sat.-Sun. 6:05.

Visiting Club Hotel: Holiday Inn Hotel and Conference Center, 101 128th St. SE, Everett, WA 98208. Telephone: (425) 337-2900.

Portland
ROCKIES

Office Address: 1844 SW Morrison, Portland, OR 97205. Mailing Address: P.O. Box 998, Portland, OR 97207. Telephone: (503) 223-2837. FAX: (503) 223-2948. E-Mail Address: rockies@telport.com. Website: www.portlandrockies.com.

Affiliation (first year): Colorado Rockies (1995). Years in League: 1973-77, 1995-.

Ownership, Management
Operated by: Portland Baseball, Inc.

Principal Owners: Jack Cain, Mary Cain. President: Jack Cain.

General Manager: Mark Helminiak. Director, Merchandising: Bob Cain. Director, Ticket Sales: Corey Kearsley. Director, Group Sales: Brad Arnsmeier. Sales Manager: Kevin Robinson. Marketing Assistant: Katy Kurtz. Account Executives: J.D. Bigelow, Matt Brubaker, Greg Herbst, Kevin Herbst, Dick Johnson, Wade Lockett, Derek Milholland, Jeff Robbins, Hank Sadorus, Tom Shepherd. Clubhouse Operations: Doug Beaty.

Field Staff
Manager: Alan Cockrell. Coach: Stu Cole. Pitching Coach: Tom Edens. Trainer: Jeremy Moeller.

Game Information
Radio Announcer: Unavailable. No. of Games Broadcast: Home-38, Away-38. Flagship Station: 1520-AM.

PA Announcer: Unavailable. Official Scorers: Chuck Charnquist, John Hilsenteger.

Stadium Name (year opened): Civic Stadium (1926). Location: I-405 to West Burnside exit, SW 20th Street to stadium. Standard Game Times: 7:05 p.m.; Sun. 2:05.

Visiting Club Hotel: Ramada Plaza Hotel, 1441 SE Second Ave., Portland, OR 97232. Telephone: (503) 233-2401.

Salem-Keizer
VOLCANOES

Street Address: 6700 Field of Dreams Way NE, Keizer, OR 97307. **Mailing Address:** P.O. Box 20936, Keizer, OR 97307. **Telephone:** (503) 390-2225. **FAX:** (503) 390-2227. **E-Mail Address:** probasebal@aol.com. **Website:** www.volcanoesbaseball.com.

Affiliation (first year): San Francisco Giants (1997). **Years in League:** 1997-.

Ownership, Management
Operated By: Sports Enterprises, Inc.
Principal Owners: Jerry Walker, Bill Tucker.
President/General Manager: Jerry Walker.
Manager, Corporate Sales/Director, Promotions: Lisa Walker. **Controller:** Rick Nelson. **Director, Stadium Operations/Marketing:** Katrinka Rau. **Director, Sales/Media Relations:** Pat Lafferty. **Director, Community Relations/Marketing:** Holly Duckworth. **Director, Ticket Sales/Publications:** Kendahl Johnson. **Ticket Sales:** Aaron Price. **Director, Food Services:** Carol Unruh. **Facility Management:** Lois Holeman, Nate Holeman.

Field Staff
Manager: Frank Reberger. **Coach:** Bert Hunter. **Pitching Coach:** Gabe Luckert. **Trainer:** Eric Reisinger.

Game Information
Radio Announcer: Pat Lafferty. **No. of Games Broadcast:** Home-38, Away-38. **Flagship Station:** KYKN 1430-AM.
PA Announcer: Dave Jarvis. **Official Scorer:** Unavailable.
Stadium Name (year opened): Volcanoes Stadium (1997). **Location:** I-5 at exit 260 (Chemawa Road), west one block to Radiant Drive, north six blocks to stadium. **Standard Game Times:** 7:05 p.m.
Visiting Club Hotel: Ramada Inn, 200 Commercial St. SE, Salem, OR 97301. Telephone: (503) 363-4123.

Southern Oregon
TIMBERJACKS

Office Address: 1801 South Pacific Hwy., Medford, OR 97501. **Mailing Address:** P.O. Box 1457, Medford, OR 97501. **Telephone:** (541) 770-5364. **FAX:** (541) 772-4466. **E-Mail Address:** sotjacks@aol.com. **Website:** www.tjacks.com.

Affiliation (first year): Oakland Athletics (1979). **Years in League:** 1967-71, 1979-.

Ownership, Management
Operated by: National Sports Organization, Inc.
Principal Owners: Dwain Cross, Fred Herrmann, Bud Kaufman, John LeCompte.
President: Fred Herrmann.
General Manager: Dan Kilgras. **Assistant General Manager:** Jamie Brown. **Director, Operations:** Daniel Smith. **Marketing/Promotions:** Toby Hess, Jennifer Scutella. **Director, Business Operations:** Kate Hicks. **Director, Ticket Sales:** Jordell Hasha. **Head Groundskeeper:** Richard Steinmuller. **Clubhouse Operations:** Eddie Bolanos. **Office Manager:** Carol Miner.

Field Staff
Manager: Greg Sparks. **Coach:** Billy Owens. **Pitching Coach:** Gil Lopez. **Trainer:** Jeff Collins.

Game Information
Radio Announcer: Unavailable. **No. of Games Broadcast:** Home-38, Away-38. **Flagship Station:** KRRM 94.7-FM.
PA Announcer: Bobby Heiken. **Official Scorer:** B.G. Gould.
Stadium Name (year opened): Jackson and Perkins Gardens at Miles Field (1951). **Location:** I-5 to exit 27, east on Barnett Road one block to South Pacific Highway, south two blocks to stadium. **Standard Game Times:** 7:05 p.m.; Sun. 6:05.
Visiting Club Hotel: Doubletree-Medford, 200 N Riverside, Medford, OR 97501. Telephone: (541) 779-5811.

Spokane
INDIANS

Office Address: 602 N Havana, Spokane, WA 99202. Mailing Address: P.O. Box 4758, Spokane, WA 99202. Telephone: (509) 535-2922. FAX: (509) 534-5368.

Affiliation (first year): Kansas City Royals (1995). Years in League: 1972, 1983-.

Ownership, Management

Operated by: Longball, Inc.

Principal Owners: Bobby Brett, George Brett, J.B. Brett, Ken Brett.

Chairman: Bobby Brett. President: Andrew Billig.

General Manager: Paul Barbeau. Executive Director, Sponsorships: Otto Klein. Assistant GM, Tickets: Brent Miles. Controller: Carol Dell. Executive Administrative Assistant: Barbara Klante. Director, Operations: Chad Smith. Marketing Assistant: Michael Lindskog. Promotions Assistant: Andrea Feider. Director, Public Relations: Rob Leslie. Account Executives: Marc Neale, Grant Riddle, Scott Salter. Coordinator, Group Sales: Jonathan Goldstein. Head Groundskeeper: Anthony Lee.

Field Staff

Manager: Kevin Long. Coach: Joe Szekely. Pitching Coach: Randy Smith.. Trainer: Matt Medeiros.

Game Information

Radio Announcer: Bob Robertson. No. of Games Broadcast: Home-38, Away-38. Flagship Station: Unavailable.

PA Announcer: Unavailable. Official Scorer: Dave Edwards.

Stadium Name (year opened): Seafirst Stadium at Interstate Fairgrounds (1958). Location: I-90 to Havana exit, follow directions to Interstate Fairgrounds.

Standard Game Times: 7 p.m.; Sun. 6.

Visiting Club Hotel: Cavanaugh's 4th Avenue, 110 E Fourth Ave., Spokane, WA 99202. Telephone: (509) 838-6101.

Yakima
BEARS

Office Address: 810 W Nob Hill Blvd., Yakima, WA 98902. Mailing Address: P.O. Box 483, Yakima, WA 98907. Telephone: (509) 457-5151. FAX: (509) 457-9909.

Affiliation (first year): Los Angeles Dodgers (1990). Years in League: 1955-66, 1990-.

Management

General Manager: Bob Romero. Director, Stadium Operations: Gerry Sayler. Director, Sales/Food Services: Todd Kent. Director, Ticket Sales: Max Flower. Office Manager: DeAnne Munson. Head Groundskeeper: Bob Garretson. Clubhouse Operations: Craig Hyatt. Administrative Assistants: Ryan Barger, Anthony Viega.

Field Staff

Manager: Dino Ebel. Coach: Mitch Webster. Pitching Coach: Max Leon. Trainer: Beau Clay.

Game Information

Radio Announcer: Unavailable. No. of Games Broadcast: Home-38, Away-38. Flagship Station: Unavailable.

PA Announcer: Todd Lyons. Official Scorers: Doug Evans, Gene Evans.

Stadium Name (year opened): Yakima County Stadium (1993). Location: I-82 to exit 34 (Nob Hill Boulevard), west to Fair Avenue, right on Fair, right on Pacific Avenue. Standard Game Times: 7:05 p.m.; Sun. 6:05.

Visiting Club Hotel: Days Inn, 2408 Rudkin Rd., Union Gap, WA 98903. Telephone: (509) 248-9700.

APPALACHIAN LEAGUE

Rookie Advanced Classification

Mailing Address: 283 Deerchase Circle, Statesville, NC 28625. **Telephone:** (704) 873-5300. **FAX:** (704) 873-4333. **E-Mail Address:** appylg@i-america.net.

Years League Active: 1921-25, 1937-55, 1957-.

President/Treasurer: Lee Landers. **Corporate Secretary:** Dan Moushon (Burlington).

Directors: Jim Duquette (Kingsport), Tom Foley (Princeton), Neal Huntington (Burlington), Len Johnston (Bluefield), Mike Jorgensen (Johnson City), Deric Ladnier (Danville), Reid Nichols (Pulaski), Tim Purpura (Martinsville), Jim Rantz (Elizabethton), Ken Williams (Bristol).

Administrative Assistant: Bobbi Landers.

1999 Opening Date: June 18. **Closing Date:** Aug. 29.

Lee Landers

Regular Season: 70 games.

Division Structure: East—Bluefield, Burlington, Danville, Martinsville, Princeton. **West**—Bristol, Elizabethton, Johnson City, Kingsport, Pulaski.

Playoff Format: Division winners meet in best-of-3 series for league championship.

All-Star Game: None.

Roster Limit: 30 active. **Player Eligibility Rule:** No more than 12 players who are 21 or older; no more than two of the 12 may be 23 or older; no more than two years of prior service.

Brand of Baseball: Rawlings.

Statistician: Howe Sportsdata, Boston Fish Pier, West Bldg. #1, Suite 302, Boston, MA 02210.

Umpires: Tyler Bolick (Roswell, GA), Ron Chamberlain (Knoxville, TN), Ben Clanton (Nesbit, MS), Blake Estes (Houston, TX), Larry Galloway (Roanoke, AL), Ray Gregson (River Ridge, LA), Rusty Griffin (Gillsville, GA), Chris Keffner (Chester, VA), James Roebuck (Connelly Springs, NC), Tony Wilder (Shelbyville, KY).

Stadium Information

Club	Stadium	Dimensions			Capacity	'98 Att.
		LF	CF	RF		
Bluefield	Bowen Field	335	365	335	2,250	39,940
Bristol	DeVault Memorial	325	400	310	2,000	27,002
Burlington	Burlington Athletic	335	410	335	3,000	45,495
Danville	Dan Daniel Memorial	330	400	330	2,588	50,711
Elizabethton	Joe O'Brien Field	335	414	326	1,500	10,665
Johnson City	Howard Johnson	320	410	320	2,500	19,684
Kingsport	Hunter Wright	330	410	330	2,500	49,579
Martinsville	Hooker Field	330	402	330	3,200	44,501
Princeton	Hunnicutt Field	330	396	330	1,537	36,548
Pulaski	Calfee Park	335	405	310	2,500	8,812

Bluefield
ORIOLES

Office Address: 2001 Stadium Dr., Bluefield, WV 24701. **Mailing Address:** P.O. Box 356, Bluefield, WV 24701. **Telephone:** (540) 326-1326. **FAX:** (540) 326-1318.

Affiliation (first year): Baltimore Orioles (1958). **Years in League:** 1946-55, 1957-.

Ownership, Management

Operated by: Bluefield Baseball Club, Inc.
Director: Tom Trebelhorn.
President/General Manager: George McGonagle. **Assistant General Manager:** Kim Long. **Director, Business Operations:** Chandra Bostic. **Controller:** Charles Peters. **Directors, Special Projects:** John Duffy, Tuillio Ramella.

Field Staff

Manager: Duffy Dyer. **Coach:** Unavailable. **Pitching Coach:** Charlie Puleo. **Trainer:** P.J. Mainville.

Game Information

Radio Announcer: Larry McKay. **No. of Games Broadcast:** Unavailable. **Flagship Station:** WHIS 1440-AM.
PA Announcer: James Shott. **Official Scorer:** Kristi Maupin.
Stadium Name (year opened): Bowen Field (1939). **Location:** I-77 to Bluefield exit, Route 290 to Route 460 West, right onto Leatherwood Lane, left at first light, past Chevron station and turn right, stadium ¼ mile on left. **Standard Game Times:** 7 p.m., Sun. 6.
Visiting Club Hotel: Ramada Inn-East River, 3175 E Cumberland Rd., Bluefield, WV 24701. Telephone: (304) 325-5421.

Bristol
SOX

Office Address: 1501 Euclid Ave., Bristol, VA 24201. **Mailing Address:** P.O. Box 1434, Bristol, VA 24203. **Telephone:** (540) 645-7275. **FAX:** (540) 645-7377, (540) 669-7686. **E-Mail Address:** bwsox@3wave.com. **Website:** www.3wave.com/brisox.

Affiliation (first year): Chicago White Sox (1995). **Years in League:** 1921-25, 1940-55, 1969-.

Ownership, Management

Operated by: Bristol Baseball, Inc.
Director: Ken Williams (Chicago White Sox).
President: Boyce Cox. **General Manager:** R.E. Childress.

Field Staff

Manager: Mark Haley. **Coach:** Dallas Williams. **Pitching Coach:** Sean Snedeker. **Trainer:** Unavailable.

Game Information

Radio: None.
PA Announcer: Boyce Cox. **Official Scorer:** Allen Shepherd.
Stadium Name (year opened): DeVault Memorial Stadium (1969). **Location:** I-81 to exit 3 onto Commonwealth Ave., right on Euclid Ave. for ½ mile. **Standard Game Times:** 7 p.m.
Visiting Club Hotel: Ramada Inn, 2122 Euclid Ave., Bristol, VA 24201. Telephone: (540) 669-7171.

Burlington
INDIANS

Office Address: 1450 Graham St., Burlington, NC 27217. **Mailing Address:** P.O. Box 1143, Burlington, NC 27216. **Telephone:** (336) 222-0223. **FAX:** (336) 226-2498. **E-Mail Address:** bindians@aol.com.

Affiliation (first year): Cleveland Indians (1986). **Years in League:** 1986-.

Ownership, Management
Operated by: Burlington Baseball Club, Inc.
Director: Neal Huntington (Cleveland Indians).
President: Miles Wolff. **Vice President:** Dan Moushon.
General Manager: Mike Edwards. **Assistant General Manager:** Lisa LaRosa. **Head Groundskeeper:** Mike Thompson.

Field Staff
Manager: Jack Mull. **Coach:** Billy Williams. **Pitching Coach:** Sam Militello. **Trainer:** Unavailable.

Game Information
Radio Announcer: Unavailable. **No. of Games Broadcast:** Home-35, Away-35. **Flagship Station:** WBAG 1150-AM.
PA Announcer: Byron Tucker. **Official Scorer:** Karen Atwater.
Stadium Name (year opened): Burlington Athletic Stadium (1960). **Location:** I-40/85 to exit 145, north on Route 100 (Maple Avenue) for 1½ miles, right on Mebane Street for 1½ miles, right on Beaumont, left on Graham. **Standard Game Times:** 7 p.m.
Visiting Club Hotel: Holiday Inn, 2444 Maple Ave., Burlington, NC 27215. Telephone: (336) 229-5203.

Danville
BRAVES

Office Address: Dan Daniel Memorial Park, 302 River Park Dr., Danville, VA 24540. **Mailing Address:** P.O. Box 3637, Danville, VA 24543. **Telephone:** (804) 791-3346. **FAX:** (804) 791-3347. **E-Mail:** dbraves@gamewood.net. **Website:** www.danvillebraves.com.
Affiliation (first year): Atlanta Braves (1993). **Years in League:** 1993-.

Ownership, Management
Operated by: Danville Braves, Inc.
Director: Deric Ladnier (Atlanta Braves).
President/General Manager: Tim Cahill. **Head Groundskeeper:** Dick Gieselman. **Director, Special Projects:** Bob Kitzmiller.

Field Staff
Manager: J.J. Cannon. **Coach:** Ralph Henriquez. **Pitching Coach:** Jerry Nyman. **Trainer:** Unavailable.

Game Information
Radio: None.
PA Announcer: Unavailable. **Official Scorers:** Danny Miller, Stan Mitchell.
Stadium Name (first year): Dan Daniel Memorial Park (1993). **Location:** US 58 to Rivermont Road, follow signs to park; US 29 bypass to Dan Daniel Park exit (U.S. 58 East), to Rivermont Road, follow signs. **Standard Game Times:** 7 p.m.
Visiting Club Hotel: Innkeeper-West, 3020 Riverside Dr., Danville, VA 24541. Telephone: (804) 799-1202.

Elizabethton
TWINS

Office Address: 208 N Holly Lane, Elizabethton, TN 37643. **Mailing Address:** 136 S Sycamore St., Elizabethton, TN 37643. **Telephone:** (423) 547-6440. **FAX:** (423) 547-6441.
Affiliation (first year): Minnesota Twins (1974). **Years in League:** 1937-42, 1945-51, 1974-.

Ownership, Management
Operated by: City of Elizabethton.
Director: Jim Rantz (Minnesota Twins).
President: Harold Mains.
General Manager: Mike Mains. **Assistant General Manager:** Lisa Story. **Head Groundskeeper:** Willie Church. **Director, Sales/Marketing:** Shelley Cornett. **Director, Promotions:** Jim Jones. **Director, Ticket Sales:** Jane Crow. **Director, Group Sales:** Harold Ray. **Director, Merchandising:** Linda Church. **Director, Food Services:** Jane Hardin. **Clubhouse Operations:** David McQueen.

Field Staff
Manager: Jon Mathews. **Coach:** Ray Smith. **Pitching Coach:** Jim Shellenback. **Trainer:** Unavailable.

Game Information
Radio Announcer: Frank Santore. **No. of Games Broadcast:** Home-35, Away-6. **Flagship Station:** WBEJ 1240-AM.

PA Announcer: Tom Banks. **Official Scorer:** Bill Crow.

Stadium Name (year opened): Joe O'Brien Field (1974). **Location:** I-81 to I-181, exit at Highway 321/67, left at Holly Lane. **Standard Game Times:** 7 p.m.

Visiting Club Hotel: Days Inn, 505 W Elk Ave., Elizabethton, TN 37643. Telephone: (423) 543-3344.

Johnson City CARDINALS

Office Address: 111 Legion St., Johnson City, TN 37601. **Mailing Address:** P.O. Box 179, Johnson City, TN 37605. **Telephone:** (423) 461-4866. **FAX:** (423) 461-4864. **E-Mail Address:** jccardinals@worldnetatt.net.

Affiliation (first year): St. Louis Cardinals (1975). **Years in League:** 1921-24, 1937-55, 1957-61, 1964-.

Ownership, Management
Operated By: City of Johnson City.

Director: Mike Jorgensen (St. Louis Cardinals).

General Manager: Harry Gibson. **Assistant General Manager:** Mary Ann Marsh. **Intern, Sales/Marketing:** Amy Wiggs. **Clubhouse Operations:** Carl Black. **Head Groundskeeper:** Eddie Teague.

Field Staff
Manager: Steve Turco. **Coach:** Unavailable. **Pitching Coach:** Elias Sosa. **Trainer:** Unavailable.

Game Information
Radio: Unavailable.

PA Announcer: Kenneth Arrowood. **Official Scorer:** Joe Todd.

Stadium Name (year opened): Howard Johnson Field (1956). **Location:** I-181 to exit 32, left on East Main, right on Legion Street. **Standard Game Times:** 7 p.m.

Visiting Club Hotel: Ramada Inn, 2406 N Roan St., Johnson City, TN 37602. Telephone: (423) 282-2161.

Kingsport METS

Office Address: 433 E Center St., Kingsport, TN 37662. **Mailing Address:** P.O. Box 1128, Kingsport, TN 37662. **Telephone:** (423) 378-3744. **FAX:** (423) 392-8538. **E-Mail Address:** info@kmets.com. **Website:** www.kmets.com.

Affiliation (first year): New York Mets (1980). **Years in League:** 1921-25, 1938-52, 1957, 1960-63, 1969-82, 1984-.

Ownership, Management
Operated by: S&H Baseball, LLC.
Director: Jim Duquette (New York Mets).

Principal Owners: Steve Harville, Rick Spivey.

President: Rick Spivey. **Vice President:** Steve Harville.

General Manager: Jim Arnold.

Field Staff
Manager: Guy Conti. **Coach:** Juan Lopez. **Pitching Coach:** Bill Champion. **Trainer:** Jason Wulf.

Game Information
Radio Announcer: Tom Taylor. **No. of Games Broadcast:** Unavailable. **Flagship Station:** WKIN 1320-AM.

PA Announcer: Don Spivey. **Official Scorer:** Eddie Durham.

Stadium Name (year opened): Hunter Wright Stadium (1995). **Location:** I-81 to I-181 North, exit 11E (Stone Drive), left on West Stone Drive (U.S. 11W) for 1½ miles, right on Granby Road for ½ mile.

Standard Game Times: 7 p.m.
   Visiting Club Hotel: Comfort Inn, Hwy. 93 and Hwy. 11W, Kingsport, TN 37660. Telephone: (423) 246-5249.

Martinsville
ASTROS

   Office Address: Hooker Field, Commonwealth Blvd. and Chatham Heights Rd., Martinsville, VA 24112. **Mailing Address:** P.O. Box 3614, Martinsville, VA 24115. **Telephone:** (540) 666-2000. **FAX:** (540) 666-2139. **E-Mail Address:** mastros@kimbanet.com.
   Affiliation (first year): Houston Astros (1999). **Years in League:** 1988-.

Ownership, Management
   Operated by: Houston Astros Baseball Club.
   Director: Tim Purpura (Houston Astros).
   General Manager: Carper Cole. **Assistant General Manager:** Rachel Byrd. **Head Groundskeeper:** Sam Pickeral. **Clubhouse Operations:** Troy Wells.

Field Staff
   Manager: Brad Wellman. **Coach:** Gordy MacKenzie. **Pitching Coach:** Stan Boroski. **Trainer:** Unavailable.

Game Information
   Radio: None.
   PA Announcer: Unavailable. **Official Scorer:** Unavailable.
   Stadium Name (year opened): Hooker Field (1988). **Location:** US 220 Business to Commonwealth Boulevard, east for three miles; US 58 to Chatham Heights Road, north two blocks, stadium is located at intersection of Commonwealth and Chatham Heights. **Standard Game Times:** 7 p.m.
   Visiting Club Hotel: Dutch Inn, 2360 Virginia Ave., Collinsville, VA 24078. Telephone: (540) 647-3721.

Princeton
DEVIL RAYS

   Office Address: Hunnicutt Field, Old Bluefield Road, Princeton, WV 24740. **Mailing Address:** P.O. Box 5646, Princeton, WV 24740. **Telephone:** (304) 487-2000. **FAX:** (304) 487-8762. **E-Mail Address:** devilrays@inetone.net. **Website:** www.inetone.net/devilrays.
   Affiliation (first year): Tampa Bay Devil Rays (1997). **Years in League:** 1988-.

Ownership, Management
   Operated by: Princeton Baseball Association, Inc.
   Director: Tom Foley (Tampa Bay Devil Rays).
   President: Dewey Russell.
   General Manager: Jim Holland. **Account Representative:** Paul Lambert. **Director, Stadium Operations:** Mick Bayle. **Head Groundskeeper:** Frankie Bailey. **Administrative Assistants:** Daniella Hatfield, Samantha Craig.

Field Staff
   Manager: Bobby Ramos. **Coach:** Mike Tosar. **Pitching Coach:** Steve Mumaw. **Trainer:** Unavailable.

Game Information
   Radio: None.
   PA Announcer: Melanie Roth. **Official Scorer:** Dick Daisey.
   Stadium Name (year opened): Hunnicutt Field (1988). **Location:** Exit 9 off I-77, US 460 West to downtown exit, left on Stafford Drive, stadium located behind Mercer County Technical Education Center. **Standard Game Times:** 7 p.m.
   Visiting Club Hotel: Days Inn, I-77 and Ambrose Lane, Princeton, WV 24740. Telephone: (304) 425-8100.

Pulaski
RANGERS

Office Address: 700 S Washington Ave., Pulaski, VA 24301. **Mailing Address:** P.O. Box 676, Pulaski, VA 24301. **Telephone:** (540) 980-1070. **FAX:** (540) 994-0847. **E-Mail Address:** hnicely@swva.net.

Affiliation (first year): Texas Rangers (1997). **Years in League:** 1946-50, 1952-55, 1957-58, 1969-77, 1982-92, 1997-.

Ownership, Management
Operated by: Pulaski Baseball, Inc.
Principal Owners: Wayne Carpenter, Hi Nicely, Dr. Rick Mansell.
Director: Reid Nichols (Texas Rangers).
President: Hi Nicely.
General Manager: Chad Brisco. **Director, Business Operations:** Wayne Carpenter. **Director, Stadium Operations:** Dave Hart. **Director, Sales/Promotions:** Tom Wallace. **Director, Ticket Sales:** Rick Mansell. **Head Groundskeeper:** Don Newman. **Assistant Groundskeeper:** Gary Martin.

Field Staff
Manager: Bruce Crabbe. **Coaches:** Unavailable. **Trainer:** Brian Ball.

Game Information
Radio: None.
PA Announcer: Unavailable. **Official Scorer:** Unavailable.
Stadium Name (year opened): Calfee Park (1935). **Location:** I-81 to exit 89 (Route 11), north to Pulaski, right on Pierce Avenue. **Standard Game Times:** 7 p.m.
Visiting Club Hotel: Unavailable.

PIONEER LEAGUE

Rookie Advanced Classification

Office Address: 812 W 30th Ave., Spokane, WA 99203. **Mailing Address:** P.O. Box 2564, Spokane, WA 99220. **Telephone:** (509) 456-7615. **FAX:** (509) 456-0136. **E-Mail Address:** baseball@ior.com. **Website:** www.pioneerleague.com.

Years League Active: 1939-42, 1946-.

President/Secretary-Treasurer: Jim McCurdy.

Vice President: Mike Ellis (Missoula).

Directors: Dave Baggott (Ogden), Mike Ellis (Missoula), Larry Geske (Great Falls), Kevin Greene (Idaho Falls), Rob Owens (Helena), Tom Whaley (Butte), Bob Wilson (Billings), Bill Yuill (Medicine Hat).

Administrative Assistant: Teryl MacDonald.

Jim McCurdy

1999 Opening Date: June 16. **Closing Date:** Sept. 3.

Regular Season: 76 games (split schedule).

Division Structure: North—Great Falls, Helena, Medicine Hat, Missoula. **South**—Butte, Billings, Idaho Falls, Ogden.

Playoff Format: First-half division winners play second-half division winners in best-of-3 series. Winners meet in best-of-3 series for league championship.

All-Star Game: None.

Roster Limit: 30 active. **Player Eligibility Rule:** No more than 17 players 21 and older, provided that no more than three are 23 or older. No player on active list may have more than three years of prior service.

Brand of Baseball: Rawlings.

Statistician: Howe Sportsdata, Boston Fish Pier, West Bldg. #1, Suite 302, Boston, MA 02210.

Umpires: Tim Cordill (Kansas City, KS), Bill Dishman (Coweta, OK), Peter Durfee (Tucson, AZ), Jimmy Forbis (Lawrence, KS), Chris Hamburg (Troutdale, OR), Adrian Johnson (Houston, TX), Dan Moore (Yucaipa, CA), Andrew Wendel (San Marcos, TX).

Stadium Information

Club	Stadium	LF	CF	RF	Capacity	'98 Att.
Billings	Cobb Field	335	405	325	4,200	95,553
Butte	Alumni Coliseum	335	450	355	1,500	26,061
Great Falls	Legion Park	335	414	335	3,800	74,369
Helena	Kindrick Field	335	400	325	2,010	36,516
Idaho Falls	McDermott Field	340	400	350	2,800	62,087
Medicine Hat	Athletic Park	350	400	350	3,000	34,631
Missoula*	Lindborg-Cregg	330	410	330	1,900	—
Ogden	Lindquist Field	335	399	335	5,000	99,443

*Club operated in Lethbridge in 1998

Billings
MUSTANGS

Office Address: Cobb Field, 901 N 27th St., Billings, MT 59103. **Mailing Address:** P.O. Box 1553, Billings, MT 59103. **Telephone:** (406) 252-1241. **FAX:** (406) 252-2968. **E-Mail Address:** mustangs@wtp.net. **Website:** www.wtp.net/mustangs.

Affiliation (first year): Cincinnati Reds (1974). **Years in League:** 1948-63, 1969-.

Ownership, Management

Operated by: Billings Pioneer Baseball Club, Inc.

Chairman: Ron May.

President/General Manager: Bob Wilson. **Assistant General Manager:** Gary Roller. **Head Groundskeeper:** Francis Rose. **Director, Broadcasting:** Joe Dominey.

Field Staff

Manager: Russ Nixon. **Coach:** Brian Wilson. **Pitching Coach:** Terry Abbott. **Trainer:** Unavailable.

Game Information

Radio Announcer: Joe Dominey. **No. of Games Broadcast:** Home-38, Away-38. **Flagship Station:** KCTR 970-AM.

PA Announcer: Hank Cox. **Official Scorer:** Jack Skinner.

Stadium Name (year opened): Cobb Field (1948). **Location:** I-90 to 27th Street North exit, north to Ninth Avenue North. **Standard Game Times:** 7 p.m., Sun. 6.

Visiting Club Hotel: Rimrock Inn, 1203 N 27th St., Billings, MT 59101. Telephone: (406) 252-7107.

Butte
COPPER KINGS

Office Address: West Park Street, Butte, MT 59701. **Mailing Address:** P.O. Box 888, Butte, MT 59703. **Telephone:** (406) 723-8206. **FAX:** (406) 723-3376. **E-Mail Address:** copkings@montana.com. **Website:** www.copperkings.com.

Affiliation: Anaheim Angels (1997). **Years in League:** 1978-85, 1987-.

Ownership, Management

Operated by: Silverbow Baseball Corp.

Principal Owners: Mike Veeck, Bill Murray, Bill Fanning, Annie Huidekoper, Rich Taylor, Cynthia Gitt, Miles Wolff.

Chairman: Mike Veeck. **President:** Bill Fanning.

General Manager: Unavailable.

Field Staff

Manager: Joe Urso. **Coach:** Orlando Mercado. **Pitching Coach:** Zeke Zimmerman. **Trainer:** Jaime Macias.

Game Information

Radio Announcer: Unavailable. **No. of Games Broadcast:** Home-38, Away-38. **Flagship Station:** KXTL 1370-AM.

PA Announcer: Unavailable. **Official Scorer:** Unavailable.

Stadium Name (year opened): Alumni Coliseum (1962). **Location:** I-90 to Montana Street exit, north to Park Street, west to stadium (on Montana Tech campus). **Standard Game Times:** 7:05 p.m., Sun. (June-July) 2:05, (Aug.-Sept.) 5:05.

Visiting Club Hotel: War Bonnet Inn, 2100 Cornell, Butte, MT 59701. Telephone: (406) 494-7800.

Great Falls
DODGERS

Office Address: 10 Third St. NW, Great Falls, MT 59401. **Mailing Address:** P.O. Box 1621, Great Falls, MT 59403. **Telephone:** (406) 452-5311. **FAX:** (406) 454-0811.

Affiliation (first year): Los Angeles Dodgers (1984). **Years in League:**

1948-63, 1969-.

Ownership, Management
Operated by: Great Falls Baseball Club, Inc.
President: Larry Geske.
General Manager: Jim Keough. Director, Stadium Operations: Billy Chaffin. Director, Media/Public Relations: Gene Black. Director, Merchandising: Sandy Geske. Director, Food Services: Larry Lucero. Office Manager: Ginger Robbins.

Field Staff
Manager: Tony Harris. Coach: Quinn Mack. Pitching Coach: Greg Gohr. Trainer: Unavailable.

Game Information
Radio Announcer: Gene Black. No. of Games Broadcast: Home-38, Away-38. Flagship Station: KFIN 1310-AM.
PA Announcer: Tim Paul. Official Scorer: Tim Paul.
Stadium Name (year opened): Legion Park (1956). Location: From I-15, take 10th Ave. South (exit 281) for four miles to 26th Street, left to 8th Ave. North, left to 25th Street North, right to ballpark. Standard Game Times: 7 p.m., Sun. 4.
Visiting Club Hotel: Midtowne Hotel, 526 Second Ave. N, Great Falls, MT 59401. Telephone: (406) 453-2411.

Helena
BREWERS

Office Address: 1103 N Main, Helena, MT 59601. Mailing Address: P.O. Box 4606, Helena, MT 59604. Telephone: (406) 449-7616. FAX: (406) 449-6979. E-mail Address: helbrewers@aol.com.
Affiliation (first year): Milwaukee Brewers (1985). Years in League: 1978-.

Ownership, Management
Operated by: Never Say Never, Inc.
Principal Owners: Rob Owens, Stanley Owens, Linda Gach Ray.
General Manager: Jessica Berry. Head Groundskeeper: Brian Wiek. Director, Media/Public Relations: Joel White. Director, Marketing/Food Services: Christi Burget. Account Representative: Dan Peterson. Clubhouse Operations: Todd Piper.

Field Staff
Manager: Carlos Lezcano. Coach: Unavailable. Pitching Coach: R.C. Lichtenstein. Trainer: Greg Barajas.

Game Information
Radio Announcer: Dan Peterson. No. of Games Broadcast: Home-38, Away-38. Flagship Station: KBLL 1240-AM.
PA Announcer: Brett Charvat. Official Scorer: Dan Peterson.
Stadium Name (year opened): Kindrick Legion Field (1939). Location: Cedar Street exit off I-15, west to Main Street, left at Memorial Park. Standard Game Times: 7:05 p.m.
Visiting Club Hotel: Super 8, 2201 11th Ave., Helena, MT 59601. Telephone: (406) 443-2450.

Idaho Falls
BRAVES

Office Address: 568 W Elva, Idaho Falls, ID 83402. Mailing Address: P.O. Box 2183, Idaho Falls, ID 83403. Telephone: (208) 522-8363. FAX: (208) 522-9858. E-Mail Address: braves@ifbraves.com. Website: ifbraves.com.
Affiliation (first year): San Diego Padres (1995). Years in League: 1940-42, 1946-.

Ownership, Management
Operated by: The Elmore Group.
Principal Owner: David Elmore.
President/General Manager: Kevin Greene. Vice President/Director, Administration: Paul Fetz. Assistant General Manager: Marcus Loyola. Director, Media/Public Relations: Michael James. Head Groundskeeper: Craig Evans.

Field Staff

Manager: Don Werner. **Coach:** Gary Kendall. **Pitching Coach:** Darryl Milne. **Trainer:** John Maxwell.

Game Information

Radio Announcer: Unavailable. **No. of Games Broadcast:** Home-38, Away-38. **Flagship Station:** KUPI 980-AM.

PA Announcer: Kelly Beckstead. **Official Scorer:** John Balginy.

Stadium Name (year opened): McDermott Field (1976). **Location:** I-15 to West Broadway exit, left onto Memorial Drive, right on Mound Avenue, ¼ mile to stadium. **Standard Game Times:** 7:15 p.m., Sun. 5.

Visiting Club Hotel: Best Western Stardust, 700 Lindsay Blvd., Idaho Falls, ID 83402. Telephone: (208) 522-2910.

Medicine Hat
BLUE JAYS

Mailing Address: 361 First St. SE, Medicine Hat, Alberta T1A 0A5. **Telephone:** (403) 526-0404. **FAX:** (403) 526-4000.

Affiliation (first year): Toronto Blue Jays (1978). **Years in League:** 1977-.

Ownership, Management

Operated By: Whycom Holdings Ltd.

Principal Owner/President: Bill Yuill.

General Manager: Larry Plante. **Controller:** Katherine Kirkup. **Director, Sales/Marketing:** Dave Bender. **Account Representative:** Raymond Christensen. **Director, Ticket Sales:** Peggy Plante. **Office Manager:** Barb Ayling.

Field Staff

Manager: Paul Elliott. **Coach:** Geovany Miranda. **Pitching Coach:** Unavailable. **Trainer:** Unavailable.

Game Information

Radio: None.

PA Announcer: Eric Baadsgaard. **Official Scorer:** Hubie Schlenker.

Stadium Name: Athletic Park (1977). **Location:** First Street SW exit off Trans Canada Highway, left on River Road. **Standard Game Times:** 7:05 p.m.

Visiting Club Hotel: Unavailable.

Missoula
OSPREY

Office Address: 137 E Main St., Missoula, MT 59802. **Telephone:** (406) 543-3300. **FAX:** (406) 543-9463. **E-Mail Address:** info@missoulaosprey.com. **Website:** www.missoulaosprey.com.

Affiliation (first year): Arizona Diamondbacks (1999). **Years in League:** 1956-60, 1999.

Ownership, Management

Operated by: Mountain Baseball, LLC

Chairman: Horn Chen. **President:** Mike Ellis.

General Manager: Joe Easton. **Office Manager:** Terri Orser.

Field Staff

Manager: Joe Almaraz. **Coach:** Rafael Landestoy. **Pitching Coach:** Royal Clayton. **Trainer:** Unavailable.

Game Information

Radio Announcer: Unavailable. **No. of Games Broadcast:** Home-38, Away-38. **Flagship Station:** Unavailable.

PA Announcer: Unavailable. **Official Scorer:** Unavailable.

Stadium Name (year opened): Lindborg-Cregg Field (1999). **Location:** I-90 to Reserve exit, south on Reserve, right on Spurgin Road, left on Tower Road, stadium on left. **Standard Game Times:** 7 p.m., Sun. 2.

Visiting Club Hotel: Unavailable.

Ogden
RAPTORS

Office Address: 2330 Lincoln Ave., Ogden, UT 84401. **Telephone:** (801) 393-2400. **FAX:** (801) 393-2473. **E-Mail Address:** homerun@ogden-raptors.com. **Website:** www.ogden-raptors.com.

Affiliation: Milwaukee Brewers (1996). **Years in League:** 1939-42, 1946-55, 1966-74, 1994-.

Ownership, Management

Operated by: Ogden Professional Baseball, Inc.

Principal Owners: Dave Baggott, John Lindquist.

Chairman/President: Dave Baggott.

General Manager: John Stein. **Head Groundskeeper:** Ken Kopinski. **Director, Media/Public Relations:** Pete Diamond. **Director, Group Sales:** Steve Oates. **Director, Merchandising:** Geri Kopinski. **Office Manager:** Jill Steenburg.

Field Staff

Manager: Jon Pont. **Coach:** Tom Houk. **Pitching Coach:** Steve Cline. **Trainer:** Unavailable.

Game Information

Radio Announcer: Phill Ellson. **No. of Games Broadcast:** Home-38, Away-38. **Flagship Station:** KSOS 800-AM.

PA Announcer: Dave Baggott. **Official Scorer:** Holly Knudsen.

Stadium Name: Lindquist Field (1997). **Location:** I-15 North to 21st Street exit, east to Lincoln Avenue, south three blocks to park. **Standard Game Times:** 7:11 p.m., Sun. 1:30.

Visiting Club Hotel: Days Inn of Ogden, 3306 Washington Blvd., Odgen, UT 84401. Telephone: (801) 399-5671.

ARIZONALEAGUE

Rookie Classification

Street Address: 5900 N Granite Reef Rd., Suite 105, Scottsdale, AZ 85250. **Mailing Address:** P.O. Box 4941, Scottsdale, AZ 85261. **Telephone:** (602) 483-8224. **FAX:** (602) 443-3450.

Years League Active: 1988-.

President/Treasurer: Bob Richmond.

Vice President: Tommy Jones (Diamondbacks). **Corporate Secretary:** Ted Polakowski (Athletics).

Administrative Assistant: Rob Richmond.

1999 Opening Date: June 23. **Closing Date:** August 31. **Game Times:** 10 a.m.; night games—7 p.m.

Division Structure: None.

Regular Season: 56 games.

Playoff Format: Phoenix-area team with best record plays Tucson-area team with best record in one-game championship.

All-Star Game: None.

Roster Limit: 30 active, 35 under control. **Player Eligibility Rule:** No more than eight players 20 or older, and no more than two players 21 or older. At least 10 pitchers. No more than two years of prior service, excluding Rookie leagues outside the United States and Canada.

Brand of Baseball: Rawlings.

Statistician: Howe Sportsdata, Boston Fish Pier, West Bldg. #1, Suite 302, Boston, MA 02210.

Clubs	Playing Site	Manager
Athletics	Papago Park Sports Complex, Phoenix	John Kuehl
Cubs	Fitch Park, Mesa	Carmelo Martinez
Diamondbacks	Kino Baseball Complex, Tucson	Roly de Armas
Mariners	Peoria Sports Complex, Peoria	Gary Thurman
Mexico All-Stars	Kino Baseball Complex, Tucson	Unavailable
Padres	Peoria Sports Complex, Peoria	Randy Whisler
Rockies	Hi Corbett Field, Tucson	P.J. Carey
White Sox	Tucson Electric Park, Tucson	Jerry Hairston

GULFCOASTLEAGUE

Rookie Classification

Mailing Address: 1503 Clower Creek Dr., Suite H-262, Sarasota, FL 34231. **Telephone:** (941) 966-6407. **FAX:** (941) 966-6872.

Years League Active: 1964-.

President/Secretary-Treasurer: Tom Saffell.

First Vice President: Steve Noworyta (Phillies). **Second Vice President:** Jim Rantz (Twins).

Executive Secretary: Anne Doyle.

1999 Opening Date: June 18. **Closing Date:** Aug. 26.

Regular Season: 60 games.

Division Structure: East—Braves, Expos, Marlins, Mets. **North**—Phillies, Royals, Tigers, Yankees. **West**—Orioles, Pirates, Rangers, Reds, Red Sox, Twins.

Playoff Format: Northern and Eastern Division winners play one game. Top two teams in Western Division play one game. Winners advance to best-of-3 series for league championship.

All-Star Game: None.

Roster Limit: 30 active. **Player Eligibility Rule:** No more than eight players 20 or older, and no more than two players 21 or older. No more than two years of prior service, excluding Rookie leagues outside the United States and Canada.

Brand of Baseball: Rawlings.

Statistician: Howe Sportsdata, Boston Fish Pier, West Bldg. #1, Suite 302, Boston, MA 02210.

Clubs	Playing Site	Manager
Braves	Disney's Wide World of Sports, Orlando	Rick Albert
Expos	Roger Dean Stadium, Jupiter	Bill Masse
Marlins	Carl Barger Baseball Complex, Melbourne	Jon Deeble

Mets	St. Lucie County Sports Complex	John Stephenson
Orioles	Twin Lakes Park, Sarasota	Jesus Alfaro
Phillies	Carpenter Complex, Clearwater	Ramon Aviles
Pirates	Pirate City Complex, Bradenton	Woody Huyke
Rangers	Charlotte County Stadium, Port Charlotte	Darryl Kennedy
Reds	Ed Smith Stadium, Sarasota	Donnie Scott
Red Sox	Red Sox minor league complex, Fort Myers	John Sanders
Royals	Baseball City Sports Complex	Andre David
Tigers	Tigertown, Lakeland	Unavailable
Twins	Lee County Stadium, Fort Myers	Al Newman
Yankees	Yankee Complex, Tampa	Ken Dominguez

TEAM best ™

THE LEADER IN MINOR LEAGUE BASEBALL™ TRADING CARDS FOR OVER 10 YEARS.

Minor League Schedules

CLASSAAA

International League

Buffalo

APRIL
8-9-10-11 .... Ottawa
12-13 .... Pawtucket
22-23 .... Rochester
24-25 .... Syracuse
26-27-28-29 .... Scranton

MAY
7-8-9-10 .... Richmond
20-21-22-23 .... Charlotte

JUNE
1-2-3-4 .... Durham
5-6-7-8 .... Pawtucket
18-19-20-21 .... Louisville
22-23-24-25 . Indianapolis
30 .... Toledo

JULY
1-2-3 .... Toledo
10-11 .... Rochester
15-16 .... Ottawa
17-18 .... Scranton
31 .... Syracuse

AUGUST
1-2 .... Syracuse
3-4 .... Pawtucket
9-10-11-12 ...... Norfolk
13-14-15-16 .. Columbus
19-20 .... Scranton
23-24-25 .... Syracuse
30-31 .... Ottawa

SEPTEMBER
1-2 .... Rochester
5-6 .... Rochester

Charlotte

APRIL
8-9-10 .... Norfolk
11-11-13 .... Richmond
20-21-22 .... Toledo
23-24-25-26 .. Columbus

MAY
3-4-5-6 .... Pawtucket
7-8-9-10 .... Syracuse
11-12 .... Durham
15-16-17-18 .. Rochester
28-29-30-31 ...... Buffalo

JUNE
1-2-3-4 .... Louisville
10-11-12-13 .... Ind.
23-24-25 .... Richmond
26-27-28-29 ...... Ottawa

JULY
4 .... Durham
5-6 .... Norfolk
15-16 .... Columbus
17-18 .... Indianapolis
28-29-30 .... Toledo
31 .... Scranton

AUGUST
1-2-3 .... Scranton
17-18 .... Durham
21-22-23 .... Norfolk
24-25 .... Louisville
31 .... Richmond

SEPTEMBER
1 .... Richmond
4-5-6 .... Durham

Columbus

APRIL
14-15 .... Durham
16-17-18-19 .... Charlotte
28-29.......... Indianapolis
30 .... Louisville

MAY
1-2-3 .... Louisville
9-10 .... Louisville
11-12-13-14....... Buffalo
22-23-24 .... Norfolk
25-26-27 .... Richmond
28-29-30-31 .... Scranton

JUNE
10-11-12-13 .... Ottawa
14-15-16-17 ... Rochester
26-27 .... Toledo
30 .... Syracuse

JULY
1-2-3 .... Syracuse
4-5-6-7 .... Pawtucket
10-11 .... Indianapolis
21-22 .... Louisville
23-24-25-26 ...... Durham

AUGUST
2-3-4 .... Norfolk
5-6............. Indianapolis
7-8 .... Charlotte
11-12 .... Toledo
21-22-23 .... Richmond
24-25 .... Toledo
26-27.......... Indianapolis

SEPTEMBER
3-4 .... Toledo

Durham

APRIL
8-9-10 .... Richmond
11-12 .... Norfolk
20-21-22 .... Columbus
23-24-25-26 .... Toledo

MAY
3-4-5-6 .... Syracuse
7-8-9-10 .... Pawtucket
13-14 .... Charlotte
24-25-26-27 ...... Buffalo

JUNE
5-6-7 .... Louisville
14-15-16-17 .... Ind.
18-19-20 .... Norfolk

JULY
3 .... Charlotte
5-6-7 .... Richmond
11-12 .... Charlotte
15-16 .... Indianapolis
17-18-19 .... Columbus
27-28-29-30 .... Scranton
31 .... Toledo

AUGUST
1 .... Toledo
2-3-4-5 .... Rochester
13-14-15-16 ..... Ottawa
19-20 .... Charlotte
21-22-23...... Louisville
24-25 .... Richmond
30 .... Charlotte

SEPTEMBER
1-2-3 .... Norfolk

Indianapolis

APRIL
8-9-10-11 .... Toledo
12-13 .... Columbus
19...................... Norfolk
20-21-22 .... Richmond
23-24-25 .... Norfolk

Louisville

APRIL
8-9-10-11 ...... Columbus
12-13 .... Toledo
20-21-22 .... Norfolk
23-24-25 .... Richmond

MAY
5-6............. Indianapolis
7-8............... Columbus
11-12-13-14 .... Ottawa
24-25-26-27 .. Pawtucket
28-29-30-31 .. Rochester

JUNE
8-9 .... Charlotte
11-12-13 .... Durham
14-15-16-17 ... Syracuse
26-27-28-29 .... Scranton

JULY
2-3............. Indianapolis
15-16-17 .... Richmond
18-19-20 .... Norfolk
23-24-25-26 ...... Buffalo
27-28............ Columbus
31 .... Indianapolis

AUGUST
1 .... Indianapolis
6-7-8............... Durham
9-10-11-12 .... Charlotte
13-14-15 .... Toledo
31 .... Indianapolis

SEPTEMBER
1-2 .... Toledo
5-6............ Indianapolis

Norfolk

APRIL
14-15 .... Louisville
16-17-18-18 .... Ind.
28-29 .... Charlotte
30 .... Durham

MAY
1-2 .... Durham
11-12-13-14 .... Scranton
15-16-17-18 .. Columbus
25-26-27 .... Toledo

28-29-30-31 ... Syracuse
JUNE
10-11-12-13....... Buffalo
14-15-16-17... Pawtucket
22-23-24-25...... Ottawa
26-27............ Richmond
30 .... Durham
JULY
1-2 .... Durham
4 .... Richmond
7-8-9-10......... Charlotte
22.................... Richmond
23-24......... Indianapolis
25-26-27 .... Toledo
29-30-31 ...... Rochester
AUGUST
1.................... Rochester
13.................... Richmond
16.................... Richmond
17-18-19-20.... Louisville
26-27............ Charlotte
28-29 .... Durham
30-31............ Columbus
SEPTEMBER
4-5.................. Richmond

Ottawa
APRIL
14-15-16 .... Scranton
17-18.............. Buffalo
19-20-21 ...... Pawtucket
30.................... Rochester
MAY
1-2 .... Rochester
3-4-5-6 .... Norfolk
15-16-17-18 .... Ind.
20-21-22-23 ... Syracuse
28-29-30-31 .... Durham
JUNE
1-2-3-4 .... Columbus
14-15-16-17....... Toledo
18-19-20-21 .. Charlotte
JULY
1-2-3 .... Rochester
4-5-6-7 .... Louisville
8-9-10-11 ...... Louisville
23-24-25 ...... Pawtucket
AUGUST
3-4 .... Syracuse
5-6-7-8 .... Richmond
9-10 .... Pawtucket
11-12 .... Rochester
23-24-25 .... Scranton
26-27.............. Buffalo
SEMPTEMBER
1-2 .... Scranton
5-6 .... Syracuse

Pawtucket
APRIL
14-15-16 .... Rochester
17-18.............. Syracuse
27-28-29 .... Ottawa
30.................... Buffalo
MAY
1-2 .... Buffalo
11-12-13-14 .... Toledo
15-16-17-18... Louisville
28-29-30-31 .... Ind.
JUNE
1-1-2-4 .... Norfolk
10-11-12-13 .. Richmond
22-23-24-25 .. Columbus
26-27-28-29...... Durham
JULY
1-2-3 .... Scranton
15-16-17-18 ... Syracuse
19-20-21-22.... Charlotte
28-29-30 .... Buffalo
31...................... Ottawa

AUGUST
1-2 .... Ottawa
12-13-14 .... Scranton
15-16 .... Rochester
21-22................ Buffalo
23-24-25 ...... Rochester
SEPTEMBER
1-2 .... Syracuse
3-4 .... Ottawa
5-6 .... Scranton

Richmond
APRIL
14-15......... Indianapolis
16-17-18-19..... Louisville
27-28-29 .... Durham
30 .... Charlotte
MAY
1-2 .... Charlotte
12-12-13-14 .. Rochester
15-16-17-18 ... Scranton
20-21.............. Columbus
28-29-30-31 ...... Toledo
JUNE
1-2-3-4 .... Syracuse
14-15-16-17 .... Buffalo
18-19-20-21 .. Pawtucket
28-29 .... Norfolk
30 .... Charlotte
JULY
1-2 .... Charlotte
3...................... Norfolk
8-9-10............. Durham
11-12................ Norfolk
23-24 .... Toledo
25-26-27-28 .... Ind.
29-30 .... Louisville
31.................... Columbus
AUGUST
1 .... Columbus
14-15 .... Norfolk
17-18-19-20 ...... Ottawa
26-27................ Durham
28-29 .... Columbus
SEPTEMBER
2-3.................. Charlotte
6...................... Norfolk

Rochester
APRIL
10-11 .... Syracuse
17-18 .... Scranton
19-20-21 .... Buffalo
24-25 .... Pawtucket
27.................... Syracuse
MAY
3-4-5-6 .... Richmond
7-8-9-10 .... Norfolk
20-21-22-23..... Louisville
24-25-26-27 ...... Ottawa
JUNE
5-6-7-8 .... Columbus
10-11-12-13 .... Scranton
22-23-24-25...... Durham
26-27-28-29 .... Ind.
JULY
4-5-6-7 .... Toledo
15-16 .... Scranton
17-18 .... Ottawa
23-24-25 ...... Charlotte
27-28 .... Ottawa
AUGUST
6-7-8 .... Buffalo
13-14............ Syracuse
17-18................ Buffalo
19-20 .... Pawtucket
21-22 .... Syracuse
27.................... Syracuse
28-29-30-31........... Paw.

Scranton/W-B
APRIL
8-9-10-11 ...... Pawtucket
12-13 .... Rochester
19-20-21...... Syracuse
22-23-24-25 .... Ottawa
MAY
4-5-6 .... Buffalo
7-8-9-10 .... Toledo
19-21-22-23..... Durham
24-25-26-27 .... Ind.
JUNE
5-6-7-8 .... Richmond
14-15-16-17 ... Charlotte
18-19-20-21 .. Columbus
JULY
4-5-6-7........... Louisville
8-9-9 .... Buffalo
19-20-21-22.. Rochester
23-24-25...... Syracuse
AUGUST
5-6-7-8 .... Norfolk
9-10 .... Rochester
15-16 .... Syracuse
17-18 .... Pawtucket
21-22 .... Ottawa
26-27 .... Pawtucket
28-29 .... Ottawa
SEPTEMBER
3-4.................... Buffalo

Syracuse
APRIL
8-9 .... Rochester
12-13 .... Ottawa
14-15-16 .... Buffalo
22-23 .... Pawtucket
28-29 .... Rochester
30 .... Scranton
MAY
1-2 .... Scranton
11-12-13-14........... Ind.
15-16-17-18.... Durham
24-25-26-27 ... Charlotte
JUNE
5-6-7-8 .... Norfolk
10-11-12-13 .... Toledo
22-23-24-25.... Louisville
26-27-28 .... Buffalo
JULY
8-9 .... Rochester
10-11-12 .... Scranton
19-20-21-22 ...... Ottawa
26-27 .... Pawtucket
29-30 .... Ottawa
AUGUST
5-6-7-8........... Pawtucket
9-10-11-12 ... Richmond
17-18-19-20 .. Columbus
28-29................ Buffalo
30-31 .... Scranton
SEPTEMBER
3-4 .... Rochester

Toledo
APRIL
14-15 .... Charlotte
16-17-18-19...... Durham
27-28-29....... Louisville
30.............. Indianapolis
MAY
1-2.............. Indianapolis
4-5-6 .... Columbus
15-16-17-18 ...... Buffalo
19-20-21 .... Norfolk
22-23-24 .... Richmond
JUNE
1-2-3-4 .... Rochester
5-6-7-8 .... Ottawa
18-19-20-21 ... Syracuse

22-23-24-25 .... Scranton	
28-29............ Columbus	
JULY	
8-9-10-11 ...... Pawtucket	
15-16-17 .... Norfolk	
18-19-20 ...... Richmond	

21-22 .... Durham
AUGUST
2-3-4 .... Louisville
5-6 .... Charlotte
7-8 .... Indianapolis
10 .... Columbus

17-18-19 .... Ind.
26-27 .... Louisville
28-29 .... Charlotte
SEPTEMBER
5-6 .... Columbus

Pacific Coast League

Albuquerque
APRIL
8-9-10-11 .... Tacoma
12-13-14 ...... Oklahoma
23-24-25-26 ...... Calgary
MAY
1-2-3-4 .... Fresno
6-7-8-9 .... Omaha
18-19-20-21 ...... N.O.
22-23-24-25 .... Nash.
30-31 .... Las Vegas
JUNE
1-2 .... Las Vegas
3-4-5-6 .... Iowa
12-13-14-15 .... Memphis
26-27-28-29 ...... Tucson
30 .... Colo. Springs
JULY
1-2-3 .... Colo. Springs
19-20-21-22 .. Colo. Spr.
23-24-25-26 .... Iowa
AUGUST
5-6-7-8 .... Edmonton
21-22-23-24 . Vancouver
26-27-28-29 ...... Omaha
SEPTEMBER
3-4-5-6 .... Salt Lake

Calgary
APRIL
16-17-18 .... N.O.
19-20-21-22 ...... Tucson
MAY
1-2-3-4 .... Nashville
6-7-8-9 ...... Las Vegas
18-19-20-21 .... Van.
22-23-24-25 ...... Tacoma
30-31 .... Salt Lake
JUNE
1-2 .... Salt Lake
12-13-14-15 .. Colo. Spr.
17-18-19-20 . Vancouver
26-27-28-29 ...... Omaha
30 .... Memphis
JULY
1-2-3 .... Memphis
19-20 .... Edmonton
23-24-25-26 ...... Tacoma
27-28-29-30 .... Okla.
AUGUST
9-10-11-12 Albuquerque
19-20 .... Edmonton
26-27-28-29 . Edmonton
30-31 .... Iowa
SEPTEMBER
1-2 .... Iowa
3-4-5-6 .... Fresno

Colo. Springs
APRIL
16-17-18 .... Tacoma
19-20-21-22.... Nashville
MAY
1-2-3-4 ..... New Orleans
6-7-8-9 .... Oklahoma
14-15-16-17 .... Fresno
18-19-20-21 ...... Omaha
26-27-28-29 .... L.V.
JUNE
8-9-9-11 .... Memphis

22-23-24-25 .... Calgary
JULY
4-5-6-7 .... Iowa
8-9-10-11 .. Albuquerque
27-28-29-30.. Omaha
31 .... Albuquerque
AUGUST
1-2-3 .... Albuquerque
9-10-11-12 .... Edmonton
13-14-15-16 .. Salt Lake
17-18-19-20 .... Iowa
30-31 .... Tucson
SEPTEMBER
1-2 .... Tucson
3-4-5-6 .... Vancouver

Edmonton
APRIL
16-17-18 .... Tucson
19-20-21-22 .... N.O.
MAY
1-2-3-4 .... Las Vegas
6-7-8-9 .... Nashville
18-19-20-21 ...... Tacoma
22-23-24-25 . Vancouver
26-27-28-29 .... Salt Lake
JUNE
8-9-10-11 ...... Calgary
17-18-19-20 .. Colo. Spr.
26-27-28-29 .... Memphis
30 .... Omaha
JULY
1-2-3 .... Omaha
21-22 .... Calgary
23-24-25-26 ...... Van.
31 .... Oklahoma
AUGUST
1-2-3 .... Oklahoma
13-14-15-16 .... Alb.
17-18 .... Calgary
21-22-23-24 .... Fresno
30-31 .... Tacoma
SEPTEMBER
1-2 .... Tacoma
3-4-5-6 .... Iowa

Fresno
APRIL
13-14-15 .... Iowa
23-24-25-26 .. Oklahoma
MAY
6-7-8-9 .... Vancouver
10-11-12-13 .... Calgary
26-27-28-29 .... Nashville
30-31 .... Edmonton
JUNE
1-2 .... Edmonton
8-9-10-11 .. Albuquerque
16-17-18-20...... Omaha
22-23-24-25 ...... Tacoma
26-27-28-29 .... N.O.
JULY
4-5-6-7 .... Tucson
8-9-10-11 ...... Las Vegas
15-16-17-18 .. Salt Lake
31 .... Tucson
AUGUST
1-2-3 .... Tucson
5-6-7-8 ..... Colo. Springs
9-10-11-12 ...... Memphis

26-27-28-29 .... L.V.
30-31 .... Salt Lake
SEPTEMBER
1-2 .... Salt Lake

Iowa
APRIL
16-17-18 ...... Las Vegas
19-20-21-22.... Memphis
MAY
2-3-4 .... Omaha
6-7-8-9 .... Salt Lake
10-11-12-13 .... Tucson
22-23-24-25 .. Colo. Spr.
26-27-28-29 .... Alb.
JUNE
8-9-10-11 ...... Nashville
12-13-14-15 .. Edmonton
26-27-28-29 .. Colo. Spr.
30 .... New Orleans
JULY
1-2-3 .... New Orleans
15-16-17-18 .... Alb.
19-20-21-22 .... Fresno
31 .... Tacoma
AUGUST
1-2-3 .... Tacoma
5-6-7-8 .... Calgary
9-10-11-12.... Vancouver
13 .... Omaha
21-22-23-24........ Omaha
26-27-28-29 .. Oklahoma

Las Vegas
APRIL
8-9-10-11 .... Omaha
12-13-14 .. Colo. Springs
23-24-25-26 .. Edmonton
27-28-29-30 .... Calgary
MAY
14-15-16-17 ... Salt Lake
18-19-20-21 ...... Fresno
22-23-24-25 .... Memphis
JUNE
3-4-5-6 .... Vancouver
12-13-14-15 .... Tacoma
17-18-19-20 .... Tucson
22-23-24-25 .... Iowa
30 .... Fresno
JULY
1-2-3 .... Fresno
15-16-17-18 .. Oklahoma
27-28-29-30 .... N.O.
31 .... Nashville
AUGUST
1-2-3 .... Nashville
9-10-11-12.... Salt Lake
21-22-23-24 ...... Tucson
30-31......... Albuquerque
SEPTEMBER
1-2 .... Albuquerque

Memphis
APRIL
8-9-10-11 .... Calgary
12-13-14 ...... Edmonton
23-24-25-26 .. Colo. Spr.
27-28-29-30 ... Salt Lake
MAY
10-11-12-13 Albuquerque
14-15-16-17 .... N.O.

26-27-28-29....... Tucson
30-31 .... Omaha
JUNE
1-2 .... Omaha
17-18-19-20...... Iowa
22-23-24-25.... Oklahoma
JULY
4-5-6-7.............. Tacoma
8-9-10-11........ Vancouver
19-20-21-22 .. Las Vegas
27-28-29-30.... Nashville
31 .... New Orleans
AUGUST
1-2-3........ New Orleans
13-14-15-16 .. Oklahoma
17-18-19-20 ...... Fresno
SEPTEMBER
3-4-5-6 .... Nashville

Nashville
APRIL
8-9-10-11 ...... Edmonton
12-13-14 .... Calgary
23-24-25-26 .. Salt Lake
27-28-29-30 .. Colo. Spr.
MAY
10-11-12-13 .. Oklahoma
14-15-16-17 .... Alb.
18-19-20-21 .... Iowa
30-31 .... Tucson
JUNE
1-2 .... Tucson
4-5-6 .... Memphis
12-14-14-15 .. Oklahoma
17-18-19-20 .... N.O.
JULY
4-5-6-7 .... Vancouver
8-9-10-11........... Tacoma
15-16-16-17-18 Memphis
23-24-25-26 .. Las Vegas
AUGUST
9-10-11-12 .... N.O.
13-14-15-16 .... Fresno
30-31 .... Omaha
SEPTEMBER
1-2 .... Omaha

New Orleans
APRIL
8-9-10-11 .... Fresno
12-13-14 .... Vancouver
23-24-25-26 ...... Omaha
MAY
6-7-8-9 .... Memphis
10-11-12-13 .. Colo. Spr.
26-27-28-29 .. Oklahoma
30-31 .... Iowa
JUNE
1-2 .... Iowa
12-13-14-15 .... Salt Lake
22-23-24-25 Albuquerque
JULY
4-5-6-7 .... Edmonton
8-9-10-11 .... Calgary
19-20-21-22.... Nashville
23-24-25-26.... Tucson
AUGUST
5-6-7-8 .... Oklahoma
13-14-15-16 .. Las Vegas
21-22-23-24.... Nashville
26-27-28-29.... Nashville
SEPTEMBER
3-4-5-6 .... Tacoma

Oklahoma
APRIL
8-9-10-11...... Vancouver
16-17-18 .... Nashville
19-20-21-22...... Tacoma
28-29-29-30 .... N.O.

MAY
2-3-3-4 .... Memphis
14-15-16-17........ Iowa
31-31 .... Colo. Springs
JUNE
1-2 .... Colo. Springs
3-4-5-6 .... Fresno
8-9-10-11........ Salt Lake
17-18-19-20 Albuquerque
JULY
4-5-6-7 .... Calgary
8-9-10-11 .... Edmonton
19-20-21-22.... Tucson
23-24-25-26.... Memphis
AUGUST
9-10-11-12........ Omaha
17-18-19-20 . Las Vegas
21-22-23-24.... Nashville
30-31 .... New Orleans
SEPTEMBER
1-2 .... New Orleans

Omaha
APRIL
16-17-18 .... Memphis
19-20-20-21 . Las Vegas
27-28-29-30 .... Alb.
MAY
1 .... Iowa
10-11-12 ...... Salt Lake
14-15-16-17........ Tucson
22-23-24-25 .... N.O.
26-27-28-29 ...... Tacoma
JUNE
3-4-5-6..... Colo. Springs
22-23-24-25 .. Edmonton
JULY
4-5-6-7 ...... Albuquerque
8-9-10-11 .... Iowa
15-16-17-18.... Colo. Springs
23-24-25-26 .... Fresno
31 .... Calgary
AUGUST
1-2-3 .... Calgary
5-6-7-8 .... Vancouver
14-15-16 .... Iowa
17-18-19-20.... Nashville
SEPTEMBER
3-4-5-6 .... Oklahoma

Salt Lake
APRIL
8-9-10-11 .... Iowa
16-17-18 .... Fresno
19-20-21-22 Albuquerque
MAY
1-2-3-4 .... Tucson
18-19-20-21 .... Memphis
22-23-24-25 .. Oklahoma
JUNE
3-4-5-6 .... Edmonton
17-18-19-20 ...... Tacoma
22-23-24-25 . Vancouver
26-27-28-29 . Las Vegas
JULY
4-5-6-7 ...... Las Vegas
8-9-10-11 .... Tucson
19-20-21-22...... Omaha
23-24-25-26 .. Colo. Spr.
27-28-29-30 ...... Fresno
AUGUST
5-6-7-8 .... Nashville
17-18-19-20 .... N.O.
21-22-23-24 ...... Calgary

Tacoma
APRIL
13-14-15 .... Salt Lake
23-24-25 .... Iowa
27-28-29-30 .... Fresno

MAY
10-11-12-13 .. Edmonton
14-15-16-17 ...... Calgary
30-31 .... Vancouver
JUNE
1-2 .... Vancouver
4-5-6-7 ..... New Orleans
8-9-10-11 .... Omaha
26-27-28-29 .. Oklahoma
30 .... Nashville
JULY
1-2-3 .... Nashville
15-16-17-18 .. Edmonton
19-20-21-22 . Vancouver
27-28-29-30 .... Alb.
AUGUST
5-6-7-8 .... Las Vegas
9-10-11-12 .... Tucson
13-14-15-16 ...... Calgary
21-22-23-24 .. Colo. Spr.
26-27-28-29.... Memphis

Tucson
APRIL
8-9-10-11. Colo. Springs
23-24-25-26 . Vancouver
27-28-29-30.. Edmonton
MAY
6-7-8-9 .... Tacoma
13-14-15.............. Omaha
18-19-20-21 .. Oklahoma
22-23-24-25 .... Fresno
JUNE
3-4-5-6 .... Calgary
8-9-10-11 ...... Las Vegas
12-13-14-15 ...... Fresno
22-23-24-25.... Nashville
30................... Salt Lake
JULY
1-2-3 .... Salt Lake
15-16-17-18 .... N.O.
27-28-29-30........ Iowa
AUGUST
5-6-7-8............. Memphis
17-18-19-20 .... Alb.
26-27-28-29 .. Salt Lake
SEPTEMBER
3-4-5-6 .... Las Vegas

Vancouver
APRIL
16-17-18 ... Albuquerque
19-20-21-22 .... Fresno
27-28-29-30........ Iowa
MAY
1-2-3-4 .... Tacoma
10-11-12-13.. Las Vegas
14-15-16-17 .. Edmonton
26-27-28-29 ...... Calgary
JUNE
8-9-10-11.. New Orleans
12-13-14-15....... Omaha
26-27-28-29.... Nashville
30................. Oklahoma
JULY
1-2-3 .... Oklahoma
15-16-17-18 ...... Calgary
27-28-29-30 .. Edmonton
31 .... Salt Lake
AUGUST
1-2-3 .... Salt Lake
13-14-15-16 ...... Tucson
17-18-19-20 ...... Tacoma
26-27-28-29 .. Colo. Spr.
30-31 .... Memphis
SEPTEMBER
1-2 .... Memphis

CLASSAA

Eastern League

Akron
APRIL
12-13-14 .... Reading
15-16-17-18.. Harrisburg
27-28-29 .... Bowie
30 .... Erie
MAY
1-2 .... Erie
3-4-5 .... Altoona
10-11-12 .... Altoona
24-25-26 ..... New Britain
27-28-29-30 ...... Trenton
JUNE
8-9-10 .... Harrisburg
14-15-16 .... Portland
17-18-19-20 New Haven
JULY
2-3-4 .... Bowie
5-6-7-8 .... Reading
15-16-17-18 .... Altoona
22-23-24-25 ..... Altoona
26-27-28 .... Harrisburg
AUGUST
6-7-8 .... Reading
16-17-18 .... Binghamton
19-20-21-22 .... Norwich
27-28-29 .... Erie
SEPTEMBER
3-4-5-6 .... Bowie

Altoona
APRIL
15-16-17-18 .... Bowie
19-20 .... Harrisburg
27-28-29 .... Reading
30 .... Bowie
MAY
1-2 .... Bowie
6-7-8-9 .... Erie
13-14-15-16-17 ..... Harr.
21-22-23 .... Akron
24-25-26 ..... New Haven
27-28-29-30 ..... Portland
JUNE
7-8-9 .... Bowie
14-15-16 .... Binghamton
17-18-19-20 ... Norwich
28-29-30 .... Erie
JULY
9-10-11-12 .... Akron
19-20-21 .... Erie
29-30-31 .... Akron
AUGUST
1 .... Akron
6-7-8 .... Erie
9-10-11 .... New Britain
19-20-21-22 .... Trenton
24-25-26 .... Akron
30-31 .... Reading
SEPTEMBER
1 .... Reading

Binghamton
APRIL
12-13-14 .... Portland
15-16-17-18 ...... Norwich
27-28-29 .... Portland
30 .... Norwich
MAY
1-2 .... Norwich

13-14-15-16 New Haven
18-19-20 .... Trenton
24-25-26 .... Harrisburg
31 .... Erie
JUNE
1-2 .... Erie
3-4-5-6 .... Altoona
8-9-10 .... Trenton
21-22-23-24 ...... Altoona
25-26-27 .... Reading
JULY
2-3-4 .... New Britain
18-19-20-21 ..... Portland
22-23-24-25 .... Reading
29-30-31 .... Trenton
AUGUST
1 .... Trenton
6-7-8 .... Norwich
9-10-11 .... Bowie
12-13-14-15.. Harrisburg
24-25-26 ..... New Britain
30-31 .... New Haven
SEPTEMBER
1 .... New Haven

Bowie
APRIL
9-10-11 .... Akron
20-21 .... Erie
22-23-24-25 ...... Altoona
MAY
3-4-5 .... Harrisburg
7-8-9 .... Akron
13-14-15-16 .... Reading
18-19-20 .... Altoona
24-25-26 .... Norwich
27-28-29-30 ...... Bing.
JUNE
11-12-13 .... Reading
14-15-16 .... Trenton
17-18-19-20 New Britain
28-29-30 .... Akron
JULY
1 .... Akron
5-6-7-8 .... Erie
19-20-21 .... Akron
29-30-31 .... Erie
AUGUST
1 .... Erie
6-7-8 .... Harrisburg
16-17-18 .... New Haven
20-21-22-23 ..... Portland
27-28-29............ Altoona
30-31 .... Erie
SEPTEMBER
1-2 .... Erie

Erie
APRIL
12-13-14.............. Bowie
15-16-17-18 ...... Reading
27-28-29 .... Harrisburg
MAY
3-4-5 .... Reading
10-11-12 .... Bowie
13-14-15-16 .... Akron
21-22-23 .... Reading
24-25-26 .... Portland
27-28-29-30 New Haven

JUNE
11-12-13 .... Akron
14-15-16 .... Norwich
17-18-19-20 ...... Bing.
JULY
2-3-4 .... Altoona
9-10-11-12 .... Harrisburg
22-23-24-25........ Bowie
26-27-28 .... Altoona
AUGUST
2-3-4 .... Akron
16-17-18 .... Trenton
20-21-22-23 New Britain
24-25-26 .... Harrisburg
SEPTEMBER
3-4-5-6 .... Altoona

Harrisburg
APRIL
9-10-11 .... Erie
12-13-14 .... Altoona
22-23-24-25 .... Akron
MAY
6-7-8-9 .... Binghamton
10-11-12 .... Trenton
18-19-20 .... Erie
21-22-23 .... Bowie
27-28-29-30 .... Norwich
JUNE
11-12-13 .... Altoona
14-15-16 .... New Britain
17-18-19-20 ...... Trenton
29-30 .... Binghamton
JULY
1 .... Binghamton
5-6-7-8 .... Altoona
15-16-17-18......... Bowie
19-20-21 .... Reading
29-30-31 .... Reading
AUGUST
1 .... Reading
3-4-5 .... Bowie
9-10-11 .... Portland
19-20-21-22 New Haven
27-28-29 .... Reading
30-31 .... Akron
SEPTEMBER
1 .... Akron

New Britain
APRIL
15-16-17-18 ...... Trenton
19-20-21 .... Norwich
27-28-29 ..... New Haven
30 .... Portland
MAY
1-2 .... Portland
13-14-15-16 ..... Norwich
21-22-23 .... Trenton
31 .... Bowie
JUNE
1-2 .... Bowie
3-4-5-6.......... Harrisburg
11-12-13..... Binghamton
22-22-23 .... Erie
24-25-26-27 ...... Altoona
28-29-30 .... Portland
JULY
1 .... Portland
5-6-7-8 .... Binghamton

20-21-22	New Haven
23-24-25	Norwich
29-30-31	New Haven

AUGUST

1	New Haven
3-4-5	Binghamton
12-13-14-15	Akron
16-17-18	Reading
27-28-29	Trenton
30-31	Portland

SEPTEMBER

1	Portland

New Haven

APRIL

12-13-14	Trenton
15-16-17-18	Portland
30	Trenton

MAY

1-2	Trenton
3-4-5	Binghamton
6	Norwich
18-19-20	New Britain
21-22-23	Binghamton
31	Akron

JUNE

1-2	Akron
3-4-5-6	Reading
8-9-10	Norwich
21-22-23-24	Bowie
25-26-27	Harrisburg
30	Norwich

JULY

1	Norwich
2-3-4	Portland
9-10-11-12	New Britain
15-16-17-18	Trenton
26-27-28	Portland

AUGUST

6-7-8	New Britain
9-10-11	Erie
12-13-14-15	Altoona
23-24-25-26	Norwich

SEPTEMBER

3-4-5-6	Binghamton

Norwich

APRIL

9-10-11	New Haven
12-13-14	New Britain
22-23-24-25	Bing.

MAY

3-4-5	Portland
7-8-9	New Haven
10-11-12	New Britain
21-22-23	Portland
31	Altoona

JUNE

1-2	Altoona
3-4-5-6	Erie
11-12-13	New Haven
21-22-23-24	Reading
25-26-27	Akron
28-29	New Haven

JULY

5-6-7	New Haven
15-16-17-18	New Britain
19-20-21	Trenton
26-27-28	New Britain
29-30-31	Portland

AUGUST

1	Portland
12-13-14-15	Bowie
16-17-18	Harrisburg
27-28-29	Binghamton
30-31	Trenton

SEPTEMBER

1	Trenton

Portland

APRIL

9-10-11	New Britain
19-20-21	Binghamton
22-23-24-25	New Haven

MAY

6-7-8-9	New Britain
10-11-12	New Haven
18-19-20	Norwich
31	Reading

JUNE

1-2	Reading
3-4-5-6	Akron
8-9-10	New Britain
21-22-23-24	Harrisburg
25-26-27	Bowie

JULY

5-6-7-8	Trenton
9-10-11-12	Norwich
15-16-17	Binghamton
23-24-25	New Haven

AUGUST

3-4-5	Norwich
6-7-8	Trenton
12-13-14-15	Erie
16-17-18	Altoona
27-28-29	New Haven

SEPTEMBER

3-4-5-6	New Britain

Reading

APRIL

9-10-11	Altoona
19-20-21	Akron

22-23-24-25	Erie
30	Harrisburg

MAY

1-2	Harrisburg
7-8-9	Trenton
10-11-12	Binghamton
18-19-20	Akron
27-28-29-30	New Britain

JUNE

7-8-9	Erie
14-15-16	New Haven
17-18-19-20	Portland
28-29-30	Trenton

JULY

1	Trenton
2-3-4	Harrisburg
9-10-11-12	Bowie
15-16-17-18	Altoona
26-27-28	Bowie

AUGUST

3-4-5	Altoona
9-10-11	Norwich
19-20-21-22	Bing.
24-25-26	Bowie

SEPTEMBER

3-4-5-6	Harrisburg

Trenton

APRIL

9-10-11	Binghamton
19-20-21	New Haven
22-23-24-25	New Britain
27-28-29	Norwich

MAY

3-4-5	New Britain
13-14-15-16	Portland
24-25-26	Reading
31	Harrisburg

JUNE

1-2	Harrisburg
3-4-5-6	Bowie
11-12-13	Portland
21-22-23	Altoona
24-25-26-27	Erie

JULY

2-3-4	Norwich
9-10-11-12	Binghamton
22-23-24-25	Harrisburg
26-27-28	Binghamton

AUGUST

3-4-5	New Haven
9-10-11	Akron
12-13-14-15	Reading
24-25-26	Portland

SEPTEMBER

3-4-5-6	Norwich

Southern League

Birmingham

APRIL

8-9-10-11	Mobile
12-13-14	Carolina
23-24-25-26	Knoxville
27-28-29-30	Greenville

MAY

10-11-12-13	Jacksonville
14-15-16-17	Huntsville
28-29-30-31	Chatta.

JUNE

1-2-3-4	Orlando
19-20-21-22	West Tenn

JULY

3-4-5	Knoxville
9-10-11-12	Carolina
19-20-21-22	Huntsville

23-24-25-26	Mobile

AUGUST

1-2-3-4	Greenville
5-6-7-8	Jacksonville
21-22-23-24	Chatta.
26-27-28-29	West Tenn
30-31	Orlando

SEPTEMBER

1-2	Orlando

Carolina

APRIL

16-17-18	West Tenn
19-20-21-22	Greenville

MAY

6-7-8-9	Huntsville
14-15-16-17	Chatta.
28-29-30-31	Mobile

JUNE

1-2-3-4	Knoxville
5-6-7-8	Birmingham
15-16-17-18	Orlando
19-20-21-22	Jacksonville

JULY

3-4-5	Jacksonville
15-16-17-18	Orlando
19-20-21-22	Chatta.
28-29-30-31	West Tenn

AUGUST

1-2-3-4	Huntsville
9-10-11-12	Greenville
13-14-15-16	Birmingham
26-27-28-29	Mobile

SEPTEMBER

3-4-5-6	Knoxville

Chattanooga

APRIL
16-17-18.......... Orlando
19-20-21-22 Jacksonville

MAY
1-2-3-4 .... West Tenn
6-7-8-9 .... Birmingham
10-11-12-13 .... Huntsville
19-20-21-22 .... Knoxville

JUNE
1-2-3-4 .... Mobile
5-6-7-8 .... Greenville
10-11-12-13 ..... Carolina
24-25-26-27 . West Tenn
29-30 .... Mobile

JULY
1-2 .... Mobile
6-7-8 .... Carolina
15-16-17-18 ... Knoxville
23-24-25-26... Huntsville

AUGUST
9-10-11-12 . Birmingham
13-14-15-16 Jacksonville
17-18-19-20.... Orlando

SEPTEMBER
3-4-5-6 .... Greenville

Greenville

APRIL
8-9-10-11 .. Chattanooga
12-13-14 .... Mobile
23-24-25-26... Huntsville

MAY
6-7-8-9 .... Knoxville
10-11-12-13 ..... Orlando
23-24-25-26 ..... Carolina
28-29-30-31 . West Tenn

JUNE
1-2-3-4 .... Jacksonville
15-16-17-18 Birmingham
24-25-26-27 .... Knoxville
29-30 .... West Tenn

JULY
1-2 .... West Tenn
6-7-8 .... Birmingham
23-24-25-26 ..... Carolina
28-29-30-31 .... Mobile

AUGUST
5-6-7-8 .... Huntsville
13-14-15-16...... Orlando
17-18-19-20 Jacksonville
30-31 .... Chattanooga

SEPTEMBER
1-2 .... Chattanooga

Huntsville

APRIL
16-17-18 .... Jacksonville
19-20-21-21 .... Birm.
27-28-29-30....... Mobile

MAY
1-2-3-4 .... Greenville
19-20-21-22 ..... Carolina
23-24-25-26 .... Knoxville
28-29-30-31...... Orlando

JUNE
15-16-17-18 . West Tenn
19-20-21-22 .... Chatta.
24-25-26-27 Jacksonville

JULY
3-4-5 .... Greenville
15-16-17-18 . West Tenn

28-29-30-31 .... Birm.

AUGUST
9-10-11-12 ...... Knoxville
17-18-19-20 .... Carolina
21-22-23-24 .... Mobile
26-27-28-29....... Chatta.

SEPTEMBER
3-4-5-6............. Orlando

Jacksonville

APRIL
8-9-10-11 ...... Huntsville
12-13-14 ...... Knoxville
23-24-25-26 .... Carolina
27-28-29-30...... Chatta.

MAY
1-2 .... Orlando
14-15 .... Orlando
19-20-21-22 .... Birm.
23-24-25-26 . West Tenn

JUNE
10-11-12-13 .. Greenville
15-16-17-18........ Mobile
29-30.......... Birmingham

JULY
1-2 .... Birmingham
6-7-8 .... Mobile
9-10-11-12.... Huntsville
15-16-17-18 .. Greenville
28-29-30-31....... Chatta.

AUGUST
1-2-3-4 .... West Tenn
9-10-11-12........ Orlando
21-22-23-24 .... Knoxville
30-31 .... Carolina

SEPTEMBER
1-2 .... Carolina

Knoxville

APRIL
16-17-18 ...... Greenville
19-20-21-22 . West Tenn

MAY
1-2-3-4 ...... Birmingham
10-11-12-13 .... Carolina
14-15-16-17....... Mobile
28-29-30-31 Jacksonville

JUNE
5-6-7-8............. Orlando
10-11-12-13 ... Huntsville
15-16-17-18...... Chatta.
29-30 .... Huntsville

JULY
1-2 .... Huntsville
6-7-8............ West Tenn
9-10-11-12 Chattanooga
19-20-21-22...... Orlando
23-24-25-26 .... Jack.

AUGUST
6-6-7-8 .... Carolina
17-18-19-20 Birmingham
26-27-28-29 .. Greenville
30-31 .... Mobile

SEPTEMBER
1-2 .... Mobile

Mobile

APRIL
16-17-18 .... Birmingham
19-20-21-22...... Orlando

MAY
1-2-3-4 .... Carolina

28-29-30-31 .... Birm.

AUGUST
9-10-11-12 ...... Knoxville
17-18-19-20 .... Carolina
21-22-23-24 ...... Mobile
26-27-28-29....... Chatta.

SEPTEMBER
3-4-5-6............. Orlando

Orlando

APRIL
8-9-10-11 .... Knoxville
12-13-14 .... Huntsville
23-24-25-26....... Chatta.
27-28-29-30 ..... Carolina

MAY
3-4 .... Jacksonville
16-17 .... Jacksonville
19-20-21-22 . West Tenn
23-24-25-26 .... Birm.

JUNE
10-11-12-13........ Mobile
19-20-21-22 .. Greenville
24-25-26-27 .... Birm.
29-30 .... Carolina

JULY
1-2 .... Carolina
6-7-8 .... Huntsville
9-10-11-12 .... Mobile
28-29-30-31 .... Knoxville

AUGUST
1-2-3-4...... Chattanooga
5-6-7-8 ...... West Tenn
21-22-23-24 .. Greenville
26-27-28-29 .... Jack.

West Tenn

APRIL
8-9-10-11 .... Carolina
12-13-14 .... Chattanooga
23-24-25-26........ Mobile
27-28-29-30 .... Knoxville

MAY
6-7-8-9............. Orlando
14-15-16-17 .. Greenville

JUNE
1-2-3-4 .... Huntsville
5-6-7-8 .... Jacksonville
10-11-12-13 .... Birm.

JULY
3-4-5 .... Chattanooga
9-10-11-12 .. Greenville
19-20-21-22 .... Jack.
23-24-25-26...... Orlando

AUGUST
9-10-11-12 .... Mobile
13-14-15-16 .... Carolina
21-22-23-24 ...... Carolina
30-31 .... Huntsville

SEPTEMBER
1-2 .... Huntsville
3-4-5-6 .... Birmingham

28-29-30-31 .... Birm.

AUGUST
9-10-11-12 ...... Knoxville
17-18-19-20 .... Carolina
21-22-23-24 ...... Mobile
26-27-28-29....... Chatta.

SEPTEMBER
3-4-5-6............. Orlando

Texas League

Arkansas

APRIL
8-9-10-10-12.... Jackson
13-14-15-16-17..... Tulsa
24-24-25-26-27. Shreve.

MAY
10-11-12-13-14. El Paso
15-15-16-17-18. Midland

JUNE
1-2-3-4-5-5 .. Shreveport
7-8-9-10-11-12...... Tulsa
25-26-26-27-28-29 Jack.

JULY
8-9-10-10-12-13 Wichita
15-16-17-17-19-20. S.A.

AUGUST
5-6-7-7-9...... Shreveport
20-21-21-23-24..... Tulsa
25-26-27-28-28 Jackson

El Paso

APRIL
14-15-16-17-18 ...... S.A.
29-30 .... Midland

MAY
1-2-3................ Midland
5-6-7-8-9 .... Wichita
21-22-23-24-25 .... Ark.
26-27-28-29-30..... Tulsa

JUNE
7-8-8-9-11-12 .... Wichita
13-14-15-16-17-18 . Mid.
25-26-27-28-29-30 . S.A.

JULY
8-9-10-11-12-13.... Jack.
15-16-17-18-19-20.. Shr.

AUGUST
5-6-7-8-9 .... Wichita
10-11-12-13-14. Midland
25-26-27-28-29 ...... S.A.

Jackson

APRIL
19-20-21-22-23...... Ark.
29-30 .... Shreveport

MAY
1-2-3................ Shreveport
4-5-6-7-8............... Tulsa
20-21-22-23-24 ..... S.A.*
26-27-28-29-30 . Wichita

JUNE
13-14-15-16-17-18.. Ark.
19-20-21-22-23-24 . Shr.

JULY
2-3-4-5-6-7 .... Tulsa
21-22-23-24-25-26 . El P
29-30-31 .... Midland

AUGUST
1-2-3................ Midland

10-11-12-13-14 . Shreve.
15-16-17-18-19 .... Ark.
31 .... Tulsa

SEPTEMBER
1-2-3-4................... Tulsa
*Games played in Austin

Midland

APRIL
19-20-21-22-23. El Paso
24-25-26-27-28 . Wichita

MAY
4-5-6-7-8.... San Antonio
21-22-23-24-25..... Ark.
26-27-28-29-30 .... Ark.

JUNE
7-8-9-10-11-12. San Ant.
19-20-21-22-23-24 . El P
25-26-27-28-29-30 Wich.

JULY
8-9-10-11-12-13 Shreve.
15-16-17-18-19-20 Jack.

AUGUST
5-6-7-8-9.... San Antonio
15-16-17-18-19 . Wichita
20-21-22-23-24. El Paso

San Antonio

APRIL
8-9-10-11-12..... Midland
24-25-26-27-28. El Paso
29-30 .... Wichita

MAY
1-2-3................ Wichita
10-11-12-13-14 . Shreve.
15-16-17-18-19 Jackson
31 .... El Paso

JUNE
1-2-3-4-5 .... El Paso
19-20-21-22-23-24 Wich.

JULY
2-3-4-5-6-7 ...... Midland
21-22-23-24-25-26 Tulsa
29-30-31 .... Arkansas

AUGUST
1-2-3............... Arkansas
10-11-12-13-14.. Wichita
15-16-17-18-19. El Paso
31 .... Midland

SEPTEMBER
1-2-3-4.............. Midland

Shreveport

APRIL
13-14-15-16-17 Jackson
19-20-21-22-23..... Tulsa

MAY
4-5-6-7-8 .... Arkansas
21-22-23-24-25 . Wichita
26-27-28-29-30 ...... S.A.

JUNE

JUNE
7-8-9-10-11-12 . Jackson
13-14-15-16-17-18 Tulsa

JULY
2-3-4-5-6-7 ..... Arkansas
21-22-23-24-25-26 . Mid.
29-30-31 .... El Paso

AUGUST
1-2-3 .... El Paso
15-16-17-18-19..... Tulsa
20-21-22-23-24 Jackson
31 .... Arkansas

SEPTEMBER
1-2-3-4............. Arkansas

Tulsa

APRIL
8-9-10-11-12 Shreveport
24-25-26-27-28 Jackson
29 .... Arkansas

MAY
1-1-2-3............. Arkansas
10-11-12-13-14. Midland
15-16-17-18-19..... Tulsa

JUNE
1-2-3-4-5-6....... Jackson
19-20-21-22-23-24 .. Ark.
25-26-27-28-29-30.. Shr.

JULY
8-9-10-11-12-13 ..... S.A.
15-16-17-18-19-20 Wich.

AUGUST
5-6-7-8-9 .... Jackson
10-11-12-13-14 .... Ark.
25-26-27-28-29. Shreve.

Wichita

APRIL
8-9-10-11-12..... El Paso
13-14-15-16-17. Midland
19-20-21-22-23 ..... S.A.

MAY
10-11-12-13-14 Jackson
15-16-17-18-19. Shreve.

JUNE
1-2-3-4-5-6 .... Midland
13-14-15-16-17-18 . S.A.

JULY
2-3-4-5-6-7 .... El Paso
21-22-23-24-25-26.. Ark.
29-30-31 .... Tulsa

AUGUST
1-1-2.................... Tulsa
20-21-22-23-24 ...... S.A.
26-27-28-29-30. Midland
31 .... El Paso

SEPTEMBER
1-2-3-4.............. El Paso

240 • 1999 DIRECTORY

CLASS A

California League

Bakersfield
APRIL
8-9-10............. Lancaster
11-12-13......... San Jose
20-21-22.. Lake Elsinore
27-28-29 .... Visalia
MAY
6-7-8................. Stockton
9-10-11 .... Modesto
19-20-21 .... San Jose
25-26-27 .... Modesto
JUNE
9 .... Visalia
11-12-13..... High Desert
15-16-17 .... R. Cuca.
18-19-20 ...... San Bern.
JULY
1-2-3 .... High Desert
7-8-9 .... Visalia
10-11-12......... San Bern.
17-18-19 .... R. Cuca.
26-27-28 .... Lancaster
29-30-31 .... Modesto
AUGUST
3-4-5-6-7 .... Stockton
12-13-14.. Lake Elsinore
17 .... Modesto
18-19-20 .... San Jose
24-25-26 .... Visalia
27-28-28-29 .... Stockton

High Desert
APRIL
14-15-16........... Modesto
17-18-19 .... San Bern.
20-21-22 .... Lancaster
MAY
3-4-5............. Bakersfield
6-7-8 ..... R. Cucamonga
12-13-14 ...... San Bern.
15.......... R. Cucamonga
16-17-18........... Lancaster
21 .... Lake Elsinore
22-23-24 .... San Jose
28-29-30........... Stockton
JUNE
4-5-6 .... Visalia
15-16-17.. Lake Elsinore
24-25-26.. Lake Elsinore
27-28-29 .... Modesto
30 .... San Bernardino
JULY
4-5-6 .... San Jose
14-15-16.......... Stockton
17-18-19.. Lake Elsinore
26-27-28 .... Visalia
29-30-31 .... R. Cuca.
AUGUST
10 .... Lancaster
12-13-14 .... San Bern.
15-16-17 .... R. Cuca.
18-19-20........... Lancaster
SEPTEMBER
3-4-5............. Bakersfield

Lake Elsinore
APRIL
14-15-16 .... Visalia
17-18-19.......... Modesto
27-28-29 .... San Bern.

30 .... Bakersfield
MAY
1-2 .... Bakersfield
9-10-11....... High Desert
12-13-14-15... Lancaster
16-17-18 .... R. Cuca.
25-26-27.......... Stockton
28-29-30 .... San Jose
JUNE
7-8-10 .... High Desert
11-12-13 R. Cucamonga
14................. San Bern.
30......... R. Cucamonga
JULY
1-2-3 .... San Bern.
10-11-12 R. Cucamonga
14-15-16........ Lancaster
20-21-22 .... Visalia
23-24-25 .... High Desert
AUGUST
1 .... High Desert
4-5-6 .... Lancaster
7-10-11 .... San Bern.
18-19-20.......... Stockton
21-22-23.......... Modesto
31 .... Bakersfield
SEPTEMBER
1-2 .... Bakersfield
3-4-5 .... San Jose

Lancaster
APRIL
14-15-16 ...... San Bern.
17-18-19 .... Visalia
23-24-25.......... Stockton
MAY
3-4-5........ Lake Elsinore
6-7-8 .... San Jose
20 .... High Desert
21 .... R. Cucamonga
22-23-24....... Bakersfield
25-26-27 .... High Desert
JUNE
1-2-3................. Modesto
8-9-14 ... R. Cucamonga
15-16-17 ...... San Bern.
18-19-20.. Lake Elsinore
30 .... Bakersfield
JULY
1-2-3 ..... R. Cucamonga
7-8-9................. Modesto
10-11-12..... High Desert
17-18-19.......... Stockton
29-30-31 .... San Jose
AUGUST
1-2 .... Bakersfield
8................... San Bern.
9 .... Lake Elsinore
12-13-14 .... R. Cuca.
15-16-17.. Lake Elsinore
24-25-26 ...... San Bern.
27-28-29 .... Visalia
31 .... High Desert
SEPTEMBER
1-2............... High Desert

Modesto
APRIL
8-9-10 .... San Jose
11-12-13..... High Desert
20-21-22 .... R. Cuca.

23-24-25.. Lake Elsinore
MAY
3-4-5 .... San Jose
6-7-8 .... San Bern.
16-17-17 .... Visalia
22-23-24.......... Stockton
28-29-30........ Lancaster
JUNE
4-5-6-7........ Bakersfield
8 .... Stockton
18-19-20 .... Visalia
30 .... Visalia
JULY
1-2-3................. Stockton
10-11-12 .... Visalia
14-15-16 .... San Bern.
19...................... San Jose
20-21-22....... Bakersfield
23-24-25 .... Lancaster
AUGUST
4-5-6-7 .... San Jose
8 .... Stockton
9 .... Bakersfield
10 .... Stockton
15-16 .... Bakersfield
24-25-26 .... High Desert
27-28-29.. Lake Elsinore
31 .... R. Cucamonga
SEPTEMBER
1-2.......... R. Cucamonga

R. Cucamonga
APRIL
8-9-10 .... Stockton
11-12-13.. Lake Elsinore
23-24-25 .... San Jose
27-28-29 .... Modesto
30 .... Visalia
MAY
1-2 .... Visalia
9-10-11 .... Lancaster
12-13-14....... Bakersfield
20 .... Lake Elsinore
28-29-30 ...... San Bern.
JUNE
1-2-3 .... High Desert
4-5-6 .... Lancaster
7....................... San Bern.
18-19-20 ...... High Desert
24-25-26....... Bakersfield
27-28-29.. Lake Elsinore
JULY
4-5-6................. Modesto
7-8-9 .... San Jose
20-21-22........ Lancaster
23-24-25 .... Visalia
26-27-28.. Lake Elsinore
AUGUST
3-4-5-6 .... High Desert
7 .... Lancaster
18-19-20 ...... San Bern.
24-25-26.......... Stockton
27-28-29 ...... San Bern.

San Bernardino
APRIL
8-9-10...... Lake Elsinore
11-12-13.......... Stockton
20-21-22 .... San Jose
23-24-25 .... High Desert
30 .... Modesto

MAY
- 1-2 .... Modesto
- 3-4-5 .... R. Cucamonga
- 15-16-17 ...... Bakersfield
- 22-23-24 .. Lake Elsinore
- 25-26-27 .... R. Cuca.

JUNE
- 1-2-3 .... Visalia
- 9 .... High Desert
- 10-11-12-13 ..... Lancaster
- 24-25-26 .... Modesto
- 27-28-29 .... Bakersfield

JULY
- 4-5-6 .... Lancaster
- 7-8-9 .... High Desert
- 20-21-22 .... High Desert
- 29-30-31 .. Lake Elsinore

AUGUST
- 1 .... R. Cucamonga
- 3 .... Lake Elsinore
- 4-5-6 .... Visalia
- 15-16-17 .... Stockton
- 21-22-23 .... R. Cuca.
- 31 .... San Jose

SEPTEMBER
- 1-2 .... San Jose
- 3-4-5 .... Lancaster

San Jose
APRIL
- 14-15-16 .... R. Cuca.
- 17-18-19 .... Bakersfield
- 27-28-29 .... Lancaster
- 30 .... High Desert

MAY
- 1-2 .... High Desert
- 9-10-11 .... Visalia
- 13-14-15 .... Modesto
- 31 .... Modesto

JUNE
- 1-2-3 .... Lake Elsinore
- 4-5-6 .... San Bern.
- 8 .... Bakersfield

- 11-12-13 .... Stockton
- 15-16-17 .... Visalia
- 18-19-20 .... Stockton
- 30 .... Stockton

JULY
- 1-2-3 .... Visalia
- 10-11-12 .... Stockton
- 14-15-16 ...... Bakersfield
- 17-18 .... Modesto
- 23-24-25 .... Bakersfield
- 26-27-28 .... San Bern.

AUGUST
- 1 .... Modesto
- 8-9-10 ... R. Cucamonga
- 11 .... Visalia
- 12-13-14 .... Modesto
- 21-22-23 .... Lancaster
- 24-25-26 .. Lake Elsinore
- 27-28-29 ...... High Desert

Stockton
APRIL
- 15-16 .... Bakersfield
- 17-18-19 .... R. Cuca.
- 27-28-29 .... High Desert
- 30 .... Lancaster

MAY
- 1-2 .... Lancaster
- 9-10-11 .... San Bern.
- 12-13-14-15 .... Visalia
- 16-17 .... San Jose
- 19-20-21 .... Modesto
- 31-31 .... Bakersfield

JUNE
- 1-2-3 .... Bakersfield
- 4-5-6 .... Lake Elsinore
- 7-14 .... San Jose
- 15-16-17 .... Modesto
- 24-25-26 .... Lancaster
- 27-28-29 .... San Jose

JULY
- 4-5-5 .... Bakersfield
- 7-8-9 .... Lake Elsinore

- 20-21-22 .... San Jose
- 23-24-25 ...... San Bern.
- 26-27-28 .... Modesto

AUGUST
- 11 .... Modesto
- 12-13-14 .... Visalia
- 21-22-23 .... High Desert
- 31 .... Visalia

SEPTEMBER
- 1-2 .... Visalia
- 3-4-5 ..... R. Cucamonga

Visalia
APRIL
- 8-9-10 .... High Desert
- 11-12-13 .... Lancaster
- 20-21-22 .... Stockton
- 23-24-25 .... Bakersfield

MAY
- 3-4-5 .... Stockton
- 6-7-8 .... Lake Elsinore
- 19-20-21 .... San Bern.
- 22-23-24 .... R. Cuca.
- 25-26-26-27 ... San Jose
- 28-29-30 ...... Bakersfield

JUNE
- 10-11-12-13 ...... Modesto
- 24-25-26 .... San Jose
- 27-28-29 .... Lancaster

JULY
- 4-5-6 .... Lake Elsinore
- 14-15-16 .... R. Cuca.
- 17-18-19 .... San Bern.
- 29-30-31 .... Stockton

AUGUST
- 1 .... Stockton
- 7-8-9 .... High Desert
- 10 .... Bakersfield
- 15-16-17 .... San Jose
- 18-19-20 .... Modesto
- 21-22-23 .... Bakersfield

SEPTEMBER
- 3-4-5 .... Modesto

Carolina League

Frederick
APRIL
- 9-10-11 ..... Myrtle Beach
- 15-16-17-18 .... Salem
- 27-28-29 .... Potomac
- 30 .... Lynchburg

MAY
- 1-2 .... Lynchburg
- 7-8-9 .... W-S
- 10-11-12-13 . Wilmington
- 18-19-20 .... Kinston
- 27-28-29-30 .... M.B.

JUNE
- 3-4-5 .... Wilmington
- 14-15-16-17 .... Potomac
- 18-19-20 .... Lynchburg
- 28-29-30 .... W-S

JULY
- 1-2-3 .... Salem
- 7-8-9 .... Kinston
- 17-18-19 .. Myrtle Beach
- 24-25-26 ..... Wilmington

AUGUST
- 3-4-5 .... Potomac
- 6-7-8-9 .... Lynchburg
- 13-14-15-16 .... W-S
- 18-19-20 .... Salem
- 25-26-27-28 ... Kinston

Kinston
APRIL
- 9-10-11 .... Potomac

- 19-20-21-22.. Wilmington
- 23-24-25 .... W-S
- 30 .... Salem

MAY
- 1-2 .... Salem
- 10-11-12-13 .. Lynchburg
- 14-15-16 .. Myrtle Beach
- 24-25-26 .... Frederick
- 27-28-29-30 .... Potomac

JUNE
- 6-7-8 .... Wilmington
- 9-10-11-12 .... W-S
- 18-19-20 .... Salem

JULY
- 1-2-3 .... Lynchburg
- 4-5-6 ...... Myrtle Beach
- 14-15-16 .... Frederick
- 17-18-19 .... Potomac
- 27-28-29 ..... Wilmington
- 30-31 .... W-S

AUGUST
- 1 .... W-S
- 6-7-8-9 .... Salem
- 18-19-20 .... Lynchburg
- 21-22-23-24 .... M.B.

SEPTEMBER
- 2-3-4-5 .... Frederick

Lynchburg
APRIL
- 9-10-11 .... W-S
- 12-13-14 .... Frederick

- 19-20-21-22 .... M.B.
- 23-24-25 .... Potomac

MAY
- 3-4-5-6 .... Kinston
- 14-15-16 ...... Wilmington
- 18-19-20 .... Salem
- 27-28-29-30 .... W-S
- 31 .... Frederick

JUNE
- 1-2 .... Frederick
- 6-7-8 .... Myrtle Beach
- 9-10-11-12 ...... Potomac
- 25-26-27 .... Kinston

JULY
- 4-5-6 .... Wilmington
- 7-8-9 .... Salem
- 17-18-19 .... W-S
- 20-21-22-23 ... Frederick
- 27-28-29 .. Myrtle Beach
- 30-31 .... Potomac

AUGUST
- 1 .... Potomac
- 10-11-12 .... Kinston
- 21-22-23-24 . Wilmington
- 27-28 .... Salem

SEPTEMBER
- 4-5 .... Salem

Myrtle Beach
APRIL
- 12-13-14 .... Potomac
- 15-16-17-18 . Wilmington

27-28-29 .... Kinston
MAY
7-8-9 .... Lynchburg
10-11-12-13 .... Salem
18-19-20 .... W-S
21-22-23 .... Frederick
31 .... Salem
JUNE
1-2 .... Salem
3-4-5 .... W-S
14-15-16-17 ...... Kinston
28-29-30 ...... Lynchburg
JULY
1-2-3 .... Wilmington
7-8-9 .... Potomac
10-11-12 .... Frederick
20-21-22-23 .... Potomac
24-25-26 .... Salem
AUGUST
3-4-5 .... Kinston
13-14-15-16 .. Lynchburg
18-19-20 ...... Wilmington
25-26-27-28 .... W-S
29-30-31 .... Frederick
SEPTEMBER
1 .... Frederick

Potomac
APRIL
15-16-17-18 .. Lynchburg
19-20-21-22 .... Salem
30 .... Wilmington
MAY
1-2 .... Wilmington
3-4-5-6 .... W-S
14-15-16 .... Frederick
21-22-23 .... Kinston
24-25-26 .. Myrtle Beach
JUNE
3-4-5 .... Lynchburg
6-7-8 .... Salem
18-19-20 ...... Wilmington
25-26-27 .... W-S
JULY
4-5-6 .... Frederick
10-11-12 .... Kinston
14-15-16 .. Myrtle Beach
24-25-26 ...... Lynchburg
27-28-29 .... Salem
AUGUST
6-7-8-9 ...... Wilmington

10-11-12 .... W-S
21-22-23-24 .. Frederick
29-30-31 .... Kinston
SEPTEMBER
1 .... Kinston
2-3-4-5 .. Myrtle Beach

Salem
APRIL
8-9-10-11 ..... Wilmington
12-13-14 .... Kinston
23-24-25 .... Frederick
27-28-29 .... W-S
MAY
3-4-5-6 .. Myrtle Beach
7-8-9 .... Potomac
21-22-23 ...... Wilmington
24-25-26 ...... Lynchburg
JUNE
3-4-5 .... Kinston
9-10-11-12 .... Frederick
14-15-16-17 .... W-S
25-26-27 .. Myrtle Beach
28-29 .... Potomac
JULY
14-15-16 ...... Lynchburg
17-18-19 ...... Wilmington
20-21-22-23 .... Kinston
30-31 .... Frederick
AUGUST
1 .... Frederick
3-4-5 .... W-S
10-11-12 .. Myrtle Beach
13-14-15-16-17 ..... Poto.
25-26 .... Lynchburg
SEPTEMBER
2-3 .... Lynchburg

Wilmington
APRIL
12-13-14 .... W-S
23-24-25 .. Myrtle Beach
27-28-29 ...... Lynchburg
MAY
3-4-5-6 .... Frederick
7-8-9 .... Kinston
18-19-20 .... Potomac
27-28-29 .... Salem
31 .... Potomac
JUNE
1-2 .... Potomac

9-10-11-12 Myrtle Beach
14-15-16-17 .. Lynchburg
25-26-27 .... Frederick
28-29-30 .... Kinston
JULY
7-8-9 .... W-S
10-11-12 .... Salem
20-21-22-23 .... W-S
30-31 .... Myrtle Beach
AUGUST
1 .... Myrtle Beach
3-4-5 .... Lynchburg
10-11-12 .... Frederick
13-14-15-16 ...... Kinston
25-26-27-28 .... Potomac
29-30-31 .... Salem
SEPTEMBER
1 .... Salem

Winston-Salem
APRIL
15-16-17-18 ...... Kinston
19-20-21-22 ... Frederick
30 .... Myrtle Beach
MAY
1-2 .... Myrtle Beach
10-11-12-13 . Potomac
14-15-16 .... Salem
21-22-23 .... Lynchburg
24-25-26 ...... Wilmington
31 .... Kinston
JUNE
1-2 .... Kinston
6-7-8 .... Frederick
18-19-20 .. Myrtle Beach
JULY
1-2-3 .... Potomac
4-5-6 .... Salem
10-11-12 .... Lynchburg
14-15-16 ...... Wilmington
24-25-26 .... Kinston
27-28-29 .... Frederick
AUGUST
6-7-8-9 .. Myrtle Beach
18-19-20 .... Potomac
21-22-23-24 .... Salem
29-30-31 .... Lynchburg
SEPTEMBER
1 .... Lynchburg
2-3-4-5 ...... Wilmington

Florida State League

Brevard County
APRIL
8 .... Vero Beach
17-18-19-20 .... Lakeland
21-22-23-23 . Clearwater
29-30 .... Dunedin
MAY
1-2 .... Dunedin
3-4-5-6 .... Tampa
8-10 .... Vero Beach
11-12 .... Jupiter
13-14-15-15 .... Daytona
18-19 .... Jupiter
23-24 .... Kissimmee
27-28 .... St. Lucie
JUNE
7-8 .... Kissimmee
14-15 .... Vero Beach
30 .... Kissimmee
JULY
3 .... Kissimmee
4-5-6-7 ... St. Petersburg
8-9-10-11 ..... Fort Myers
22-23-24 .... St. Lucie

29-30 .... Vero Beach
31 .... Kissimmee
AUGUST
4 .... St. Lucie
6 .... Kissimmee
10-11-12-13 .... Sarasota
14-15-16-17 .... Charlotte
20 .... Vero Beach
23-24 .... Daytona
30-31 .... Daytona
SEPTEMBER
1-2-3-4 .... Jupiter

Charlotte
APRIL
8 .... Fort Myers
13-14-15-16 ...... Brevard
19-20 ..... St. Petersburg
21-22-23-23 ...... Daytona
24-25 .... Dunedin
MAY
3 .... Sarasota
5-6 .... Clearwater
9-10-11-12 ...... Lakeland
14 .... Fort Myers

15-15 ...... St. Petersburg
19-20 .... Tampa
21-22 .... Clearwater
23-27 .... Sarasota
29-30-31 .... Kissimmee
JUNE
1 .... Kissimmee
11 .... Fort Myers
12 .... Sarasota
21-22-23-24 .... St. Lucie
JULY
2-3 .... Sarasota
12 .... Fort Myers
14-15 .... Lakeland
16-17 ...... St. Petersburg
18-19-20-21 Vero Beach
27-28-29-30 .... Jupiter
31 .... Fort Myers
AUGUST
5 .... Sarasota
7 .... Fort Myers
10-11 .... Dunedin
12-13 .... Clearwater
18-19 .... Dunedin
20-21 .... Tampa

23.................. Sarasota
27.................. Fort Myers
SEPTEMBER
1-2.................. Tampa
5.................... Fort Myers

Clearwater
APRIL
9-10 .... Sarasota
11-12 .... Charlotte
15-16 .... Lakeland
24 .... St. Petersburg
28 .... Tampa
29 .... Lakeland
MAY
2..................... Sarasota
3-4 .... Fort Myers
8 .... Tampa
9-10-11-12...... St. Lucie
19................... Dunedin
23-24-25-26 Vero Beach
27-28-29-30....... Jupiter
JUNE
3 .... St. Petersburg
4-5 .... Dunedin
6-7 .... Tampa
9-10 .... Fort Myers
13.................. Sarasota
14.................. Dunedin
25-26-27-28 .... Brevard
JULY
9..................... Dunedin
12...................... Tampa
14-15...... St. Petersburg
16-17 .... Lakeland
21.................. Sarasota
22-23-24-25 .... Charlotte
29-30 .... Fort Myers
AUGUST
2 .... St. Petersburg
3-4 .... Tampa
5.................... Dunedin
9 .... St. Petersburg
14-15-16-17 ..... Daytona
18-19-20-21. Kissimmee
24-25 .... Dunedin
26 .... Lakeland
28 .... Sarasota
SEPTEMBER
5 .... Tampa

Daytona
APRIL
8 .... Kissimmee
13-14-15-16 ..... Dunedin
17-18-19-20 . Clearwater
29-30 .... Tampa
MAY
1-2 .... Tampa
4 .... Kissimmee
5-6 .... St. Lucie
7-8-9-10............ Jupiter
11-12 .... Vero Beach
17-18-19-20.... Lakeland
21-22.... Brevard County
25-26....Brevard County
JUNE
4-5 .... Vero Beach
15 .... Kissimmee
16-17 .... St. Lucie
21-22-23-24 .... Sarasota
25-26-27-28 .... St. Pete.
JULY
6-7 .... Vero Beach
8-9-10-11 .... Charlotte
12 .... Kissimmee
22-23-24-25. Fort Myers
27 .... Brevard County
28-29-30-31 .... St. Lucie

AUGUST
3-4 .... Kissimmee
5.......... Brevard County
18-19 ..... Brevard County
20-21 .... Jupiter
25-26 .... Vero Beach
27 .... Kissimmee
SEPTEMBER
1 .... Kissimmee

Dunedin
APRIL
8 .... Tampa
17-18-19-20 Vero Beach
21-22-23-23...... Jupiter
MAY
3 .... Lakeland
5-6 .... Fort Myers
9 .... St. Petersburg
13-14-15-15 .... St. Lucie
17-18 .... Clearwater
20 .... Clearwater
21-22-23 . St. Petersburg
24-25-26 .... Charlotte
29 .... Sarasota
JUNE
1 .... Sarasota
7-8-9 .... Lakeland
11 .... Clearwater
15 .... Charlotte
16-17 .... Clearwater
21-22-23-24 . Fort Myers
25-29 .... Tampa
JULY
8 .... Lakeland
10 .... Clearwater
14-15-16-17 .... Daytona
18-19-20-21 .... Brevard
27 .... Kissimmee
28 .... Sarasota
AUGUST
2 .... Tampa
3-4 .... Charlotte
6.................... Clearwater
7 .... Sarasota
14-15-16-17. Vero Beach
20-21 .... St. Petersburg
27-28 .... Lakeland
30-31 .... Clearwater
SEPTEMBER
3-4 .... Sarasota

Fort Myers
APRIL
9-10-11-12 .... Brevard
21-22-23-23 ... St. Pete.
24-25-26-27 .... Daytona
MAY
7-8 .... Charlotte
9-10-11-12 ... Kissimmee
13 .... Charlotte
23-24 .... Tampa
25-26 .... Sarasota
29-30 .... Lakeland
31................ Clearwater
JUNE
1.................... Clearwater
2-3 .... Dunedin
4-5 .... Tampa
12-13 .... Dunedin
16-17 .... Charlotte
25-26-27-28 .... St. Lucie
30 .... Lakeland
JULY
1-2-3 .... Lakeland
4-5 .... Sarasota
14-15-16-17....... Jupiter
27-28 .... Clearwater

AUGUST
2-9 .... Charlotte
10-11-12-13 Vero Beach
14-15 .... Tampa
18-19 .... Sarasota
23-24-25-26 .... St. Pete.
28 .... Charlotte
SEPTEMBER
1-2 .... Dunedin
3-4 .... Clearwater

Jupiter
APRIL
8...................... St. Lucie
9-10-11-12 ...... Daytona
13-14-15-16 . Fort Myers
24-25-26-27 .... Sarasota
29-30 .... Kissimmee
MAY
3-4-5-6 ... St. Petersburg
13-14 .... Vero Beach
20-21 .... Kissimmee
JUNE
1...................... St. Lucie
2-3 .... Vero Beach
6-7-8-9 .... Charlotte
11-12 ...... Brevard County
13-14-15 .... St. Lucie
21-22-23-24 . Clearwater
25-26 .... Vero Beach
30.................... Daytona
JULY
1-2-3 .... Daytona
4-5-6-7 .... Dunedin
12 .... St. Lucie
22-23-24-25... Tampa
AUGUST
6-7 .... St. Lucie
10-11 .... Kissimmee
14-15-16-17... Lakeland
19 .... Vero Beach
25-26-27-28 ..... Brevard
30-31 .... Kissimmee
SEPTEMBER
5 .... Vero Beach

Kissimmee
APRIL
9-10-11-12 .... Dunedin
21-22-23-23........ Tampa
24-25............... St. Lucie
27-28 .... Vero Beach
MAY
1-2 .... Jupiter
3...................... Daytona
13-14-15-15 . Clearwater
17 .... Brevard County
25-26.............. St. Lucie
27-28 .... Daytona
JUNE
2-3 .... Daytona
4-5 .... Jupiter
9 .... Brevard County
11-12-13-14 .... Lakeland
16-17........ Brevard County
21-22-23-24 ... St. Pete.
25-26-27-28 .... Sarasota
JULY
1-2........ Brevard County
4-5-6-7 .... Charlotte
8-9 .... Jupiter
16-17 .... St. Lucie
18-19-20-21 . Fort Myers
AUGUST
2...................... Daytona
5 .... Vero Beach
7 .... Brevard County
9...................... Daytona
12-13 .... Jupiter

23-24	Vero Beach
25-26..............	St. Lucie
28.....................	Daytona

SEPTEMBER

2	Vero Beach
5..........	Brevard County

Lakeland

APRIL

9-10-11-12....	St. Lucie
13-14	Clearwater
21-22-23-23	Vero Beach
25	Tampa
27-28	Charlotte
30...............	Clearwater

MAY

1-2................	Fort Myers
4....................	Dunedin
13-14-15-15	Sarasota
21-22	Fort Myers
23-24-25-26.......	Dunedin
27-28	Dunedin

JUNE

1-2-3..............	Tampa
4-5.........	St. Petersburg
15...............	Clearwater
21-22-23-24.....	Brevard
25-26-27-28....	Charlotte

JULY

4	Tampa
11-12.............	Sarasota
18-19-20-21	Daytona
22-23-24-25.	Kissimmee
28...........	St. Petersburg

AUGUST

6-7-9..................	Tampa
10-11............	Clearwater
12-13	Dunedin
23....................	Dunedin
30-31	Fort Myers

SEPTEMBER

1-2	Clearwater
3-4-5	St. Petersburg

St. Lucie

APRIL

17-18-19-20.	Fort Myers
21-22-23-23	Sarasota
27-28....	Brevard County
29-30....	St. Petersburg

MAY

1-2........	St. Petersburg
3	Vero Beach
7-8	Kissimmee
17	Jupiter
18-19	Kissimmee
20........	Brevard County
21	Vero Beach
22	Jupiter
23-24-29-30	Daytona
31	Jupiter

JUNE

2-3-4-5............	Charlotte
10........	Brevard County
11-12	Vero Beach
30....................	Dunedin

JULY

1-2-3	Dunedin
4-5-6-7	Clearwater
9	Vero Beach
10-11	Jupiter
14-15	Kissimmee
18-19-20-21.......	Tampa
26........	Brevard County
27.........	Vero Beach

AUGUST

2-3.......	Brevard County
5	Jupiter
9	Brevard County

18-19-20-21....	Lakeland
23-24	Jupiter
27	Vero Beach

SEPTEMBER

1	Vero Beach
2-3-4-5	Daytona

St. Petersburg

APRIL

8	Lakeland
13-14-15-16.	Kissimmee
17-18	Charlotte
26..................	Clearwater
27-28	Dunedin

MAY

7-8	Lakeland
10....................	Sarasota
13	Tampa
17-18	Clearwater
19-20	Sarasota
27-28	Fort Myers
29-30-31	Brevard Co.

JUNE

1	Brevard Co.
2....................	Clearwater
7-8.................	Fort Myers
9	Tampa
10	Lakeland
11-12-13-14	Daytona
16-17	Sarasota
30	Charlotte

JULY

1	Charlotte
2-3	Tampa
9-10	Lakeland
11-12.............	Dunedin
18-19-20-21	Jupiter
22-24	Sarasota
29-30	Dunedin
31	Clearwater

AUGUST

3-4-5-6	Fort Myers
7...................	Clearwater
10-11-12-13....	St. Lucie
14-15-16-17	Vero Beach
27-28	Tampa
30-31	Charlotte

SEPTEMBER

2......................	Sarasota

Sarasota

APRIL

8..................	Clearwater
11-12	Tampa
17-18-19-20.	Kissimmee
29-30	Fort Myers

MAY

1...................	Clearwater
4	Charlotte
5-6	Lakeland
7-8	Dunedin
11-12......	St. Petersburg
17-18	Charlotte
21-22	Tampa
24	St. Petersburg
28	Charlotte
30-31	Dunedin

JUNE

2-3-4-5	Brevard Co.
7-8-9-10	Daytona
14-15	Fort Myers
30	Tampa

JULY

6-7	Lakeland
8.............	St. Petersburg
9	Tampa
14-15-16-17	Vero Beach
18-19-20	Clearwater
23-26-27	St. Petersburg

29-30	Lakeland
31	Jupiter

AUGUST

1-2-3..................	Jupiter
6	Charlotte
9......................	Dunedin
14-15-16-17	St. Lucie
20-21	Fort Myers
24-25-26	Charlotte
27	Clearwater

SEPTEMBER

1	St. Petersburg
5......................	Dunedin

Tampa

APRIL

9-10	Charlotte
13-14-15-16	St. Lucie
17-18-19-20....	Jupiter
24	Lakeland
27	Clearwater

MAY

7....................	Clearwater
9......................	Sarasota
10-11-12	Dunedin
14..........	St. Petersburg
15-15	Fort Myers
25-26	St. Petersburg
27-28-29-30	Vero Beach
31	Lakeland

JUNE

10....................	Dunedin
11	Sarasota
12..................	Clearwater
13-14	Charlotte
15..........	St. Petersburg
16-17	Lakeland
26-28	Dunedin

JULY

1......................	Sarasota
5	Lakeland
6-7...............	Fort Myers
8...................	Clearwater
10....................	Sarasota
11	Clearwater
14-15-16-17......	Brevard
27-28-29-30.	Kissimmee
31......................	Dunedin

AUGUST

5	Lakeland
10-11-12-13	Daytona
16-17	Fort Myers
18-19......	St. Petersburg
23..................	Clearwater
24-25	Lakeland
26....................	Dunedin
30-31	Sarasota

SEPTEMBER

3-4	Charlotte

Vero Beach

APRIL

9-10-11-12......	St. Pete.
13-14-15-16....	Sarasota
24-25....	Brevard County
29-30	Charlotte

MAY

1-2	Charlotte
4......................	St. Lucie
5-6	Kissimmee
7-9............	Brevard County
15-15...................	Jupiter
17-18-19-20 .	Fort Myers
22	Kissimmee
31....................	Daytona

JUNE

1	Daytona
7-8-9	St. Lucie
10	Kissimmee

13......... Brevard County
16-17.............. Jupiter
21-22-23-24....... Tampa
28-29.............. Jupiter
30............... Clearwater
JULY
1-2-3 .... Clearwater
5-5 .... Daytona

8..................... St. Lucie
10-11 .... Kissimmee
12........... Brevard County
22-23-24-25..... Dunedin
28........ Brevard County
31 .... Lakeland
AUGUST
1-2-3 .... Lakeland

6-7 .... Daytona
9-18 .... Jupiter
21 .... Brevard County
28-30-31 .... St. Lucie
SEPTEMBER
3-4 .... Kissimmee

Midwest League

Beloit
APRIL
8-9-10-11 ... Wisconsin
16-17-18-19 .. Kane Co.
24-25-26-27 Cedar Rap.
MAY
7-8-9-10 .... Burlington
11-12-13-14 ...... Clinton
23-24-25-26 .... Peoria
27-28-29-30 .. Quad City
JUNE
9-10-12 .... Rockford
13-14-15-16 .. S. Bend
25-26-27 .... Wisconsin
JULY
4-5-6-7 .... Rockford
8-9 .... Peoria
14-15........ Kane County
18-19 .... West Mich.
22-23 .... Kane County
26-27 .... West Mich.
AUGUST
9-10 .... Peoria
11-12-13-14...... Michigan
19-20-21-22...... Lansing
27-28 .... Rockford
29-30 .... Wisconsin
SEPTEMBER
1-2-3-4........ Fort Wayne

Burlington
APRIL
8-9-11 .... Quad City
20-21-22-23 .. Rockford
24 .... Quad City
28-29-30...... West Mich.
MAY
1 .... West Mich.
2-3-4-5........... Michigan
15-16-17-18 .... Beloit
19-20-21-22 ... Kane Co.
JUNE
1-2-3-4 .... Clinton
5-6-7 .... Cedar Rapids
9-10-11-12 ... Wisconsin
24............ Cedar Rapids
27-28-29 .... Quad City
JULY
2-3........... Cedar Rapids
8-9-10-11.... South Bend
14-15-16-17 Fort Wayne
18-19-20-21 ... Lansing
27-29............. Quad City
30-31......... Cedar Rapids
AUGUST
7-8-9 .... Clinton
12 .... Quad City
15-16-17-18 ...... Peoria
SEPTEMBER
2-3.......... Cedar Rapids
4-5-6 .... Clinton

Cedar Rapids
APRIL
10-11 .... Clinton
16-17-18-19 .. Burlington
22-23................. Clinton
28-29-30 .... Michigan

MAY
1 .... Michigan
2-3-4-5 .... Clinton
12-13-14 .... Quad City
15-16-17-18...... Peoria
28-29-30-31 ... Lansing
JUNE
1-2-3-4 ... Kane County
17-18-19-20 .... Rockford
25-26 .... Burlington
30................... Burlington
JULY
1 .... Burlington
4-5-6-7 .... Quad City
18-19-20-21 .... S. Bend
22-23-24-25..... Wisc.
AUGUST
1-2 .... Burlington
3-4-5-6........... West Mich.
15-16-17-18 .... Beloit
19-20-21-22 Fort Wayne
27-28-29 .... Quad City
30-31.................. Clinton

Clinton
APRIL
8-9............. Cedar Rapids
13-14-15 .... Burlington
20-21...... Cedar Rapids
24-25-26-27 ...... Peoria
MAY
7-8-9-10 ...... Quad City
15-16-17-18....... S.Bend
23-24-25-26. West Mich.
28-29-30-31 .. Wisconsin
JUNE
9-10-11-12 .. Fort Wayne
17-18-19-20 ..... Lansing
24-25-26 ...... Quad City
27-28-29 . Cedar Rapids
JULY
4-5-6-7 .... Burlington
18-19-20-21 .... Michigan
26-27-28-29 ... Kane Co.
30-31 .... Rockford
AUGUST
1-2 .... Rockford
12-13-14 . Cedar Rapids
23-24-25-26 .... Beloit
27-28-29 .... Burlington
SEPTEMBER
1-2-3 .... Quad City

Fort Wayne
APRIL
8-9-10-11 .... Lansing
16-17-18-19 .... Clinton
28-29-30............. Beloit
MAY
1 .... Beloit
7-8-9-10 .... Peoria
14..................... Michigan
20-21-22........ South Bend
23-24-25-26 Cedar Rap.
28-28-29 ...... Michigan
JUNE
1-2 .... West Mich.

13-14-15-16 .. Burlington
17-18 .... West Mich.
24-25 .... Lansing
28-29 .... South Bend
JULY
5.................... Michigan
6-7 .... Lansing
8-9-10-11 ... Wisconsin
18-19-20-21 .. Quad City
29 .... South Bend
30-31 .... Michigan
AUGUST
1..................... Michigan
3-4-5-6 .... Rockford
11-12-13-14.... Kane Co.
15-16-17........ South Bend
26 .... Michigan
27-28-29-30. West Mich.

Kane County
APRIL
12-13-14-15 ..... S. Bend
20-21-22-23 Fort Wayne
24-25-26-27 .... Rockford
MAY
7-8-9-10 .. Cedar Rapids
11-12-12-14 .. Burlington
23-24-25-26 .... Michigan
28-29-30-31 ..... Peoria
JUNE
5-6-7-8 .... Wisconsin
18-19-20 .... Beloit
28-29 .... Beloit
JULY
4-5-6 .... Peoria
10-11............... Rockford
16-17................... Beloit
18-19 .... Rockford
24-25 .... Beloit
30-31 .... West Mich.
AUGUST
1-2 .... West Mich.
3-4-5-6 .... Quad City
9-10 .... Wisconsin
15-16-17-18 .... Clinton
21-22 .... Wisconsin
23-24-25-26..... Lansing
SEPTEMBER
3-4 .... Peoria

Lansing
APRIL
13-14-15 .... Michigan
20-21-22-23 ..... S. Bend
24................... Michigan
28-29-30... Kane County
MAY
1 .... Kane County
2-3-4-5 .... Beloit
15-16-17-18 .. Wisconsin
22 .... West Mich.
23-24-25-26 .. Burlington
JUNE
5-6-7 .... Fort Wayne
10-11-12 ...... West Mich.
13-14-15-16 .. Quad City
26-27 .... Fort Wayne
28-29 .... West Mich.

JULY

1-2	Michigan
8-9-10-11	Cedar Rapids
14-15	Peoria
22-23-24-25	Fort Wayne
26-27	Peoria

AUGUST

3-4-5-6	Clinton
7-8	Michigan
13-14	West Mich.
15-16-17-18	Rockford
27-28-29-30	S. Bend

SEPTEMBER

4	West Mich.

Michigan

APRIL

8-9-10-11	West Mich.
12	Lansing
16-17-18-19	Wisconsin
25-26-27	Lansing

MAY

7-8-9-10	South Bend
11-12	Fort Wayne
15-16-18	West Mich.
30-31	Fort Wayne

JUNE

1-2-3-4	Beloit
9-10-11-12	Quad City
13-14-15-16	Clinton
26-27	Rockford

JULY

1	Lansing
4	Fort Wayne
6-7	South Bend
8-9	West Mich.
16-17	Rockford
26-27-28-29	Cedar Rap.

AUGUST

2	Fort Wayne
3-4-5-6	Peoria
9-10	Lansing
19-20-21-22	Burlington
24-25	Fort Wayne
27-28-29-30	Kane Co.

SEPTEMBER

3-4	South Bend
5-6	Lansing

Peoria

APRIL

12-13-14-15	Beloit
16-17-18-19	Lansing
29-30	Wisconsin

MAY

1	Wisconsin
2-3-4-5	Kane County
11-12-13-14	Rockford
19-20-21-22	Michigan

JUNE

5-6-7-8	Clinton
9-10-11-12	Kane County
17-18-19-20	Burlington
24-25	Rockford
30	Fort Wayne

JULY

1-2-3	Fort Wayne
10-11	Beloit
18-19	Wisconsin
20-21	West Mich.
28-29	Wisconsin
30-31	South Bend

AUGUST

1-2	South Bend
7-8	Beloit
12-13-14	Rockford
19-20-21-22	Quad City
23-24-25-26	Cedar Rap.

SEPTEMBER

1-2	Wisconsin
5-6	West Mich.

Quad City

APRIL

10	Burlington
12-13-14-15	Cedar Rap.
20-21-22-23	Peoria
25-26-27	Burlington

MAY

2-3-4-5	West Mich.
15-16-17-18	Kane Co.
19-21-22	Clinton

JUNE

1-2-3-4	South Bend
5-6-7-8	Rockford
17-18-19-20	Michigan
30	Beloit

JULY

1-2-3	Beloit
8-9-10-11	Clinton
15-16-17	Cedar Rapids
23-24-25	Clinton
28	Burlington
30-31	Lansing

AUGUST

1-2	Lansing
7-8-9-10	Fort Wayne
11-13-14	Burlington
23-24-25-26	Wisconsin
30-31	Burlington

SEPTEMBER

4-5-6	Cedar Rapids

Rockford

APRIL

8-9-10-11	Kane County
16-17-18-19	Quad City
28-29-30	Clinton

MAY

1	Clinton
2-3-4-5	Wisconsin
15-16-17-18	Fort Wayne
19-20-21-22	Beloit
28-29-30-31	West Mich.

JUNE

1-2-3-4	Lansing
13-14-15	Peoria
28-29	Michigan
30	Wisconsin

JULY

1-2-3	Wisconsin
9	Kane County
14-15	Michigan
20-21	Beloit
23-24-25	Peoria
28-29	Beloit

AUGUST

7-8-9-10	Cedar Rapids
19-20-21-22	S. Bend
23-24-25-26	Burlington
29-30-31	Peoria

SEPTEMBER

1-2	Kane County
5-6	Kane County

South Bend

APRIL

8-9-10-11	Peoria
16-17-18-19	West Mich.
28-29-30	Quad City

MAY

1	Quad City
2-3-4-5	Fort Wayne
11-12-13	Lansing
23-24-25-26	Rockford
27-28-29-30	Burlington

JUNE

5-6-7-8	Michigan
9-10-11-12	Cedar Rap.
24-25-26-27	Kane Co.
30	Clinton

JULY

1-2-3	Clinton
4-5	Lansing
16-17	Lansing
22-23-24-25	Michigan
26-27-28	Fort Wayne

AUGUST

3-4-5-6	Beloit
11-12-13-14	Wisconsin
23-24-25-26	West Mich.
31	Lansing

SEPTEMBER

1	Lansing
5-6	Fort Wayne

West Michigan

APRIL

12-13-14-15	Fort Wayne
21-22-23	Michigan
24-25-26-27	S. Bend

MAY

7-8-9-10	Rockford
11-12-13-14	Wisconsin
19-20-21	Lansing

JUNE

3-4	Fort Wayne
5-6-7-8	Beloit
9	Lansing
13-14-15-16	Cedar Rap.
19-20	Fort Wayne
24-25	Michigan
26-27	Peoria
30	Kane County

JULY

1-2-3	Kane County
10-11	Michigan
14-15	South Bend
16-17	Peoria
22-23-24-25	Burlington
28-29	Lansing

AUGUST

7-8-9	South Bend
12	Lansing
15-16-17-18	Quad City
19-20-21-22	Clinton

SEPTEMBER

1-2	Michigan
3	Lansing

Wisconsin

APRIL

12-13-14-15	Rockford
20-21-22-23	Beloit
24-25-26-27	Fort Wayne

MAY

7-8-9-10	Lansing
19-20-21-22	Cedar Rap.
23-24-25-26	Quad City

JUNE

1-2-3-4	Peoria
13-14-15	Kane County
17-18-19-20	S. Bend
28-29	Peoria

JULY

4-5-6-7	West Mich.
14-15-16-17	Clinton
20-21	Kane County
26-27	Rockford
30-31	Beloit

AUGUST

1	Beloit
3-4-5-6	Burlington
7-8	Kane County
15-16-17-18	Michigan

SOUTH ATLANTIC LEAGUE 1999 SCHEDULE

19-20........ Kane County
27-28 .... Peoria

SEPTEMBER
3-4 .... Rockford

5-6 ....Beloit

South Atlantic League

Asheville
APRIL
10-11........ Capital City
16-17-18-19 .. Savannah
20-21-22.... Char., SC
26-27-28-29.... G'boro
30 .... Capital City
MAY
1 .... Capital City
4-5-6-7 .... Columbus
10-11-12.... Piedmont
22-23-24-25... Hag.
26-27 .... Greensboro
JUNE
1-2 .... Hickory
3-4-5-6 .... Cape Fear
12-13 .... Hickory
24-25 .... Capital City
JULY
3-4-5-6 .... Delmarva
7-8 .... Capital City
11-12 .... Piedmont
15 .... Hickory
21-22-23-24.. Char., WV
26-27-28-29 ..... Augusta
AUGUST
4-5-6 .... Piedmont
7-8 .... Greensboro
9-10-11 .... Char., SC
26-27-28-29....... Macon
30-31 .... Char., SC
SEPTEMBER
5-6.................... Hickory

Augusta
APRIL
12-13-14-15.. Char., WV
16-17-18-19 ...... Hickory
22-23-24 ...... Columbus
MAY
2-3.................. Piedmont
4-5-6-7 .... Capital City
8-9.................. Savannah
15-16.............. Piedmont
26-27 .... Macon
JUNE
1-2 .... Macon
3-4.................... Savannah
10-11 .... Savannah
14-15-16............ Macon
17-18-19-20 . Cape Fear
26-27-28 ...... Columbus
JULY
1-2 .... Char., SC
7-8.................. Savannah
14-15-16 ...... Columbus
17-18 .... Char., SC
21-22-23-24... Hag.
30-31 .... Greensboro
AUGUST
1-2 .... Greensboro
7-8.................. Savannah
17-18-19-20 .... Asheville
21-22-23-24.... Delmarva
SEPTEMBER
2-3-4................... Macon
5-6................ Savannah

Cape Fear
APRIL
8-9-10-11 .... Piedmont
12-13-14-15 .... Asheville
23-24 .... Char., WV

30 .... Macon
MAY
1-2-3 .... Macon
8-9 .... Char., WV
10-11-12..... Hagerstown
13-14-15-16 .. Delmarva
22-23-24-25... Char., SC
JUNE
1-2 .... Char., WV
10-11-12-13 .. Columbus
14-15-16 ...... Delmarva
24-25 .... Char., WV
JULY
3-4-5-6 .... Augusta
7-8 .... Char., WV
17-18-19-20 .... Hickory
21-22-23-24 .. Savannah
30-31 .... Capital City
AUGUST
1-2 .... Capital City
4-5-6 .... Hagerstown
9-10-11 .... Delmarva
21-22-23-24....... G'boro
30-31 .... Char., WV
SEPTEMBER
1-2-3 .... Hagerstown

Capital City
APRIL
10-11 .... Asheville
12-13-14-15 ... Delmarva
23-24 .... Char., SC
MAY
2-3.................. Asheville
10-11-12..... Greensboro
13-14................ Hickory
18-19-20-21........ Macon
22-23-24-25 ..... Augusta
JUNE
1-2 .... Greensboro
3-4-5-6 .... Piedmont
10-11-12-13 .. Char., WV
14-15-16 ...... Piedmont
26-27-28 ...... Char., SC
JULY
3-4-5-6 .... Hagerstown
9-10-11-12.... Cape Fear
17-18-19-20 .. Savannah
28-29 .... Greensboro
AUGUST
4-5-6 .... Hickory
12-13-14-15 .. Columbus
17-18................ Hickory
19-20................ Piedmont
23-24 .... Char., SC
30-31................ Hickory
SEPTEMBER
1-2-3 .... Asheville

Charleston, SC
APRIL
16-17-18-19 .. Columbus
26-27-28-29 .. Cape Fear
MAY
4-5-6-7 .... Char., WV
8-9 .... Piedmont
15-16.............. Hickory
26-27.............. Piedmont
28-29-30-31 .... Asheville
JUNE
3-4-5-6............. Macon
7-8-9 .... Capital City
14-15-16..... Greensboro

17-18.............. Piedmont
19-20................ Hickory
24-25................ Hickory
29-30.............. Augusta
JULY
3-4-5-6 ...... Savannah
14-15-16..... Greensboro
19-20................ Augusta
21-22-23-24 ... Delmarva
30-31 .... Asheville
AUGUST
1-2.................... Asheville
7-8.................... Piedmont
17-18-19-20....... Hag.
21-22 .... Capital City
SEPTEMBER
1-2-3 .... Greensboro
4-5-6 .... Capital City

Charleston, WV
APRIL
16-17-18-19 . Cape Fear
20-21-22.... Hagerstown
26-27-28-29 Capital City
30 .... Hagerstown
MAY
1-2-3 .... Hagerstown
13-14-15-16 .. Columbus
18-19-20-21... Char., SC
26-27.............. Cape Fear
28-29-30-31.... G'boro
JUNE
7-8-9 .... Delmarva
17-18-19-20..... Macon
26-27-28 .... Hagerstown
29-30.............. Asheville
JULY
1-2.................... Asheville
9-10-11-12........ Hickory
17-18-19-20 .. Delmarva
26-27-28-29 .. Piedmont
AUGUST
4-5-6 .... Delmarva
7-8.................... Cape Fear
12-13-14-15 .. Savannah
26-27-28-29 ..... Augusta
SEPTEMBER
4-5-6 .... Cape Fear

Columbus
APRIL
8-9-10-11 ... Hagerstown
12-13-14-15 .. Savannah
20-21 .... Macon
30 .... Char., SC
MAY
1-2-3 .... Char., SC
8-9 .... Macon
18-19-20-21 .... Asheville
24-25 .... Macon
28-29-29-30 ...... Hickory
JUNE
7-8-9................. Augusta
14-15-16 .... Savannah
17-18-19-20 .. Delmarva
24-25 .... Macon
29-30................ Piedmont
JULY
1-2 .... Piedmont
7-8 .... Macon
17-18-19-20....... G'boro
21-22-23-24 Capital City

AUGUST
4-5-6................. Augusta
7-8 .... Macon
9-10-11 .... Augusta
17-18-19-20 . Cape Fear
21-22-23-24 .. Char., WV
SEPTEMBER
2-3-4 .... Savannah

Delmarva
APRIL
16-17-18-19 ... Piedmont
20-21-22 ...... Cape Fear
26-27-28-29 .. Savannah
30 .... Hickory
MAY
1-2-3................. Hickory
10-11-12 ...... Char., WV
18-19-20-21 ... Augusta
26-27 .... Hagerstown
28-29-30-31 Capital City
JUNE
3-4-5-6 .... Char., WV
10-11-12-13 .... Hag.
26-27-28 ...... Cape Fear
29-30 .... Greensboro
JULY
1-2................. Greensboro
7-8............. Hagerstown
14-15-16 ...... Cape Fear
26-27-28-29.. ... Macon
30-31 .... Columbus
AUGUST
1-2................. Columbus
7-8............. Hagerstown
12-13-14-15 .... Asheville
26-27-28-29... Char., SC
30-31............. Hagerstown
SEPTEMBER
1-2-3 .... Char., WV

Greensboro
APRIL
8-9-10-11 .... Char., SC
12-13-14-15........ Macon
20-21-22............ Hickory
30 .... Savannah
MAY
1-2-3 .... Savannah
8-9.................. Asheville
13-14 .... Char., SC
15-16 .... Capital City
18-19 .... Hickory
22-23-24-25... Char., WV
JUNE
3-4-5-6 .... Hagerstown
7-8-9 .... Asheville
26-27-28 .... Asheville
12-13 .... Piedmont
JULY
3-4-5-6 .... Columbus
9-10-11-12 .... Delmarva
23-24 .... Hickory
26-27 .... Capital City
AUGUST
4-5-6 .... Char., SC
9-10-11 .... Capital City
12-13-14-15 ... Augusta
17-18 .... Piedmont
19-20 .... Hickory
26-27-28-29 . Cape Fear
30-31 .... Piedmont

Hagerstown
APRIL
16-17-18-19...... G'boro
23-24 .... Delmarva
26-27-28-29 .. Augusta

MAY
4-5-6-7 .... Hickory
8-9 .... Delmarva
18-19-20-21 .. Savannah
28-29-30-31 . Cape Fear
JUNE
1-2 .... Delmarva
7-8-9 .... Cape Fear
14-15-16 ...... Char., WV
17-18-19-20 .... Asheville
24-25 .... Delmarva
29-30............ Cape Fear
JULY
1-2................. Cape Fear
9-10-11-12..... Char., SC
14-15-16 ...... Char., WV
26-27-28-29 .. Columbus
30-31 .... Macon
AUGUST
1-2 .... Macon
9-10-11 ...... Char., WV
12-13-14-15 ... Piedmont
26-27-28-29 Capital City
SEPTEMBER
4-5-6 .... Delmarva

Hickory
APRIL
8-9-10-11.......... Augusta
12-13-14-15.......... Hag.
23-24................... Asheville
28-29................... Piedmont
MAY
8-9 .... Capital City
10-11-12 .... Char., SC
20-21 .... Greensboro
22-23-24-25... Delmarva
26-27 .... Capital City
JUNE
3-4-5-6 .... Columbus
10-11 .... Greensboro
14-15-16 .... Asheville
17-18 .... Capital City
26-27-28 .... Piedmont
JULY
3-4-5-6 .... Char., WV
7-8 .... Greensboro
14-16 .... Asheville
21-22 .... Greensboro
26-27-28-29 . Cape Fear
AUGUST
7-8 .... Capital City
12-13-14-15... Char., SC
21-22-23-24....... Macon
26-27-28-29 .. Savannah
SEPTEMBER
1-2-3 .... Piedmont
4 .... Asheville

Macon
APRIL
8-9-10-11 ...... Delmarva
16-17-18-19 Capital City
26-27-28-29 .. Columbus
MAY
4-5-6-7 .... Greensboro
10-11-12........... Augusta
13-14-15-16.......... Hag.
22-23................. Columbus
28-29-30-31 ..... Augusta
JUNE
7-8-9 .... Savannah
10-11-12-13 ... Char., WV
26-27-28 .... Savannah
29-30 .... Hickory
JULY
1-2 .... Hickory

9-10-11-12....... Augusta
17-18-19-20 .... Asheville
21-22-23-24 ... Piedmont
AUGUST
4-5-6 .... Savannah
12-13-14-15 . Cape Fear
17-18-19-20 .. Char., WV
30-31............. Columbus
SEPTEMBER
1-5-6 .... Columbus

Piedmont
APRIL
12-13-14-15... Char., SC
20-21-22 ...... Capital City
23-24.......... Greensboro
26-27 .... Hickory
30 .... Augusta
MAY
1 .... Augusta
4-5-6-7 .... Delmarva
13-14............... Augusta
18-19-20-21 . Cape Fear
22-23-24-25 .. Savannah
JUNE
1-2 .... Char., SC
7-8-9............... Hickory
10-11 .... Asheville
19-20 .... Capital City
24-25 .... Greensboro
JULY
3-4-5-6................. Macon
7-8 .... Char., SC
9-10 .... Asheville
14-15-16 ..... Capital City
17-18-19-20 .... Hag.
30-31 .... Char., WV
AUGUST
1-2 .... Char., WV
9-10-11 .... Hickory
21-22-23-24 .... Asheville
26-27-28-29 .. Columbus
SEPTEMBER
4-5-6.......... Greensboro

Savannah
APRIL
8-9-10-11 ...... Char., WV
20-21 .... Augusta
22-23-24............. Macon
MAY
4-5-6-7 .... Cape Fear
10-11-12.......... Columbus
13-14-15-16 .. Asheville
26-27 .... Columbus
28-29-30-31 .. Piedmont
JUNE
1-2 .... Columbus
5-6 .... Augusta
12-13 .... Augusta
17-18-19-20...... G'boro
24-25 .... Augusta
29-30 .... Capital City
JULY
1-2 .... Capital City
9-10-11-12 .... Columbus
14-15-16 .... Macon
26-27-28-29 ... Char., SC
30-31 .... Hickory
AUGUST
1-2 .... Hickory
9-10-11 .... Macon
17-18-19-20 .. Delmarva
21-22-23-24 .... Hag.
30-31 .... Augusta
SEPTEMBER
1 .... Augusta

SHORTSEASON

CLASS A

New York-Penn League

Auburn
JUNE
16-17 .... Mah. Valley
21-22-23-24 .... Williams.
28 .... Batavia
30 .... Jamestown
JULY
1-2 .... Jamestown
8-10 .... Batavia
12-13 ...... St. Catharines
14-15 .... Jamestown
20-21-22-23 .... St. Cath.
24-25-26 .... Williamsport
AUGUST
2 .... Batavia
4-5-6-7 ...... Mah. Valley
10-12 .... Batavia
19 .... Batavia
21-22 ...... St. Catharines
24-25 ...... Mah. Valley
26 .... Batavia
SEPTEMBER
1-2 .... Jamestown

Batavia
JUNE
16 .... Jamestown
18-19-20 ...... Mah. Valley
22-24 ...... St. Catharines
29 .... Auburn
30 .... St. Catharines
JULY
2 .... St. Catharines
3-4 .... Mah. Valley
6 .... Jamestown
9-11 .... Auburn
12 .... Jamestown
17 .... St. Catharines
18-19 .... Mah. Valley
20-21-22-23 .... Williams.
25 .... Jamestown
28-30 ...... St. Catharines
AUGUST
3 .... Auburn
5-6-7-8 .... Williams.
9-11 .... Auburn
20 .... Auburn
22-24 .... Jamestown
27 .... Auburn
30-31 .... Jamestown

Hudson Valley
JUNE
16-17 .... Lowell
19 .... New Jersey
23-24 .... Vermont
25-26-27 .... Utica
JULY
2-3-4 .... Lowell
10-11-12-13 ..... Oneonta
16-18-20-22 ... N. Jersey
26-27 .... Vermont
28-29 .... Pittsfield
AUGUST
4-5-6 .... Pittsfield
7-8 .... Oneonta
12 .... New Jersey
16-17 .... Staten Island

Jamestown
JUNE
17 .... Batavia
21-22-23-24 Mah. Valley
25-26-27 .... St. Cath.
JULY
3-4 .... Auburn
7 .... Batavia
8-9-10-11 .... Williams.
13 .... Batavia
20-21-22-23 Mah. Valley
24-26 .... Batavia
AUGUST
5-6-7-8 .... St. Cath.
11-12 .... Williamsport
13-14 .... Auburn
17-18 .... Auburn
21-23 .... Batavia
26-27 .... Williamsport
28-29 .... Auburn

Lowell
JUNE
18-19 .... Utica
20-21-22 ...... New Jersey
28-29 ...... Hudson Valley
30 .... New Jersey
JULY
I .... New Jersey
8-9 .... Oneonta
16-17-18 .... Oneonta
19-20 .... Staten Island
21-22 .... Pittsfield
28-29-30 .... Vermont
31 ....Utica
AUGUST
1-2-3 .... Utica
12-13-14-15 ... Staten Is.
18-19-20 ..... Hud. Valley
24-25 .... Vermont
26-27 .... Pittsfield
SEPTEMBER
1-2 .... Pittsfield

Mahoning Valley
JUNE
25-26-27 .... Auburn
28-29 .... Jamestown
30 .... Williamsport
JULY
1-2 .... Williamsport
8-9-10-11 St. Catharines
12-13 .... Williamsport
16-17 .... Jamestown
27-28-29-30 .... Auburn
31 .... Batavia
AUGUST
1 .... Batavia
2-3 .... Jamestown
9-10 .... Jamestown
15-16 .... Batavia
17-18 ...... St. Catharines
21-22 .... Williamsport
26-27 ...... St. Catharines
28-29 .... Batavia
SEPTEMBER
1-2 .... Batavia

New Jersey
JUNE
16-17 .... Pittsfield
18 .... Hudson Valley
23-24 .... Oneonta
25-26-27 .... Pittsfield
JULY
2-3-4 .... Vermont
5-6 .... Lowell
8 .... Staten Island
10-11-12-13 .... Utica
14 .... Staten Island
17-19-21 ..... Hud. Valley
26-27 .... Oneonta
31 .... Staten Island
AUGUST
5-6 .... Vermont
10 .... Staten Island
13 .... Hudson Valley
16-17 .... Lowell
21-22 .... Lowell
29 .... Staten Island
30-31 .... Utica
SEPTEMBER
1-2 .... Oneonta

Oneonta
JUNE
16-17 .... Staten Island
20-22 .... Utica
25-26-27 .... Vermont
28-29 ....Pittsfield
JULY
2-3-4 .... Staten Island
5-6 .... Vermont
14-15 ...... Hudson Valley
19 .... Utica
23-24-25 ..... Hud. Valley
28-29-30 ..... New Jersey
AUGUST
3-4 .... New Jersey
5-6 .... Lowell
14-15 .... Pittsfield
17 .... Utica
22 .... Utica
24-25 .... Pittsfield
26 .... Utica
28-29-30-31 ...... Lowell

Pittsfield
JUNE
18-19 .... Oneonta
23-24 .... Lowell
30 .... Staten Island
JULY
1 .... Staten Island
2-3-4 .... Utica
10-11-12-13 .... St. Island
14-15 .... Vermont
19-20 .... Vermont
23-24-25 .... Lowell
30-31 ...... Hudson Valley
AUGUST
1-2 .... Hudson Valley
7-8 .... New Jersey

9-10-11 .... Oneonta
12-13 .... Utica
16-17 .... Vermont
18-19-20 ..... New Jersey
30-31 ...... Hudson Valley

St. Catharines
JUNE
18-19-20 .... Auburn
21-23 .... Batavia
28-29 .... Williamsport
JULY
1 .... Batavia
6-7 .... Auburn
14-15 .... Mah. Valley
16 .... Batavia
18-19 .... Jamestown
24-25-26 ..... Mah. Valley
27-29 .... Batavia
31 .... Jamestown
AUGUST
1 .... Jamestown
3-4 .... Williamsport
11-12 .... Mah. Valley
13-14 .... Batavia
15-16 .... Jamestown
19-20 .... Jamestown
24-25 .... Williamsport
28-29 .... Williamsport
30-31 ....Auburn

Staten Island
JUNE
20-21-22. Hudson Valley
25-26-27 .... Lowell
28-29 .... Utica
JULY
6-7 .... Pittsfield
9 .... New Jersey
15 .... New Jersey
16-17-18 .... Pittsfield
21-22 .... Oneonta

26-27 .... Lowell
28-29-30 .... Utica
AUGUST
1 .... New Jersey
3-4 .... Vermont
9-11 .... New Jersey
18-19-20 .... Oneonta
24-25-26. Hudson Valley
28 .... New Jersey
30-31 .... Vermont
SEPTEMBER
1-2 .... Vermont

Utica
JUNE
16-17 .... Vermont
21 .... Oneonta
23-24 .... Staten Island
30 .... Hudson Valley
JULY
1 .... Hudson Valley
6-7 .... Hudson Valley
8-9 .... Pittsfield
14-15 .... Lowell
16-17-18 .... Vermont
20 .... Oneonta
23-24-25 ..... New Jersey
26-27 .... Pittsfield
AUGUST
5-6-7-8 ..... Staten Island
9-10-11 .... Lowell
14-15 ...... Hudson Valley
16 .... Oneonta
23 .... Oneonta
24-25 .... New Jersey
27 .... Oneonta
28-29 .... Pittsfield

Vermont
JUNE
18-19 .... Staten Island
20-21-22 .... Pittsfield

28-29 .... New Jersey
30 .... Oneonta
JULY
1 .... Oneonta
8-9 .... Hudson Valley
10-11-12-13 .... Lowell
21-22 .... Utica
23-24-25 .. Staten Island
31 .... Oneonta
AUGUST
1 .... Oneonta
7-8 .... Lowell
9-10-11 .. Hudson Valley
12-13 .... Oneonta
14-15 .... New Jersey
18-19-20 .... Utica
21-22 .... Pittsfield
26-27 .... New Jersey

Williamsport
JUNE
16-17 ...... St. Catharines
18-19-20 ..... Jamestown
25-26-27 .... Batavia
JULY
3-4 .... St. Catharines
5-6 .... Mah. Valley
14-15 .... Batavia
16-17-18-19 .... Auburn
27-28-29-30 Jamestown
31 .... Auburn
AUGUST
1 .... Auburn
9-10 .... St. Catharines
13-14 .... Mah. Valley
15-16 .... Auburn
17-18 .... Batavia
19-20 .... Mah. Valley
30-31 .... Mah. Valley
SEPTEMBER
1-2 .... St. Catharines

Northwest League

Boise
JUNE
18-19-20 .... Spokane
26-27-28-29-30 .. Salem
JULY
4-5-6 .... Yakima
14-15-16-17-18 Portland
22-23-24 .... Yakima
30-31 .... Eugene
AUGUST
1-2-3 .... Eugene
8-9-10 .... Spokane
14-15-16-17-18.. S. Ore.
31 .... Everett
SEPTEMBER
1-2-3-4-5 .... Everett

Eugene
JUNE
18-19-20 .... S. Oregon
26-27-28-29-30.. Yakima
JULY
4-5-6 .... Portland
7-8-9-10-11 .... Boise
19-20-21 .... Salem
25-26-27-28-29 .. Everett
AUGUST
5-6-7 .... S. Oregon
14-15-16-17-18 ..... Spo.
28-29-30 .... Portland
SEPTEMBER
3-4-5 .... Salem

Everett
JUNE
18-19-20 .... Yakima
26-27-28-29-30.. S. Ore.
JULY
4-5-6 .... Spokane
10-11 .... Portland
14-15-16-17-18. Eugene
19-20-21 .... Boise
30-31 .... Portland
AUGUST
1 .... Portland
5-6-7 .... Boise
14-15-16-17-18 ... Salem
25-26-27 .... Yakima
28-29-30 .... Spokane

Portland
JUNE
26-27-28-29-30 ...... Spo.
JULY
1-2-3 .... Salem
7-8-9 .... Everett
19-20-21 ...... S. Oregon
25-26-27-28-29 .... Boise
AUGUST
2-3 ....Everett
5-6-7 .... Salem
8-9-10 .... Eugene
14-15-16-17-18.. Yakima
25-26-27 .... Eugene
SEPTEMBER
3-4-5 .... S. Oregon

Salem
JUNE
18-19-20 .... Portland
21-22-23-24-25 .. Everett
JULY
4-5-6 .... S. Oregon
14-15-16-17-18 ...... Spo.
22-23-24 .... Eugene
30-31 .... Yakima
AUGUST
1-2-3 .... Yakima
11-12-13 .... Boise
20-21-22-23-24 .... Boise
28-29-30 .... S. Oregon
31 .... Portland
SEPTEMBER
1-2 .... Portland

So. Oregon
JUNE
21-22-23-24-25 .... Boise
JULY
1-2-3 .... Eugene
14-15-16-17-18.. Yakima
22-23-24 .... Portland
30-31 .... Spokane
AUGUST
1-2-3 .... Spokane
8-9-10 .... Salem
11-12-13 .... Portland
20-21-22-23-24.. Everett
25-26-27 .... Salem
31 .... Eugene

SEPTEMBER
1-2 .... Eugene

Spokane
JUNE
21-22-23-24-25. Eugene
JULY
1-2-3................... Boise
8-9-10-11-12. S. Oregon
22-23-24 .... Everett
25-26-27-28-29 ... Salem
AUGUST
5-6-7 .... Yakima

11-12-13 .... Everett
20-21-22-23-24 Portland
25-26-27............. Boise
31 .... Yakima

SEPTEMBER
1-2 .... Yakima

Yakima
JUNE
21-22-23-24-25 Portland
JULY
1-2-3 .... Everett

8-9-10-11-12 .... Salem
19-20-21 .... Spokane
25-26-27-28-29.. S. Ore.
AUGUST
8-9-10 .... Everett
11-12-13 .... Boise
20-21-22-23-24.. Eugene
28-29-30............. Boise
SEPTEMBER
3-4-5 .... Spokane

ROOKIE LEAGUES

Appalachian League

Bluefield
JUNE
19.................... Princeton
26-27-28.......... Danville
29-30 .... Martinsville
JULY
1 .... Martinsville
4-5 .... Danville
13-14............... Princeton
16-17-18 .... Pulaski
22-23-24.. Johnson City
26-27-28............. Bristol
AUGUST
1-2-3 .... Kingsport
10-11-12........ Burlington
13-14............... Princeton
17-18 .... Pulaski
20.................... Princeton
23.................... Princeton
24-25-26 .... Elizabethton

Bristol
JUNE
18 .... Elizabethton
23-24-25 .... Bluefield
29-30 .... Elizabethton
JULY
1 .... Elizabethton
2..................... Kingsport
5..................... Kingsport
7-8-9 .... Johnson City
16-17-18 .... Danville
19-20-21 ...... Burlington
22-23-24 .... Kingsport
29-30-31...... Martinsville
AUGUST
7-8-9 .... Pulaski
10-11-12........... Princeton
13.................... Kingsport
18-19 .... Elizabethton
22-23 .... Johnson City

Burlington
JUNE
19 .... Danville
23-24-25.. Johnson City
26-27-28 .... Elizabethton
JULY
1 .... Danville
4-5 .... Martinsville
10-11-12 .... Bluefield
14-15 .... Martinsville
22-23-24 .... Pulaski
AUGUST
1-2-3 .... Princeton
4-5-6 .... Danville
7 .... Martinsville
17 ....Danville
20-21 .... Pulaski
23 .... Danville
24-25-26............. Bristol

27-28-29 .... Kingsport

Danville
JUNE
18 .... Burlington
23-24-25 .... Pulaski
29-30............ Burlington
JULY
2-3 .... Bluefield
10-11-12 .. Johnson City
13-14-15 .... Kingsport
22-23-24 .... Elizabethton
29-30-31 .... Bluefield
AUGUST
1-2-3............ Martinsville
13-14 .... Martinsville
16-18-19 ..... Burlington
22.................. Burlington
24-25-26 .... Princeton
27-28-29............. Bristol

Elizabethton
JUNE
19 .... Bristol
20-21-22 .... Danville
JULY
2-3 .... Johnson City
7-8-9 .... Pulaski
10-11 .... Kingsport
15 .... Johnson City
16-17-18..... Martinsville
19-20-21 .... Bluefield
26-27-28 .... Princeton
29-30-31 .... Burlington
AUGUST
4-5-6.................. Bristol
7 .... Kingsport
11-12-13.... Johnson City
16-17 .... Bristol
22-23 .... Kingsport

Johnson City
JUNE
19 .... Kingsport
20-21-22...... Bluefield
26-27-28 .... Kingsport
29-30 .... Pulaski
JULY
1 .... Pulaski
4-5 .... Elizabethton
13-14 .... Elizabethton
16-17-18 .... Princeton
19 .... Martinsville
26-27-28 ...... Burlington
AUGUST
1-2-3................... Bristol
7-8-9................. Danville
10 .... Elizabethton
14 .... Bristol
18-19 .... Kingsport
20-21 .... Bristol

24-25.......... Martinsville

Kingsport
JUNE
18 .... Johnson City
20-21-22............. Bristol
29-30............. Princeton
JULY
1 .... Princeton
3-4 .... Bristol
7-8-9.............. Bluefield
12 .... Elizabethton
16-17-18 ...... Burlington
19-20-21 .... Pulaski
26-27-28........ Martinsville
29-30-31.... Johnson City
AUGUST
8-9 .... Elizabethton
10-11-12 .... Danville
14 .... Elizabethton
16-17 .... Johnson City
20-21 .... Elizabethton

Martinsville
JUNE
18 .... Pulaski
23-24-25 .... Kingsport
26-27-28............. Bristol
JULY
2-3................. Burlington
7-8-9 .... Danville
13 .... Burlington
20-21 .... Johnson City
22-23-24 .... Princeton
AUGUST
4-5-6 .... Bluefield
8-9 .... Burlington
10-11-12 .... Pulaski
18-19 .... Princeton
20-21 .... Danville
22 .... Pulaski
26 .... Johnson City
27-28-29 .... Elizabethton

Princeton
JUNE
18 .... Bluefield
20-21-22.... Martinsville
23-24-25 .... Elizabethton
28 .... Pulaski
JULY
2-3 .... Pulaski
7-8-9 .... Burlington
10-11-12 .... Bristol
15 .... Bluefield
19-20-21 .... Danville
29-31 .... Pulaski
AUGUST
4-5-6 .... Kingsport
7-8-9 .... Bluefield
16-17.......... Martinsville

21-22 .... Bluefield
27-28-29 ... Johnson City

Pulaski

JUNE
19 .... Martinsville
20-21-22 .... Burlington
26-27 .... Princeton

JULY
4-5 .... Princeton
10-11-12 ..... Martinsville
13-14-15 .... Bristol
26-27-28 .... Danville
30 .... Princeton

AUGUST
1-2-3 .... Elizabethton

4-5-6 .... Johnson City
13-14 .... Burlington
16 .... Bluefield
19 .... Bluefield
23 .... Martinsville
24-25-26 ...... Kingsport
27-28-29 .... Bluefield

Pioneer League

Billings

JUNE
19-20-21 .... Ogden
22-23-24 .... Butte
30 .... Idaho Falls

JULY
1 .... Idaho Falls
4-5 .... Ogden
18-19-20-21 .... Med. Hat
22-23-24-25 .... Helena
31 .... Butte

AUGUST
1-2 .... Butte
3-4 .... Idaho Falls
14-15-16-17. Great Falls
18-19-20-21 .... Missoula
27-28 .... Ogden
30-31 .... Idaho Falls

SEPTEMBER
1 .... Idaho Falls
2-3 .... Butte

Butte

JUNE
16-17-18 .... Billings
19-20-21 ...... Idaho Falls
25-26-27 .... Ogden

JULY
2-3 .... Billings
6-7 .... Idaho Falls
9-10-11-12 .... Missoula
14-15-16-17. Great Falls
26-27-28 .... Billings
29-30 .... Ogden

AUGUST
5-6-7-8 .... Helena
14-15-16-17.... Med. Hat
22-23 .... Ogden
24-25 .... Idaho Falls

Great Falls

JUNE
16-17-18 .... Missoula
25-26 .... Helena
27-28-29 .. Medicine Hat

JULY
3-4-5 .... Helena
9-10-11-12 .... Billings
18-19-20-21 .... Ogden
26-27 .... Missoula
28-29-30 .. Medicine Hat

AUGUST
5-6-7-8 .... Idaho Falls

18-19-20-21 .... Butte
23-24 .... Medicine Hat
29-30 .... Missoula
31 .... Helena

SEPTEMBER
1 .... Helena

Helena

JUNE
16-17-18 .. Medicine Hat
19-20-21 ..... Great Falls
27-28-29 .... Missoula

JULY
6-7 .... Missoula
14-15-16-17. Idaho Falls
18-19-20-21 .... Butte
28-29-30 .... Great Falls
31 .... Great Falls

AUGUST
1 .... Great Falls
10-11-12-13 ...... Billings
14-15-16-17........ Ogden
25-26-27-28..... Med.Hat

SEPTEMBER
1-2 .... Great Falls

Idaho Falls

JUNE
16-17-18 .... Ogden
25-26-27 .... Billings
28-29 .... Butte

JULY
2-3 .... Ogden
4-5 .... Butte
18-19-20-21 .... Missoula
22-23-24-25. Great Falls
29-30 .... Billings
31 .... Ogden

AUGUST
1-2 .... Ogden
10-11-12-13 .... Med. Hat
18-19-20-21 ...... Helena
22-23 .... Billings
27-28-29 .... Butte

Medicine Hat

JUNE
19-20-21 .... Missoula
22-23-24 ...... Great Falls
30 .... Helena

JULY
1-2 .... Helena
6-7 .... Great Falls

9-10-11-12 ... Idaho Falls
22-23-24-25 .... Butte
26-27 .... Helena

AUGUST
2-3-4 .... Great Falls
5-6-7-8 .... Billings
18-19-20-21....... Ogden
29-30 .... Helena
31 .... Missoula

SEPTEMBER
1-2-3 .... Missoula

Missoula

JUNE
22-23-24 .... Helena
25-26........ Medicine Hat
30 .... Great Falls

JULY
1-2 .... Great Falls
3-4-5 .... Medicine Hat
14-15-16-17 ...... Billings
22-23-24-25........ Ogden
31 .... Medicine Hat

AUGUST
1 .... Medicine Hat
2-3-4 .... Helena
10-11-12-13 .... Butte
14-15-16-17. Idaho Falls
23-24 .... Helena
25-26-27-28. Great Falls

Ogden

JUNE
22-23-24 ...... Idaho Falls
28-29 .... Billings
30.......................... Butte

JULY
1.......................... Butte
6-7 .... Billings
9-10-11-12 .... Helena
14-15-16-17.... Med. Hat
26-27-28...... Idaho Falls

AUGUST
3-4 .... Butte
5-6-7-8 .... Missoula
10-11-12-13. Great Falls
24-25-26 .... Billings
30-31 .... Butte

SEPTEMBER
1 .... Butte
2-3 .... Idaho Falls

Independent Leagues

1998 STANDINGS

ATLANTIC LEAGUE

	W	L	PCT	GB		W	L	PCT	GB
Bridgeport	64	36	.640	—	Newburgh	42	58	.420	22
Atlantic City	60	40	.600	4	Somerset	40	60	.400	24
Nashua	59	41	.590	5	Newark	35	65	.350	29

PLAYOFFS: Finals (best-of-5)—Atlantic City defeated Bridgeport 3-1.

FRONTIER LEAGUE

EAST	W	L	PCT	GB	WEST	W	L	PCT	GB
**Chillicothe	48	31	.608	—	*Springfield	48	29	.623	—
Canton	41	38	.519	7	Richmond	49	31	.613	½
Johnstown	34	43	.442	13	*Evansville	43	36	.544	6
Ohio Valley	26	52	.333	21½	Kalamazoo	25	54	.316	24

PLAYOFFS: Semifinals (best-of-3)—Chillicothe defeated Canton 2-1; Springfield defeated Evansville 2-1. **Finals** (best-of-3)—Springfield defeated Chillicothe 2-1.

HEARTLAND LEAGUE

	W	L	PCT	GB		W	L	PCT	GB
**Tennesee	43	21	.672	—	Dubois County	15	19	.441	13
Cook County	37	29	.561	7	#Huntington	12	28	.300	DNF
Lafayete	35	39	.473	13	#Tupelo	4	10	.286	DNF

#Suspended operations; did not finish season
PLAYOFFS: Finals (best-of-3)—Cook County defeated Tennesee 2-0.

NORTHEAST LEAGUE

NORTH	W	L	PCT	GB	SOUTH	W	L	PCT	GB
*Albany	47	37	.560	—	*New Jersey	53	31	.631	—
*Waterbury	42	42	.500	5	*Allentown	52	32	.619	1
Massachusetts	39	45	.464	8	Catskill	36	47	.434	16½
Adirondack	34	50	.405	13	Elmira	32	51	.386	20½

PLAYOFFS: Semifinals (best-of-3)—Abany defeated Waterbury 2-0; New Jersey defeated Allentown 2-0. **Finals** (best-of-3)—New Jersey defeated Albany 2-0.

NORTHERN LEAGUE

EAST	W	L	PCT	GB	WEST	W	L	PCT	GB
*Thunder Bay	40	45	.471	—	*Fargo-Moorhead	64	21	.753	—
*St. Paul	40	46	.465	½	*Winnipeg	58	28	.674	6½
Madison	35	51	.407	5½	Sioux City	40	46	.465	24½
Duluth-Superior	29	56	.341	11	Sioux Falls	36	49	.424	28

PLAYOFFS: Semifinals (best-of-5)—St. Paul defeated Thunder Bay 3-2; Fargo-Moorhead defeated Winnipeg 3-1. **Finals** (best-of-5)—Fargo-Moorhead defeated St. Paul 3-0.

TEXAS-LOUISIANA LEAGUE

	W	L	PCT	GB		W	L	PCT	GB
**Amarillo	64	20	.762	—	Rio Grande Valley	36	48	.429	28
Alexandria	58	26	.690	6	Bayou	36	48	.428	28
Lubbock	39	45	.464	25	Greenville	22	62	.262	42
Abilene	39	45	.464	25					

PLAYOFFS: finals (best-of-5)—Alexandria defeated Amarillo 3-0.

WESTERN LEAGUE

NORTH	W	L	PCT	GB	SOUTH	W	L	PCT	GB
*Reno	45	45	.500	—	**Chico	63	26	.708	—
Bend	43	46	.483	1½	Sonoma County	49	41	.544	14½
*Western	43	47	.478	2	Mission Viejo	49	41	.544	14½
Tri-City	39	51	.433	6	Pacific	28	62	.311	35½

PLAYOFFS: Semifinals (best-of-5)—Sonoma County defeated Chico 3-0; Western defeated Reno 3-1. **Finals** (best-of-5)—Sonoma County defeated Western 3-0.

*Split-season champion

INDEPENDENTLEAGUES

Atlantic
LEAGUE

Mailing Address: 31 Turner Ln., West Chester, PA 19380. **Telephone:** (610) 696-8662. **FAX:** (610) 696-8667. **E-Mail Address:** atlge@aol.com. **Website:** www.atlanticleague.com.
Year Founded: 1998.
Chief Executive Officer: Frank Boulton. **President:** Bud Harrelson.
Executive Director: Joe Klein.
Directors: Frank Boulton (Atlantic City), Rick Cerone (Newark), Chris English (Nashua), Tom Flaherty (Lehigh Valley), Mickey Herbert (Bridgeport), Steven Kalafer (Somerset).
1999 Opening Date: May 5. **Closing Date:** Sept. 12.
Regular Season: 120 games (split schedule).
Playoff Format: First-half winner meets second-half winner in best-of-5 series for league championship.
All-Star Game: July 14 at Bridgeport.
Roster Limit: 25. **Eligibility Rule:** No restrictions.
Brand of Baseball: Rawlings.
Statistician: Howe Sportsdata, Boston Fish Pier, West Bldg. #1, Suite 302, Boston, MA 02210.

ATLANTIC CITY SURF
Office Address: 545 N Albany Ave., Atlantic City, NJ 08401. **Telephone:** (609) 344-8873. **FAX:** (609) 344-7010. **Website:** www.acsurf.com.
Operated by: Atlantic City Surf Professional Baseball Club, Inc.
Principal Owners: Frank Boulton, Tony Rosenthal, Ken Shepard. **Chairman:** Frank Boulton.
President/General Manager: Ken Shepard. **Director, Stadium Operations:** Todd Garrison. **Head Groundskeeper:** Rob Prettyman. **Director, Media Relations/Broadcasting:** Kelly Klunk. **Director, Ticket Sales:** Mark Porch. **Director, Group Sales:** John Kiphorn. **Assistant Director, Group Sales:** Brendan Fairfield. **Director, Merchandising:** Scott Eafrati. **Director, Food Services:** Matt Perachi. **Director, Special Projects:** Jeff Kleeman. **Account Representatives:** Chuck Betson, Frank Dougherty, Mario Perucci. **Office Manager:** Patty MacLuckie.
Manager: Doc Edwards. **Coach:** Bert Pena.
Stadium Name: The Sandcastle. **Standard Game Times:** 7:05 p.m.; Sun. 4:05, 2:05.

BRIDGEPORT BLUEFISH
Office Address: 500 Main St., Bridgeport, CT 06604. **Telephone:** (203) 345-4800. **FAX:** (203) 345-4830. **E-Mail Address:** sschoenfeld@bridgeportbluefish.com **Website:** www.bridgeportbluefish.com.
Operated by: Bridgeport Bluefish Professional Baseball Club, LLC.
Managing General Partner: Mickey Herbert.
General Manager: Charlie Dowd. **Assistant General Manager:** John Brandt. **Manager, Sales/Marketing:** Mike Burke. **Office Manager:** Diane Coniglio. **Manager, Food/Beverage:** Rick DelVecchio. **Manager, Promotions:** Rachael DiLauro. **Manager, Community Outreach:** John Farrell. **Manager, Ticket Subscriptions:** Laurence Grotheer. **Account Executive:** W.H. Mebane. **Coordinator, Accounting:** Tish Pizarro. **Manager, Ballpark Operations:** Michael Rogers. **Manager, Communications:** Steve Schoenfeld. **Controller:** Tony Scott. **Manager, Ticket Operations:** Chris Slawsky. **Coordinator, Special Events:** John Taccone. **Project Manager:** Jay Zammiello.
Manager: Willie Upshaw. **Coach:** Unavailable. **Trainer:** Tom Holton.
Stadium Name: The Ballpark at Harbor Yard. **Standard Game Times:** 7:05 p.m., (May) 6:35; Sun. 1:05.

LEHIGH VALLEY BLACK DIAMONDS
Office Address: 800 Cedarville Rd., Easton, PA 18042. **Mailing Address:** P.O. Box 4000, Easton, PA 18043. **Telephone:** (610) 250-2273. **FAX:** (610) 250-6552. **E-Mail Address:** blkdiamnds@aol.com. **Website:** www.blackdiamondsbaseball.com.
Operated by: Lehigh Valley Professional Sports Clubs, Inc.
Principal Owner: Tom Flaherty. **Chief Executive Officer:** Dilip Petigara.

President/General Manager: Ross Vecchio. **Sales/Promotions Team Leader:** Kristen Beernink. **Operations Assistant:** Doug Kleintop.

Manager: Wayne Krenchicki. **Pitching Coach:** Steve Foucault.

Stadium Name: Lehigh Valley Multi-Purpose Sport Complex. **Standard Game Times:** 7:05 p.m., Sun. 1:35.

NASHUA PRIDE

Office Address: 100 Main St. #1, Nashua, NH 03060. **Telephone:** (603) 883-2255. **FAX:** (603) 883-0880. **E-Mail Address:** pride@nashuabaseball.com. **Website:** nashuabaseball.com.

Operated by: Nashua Pride Professional Baseball, LLC.

Principal Owner/President: Chris English.

General Manager: Billy Johnson. **Manager, Group Events:** Chris Ames. **Manager, Community/Client Relations:** Kim Anastasiou. **Manager, Baseball Operations:** Jim Cardello. **Manager, Public/Media Relations:** Paul Hemingway. **Manager, Promotions/Merchandise:** Todd Marlin. **Assistant, Promotions/Merchandise:** Scott Reeds. **Assistant, Ticketing:** Beverly Taylor.

Manager: Unavailable. **Coach:** Unavailable.

Stadium Name: Holman Stadium. **Standard Game Times:** 7:05 p.m., Sun. 6:05.

NEWARK BEARS

Office Address: 10 Bridge St., Newark, NJ 07102. **Telephone:** (973) 483-6900. **FAX:** (973) 483-6975. **Website:** www.newarkbears.com.

Operated by: Newark Bears, Inc.

Owner/President: Rick Cerone.

General Manager: Kevin Reynolds. **Director, Business Operations:** Greg Aroneo. **Director, Sales:** J.G. Robilotti. **Director, Merchandising:** Jennifer Bauer.

Manager: Unavailable. **Coach:** Unavailable.

Stadium Name: Riverfront Stadium. **Standard Game Times:** 7:11 p.m.; Sun. 2:05.

SOMERSET PATRIOTS

Office Address: 20 W Main St., Somerville, NJ 08876. **Telephone:** (908) 252-0700. **FAX:** (908) 252-0776. **Website:** www.somersetpatriots.com.

Operated by: Somerset Patriots Baseball Club, LLC.

Principal Owners: Steven Kalafer, Michael Kalafer, Jack Cust, Byron Brisby.

Chairman: Steven Kalafer. **President:** Michael Kalafer.

General Manager: David Gasaway. **Assistant General Manager:** Matt O'Brien. **Director, Business Operations:** Ian Allena. **Director, Stadium Operations:** Chris Bryan. **Head Groundskeeper:** Ray Cipperly. **Director, Media Relations:** Rich Beitman. **Director, Sales/Marketing:** Patrick McVerry. **Account Representatives:** Dane Lyle, Paul Nardoni, Marc Skowronek. **Director, Ticket Sales:** Robert Patton. **Director, Group Sales:** Tristan Wallack. **Director, Food Services:** Michael McDermott. **Office Manager:** Michele DaCosta.

Director, Player Procurement: Jim Frey.

Manager: Sparky Lyle. **Pitching Coach:** Jeff Capriotti. **Trainer:** Paul Kolody.

Stadium Name: Somerset County Ballpark. **Standard Game Times:** 7:05 p.m.; Sun. 2:05.

Frontier
LEAGUE

Office Address: 727 Market St., Zanesville, OH 43701. **Mailing Address:** P.O. Box 2662, Zanesville, OH 43702. **Telephone:** (740) 452-7400. **FAX:** (740) 452-2999. **E-Mail Address:** klee@y-city.net. **Website:** www.frontierleague.com.

Year Founded: 1993.

Commissioner: Bill Lee. **President:** Chris Hanners (Chillicothe). **Vice President:** Duke Ward (Richmond). **Corporate Secretary/Treasurer:** Bob Wolfe.

Directors: David Arch (Cook County), Harry Figgie (Canton), Charles Jacob (Evansville), John Kuhn (London), Bill Lett (Dubois County), Rich Sauget (Gateway), Tom Sullivan (Johnstown), John Wallenstein (Springfield), Ken Wilson (River City).

Administrative Assistant: Kathy Lee.

1999 Opening Date: June 2. **Closing Date:** Aug. 30.

Regular Season: 84 games.

Division Structure: East—Canton, Chillicothe, Johnstown, London, Richmond. **West**—Cook County, Dubois County, Evansville, River City, Springfield.

Playoff Format: Division winners plus next two highest finishers meet in best-of-3 semifinals. Winners meet in best-of-3 series for league championship.

All-Star Game: July 14 at Huntingburg, IN (Dubois County).

Roster Limit: 24. **Eligibility Rule:** Minimum of 11 first-year players; maximum of eight players with one year professional experience; maximum of three with unlimited experience. No player may be 27 before June 1, 1999.

Brand of Baseball: Wilson.

Statistician: Howe Sportsdata, Boston Fish Pier, West Bldg. #1, Suite 302, Boston, MA 02210.

CANTON CROCODILES

Office Address: 2501 Allen Ave. SE, Canton, OH 44707. **Telephone:** (330) 455-2255. **FAX:** (330) 454-4835.

Operated by: Canton Frontier League Baseball, LLC.

General Manager: Robert Jones. **Director, Media/Public Relations:** Frank Derry. **Director, Sales:** Stacy Golub. **Director, Community Relations:** Julie Rose. **Director, Group Sales:** Marlene Smart. **Director, Food Services:** Paul Keller. **Head Groundskeeper:** Kevin Lindsey. **Clubhouse Operations:** Carl Crowl. **Office Manager:** Linda Crowl.

Manager: John Zizzo. **Coach:** Unavailable.

Stadium Name: Thurman Munson Memorial Stadium. **Standard Game Times:** 7:11 p.m.; Sun. 6:11.

CHILLICOTHE PAINTS

Office Address: 59 N Paint St., Chillicothe, OH 45601. **Telephone:** (740) 773-8326. **FAX:** (740) 773-8338. **E-Mail Address:** paints@bright.net. **Website:** www.bright.net/~paints.

Operated by: Chillicothe Paints Professional Baseball Association, Inc.

Principal Owner/President: Chris Hanners.

General Manager: Bryan Wickline. **Director, Business Operations:** Shirley Bandy. **Director, Stadium Operations:** Ralph Moore. **Stadium Superintendent/Head Groundskeeper:** Jim Miner. **Director, Public Relations/Promotions:** John Wend. **Director, Community Relations:** Harry Chenault. **Director, Ticket Sales:** Kelly Mickelson. **Director, Merchandising:** Dawn Holton. **Directors, Special Projects:** Dan Clary, Paul Pollard. **Clubhouse Operations:** Butch Atteberry.

Manager/Director, Player Procurement: Roger Hanners. **Coaches:** Steve Dawes, Marty Dunn, Brian Mannino, Eric Welch. **Trainer:** Scott Kaser.

Stadium Name: V.A. Memorial Stadium. **Standard Game Times:** 7:05 p.m.; Sun. 6:05.

COOK COUNTY CHEETAHS

Office Address: 4545 Midlothian Turnpike, Crestwood, IL 60445. **Telephone:** (708) 489-2255. **FAX:** (708) 489-2999. **Website:** www.cookcocheetahs.com.

Operated by: Cheetah Professional Sports II LLC.

Chairman: David Arch. **President:** Leon Steinberg.

Vice President, General Manager: Gerald Clarke. **Assistant General Manager:** Steve Arch. **Head Groundskeeper:** Marty Pelicore. **Director, Public Relations:** Dick Fredrickson. **Account Representatives:** Laura Bland, George King. **Director, Ticket Sales:** Dave Fitzgerald. **Personnel Manager:** Laura Bland. **Clubhouse Operations:** Tom Guare.

Manager: Chico Walker. **Coaches:** Ron LeFlore, Carlos May. **Pitching Coach:** Peter Gahan. **Trainer:** Rob Lacey.

Stadium Name: Hawkinson Ford Field. **Standard Game Times:** 7 p.m.; Sun. 5:30.

DUBOIS COUNTY DRAGONS

Office Address: 426 E Fourth St., Huntingburg, IN 47542. **Mailing Address:** P.O. Box 301, Huntingburg, IN 47542. **Telephone:** (812) 683-4405. **FAX:** (812) 683-4299. **E-Mail Address:** dragons@psci.net. **Website:** www.dragonsbaseball.com.

Operated by: Dragons Baseball, LLC.

Chairman: Bill Lett.

Vice President, Marketing and Sales/Director, Operations: Don Campbell. **Controller:** Ken Craig. **Director, Promotions/Representative, Marketing and Sales:** Chris Johnson. **Head Groundskeeper:** Jim Gunselman. **Office Manager:** Courtney Palmer.

Manager: Unavailable.

Stadium Name: Huntingburg League Stadium. **Standard Game Times:** 7:05 p.m.; Sun. 6:05.

EVANSVILLE OTTERS

Office Address: 1701 N Main St., Evansville, IN 47711. **Telephone:** (812) 435-8686. **FAX:** (812) 435-8688. **E-Mail Address:** ottersbb@evansville.net. **Website:** www.evansville.net/~ottersbb/otters1.htm.

Operated by: Old Time Sports I, LLC.

President: Charles Jacey Jr.

Executive Vice President/Chief Operating Officer: Curt Jacey.

Vice President/General Manager: Jim Miller. **Vice President/Director, Sales and Marketing:** Jack Tracz. **Director, Baseball Operations:** Greg Tagert. **Assistant General Manager:** Pam Miller. **Director, Operations:** Steve Tahsler. **Director, Group/Advance Sales:** John McDonnell. **Souvenir Manager:** Angie Embry.

Manager: Greg Tagert. **Coaches:** Mike Kass, Jeff Leystra.

Stadium Name: Bosse Field. **Standard Game Time:** 7:05 p.m.; Sun. 6:05.

GATEWAY GRIZZLIES
(Expansion team, 2000)

Office Address: 1403 Nickell St., Sauget, IL 62206. **Mailing Address:** P.O. Box 1053, O'Fallon, IL 62269. **Telephone:** (618) 632-0100. **FAX:** (618) 632-0550. **E-Mail Address:** emarglous@gatewaygrizzlies.com. **Website:** www.gatewaygrizzlies.com.

Operated by: Gateway Baseball, LLC.

Principal Owners: Richard Sauget, Ken Wilson.

General Manager: Eric Marglous.

JOHNSTOWN JOHNNIES

Office Address: 345 Main St., Johnstown, PA 15901. **Telephone:** (814) 536-8326. **FAX:** (814) 539-0056. **E-Mail Address:** gmpas@johnniesbaseball.com. **Website:** www.johnniesbaseball.com.

Operated by: Johnstown Professional Baseball, Inc.

President: Tom Sullivan.

General Manager: Patty Sladki. **Director, Public Relations:** Barbara Bailey. **Director, Community Relations:** Edward Zimmerman. **Director, Ticket Sales:** Courtney Brydon. **Director, Merchandising/Office Manager:** Chastity Wills. **Director, Food Services:** Mike Philibin. **Account Representatives:** Barbara Bailey, Karen Charney, Rick Hull, Rick Satcho. **Head Groundskeeper:** Greg Avramis.

Manager/Director, Player Procurement: Mal Fichman. **Coach:** Tom Tornicasa.

Stadium Name: Point Stadium. **Standard Game Times:** 7:05 p.m.; Sun. 6:05.

LONDON WEREWOLVES

Office Address: 25 Wilson Ave., London, ON N6H 1X2. **Telephone:** (519) 679-7337. **FAX:** (519) 679-5713. **E-Mail Address:** londonbaseball@lon.imag.net. **Website:** www.londonwerewolves.com.

Operated by: London Professional Baseball, Inc.

Principal Owner/Chairman: James Kuhn.

President/General Manager: John Kuhn. **Director, Stadium Operations:** Ric Telfer. **Director, Sales/Marketing:** Stephanie Dakins. **Director, Community Relations:** Francee Ender. **Director, Merchandising:** Darrell Bradbury. **Account Representative:** Bruce Maxim. **Groundskeepers:** Mike Reagan, Ryan Williams. **Clubhouse Operations:** Paul Folkad.

Manager: Andy McCauley. **Pitching Coach:** Bruce Gray. **Director, Player Procurement:** Paul Hoines.

Stadium Name: Labatt Memorial Park. **Standard Game Times:** 7:05 p.m.; Sun. 2:05.

RICHMOND ROOSTERS

Mailing Address: 201 NW 13th St., Richmond, IN 47374. **Telephone:** (765) 935-7529. **FAX:** (765) 962-7047. **E-Mail Address:** roosters@infocom.com. **Website:** www.richmondroosters.com.

Operated by: Richmond Baseball, LLC.

Managing Partner: John Cate.

General Manager: Brent Martin. **Assistant General Manager:** Deanna Beamon. **Director, Business Operations:** Duke Ward. **Marketing Representative:** Sam Hodges. **Administrative Assistant:** Becky Luebbe. **Head Groundskeeper:** Cindy Blunk. **Clubhouse Operations:** John Mann.

Manager: John Cate. **Pitching Coach:** Bill Richardson. **Trainer:** Scott Lambert.

Stadium Name: Don McBride Stadium. **Standard Game Times:** 7:05 p.m.; Sun. 5:05.

RIVER CITY RASCALS

Office Address: 900 Ozzie Smith Dr., O'Fallon, MO 63366. **Mailing Address:** P.O. Box 662, O'Fallon, MO 63366. **Telephone:** (314) 240-2287. **FAX:** (314) 240-7313. **Website:** www.rivercityrascals.com.

Operated by: Missouri River Baseball, LLC.

Principal Owner: Ken Wilson.

General Manager: Patrick Daly. **Director, Stadium Operations:** Matt Jones. **Director, Sales/Marketing:** Keith Lucier. **Director, Merchandising:** Bobby Rhoden. **Director, Public Relations:** David Ellington. **Director, Office/Ticket Operations:** Becky Painter.

Manager: Jack Clark. **Coach:** Dick Schofield. **Pitching Coach:** Greg Mathews. **Trainer:** Unavailable.

Stadium Name: T.R. Hughes Ballpark. **Standard Game Times:** 7:05 p.m.; Sun. 6:05.

SPRINGFIELD CAPITALS

Office Address: 1351 N Grand Ave. E, Springfield, IL 62702. **Telephone:** (217) 525-5500. **FAX:** (217) 525-5508. **Website:** www.springfieldcapitals.com.

Operated by: Springfield Capitals Professional Baseball LLC.

General Manager: John Wallenstein. **Director, Business Operations:** Todd Fulk. **Head Groundskeeper:** Larry Rockford. **Director, Broadcasting:** Steve Shannon. **Account Representative:** Brent Zampier. **Director, Food Service:** Lanny Higgins. **Clubhouse Operations:** Mike Fletcher.

Manager: Paul Fletcher. **Coach:** Ed Gillis. **Pitching Coach:** Don Herron. **Director, Player Procurement:** Jim Belz.

Stadium Name: Robin Roberts Stadium. **Standard Game Times:** 7:05 p.m.; Sun. 2:05.

Northern LEAGUE

CENTRAL DIVISION

Office Address: 524 S Duke St., Durham, NC 27701. **Mailing Address:** P.O. Box 1282, Durham, NC 27702. **Telephone:** (919) 956-8150. **FAX:** (919) 683-2693.

E-Mail Address: northernlg@earthlink.net. **Website:** www.northern-league.com.

Year Founded: 1993.

Commissioner: Miles Wolff. **President:** Dan Moushon.

Director, Baseball Operations: Nick Belmonte (16395 Malibu Dr., Fort Lauderdale, FL 33326. Telephone: 954-389-5286). **Supervisor, Umpires:** Butch Fisher.

1999 Opening Date: May 28. **Closing Date:** Sept. 1.

Regular Season: 86 games (split schedule).

Division Structure: East—Duluth-Superior, Madison, St. Paul, Schaumburg. West—Fargo-Moorhead, Sioux City, Sioux Falls, Winnipeg.

All-Star Game: Aug. 2 at Fargo.

Playoff Format: First-half division winners (East, West, North, South) play second-half division winners in best-of-5 playoff series. Winners meet in best-of-5 division (Central, East) championship series. Winners meet in best-of-5 series for league championship.

Roster Limit: 22. **Eligibility Rule:** Minimum of five first-year players; maximum of four veterans (at least four years of professional service).

Brand of Baseball: Rawlings.

Statistician: Howe Sportsdata, Boston Fish Pier, West Bldg. #1, Suite 302, Boston, MA 02210.

DULUTH-SUPERIOR DUKES

Office Address: 207 W Superior St., Suite 206, Duluth, MN 55802. **Mailing Address:** P.O. Box 205, Duluth, MN 55801. **Telephone:** (218) 727-4525. **FAX:** (218) 727-4533. **E-Mail Address:** hitnrun@dsdukes.com. **Website:** www.dsdukes.com.

Operated By: Dukes Baseball Inc.

Principal Owners: Ted Cushmore, Jim Wadley.

President: Jim Wadley.

Vice President/General Manager: Bob Gustafson. Director, Stadium Operations: Rob Hargraves. Director, Media Relations: Mike Bernier. Head Groundskeeper: Ray Adameak.

Manager/Director, Player Procurement: Larry See. Coach: Al Barsoom. Pitching Coach: Steve Shirley.

Stadium Name: Wade Stadium. Standard Game Times: 7:05 p.m.; Sun. 2:05.

FARGO-MOORHEAD REDHAWKS

Office Address: 1515 15th Ave. N, Fargo, ND 58102. Mailing Address: P.O. Box 5258, Fargo, ND 58105. Telephone: (701) 235-6161. FAX: (701) 297-9247. E-Mail Address: redhawks@fmredhawks.com. Website: www.fmredhawks.com.

Operated by: Fargo Baseball, LLC.

Principal Owners: Varistar Corp., Gene Allen.

President: Bruce Thom.

General Manager: Tim Flakoll. Assistant General Manager: Lee Schwartz. Director, Promotions: Kris Breuer. Assistant Director, Promotions: Josh Krueger. Director, Media Relations: Josh Buchholz. Director, Advertising: Nate Hancock. Ticket Manager: Paula Cihla. Accounting Manager: Chuck Lundgren. Assistant Accounting Manager: Jeremy Lewis. Director, Stadium Operations/Head Groundskeeper: Blair Tweet. Administrative Assistant: Tina Ross. Clubhouse Operations: Brent Tehven.

Manager/Director, Player Procurement: Doug Simunic. Coaches: Tom Carcione, Tony Kunka. Pitching Coach: Jeff Bittiger. Trainer: Jeff Bjerke.

Stadium Name: Newman Outdoor Field. Standard Game Times: 7:05 p.m.; Sun. 2:05.

MADISON BLACK WOLF

Office Address: 2920 N Sherman Ave., Madison, WI 53704. Telephone: (608) 244-5666. FAX: (608) 244-6996. E-Mail Address: madwolf@madwolf.com. Website: www.madwolf.com.

Operated by: Madison Baseball, LLC.

Principal Owners: Miles Wolff, Patrick Sweeney, Jimmy Buffett.

Chairman: Patrick Sweeney. President: Bill Terlecky.

General Manager: George Stavrenos. Director, Stadium Operations: Tim Arseneau. Director, Media/Public Relations: Jennifer Watkins. Account Representative: John LaRue. Computer Services: Jacques Besent.

Manager: Al Gallagher. Trainer: Justin Byers.

Stadium Name: Warner Park. Standard Game Times: 7 p.m.; Sun. 1:30.

ST. PAUL SAINTS

Office Address: 1771 Energy Park Dr., St. Paul, MN 55108. Telephone: (651) 644-3517. FAX: (651) 644-1627. E-Mail Address: funsgood@spsaints.com. Website: www.spsaints.com.

Operated by: St. Paul Saints Baseball Club, Inc.

Principal Owners: Marvin Goldklang, Mike Veeck, Bill Murray, Van Schley.

Chairman: Marvin Goldklang. President: Mike Veeck.

Vice President/General Manager: Bill Fanning. Vice President: Marty Scott. Director, Sales: Bob St. Pierre. Director, Promotions: Elizabeth Adams. Director, Public Relations: Eric Webster. Director, Ticket Sales: J.J. Lally. Director, Food Services: Steve Marso. Controller: Wayne Engel. Office Manager: Kelly Komppa. Clubhouse Operations: Brent Proulx. Director, Stadium Operations: Bob Klepperich. Head Groundskeeper: Connie Rudolph.

Manager/Director, Player Procurement: Marty Scott. Coaches: Barry Moss, Wayne Terwilliger. Pitching Coach: Ray Korn.

Stadium Name: Midway Stadium. Standard Game Times: 7:05 p.m.; Sun. 1:05.

SCHAUMBURG FLYERS

Office Address: 1144 S Roselle Rd., Schaumburg, IL 60193. Mailing Address: P.O. Box 68905, Schaumburg, IL 60168. Telephone: (847) 891-2255. FAX: (847) 891-6441. E-Mail Address: info@flyersbaseball.com. Website: www.flyersbaseball.com.

Operated by: Schaumburg Professional Baseball, LLC

Managing Owner: Richard Ehrenreich.

Vice President/General Manager: John Dittrich. Assistant General Manager: Rick Rungaitis. Director, Operations: Fred Rosenthal. Director, Community Relations: Sara Odland. Director, Media

Relations: Matt McLaughlin. **Director, Marketing:** Tom O'Reilly. **Director, Advertising:** Jan Plaude. **Business/Ticket Manager:** Lois Dittrich. **Head Groundskeeper:** Steve Erickson. **Clubhouse Manager:** Alan Taraszka.

Manager: Ron Kittle. **Director, Baseball Operations/Coach:** Pete Caliendo. **Pitching Coach:** Greg Hibbard.

Stadium Name: Schaumburg Baseball Stadium. **Standard Game Times:** 7:20 p.m.; Sun. 1:20.

SIOUX CITY EXPLORERS

Office Address: 3400 Line Dr., Sioux City, IA 51106. **Telephone:** (712) 277-9467. **FAX:** (712) 277-9406. **E-Mail Address:** xsbaseball@aol.com.

Operated by: Sioux City Explorers Baseball Club, LLC.

Principal Owner/President: Ed Nottle.

Vice President/General Manager: Tim Utrup. **Controller:** Donna Hopley. **Director, Stadium Operations:** Eugene Carlson. **Director, Sales/Marketing:** Kevin Farlow. **Director, Community Relations:** Todd Jamison. **Director, Ticket Sales:** Shane Codwell. **Director, Group Sales:** Kerry White.

Manager: Ed Nottle. **Coach:** Steve Shoemaker. **Pitching Coach:** Pat Tilmon. **Trainer:** Mike Wright. **Director, Player Procurement:** Harry Stavrenos.

Stadium Name: Lewis and Clark Park. **Standard Game Times:** 7:05 p.m.; Sun. 6:05.

SIOUX FALLS CANARIES

Office Address: 1001 N West Ave., Sioux Falls, SD 57104. **Mailing Address:** P.O. Box 84412, Sioux Falls, SD 57118. **Telephone:** (605) 333-0179. **FAX:** (605) 333-0139. **E-Mail Address:** canaries@iw.net. **Website:** www.iw.net/canaries.

Operated By: Sioux Falls Canaries Professional Baseball Club, LLC.

Principal Owners: Marvin Goldklang, Mike Veeck.

Chairman: Marvin Goldklang. **President:** Mike Veeck.

General Manager: Ripper Hatch. **Assistant General Managers:** Bill Fisher, Larry McKenney. **Director, Business Operations:** Brad Seymour. **Director, Public Relations:** Elizabeth Arnold. **Director, Ticket Sales:** Matt Brown. **Director, Group Sales:** Darcey Otter. **Account Executive:** Joe Wagoner.

Manager: Unavailable. **Coach:** Unavailable.

Stadium Name: Sioux Falls Stadium. **Standard Game Times:** 7:05 p.m.; Sun. 2:05, 6:05.

Visiting Club Hotel: Comfort Inn, 3216 S Carolyn Ave., Sioux Falls, SD 57106. Telephone: (605) 361-2822.

WINNIPEG GOLDEYES

Office Address: 200-177 McDermot Ave., Winnipeg, Manitoba R3B 0S1. **Telephone:** (204) 982-2273. **FAX:** (204) 982-2274. **E-Mail Address:** goldeyes@mts.net. **Website:** www.goldeyes.aroundmanitoba.com.

Operated by: Winnipeg Goldeyes Baseball Club Inc.

Principal Owner/President: Sam Katz.

Vice President, General Manager: John Hindle. **Vice President, Finance:** Andrew Collier. **Vice President, Sales/Marketing:** Kevin Moore. **Director, Public Relations:** Jonathan Green. **Director, Promotions:** Barb McTavish. **Director, Group Sales:** Lorraine Maciboric. **Account Representatives:** Dave Loat, Dennis McLean, Tracy Smith. **Bookkeeper:** Judy Jemson. **Receptionist:** Lisa Major.

Manager/Director, Player Procurement: Hal Lanier. **Coach:** Scott Neiles. **Trainer:** Brad Hall.

Stadium Name: Canwest Global Park. **Standard Game Times:** 7:05 p.m.; Sun. 1:35.

EASTERN DIVISION

(Formerly Northeast League)

Office Address: 1308 Davos Pointe, Woodridge, NY 12789. **Telephone:** (914) 436-0411. **FAX:** (914) 436-6864.

Executive Director: Mike McGuire.

Division Structure: North—Adirondack, Albany, Massachusetts, Quebec. **South**—Allentown, Elmira, New Jersey, Waterbury.

Brand of Baseball: Wilson.

ADIRONDACK LUMBERJACKS

Office Address: 15 Dix Ave., Glens Falls, NY 12801. **Telephone:** (518) 743-9618. **FAX:** (518) 743-9721. **E-Mail Address:** baseball@superior.net. **Website:** www.adirondacklumberjack.com.

Operated by: Old Time Sports, LLC.

Principal Owner: Charles Jacey.

General Manager: Curt Jacey. Director, Media/Special Projects: Junina Nacua. Director, Community Relations: Heather LaVine. Director, Merchandising: Kristen Jacey. Director, Food Services: Sue Didio.

Manager: Les Lancaster. Director, Player Procurement: Doug Kindler.

Stadium Name: East Field. Standard Game Times: 7 p.m., Sun. 2.

ALBANY-COLONIE DIAMOND DOGS

Office Address: Heritage Park, 780 Watervliet-Shaker Rd., Albany, NY 12211. Telephone: (518) 869-9234. FAX: (518) 869-5291. E-Mail Address: acdogs@acmenet.net. Website: www.diamonddogs.com.

Operated by: Diamond Dogs Sports, Inc.

President: Tom Sullivan.

Vice President/General Manager: Charlie Voelker. Vice President, Sales: Rip Rowan. Director, Stadium Operations: Kevin Forrester. Head Groundskeeper: Dave Hildebrandt. Director, Promotions: Mike DiGildramo. Director, Merchandising: Erinn McNeil. Director, Group Sales: Robert Totaro.

Manager/Director, Player Procurement: Charlie Sullivan. Pitching Coach: Dane Johnson.

Stadium Name: Heritage Park. Standard Game Times: 7:05 p.m.; Sun. 2:05.

ALLENTOWN AMBASSADORS

Office Address: 1511-1525 Hamilton St., Allentown, PA 18102. Telephone: (610) 437-6800. FAX: (610) 437-6804. Website: www.ambassadorsbaseball.com.

Operated by: Allentown Ambassadors Professional Baseball Team, Inc.

Principal Owner: Peter Karoly.

General Manager: Dean Gyorgy. Assistant General Manager: David Hieter. Director, Group Events: Carol Hecht. Director, Communications: Karin Crossley.

Manager: Ed Ott. Director, Player Development: Joe Calsapietra.

Stadium Name: Bicentennial Park. Standard Game Times: 7:05 p.m.; Sun. 5:05.

ELMIRA PIONEERS

Office Address: 546 Luce St., Elmira, NY 14904. Telephone: (607) 734-1270. FAX: (607) 734-0891. Website: www.elmirapioneers.com.

Operated by: Elmira Baseball, LLC.

President: John Ervin.

General Manager: Ric Sisler. Assistant General Manager: Matt Hufnagel. Director, Business Operations: Steve Ervin. Director, Sales/Marketing: Jennifer Booth. Account Representative: Joe Kosmicki. Head Groundskeeper: Dale Storch. Office Manager: Penny Riker.

Manager: Dan Shwam. Batting Coach: John Booher. Director, Player Procurement: Jeff Kunion.

Stadium Name: Dunn Field. Standard Game Times: 7:05 p.m.; Sun. 5:05.

MASSACHUSETTS MAD DOGS

Office Address: 359 Western Ave., Lynn, MA 01904. Mailing Address: P.O. Box 8292, Lynn, MA 01904. Telephone: (781) 592-2255. FAX: (781) 592-8814. E-Mail Address: maddogs@shorenet.com. Website: www.maddogs.com.

Operated by: Flyball, Inc.

Principal Owner: Jonathan Fleisig.

President/General Manager: Michael Kardamis. Director, Business Operations: Vikki Enos. Director, Stadium Operations: Ernie Sharpe.

Manager/Director, Player Procurement: George Scott. Coach: Tom Donahue.

Stadium Name: Fraser Field. Standard Game Times: 7:05 p.m.; Sun. 6:05.

NEW JERSEY JACKALS

Office Address: One Hall Dr., Little Falls, NJ 07424. Telephone: (973) 746-7434. FAX: (973) 655-8021. E-Mail Address: njjackals@aol.com. Website: www.jackals.com.

Operated by: Floyd Hall Enterprises, LLC.

Principal Owner: Floyd Hall. President: Greg Lockard. Executive Vice President: Larry Hall.

General Manager: Leo Kirk. Assistant General Manager: Hank Manning. Director, Business Operations: Jennifer Fertig. Director, Public Relations: Jim Cerny. Head Groundskeeper: Larry Castoro.

Director, Ticket Sales: Elisabeth Unley. Director, Group Sales: Ken Yudman. Office Manager: Anita Wall.

Manager: Kash Beauchamp. Pitching Coach: Vance Lovelace.

Stadium Name: Yogi Berra Stadium. Standard Game Times: 7:10 p.m.; Sun. 6:10.

LES CAPITALES DE QUEBEC

Office Address: 100 rue du Cardinal Maurice-Roy, Quebec City, Quebec G1K 8Z1. Telephone: (418) 521-2255. FAX: (418) 521-2266. E-Mail Address: webmaster@capitalesdequebec.com. Website: capitalesdequebec.com.

Operated by: Club de Baseball Professional de Quebec, Inc.

Principal Owners: Vince Burns, Miles Wolff.

President/General Manager: Miles Wolff.

Director, Business Operations: Jeff Cote. Director, Stadium Operations: Jean Gagnon. Director, Sales/Marketing: Michel Laplante. Director, Ticket Sales: Stephone Dionne. Director, Food Services: Herve Lapointe.

Manager/Director, Player Procurement: Jay Ward. Trainer: Dennis Laberge.

Stadium Name: Le Stade de Quebec. Standard Game Times: 7:05 p.m.; Sun 2:05.

WATERBURY SPIRIT

Office Address: 1200 Watertown Rd., Waterbury, CT 06708. Telephone: (203) 419-0393. FAX: (203) 419-0396. E-Mail Address: info@waterburyspirit.com. Website: waterburyspirit.com.

Operated by: WC Sports, LLC.

Principal Owners: David Carpenter, Bob Wirz.

Chairman: David Carpenter. President: Bob Wirz.

General Manager: Russ Ardolina. Assistant General Manager: Jay Baldacci. Assistant GM, Sales/Marketing: Terry Cole. Controller: Ginny Kozlowski. Director, Food Services: Joe Caiazzo. Director, Group Sales: David Rodriguez. Account Representative: William McMinn.

Manager: George Tsamis. Trainer: Liz Gale.

Stadium Name: Municipal Stadium. Standard Game Times: 7:05 p.m.; Sun 5:05.

Texas-Louisiana
LEAGUE

Mailing Address: 2801 N Third St., Abilene, TX 79601. Telephone: (915) 673-7364. FAX: (915) 673-5150. E-Mail Address: txlaops@txproball.com. Website: txproball.com.

Year Founded: 1994.

President: Byron Pierce. Director, Operations: Travis Hartgraves. Chief Financial Officer: Rick Ivey. Director, Marketing: Bruce Unrue.

Administrative Assistant: Mindy Cheek.

1999 Opening Date: May 27. Closing Date: Aug. 31.

Regular Season: 84 games (split schedule).

All-Star Game: Unavailable.

Playoff Format: First-half and second-half champions meet in best-of-5 series for league championship.

Roster Limit: 22. Player Eligibility Rule: None.

Statistician: Howe Sportsdata, Boston Fish Pier, West Bldg. #1, Suite 302, Boston, MA 02110.

ABILENE PRAIRIE DOGS

Office Address: 2801 N Third, Abilene, TX 79601. Telephone: (915) 673-7364. FAX: (915) 673-5150.

Operated by: Texas-Louisiana Baseball League.

General Manager: Unavailable. Assistant General Manager: Mindy Cheek. Director, Public Relations: Scott Kirk. Director, Community Relations/Ticket Sales: Dusty Moore. Clubhouse Operations: Blake Burton.

Manager: Dan Madsen.

Stadium Name: Crutcher-Scott Field. Standard Game Time: 7:05 p.m.

ALEXANDRIA ACES

Office Address: 1 Babe Ruth Dr., Alexandria, LA 71301. Mailing Address: P.O. Box 6005, Alexandria, LA 71307. Telephone: (318) 473-2237. FAX: (318) 473-2229.

Operated by: Alexandria Baseball Club, LC.
General Manager: Craig Brasfield. **Assistant General Manager:** Chet Carey. **Director, Business Operations/Merchandising:** Carrie Brasfield. **Director, Stadium Operations:** Jodie White. **Head Groundskeeper/Clubhouse Operations:** John Hickman. **Director, Public Relations:** Ryan Sachs. **Director, Ticket/Group Sales:** Dave Bengert. **Director, Food Services:** Fred Eloi.
Manager: Stan Cliburn. **Trainer:** Mike Palombo.
Stadium Name: Bringhurst Field. **Standard Game Time:** 6:35 p.m.

AMARILLO DILLAS
Street Address: 501 W Ninth St., Amarillo, TX 79101. **Mailing Address:** P.O. Box 31241, Amarillo, TX 79120. **Telephone:** (806) 342-3455. **FAX:** (806) 374-2269.
Operated by: Amarillo Baseball Club, LC.
President: Byron Pierce.
General Manager: John Cook. **Director, Marketing:** Chris Miller. **Account Representatives:** Daren Brown, Jamille Mann. **Office Manager:** Jamille Mann. **Director, Community Relations/Group Sales:** Allison Rickles. **Director, Ticket Sales:** Rita Ecker. **Director, Special Projects:** Cindy Withrow. **Clubhouse Operations:** George Escamilla.
Manager: Daren Brown.
Stadium Name: Potter County Memorial Stadium. **Standard Game Times:** 7:05 p.m.; Sun. 5:05.

BAYOU BULLFROGS
Mailing Address: 801 W Congress St., Lafayette, LA 70501. **Telephone:** (318) 233-0998. **FAX:** (318) 237-3539.
Operated by: Bayou Baseball Club, LC.
Chairman: Horn Chen.
General Manager: Scott Clause. **Director, Operations:** Anthony De Vincenzo. **Director, Sales/Marketing:** Lydia Bergeron. **Director, Group Sales:** Brenda Kowalski.
Manager: John Harris. **Coach:** L.J DuPuy. **Pitching Coach:** Ron Guidry.
Stadium Name: Moore Field (University of Southwestern Louisiana). **Standard Game Times:** 7:05 p.m.; Sat., Sun. 6:05.

GREENVILLE BLUESMEN
Mailing Address: 1040 S Raceway Rd., Greenville, MS 38701. **Telephone:** (601) 335-2583. **FAX:** (601) 335-7742. **E-Mail Address:** bluesmen@tecinfo.com. **Website:** www.tecinfo.com/~bluesmen.
Operated by: Greenville Bluesmen Professional Baseball Club, LLC.
President/General Manager: George Hood. **Assistant General Manager:** Jeff Brown. **Office Manager:** Darline Rodgers.
Manager: Bob Lacey.
Stadium Name: Legion Field. **Standard Game Times:** 7:05 p.m.; Sun. 5:05.

OZARK MOUNTAIN DUCKS
Office Address: 5245 N 17th St., Ozark, MO 65721. **Mailing Address:** P.O. Box 1472, Ozark, MO 65721. **Telephone:** (417) 581-2868. **FAX:** (417) 581-8342.
General Manager: Brad Eldridge. **Assistant General Manager:** Sherri Lippoldt. **Director, Stadium Operations:** Brock Phipps. **Director, Sales/Broadcasting:** Len Smith. **Director, Food Services:** Bradley Moncado.
Manager: Barry Jones.
Stadium Name: Unavailable. **Standard Game Times:** 7:05 p.m.; Sun. 6:05.

RIO GRANDE VALLEY WHITEWINGS
Mailing Address: 1216 Fair Park Blvd., Harlingen, TX 78550. **Telephone:** (956) 412-9464. **FAX:** (956) 412-9479. **E-Mail Address:** homerun@rgvwhitewings.com. **Website:** www.rgvwhitewings.com.
Operated by: Rio Grande Valley Baseball Club, LC.
General Manager: Mike Babcock. **Assistant General Manager:** Mike Lieberman. **Director, Business Operations:** John Cannon. **Head Groundskeeper:** Omar Benavides. **Director, Sales/Marketing:** Clay Stanton. **Office Manager:** Marilyn Farley.
Manager: Eddie Dennis.
Stadium Name: Harlingen Field. **Standard Game Times:** 7:05 p.m.

Western LEAGUE

Office Address: 426 Broadway, Suite 208, Chico, CA 95928.
Telephone: (530) 897-6125. FAX: (530) 897-6124. E-Mail Address:
office@westernbaseball.com. Website: www.westernbaseball.com.
Year Founded: 1995.
President/Treasurer: Bob Linscheid. Marketing Director: Margaret
Schmidt. Administrative Assistant: Corey King.
Directors: Pat Elster (Zion), Teri Engel (Reno), Bob Fletcher (Sonoma
County), John Montero (Tri-City), Steve Nettleton (Chico), Bruce Portner
(Sacramento).
1999 Opening Date: May 21. Closing Date: Sept. 2.
Regular Season: 90 games.
Playoff Format: Top four teams qualify for best-of-3 semifinal series.
Winners meet in best-of-5 series for league championship.
All-Star Game: July 12 at Chico.
Roster Limit: 22. Player Eligibility Rule: Minimum of five first-year play-
ers; maximum of eight veterans (five or more years of professional service).
Brand of Baseball: Wilson.
Statistician: Howe Sportsdata, Boston Fish Pier, West Bldg. #1, Suite
302, Boston, MA 02210.

CHICO HEAT
Street Address: 250 Vallombrosa Ave., Suite 200, Chico, CA 95926.
Telephone: (530) 343-4328. FAX: (530) 894-1799. E-Mail Address:
steven@chicoheat.com. Website: www.chicoheat.com.
Operated by: Chico Heat Baseball Club, LLC.
President/General Manager: Steve Nettleton.
Assistant General Manager: Brian Ceccon. Director, Sales/Market-
ing: Jeff Kragel. Director, Stadium Operations: Ken Shamburg. Con-
troller: Alan Guidi. Director, Media Relations/Group Sales: Rory Miller.
Director, Ticket Sales: Heather Schmidt. Director, Merchandising: Jeff
Miller. Director, Food Services: Bob Pinocchio. Office Manager: Tracey
Perotti.
Manager: Bill Plummer. Coach: Ken Shamburg. Pitching Coach: Jeff
Pico. Directors, Player Procurement: Brian Ceccon, Bill Plummer.
Stadium Name: Nettleton Stadium. Standard Game Times: 7:05 p.m.

RENO CHUKARS
Office Address: 240 W Moana Ln., Reno, NV 89509. Telephone: (702)
829-7890. FAX: (702) 829-7895. E-Mail Address: info@renochukars.com.
Website: www.renochukars.com.
Operated By: Reno Chukars, LLC.
President: Bruce Engel.
General Manager: Teri Engel. Assistant General Manager: Terry
Donovan. Director, Media Relations: Corey Alan Forgue. Director,
Group Sales: Adam Colby. Head Groundskeeper: Ron Malcolm.
Manager: Charlie Kerfeld. Pitching Coach: Bob Ayrault.
Stadium Name: Moana Stadium. Standard Game Times: 7:05 p.m.;
Sat. 5:05; Sun. 1:35.

SACRAMENTO STEELHEADS
Office Address: 2527 J St., Sacramento, CA 95816. Telephone: (916)
553-4500. FAX: (916) 448-3517.
Operated By: Sacramento Steelheads, LLC.
President: Bruce Portner.
Assistant General Manager: Frank Banales. Director, Sales/
Marketing: Roger Ditteshi. Account Representatives: Melissa Arnsten,
Brett Jenkins. Director, Community Relations: Emily Horton. Director,
Promotions/Special Projects: T.C. Martin. Director, Group Sales: Gary
Wilson. Director, Food Services: Mark Scribner. Office Manager: David
Gull.
Manager/Director, Player Procurement: Butch Hughes. Coach: John
Noce.
Stadium Name: Union Stadium. Standard Game Times: 7:05 p.m.

SONOMA COUNTY CRUSHERS
Office Address: 5900 Labath Ave., Rohnert Park, CA 94928.
Telephone: (707) 588-8300. FAX: (707) 538-9339. E-Mail Address:
rbfletch@aol.com.
Operated by: Sonoma County Professional Baseball, Inc.

President/General Manager: Robert Fletcher.
Director, Business Operations: Susan Fletcher. Director, Stadium Operations: Steve Fraire. Head Groundskeeper: Dolf Hes. Director, Media/Public Relations: David Raymond. Director, Sales/Marketing: Kevin Wolski. Director, Group Sales: Chris Corda.
Manager: Dick Dietz. Pitching Coach: Dolf Hes.
Stadium Name: Rohnert Park Stadium. Standard Game Times: 7:05 p.m.; Wed. 1:30; Sat. 5:05; Sun. 1:30.

TRI-CITY POSSE

Office Address: 6200 Burden Rd., Pasco, WA 99301. Telephone: (509) 547-6773. FAX: (509) 547-4008.
Operated By: Tri-City Posse Baseball, Inc.
President/Baseball Operations: John Montero. Vice President/General Manager: Sean Kelly. Assistant General Manager: Rich Buel. Ticket Manager: Rick Marple. Account Executive: Brandon Cruz. Head Groundskeeper: Gordi Franti.
Manager: Wally Backman. Coach: Chris Catanoso. Pitching Coach: Floyd Youmans. Trainer: Leo Combs.
Stadium Name: Tri-Cities Stadium. Standard Game Times: 7:05 p.m.; Sun. 6:05.

ZION PIONEERZZ

Office Address: 1240 E 100 S, Suite 16B, St. George, UT 84790. Telephone: (435) 656-9000. FAX: (435) 628-8389. E-Mail Address: info@zionpioneerzz.com. Website: www.zionpioneerzz.com.
Operated by: Red Rock Professional Baseball Club.
Principal Owner: Shugart Corporation.
President: Pat Elster.
General Manager: Rob White. Director, Media Relations: Randy Miller.
Manager/Director, Player Development: Bruce Hurst. Coaches: Jake Jenkins, Mike Littlewood, Randy Wilstead.
Stadium Name: Bruce Hurst Field. Standard Game Times: 7:05 p.m.

INDEPENDENT SCHEDULES

Atlantic League

Atlantic City

MAY
6-7-8 .... Newark
9-10-11 .... Lehigh Valley
13-14-15 .... Nashua
29-30-31 .... Bridgeport

JUNE
1-2-3 .... Lehigh Valley
4-5-6 .... Somerset
11-12-13 .... Bridgeport
15-16-17 .... Newark
18-19-20 .. Lehigh Valley
24-25-26 ...Lehigh Valley
27-28-29 .... Somerset

JULY
1-2-3 .... Nashua
7-8-9 .... Newark
16-17-18 .... Nashua
19-20-21 .... Bridgeport
31 .... Newark

AUGUST
1-2.................... Newark
3-4-5 .... Nashua
6-7-8 .... Bridgeport
16-17-18 .... Somerset
19-20-21 .. Lehigh Valley
28-29-30 .... Somerset

SEPTEMBER
1-2-3 .... Newark
10-11-12 .. Lehigh Valley

Bridgeport

MAY
5-6 .... Nashua
11 .... Nashua
13-14-15 .... Somerset
16-17-18..... Atlantic City
19-20-21 .... Newark
22-23-24 .. Lehigh Valley

JUNE
1-2-3 .... Nashua
4-5-6 .... Lehigh Valley
15-16-17 .. Lehigh Valley
18-19-20 .... Somerset
21-22-23 .... Newark
27-28-29 .. Lehigh Valley

JULY
1-2-3 .... Newark
4-5-6........... Atlantic City
10-11-12 .... Nashua
16-17-18 .... Somerset
28-29-30..... Atlantic City
31............. Lehigh Valley

AUGUST
1-2 .... Lehigh Valley
10-11-12 .. Lehigh Valley
16-17-18 .... Newark
19-20-21 .... Somerset
28-29-30 .... Newark

SEPTEMBER
1-2-3 .... Nashua
4-5-6 .... Atlantic City

Lehigh Valley

JULY
4-5-6 .... Newark
10-11-12 .... Atlantic City
19-20-21 .... Nashua
22-23-24 .... Bridgeport
25-26-27 .... Somerset

AUGUST
3-4-5 .... Newark
13-14-15.... Atlantic City
16-17-18 .... Nashua
22-23-24 .... Bridgeport

SEPTEMBER
1-2-3 .... Somerset
4-5-6 .... Newark

Nashua

MAY
7-8-9 .... Bridgeport
16-17-18 .... Somerset
19-20-21.... Atlantic City
26-27-28 .. Lehigh Valley
29-30-31 ...... Somersot

JUNE
4-5-6 .... Newark
8-9-10 .... Atlantic City
11-12-13 .. Lehigh Valley
18-19-20 .... Newark
21-22-23 .. Lehigh Valley
24-25-26 .... Bridgeport

JULY
7-8-9 .... Lehigh Valley
22-23-24 .... Newark
25-26-27.... Atlantic City
28-29-30 .. Lehigh Valley

AUGUST
10-11-12 .... Somerset
13-14-15 .... Bridgeport
22-23-24 .... Newark
25-26-27.... Atlantic City
28-29-30 .. Lehigh Valley

SEPTEMBER
7-8-9 .... Bridgeport
10-11-12 .... Somerset

Newark

MAY
13-14-15-16-17-18. L.V.*
22-23-24......... Nashua*
26-27-28 .. Atlantic City*
29-30-31. Lehigh Valley*

JUNE
8-9-10.... Bridgeport*
27-28-29 .... Nashua*

JULY
16-17-18 .. Lehigh Valley
19-20-21 .... Somerset
25-26-27 .... Bridgeport
28-29-30 .... Somerset

AUGUST
6-7-8 .... Nashua
10-11-12.... Atlantic City
19-20-21 .... Nashua
25-26-27 .. Lehigh Valley

SEPTEMBER
7-8-9.......... Atlantic City
10-11-12 .... Bridgeport

Somerset

MAY
7-8......... Lehigh Valley**
9-10-11............... Newark
19-20-21 .. Lehigh Valley
22-23-24.... Atlantic City
26-27-28 .... Bridgeport

JUNE
1-2-3 .... Newark
7-8-9-10... Lehigh Valley
11-12-13........... Newark
15-16-17 .... Nashua
21-22-23.... Atlantic City
24-25-26 .... Newark

JULY
1-2-3 .... Lehigh Valley
4-5-6 .... Nashua
7-8-9 .... Bridgeport
10-11-12............. Newark
22-23-24.... Atlantic City
31..................... Nashua

AUGUST
1-2 .... Nashua
3-4-5 .... Bridgeport
6-7-8 .... Lehigh Valley
13-14-15 .... Newark
22-23-24.... Atlantic City
25-26-27 .... Bridgeport

SEPTEMBER
4-5-6 .... Nashua
7-8-9 .... Lehigh Valley

Below for Atlantic City AUGUST:
AUGUST
1-2 .... Lehigh Valley
10-11-12 .. Lehigh Valley
16-17-18 .... Newark
19-20-21 .... Somerset
28-29-30 .... Newark

SEPTEMBER
1-2-3 .... Nashua
4-5-6 .... Atlantic City

NOTE: Lehigh Valley and Newark ballparks will not be completed until the end of June.

*Games at Skylands Park, home of New Jersey Cardinals of New York-Penn League

**Games at Atlantic City

Frontier League

Canton

JUNE
8-9-10 .... Evansville
11-12-13........... London
21-22-23 .... River City

JULY
1-2-3 .... Johnstown
4-5-6 .... Chillicothe
7-8-9 .... Richmond
21-22-23............ London
27-28-29 .... Richmond
30-31............. Evansville

AUGUST
1.................... Evansville
3-4-5............. Springfield

10-11-12.... Cook County
13-14-15 Dubois County
19-20-21 .... Chillicothe
25-26-27 .... Johnstown

Chillicothe

JUNE
2-3-4............. Springfield

268 • 1999 DIRECTORY

JULY
1-2-3 .... London
15-16-17 ..... Johnstown
18-19-20 .... London
24-25-26 .... Canton
27-28-29 ... Johnstown

AUGUST
3-4-5 .... River City
6-7-8 ..... Cook County
16-17-18 ..... Springfield
22-23-24 .... Richmond

Cook County

JUNE
2-3-4 .... River City
11-12-13 Dubois County
18-19-20 .... Richmond
21-22-23 .... Chillicothe
24-25-26 .... Canton

JULY
4-5-6 .... London
10-11-12 .... River City
18-19-20 .... Evansville
27-28-29 .... London
30-31 .... Springfield

AUGUST
1 .... Springfield
13-14-15 .... Johnstown
16-17-18 Dubois County
22-23-24 ...... Springfield
25-26-27 .... Evansville

Dubois County

JUNE
5-6-7 .... Springfield
15-16-17 ...... Johnstown
28-29-30 .... Canton

JULY
4-5-6 .... Evansville
7-8-9 .... Cook County
15-16-17 ...... River City
18-19-20 ...... Springfield
21-22-23 ... Cook County
27-28-29 ..... Evansville

AUGUST
3-4-5 .... London
6-7-8 ...... Richmond
10-11-12 .... Chillicothe
19-20-21 ...... Johnstown
22-23-24 ...... River City

Evansville

JUNE
2-3-4 ...... Dubois County

5-6-7 .... River City
15-16-17 ... Cook County
24-25-26 ...... Richmond

JULY
1-2-3 .... Cook County
10-11-12 .... Springfield
15-16-17 .... Canton
24-25-26 ...... Springfield

AUGUST
3-4-5 .... Johnstown
6-7-8 .... London
13-14-15 .... Chillicothe
16-17-18 ...... River City
22-23-24 .... Canton
28-29-30 .. Dubois County

Johnstown

JUNE
2-3-4 .... London
5-6-7 .... Canton
11-12-13 .... Chillicothe
18-19-20 .... Evansville
24-25-26 .... River City
28-29-30 ... Cook County

JULY
4-5-6 .... Richmond
10-11-12 .. Dubois County
18-19-20 .... Canton
24-25-26 .. Dubois County

AUGUST
6-7-8 .... Springfield
16-17-18 ...... Richmond
22-23-24 .... London
28-29-30 ..... Chillicothe

London

JUNE
5-6-7 ...... Cook County
8-9-10 .... Chillicothe
15-16-17 ...... Richmond
18-19-20 .. Dubois County
21-22-23 ...... Evansville
24-25-26 ...... Springfield

JULY
7-8-9 .... Johnstown
10-11-12 .... Canton
24-25-26 ...... Richmond
30-31 .... Johnstown

AUGUST
1 .... Johnstown
13-14-15 .... River City
16-17-18 .... Canton
25-26-27 .... Chillicothe
28-29-30 ... Cook County

Richmond

JUNE
2-3-4 .... Canton

8-9-10 .... Johnstown
11-12-13 ...... River City
21-22-23 Dubois County

JULY
1-2-3 .... River City
10-11-12 .... Chillicothe
15-16-17 .... London
21-22-23 ...... Johnstown
30-31 .... Chillicothe

AUGUST
1 .... Chillicothe
3-4-5 .... Cook County
10-11-12 ..... Evansville
13-14-15 .... Springfield
19-20-21 .... London
28-29-30 .... Canton

River City

JUNE
8-9-10 .... Dubois County
15-16-17 ...... Springfield
18-19-20 .... Chillicothe
28-29-30 .... London

JULY
4-5-6 .... Springfield
7-8-9 .... Evansville
18-19-20 ...... Richmond
21-22-23 ..... Evansville
24-25-26 ... Cook County
30-31 ..... Dubois County

AUGUST
1 .... Dubois County
6-7-8 .... Canton
10-11-12 ..... Johnstown
19-20-21 ... Cook County
25-26-27 ...... Richmond

Springfield

JUNE
8-9-10 .... Cook County
11-12-13 ..... Evansville
18-19-20 .... Canton
21-22-23 ...... Johnstown
27-28-29 ...... Richmond

JULY
1-2-3 ... Dubois County
7-8-9 .... Chillicothe
15-16-17 ... Cook County
21-22-23 ..... Chillicothe
27-28-29 ..... River City

AUGUST
9-10-11 .... London
19-20-21 .... Evansville
25-26-27 Dubois County
28-29-30 .... River City

Northern League

Duluth

MAY
28-29-30 .... Fargo

JUNE
1-2-3 .... Schaumburg
7-8-9-10 .... St. Paul
11-12-13 .... Winnipeg
21-22-23 .... Sioux City

JULY
2-3-4 ...... Madison
6-7-8 .... Sioux Falls
16-17-18 .... Fargo

CENTRAL DIVISION
19-20-21 .... Sioux City
29-30-31 ... Schaumburg

AUGUST
10-11-12 .... Madison
20-21-22 .... Winnipeg
24-25-26 ..... Sioux Falls
30-31 .... St. Paul

SEPTEMBER
1 .... St. Paul

Fargo-Moorhead

JUNE
1-2-3 .... Sioux Falls

4-5-6 .... Duluth
11-12-13 .... St. Paul
15-16-17 .... Madison
25-26-27-28 ... Winnipeg

JULY
6-7-8 .... Schaumburg
9-10-11 ...... Sioux City
22-23-24 .... Madison
26-27-28 ...... Sioux Falls

AUGUST
7-8-9 .... Sioux City
10-11-12 .... St. Paul
17-18-19 .... Duluth

27-28-29 ... Schaumburg
30-31 .... Winnipeg
SEPTEMBER
1 .... Winnipeg

Madison
MAY
31 .... St. Paul
JUNE
1-2 .... St. Paul
4-5-6 .... Sioux City
11-12-13 ...... Sioux Falls
21-22-23 .... Fargo
25-26-27 ... Schaumburg
JULY
5-6-7 .... Winnipeg
9-10-11 .... Duluth
16-17-18 .... St. Paul
26-27-28 .... Winnipeg
AUGUST
3-4-5 .... Duluth
6-7-8 .... Sioux Falls
13-14-15-16 ... Schaum.
23-24-25 .... Fargo
26-28-29 ...... Sioux City

St. Paul
JUNE
4-5-6 .... Schaumburg
14-15-16........ Winnipeg
18-19-20 ...... Sioux City
25-26-27 .... Duluth
29-30 .... Madison
JULY
1 .... Madison
9-10-11 ...... Sioux Falls
12-13-14 .... Fargo
19-20-21 ... Schaumburg
22-23-24 ...... Sioux City
29-30-31......... Madison
AUGUST
4-5-6 .... Fargo
13-14-15-16....... Duluth
17-18-19 ...... Winnipeg
27-28-29 ...... Sioux Falls

Adirondack
MAY
28-29-30 .... Elmira
JUNE
1-2-3 .... Adirondack
7-8-9-10 .... Quebec
11-12-13 ...... Waterbury
21-22-23 .... Allentown
JULY
2-3-4 ..... Massachusetts
6-7-8 .... New Jersey
16-17-18 ...... Waterbury
20-21-22 .... Allentown
29-30-31 .... Elmira
AUGUST
10-11-12 .... Albany
13-14-15 .... Quebec
20-21-22 ...... New Jersey
24-25-26 .... Mass.

Albany
MAY
29-29-30 .... Quebec
JUNE
7-8-9-10.............. Mass.
11-12-13 .... Allentown
18-19-20 .... Elmira
22-23-24..... New Jersey
JULY
2-3-4 .... Waterbury

Sioux City
MAY
28-29-30 .... Madison
31 .... Winnipeg
JUNE
1-2 .... Winnipeg
7 .... Sioux Falls
11-12-13 ... Schaumburg
15-16-17 .... Duluth
25-26-27 ...... Sioux Falls
JULY
2-3-4 .... Fargo
5-6-7 .... St. Paul
16-17-18 ... Schaumburg
26-27-28 .... Duluth
29-30-31 .... Fargo
AUGUST
10-11-12 ...... Winnipeg
14-16 .... Sioux Falls
20-21-22 .... Madison
23-24-25 .... St. Paul
30 .... Sioux Falls

Sioux Falls
MAY
28-29-30... Winnipeg
JUNE
8-9-10 .... Sioux City
14-15-16 ... Schaumburg
18-19-20 .... Duluth
29-30 .... Fargo
JULY
1 .... Fargo
2-3-4 .... St. Paul
12-13-14 .... Madison
19-20-21 .... Fargo
23-24-25 .... Duluth
29-30-31......... Winnipeg
AUGUST
10-11-12 ... Schaumburg
13-15 .... Sioux City
17-18-19 .... Madison
20-21-22 .... St. Paul
31 .... Sioux City

EASTERN DIVISION
12-13-14...... Adirondack
20-21-22............. Albany
23-24-25..... New Jersey
AUGUST
3-4-5............. Adirondack
13-14-15 .... Mass.
17-18-19 .... Allentown
23-24-25 .... Quebec
27-28-29 ...... Waterbury

Allentown
JUNE
1-2-3 .... Waterbury
4-5-6 .... Mass.
15-16-17.... Adirondack
25-26-27.... New Jersey
29-30 .... Albany
JULY
1 .... Albany
2-3-4 .... Elmira
5-6-7 .... Quebec
16-17-18 .... Quebec
26-27-28.... Adirondack
29-30-31......... Albany
AUGUST
6-7-8-9......... Waterbury
10-11-12 .... Mass.
20-21-22 .... Elmira
30-31 .... New Jersey
SEPTEMBER
1 .... New Jersey

SEPTEMBER
1................... Sioux City

Schaumburg
MAY
28-29-30 .... St. Paul
JUNE
7-8-9-10 .... Madison
18-19-20 .... Fargo
22-23-24 ...... Sioux Falls
29-30 .... Sioux City
JULY
1 .... Sioux City
2-3-4............... Winnipeg
12-13-14 .... Duluth
23-24-25........... Winnipeg
26-27-28 .... St. Paul
AUGUST
3-4-5 .... Sioux Falls
6-7-8 .... Duluth
17-18-19 ...... Sioux City
20-21-22 .... Fargo
30-31 .... Madison
SEPTEMBER
1 .... Madison

Winnipeg
JUNE
4-5-6 .... Sioux Falls
7-8-9 .... Fargo
18-19-20 .... Madison
22-23-24 .... St. Paul
29-30 .... Duluth
JULY
1 .... Duluth
9-10-11 ..... Schaumburg
12-13-14 ...... Sioux City
16-17-18 ...... Sioux Falls
19-20-21 .... Madison
AUGUST
4-5-6 .... Sioux City
7-8-9 .... St. Paul
13-14-15-16 .... Fargo
24-25-26 ... Schaumburg
27-28-29 .... Duluth

Elmira
JUNE
1-2-3 .... New Jersey
4-5-6 .... Adirondack
11-12-13 .... Quebec
15-16-17 .... Mass.
25-26-27 ...... Waterbury
JULY
6-7-8 .... Albany
9-10-11 .... Allentown
23-24-25 .... Mass.
26-27-28 .... Albany
AUGUST
6-7-8-9 ...... New Jersey
10-11-12 .... Quebec
17-18-19..... Adirondack
27-28-29 .... Allentown
30-31 .... Waterbury
SEPTEMBER
1..................... Waterbury

Massachusetts
MAY
28-29-30 .... Allentown
31 .... Quebec
JUNE
1-2 .... Quebec
11-12-13 ...... New Jersey
21-22-23 .... Elmira
25-26-27 .... Albany

JULY
6-7-8 .... Waterbury
9-10-11 ...... Adirondack
16-17-18 .... Elmira
26-27-28 ..... New Jersey
AUGUST
3-4-5 .... Allentown
6-7-8-9 .... Adirondack
17-18-19 .... Waterbury
20-21-22 .... Quebec
30-31 .... Albany
SEPTEMBER
1 .... Albany

New Jersey
MAY
28-29-30 .... Waterbury
JUNE
7-8-9-10 .... Allentown
15-16-17 .... Albany
18-19-20 ...... Adirondack
29-30 .... Elmira
JULY
1 .... Elmira
2-3-4 .... Quebec

12-13-14 .... Mass.
16-17-18 .... Albany
20-21-22 .... Mass.
29-30-31 .... Quebec
AUGUST
10-11-12 .... Waterbury
13-14-15 .... Allentown
24-25-26 .... Elmira
27-28-29 ...... Adirondack

Quebec
JUNE
4-5-6 .... Albany
14-15-16 .... Waterbury
18-19-20 .... Allentown
25-26-27 ...... Adirondack
29-30 .... Mass.
JULY
1 .... Massachusetts
9-10-11 .... New Jersey
12-13-14 .... Elmira
23-24-25 .... Allentown
26-27-28 .... Waterbury
AUGUST
3-4-5 .... Elmira

6-7-8-9 .... Albany
17-18-19 ...... New Jersey
27-28-29 .... Mass.
30-31 .... Adirondack
SEPTEMBER
1 .... Adirondack

Waterbury
JUNE
4-5-6 .... New Jersey
7-8-9-10 .... Elmira
18-19-20 .... Mass.
22-23-24 .... Quebec
29-30 .... Adirondack
JULY
1 .... Adirondack
9-10-11 .... Albany
12-13-14 .... Allentown
19-20-21 .... Quebec
23-24-25 ...... Adirondack
29-30-31 .... Mass.
AUGUST
3-4-5 .... New Jersey
13-14-15 .... Elmira
20-21-22 .... Albany
24-25-26 .... Allentown

Texas-Louisiana League

Abilene
MAY
31 .... Ozark
JUNE
1-2 .... Ozark
10-11-12-13 .. Greenville
21-22-23 ...... Alexandria
JULY
2-3-4-5 .... Bayou
6-7-8 .... Amarillo
15-16-17-17 .... Alex.
20-21-22-23 .... Ozark
24-25-26 ..... Rio Grande
AUGUST
3-4-5 .... Bayou
14-15-16-17 Rio Grande
18-19-20-21 ...... Amarillo
31 .... Greenville
SEPTEMBER
1-2 .... Greenville

Alexandria
MAY
27-28 .... Bayou
31 .... Rio Grande
JUNE
1-2 .... Rio Grande
3-4-5-6 .... Ozark
14-15-16-17 .. Greenville
18-19-20 .... Abilene
24-25-26-27 ...... Amarillo
JULY
9-10-11 .... Amarillo
21-22 .... Bayou
23-24-25 .... Greenville
AUGUST
3-4-5-6 .... Rio Grande
7-8-9-10 .... Abilene
22-23-24 .... Bayou
31 .... Ozark
SEPTEMBER
1-2 .... Ozark

Amarillo
MAY
27-28-29-30 .... Ozark
31 .... Greenville

JUNE
1-2 .... Greenville
14-15-16-17 .... Bayou
28-29-30 .... Abilene
JULY
1 .... Abilene
2-3-4-5 .... Greenville
12-13-14 ...... Rio Grande
20-21-22-23 Rio Grande
24-25-26 .... Ozark
30-31 .... Abilene
AUGUST
1 .... Abilene
11-12-13-14 .. Alexandria
26-27-28 .... Alexandria
SEPTEMBER
2-3-4 .... Bayou

Bayou
MAY
29-30 .... Alexandria
JUNE
3-4-5-6 .... Amarillo
7-8-9 .... Abilene
18-19-20 .... Greenville
21-22-23 .... Ozark
28-29-30 ..... Rio Grande
JULY
1 .... Rio Grande
12-13-14 .... Abilene
15-16-17-17 .. Greenville
20 .... Alexandria
AUGUST
7-8-9 .... Amarillo
18-19-20-21 .... Ozark
25-26-27-28 ...... Abilene
29-30-31 ..... Rio Grande
SEPTEMBER
6 .... Alexandria

Greenville
MAY
27-28-29-30 .... Abilene
JUNE
3-4-5-6 ...... Rio Grande
7-8-9 .... Amarillo
28-29-30 .... Alexandria
JULY
1 .... Alexandria

10-11-12-13 .... Ozark
26-27-28 .... Bayou
AUGUST
3-4-5-6 .... Amarillo
11-12-13 .... Abilene
14-15-16-17 .... Bayou
23-24-25 .... Ozark
26-27-28 ..... Rio Grande
SEPTEMBER
3-4-5 .... Alexandria

Ozark
JUNE
10-11-12-13 .... Amarillo
14-15-16-17 .... Abilene
18-19-20 ...... Rio Grande
24-25-26-27 .. Greenville
JULY
2-3-4-5 .... Alexandria
6-7-8-9 .... Bayou
27-28-29 .... Amarillo
30-31 .... Greenville
AUGUST
1 .... Greenville
6 .... Abilene
7-8-9-10 ...... Rio Grande
11-12-13 .... Bayou
15-16-17 .... Alexandria
29-30 .... Abilene

Rio Grande Valley
JUNE
7-8-9 .... Alexandria
10-11-12-13 .... Bayou
21-22-23 .... Amarillo
24-25-26-27 ...... Abilene
JULY
6-7-8 .... Greenville
9-10-11 .... Abilene
15-16-17 .... Ozark
27-28-29-30 . Alexandria
31 .... Bayou
AUGUST
1-2 .... Bayou
18-19-20-21 .. Greenville
22-23-24-25 ...... Amarillo
SEPTEMBER
3-4-5-6 .... Ozark

Western League

Chico

MAY
25-26 .... Sacramento
28-29-30 .... Reno

JUNE
4-5-6-7 .... Zion
19-20 .... Sonoma
29-30 .... Sacramento

JULY
1-2-3 .... Reno
4-5 .... Tri-City
14-15-16 .... Tri-City
17-18-19-20-21 ...... Zion
27-28-29 .... Sonoma
31 .... Sacramento

AUGUST
1................. Sacramento
13-14-15 .... Reno
17-18-19 .... Sacramento
26-27-28-29 ...... Tri-City
30-31 .... Sonoma

SEPTEMBER
1-2 .... Sonoma

Reno

MAY
21-22-23 .... Chico
24-25-26 .... Sonoma

JUNE
4-5-6 .... Sacramento
11-12-13................ Zion
14-15-16-17 .... Chico
18-19-20 .... Tri-City
28-29-30 .... Sonoma

JULY
4-5-6...................... Zion
8-9 .... Sacramento
17-18-19-20..... Sacram.
23-24-25................. Zion
30..................... Sonoma

AUGUST
9-10-11 .... Tri-City
16-17-18 .... Tri-City
23-24................... Chico
27-28 .... Sonoma

Sacramento

MAY
28-29-30 .... Tri-City
31 .... Chico

JUNE
1-2-3 .... Chico
8-9-10...................... Zion
14-15-16 .... Tri-City
21-22-23 .... Chico
26...................... Sonoma
27-28...................... Chico

JULY
4-5-6 .... Sonoma
10-11 .... Reno
15-16 .... Sonoma
21-22 .... Reno
23-24-25 .... Sonoma

AUGUST
4-5-6-7-8.............. Reno
9-10-11.................. Zion
20-21-22 .... Tri-City
27-28-29................. Zion

Sonoma County

MAY
21-22-23 .... Sonoma
31 .... Reno

JUNE
1-2-3 .... Reno
4-5-6 .... Tri-City
8-9........................ Chico
11-12-13 ..... Sacramento
22-23 .... Reno
24-25 .... Sacramento

JULY
1-2-3...................... Zion
14............. Sacramento
17-18-19-20-21-22 .. T-C
31 .... Reno

AUGUST
1 .... Reno
9-10-11-12 .... Chico
13-14-15................ Zion
20-21-22 .... Chico
24-25-26 .... Sacramento
29 .... Reno

Tri-City

MAY
21-22-23 .... Sacramento
24-25-26.................. Zion

JUNE
7-8-9...................... Reno
11-12-13.............. Chico
25-26................... Chico
28-29-30................ Zion

JULY
1-2-3 .... Sacramento
8-9-10-11 .... Sonoma
23-24-25-26 ...... Chico
27-28 .... Reno

AUGUST
4-5-6-7-8......... Sonoma
13-14-15 .... Sacramento
23-24-25................ Zion
30-31 .... Reno

SEPTEMBER
1-2 .... Reno

Zion

MAY
28-29 .... Sonoma
31...................... Tri-City

JUNE
1-2 .... Tri-City
14-15-16-17 ..... Sonoma
18-19 .... Sacramento
21-22-23 .... Tri-City
24-25-26 .... Reno

JULY
7-8-9-10 .... Chico
14-15-16 .... Reno
27-28-29 .... Sacramento
30-31 .... Tri-City

AUGUST
2........................ Tri-City
3-4-5-6-7 .... Chico
16-17-18 .... Sonoma
19-20-21 .... Reno
30-31 .... Sacramento

SEPTEMBER
1-2 .... Sacramento

Foreign Leagues

1998 STANDINGS

MEXICAN LEAGUE

Triple-A Classification

CENTRAL	W	L	PCT	GB	SOUTH	W	L	PCT	GB
**Mexico City Reds	81	41	.664	—	*Tabasco	66	54	.550	—
Mexico City Tigers	72	48	.600	8	*Cancun	62	56	.525	3
Oaxaca	68	50	.576	11	Yucatan	57	63	.475	9
Aguascalientes	57	63	.475	23	Chetumal	51	67	.432	14
Cordoba	37	83	.308	43	Campeche	47	73	.392	19

NORTH	W	L	PCT	GB		W	L	PCT	GB
**Monterrey	80	39	.672	—	Reynosa	51	69	.425	29½
*Monclova	75	46	.620	6	Saltillo	50	69	.420	30
Union Laguna	55	67	.451	26½	Laredo	50	71	.413	31

PLAYOFFS: Quarterfinals (best-of-7)—Oaxaca defeated Mexico City Reds 4-2; Mexico City Tigers defeated Tabasco 4-2; Monterrey defeated Yucatan 4-0; Monclova defeated Cancun 4-2. **Semifinals** (best-of-7)—Oaxaca defeated Monterrey 4-3; Monclova defeated Mexico City Tigers 4-3. **Finals** (best-of-7)—Oaxaca defeated Monclova 4-0.

JAPAN LEAGUES

CENTRAL	W	L	PCT	GB	PACIFIC	W	L	PCT	GB
Yokohama	79	56	.585	—	Seibu	70	61	.534	—
Chunichi	75	60	.556	4	Nippon Ham	67	65	.508	3½
Yomiuri	73	62	.541	6	Fukuoka	67	67	.500	4½
Yakult	66	69	.489	13	Orix	66	66	.500	4½
Hiroshima	60	75	.444	19	Kintetsu	66	67	.496	5
Hanshin	52	83	.385	27	Chiba Lotte	61	71	.462	9½

PLAYOFFS: Finals (best-of-7)—Yokohama defeated Seibu 4-2.

TAIWAN LEAGUES

CPBL	W	L	PCT	GB		W	L	PCT	GB
Sinon	58	45	.563	—	China Trust	54	49	.524	4
President	57	45	.559	½	Mercury	50	52	.490	7½
Weichuan	56	48	.538	2½	Brother	33	69	.324	24½

PLAYOFFS: Semifinals (best-of-3)—Weichuan defeated President 2-1. **Finals** (best-of-7)—Weichuan defeated Sinon 4-3.

TAIWAN MAJOR	W	L	PCT	GB		W	L	PCT	GB
Kao-ping	62	45	.579	—	Taipei	53	53	.500	8½
Chia-nan	57	48	.543	4	Taichung	40	66	.377	21½

PLAYOFFS: Semifinals (best-of-3)—Taipei defeated Chia-nan 2-1. **Finals** (best-of-7)—Taipei defeated Kao-ping 4-3.

KOREAN BASEBALL ORGANIZATION

	W	L	PCT	GB		W	L	PCT	GB
Hyundai	81	45	.643	—	Haitai	61	64	.488	19½
Samsung	66	58	.532	14	Ssangbangwool	58	66	.468	22
LG Twins	63	62	.504	17½	Hanwha	55	66	.455	23½
OB Bears	61	62	.496	18½	Lotte	50	72	.410	29

DOMINICAN SUMMER LEAGUE

Rookie Classification

S.D. EAST	W	L	PCT	GB	S.D. WEST	W	L	PCT	GB
Diamondbacks	48	23	.676	—	Athletics West	57	12	.826	—
Dodgers I	44	23	.657	2	Yankees	42	26	.618	14½
Brewers	43	26	.623	4	Mets I	43	27	.614	14½
Mariners	40	28	.588	6½	Reds	38	30	.559	18½
Tigers	40	28	.588	6½	Rangers	37	32	.536	20
Marlins	30	36	.455	15½	Devil Rays	34	35	.493	23
Athletics East	26	42	.382	20½	Cubs	25	44	.362	32
Cardinals	25	43	.368	21½	Pirates	23	49	.319	35½
Expos	23	45	.338	23½	Padres	13	57	.186	44½
Twins/Co-op	21	46	.313	25					

SAN PEDRO	W	L	PCT	GB			W	L	PCT	GB
Dodgers II	50	14	.781	—		Angels/White Sox	28	38	.424	23
Blue Jays	50	16	.758	1		Astros	26	38	.406	24
Red Sox	37	30	.552	14½		Orioles	22	42	.344	28
Braves	30	36	.455	18		Giants	17	46	.270	32½

CIBAO	W	L	PCT	GB			W	L	PCT	GB
Indians	46	25	.648	—		Phillies	33	37	.471	12½
Mets II	44	28	.611	2½		Rockies	14	55	.203	31
Royals	39	31	.557	6½						

PLAYOFFS: Semifinals (best-of-3)—Athletics West defeated Indians 2-1; Dodgers II defeated Diamondbacks 2-1. **Finals** (best-of-5)—Athletics West defeated Dodgers II 3-2.

VENEZUELEAN SUMMER LEAGUE

Rookie Classification

	W	L	PCT	GB			W	L	PCT	GB
Guacara I	42	18	.700	—		Guacara II	28	32	.467	14
Montalban	38	21	.642	3½		San Joaquin I	25	34	.425	16½
La Pradera	27	30	.475	13½		Miranda	25	35	.417	17
San Joaquin II	28	32	.467	14		Universidad	24	35	.408	17½

PLAYOFFS: None.

*Split-season champion

MEXICANLEAGUE

Class AAA

NOTE: The Mexican League is a member of the National Association of Professional Baseball Leagues and has a Triple-A classification. However, its member clubs operate largely independent of the 30 major league teams, and for that reason the league is listed in the international and winter league section.

Mailing Address: Angel Pola No. 16, Col. Periodista, CP 11220, Mexico, D.F. **Telephone:** 011-525-557-10-07, 011-525-557-14-08. **FAX:** 011-525-395-24-54. **E-Mail Address:** lmb@lmb.com.mx. **Website:** www.lmb.com.mx.

Years League Active: 1955-.

President: Pedro Treto Cisneros. **Vice President:** Roberto Mansur Galan. **Assistant to President/Public Relations:** Nestor Alva Brito. **Treasurer:** Salvador Velazquez Andrade. **Secretary:** Socorro Becerra Campos.

1999 Opening Date: March 17. **Closing Date:** August 4.

Regular Season: 122 games.

Division Structure: Central—Aguascalientes, Cordoba, Mexico City Red Devils, Mexico City Tigers, Oaxaca. **North**—Laredo, Monclova, Monterrey, Reynosa, Saltillo, Union Laguna. **South**—Campeche, Cancun, Tabasco, Veracruz, Yucatan.

Playoff Format: Three-tier playoffs involving top two teams in each zone, plus two wild-card teams. Two finalists meet in best-of-7 series for league championship.

All-Star Game: May 31 at Oaxaca.

Roster Limit: 25. **Roster Limit, Imports:** 4.

Statistician: Ana Luisa Perea Talarico, Angel Pola No. 16, Col. Periodista, CP 11220, Mexico, D.F.

AGUASCALIENTES RAILROADMEN

Office Address: General Manuel Madrigal No. 110, Col. Heroes, CP 20190, Aguascalientes, Aguascalientes. **Telephone:** (49) 15-84-22, 15-80-33. **FAX:** (49) 18-77-78. **E-Mail Address:** rieleros@rieleros.com.mx. **Website:** www.rieleros.com.mx.

President: Oscar Lomelin Ibarra. **General Manager:** Felipe Rodriguez. **Manager:** Enrique Reyes Garcia.

CAMPECHE PIRATES

Office Address: Unidad Deportiva 20 de Noviembre, Local 4, CP 24000, Campeche, Campeche. **Telephone:** (981) 6-60-71. **FAX:** (981) 638-07. **E-Mail Address:** injudeca@camp1.telmex.net.mx.

President: Gustavo Ortiz Avila. **General Manager:** Socorro Morales. **Manager:** Unavailable.

CANCUN LOBSTERMEN

Office Address: Av. Kabah, Super Manzana 31, Manzana 6 Lote 25, Col. Altos, CP 77500, Cancun, Quintana Roo. **Telephone/FAX:** (98) 87-40-11.

President: Ariel Magana Carrillo.
Manager: Francisco Estrada.

CORDOBA COFFEEGROWERS

Office Adress: Av. 1, Esq. Calle 24 S/N, CP 94500, Cordoba, Veracruz. **Telephone:** (271) 6-54-11, 6-55-35, 6-55-70.

Presidents: Jose Antonio Mansur Galan, Francisco Garcia Gonzalez. **General Manager:** Antelmo Hernandez Quirasco.
Manager: Ramon Arano.

OWLS OF THE TWO LAREDOS

Office Address: Av. Degollado #235-G, Col. Independencia, CP 88020, Nuevo Laredo, Tamaulipas. **Telephone/FAX:** (87) 12-07-36. **E-Mail Address:** tecolotes@nlaredo.globalpc.net. **Website:** www.t2l.com.mx.

President: Martin Reyes Madrigal. **General Manager:** Samuel Lozano. **Manager:** Andres Mora.

MEXICO CITY RED DEVILS

Office Address: Av. Cuauhtemoc No. 451-101, Col. Narvarte, CP 03020, Mexico, D.F. **Telephone:** (563) 9-87-22. **FAX:** (563) 9-97-22. **E-Mail Address:** diablos@mail.cpesa.com.mx. **Website:** www.diablos.-com.mx.

Co-Presidents: Roberto Mansur Galan, Alfredo Harp Heluy. **General Manager:** Pedro Mayorquin Aguilar.
Manager: Marco Vazquez.

MEXICO CITY TIGERS
Office Address: Tuxpan No. 45-A, 5o. Piso, Col. Roma Sur, CP 06760, Mexico, D.F. **Telephone:** (905) 584-02-16, 584-02-49. **FAX:** (905) 584-02-16. **E-Mail Address:** tigres@tigrescapitalinos.com.mx. **Website:** tigrescapitalinos.com.mx.
President: Cuauhtemoc Rodriguez. **General Manager:** Alfonso Lopez. **Manager:** Dan Firova.

MONCLOVA STEELERS
Office Address: Cuauhtemoc #1002, Col. Ciudad Deportiva, CP 25750, Monclova, Coahuila. **Telephone:** (86) 34-21-72. **FAX:** (86) 34-21-76.
President: Alonso Ancira Gonzalez. **General Manager:** Carlos de la Garza Barajas.
Manager: Aurelio Rodriguez.

MONTERREY SULTANS
Office Address: Av. Manuel L. Barragan S/N, Estadio Monterrey, CP 64460, Monterrey, Nuevo Leon. **Telephone:** (8) 351-86-34, 351-80-22. **FAX:** (08) 351-02-09. **E-Mail Address:** beisbol@intercable.net.
President: Jose Garcia. **General Manager:** Roberto Magdelano Ramirez.
Manager: Juan Francisco Rodriguez.

OAXACA WARRIORS
Office Address: Privada del Chopo No. 105, Fraccionamiento El Chopo, CP 68050, Oaxaca, Oaxaca. **Telephone:** (951) 555-22. **FAX:** (951) 549-66.
President: Vicente Perez Avella. **General Manager:** Roberto Castellon. **Manager:** Nelson Barrera.

REYNOSA BRONCOS
Office Address: Blvd. Hidalgo Km 102, Col. Privada Adolfo Lopez Mateos, CP 88650, Reynosa, Tamaulipas. **Telephone:** (89) 25-28-08. **FAX:** (89) 24-26-95. **E-Mail Address:** broncos1@fan.com.
President: Carlos Torres. **General Manager:** Rogelio Treto Cisneros. **Manager:** Leo Clayton.

SALTILLO SARAPE MAKERS
Office Address: Blvd. Nazario S. Ortiz Garza, Col. Ciudad Deportiva, CP 25280, Saltillo, Coahuila. **Telephone:** (84) 16-94-55, 16-97-55. **E-Mail Address:** saraperos@tomateros.com.mx.
President: Juan Lopez. **General Manager:** Jaime Blancarte Pimentel. **Manager:** Houston Jimenez.

TABASCO CATTLEMEN
Office Address: Explanada de la Cd. Deportiva, Parque de Beisbol Centenario del 27 de Febrero, Col. Atasta de Serra, CP 86100, Villahermosa, Tabasco. **Telephone/FAX:** (93) 15-32-37. **E-Mail Address:** colmecas@tabasco.podernet.com.mx. **Website:** www.tabasco.gob.mx/olmecas/bien.htm.
President: Diego Rosique Palavicini. **General Manager:** Juan Alberto Nava.
Manager: Unavailable.

UNION LAGUNA COTTON PICKERS
Office Address: Calle Gutemberg, S/N Zona Centro, CP 27000, Torreon, Coahuila. **Telephone:** (17) 17-43-35. **FAX:** (17) 18-55-15.
President: Javier Cavazos Gomez. **General Manager:** Moises Camacho Muniz.
Manager: Pompeyo Davalillo.

VERACRUZ EAGLES
Office Address: Jacarandas Esq. Espana, Fracc. Virginia, CP 94294, Boca del Rio, Veracruz. **Telephone:** (92) 35-50-04, 35-50-08.
President: Antonio Chedraui Mafud. **General Manager:** Rafael Duran. **Manager:** Raul Cano.

YUCATAN LIONS
Office Address: Calle 50 #406-B, X35 Y37, Col. Jesus Carranza, CP 97109, Merida, Yucatan. **Telephone:** (99) 26-30-22. **FAX:** (99) 26-36-31.
President: Gustavo Ricalde Duran. **Vice President:** Wilbert Valle Acevedo.
Manager: Ramiro Rubio Harrison.

MEXICAN ACADEMY

Rookie Classification
Mailing Address: Angel Pola No. 16 Col. Periodista, CP 11220, Mexico, D.F. **Telephone:** 011-525-577-10-07, 557-14-08. **FAX:** 011-525-395-24-54.
Years League Active: 1997-.
Commissioner: Unavailable.
Member Clubs: Unavailable.

JAPANESE LEAGUES

Mailing Address: Imperial Tower, 10F, 1-1-1 Uchisaiwai-cho, Chiyoda-ku, Tokyo 100-0011, Japan. **Telephone:** 03-3502-0022. **FAX:** 03-3502-0140.

Commissioner: Hiromori Kawashima.

Executive Secretary: Yoshiaki Kanai. **Assistant Director, International Affairs:** Nobuhisa "Nobby" Ito.

Japan Series: Best-of-7 series between Central and Pacific League champions, begins Oct. 23 at home of Pacific League club.

All-Star Series: July 24 at Seibu Dome, July 25 at Koshien Stadium, July 27 at Muscat Stadium, Kurashiki.

Roster Limit: 70 per organization (one major league club, one minor league club). Major league club is permitted to register 28 players at a time, though only 25 may be available for each game. **Roster Limit, Imports:** 4 (2 position players, 2 pitchers) in majors; unlimited in minors.

CENTRAL LEAGUE

Mailing Address: Asahi Bldg. 3F, 6-6-7 Ginza, Chuo-ku, Tokyo 104-0061. **Telephone:** 03-3572-1673. **FAX:** 03-3571-4545.

Years League Active: 1950-.

President: Sumiko Takahara.

Secretary General: Ryoichi Shibusawa. **Planning Department:** Masaaki Nagino.

1999 Opening Date: April 2. **Closing Date:** Sept. 30.

Regular Season: 135 games.

Playoff Format: None.

CHUNICHI DRAGONS

Mailing Address: Chunichi Bldg. 6F, 4-1-1 Sakae, Naka-ku, Nagoya 460-0008. **Telephone:** 052-252-5226. **FAX:** 052-263-7696.

Chairman: Hirohiko Oshima. **President:** Tsuyoshi Sato. **General Manager:** Osamu Ito.

Field Manager: Senichi Hoshino.

1998 Attendance: 2,537,000.

1999 Foreign Players: Leo Gomez, Jeong Bum Lee (Korea), San Hoon Lee (Korea), Sun Dong Yol (Korea).

HANSHIN TIGERS

Mailing Address: 1-47 Koshien-cho, Nishinomiya-shi, Hyogo-ken 663-8152. **Telephone:** 0798-46-1515. **FAX:** 0798-40-0934.

Chairman: Shunjiro Kuma. **President:** Yoshihiro Takada. **General Manager:** Katsuyoshi Nozaki.

Field Manager: Katsuya Nomura.

1998 Attendance: 1,980,000.

1999 Foreign Players: Mike Blowers, Mark Johnson, Darrell May, Ben Rivera.

HIROSHIMA TOYO CARP

Mailing Address: 5-25 Motomachi, Naka-ku, Hiroshima 730-8508. **Telephone:** 082-221-2040. **FAX:** 082-228-5013.

Chairman: Kohei Matsuda. **General Manager:** Chitomi Takahashi.

Field Manager: Mitsuo Tatsukawa.

1998 Attendance: 1,140,000.

1999 Foreign Players: Eddy Diaz, Nate Minchey, Felix Perdomo.

YAKULT SWALLOWS

Mailing Address: Shimbashi MDV Bldg. 5F, 5-13-5 Shimbashi, Minato-ku, Tokyo 105-0004. **Telephone:** 03-5470-8915. **FAX:** 03-5470-8916.

Chairman: Naomi Matsuzono. **President/General Manager:** Itaru Taguchi.

Field Manager: Tsutomu Wakamatsu.

1998 Attendance: 1,856,000.

1999 Foreign Players: Mark Acre, Jason Jacome, Daniel Matsumoto (Brazil), Roberto Petagine, Leonardo Sato (Brazil), Mark Smith.

YOKOHAMA BAYSTARS

Mailing Address: Nihon Seimei Yokohama Hon-machi Bldg. 6F, 2-22 Hon-machi, Naka-ku, Yokohama 231-0005. **Telephone:** 045-681-0811. **FAX:** 045-661-2500.

Chairman: Keijiro Nakabe. **President:** Takashi Ohori. **General Manager:** Takeo Minatoya.

Field Manager: Hiroshi Gondo.

1998 Attendance: 1,857,000.

1999 Foreign Players: Arquimedez Pozo, Bobby Rose.

YOMIURI GIANTS

Mailing Address: Takebashi 3-3 Bldg., 3-3 Kanda Nishiki-cho, Chiyoda-ku, Tokyo 101-0054. **Telephone:** 03-3295-7711. **FAX:** 03-3295-7708.

Chairman: Tsuneo Watanabe. **General Manager:** Hiroyuki Yamamuro.

Field Manager: Shigeo Nagashima.

1998 Attendance: 3,634,000.

1999 Foreign Players: Balvino Galvez, Cho Sung Min (Korea), Jose Parra.

PACIFIC LEAGUE

Mailing Address: Asahi Bldg. 9F, 6-6-7 Ginza, Chuo-ku, Tokyo 104-0061. **Telephone:** 03-3573-1551. **FAX:** 03-3572-5843.

Years League Active: 1950-.

President: Kazuo Harano.

Secretary General: Shigeru Murata.

1999 Opening Date: April 3. **Closing Date:** Sept. 30.

Regular Season: 135 games.

Playoff Format: None.

CHIBA LOTTE MARINES

Mailing Address: WBG Marive West 25F, 2-6 Nakase, Mihama-ku, Chiba-shi, Chiba-ken 261-7125. **Telephone:** 043-297-2101. **FAX:** 043-297-2181.

Chairman: Takeo Shigemitsu. **General Manager:** Mitsumasa Mitsuno.

Field Manager: Koji Yamamoto.

1998 Attendance: 946,000.

1999 Foreign Players: Frank Bolick, Brent Brede, Dean Hartgraves, Brian Warren.

FUKUOKA DAIEI HAWKS

Mailing Address: Fukuoka Dome 6F, 2-2-2 Jigyohama, Chuo-ku, Fukuoka 810-0065. **Telephone:** 092-844-1189. **FAX:** 092-844-4600.

Chairman: Isao Nakauchi. **President:** Rikuo Nemoto. **General Manager:** Yasuharu Kishitani.

Field Manager: Sadaharu Oh.

1998 Attendance: 2,163,000.

1999 Foreign Players: None.

KINTETSU BUFFALOES

Mailing Address: Midosuji Grand Bldg. 5F, 2-2-3 Namba, Chuo-ku, Osaka 542-0076. **Telephone:** 06-6212-9744. **FAX:** 06-6212-6834.

Chairman: Shigeichiro Kanamori. **President:** Kenzo Fujii. **General Manager:** Isami Okamoto.

Field Manager: Kyosuke Sasaki.

1998 Attendance: 1,250,000.

1999 Foreign Players: Phil Clark, Fernando de la Cruz, Phil Leftwich, Rob Mattson, Tuffy Rhodes, Carlos Valdez.

NIPPON HAM FIGHTERS

Mailing Address: Roppongi Denki Bldg. 6F, 6-1-20 Roppongi, Minato-ku, Tokyo 106-0032. **Telephone:** 03-3403-9131. **FAX:** 03-3403-9143.

Chairman: Yoshinori Okoso. **President/General Manager:** Takeshi Kojima.

Field Manager: Toshiharu Ueda.

1998 Attendance: 1,572,000.

1999 Foreign Players: Micah Franklin, Rafael Orellano, Erik Schullstrom, Nigel Wilson, Shannon Withem.

ORIX BLUEWAVE

Mailing Address: Sumitomo Kaijo Kobe Bldg. 2F, 1-1-18 Sakae-machi Dori, Chuo-ku, Kobe 650-0023. **Telephone:** 078-333-0065. **FAX:** 078-333-0084.

Chairman: Yoshihiko Miyauchi. **President:** Yoshinori Tsukiji. **General Manager:** Shigeyoshi "Steve" Ino.

Field Manager: Akira Ogi.

1998 Attendance: 1,345,000.

1999 Foreign Players: Chris Donnels, Paul Gonzalez, Edwin Hurtado, Mark Mimbs, Troy Neel, Harvey Pulliam.

SEIBU LIONS

Mailing Address: Seibu Lions Stadium, 2135 Kami-Yamaguchi, Tokorozawa-shi, Saitama-ken 359-1189. **Telephone:** 042-924-1155. **FAX:** 042-928-1919.

Chairman: Yoshiaki Tsutsumi. **President/General Manager:** Kenji Ono.

Field Manager: Osamu Higashio.

1998 Attendance: 1,384,500.

1999 Foreign Players: Greg Blosser, Terry Bross, Archi Cianfrocco, Barry Manuel.

OTHERLEAGUES

DOMINICAN SUMMER LEAGUE
Member, National Association
Rookie Classification

Mailing Address: Calle Segundo No. 14, Reparto Antilla, Santo Domingo, Dominican Republic. **Telephone/FAX:** (809) 532-3619.

Years League Active: 1985-.

President: Freddy Jana. **Administrative Assistant:** Orlando Diaz.

Member Clubs, Division Structure (tentative)**: Santo Domingo East**—Athletics East, Brewers, Cardinals, Diamondbacks, Dodgers I, Expos, Mariners, Marlins, Tigers, Twins. **Santo Domingo West**—Athletics West, Cubs, Devil Rays, Mets I, Padres, Pirates, Rangers, Reds, Yankees. **San Pedro de Macoris**—Angels, Astros, Blue Jays, Braves, Dodgers II, Giants, Orioles, Red Sox. **Cibao**—Indians, Mets II, Phillies, Rockies, Royals, White Sox.

1999 Opening Date: June 1. **Closing Date:** Aug. 30.

Regular Season: 72 games.

Playoff Format: Four division winners meet in best-of-3 series. Winners meet in best-of-5 series for league championship.

Roster Limit: 30 active. **Player Eligibility Rule:** No more than eight players 20 or older and no more than two players 21 or older. At least 10 players must be pitchers. No more than two years of prior service, excluding Rookie leagues outside the U.S. and Canada.

VENEZUELA

VENEZUELAN SUMMER LEAGUE
Member, National Association
Rookie Classification

Address: Estadio Jose Perez Colmenares, Maracay, Aragua, Venezuela. **Telephone:** 011-58-41-24-0321. **FAX:** 011-58-41-24-0705.

Years League Active: 1997-.

Administrator: Saul Gonzalez. **Coordinator:** Ramon Fereira.

Member Clubs, 1999: Unavailable (10 tentative).

1999 Opening Date: June 7. **Closing Date:** Aug. 27.

Regular Season: 60 games.

Playoffs: None.

Roster Limit: 30 active. **Player Eligibility Rule:** No player on active list may have more than three years of minor league service. Open to players from all Latin American Spanish-speaking countries except Mexico, the Dominican Republic and Puerto Rico.

TAIWAN

CHINESE PROFESSIONAL BASEBALL LEAGUE
Mailing Address: 2F, No. 32, Pateh Road, Sec. 3, Taipei, Taiwan. **Telephone:** 886-2-2577-6992. **FAX:** 886-2-2577-2606. **Website:** www. cpbl.com.tw.

Years League Active: 1990-.

Commissioner: T.C. Huang. **Secretary General:** Wayne Lee.

Member Clubs: Brother Elephants (Taipei), China Trust Whales (Chiayi City), Mercury Tigers (Taipei), President Lions (Tainan), Sinon Bulls (Taichung), Weichuan Dragons (Taipei).

Regular Season: 100 games (split schedule).

1999 Opening Date: March 13. **Closing Date:** Oct. 24.

Import Rule: Unlimited number of import players may be registered during a season, with a maximum of eight active (only three import players on field at one time).

TAIWAN MAJOR LEAGUE
Mailing Address: 5F, No. 214, Tunhua North Rd., Taipei, Taiwan. **Telephone:** 886-2-2545-9566. **FAX:** 886-2-2514-0802. **Website:** www.naluwan.com.tw.

Years League Active: 1997-.

President: Felix S.T. Chen. **General Manager:** Joey Chen. **Secretary General:** Huang Ying-po.

Member Clubs: Chia-nan Luka, Kao-ping Fala, Taichung Agan, Taipei Gida.

Regular Season: 96 games.

1999 Opening Date: March 20. **Closing Date:** Oct. 11.
Import Rule: Six (three on field at one time).

SOUTH KOREA

KOREA BASEBALL ORGANIZATION
Mailing Address: The Hall of Baseball, 946-16 Dogok-Dong, Kangnam-Ku, Seoul, South Korea. **Telephone:** (82) 2-3461-7887. **FAX:** (82) 2-3462-7800/7860.
Years League Active: 1982-.
Commissioner: Yong Oh Park. **Secretary General:** Young Eun Choi.
Manager, International Affairs/Public Relations: Sang-Hyun Lee.
Assistant Manager: Smiley Kim.
1999 Opening Date: Unavailable. **Closing Date:** Unavailable.
Regular Season: 132 games.
Division Structure: Dream League—Doosan, Haitai, Hyundai, Lotte.
Magic League—Hanhwa, LG, Samsung, Ssangbangwool.
Korean Series: Best-of-7 series between winners of best-of-7 semifinal playoffs.
Roster Limit: 25 active through Aug. 31, when rosters expand to 30.
Imports: 2 active.

DOOSAN BEARS
Mailing Address: Chamsil Baseball Stadium, Chamsil-1 Dong, Songpa-Ku, Seoul, Korea. **Telephone:** 2-2401-777. **FAX:** 2-2401-788.
General Manager: Kun Koo Kang.

HAITAI TIGERS
Mailing Address: 622 Lim-Dong, Puk-Ku, Kwangju, Korea. **Telephone:** 62-525-1950. **FAX:** 62-525-5350.
General Manager: Yoon Bum Choi.

HANHWA EAGLES
Mailing Address: 22-1 Young-Jeon-Dong, Daejeon, Korea. **Telephone:** 42-631-6331-3. **FAX:** 42-632-2929.
General Manager: Kyung Yon Hwang.

HYUNDAI UNICORNS
Mailing Address: 1128-10 Hyundai Building, 12th Floor, Kuwol-Dong, Namdong Ku, Inchon, Korea. **Telephone:** 32-433-7979. **FAX:** 32-435-3108.
General Manager: Yong Hwi Kim.

LG TWINS
Mailing Address: 891 LG Young Dong Building, 10th Floor, Dae-Chi-Dong, Kangnam-Ku, Seoul, Korea. **Telephone:** 2-3459-5345. **FAX:** 2-3459-5354.
General Manager: Jong Jun Choi.

LOTTE GIANTS
Mailing Address: 930 Sajik-Dong Dongrae-Ku, Pusan, Korea. **Telephone:** 51-505-7422-3. **FAX:** 51-506-0090.
General Manager: Chul Hwa Lee.

SAMSUNG LIONS
Mailing Address: 184-3 Sunhwari, Jinliangeup, Kyungsan, Kyung-Buk, Korea. **Telephone:** 53-859-3111-3. **FAX:** 53-859-3117.
General Manager: Jong Man Kim.

SSANGBANGWOOL RAIDERS
Mailing Address: 1-1220 Dokjin-Dong 1GA, Dokjin-Ku, Jeonju, Korea. **Telephone:** 652-275-2014/5. **FAX:** 652-275-2113.
General Manager: Eun Su Yoo.

Winter Baseball

1998-99 STANDINGS

CARIBBEAN WORLD SERIES

	W	L	PCT	GB		W	L	PCT	GB
Dominican Republic	5	2	.714	—	Venezuela	2	4	.333	2½
Puerto Rico	4	3	.571	1	Mexico	2	4	.333	2½

DOMINICAN LEAGUE

	W	L	PCT	GB		W	L	PCT	GB
Escogido	40	21	.656	—	Licey	33	27	.550	6½
Aguilas	39	22	.639	1	Northern	9	51	.150	30½

PLAYOFFS: Semifinals (best-of-5)—Licey defeated Aguilas 3-1. **Finals** (best-of-9)—Licey defeated Escogido 5-4.

MEXICAN PACIFIC LEAGUE

	W	L	Pct.	GB		W	L	Pct.	GB
*Hermosillo	38	29	.567	—	Mexicali	35	32	.522	3
Los Mochis	38	29	.567	—	*Culiacan	32	35	.478	6
*Obregon	38	29	.567	—	Mazatlan	28	40	.412	10½
Guasave	35	32	.522	3	Navojoa	25	43	.368	13½

*Split-season champions

PLAYOFFS: Quarterfinals (best-of-7)—Culiacan defeated Obregon 4-1; Hermosillo defeated Guasave 4-2; Mexicali defeated Los Mochis 4-2. **Semifinals** (best-of-7)—Mexicali defeated Guasave 4-0; Culiacan defeated Hermosillo 4-3. **Finals** (best-of-7)—Mexicali defeated Culiacan 4-1.

PUERTO RICAN LEAGUE

	W	L	Pct.	GB		W	L	Pct.	GB
Ponce	29	18	.617	—	Arecibo	23	26	.469	7
Santurce	26	22	.542	3½	Caguas	21	28	.429	9
Mayaguez	26	24	.520	4½	San Juan	21	28	.429	9

PLAYOFFS: Semifinals (best-of-7)—Mayaguez defeated Santurce 4-0; Ponce defeated Arecibo 4-0. **Finals** (best-of-9)—Mayaguez defeated Ponce 5-1.

VENEZUELAN LEAGUE

EAST	W	L	Pct.	GB	WEST	W	L	Pct.	GB
Magallanes	35	27	.565	—	Lara	35	26	.574	—
Caracas	34	28	.548	1	Aragua	34	28	.548	1½
La Guaira	30	33	.476	5½	Zulia	31	32	.492	5
Oriente	24	37	.393	10½	Occidente	25	37	.403	10½
Round-Robin	W	L	Pct.	GB		W	L	Pct.	GB
Caracas	10	6	.625	—	Zulia	9	7	.563	1
Lara	10	6	.625	—	Magallanes	7	9	.438	3

PLAYOFFS: Finals (best-of-7)—Lara defeated Caracas 4-2.

ARIZONA FALL LEAGUE

NATIONAL	W	L	Pct.	GB	AMERICAN	W	L	Pct.	GB
Sun Cities	22	22	.500	—	Grand Canyon	26	18	.591	—
Scottsdale	20	23	.465	1½	Peoria	23	21	.523	3
Maryvale	19	25	.432	3	Phoenix	21	22	.488	4½

PLAYOFFS: Finals (best-of-3)—Sun Cities defeated Grand Canyon 2-0.

AUSTRALIAN BASEBALL LEAGUE

	W	L	Pct.	GB		W	L	Pct.	GB
Adelaide	28	17	.622	—	Sydney	21	22	.488	6
Gold Coast	24	20	.545	3½	Mel. Reds	20	23	.465	7
Mel. Monarchs	22	22	.500	5½	Perth	17	28	.378	11

PLAYOFFS: Semifinals (best-of-3)—Sydney defeated Adelaide 2-0; Gold Coast defeated Melbourne Monarchs 2-1. **Finals** (best-of-3)—Gold Coast defeated Sydney 2-0.

MARYLAND FALL LEAGUE

	W	L	Pct.	GB		W	L	Pct.	GB
Frederick	23	19	.548	—	Delaware	21	20	.512	1½
Delmarva	21	20	.512	1½	Bowie	18	24	.429	5

PLAYOFFS: None.

WINTERBASEBALL

Mailing Address: Frank Feliz Miranda No. 1 Naco, Santo Domingo, Dominican Republic. **Telephone:** (809) 562-4737, 562-4715. **FAX:** (809) 565-4654.

Commissioner: Juan Fco. Puello Herrera.

Member Leagues: Dominican Republic, Mexican Pacific, Puerto Rican, Venezuelan.

2000 Caribbean World Series: Feb. 1-6 at Santo Domingo, Dominican Republic.

DOMINICAN LEAGUE

Office Address: Estadio Quisqueya, Santo Domingo, Dominican Republic. **Mailing Address:** Apartado Postal 1246, Santo Domingo, Dominican Republic. **Telephone:** (809) 567-6371, 563-5085. **FAX:** (809) 567-5720.

Years League Active: 1951-.

President: Dr. Leonardo Matos. **Vice President:** Marcos Rodriguez. **Public Relations Director:** Jorge Torres.

1998-99 Opening Date: Oct. 23. **Closing Date:** Jan. 13.

Regular Season: 60 games.

Playoff Format: Top four teams meet in best-of-5 semifinals. Winners advance to best-of-9 series for league championship. Winner advances to Caribbean World Series.

Roster Limit: 30. **Roster Limit, Imports:** 7.

AGUILAS CIBAENAS

Street Address: Estadio Cibao, Ave. Imbert, Santiago, Dom. Rep. **Mailing Address:** EPS B-225, P.O. Box 02-5360, Miami, FL 33102. **Telephone:** (809) 575-4310, 575-1810. **FAX:** (809) 575-0865.

Primary Working Agreement: None.

President: Winston Llenas. **General Manager:** Reynaldo Bisono.

1998-99 Manager: Tony Pena.

AZUCAREROS DEL ESTE
(Did not operate in 1998-99)

Mailing Address: Estadio Francisco Micholi, La Romana, Dom. Rep. **Telephone:** (809) 556-6188. **FAX:** (809) 550-1550.

Primary Working Agreement: Arizona Diamondbacks.

President: Arturo Gil. **General Manager:** Pablo Peguero.

ESCOGIDO LIONS

Street Address: Estadio Quisqueya, Ens. la Fe, Santo Domingo, Dom. Rep. **Mailing Address:** P.O. Box 1287, Santo Domingo, Dom. Rep. **Telephone:** (809) 565-1910. **FAX:** (809) 567-7643. **Website:** www.escogi-do.do.

Primary Working Agreement: Cincinnati Reds.

President: Daniel Aquino-Mendez. **General Manager:** Mario Soto.

1998-99 Manager: Dave Miley.

ESTRELLAS ORIENTALES
(Did not operate in 1998-99)

Street Address: Av. Lope de Vega No. 46, Altos, Enz. Piantini, Santo Domingo, Dom. Rep. **Telephone:** (809) 476-0080. **FAX:** (809) 476-0084.

Primary Working Agreement: None.

President: Eduardo Antun. **General Manager:** Fitzgerald Astacio.

LICEY TIGERS

Mailing Address: Estadio Quisqueya, Santo Domingo, Dom. Rep. **Telephone:** (809) 567-3090. **FAX:** (809) 542-7714. **Website:** www.licey.com.

Primary Working Agreement: None.

President: Miguel Heded. **General Manager:** Rafael Landestoy.

1998-99 Manager: Dave Jauss.

NORTHERN GIANTS

Street Address: Estadio Julian Javier, San Francisco de Macoris, Dom. Rep. **Mailing Address:** EPS No. F-1447, P.O. Box 02-5301, Miami, FL 33102. **Telephone:** (809) 588-8882. **FAX:** (809) 588-8733.

Primary Working Agreement: Kansas City Royals.

President: Angel Miguel Almanzar. **General Manager:** Luis Silverio.

1998-99 Managers: Ron Johnson, Alex Taveras, Miguel Dilone.

Mailing Address: Pesqueira 401-R Altos, Navojoa, Sonora, Mexico. **Telephone:** (52-642) 2-3100. **FAX:** (52-642) 2-7250. **Website:** www.lig-adelpacifico.com.mx.

Years League Active: 1958-.

President: Dr. Arturo Leon Lerma. **Vice President:** Victor Cuevas. **General Manager:** Obiel Denis Gonzalez.

1999 Opening Date: Oct. 14. **Closing Date:** Dec. 30.

Regular Season: 64 games.

Playoff Format: Six teams advance to best-of-7 quarterfinals. Three winners and losing team with best record advance to best-of-7 semifinals. Winners meet in best-of-7 series for league championship. Winner advances to Caribbean World Series.

Roster Limit: 27. **Roster Limit, Imports:** 5.

CULIACAN TOMATO GROWERS

Street Address: Av. Alvaro Obregon 348 Sur, CP 80200, Culiacan, Sinaloa, Mexico. **Telephone:** (67) 13-33-69. **FAX:** (67) 15-68-28. **E-Mail Address:** administracion@tomateros.com.mx. **Website:** www.tomateros.com.mx.

President: Juan Manuel Ley Lopez. **General Manager:** Jaime Blancarte.

1998-99 Manager: Jorge Orta.

GUASAVE COTTONEERS

Mailing Address: Ave. Obregon No. 43, Guasave, Sinaloa, Mexico. **Telephone:** (68) 72-14-31. **FAX:** (68) 72-29-98.

President: Carlos Chavez. **General Manager:** Sebastian Sandoval.

1998-99 Manager: Aurelio Rodriguez.

HERMOSILLO ORANGE GROWERS

Mailing Address: Blvd. Navarrete No. 309, Esq. Torreon Y Atenas, Hermosillo, Sonora, Mexico. **Telephone:** (62) 60-69-32, 60-69-33. **FAX:** (62) 60-69-31.

President: Enrique Mazon Rubio. **General Manager:** Marco Antonio Manzo.

1998-99 Manager: Derek Bryant.

LOS MOCHIS SUGARCANE GROWERS

Mailing Address: Madero No. 116 Ote., CP 81200, Los Mochis, Sinaloa, Mexico. **Telephone:** (68) 12-86-02. **FAX:** (68) 12-67-40.

President: Mario Lopez Valdez. **General Manager:** Antonio Castro Chavez.

1998-99 Manager: Juan Navarrete.

MAZATLAN DEER

Street Address: Gutierrez Najera No. 821, Col. Montuosa, Mazatlan, Sinaloa, Mexico. **Telephone:** (69) 81-17-10. **FAX:** (69) 81-17-11.

President: Hermilo Diaz Bringas. **General Manager:** Alejandro Vega.

1998-99 Manager: Raul Cano.

MEXICALI EAGLES

Street Address: Estadio De Beisbol De La Ciudad. Deportiva Calz. Ex-Aviacion S/N, Mexicali, Baja California. **Mailing Address:** P.O. Box 7844, Calexico, CA 92231. **Telephone:** (65) 67-00-40, 67-00-10. **FAX:** (65) 67-00-95.

President: Mario Hernandez Maytorena. **General Manager:** Leonardo Ovies.

1998-99 Manager: Paquin Estrada.

NAVOJOA MAYOS

Mailing Address: Allende No. 208, Dpto. 2, CP 85800, Novojoa, Sonora, Mexico. **Telephone:** (64) 22-14-33. **FAX:** (64) 22-89-97.

Primary Working Agreement: Boston Red Sox.

President: Victor Cuevas Garibay. **General Manager:** Lauro Villalobos.

1998-99 Managers: Dave Hilton/Gomer Hodge.

OBREGON YAQUIS

Mailing Address: Yucatan y Nainari No. 294, Edificio C. Depto. 11, Ciudad Obregon, Sonora, Mexico. **Telephone:** (64) 14-11-56. **FAX:** (64) 14-11-56.

President: Luis Felipe Garcia DeLeon. **General Manager:** Luis Carlos Joffroy.

1998-99 Manager: Tony Oliva.

PUERTO RICAN LEAGUE

Mailing Address: P.O. Box 1852, Hato Rey, PR 00919. **Telephone:** (787) 765-6285, 765-7285. **FAX:** (787) 767-3028.

Years League Active: 1938-.

President: Elpidio Batista. **Executive Director/Administrator:** Benny Agosto.

1998-99 Opening Date: Nov. 6. **Closing Date:** Jan. 12.

Regular Season: 50 games.

Playoff Format: Top four teams meet in best-of-7 semifinal series. Winners meet in best-of-9 series for league championship. Winner advances to Caribbean World Series.

Roster Limit: 26. **Roster Limit, Imports:** 4. Up to six more may be used to replace native players who are injured or are major leaguers who opt not to play.

ARECIBO WOLVES

Street Address: Road #10, Rodriguez Olmo Stadium, Arecibo, PR 00613. **Mailing Address:** P.O. Box 141425, Arecibo, PR 00613. **Telephone:** (787) 879-0309. **FAX:** (787) 817-2323.

Primary Working Agreement: None.

President: Josue Vega. **General Manager:** Che Conde.

1998-99 Manager: Pat Kelly.

CAGUAS CRIOLLOS

Mailing Address: P.O. Box 1415, Caguas, PR 00726. **Telephone:** (787) 258-2222. **FAX:** (787) 743-0545.

Primary Working Agreement: None.

General Manager: Guy Hansen.

1998-99 Maanager: Juan Nieves.

MAYAGUEZ INDIANS

Mailing Address: 3089 Marina Station, Mayaguez, PR 00681. **Telephone:** (787) 834-6111, 834-5211. **FAX:** (787) 834-7480.

Primary Working Agreement: None.

President/General Manager: Luis Ivan Mendez.

1998-99 Manager: Al Newman.

PONCE LIONS

Mailing Address: P.O. Box 7444, Ponce, PR 00732. **Telephone:** (787) 848-0050. **FAX:** (787) 848-8884.

Primary Working Agreement: None.

President: Antonio Munoz Jr. **General Manager:** Ramon Conde.

1998-99 Manager: Carlos Lezcano.

SAN JUAN SENATORS

Street Address: Estadio Hiram Bithorn, Roosevelt Avenue, Hato Rey, PR 00927. **Mailing Address:** P.O. Box 366246, San Juan, PR 00936. **Telephone:** (787) 754-1300. **FAX:** (787) 763-2217.

Primary Working Agreement: Kansas City Royals.

President: Benjamin Rivera. **General Manager:** Unavailable.

1998-99 Manager: Ed Romero.

SANTURCE CRABBERS

Mailing Address: P.O. Box 1077, Hato Rey, PR 00919. **Telephone:** (787) 274-0240, 274-0241. **FAX:** (787) 765-0410.

Primary Working Agreement: Houston Astros.

General Manager/1998-99 Manager: Frankie Thon.

VENEZUELAN LEAGUE

Mailing Address: Avenida Casanova, Centro Comercial El Recreo, Torre Sur, Piso 3, Oficinas 36-37, Caracas, Venezuela. **Telephone:** (011-58-2) 761-2750, 761-4817. **FAX:** (011-58-2) 761-7661.

Years League Active: 1946-.

President: Carlos Cordido. **Vice President:** Jesus Efrain Munoz. **General Manager:** Domingo Alvarez.

Division Structure: East—Caracas, La Guaira, Magallanes, Oriente. **West**—Aragua, Lara, Pastora, Zulia.

1998-99 Opening Date: Oct. 14. **Closing Date:** Dec. 30.

Regular Season: 62 games.

Playoff Format: Top two teams in each division, plus a wild-card team, meet in 16-game round-robin series. Top two finishers meet in a best-of-7 series for league championship. Winner advances to Caribbean World Series.

Roster Limit: 26. **Roster Limit, Imports:** 7.

ARAGUA TIGERS

Address: Estadio Jose Perez Colmenares, Calle Campo Elias, Barrio Democratico, Maracay, Aragua, Venezuela. **Telephone:** (58-043) 54-4632. **FAX:** (58-43) 53-8655. **E-Mail Address:** tigres@telcel.net.ve.

Primary Working Agreement: None.

President/General Manager: Jose Pages.

1998-99 Manager: Alfredo Ortiz.

CARACAS LIONS

Street Address: Av. Francisco de Miranda, Centro Seguros La Paz, Piso 4, La California, Municipio Sucre, Caracas, Venezuela 1070. **Telephone:** (582) 238-7733. **FAX:** (582) 238-0691.

Primary Working Agreement: None.

President: Pablo Morales. **Vice President/General Manger:** Oscar Prieto.

1998-99 Manager: Jim Pankovits.

LA GUAIRA SHARKS

Mailing Address: Primera Avenida, Urbanizacion Miramar, Detras del Periferico de Pariata, Maiquetia, Vargas, Venezuela. **Telephone:** (58-31) 25-579. **FAX:** (58-31) 23-116.

Primary Working Agreement: None.

President/General Manager: Pedro Padron Panza.

1998-99 Manager: John McLaren.

LARA CARDINALS

Mailing Address: Av. Rotaria, Estadio Antonio Herrera, Barquisimeto, Venezuela 3001. **Telephone:** (58-51) 42-3132 or 4543. **FAX:** (58-51) 42-1921. **E-Mail Address:** cardenal@cardenales.org. **Website:** www.cardenales.org.

Primary Working Agreement: Toronto Blue Jays.

President: Adolfo Alvares. **General Manager:** Humberto Oropeza.

1998-99 Manager: Omar Malave.

MAGALLANES NAVIGATORS

Address: Centro Comercial Caribbean Plaza, Modulo 8, Local 173, Valencia, Carabobo, Venezuela. **Telephone:** (58-041) 24-0321 or 0980. **FAX:** (58-041) 24-0705.

Primary Working Agreements: Houston Astros, New York Mets.

President: Alfredo Guadarrama.

1998-99 Manager: Al Pedrique.

OCCIDENTE PASTORA

Mailing Address: Estadio Bachiller Julio Hernandez Molina, Avenida Romulo Gallegos, Aruare, Venezuela. **Telephone:** (055) 22-2945. **FAX:** (055) 21-8595.

Primary Working Agreement: None.

President: Enrique Finol. **General Manager:** Carlos Jimenez.

1998-99 Manager: Domingo Carrasquel.

ORIENTE CARIBBEANS

Mailing Address: Avenida Estadium Alfonso Carrasquel, Oficina del Equipo de Caribes de Oriente, Centro Comercial Novocentro, Piso 2, Local 2-4, Puerto la Cruz, Anzoategui, Venezuela. **Telephone:** (081) 66-2536 or 66-7054. **FAX:** (081) 66-7054.

Primary Working Agreement: Cleveland Indians.

President: Gioconda de Marquez. **Vice President:** Pablo Ruggeri.

1998-99 Manager: Pompeyo Davalillo.

ZULIA EAGLES

Mailing Address: Avenida 8, Urb. Santa Rita, Edificio Las Carolinas, Local M-10, Maracaibo, Zulia, Venezuela. **Telephone:** (58-061) 97-9834 or 97-9839. **FAX:** (58-061) 98-0210.

Primary Working Agreement: None.

President: Lucas Rincon. **Vice President/General Manager:** Luis Rodolfo Machado Silva.

1998-99 Manager: Greg Biagini.

OTHER WINTER LEAGUES

ARIZONA FALL LEAGUE

Mailing Address: 10201 S 51st St., Suite 230, Phoenix, AZ 85044. **Telephone:** (602) 496-6700. **FAX:** (602) 496-6384. **E-Mail Address:** afl@goodnet.com. **Website:** www.majorleaguebaseball.com/arizona.

Years League Active: 1992-.

Operated by: Major League Baseball.

Executive Vice President: Steve Cobb. **Administrative Assistant:** Joan McGrath.

Division Structure: North—Maryvale, Scottsdale, Sun Cities. **South**—Grand Canyon, Peoria, Phoenix.

1999 Opening Date: Unavailable. **Closing Date:** Unavailable.

Regular Season: 52 games.

Playoff Format: Division champions meet in best-of-3 series for league championship.

Roster Limit: 30. Players with less than one year of major league service are eligible.

GRAND CANYON RAFTERS
Mailing Address: See league address.
Working Agreement: Baltimore Orioles, Boston Red Sox, New York Yankees, Tampa Bay Devil Rays, Toronto Blue Jays.
1998 Manager: Gerald Perry (Red Sox).

MARYVALE SAGUAROS
Mailing Address: See league address.
Working Agreements: Chicago Cubs, Cincinnati Reds, Houston Astros, Milwaukee Brewers, Pittsburgh Pirates.
1998 Manager: Ken Griffey Sr. (Reds).

PEORIA JAVELINAS
Mailing Address: See league address.
Working Agreements: Anaheim Angels, Oakland Athletics, St. Louis Cardinals, Seattle Mariners, Texas Rangers.
1998 Manager: Dan Rohn (Mariners).

PHOENIX DESERT DOGS
Mailing Address: See league address.
Working Agreements: Chicago White Sox, Cleveland Indians, Detroit Tigers, Kansas City Royals, Minnesota Twins.
1998 Manager: Bruce Fields (Tigers).

SCOTTSDALE SCORPIONS
Mailing Address: See league address.
Working Agreements: Arizona Diamondbacks, Colorado Rockies, Los Angeles Dodgers, San Diego Padres, San Francisco Giants.
1998 Manager: Chris Speier (Diamondbacks).

SUN CITIES SOLAR SOX
Mailing Address: See league address.
Working Agreements: Atlanta Braves, Florida Marlins, Montreal Expos, New York Mets, Philadelphia Phillies.
1998 Manager: Fredi Gonzalez (Marlins).

AUSTRALIAN BASEBALL LEAGUE

Mailing Address: Level 2, 48 Atchison St., St. Leonards, New South Wales 2065 Australia. **Telephone:** (011-61-2) 9437-4622. **FAX:** (011-61-2) 9437-4155.
Chairman: Rod Byrne. **Manager, Baseball Operations:** Don Knapp.
1998-99 Opening Date: Oct. 17. **Closing Date:** Feb. 5.
Regular Season: 46 games.
Playoff Format: Top four teams meet in best-of-3 series. Winners meet in best-of-3 final for league championship.
Import Rule: 4 players.

ADELAIDE GIANTS
Mailing Address: P.O. Box 2628 Kent Town, SA 5071, Australia. **Telephone:** (08) 8364-3231. **FAX:** (08) 8364-3237. **Website:** www.adelaidegiants.com.au.
Primary Working Agreement: Los Angeles Dodgers.
Chief Executive Officer: Neil Sheere. **Baseball Operations Manager:** Ron Harvey.
1998-99 Manager: Tony Harris.

GOLD COAST COUGARS
Address: Carrara Sports Stadium, Broadbeach Road, Nerang, Queensland 4211 Australia.
Telephone: (075) 57-99972. **FAX:** (075) 57-99983.
Primary Working Agreement: Boston Red Sox.
General Manager: Glen Partridge.
1998-99 Manager: Unavailable.

MELBOURNE MONARCHS
Address: P.O. Box 447, Berwick, Victoria 3806, Australia.
Telephone: (03) 9705-1533. **FAX:** (03) 9705-1577. **Website:** www.monarchs.com.au.
Primary Working Agreement: Atlanta Braves.
Chief Executive Officer: Don Fenwick. **Director, Baseball Operations:** Phil Dale.
1998-99 Manager: Jon Deeble.

MELBOURNE REDS
Street Address: Moorabbin Reserve, 10 Linton St., Moorabbin, Victoria 3189, Australia. **Mailing Address:** P.O. Box 2143, Moorabbin, Victoria 3189, Australia. **Telephone:** (03) 9553-3202. **FAX:** (03) 9553-3257.
Primary Working Agreement: Tampa Bay Devil Rays.
President: Geoff Pearce. **Operations Manager:** Bruce Utting.
1998-99 Manager: Steve Livesey.

PERTH HEAT

Mailing Address: P.O. Box 238, Bassendean, Western Australia, 6054, Australia. **Telephone:** (08) 9279-8473. **FAX:** (08) 9378-3109. **Website:** www.perthheat.aust.com.

Primary Working Agreement: Baltimore Orioles.
General Manager: Unavailable.
1998-99 Manager: John Tourville.

SYDNEY STORM

Street Address: 32 George St., Homebush, New South Wales 2140, Australia. **Mailing Address:** P.O. Box S 63, Homebush, New South Wales 2140, Australia. **Telephone:** (02) 9763-5011. **FAX:** (02) 9763-5158. **E-Mail:** storm@hartingdale.com.au. **Website:** www.storm.aapt.com.au.

Primary Working Agreement: Toronto Blue Jays.
President: Trevor Jarrett. **General Manager:** David Balfour.
1998-99 Manager: Dennis Holmberg.

MARYLAND FALL LEAGUE

Mailing Address: 4101 NE Crain Hwy., Bowie, MD 20716. **Telephone:** (301) 805-6012. **FAX:** (301) 805-6011. **Website:** www.mdfallbaseball.com.

Years League Active: 1998-.
President: Keith Lupton. **Administrative Assistant:** Jan Varney.
1999 Opening Date: Unavailable. **Closing Date:** Unavailable.
Regular Season: 42 games.
Playoff Format: Unavailable.
Roster Limit: 28 (Class AA and Class A players are eligible).

BOWIE NATIONALS

Office Address: 4101 NE Crain Hwy., Bowie, MD 20716. **Mailing Address:** P.O. Box 1661, Bowie, MD 20717. **Telephone:** (301) 805-6000. **FAX:** (301) 805-6008. **E-Mail Address:** nationals@mdfallbaseball.com. **Website:** nationals.mdfallbaseball.com.

Working Agreements: Baltimore Orioles, Cincinnati Reds, Florida Marlins, Houston Astros, New York Yankees, Pittsburgh Pirates.
President: Peter Kirk. **General Manager:** John Danos.
1998 Manager: John Tamargo.

DELAWARE STARS

Mailing Address: 801 S Madison St., Wilmington, DE 19801. **Telephone:** (302) 888-2015. **FAX:** (302) 888-2032. **E-Mail Address:** stars@mdfallbaseball.com. **Website:** stars.mdfallbaseball.com.

Working Agreements: Chicago White Sox, Detroit Tigers, Kansas City Royals, Minnesota Twins, Philadelphia Phillies, St. Louis Cardinals, San Diego Padres.
President: Matt Minker. **General Manager:** Chris Kemple.
1998 Manager: John Mizerock.

DELMARVA ROCKFISH

Office Address: 6400 Hobbs Rd., Salisbury, MD 21804. **Mailing Address:** P.O. Box 1557, Salisbury, MD 21802. **Telephone:** (410) 219-3112. **FAX:** (410) 219-9164. **E-Mail Address:** rockfish@mdfallbaseball.com. **Website:** rockfish.mdfallbaseball.com.

Working Agreements: Atlanta Braves, Boston Red Sox, Cleveland Indians, Montreal Expos, San Francisco Giants, Tampa Bay Devil Rays.
President: Peter Kirk. **General Manager:** Jim Terrill.
1998 Manager: Randy Ingle.

FREDERICK REGIMENT

Office Address: 6201 New Design Rd., Frederick, MD 21703. **Mailing Address:** P.O. Box 3169, Frederick, MD 21705. **Telephone:** (301) 662-0013. **FAX:** (301) 662-0018. **E-Mail Address:** regiment@mdfallbaseball.com. **Website:** regiment.mdfallbaseball.com.

Working Agreements: Anaheim Angels, Colorado Rockies, Milwaukee Brewers, New York Mets, Seattle Mariners, Texas Rangers, Toronto Blue Jays.
President: Pete Simmons. **General Manager:** Joe Preseren.
1998 Manager: Doug Davis.

COLLEGEBASEBALL

NATIONAL COLLEGIATE
ATHLETIC ASSOCIATION

Mailing Address: 6201 College Blvd., Overland Park, KS 66211. **Telephone:** (913) 339-1906. **FAX:** (913) 339-0043.

President: Cedric Dempsey. **Director, Championships:** Dennis Poppe. **Contact, College World Series:** Jim Wright. **Contact, Statistics:** John Painter.

Chairman, Division I Baseball Committee: Dick Rockwell (athletic director, LeMoyne). **Division I Baseball Committee:** Rich Alday (baseball coach, New Mexico), Jay Bergman (baseball coach, Central Florida), Joe Durant (baseball coach, Florida A&M), John Easterbrook (athletic director, Cal State Fullerton), Paul Fernandes (associate athletic director, Columbia), Wally Groff (athletic director, Texas A&M), Mike Knight (athletic director, Nicholls State), Bob Todd (baseball coach, Ohio State).

Chairman, Division II Baseball Committee: Mark Ekeland (baseball coach, South Dakota State). **Chairman, Division III Baseball Committee:** Randy Town (baseball coach, Claremont McKenna-Mudd/Scripps, Calif.).

2000 National Convention: Jan. 8-11 at San Diego.

1999 Championship Tournaments
NCAA Division I

53rd College World Series	Omaha, NE, June 11-19
Super Regionals(16)	Campus sites, June 4-6
Regionals (8)	Campus sites, May 28-30

NCAA Division II

32nd World Series	Montgomery, AL, May 22-29
Regionals (8)	Campus sites, May 13-15

NCAA Division III

24th World Series	Salem, VA, May 28-June 1
Regionals (8)	Campus sites, May 19-23

NATIONAL ASSOCIATION
OF INTERCOLLEGIATE ATHLETICS

Mailing Address: 6120 South Yale Ave., Suite 1450, Tulsa, OK 74136. **Telephone:** (918) 494-8828. **FAX:** (918) 494-8841.

Chief Executive Officer: Steve Baker. **Director, Championship Events:** Tim Kramer. **Baseball Event Coordinator:** John Mark Adkison.

1999 Championship Tournament

NAIA World Series	Jupiter, FL, May 24-31

NATIONAL JUNIOR COLLEGE
ATHLETIC ASSOCIATION

Mailing Address: P.O. Box 7305, Colorado Springs, CO 80933. **Telephone:** (719) 590-9788. **FAX:** (719) 590-7324.

Executive Director: George Killian. **Director, Division I Baseball Tournament:** Sam Suplizio. **Director, Division II Tournament:** John Daigle. **Director, Division III Tournament:** Barry Bower.

1999 Championship Tournaments
Division I

World Series	Grand Junction, CO, May 29-June 5

Division II

World Series	Millington, TN, May 29-June 5

Division III

World Series	Batavia, NY, May 15-21

CALIFORNIA COMMUNITY COLLEGE
COMMISSION ON ATHLETICS

Mailing Address: 2017 O St., Sacramento, CA 95814. **Telephone:** (916) 444-1600. **FAX:** (916) 444-2616.

Commissioner of Athletics: Joanne Fortunato. **Associate Commissioner of Athletics:** Stuart Van Horn. **Sports Information Director:** Ryan Hopping.

1999 Championship Tournament

State Championship	Fresno City College, May 29-31

AMERICAN BASEBALL
COACHES ASSOCIATION

Office Address: 108 S University Ave., Suite 3, Mount Pleasant, MI 48858. **Telephone:** (517) 775-3300. **FAX:** (517) 775-3600.

Executive Director: Dave Keilitz. **Assistant to Executive Director:** Betty Rulong. **Administrative Assistant:** Nick Williams.

President: Ed Flaherty (Southern Maine). **Chairman:** Carroll Land (Point Loma Nazarene, CA).

2000 National Convention: Jan. 6-9 at Chicago (Hyatt Regency).

AMERICA EAST CONFERENCE

Mailing Address: 10 High St., Suite 860, Boston, MA 02110. **Telephone:** (617) 695-6369. **FAX:** (617) 695-6385. **E-Mail Address:** bourque@americaeast.com. **Website:** www.americaeast.org.

Baseball Members (First Year): Delaware (1992), Drexel (1992), Hartford (1990), Hofstra (1995), Maine (1990), Northeastern (1990), Towson (1996), Vermont (1990).

Assistant Commissioner/Communications: Matt Bourque.

1999 Tournament: Four teams, double-elimination. May 20-22 at Frawley Stadium, Wilmington, DE.

ATLANTIC COAST CONFERENCE

Office Address: 4512 Weybridge Lane, Greensboro, NC 27407. **Mailing Address:** P.O. Drawer ACC, Greensboro, NC 27417. **Telephone:** (336) 851-6062. **FAX:** (336) 854-8797, 547-6261.

Baseball Members (First Year): Clemson (1953), Duke (1953), Florida State (1992), Georgia Tech (1980), Maryland (1953), North Carolina (1953), North Carolina State (1953), Virginia (1955), Wake Forest (1953).

Assistant Commissioner, Media Relations: Brian Morrison. **Baseball Contact:** Emily Watkins.

1999 Tournament: Nine teams, double-elimination. May 18-23, Durham Bulls Athletic Park, Durham, NC.

ATLANTIC-10 CONFERENCE

Mailing Address: 2 Penn Center Plaza, Suite 1410, Philadelphia, PA 19102. **Telephone:** (215) 751-0500. **FAX:** (215) 751-0770. **E-Mail Address:** cmorrison@atlantic10.org. **Website:** www.atlantic10.org.

Baseball Members (First Year): East—Fordham (1996), Massachusetts (1977), Rhode Island (1981), St. Bonaventure (1980), St. Joseph's (1983), Temple (1983). **West**—Dayton (1996), Duquesne (1977), George Washington (1977), LaSalle (1996), Virginia Tech (1996), Xavier (1996).

Director, Communications: Courtney Morrison.

1999 Tournament: Four teams, double-elimination. May 20-22 at Boyertown, PA.

BIG EAST CONFERENCE

Mailing Address: 56 Exchange Terrace, Providence, RI 02903. **Telephone:** (401) 272-9108. **FAX:** (401) 751-8540. **E-Mail Address:** rcarolla@bigeast.org. **Website:** www.bigeast.org.

Baseball Members (First Year): Boston College (1985), Connecticut (1985), Georgetown (1985), Notre Dame (1996), Pittsburgh (1985), Providence (1985), Rutgers (1996), St. John's (1985), Seton Hall (1985), Villanova (1985), West Virginia (1996).

Assistant Director, Communications: Rob Carolla.

1999 Tournament: Six teams, double-elimination. May 19-22 at Mercer County Waterfront Park, Trenton, NJ.

BIG SOUTH CONFERENCE

Mailing Address: 6428 Bannington Dr., Suite A, Charlotte, NC 28226. **Telephone:** (704) 341-7990. **FAX:** (704) 341-7991. **E-Mail Address:** drewd@bigsouth.org. **Website:** www.bigsouth.org.

Baseball Members (First Year): Charleston Southern (1983), Coastal Carolina (1983), Elon (1999), High Point (1999), Liberty (1991), UNC Asheville (1985), Radford (1983), Winthrop (1983).

Director, Public Relations: Drew Dickerson.

1999 Tournament: Four teams, double-elimination. May 20-23 at Conway, SC (Coastal Carolina College).

BIG TEN CONFERENCE

Mailing Address: 1500 W Higgins Rd., Park Ridge, IL 60068. **Telephone:** (847) 696-1010. **FAX:** (847) 696-1110. **E-Mail Address:** ljuscik@bigten.org. **Website:** www.bigten.org.

Baseball Members (First Year): Illinois (1896), Indiana (1906), Iowa (1906), Michigan (1896), Michigan State (1950), Minnesota (1906), Northwestern (1898), Ohio State (1913), Penn State (1992), Purdue (1906).

Associate Director, Communications: Lisa Juscik.

1999 Tournament: Four teams, double-elimination. May 20-23 at regular season champion.

BIG 12 CONFERENCE

Mailing Address: 2201 Stemmons Freeway, 28th Floor, Dallas, TX 75207. **Telephone:** (214) 742-1212. **FAX:** (214) 753-0145. **E-Maill Address:** bo@big12-sports.com. **Website:** www.big12sports.com.

Baseball Members (First Year): Baylor (1997), Iowa State (1997), Kansas (1997), Kansas State (1997), Missouri (1997), Nebraska (1997), Oklahoma (1997), Oklahoma State (1997), Texas (1997), Texas A&M (1997), Texas Tech (1997).

Director, Media Relations: Bo Carter.

1999 Tournament: Eight teams, double-elimination. May 19-23 at Southwestern Bell Bricktown Ballpark, Oklahoma City, OK.

BIG WEST CONFERENCE

Mailing Address: 2 Corporate Park, Suite 206, Irvine, CA 92606. **Telephone:** (949) 261-2525. **FAX:** (949) 261-2528. **E-Mail Address:** mvillamor@bigwest.org. **Website:** www.bigwest.org.

Baseball Members (First Year): Cal Poly San Luis Obispo (1997), UC Santa Barbara (1970), Cal State Fullerton (1975), Long Beach State (1970), Nevada (1993), New Mexico State (1992), Pacific (1972), Sacramento State (1997).

Assistant Information Director: Mike Villamor.

1999 Tournament: None.

COLONIAL ATHLETIC ASSOCIATION

Mailing Address: 8625 Patterson Ave., Richmond, VA 23229. **Telephone:** (804) 754-1616. **FAX:** (804) 754-1830. **E-Mail Address:** svehorn@caasports.com. **Website:** www.caasports.com.

Baseball Members (First Year): East Carolina (1986), George Mason (1986), James Madison (1986), UNC Wilmington (1986), Old Dominion (1992), Richmond (1986), Virginia Commonwealth (1996), William & Mary (1985).

Sports Information Director: Steve Vehorn.

1999 Tournament: Eight teams, double-elimination. May 18-22 at Grainger Stadium, Kinston, NC.

CONFERENCE USA

Mailing Address: 35 E Wacker Dr., Suite 650, Chicago, IL 60601. **Telephone:** (312) 553-0483. **FAX:** (312) 553-0495. **E-Mail Address:** rdanderson@c-usa.org. **Website:** www.c-usa.org.

Baseball Members (First Year): Alabama-Birmingham (1996), Cincinnati (1996), Houston (1997), Louisville (1996), Memphis (1996), UNC Charlotte (1996), Saint Louis (1996), South Florida (1996), Southern Mississippi (1996), Tulane (1996).

Director, Information Services: Russell Anderson.

1999 Tournament: Ten teams, double-elimination. May 18-23 at Millington, TN.

IVY GROUP

Mailing Address: 330 Alexander St., Princeton, NJ 08544. **Telephone:** (609) 258-6426. **FAX:** (609) 258-1690.

E-Mail Address: ivygroup@princeton.edu. **Website:** www.ivyleague.princeton.edu.

Baseball Members (First Year): Rolfe—Brown (1993), Dartmouth (1993), Harvard (1993), Yale (1993). **Gehrig**—Columbia (1993), Cornell (1993), Pennsylvania (1993), Princeton (1993).

Associate Director/Communications: Chuck Yrigoyen.

1999 Tournament: Best-of-3 series between division champions. May 8-9 at Rolfe champion.

METRO ATLANTIC ATHLETIC CONFERENCE

Mailing Address: 1090 Amboy Ave., Edison, NJ 08837. **Telephone:** (732) 225-0202. **FAX:** (732) 225-5440. **E-Mail Address:** catherine.hughes@maac.org. **Website:** www.maac.org.

Baseball Members (First Year): North—Canisius (1990), LeMoyne (1990), Marist (1998), Niagara (1990), Siena (1990). **South**—Fairfield (1982), Iona (1982), Manhattan (1982), Rider (1998), St. Peter's (1982).

Director, Media Relations: Catherine Hughes.

1999 Tournament: Four teams, double-elimination. May 7-9 at Dutchess Stadium, Fishkill, NY.

MID-AMERICAN CONFERENCE

Mailing Address: Four Sea Gate, Suite 102, Toledo, OH 43604. **Telephone:** (419) 249-7177. **FAX:** (419) 242-4022. **E-Mail Address:** grichter@midamconf.com. **Website:** www.midamconf.com.

Baseball Members (First Year): East—Akron (1992), Bowling Green State (1952), Kent (1951), Marshall (1997), Miami (1947), Ohio (1946). **West**—Ball State (1973), Central Michigan (1971), Eastern Michigan (1971), Northern Illinois (1997), Toledo (1950), Western Michigan (1947).

Assistant Commissioner, Communications: Gary Richter.

1999 Tournament: Six teams, double-elimination. May 19-22 at West champion.

MID-CONTINENT CONFERENCE

Mailing Address: 340 W Butterfield Rd., Suite 3-D, Elmhurst, IL 60126. **Telephone:** (630) 516-0661. **FAX:** (630) 516-0673. **E-Mail Address:** nsmidcon@aol.com. **Website:** www.mid-con.com.

Baseball Members (First Year): Chicago State (1994), Indiana-Purdue (1999), Oral Roberts (1998), Valparaiso (1983), Western Illinois (1982), Youngstown State (1992).

Interim Director, Media Relations: Nancy Smith.

1999 Tournament: Six teams, double-elimination. May 20-23 at Tulsa, OK (Oral Roberts University).

MID-EASTERN ATHLETIC CONFERENCE

Mailing Address: 102 N Elm St., Suite 401, P.O. Box 21205, Greensboro, NC 27420. **Telephone:** (336) 275-9961. **FAX:** (336) 275-9964. **E-Mail Address:** meac@nr.infi.net. **Website:** www.meacsports.com.

Baseball Members (First Year): North—Coppin State (1985), Delaware

State (1970), Howard (1970), Maryland-Eastern Shore (1970). **South**—Bethune-Cookman (1979), Florida A&M (1979), Norfolk State (1998), North Carolina A&T (1970).

Director, Media Relations: Bradford Evans. **Baseball Contact:** Mitchell Jennings.

1999 Tournament: Eight teams, double-elimination. April 30-May 2 at Daytona Beach, FL (Bethune-Cookman College).

MIDWESTERN COLLEGIATE CONFERENCE

Mailing Address: 201 S Capitol Ave., Suite 500, Indianapolis, IN 46225. **Telephone:** (317) 237-5622. **FAX:** (317) 237-5620.

E-Mail Address: jlehman@mccnet.org. **Website:** www.mccnet.org.

Baseball Members (First Year): Butler (1979), Cleveland State (1994), Detroit (1980), Illinois-Chicago (1994), Wisconsin-Milwaukee (1994), Wright State (1994).

Director, Communications: Josh Lehman.

1999 Tournament: Six teams, double-elimination. May 14-16 at Chicago, IL (University of Illinois-Chicago).

MISSOURI VALLEY CONFERENCE

Mailing Address: 1000 St. Louis Union Station, Suite 105, St. Louis, MO 63103. **Telephone:** (314) 421-0339. **FAX:** (314) 421-3505. **Website:** www.mvc.org.

Baseball Members (First Year): Bradley (1955), Creighton (1976), Evansville (1994), Illinois State (1980), Indiana State (1976), Northern Iowa (1991), Southern Illinois (1974), Southwest Missouri State (1990), Wichita State (1945).

Assistant Commissioner: Jack Watkins.

1999 Tournament: Six teams, double-elimination. May 19-22 at Wichita, KS (Wichita State University).

NORTHEAST CONFERENCE

Mailing Address: 220 Old New Brunswick Rd., Piscataway, NJ 08854. **Telephone:** (732) 562-0877. **FAX:** (732) 562-8838. **E-Mail Address:** rratner@northeastconference.org. **Website:** www.northeastconference.org.

Baseball Members (First Year): **North**—Central Connecticut State (1999), Fairleigh Dickinson (1981), Long Island (1981), Quinnipiac (1999), St. Francis, N.Y. (1981). **South**—Maryland-Baltimore County (1999), Monmouth (1985), Mount St. Mary's (1989), Wagner (1981).

Assistant Commissioner: Ron Ratner.

1999 Tournament: Four teams, double-elimination. May 7-9 at The Ballpark at Harbor Yard, Bridgeport, CT.

OHIO VALLEY CONFERENCE

Mailing Address: 278 Franklin Rd., Suite 103, Brentwood, TN 37027. **Telephone:** (615) 371-1698. **FAX:** (615) 371-1788. **E-Mail Address:** rwashburn@ovc.org. **Website:** www.ovcsports.com.

Baseball Members (First Year): Austin Peay State (1962), Eastern Illinois (1996), Eastern Kentucky (1948), Middle Tennessee State (1952), Morehead State (1948), Murray State (1948), Southeast Missouri State (1991), Tennessee-Martin (1992), Tennessee Tech (1949).

Assistant Commissioner: Rob Washburn.

1999 Tournament: Six teams, double-elimination. May 20-22, site of highest seeded team with lights.

PACIFIC-10 CONFERENCE

Mailing Address: 800 S Broadway, Suite 400, Walnut Creek, CA 94596. **Telephone:** (925) 932-4411. **FAX:** (925) 932-4601. **E-Mail Address:** jgonzalez@pac-10.org. **Website:** www.pac-10.org.

Baseball Members (First Year): Arizona (1979), Arizona State (1979), California (1916), UCLA (1928), Oregon State (1916), Southern California (1922), Stanford (1917), Washington (1916), Washington State (1917).

Baseball Intern: Jennifer Gonzalez.

1999 Tournament: None.

PATRIOT LEAGUE

Mailing Address: 3897 Adler Pl., Bldg. C, Suite 310, Bethlehem, PA 18017. **Telephone:** (610) 691-2414. **FAX:** (610) 691-8414. **Website:** www.patriotleague.org.

Baseball Members (First Year): Army (1993), Bucknell (1991), Holy Cross (1991), Lafayette (1991), Lehigh (1991), Navy (1993).

Associate Executive Director: Todd Newcomb.

1999 Tournament: Top three teams; No. 2 plays No. 3 in one-game playoff. Winner faces No. 1 team in best-of-3 series at No. 1 seed May 15-16.

SOUTHEASTERN CONFERENCE

Mailing Address: 2201 Civic Center Blvd., Birmingham, AL 35203. **Telephone:** (205) 458-3000. **FAX:** (205) 458-3030. **E-Mail Address:** cbloom@sec.org. **Website:** www.secsports.com.

Baseball Members (First Year): **East**—Florida (1933), Georgia (1933), Kentucky (1933), South Carolina (1991), Tennessee (1933), Vanderbilt (1933). **West**—Alabama (1933), Arkansas (1991), Auburn (1933), Louisiana State (1933), Mississippi (1933), Mississippi State (1933).

Assistant Commissioner: Charles Bloom.

1999 Tournament: Eight teams, modified double-elimination. May 19-23 at Hoover Metropolitan Stadium, Birmingham, AL.

SOUTHERN CONFERENCE

Mailing Address: One West Pack Square, Suite 1508, Asheville, NC 28801. **Telephone:** (828) 255-7872. **FAX:** (828) 251-5006. **E-Mail Address:** socon@socon.org. **Website:** www.socon.org.

Baseball Members (First Year): Appalachian State (1971), Charleston (1998), The Citadel (1936), Davidson (1991), East Tennessee State (1978), Furman (1936), Georgia Southern (1991), UNC Greensboro (1997), Virginia Military Institute (1924), Western Carolina (1976), Wofford (1997).

Media Relations Assistant: Nathan Boudreaux.

1999 Tournament: Eight teams, double-elimination. May 20-23 at Charleston, SC (The Citadel).

SOUTHLAND CONFERENCE

Mailing Address: 8150 N Central Expy., Suite 930, Dallas, TX 75206. **Telephone:** (214) 750-7522. **FAX:** (214) 750-8077. **E-Mail Address:** bludlow@southland.org.

Baseball Members (First Year): Lamar (1999), McNeese State (1973), Nicholls State (1992), Northeast Louisiana (1983), Northwestern State (1988), Sam Houston State (1988), Southeastern Louisiana (1998), Southwest Texas State (1988), Texas-Arlington (1964), Texas-San Antonio (1992).

Director, Media Relations: Bruce Ludlow.

1999 Tournament: Six teams, double-elimination. May 15-18 at Monroe, LA (Northeast Louisiana University).

SOUTHWESTERN ATHLETIC CONFERENCE

Mailing Address: Louisiana Superdome, 1500 Sugar Bowl Dr., New Orleans, LA 70112. **Telephone:** (504) 523-7574. **FAX:** (504) 523-7513. **E-Mail Address:** lhardy@swac.org. **Website:** www.swac.org.

Baseball Members (First Year): East—Alabama State (1982), Alcorn State (1962), Jackson State (1958), Mississippi Valley State (1968). **West**—Arkansas-Pine Bluff (1999), Grambling State (1958), Prairie View A&M (1920), Southern (1934), Texas Southern (1954).

Associate Commissioner: Lonza Hardy Jr.

1999 Tournament: Six teams, double-elimination. May 7-9 at New Orleans, LA.

SUN BELT CONFERENCE

Mailing Address: One Galleria Blvd., Suite 2115, Metairie, LA 70001. **Telephone:** (504) 834-6600. **FAX:** (504) 834-6642. **Website:** www.sunbelt-sports.org.

Baseball Members (First Year): Arkansas-Little Rock (1991), Arkansas State (1991), Florida International (1999), Louisiana Tech (1991), New Orleans (1976), South Alabama (1976), Southwestern Louisiana (1991), Western Kentucky (1982).

Associate Commissioner: Rob Bernardi.

1999 Tournament: Eight teams, double-elimination. May 18-22 at Zephyr Field, New Orleans, LA.

TRANS AMERICA ATHLETIC CONFERENCE

Mailing Address: The Commons, 3370 Vineville Ave., Suite 108-B, Macon, GA 31204. **Telephone:** (912) 474-3394. **FAX:** (912) 476-2178. **E-Mail Address:** tsnyder@taac.org. **Website:** www.taac.org.

Baseball Members (First Year): Campbell (1994), Centenary (1978), Central Florida (1992), Florida Atlantic (1993), Georgia State (1983), Jacksonville (1999), Jacksonville State (1996), Mercer (1978), Samford (1978), Stetson (1985), Troy State (1998).

Assistant Commissioner: Tom Snyder.

1999 Tournament: Six teams, double-elimination. May 19-22 at Osceola Sports Complex, Kissimmee, FL.

WEST COAST CONFERENCE

Mailing Address: 1200 Bayhill Dr., Suite 302, San Bruno, CA 94066. **Telephone:** (650) 873-8622. **FAX:** (650) 873-7846. **E-Mail Address:** dott@westcoast.org. **Website:** www.westcoast.org.

Baseball Members (First Year): West—Loyola Marymount (1968), Portland (1996), Saint Mary's (1968), Santa Clara (1968). **Coast**—Gonzaga (1996), Pepperdine (1968), San Diego (1979), San Francisco (1968).

Assistant Commissioner: Don Ott.

1999 Tournament: None.

WESTERN ATHLETIC CONFERENCE

Mailing Address: 9250 East Costilla Ave., Suite 300, Englewood, CO 80112. **Telephone:** (303) 799-9221. **FAX:** (303) 799-3888. **E-Mail Address:** dchaffin@wac.org. **Website:** www.wac.org.

Baseball Members (First Year): Air Force (1980), Brigham Young (1963), Fresno State (1992), Hawaii (1978), Nevada-Las Vegas (1996), New Mexico (1963), Rice (1996), San Diego State (1979), San Jose State (1996), Texas Christian (1996), Utah (1963).

Associate Commissioner: Jeff Hurd. **Director, Sports Information:** Dave Chaffin.

1999 Tournament: Six teams, double-elimination. May 19-22 at Fresno, CA (Fresno State University).

CALIFORNIA COLLEGIATE ATHLETIC ASSOCIATION

Mailing Address: 40 Via di Roma Walk, Long Beach, CA 90803. **Telephone**: (310) 985-4065. **FAX**: (310) 985-8067.

Baseball Members: UC Davis, UC Riverside, Cal Poly Pomona, Cal State Chico, Cal State Dominguez Hills, Cal State Los Angeles, Cal State San Bernardino, Cal State Stanislaus, San Francisco State, Sonoma State.

CAROLINAS-VIRGINIA INTERCOLLEGIATE ATHLETIC CONFERENCE

Mailing Address: 26 Club Dr., Thomasville, NC 27360. **Telephone**: (336) 884-0482. **FAX**: (336) 884-0315.

Baseball Members: Barton, Belmont Abbey, Coker, Erskine, Limestone, Longwood, Mount Olive, Pfeiffer, Saint Andrews.

CENTRAL INTERCOLLEGIATE ATHLETIC ASSOCIATION

Mailing Address: 303 Butler Farm Rd., Suite 102, Hampton, VA 23666. **Telephone**: (757) 865-0071. **FAX**: (757) 865-8436.

Baseball Members: Bowie State, Elizabeth City State, Saint Augustine's, Saint Paul's, Shaw, Virginia State.

GREAT LAKES INTERCOLLEGIATE ATHLETIC CONFERENCE

Mailing Address: 3250 W Big Beaver, Suite 300, Troy, MI 48084. **Telephone**: (248) 649-2036. **FAX**: (248) 649-6847.

Baseball Members: Ashland, Gannon, Grand Valley State, Hillsdale, Mercyhurst, Northwood, Saginaw Valley, Wayne (Mich.) State, Westminster (Pa.).

GREAT LAKES VALLEY CONFERENCE

Mailing Address: Pan Am Plaza, Suite 560, 201 S Capitol Ave., Indianapolis, IN 46225. **Telephone**: (317) 237-5636. **FAX**: (317) 237-5632.

Baseball Members: Bellarmine, IU/PU-Fort Wayne, Indianapolis, Kentucky Wesleyan, Lewis, Missouri-Saint Louis, Northern Kentucky, Quincy, Saint Joseph's, Southern Illinois-Edwardsville, Southern Indiana, Wisconsin-Parkside.

GULF SOUTH CONFERENCE

Mailing Address: 4 Office Park Circle, Suite 218, Birmingham, AL 25223. **Telephone**: (205) 870-9750. **FAX**: (205) 870-4723.

Baseball Members: Alabama-Huntsville, Arkansas-Monticello, Arkansas Tech, Central Arkansas, Christian Brothers, Delta State, Henderson State, Lincoln Memorial, Montevallo, North Alabama, Southern Arkansas, Valdosta State, West Alabama, West Florida, West Georgia.

HEART OF TEXAS CONFERENCE

Mailing Address: 527 Dale, Waco, TX 76706. **Telephone**: (254) 662-6472. **FAX**: (254) 662-6627.

Baseball Members: Incarnate Word, Saint Edward's, Saint Mary's, Texas Lutheran, Texas Wesleyan.

LONE STAR CONFERENCE

Mailing Address: 1221 W Campbell Rd. No. 217, Richardson, TX 75080. **Telephone**: (972) 234-0033. **FAX**: (972) 234-4110.

Baseball Members: Abilene Christian, Cameron, Central Oklahoma, East Central, Eastern New Mexico, Harding, Northeastern State, Ouachita Baptist, Southeastern Oklahoma, Southwestern Oklahoma, Tarleton State, Texas A&M-Kingsville, West Texas A&M.

MID-AMERICA INTERCOLLEGIATE ATHLETICS ASSOCIATION

Mailing Address: 10551 Barkley, Suite 501, Overland Park, KS 66212. **Telephone**: (913) 341-3839. **FAX**: (913) 341-5887.

Baseball Members: Central Missouri State, Emporia State, Lincoln (Mo.), Missouri-Rolla, Missouri Southern State, Missouri Western State, Northwest Missouri State, Pittsburg State, Southwest Baptist, Truman State, Washburn.

NEW ENGLAND COLLEGIATE CONFERENCE

Mailing Address: 20 Forest Hills Dr., PO Box 1307, Farmington, CT 06034. **Telephone**: (860) 677-1269. **FAX**: (860) 674-8363.

Baseball Members: Albany, Binghamton, Bridgeport, Franklin Pierce, Massachusetts-Lowell, New Hampshire College, New Haven, Sacred Heart, Southern Connecticut State, Stony Brook.

NEW YORK COLLEGIATE ATHLETIC CONFERENCE

Mailing Address: 3031 Arrowhead Lane, Norristown, PA 19401. **Telephone**: (610) 825-5068. **FAX**: (610) 825-3676.

Baseball Members: Adelphi, Concordia (N.Y.), Dowling, Mercy, Molloy, New Jersey Institute of Technology, Philadelphia Textile, Queens, Saint Rose.

NORTH CENTRAL INTERCOLLEGIATE ATHLETIC CONFERENCE

Mailing Address: 2400 N Louise, Ramkota Inn, Sioux Falls, SD 57107. **Telephone**: (605) 338-0907. **FAX**: (605) 338-1889.

Baseball Members: Augustana (S.D.), Mankato State, Morningside, Nebraska-Omaha, North Dakota, North Dakota State, Northern Colorado, Saint Cloud State, South Dakota, South Dakota State.

NORTHEAST-10 CONFERENCE

Mailing Address: PO Box 1197, Westfield, MA 01086. **Telephone**: (413) 562-4789. **FAX**: (413) 562-2660.

Baseball Members: American International, Assumption, Bentley, Bryant, Merrimack, Saint Anselm, Saint Michael's, Stonehill.

NORTHERN SUN INTERCOLLEGIATE CONFERENCE

Mailing Address: 1901 University Ave. SE, Suite 310-F, Minneapolis, MN 55414. **Telephone**: (612) 626-7680. **FAX**: (612) 626-7682.

Baseball Members: Bemidji State, Minnesota-Duluth, Minnesota-Morris, Northern State, Southwest State, Winona State.

PEACH BELT ATHLETIC CONFERENCE

Mailing Address: PO Box 204290, Augusta, GA 30917. **Telephone**: (706) 860-8499. **FAX**: (706) 650-8113.

Baseball Members: Armstrong Atlantic, Augusta State, Columbus State, Francis Marion, Georgia College, Kennesaw State, Lander, UNC Pembroke, North Florida, South Carolina-Aiken, South Carolina-Spartanburg.

PENNSYLVANIA STATE ATHLETIC CONFERENCE

Mailing Address: 105 Zimmerli, Lock Haven U., Lock Haven, PA 17745. **Telephone**: (717) 893-2512. **FAX**: (717) 893-2650.

Baseball Members: Bloomsburg, California (Pa.), Clarion, East Stroudsburg, Edinboro, Indiana (Pa.), Kutztown, Lock Haven, Mansfield, Millersville, Shippensburg, Slippery Rock, West Chester.

ROCKY MOUNTAIN ATHLETIC CONFERENCE

Mailing Address: Copper Building, Suite B, 1631 Mesa Ave., Colorado Springs, CO 80906. **Telephone**: (719) 471-0066. **FAX**: (719) 471-0088.

Baseball Members: Colorado Mines, Fort Hays State, Mesa State, Metro State, Nebraska-Kearney, New Mexico Highlands, Regis, Southern Colorado.

SOUTH ATLANTIC CONFERENCE

Mailing Address: Gateway Plaza, Suite 130, 226 N Park Dr., Rock Hill, SC 29730. **Telephone**: (803) 981-5240. **FAX**: (803) 981-9444.

Baseball Members: Carson-Newman, Catawba, Gardner-Webb, Lenoir-Rhyne, Mars Hill, Newberry, Presbyterian, Tusculum, Wingate.

SOUTHERN INTERCOLLEGIATE ATHLETIC CONFERENCE

Mailing Address: Harris Tower, 233 Peachtree St. NE, Suite 301, Atlanta, GA 30303. **Telephone**: (404) 659-3380. **FAX**: (404) 659-7422.

Baseball Members: Albany State (Ga.), Kentucky State, Lane, LeMoyne-Owen, Miles, Paine, Savannah State, Tuskegee.

SUNSHINE STATE CONFERENCE

Mailing Address: 7061 Grand National Dr., Suite 138, Orlando, FL 32819. **Telephone**: (407) 248-8460. **FAX**: (407) 248-8325.

Baseball Members: Barry, Eckerd, Florida Southern, Florida Tech, Lynn, Rollins, Saint Leo, Tampa.

WEST VIRGINIA INTERCOLLEGIATE ATHLETIC CONFERENCE

Mailing Address: 1422 Main St., Princeton, WV 24740. **Telephone**: (304) 487-6298. **FAX**: (304) 487-6299.

Baseball Members: Alderson-Broaddus, Bluefield State, Charleston (W.Va.), Concord, Davis & Elkins, Fairmont State, Salem-Teikyo, Shepherd, West Liberty State, West Virginia State, West Virginia Tech, West Virginia Wesleyan.

INDEPENDENTS

Alabama A&M, Central Washington, Columbia Union, Hawaii Pacific, Oakland, Oakland City, Pittsburgh-Johnstown, Rockhurst, Saint Francis (Ill.), Saint Martin's, Wayne (Neb.) State

*Recruiting coordinator

AIR FORCE ACADEMY Falcons
Conference: Western Athletic.
Mailing Address: 2169 Field House Dr., USAF Academy, CO 80840.
Head Coach: Joe Giarratano. **Assistant Coach:** *Mike Saks. **Telephone:** (719) 333-2057. ■ **Baseball SID:** Dave Toller. **Telephone:** (719) 333-3950. **FAX:** (719) 333-3798.
Home Field: Falcon Field. **Seating Capacity:** 1,000. **Outfield Dimensions:** LF—349, CF—400, RF—316. **Press Box Telephone:** (719) 333-3472.

AKRON Zips
Conference: Mid-American (East).
Mailing Address: JAR Arena, Room 76, Akron, OH 44325.
Head Coach: Dave Fross. **Assistant Coach:** *Tim Berenyi. **Telephone:** (330) 972-7277. ■ **Baseball SID:** Jeff Brewer. **Telephone:** (330) 972-7468. **FAX:** (330) 374-8844.
Home Field: Lee R. Jackson Field. **Seating Capacity:** 2,500. **Outfield Dimensions:** LF—330, CF—405, RF—330. **Press Box Telephone:** (330) 972-8896.

ALABAMA Crimson Tide
Conference: Southeastern (West).
Mailing Address: P.O. Box 870391, Tuscaloosa, AL 35487.
Head Coach: Jim Wells. **Assistant Coaches:** Todd Butler, *Mitch Gaspard, Jim Gatewood. **Telephone:** (205) 348-6171. ■ **Baseball SID:** Barry Allen. **Telephone:** (205) 348-6084. **FAX:** (205) 348-8841.
Home Field: Sewell-Thomas Stadium. **Seating Capacity:** 4,107. **Outfield Dimensions:** LF—325, CF—400, RF—325. **Press Box Telephone:** (205) 348-4927.

ALABAMA-BIRMINGHAM Blazers
Conference: Conference USA.
Mailing Address: 617 13th St. S, Room 115, Birmingham, AL 35294.
Head Coach: Pete Rancont. **Assistant Coaches:** Brian Pompili, Frank Walton. **Telephone:** (205) 934-5181. ■ **Baseball SID:** Chris Pika. **Telephone:** (205) 934-0722. **FAX:** (205) 934-7505.
Home Field: Jerry D. Young Memorial Field. **Seating Capacity:** 1,000. **Outfield Dimensions:** LF—337, CF—390, RF—330. **Press Box Telephone:** (205) 934-0200.

ALABAMA STATE Hornets
Conference: Southwestern Athletic (East).
Mailing Address: P.O. Box 271, Montgomery, AL 36101.
Head Coach: Larry Watkins. **Assistant Coaches:** John Broom, James Graham. **Telephone:** (334) 229-4228. ■ **Baseball SID** Kevin Mannes. **Telephone:** (334) 229-4511. **FAX:** (334) 262-2971.

ALCORN STATE Braves
Conference: Southwestern Athletic (East).
Mailing Address: 1000 ASU Drive, No. 510, Lorman, MS 39096.
Head Coach: Willie McGowan. **Assistant Coach:** David Robinson. **Telephone:** (601) 877-6279. ■ **Baseball SID:** Peter Forest. **Telephone:** (601) 877-6466. **FAX:** (601) 877-3821.

APPALACHIAN STATE Mountaineers
Conference: Southern.
Mailing Address: Broome-Kirk Gymnasium, Boone, NC 28608.
Head Coach: Troy Huestess. **Assistant Coaches:** David Miller, Stony Wine. **Telephone:** (828) 262-6097. ■ **Baseball SID:** Bill Dyer. **Telephone:** (828) 262-2268. **FAX:** (828) 262-6106.

ARIZONA Wildcats
Conference: Pacific-10.
Mailing Address: P.O. Box 210096, Tucson, AZ 85721.
Head Coach: Jerry Stitt. **Assistant Coaches:** Tod Brown, *Bill Kinneberg, Victor Solis. **Telephone:** (520) 621-4102. ■ **Baseball SID:** David Hardee. **Telephone:** (520) 621-0914. **FAX:** (520) 621-2681.
Home Field: Frank Sancet Field. **Seating Capacity:** 6,700. **Outfield Dimensions:** LF—360, CF—400, RF—360. **Press Box Telephone:** (520) 621-4440.

ARIZONA STATE Sun Devils
Conference: Pacific-10.
Mailing Address: ICA Bldg., Room 105, Tempe, AZ 85287.
Head Coach: Pat Murphy. **Assistant Coaches:** *John Pawlowski, Mike Rooney, Jay Sferra. **Telephone:** (602) 965-6085. ■ **Baseball SID:** Aimee Dombroski. **Telephone:** (602) 965-6592. **FAX:** (602) 965-5408.
Home Field: Packard Stadium. **Seating Capacity:** 4,000. **Outfield Dimensions:** LF—340, CF—395, RF—340. **Press Box Telephone:** (602) 965-1509.

ARKANSAS Razorbacks
Conference: Southeastern (West).
Mailing Address: P.O. Box 7777, Fayetteville, AR 72702.

Head Coach: Norm DeBriyn. Assistant Coaches: Doug Clark, *Tim Montez. Telephone: (501) 575-3655. ■ Baseball SID: Chris Williams. Telephone: (501) 575-2751. FAX: (501) 575-7481.

Home Field: Baum Stadium. Seating Capacity: 3,300. Outfield Dimensions: LF—320, CF—400, RF—320. Press Box Telephone: (501) 444-0031.

ARKANSAS-LITTLE ROCK Trojans

Conference: Sun Belt.
Mailing Address: 2801 South University, Little Rock, AR 72204.
Head Coach: Brian Rhees. Assistant Coaches: Mark Coca, *Karl Kuhn. Telephone: (501) 663-8095. ■ Baseball SID: Jason Whaley. Telephone: (501) 569-3449. FAX: (501) 569-3030.

ARKANSAS-PINE BLUFF Golden Lions

Conference: Southwestern Athletic (West).
Mailing Address: 1200 N University, Pine Bluff, AR 71611.
Head Coach: Elbert Bennett. Assistant Coaches: Mike Bumpers, *George Howard, Mark Hughes. Telephone: (870) 543-8938. ■ Baseball SID: James Jackson. Telephone: (870) 543-8684. FAX: (870) 543-8013.

ARKANSAS STATE Indians

Conference: Sun Belt.
Mailing Address: P.O. Box 1000, State University, AR 72467.
Head Coach: Bill Bethea. Assistant Coaches: David Kenley, *Earl Wheeler. Telephone: (870) 972-2077. ■ Baseball SID: Scott Costello. Telephone: (870) 972-2541. FAX: (870) 972-3367.

Home Field: Tomlinson Stadium/Kell Field. Seating Capacity: 1,000. Outfield Dimensions: LF—335, CF—400, RF—335. Press Box Telephone: (870) 972-3383.

ARMY Cadets

Conference: Patriot.
Mailing Address: Howard Road, Building 639, West Point, NY 10996.
Head Coach: Dan Roberts. Assistant Coach: Joe Sottolano. Telephone: (914) 938-3712. ■ Baseball SID: Bob Beretta. Telephone: (914) 938-3512. FAX: (914) 446-2556.

AUBURN Tigers

Conference: Southeastern (West).
Mailing Address: P.O. Box 351, Auburn, AL 36830.
Head Coach: Hal Baird. Assistant Coaches: *Steve Renfroe, Tom Slater. Telephone: (334) 844-4975. ■ Baseball SID: Meredith Jenkins. Telephone: (334) 844-9806. FAX: (334) 844-9807.

Home Field: Hitchcock Field at Plainsman Park. Seating Capacity: 2,597. Outfield Dimensions: LF—315, CF—385, RF—331. Press Box Telephone: (334) 844-4138.

AUSTIN PEAY STATE Governors

Conference: Ohio Valley.
Mailing Address: P.O. Box 4515, Clarksville, TN 37044.
Head Coach: Gary McClure. Assistant Coaches: *Brian Hetland, Larry Owens. Telephone: (931) 648-6266. ■ Baseball SID: Carol Bagwell. Telephone: (931) 648-7561. FAX: (931) 648-7562.

BALL STATE Cardinals

Conference: Mid-American (West).
Mailing Address: 2000 University Ave., Muncie, IN 47306.
Head Coach: Rich Maloney. Assistant Coaches: Matt Husted, Chris Kessick, John Lowery. Telephone: (765) 285-8226. ■ Baseball SID: Bob Moore. Telephone: (765) 285-8242. FAX: (765) 285-8929.

Home Field: Ball Diamond. Seating Capacity: 1,700. Outfield Dimensions: LF—330, CF—400, RF—330. Press Box Telephone: (765) 285-8932.

BAYLOR Bears

Conference: Big 12.
Mailing Address: 150 Bear Run, Waco, TX 76711.
Head Coach: Steve Smith. Assistant Coaches: Steve Johnigan, Mike Rardin, *Mitch Thompson. Telephone: (254) 710-3029. ■ Baseball SID: Jason Archinal. Telephone: (254) 710-3066. FAX: (254) 710-1369.

Home Field: Ferrell Field. Seating Capacity: 4,100. Outfield Dimensions: LF—330, CF—400, RF—330. Press Box Telephone: (254) 754-5546.

BETHUNE-COOKMAN Wildcats

Conference: Mid-Eastern Athletic (South).
Mailing Address: 640 Dr. Mary McLeod Bethune Blvd., Daytona Beach, FL 32114.
Head Coach: Richard Skeel. Assistant Coaches: Willie Brown, Juan Goytia, *Mervyl Melendez. Telephone: (904) 255-1401, ext. 340. ■ Baseball SID: Robert Roseberry. Telephone: (904) 258-7621. FAX: (904) 253-4231.

BOSTON COLLEGE Eagles

Conference: Big East.
Mailing Address: 321 Conte Forum, Chestnut Hill, MA 02467.
Head Coach: Pete Hughes. Assistant Coaches: Rob Carpentier, Justin Cronk, Pat Mason. Telephone: (617) 552-3092. ■ Baseball SID: Simon Gray.

Telephone: (617) 552-0524. **FAX:** (617) 552-4903.
   Home Field: Commander Shea Field. **Seating Capacity:** 1,000. **Outfield Dimensions:** LF—320, CF—400, RF—320. **Press Box Telephone:** None.

BOWLING GREEN STATE Falcons

   Conference: Mid-American (East).
   Mailing Address: 201 Perry Stadium E, Bowling Green, OH 43403.
   Head Coach: Danny Schmitz. **Assistant Coaches:** L.J. Archambeau, Mark Nell. **Telephone:** (419) 372-7095. ■ **Baseball SID:** Jeff Weiss. **Telephone:** (419) 372-7077. **FAX:** (419) 372-6015.

BRADLEY Braves

   Conference: Missouri Valley.
   Mailing Address: 1501 West Bradley Ave., Peoria, IL 61625.
   Head Coach: Dewey Kalmer. **Assistant Coaches:** John Dyke, John Young. **Telephone:** (309) 677-2684. ■ **Baseball SID:** Bo Ryan. **Telephone:** (309) 677-2627. **FAX:** (309) 677-2626.
   Home Field: Vonachen Stadium. **Seating Capacity:** 6,200. **Outfield Dimensions:** LF—335, CF—383, RF—335. **Press Box Telephone:** (309) 688-2653.

BRIGHAM YOUNG Cougars

   Conference: Western Athletic.
   Mailing Address: 30 SFH, Provo, UT 84602.
   Head Coach: Gary Pullins. **Assistant Coaches:** Dave Eldredge, Bob Noel. **Telephone:** (801) 378-5049. ■ **Baseball SID:** Ralph Zobell. **Telephone:** (801) 378-9769. **FAX:** (801) 378-3520.
   Home Field: Cougar Field. **Seating Capacity:** 3,000. **Outfield Dimensions:** LF—345, CF—390, RF—345. **Press Box Telephone:** (801) 378-4041.

BROWN Bears

   Conference: Ivy League (Rolfe).
   Mailing Address: Box 1932, Providence, RI 02912.
   Head Coach: Marek Drabinski. **Assistant Coach:** Brett Borretti. **Telephone:** (401) 863-3090. ■ **Baseball SID:** Tim Chestney. **Telephone:** (401) 863-2219. **FAX:** (401) 863-1436.

BUCKNELL Bison

   Conference: Patriot.
   Mailing Address: Davis Gym, Moore Ave., Lewisburg, PA 17837.
   Head Coach: Gene Depew. **Assistant Coaches:** Brian Hoyt, Brian Reidel. **Telephone:** (570) 577-3593. ■ **Baseball SID:** Bob Behler. **Telephone:** (570) 577-1227. **FAX:** (570) 577-1660.

BUTLER Bulldogs

   Conference: Midwestern Collegiate.
   Mailing Address: 4600 Sunset Ave., Indianapolis, IN 46208.
   Head Coach: Steve Farley. **Assistant Coaches:** *Tony Baldwin, Ryan O'Donovan. **Telephone:** (317) 940-9721. ■ **Baseball SID:** Tony Hamilton. **Telephone:** (317) 940-9994. **FAX:** (317) 940-9808.

C.W. POST Pioneers

   Conference: Independent.
   Mailing Address: 720 Northern Blvd., Brookville, NY 11548.
   Head Coach: Dick Vining. **Assistant Coaches:** Dan Mascia, Pete Timmes. **Telephone:** (516) 299-2938. ■ **Baseball SID:** Brad Sullivan. **Telephone:** (516) 299-4156. **FAX:** (516) 299-3155.

CALIFORNIA Golden Bears

   Conference: Pacific-10.
   Mailing Address: 210 Memorial Stadium, Berkeley, CA 94720.
   Head Coach: Bob Milano. **Assistant Coaches:** *David Lawn, Scott Murray, Pat Shine. **Telephone:** (510) 643-6006. ■ **Baseball SID:** Scott Ball. **Telephone:** (510) 643-1741. **FAX:** (510) 643-7778.
   Home Field: Evans Diamond. **Seating Capacity:** 4,000. **Outfield Dimensions:** LF—320, CF—395, RF—320. **Press Box Telephone:** (510) 642-3098.

UCLA Bruins

   Conference: Pacific-10.
   Mailing Address: P.O. Box 24044, Los Angeles, CA 90024.
   Head Coach: Gary Adams. **Assistant Coaches:** *Vince Beringhele, Rob Hinds, Tim Leary. **Telephone:** (310) 794-8210. ■ **Baseball SID:** Jeff Blank. **Telephone:** (310) 206-7870. **FAX:** (310) 825-8664.
   Home Field: Jackie Robinson Stadium. **Seating Capacity:** 1,250. **Outfield Dimensions:** LF—365, CF—390, RF—365. **Press Box Telephone:** (310) 794-8213.

UC SANTA BARBARA Gauchos

   Conference: Big West.
   Mailing Address: 1000 Robertson Gym, Goleta, CA 93107.
   Head Coach: Bob Brontsema. **Assistant Coaches:** Shad Knighton, *Tom Myers. **Telephone:** (805) 893-3690. ■ **Baseball SID:** Gabe Rosenthal. **Telephone:** (805) 893-3428. **FAX:** (805) 893-4537.
   Home Field: Caesar Uyesaka Stadium. **Seating Capacity:** 1,000. **Outfield Dimensions:** LF—335, CF—400, RF—335. **Press Box Telephone:** (805) 893-4671/8079.

CAL POLY SAN LUIS OBISPO Mustangs

Conference: Big West.

Mailing Address: One Grand Ave., San Luis Obispo, CA 93407.

Head Coach: Ritch Price. **Assistant Coaches:** Todd Coburn, Tom Kunis, Mike Oakland. **Telephone:** (805) 756-6367. ■ **Baseball SID:** Scott Flanders. **Telephone:** (805) 756-6531. **FAX:** (805) 756-2650.

Home Field: San Luis Obispo Stadium. **Seating Capacity:** 1,500. **Outfield Dimensions:** LF—333, CF—410, RF—333. **Press Box Telephone:** (805) 756-2410.

CAL STATE FULLERTON Titans

Conference: Big West.

Mailing Address: 800 N State College Blvd., PE 133C, Fullerton, CA 92834.

Head Coach: George Horton. **Assistant Coaches:** Mike Kirby, *Dave Serrano, Rick Vanderhook. **Telephone:** (714) 278-3789. ■ **Baseball SID:** Mel Franks. **Telephone:** (714) 278-3970. **FAX:** (714) 278-3141.

Home Field: Titan Field. **Seating Capacity:** 1,500. **Outfield Dimensions:** LF—330, CF—400, RF—330. **Press Box Telephone:** (714) 278-5327.

CAL STATE NORTHRIDGE Matadors

Conference: Independent.

Mailing Address: 18111 Nordhoff St., Northridge, CA 91330.

Head Coach: Mike Batesole. **Assistant Coaches:** Jamie Nelson, Grant Hohman. **Telephone:** (818) 677-7055. ■ **Baseball SID:** Aaron Meier. **Telephone:** (818) 677-3243. **FAX:** (818) 677-4762.

Home Field: Matador Field. **Seating Capacity:** 1,200. **Outfield Dimensions:** LF—325, CF—400, RF—330. **Press Box Telephone:** (818) 677-4293.

CAMPBELL Fighting Camels

Conference: Trans America Athletic.

Mailing Address: P.O. Box 10, Buies Creek, NC 27506.

Head Coach: Chip Smith. **Assistant Coaches:** Jeff Bock, *Randy Hood. **Telephone:** (910) 893-1354. ■ **Baseball SID:** Stan Cole. **Telephone:** (910) 893-1331. **FAX:** (910) 893-1330.

CANISIUS Golden Griffins

Conference: Metro Atlantic (North).

Mailing Address: 2001 Main St., Buffalo, NY 14208.

Head Coach: Don Colpoys. **Assistant Coaches:** Joe Cagiano, Ray Hennessy. **Telephone:** (716) 888-2977. ■ **Baseball SID:** John Maddock. **Telephone:** (716) 888-2977. **FAX:** (716) 888-2980.

CENTENARY Gents

Conference: Trans America Athletic.

Mailing Address: 2911 Centenary Blvd., Shreveport, LA 71134.

Head Coach: Ed McCann. **Assistant Coaches:** Scott Leach, Justin Kern. **Telephone:** (318) 869-5095. ■ **Baseball SID:** Todd Degree. **Telephone:** (318) 869-5092. **FAX:** (318) 869-5145.

CENTRAL CONNECTICUT STATE Blue Devils

Conference: Northeast (North).

Mailing Address: Kaiser Hall, 1615 Stanley St., New Britain, CT 06050.

Head Coach: George Redman. **Assistant Coaches:** Mike Church, Craig Schmitt. **Telephone:** (860) 832-3074. ■ **Baseball SID:** Chris O'Connor. **Telephone:** (860) 832-3059. **FAX:** (860) 832-3084.

CENTRAL FLORIDA Golden Knights

Conference: Trans America Athletic.

Mailing Address: P.O. Box 163555, Orlando, FL 32816.

Head Coach: Jay Bergman. **Assistant Coaches:** Craig Cozart, *Greg Frady, Rookie Gage. **Telephone:** (407) 823-0140. ■ **Baseball SID:** Stephanie Burchill. **Telephone:** (407) 823-2464. **FAX:** (407) 823-5266.

Home Field: UCF Baseball Complex. **Seating Capacity:** 1,800. **Outfield Dimensions:** LF—325, CF—400, RF—325. **Press Box Telephone:** (407) 823-5002.

CENTRAL MICHIGAN Chippewas

Conference: Mid-American (West).

Mailing Address: 108 West Hall, Mount Pleasant, MI 48859.

Head Coach: Judd Folske. **Assistant Coaches:** *Steve Jaksa, Rick Smith. **Telephone:** (517) 774-6670. ■ **Baseball SID:** Fred Stabley Jr. **Telephone:** (517) 774-3277. **FAX:** (517) 774-7324.

Home Field: Theunissen Stadium. **Seating Capacity:** 4,100. **Outfield Dimensions:** LF—330, CF—390, RF—330. **Press Box Telephone:** (517) 774-3579.

CHARLESTON Cougars

Conference: Southern.

Mailing Address: 26 George St., Charleston, SC 29424.

Head Coach: Ralph Ciabattari. **Assistant Coaches:** Scott Foxhall, R.J. Kackley, Steve Turner. **Telephone:** (843) 953-5916. ■ **Baseball SID:** Tony Ciuffo. **Telephone:** (843) 953-5465. **FAX:** (843) 953-6534.

CHARLESTON SOUTHERN Buccaneers

Conference: Big South.

Mailing Address: P.O. Box 118087, Charleston, SC 29423.

Head Coach: Gary Murphy. **Assistant Coaches:** Austin Alexander, Jeff Cisar, Dirk Thomas. **Telephone:** (843) 863-7591. ■ **Baseball SID:** Ken Gerlinger. **Telephone:** (843) 863-7688. **FAX:** (843) 863-7676.

CHICAGO STATE Cougars
Conference: Mid-Continent.
Mailing Address: 9501 S King Dr., Chicago, IL 60628.
Head Coach: Kevin McCray. **Assistant Coach:** Terrence Jackson. **Telephone:** (773) 995-3659. ■ **Baseball SID:** Terrence Jackson. **Telephone:** (773) 995-2217. **FAX:** (773) 995-3656.

CINCINNATI Bearcats
Conference: Conference USA.
Mailing Address: Mail Location 21, Cincinnati, OH 45221.
Head Coach: Brian Cleary. **Assistant Coaches:** Jeff Ditch, Dusty Lepper. **Telephone:** (513) 556-0566. ■ **Baseball SID:** Jeremy Hartigan. **Telephone:** (513) 556-5191. **FAX:** (513) 556-0619.
Home Field: Johnny Bench Field. **Seating Capacity:** 500. **Outfield Dimensions:** LF—327, CF—385, RF—330. **Press Box Telephone:** (513) 556-0818.

THE CITADEL Bulldogs
Conference: Southern.
Mailing Address: P.O. Box 7, Citadel Station, Charleston, SC 29409.
Head Coach: Fred Jordan. **Assistant Coaches:** Chris Lemonis, *Dan McDonnell. **Telephone:** (843) 953-5901. ■ **Baseball SID:** Geoff Wiswell. **Telephone:** (843) 953-5120. **FAX:** (843) 953-5058.
Home Field: Joseph P. Riley Park (6,000). **Outfield Dimensions:** LF—305, CF—398, RF—337. **Press Box Telephone:** (843) 965-4151.

CLEMSON Tigers
Conference: Atlantic Coast.
Mailing Address: P.O. Box 31, Clemson, SC 29633.
Head Coach: Jack Leggett. **Assistant Coaches:** *Tim Corbin, Mike Hampton, Kevin O'Sullivan. **Telephone:** (864) 656-1940. ■ **Baseball SIDs:** Brian Hennessy, Brett Sowell. **Telephone:** (864) 656-2114. **FAX:** (864) 656-0299.
Home Field: Tiger Field. **Seating Capacity:** 5,000. **Outfield Dimensions:** LF—328, CF—400, RF—338. **Press Box Telephone:** (864) 656-7731.

CLEVELAND STATE Vikings
Conference: Midwestern Collegiate.
Mailing Address: 2451 Euclid Ave., Cleveland, OH 44115.
Head Coach: Jay Murphy. **Assistant Coaches:** Dennis Healy, Dave Sprochi. **Telephone:** (216) 687-4822. ■ **Baseball SID:** Julie Imes. **Telephone:** (216) 687-5115. **FAX:** (216) 523-7257.

COASTAL CAROLINA Chanticleers
Conference: Big South.
Mailing Address: P.O. Box 261954, Conway, SC 29528.
Head Coach: Gary Gilmore. **Assistant Coaches:** *Bill Jarman, Matt Schilling, Mac Smith. **Telephone:** (843) 349-2816. ■ **Baseball SID:** Matt Hogue. **Telephone:** (843) 349-2822. **FAX:** (843) 349-2819.

COLUMBIA Lions
Conference: Ivy League (Gehrig).
Mailing Address: Dodge Physical Fitness Center, 3030 Broadway, New York, NY 10027.
Head Coach: Mikio Aoki. **Assistant Coaches:** Derek England, Chris Neill. **Telephone:** (212) 854-7772. ■ **Baseball SID:** Heather Croze. **Telephone:** (212) 854-2534. **FAX:** (212) 854-8168.

CONNECTICUT Huskies
Conference: Big East.
Mailing Address: U-78, 2095 Hillside Road, Storrs, CT 06269.
Head Coach: Andy Baylock. **Assistant Coaches:** Jerry LaPenta, Jim Penders. **Telephone:** (860) 486-2458. ■ **Baseball SID:** Scott Wherley. **Telephone:** (860) 486-3531. **FAX:** (860) 486-5085.
Home Field: J.O. Christian Field. **Seating Capacity:** 2,500. **Outfield Dimensions:** LF—340, CF—405, RF—340. **Press Box Telephone:** Unavailable.

COPPIN STATE Eagles
Conference: Mid-Eastern Athletic (North).
Mailing Address: 2500 West North Ave., Baltimore, MD 21216.
Head Coach: Paul Blair. **Assistant Coach:** Andy Srebroski. **Telephone:** (410) 383-5686. ■ **Baseball SID:** Matt Burton. **Telephone:** (410) 383-5981. **FAX:** (410) 383-2511.

CORNELL Big Red
Conference: Ivy League (Rolfe).
Mailing Address: Schoellkopf House, Campus Road, Ithaca, NY 14853.
Head Coach: Tom Ford. **Assistant Coaches:** Scott Marsh, Tom Neubert. **Telephone:** (607) 255-6604. ■ **Baseball SID:** Laura Stange. **Telephone:** (607) 255-3752. **FAX:** (607) 255-9791.

CREIGHTON Blue Jays
Conference: Missouri Valley.
Mailing Address: 2500 California Plaza, Omaha, NE 68178.

Head Coach: Jack Dahm. **Assistant Coaches:** Bill Olson, Ed Servais. **Telephone:** (402) 280-5545. ■ **Baseball SID:** Bobby Parker. **Telephone:** (402) 280-2488. **FAX:** (402) 280-2495.

Home Field: Creighton Sports Complex. **Seating Capacity:** 2,000. **Outfield Dimensions:** LF—330, CF—405, RF—330. **Press Box Telephone:** Unavailable.

DARTMOUTH Big Green

Conference: Ivy League (Rolfe).

Mailing Address: 6083 Alumni Gym, Hanover, NH 03755.

Head Coach: Bob Whalen. **Assistant Coach:** Chris Dotolo. **Telephone:** (603) 646-2477. ■ **Baseball SID:** Sarah Hood. **Telephone:** (603) 646-2468. **FAX:** (603) 646-1286.

DAVIDSON Wildcats

Conference: Southern.

Mailing Address: P.O. Box 1750, Davidson, NC 28036.

Head Coach: Dick Cooke. **Assistant Coaches:** Rick Hurni, *Chris Pollard. **Telephone:** (704) 892-2368. ■ **Baseball SID:** Rick Bender. **Telephone:** (704) 892-2123. **FAX:** (704) 892-2636.

DAYTON Flyers

Conference: Atlantic-10 (West).

Mailing Address: Box 1238, 300 College Park, Dayton, OH 45469.

Head Coach: Chris Sorrell. **Assistant Coaches:** Clint Albert, Terry Bell, Jerry Salyers. **Telephone:** (937) 229-4456. ■ **Baseball SID:** Mike DeGeorge. **Telephone:** (937) 229-4460. **FAX:** (937) 229-4461.

DELAWARE Fightin' Blue Hens

Conference: America East.

Mailing Address: 631 S College Ave., Newark, DE 19716.

Head Coach: Bob Hannah. **Assistant Coaches:** Paul Gillerlain, Dan Hammer, Jim Sherman. **Telephone:** (302) 831-8596. ■ **Baseball SID:** Steve Geller. **Telephone:** (302) 831-2186. **FAX:** (302) 831-8653.

DELAWARE STATE Hornets

Conference: Mid-Eastern Athletic (North).

Mailing Address: 1200 N DuPont Hwy., Dover, DE 19901.

Head Coach: Tripp Keister. **Assistant Coaches:** *Nate Goulet, Mike Henderson. **Telephone:** (302) 739-2304. ■ **Baseball SID:** Dennis Jones. **Telephone:** (302) 739-4926. **FAX:** (302) 739-5241.

DETROIT Titans

Conference: Midwestern Collegiate.

Mailing Address: P.O. Box 19900, Detroit, MI 48219.

Head Coach: Bob Miller. **Assistant Coaches:** Lee Bjerke, Dean Rovinelli. **Telephone:** (313) 993-1725. ■ **Baseball SID:** Unavailable. **Telephone:** (313) 993-1745. **FAX:** (313) 993-1765.

DREXEL Dragons

Conference: America East.

Mailing Address: 3141 Chestnut St., Philadelphia, PA 19104.

Head Coach: Don Maines. **Assistant Coaches:** *Chris Calciano, Tom O'Connell. **Telephone:** (215) 895-1782. ■ **Baseball SID:** Chris Beckett. **Telephone:** (215) 895-1570. **FAX:** (215) 895-2038.

DUKE Blue Devils

Conference: Atlantic Coast.

Mailing Address: 115 Cameron Indoor Stadium, Durham, NC 27708.

Head Coach: Steve Traylor. **Assistant Coaches:** *Dave Koblentz, Chris McMullan. **Telephone:** (919) 684-2358. ■ **Baseball SID:** Dwayne Harrison. **Telephone:** (919) 684-2633. **FAX:** (919) 684-2489.

Home Field: Jack Coombs Field. **Seating Capacity:** 2,000. **Outfield Dimensions:** LF—330, CF—400, RF—331. **Press Box Telephone:** (919) 684-6074.

DUQUESNE Dukes

Conference: Atlantic-10 (West).

Mailing Address: A.J. Palumbo Center, 600 Forbes Ave., Pittsburgh, PA 15282.

Head Coach: Mike Wilson. **Assistant Coaches:** *Joe Hill, Jay Stoner. **Telephone:** (412) 396-5245. ■ **Baseball SID:** George Nieman. **Telephone:** (412) 396-5376. **FAX:** (412) 396-6210.

EAST CAROLINA Pirates

Conference: Colonial Athletic.

Mailing Address: Scales Field House, Greenville, NC 27858.

Head Coach: Keith LeClair. **Assistant Coaches:** Tommy Eason, *Todd Raleigh, George Whitfield. **Telephone:** (252) 328-4604. ■ **Baseball SID:** Jerry Trickie. **Telephone:** (252) 328-4522. **FAX:** (252) 328-4528.

EAST TENNESSEE STATE Buccaneers

Conference: Southern.

Mailing Address: P.O. Box 70641, Johnson City, TN 37614.

Head Coach: Ken Campbell. **Assistant Coach:** John Cloud. **Telephone:** (423) 439-4496. ■ **Baseball SID:** Sanford Rogers. **Telephone:** (423) 439-4220. **FAX:** (423) 439-6138.

EASTERN ILLINOIS Panthers

Conference: Ohio Valley.
Mailing Address: Lantz Gym, Charleston, IL 61920.
Head Coach: Jim Schmitz. **Assistant Coaches:** Matt Buczkowski, Andy Haines, Chris Hall. **Telephone:** (217) 581-2522. ■ **Baseball SID:** Pat Osterman. **Telephone:** (217) 581-6408. **FAX:** (217) 581-6434.

EASTERN KENTUCKY Colonels

Conference: Ohio Valley.
Mailing Address: 118 Alumni Coliseum, 521 Lancaster Ave., Richmond, KY 40475.
Head Coach: Jim Ward. **Assistant Coaches:** Ron Nichols, *Jason Stein, Greg Yurevich. **Telephone:** (606) 622-2128. ■ **Baseball SID:** Karl Park. **Telephone:** (606) 622-1291. **FAX:** (606) 622-1230.

EASTERN MICHIGAN Eagles

Conference: Mid-American (West).
Mailing Address: Room 307, Convocation Center, Ypsilanti, MI 48197.
Head Coach: Roger Coryell. **Assistant Coach:** Jake Boss. **Telephone:** (734) 487-0315. ■ **Baseball SID:** John Martin. **Telephone:** (734) 487-0317. **FAX:** (734) 485-3840.
Home Field: Oestrike Stadium. **Seating Capacity:** 2,500. **Outfield Dimensions:** LF—330, CF—390, RF—330. **Press Box Telephone:** (734) 484-1396.

ELON Fightin' Christians

Conference: Big South.
Mailing Address: Campus Box 2500, Elon College, NC 27244.
Head Coach: Mike Kennedy. **Assistant Coaches:** Brendan Dougherty, Greg Starbuck. **Telephone:** (336) 584-2420. ■ **Baseball SID:** David Hibbard. **Telephone:** (336) 584-2316. **FAX:** (336) 584-2443.

EVANSVILLE Purple Aces

Conference: Missouri Valley.
Mailing Address: 1800 Lincoln Ave., Evansville, IN 47722.
Head Coach: Jim Brownlee. **Assistant Coaches:** Ryan Barrett, Ryan Brownlee, Tim Brownlee. **Telephone:** (812) 479-2059. ■ **Baseball SID:** Kyle Campbell. **Telephone:** (812) 479-2350. **FAX:** (812) 479-2090.

FAIRFIELD Stags

Conference: Metro Atlantic (South).
Mailing Address: North Benson Rd., Fairfield, CT 06430.
Head Coach: John Slosar. **Assistant Coaches:** Drew Brown, *Sean Martin, Keith O'Rourke, Dennis Whalen. **Telephone:** (203) 254-4000, ext. 2605. ■ **Baseball SID:** Drew Brown. **Telephone:** (203) 254-4000, ext. 2878. **FAX:** (203) 254-4117.

FAIRLEIGH DICKINSON Knights

Conference: Northeast (North).
Mailing Address: Temple Avenue, Rothman Center, Hackensack, NJ 07601.
Head Coach: Dennis Sasso. **Assistant Coaches:** Jerry DeFabbia, Mike Mongiello. **Telephone:** (201) 692-2245. ■ **Baseball SID:** Bob Rothwell. **Telephone:** (201) 692-2204. **FAX:** (201) 692-9361.

FLORIDA Gators

Conference: Southeastern (East).
Mailing Address: P.O. Box 14485, Gainesville, FL 32604.
Head Coach: Andy Lopez. **Telephone:** (352) 375-4683, ext. 4457. ■ **Baseball SID:** Steve Shaff. **Telephone:** (352) 375-4683, ext. 6130. **FAX:** (352) 375-4809.
Home Field: McKethan Stadium at Perry Field. **Seating Capacity:** 5,000. **Outfield Dimensions:** LF—329, CF—400, RF—325. **Press Box Telephone:** (352) 375-4683, ext. 4355.

FLORIDA A&M Rattlers

Conference: Mid-Eastern Athletic (South).
Mailing Address: Room 205, Gaither Athletic Center, Tallahassee, FL 32307.
Head Coach: Joe Durant. **Assistant Coaches:** Willie Brown, Brett Richardson, Harry Sapp. **Telephone:** (850) 599-3202. ■ **Baseball SID:** Alvin Hollins. **Telephone:** (850) 599-3200. **FAX:** (850) 599-3206.

FLORIDA ATLANTIC Owls

Conference: Trans America Athletic.
Mailing Address: 777 Glades Rd., Boca Raton, FL 33431.
Head Coach: Kevin Cooney. **Assistant Coaches:** Bob Deutchman, Jim Lyttle, *John McCormack. **Telephone:** (561) 297-3956. ■ **Baseball SID:** Katrina McCormack. **Telephone:** (561) 297-3163. **FAX:** (561) 297-2996.

FLORIDA INTERNATIONAL Golden Panthers

Conference: Sun Belt.
Mailing Address: University Park Campus, Miami, FL 33199.
Head Coach: Danny Price. **Assistant Coaches:** Marc Calvi, *Rolando Casanova, Ken Foster. **Telephone:** (305) 348-3166. ■ **Baseball SID:** Rich Kelch. **Telephone:** (305) 348-3164. **FAX:** (305) 348-2963.
Home Field: University Park. **Seating Capacity:** 1,000. **Outfield Dimensions:** LF—325, CF—400, RF—325. **Press Box Telephone:** (305) 554-8694.

FLORIDA STATE Seminoles
Conference: Atlantic Coast.
Mailing Address: P.O. Box 2195, Tallahassee, FL 32316.
Head Coach: Mike Martin. **Assistant Coaches:** Chip Baker, Mike Martin Jr., *Jamey Shouppe. **Telephone:** (850) 644-1073. ■ **Baseball SID:** Amy Farnum. **Telephone:** (850) 644-0615. **FAX:** (850) 644-3820.
Home Field: Dick Howser Stadium. **Seating Capacity:** 5,000. **Outfield Dimensions:** LF—340, CF—400, RF—320. **Press Box Telephone:** (850) 644-1553.

FORDHAM Rams
Conference: Atlantic-10 (East).
Mailing Address: 441 E Fordham Rd., Bronx, NY 10458.
Head Coach: Dan Gallagher. **Assistant Coaches:** John Ceprini, Tony Mellaci, *Nick Restaino. **Telephone:** (718) 817-4290. ■ **Baseball SID:** Joe DiBari. **Telephone:** (718) 817-4240. **FAX:** (718) 817-4244.

FRESNO STATE Bulldogs
Conference: Western Athletic.
Mailing Address: 5305 N Campus Dr., Room 153, Fresno, CA 93740.
Head Coach: Bob Bennett. **Assistant Coaches:** Steve Pearse, *Mike Rupcich. **Telephone:** (559) 278-2178. ■ **Baseball SID:** Michael Smoose. **Telephone:** (559) 278-2509. **FAX:** (559) 278-4689.
Home Field: Beiden Field. **Seating Capacity:** 6,575. **Outfield Dimensions:** LF—330, CF—400, RF—330. **Press Box Telephone:** (559) 278-7678.

FURMAN Paladins
Conference: Southern.
Mailing Address: 3300 Poinsett Hwy., Greenville, SC 29613.
Head Coach: Ron Smith. **Assistant Coaches:** Jeff Massey, *Greg McVey. **Telephone:** (864) 294-2146. ■ **Baseball SID:** Kylie Inman. **Telephone:** (864) 294-3062. **FAX:** (864) 294-3061.

GEORGE MASON Patriots
Conference: Colonial Athletic.
Mailing Address: MS 3A5/Baseball Office, 4400 University Dr., Fairfax, VA 22030.
Head Coach: Bill Brown. **Assistant Coaches:** Ken Munoz, Chris Murphy, *J.J. Picollo. **Telephone:** (703) 993-3282. ■ **Baseball SID:** Ben Trittipoe. **Telephone:** (703) 993-3260. **FAX:** (703) 993-3259.

GEORGE WASHINGTON Colonials
Conference: Atlantic-10 (West).
Mailing Address: 600 22nd St. NW, Washington, DC 20052.
Head Coach: Tom Walter. **Assistant Coaches:** *Joe Raccuia, Dave Willman. **Telephone:** (202) 994-7399. ■ **Baseball SID:** Charlene Miller. **Telephone:** (202) 994-0339. **FAX:** (202) 994-2713.

GEORGETOWN Hoyas
Conference: Big East.
Mailing Address: McDonough Arena, 37th & O Streets NW, Washington, DC 20057.
Head Coach: Kirk Mason. **Assistant Coaches:** Scott DeGeorge, Russ DiMarcello, *Pete Wilk. **Telephone:** (202) 687-2462. ■ **Baseball SID:** Mark Wasik. **Telephone:** (202) 687-2492. **FAX:** (202) 687-2491.
Home Field: Georgetown Baseball Diamond. **Seating Capacity:** 900. **Outfield Dimensions:** LF—301, CF—410, RF—310. **Press Box Telephone:** None.

GEORGIA Bulldogs
Conference: Southeastern (East).
Mailing Address: P.O. Box 1472, Athens, GA 30603.
Head Coach: Robert Sapp. **Assistant Coaches:** Matt Donahue, *David Perno. **Telephone:** (706) 542-7971. ■ **Baseball SID:** Christopher Lakos. **Telephone:** (706) 542-1621. **FAX:** (706) 542-7993.
Home Field: Foley Field. **Seating Capacity:** 3,200. **Outfield Dimensions:** LF—350, CF—410, RF—320. **Press Box Telephone:** (706) 542-6162/6161.

GEORGIA SOUTHERN Eagles
Conference: Southern.
Mailing Address: P.O. Box 8095, Statesboro, GA 30460.
Head Coach: Jack Stallings. **Assistant Coaches:** *Scott Baker, Buddy Holder, Darin Van Tassell. **Telephone:** (912) 681-5187. ■ **Baseball SID:** Tom McClellan. **Telephone:** (912) 681-5239. **FAX:** (912) 681-0046.
Home Field: J.I. Clements Stadium. **Seating Capacity:** 2,000. **Outfield Dimensions:** LF—330, CF—380, RF—330. **Press Box Telephone:** (912) 681-2508.

GEORGIA STATE Panthers
Conference: Trans America Athletic.
Mailing Address: University Plaza, Atlanta, GA 30303.
Head Coach: Mike Hurst. **Assistant Coaches:** *David Hartley, Bob Keller, Ryan Lambert. **Telephone:** (404) 651-1198. ■ **Baseball SID:** Ramsey Baker. **Telephone:** (404) 651-4629. **FAX:** (404) 651-3204.

GEORGIA TECH Yellow Jackets
Conference: Atlantic Coast.

Mailing Address: 150 Bobby Dodd Way NW, Atlanta, GA 30332.
Head Coach: Danny Hall. Assistant Coaches: Jeff Guy, *Mike Trapasso.
Telephone: (404) 894-5471. ■ Baseball SID: Mike Stamus. Telephone: (404) 894-5445. FAX: (404) 894-1248.
Home Field: Russ Chandler Stadium. Seating Capacity: 2,500. Outfield Dimensions: LF—320, CF—400, RF—330. Press Box Telephone: (404) 894-3167.

GONZAGA Bulldogs
Conference: West Coast.
Mailing Address: East 502 Boone Ave, Spokane, WA 99258.
Head Coach: Steve Hertz. Assistant Coaches: Greg Gores, Travis Jewett, Mark Machtolf. Telephone: (509) 323-4226. ■ Baseball SID: Oliver Pierce. Telephone: (509) 323-6373. FAX: (509) 323-5730.

GRAMBLING STATE Tigers
Conference: Southwestern Athletic (West).
Mailing Address: Athletics Complex, Room 105, 100 Robinson St., Grambling, LA 71245.
Head Coach: Wilbert Ellis. Assistant Coach: James Randall. Telephone: (318) 274-6121. ■ Baseball SID: Stanley Lewis. Telephone: (318) 274-6199. FAX: (318) 274-2761.

GRAND CANYON Antelopes
Conference: Independent.
Mailing Address: 3300 W Camelback Rd., Phoenix, AZ 85061.
Head Coach: Gil Stafford. Assistant Coaches: Scott Snyder, Dave Stapleton, Ed Wolfe. Telephone: (602) 589-2810. ■ Baseball SID: Deron Filip. Telephone: (602) 589-2795. FAX: (602) 589-2529.
Home Field: Brazell Stadium. Seating Capacity: 1,500. Outfield Dimensions: LF—325, CF—390, RF—325. Press Box Telephone: (602) 589-2719.

HARTFORD Hawks
Conference: America East.
Mailing Address: 200 Bloomfield Ave., West Hartford, CT 06117.
Head Coach: Harvey Shapiro. Assistant Coaches: Bill Gross, John Shea. Telephone: (860) 768-4656. ■ Baseball SID: Jason Guy. Telephone: (860) 768-4620. FAX: (860) 768-4068.

HARVARD Crimson
Conference: Ivy League (Rolfe).
Mailing Address: Murr Center, 65 N Harvard St., Boston, MA 02163.
Head Coach: Joe Walsh. Assistant Coaches: *Gary Donovan, Chip Forrest, Marty Nastasia. Telephone: (617) 495-2629. ■ Baseball SID: Paul McNeeley. Telephone: (617) 495-2206. FAX: (617) 495-2130.

HAWAII Rainbows
Conference: Western Athletic.
Mailing Address: 1337 Lower Campus Dr., Honolulu, HI 96822.
Head Coach: Les Murakami. Assistant Coaches: Carl Furutani, Les Nakama. Telephone: (808) 956-6247. ■ Baseball SID: Markus Owens. Telephone: (808) 956-7523. FAX: (808) 956-4470.
Home Field: Rainbow Stadium. Seating Capacity: 4,312. Outfield Dimensions: LF—340, CF—400, RF—340. Press Box Telephone: (808) 956-6253.

HAWAII-HILO Vulcans
Conference: Independent.
Mailing Address: 200 W Kawili St., Hilo, HI 96720.
Head Coach: Joey Estrella. Assistant Coaches: Richard DeSa, Geoff Hirai, Kallen Miyataki. Telephone: (808) 974-7700. ■ Baseball SID: Kelly Leong. Telephone: (808) 974-7606. FAX: (808) 974-7711.

HIGH POINT Panthers
Conference: Big South.
Mailing Address: University Station, Montlieu Ave., High Point, NC 27262.
Head Coach: Jim Speight. Assistant Coach: Brian Kemp. Telephone: (336) 841-9190. ■ Baseball SID: Holly Jergensen. Telephone: (336) 841-4605. FAX: (336) 841-9182.

HOFSTRA Flying Dutchmen
Conference: America East.
Mailing Address: 1000 Hempstead Turnpike, PFC 230, Hempstead, NY 11549.
Head Coach: Reginal Jackson. Assistant Coaches: Patrick Anderson, Larry Minor. Telephone: (516) 463-5065. ■ Baseball SID: Rikki Dilen. Telephone: (516) 463-4933. FAX: (516) 463-5033.

HOLY CROSS Crusaders
Conference: Patriot.
Mailing Address: One College St., Worcester, MA 01610.
Head Coach: Paul Pearl. Assistant Coaches: Terrence Butt, Fran O'Brien, Tim Whalen. Telephone: (508) 793-2326. ■ Baseball SID: John Butman. Telephone: (508) 793-2583. FAX: (508) 793-2309.

HOUSTON Cougars

Conference: Conference USA.

Mailing Address: 3100 Cullen Rd., Houston, TX 77204.

Head Coach: Rayner Noble. **Assistant Coaches:** Kirk Blount, *Trip Couch, Todd Whitting. **Telephone:** (713) 743-9396. ■ **Baseball SID:** John Sullivan. **Telephone:** (713) 743-9410. **FAX:** (713) 743-9411.

Home Field: Cougar Field. **Seating Capacity:** 4,500. **Outfield Dimensions:** LF—330, CF—390, RF—330. **Press Box Telephone:** (713) 743-0840.

HOWARD Bison

Conference: Mid-Eastern Athletic (North).

Mailing Address: Sixth and Girard Street NW, Drew Hall, Washington, DC 20059.

Head Coach: Chuck Hinton. **Assistant Coach:** Chico Hinton. **Telephone:** (202) 806-5162. ■ **Baseball SIDs:** Anthony Estelle, Kevin Page. **Telephone:** (202) 806-7188. **FAX:** (202) 806-9090.

ILLINOIS Fighting Illini

Conference: Big Ten.

Mailing Address: 1700 S Fourth St., Champaign, IL 61820.

Head Coach: Itch Jones. **Assistant Coaches:** *Dan Hartleb, Eric Snider. **Telephone:** (217) 333-8605. ■ **Baseball SID:** Michelle Warner. **Telephone:** (217) 333-1391. **FAX:** (217) 333-5540.

Home Field: Illinois Field. **Seating Capacity:** 2,000. **Outfield Dimensions:** LF—330, CF—400, RF—330. **Press Box Telephone:** (217) 333-1227.

ILLINOIS-CHICAGO Flames

Conference: Midwestern Collegiate.

Mailing Address: 839 W Roosevelt Rd., Chicago, IL 60607.

Head Coach: Mike Dee. **Assistant Coaches:** J.T. Bruett, Chris Malinoski, *Sean McDermott. **Telephone:** (312) 996-8645. ■ **Baseball SID:** Anne Schoenherr. **Telephone:** (312) 996-5880. **FAX:** (312) 996-5882.

ILLINOIS STATE Redbirds

Conference: Missouri Valley.

Mailing Address: Campus Box 7130, Normal, IL 61790.

Head Coach: Jeff Stewart. **Assistant Coaches:** Tim Johnson, Mark Kingston. **Telephone:** (309) 438-5151. ■ **Baseball SID:** Andy Knapick. **Telephone:** (309) 438-3249. **FAX:** (309) 438-5634.

INDIANA Hoosiers

Conference: Big Ten.

Mailing Address: 1001 E 17th St., Bloomington, IN 47408.

Head Coach: Bob Morgan. **Assistant Coaches:** *Jeff Calcaterra, Scott Googins. **Telephone:** (812) 855-1680. ■ **Baseball SID:** Greg Greenwell. **Telephone:** (812) 855-9399. **FAX:** (812) 855-9401.

Home Field: Sembower Field. **Seating Capacity:** 3,000. **Outfield Dimensions:** LF—333, CF—380, RF—333. **Press Box Telephone:** (812) 855-4787.

INDIANA-PURDUE Metros

Conference: Mid-Continent.

Mailing Address: 901 W New York St., Suite 105, Indianapolis, IN 46202.

Head Coach: Brian Donohew. **Assistant Coaches:** *Mark Flueckiger, Kip McWilliams, Neil Schaffner. **Telephone:** (317) 278-2657. ■ **Baseball SID:** Perry Mann. **Telephone:** (317) 274-2725. **FAX:** (317) 278-2683.

INDIANA STATE Sycamores

Conference: Missouri Valley.

Mailing Address: Student Services Building, Room A-15, Terre Haute, IN 47809.

Head Coach: Bob Warn. **Assistant Coach:** *Mitch Hannahs. **Telephone:** (812) 237-4051. ■ **Baseball SID:** Doug Hoffman. **Telephone:** (812) 237-4073. **FAX:** (812) 237-4157.

Home Field: Sycamore Field. **Seating Capacity:** 2,500. **Outfield Dimensions:** LF—340, CF—402, RF—340. **Press Box Telephone:** (812) 237-4187.

IONA Gaels

Conference: Metro Atlantic (South).

Mailing Address: Mulcahy Center, 715 North Ave., New Rochelle, NY 10801.

Head Coach: Al Zoccolillo. **Assistant Coaches:** J.B. Buono, Dean Degantano, Stephan Rapaglia. **Telephone:** (914) 633-2319. ■ **Baseball SID:** Dave Cagianello. **Telephone:** (914) 633-2334. **FAX:** (914) 633-2072.

IOWA Hawkeyes

Conference: Big Ten.

Mailing Address: 340 Carver-Hawkeye Arena, Iowa City, IA 52242.

Head Coach: Scott Broghamer. **Assistant Coaches:** Ken Charipar, *Elvis Dominguez. **Telephone:** (319) 335-9390. ■ **Baseball SID:** Kristy Fick. **Telephone:** (319) 335-9411. **FAX:** (319) 335-9417.

Home Field: Iowa Field. **Seating Capacity:** 3,000. **Outfield Dimensions:** LF—330, CF—400, RF—330. **Press Box Telephone:** (319) 335-9520.

IOWA STATE Cyclones

Conference: Big 12.

Mailing Address: Jacobson Athletic Building, 1800 S Fourth St., Ames, IA 50011.

Head Coach: Lyle Smith. Assistant Coaches: Jim Murphy, Tony Trumm. Telephone: (515) 294-4201. ■ Baseball SID: Mike Green. Telephone: (515) 294-1393. FAX: (515) 294-0558.

Home Field: Cap Timm Field. Seating Capacity: 3,000. Outfield Dimensions: LF—330, CF—400, RF—330. Press Box Telephone: (515) 294-1640.

JACKSON STATE Tigers

Conference: Southwestern Athletic (East).

Mailing Address: 1325 J.R. Lynch St., Jackson, MS 39217.

Head Coach: Robert Braddy. Assistant Coaches: Lewis Braddy, Mark Salter. Telephone: (601) 968-2425. ■ Baseball SID: Sam Jefferson. Telephone: (601) 968-2273. FAX: (601) 968-2000.

JACKSONVILLE Dolphins

Conference: Trans America Athletic.

Mailing Address: 2800 University Blvd. North, Jacksonville, FL 32211.

Head Coach: Terry Alexander. Assistant Coaches: Joe Fletcher, Bob Shepherd, Les Wright. Telephone: (904) 745-7476. ■ Baseball SID: George Sorensen. Telephone: (904) 745-7402. FAX: (904) 745-7179.

Home Field: Brest Field. Seating Capacity: 2,300. Outfield Dimensions: LF—340, CF—405, RF—340. Press Box Telephone: (904) 745-7588.

JACKSONVILLE STATE Gamecocks

Conference: Trans America Athletic.

Mailing Address: Gamecock Fieldhouse, 700 Pelham Road N., Jacksonville, AL 36265.

Head Coach: Rudy Abbott. Assistant Coach: *Skipper Jones. Telephone: (256) 782-5367. ■ Baseball SID: Greg Seitz. Telephone: (256) 782-5279. FAX: (256) 782-5958.

JAMES MADISON Dukes

Conference: Colonial Athletic.

Mailing Address: South Main, Harrisonburg, VA 22807.

Head Coach: Spanky McFarland. Assistant Coaches: Chuck Bartlett, *Terry Rooney. Telephone: (540) 568-6467. ■ Baseball SID: Curt Dudley. Telephone: (540) 568-6154. FAX: (540) 568-3703.

Home Field: Long Field/Mauck Stadium. Seating Capacity: 1,200. Outfield Dimensions: LF—340, CF—400, RF—320. Press Box Telephone: (540) 568-6545.

KANSAS Jayhawks

Conference: Big 12.

Mailing Address: 104 Allen Fieldhouse, Lawrence, KS 66045.

Head Coach: Bobby Randall. Assistant Coaches: *Mike Bard, Wilson Kilmer. Telephone: (785) 864-7907. ■ Baseball SID: Mitch Germann. Telephone: (785) 864-3417. FAX: (785) 864-7944.

Home Field: Hoglund Ballpark. Seating Capacity: 2,000. Outfield Dimensions: LF—350, CF—380, RF—350. Press Box Telephone: (785) 864-4037.

KANSAS STATE Wildcats

Conference: Big 12.

Mailing Address: 1800 College Ave., Suite 134D, Manhattan, KS 66502.

Head Coach: Mike Clark. Assistant Coaches: *Mike Hensley, Robbie Moen, Darin Vaughan. Telephone: (785) 532-5723. ■ Baseball SID: Andy Bartlett. Telephone: (785) 532-6735. FAX: (785) 532-6093.

Home Field: Frank Myers Field. Seating Capacity: 5,000. Outfield Dimensions: LF—340, CF—400, RF—325. Press Box Telephone: (785) 532-6926.

KENT Golden Flashes

Conference: Mid-American (East).

Mailing Address: P.O. Box 5190, Kent, OH 44240.

Head Coach: Rick Rembielak. Assistant Coaches: *Greg Beals, Mike Birkbeck. Telephone: (330) 672-3696. ■ Baseball SID: Heather Brocious. Telephone: (330) 672-2110. FAX: (330) 672-2112.

Home Field: Gene Michael Field. Seating Capacity: 2,000. Outfield Dimensions: LF—330, CF—400, RF—330. Press Box Telephone: (330) 672-2036.

KENTUCKY Wildcats

Conference: Southeastern (East).

Mailing Address: Room 23, Memorial Coliseum, Lexington, KY 40506.

Head Coach: Keith Madison. Assistant Coaches: Doug Flynn, *Daron Shoenrock, Jan Weisberg. Telephone: (606) 257-6500. ■ Baseball SID: Holly Ratliff. Telephone: (606) 257-3838. FAX: (606) 323-4310.

Home Field: Cliff Hagan Stadium. Seating Capacity: 2,500. Outfield Dimensions: LF—340, CF—390, RF—310. Press Box Telephone: (606) 257-8027.

LAFAYETTE Leopards

Conference: Patriot.

Mailing Address: A.P. Kirby Field House, Easton, PA 18042.

Head Coach: Lloyd Brewer. Assistant Coaches: Jim Kilpatrick, John Kochmansky, Tom Stoudt. Telephone: (610) 330-5476. ■ Baseball SID: Phil LaBella. Telephone: (610) 330-5122. FAX: (610) 330-5519.

LAMAR Cardinals

Conference: Southland.

Mailing Address: Box 10066, LU Station, Beaumont, TX 77710.

Head Coach: Jim Gilligan. **Assistant Coaches:** Emerick Jagneaux, Jim Ricklefsen. **Telephone:** (409) 880-8135. ■ **Baseball SID:** Daucy Crizer. **Telephone:** (409) 880-8329. **FAX:** (409) 880-2338.

Home Field: Vincent-Beck Stadium. **Seating Capacity:** 3,500. **Outfield Dimensions:** LF—325, CF—380, RF—325. **Press Box Telephone:** (409) 880-8327.

LA SALLE Explorers

Conference: Atlantic-10 (West).

Mailing Address: 1900 W Olney Ave., Philadelphia, PA 19141.

Head Coach: Larry Conti. **Assistant Coaches:** Barry Lopoten, Brian Mills. **Telephone:** (215) 951-1995. ■ **Baseball SID:** Kevin Currie. **Telephone:** (215) 951-1605. **FAX:** (215) 951-1694.

LEHIGH Mountain Hawks

Conference: Patriot.

Mailing Address: Taylor Gym, 641 Taylor St., Bethlehem, PA 18015.

Head Coach: Sean Leary. **Assistant Coaches:** Craig Anderson, Chris Querns. **Telephone:** (610) 758-4315. ■ **Baseball SID:** Jim Marshall. **Telephone:** (610) 758-3158. **FAX:** (610) 758-6629.

LE MOYNE Dolphins

Conference: Metro Atlantic (North).

Mailing Address: Springfield Road, Syracuse, NY 13214.

Head Coach: John King. **Assistant Coaches:** Pete Hoy, Bob Nandin. **Telephone:** (315) 445-4415. ■ **Baseball SID:** Mike Tuberosa. **Telephone:** (315) 445-4412. **FAX:** (315) 445-4678.

LIBERTY Flames

Conference: Big South.

Mailing Address: 1971 University Blvd., Lynchburg, VA 24506.

Head Coach: Dave Pastors. **Assistant Coaches:** Jeff Edwards, Randy Tomlin. **Telephone:** (804) 582-2103. ■ **Baseball SID:** Mike Montoro. **Telephone:** (804) 582-2292. **FAX:** (804) 582-2076.

LONG BEACH STATE 49ers

Conference: Big West.

Mailing Address: 1250 Bellflower Blvd., Long Beach, CA 90840.

Head Coach: Dave Snow. **Assistant Coaches:** Don Barbara, Mike Weathers, *Jim Yogi. **Telephone:** (562) 985-4661. ■ **Baseball SID:** Steve Janisch. **Telephone:** (562) 985-7797. **FAX:** (562) 985-8197.

Home Field: Blair Field. **Seating Capacity:** 3,000. **Outfield Dimensions:** LF—348, CF—400, RF—348. **Press Box Telephone:** (562) 433-8605.

LONG ISLAND Blackbirds

Conference: Northeast (North).

Mailing Address: One University Plaza, Brooklyn, NY 11201.

Head Coach: Frank Giannone. **Assistant Coaches:** Chris Bagley, Mike Ryan. **Telephone:** (718) 488-1538. ■ **Baseball SID:** Greg Fox. **Telephone:** (718) 488-1420. **FAX:** (718) 488-3302.

LOUISIANA STATE Tigers

Conference: Southeastern (West).

Mailing Address: P.O. Box 25095, Baton Rouge, LA 70894.

Head Coach: Skip Bertman. **Assistant Coaches:** Dan Canevari, Bill Dailey, *Jim Schwanke. **Telephone:** (225) 388-4148. ■ **Baseball SID:** Bill Franques. **Telephone:** (225) 388-8226. **FAX:** (225) 388-1861.

Home Field: Alex Box Stadium. **Seating Capacity:** 7,020. **Outfield Dimensions:** LF—330, CF—405, RF—330. **Press Box Telephone:** (225) 388-4149.

LOUISIANA TECH Bulldogs

Conference: Sun Belt.

Mailing Address: P.O. Box 3166, Ruston, LA 71270.

Head Coach: Jeff Richardson. **Assistant Coaches:** Frank Kellner, Brian Rountree. **Telephone:** (318) 257-4111. ■ **Baseball SID:** Scott Keatts. **Telephone:** (318) 257-3144. **FAX:** (318) 257-3757.

LOUISVILLE Cardinals

Conference: Conference USA.

Mailing Address: University of Louisville Athletic Dept., Louisville, KY 40292.

Head Coach: Lelo Prado. **Assistant Coaches:** Al Lopez, *Brian Mundorf. **Telephone:** (502) 852-0103. ■ **Baseball SID:** Nancy Smith. **Telephone:** (502) 852-6581. **FAX:** (502) 852-7401.

Home Field: Cardinal Stadium. **Seating Capacity:** 20,000. **Outfield Dimensions:** LF—360, CF—405, RF—315. **Press Box Telephone:** (502) 367-5000.

LOYOLA MARYMOUNT Lions

Conference: West Coast (West).

Mailing Address: 7900 Loyola Blvd., Los Angeles, CA 90045.

Head Coach: Frank Cruz. **Assistant Coaches:** Brian Criss, Jason Gill, Kelly Nicholson. **Telephone:** (310) 338-2765. ■ **Baseball SID:** Dan Smith. **Telephone:** (310) 338-7643. **FAX:** (310) 338-2703.

MAINE Black Bears

Conference: America East.
Mailing Address: 186 Memorial Gym, Orono, ME 04469.
Head Coach: Paul Kostacopoulos. **Assistant Coaches:** Matt Haney, Mike McRae. **Telephone:** (207) 581-1096. ■ **Baseball SID:** David Lang. **Telephone:** (207) 581-3646. **FAX:** (207) 581-3297.
Home Field: Mahaney Diamond. **Seating Capacity:** 4,000. **Outfield Dimensions:** LF—330, CF—400, RF—330. **Press Box Telephone:** (207) 581-1049/4734.

MANHATTAN Jaspers

Conference: Metro Atlantic (South).
Mailing Address: Manhattan College Parkway, Riverdale, NY 10471.
Head Coach: Steve Trimper. **Assistant Coach:** Unavailable. **Telephone:** (718) 862-7486. ■ **Baseball SID:** Jeff Bernstein. **Telephone:** (718) 862-7228. **FAX:** (718) 862-8020.

MARIST Red Foxes

Conference: Metro Atlantic (North).
Mailing Address: McCann Center, 290 North Rd., Poughkeepsie, NY 12601.
Head Coach: John Szefc. **Assistant Coaches:** Al Kelly, Chris Webb. **Telephone:** (914) 575-3699, ext. 2570. ■ **Baseball SID:** Jill Skotarczak. **Telephone:** (914) 575-3000 ext. 2322. **FAX:** (914) 471-0466.

MARSHALL Thundering Herd

Conference: Mid-American (East).
Mailing Address: P.O. Box 1360, Huntington, WV 25715.
Head Coach: Dave Piepenbrink. **Assistant Coaches:** Tim Adkins, Tim Fratz, Matt Harre. **Telephone:** (304) 696-5277. ■ **Baseball SID:** Jake Keys. **Telephone:** (304) 696-2418. **FAX:** (304) 696-2325.

MARYLAND Terrapins

Conference: Atlantic Coast.
Mailing Address: P.O. Box 295, College Park, MD 20741.
Head Coach: Tom Bradley. **Assistant Coaches:** Jim Flack, *Kelly Kulina. **Telephone:** (301) 314-7122. ■ **Baseball SID:** David O'Brian. **Telephone:** (301) 314-7068. **FAX:** (301) 314-9094.
Home Field: Shipley Field. **Seating Capacity:** 2,200. **Outfield Dimensions:** LF—320, CF—360, RF—370. **Press Box Telephone:** None.

MARYLAND-BALTIMORE COUNTY Retrievers

Conference: Northeast (South).
Mailing Address: 1000 Hilltop Circle, Baltimore, MD 21250.
Head Coach: John Jancuska. **Assistant Coaches:** Evan Evans, *Bob Mumma. **Telephone:** (410) 455-2239. ■ **Baseball SID:** David Gansell. **Telephone:** (410) 455-2639. **FAX:** (410) 455-3994.

MARYLAND-EASTERN SHORE Hawks

Conference: Mid-Eastern Athletic (North).
Mailing Address: Tawes Gymnasium, Backbone Road, Princess Anne, MD 21853.
Head Coach: Kaye Pinhey. **Assistant Coach:** Brian Hollamon. **Telephone:** (410) 651-6539. ■ **Baseball SID:** Romanda Noble. **Telephone:** (410) 651-6499. **FAX:** (410) 651-7514.

MASSACHUSETTS Minutemen

Conference: Atlantic-10 (East).
Mailing Address: 248A Boyden Bldg., Commonwealth Avenue, Amherst, MA 01003.
Head Coach: Mike Stone. **Assistant Coaches:** Raphael Cerrato, *Scott Meaney. **Telephone:** (413) 545-3120. ■ **Baseball SIDs:** Mark Awdycki, Charles Bare. **Telephone:** (413) 545-2439. **FAX:** (413) 545-1566.

McNEESE STATE Cowboys

Conference: Southland.
Mailing Address: P.O. Box 92724, Lake Charles, LA 70609.
Head Coach: Mike Bianco. **Assistant Coaches:** Clint Carver, Chad Clement, *Daniel Tomlin. **Telephone:** (318) 475-5482. ■ **Baseball SID:** Louis Bonnette. **Telephone:** (318) 475-5207. **FAX:** (318) 475-5202.

MEMPHIS Tigers

Conference: Conference USA.
Mailing Address: 205 Athletic Office Building, 570 Normal, Memphis, TN 38152.
Head Coach: Jeff Hopkins. **Assistant Coaches:** Rob McDonald, *Eric Page. **Telephone:** (901) 678-2452. ■ **Baseball SID:** Jamie Bataille. **Telephone:** (901) 678-2337. **FAX:** (901) 678-4134.
Home Field: Nat Buring Stadium. **Seating Capacity:** 2,000. **Outfield Dimensions:** LF—320, CF—380, RF—320. **Press Box Telephone:** (901) 678-2862.

MERCER Bears

Conference: Trans America Athletic.
Mailing Address: 1400 Coleman Ave., Macon, GA 31207.
Head Coach: Barry Myers. **Assistant Coaches:** Rob Fitzpatrick, Craig

Gibson. **Telephone:** (912) 752-2738. ■ **Baseball SID:** Kevin Coulombe. **Telephone:** (912) 752-2735. **FAX:** (912) 752-5350.

MIAMI Hurricanes

Conference: Independent.
Mailing Address: 5821 San Amaro Dr., Coral Gables, FL 33146.
Head Coach: Jim Morris. **Assistant Coaches:** Lazaro Collazo, Gino DiMare, *Turtle Thomas. **Telephone:** (305) 284-4171. ■ **Baseball SID:** Phil de Montmollin. **Telephone:** (305) 284-3244. **FAX:** (305) 284-2387.
Home Field: Mark Light Stadium. **Seating Capacity:** 5,000. **Outfield Dimensions:** LF—330, CF—400, RF—330. **Press Box Telephone:** Unavailable.

MIAMI Redskins

Conference: Mid-American (East).
Mailing Address: 230 Millett Hall, Oxford, OH 45056.
Head Coach: Tracy Smith. **Assistant Coaches:** Don Carson, Matt Jackson, *Tom Kinkelaar. **Telephone:** (513) 529-7293. ■ **Baseball SID:** Kelby Siler. **Telephone:** (513) 529-4330. **FAX:** (513) 529-6729.
Home Field: Stanley G. McKie Field. **Seating Capacity:** 1,500. **Outfield Dimensions:** LF—330, CF—390, RF—330. **Press Box Telephone:** (513) 529-4331.

MICHIGAN Wolverines

Conference: Big Ten.
Mailing Address: 1000 S State St., Ann Arbor, MI 48109.
Head Coach: Geoff Zahn. **Assistant Coaches:** John Edman, Chris Harrison, Matt Hyde. **Telephone:** (734) 647-4550. ■ **Baseball SID:** Jim Schneider. **Telephone:** (734) 763-1381. **FAX:** (734) 647-1188.
Home Field: Ray Fisher Stadium. **Seating Capacity:** 4,000. **Outfield Dimensions:** LF—330, CF—400, RF—330. **Press Box Telephone:** (734) 647-1283.

MICHIGAN STATE Spartans

Conference: Big Ten.
Mailing Address: 401 Olds Hall, East Lansing, MI 48824.
Head Coach: Ted Mahan. **Assistant Coaches:** Greg Gunderson, Tom Hager, Eddie Turek. **Telephone:** (517) 355-4486. ■ **Baseball SID:** Matt Larson. **Telephone:** (517) 355-2271. **FAX:** (517) 353-9636.
Home Fields (Seating Capacity): Kobs Field (4,000), Oldsmobile Park (6,000). **Outfield Dimensions:** Kobs Field/LF—340, CF—400, RF—301; Oldsmobile Park/LF—330, CF—412, LF—337. **Press Box Telephone:** Kobs Field/(517) 353-3009; Oldsmobile Park/(517) 485-2616.

MIDDLE TENNESSEE STATE Blue Raiders

Conference: Ohio Valley.
Mailing Address: MTSU Box 20, Murfreesboro, TN 37132.
Head Coach: Steve Peterson. **Assistant Coaches:** Buddy Custer, *Jim McGuire. **Telephone:** (615) 898-2926. ■ **Baseball SID:** Ryan Simmons. **Telephone:** (615) 904-8209. **FAX:** (615) 898-5626.

MINNESOTA Golden Gophers

Conference: Big Ten.
Mailing Address: 516 15th Ave. SE, Minneapolis, MN 55455.
Head Coach: John Anderson. **Assistant Coaches:** *Rob Fornasiere, Todd Oakes. **Telephone:** (612) 625-4057. ■ **Baseball SID:** John Romo. **Telephone:** (612) 625-4090. **FAX:** (612) 625-0359.
Home Fields (Seating Capacity): Siebert Field (2,500), Metrodome (55,000). **Outfield Dimensions:** Siebert Field/LF—330, CF—380, RF—330; Metrodome /LF—343, CF—408, RF—327. **Press Box Telephone:** Siebert Field/(612) 625-4031; Metrodome/(612) 627-4400.

MISSISSIPPI Rebels

Conference: Southeastern (West).
Mailing Address: P.O. Box 217, University, MS 38677.
Head Coach: Pat Harrison. **Assistant Coaches:** Darby Carmichael, Doug Fortenberry, *Keith Kessinger. **Telephone:** (601) 232-7241. ■ **Baseball SID:** Rick Stupak. **Telephone:** (601) 232-7522. **FAX:** (601) 232-7006.
Home Field: Oxford University Stadium. **Seating Capacity:** 3,000. **Outfield Dimensions:** LF—330, CF—400, RF—330. **Press Box Telephone:** (601) 236-1931.

MISSISSIPPI STATE Bulldogs

Conference: Southeastern (West).
Mailing Address: P.O. Box 5308, Starkville, MS 39762.
Head Coach: Pat McMahon. **Assistant Coaches:** Charlie Anderson, Jim Case, Tommy Raffo. **Telephone:** (601) 325-3597. ■ **Baseball SID:** Joe Dier. **Telephone:** (601) 325-8040. **FAX:** (601) 325-3654.
Home Field: Dudy Noble Field/Polk-DeMent Stadium. **Seating Capacity:** 15,000. **Outfield Dimensions:** LF—325, CF—390, RF—325. **Press Box Telephone:** (601) 325-3776.

MISSISSIPPI VALLEY STATE Delta Devils

Conference: Southwestern Athletic (East).
Mailing Address: 14000 Highway 82 West, Itta Bena, MS 38941.
Head Coach: Cleotha Wilson. **Telephone:** (601) 254-3398. ■ **Baseball SID:**

Chuck Prophet. **Telephone:** (601) 254-3550. **FAX:** (601) 254-3639.

MISSOURI Tigers

Conference: Big 12.
Mailing Address: 370 Hearnes Center, Columbia, MO 65211.
Head Coach: Tim Jamieson. **Assistant Coaches:** Chal Fanning, Evan Pratte. **Telephone:** (573) 882-0731. ■ **Baseball SID:** Jeremy McNeive. **Telephone:** (573) 884-2437. **FAX:** (573) 882-4720.
Home Field: Simmons Field. **Seating Capacity:** 2,500. **Outfield Dimensions:** LF—340, CF—400, RF—340. **Press Box Telephone:** (573) 882-2112.

MONMOUTH Hawks

Conference: Northeast (South).
Mailing Address: Cedar Ave., West Long Branch, NJ 07764.
Head Coach: Dean Ehehalt. **Assistant Coaches:** *Jeff Barbalinardo, Joe Litterio. **Telephone:** (732) 263-5186. ■ **Baseball SID:** Chris Risden. **Telephone:** (732) 263-5180. **FAX:** (732) 571-3535.

MOREHEAD STATE Eagles

Conference: Ohio Valley.
Mailing Address: UPO 1023, Morehead, KY 40351.
Head Coach: John Jarnagin. **Assistant Coaches:** Mitch Dunn, Larry Lipker. **Telephone:** (606) 783-2882. ■ **Baseball SID:** Randy Stacy. **Telephone:** (606) 783-2500. **FAX:** (606) 783-2550.

MOUNT ST. MARY'S Mountaineers

Conference: Northeast (South).
Mailing Address: Route 15, Emmitsburg, MD 21727.
Head Coach: Scott Thomson. **Assistant Coaches:** Trevor Buckley, Steve Mott. **Telephone:** (301) 447-3806. ■ **Baseball SIDs:** Natalie Ciccone, Eric Kloiber. **Telephone:** (301) 447-5384. **FAX:** (301) 447-5300.

MURRAY STATE Thoroughbreds

Conference: Ohio Valley.
Mailing Address: P.O. Box 9, Stewart Stadium, Murray, KY 42071.
Head Coach: Mike Thieke. **Assistant Coaches:** Eddie Doyle, Adam Hines, *Bart Osborne. **Telephone:** (502) 762-4892. ■ **Baseball SID:** David Snow. **Telephone:** (502) 762-3351. **FAX:** (502) 762-6814.

NAVY Midshipmen

Conference: Patriot.
Mailing Address: Ricketts Hall, 566 Brownson Rd., Annapolis, MD 21402.
Head Coach: Bob MacDonald. **Assistant Coaches:** Todd Butler, Glenn Davis, Joe Kinney. **Telephone:** (410) 293-5571. ■ **Baseball SID:** Kris Kamann. **Telephone:** (410) 268-6226. **FAX:** (410) 269-6779.

NEBRASKA Cornhuskers

Conference: Big 12.
Mailing Address: 1101 Avery Ave., Lincoln, NE 68588.
Head Coach: Dave Van Horn. **Assistant Coaches:** Mike Anderson, *Rob Childress, Jeremy Talbot. **Telephone:** (402) 472-2269. ■ **Baseball SID:** Trevor Parks. **Telephone:** (402) 472-2263. **FAX:** (402) 472-2005.
Home Field: Buck Beltzer Stadium. **Seating Capacity:** 1,500. **Outfield Dimensions:** LF—330, CF—400, RF—330. **Press Box Telephone:** (402) 472-2279.

NEVADA Wolf Pack

Conference: Big West.
Mailing Address: Lawlor Annex, Mail Stop 232, Reno, NV 89557.
Head Coach: Gary Powers. **Assistant Coaches:** Justin Drizos, Gary McNamara, *Stan Stolte. **Telephone:** (702) 784-4180. ■ **Baseball SID:** Zen Mocarski. **Telephone:** (702) 784-4600. **FAX:** (702) 784-4386.
Home Field: Peccole Park. **Seating Capacity:** 1,800. **Outfield Dimensions:** LF—340, CF—401, RF—340. **Press Box Telephone:** (702) 784-1585.

NEVADA-LAS VEGAS Rebels

Conference: Western Athletic.
Mailing Address: 4505 Maryland Pkwy., Las Vegas, NV 89154.
Head Coach: Rod Soesbe. **Assistant Coaches:** Jim Pace, Mel Stottlemyre Jr. **Telephone:** (702) 895-3499. ■ **Baseball SID:** Jim Gemma. **Telephone:** (702) 895-3995. **FAX:** (702) 895-0989.
Home Field: Earl E. Wilson Stadium. **Seating Capacity:** 3,000. **Outfield Dimensions:** LF—335, CF—400, RF—335. **Press Box Telephone:** (702) 895-1595.

NEW MEXICO Lobos

Conference: Western Athletic.
Mailing Address: 1414 University Blvd., South Campus, Albuquerque, NM 87131.
Head Coach: Rich Alday. **Assistant Coaches:** Paul Huitt, *Mark Martinez. **Telephone:** (505) 925-5720. ■ **Baseball SID:** Bryan Satter. **Telephone:** (505) 925-5528. **FAX:** (505) 925-5529.
Home Field: Lobo Field. **Seating Capacity:** 500. **Outfield Dimensions:** LF—340, CF—407, RF—340. **Press Box Telephone:** (505) 925-5722.

NEW MEXICO STATE Aggies

Conference: Big West.
Mailing Address: Athletics Department MSC 3145, P.O. Box 30001, Las

Cruces, NM 88003.

Head Coach: Rocky Ward. **Assistant Coaches:** Brad Meador, *Tim Touma. **Telephone:** (505) 646-5813. ■ **Baseball SID:** Thomas Dick. **Telephone:** (505) 646-2927. **FAX:** (505) 646-2425.

Home Field: Presley Askew Field. **Seating Capacity:** 1,000. **Outfield Dimensions:** LF—330, CF—400, RF—370. **Press Box Telephone:** (505) 646-5700.

NEW ORLEANS Privateers

Conference: Sun Belt.

Mailing Address: Lakefront Arena, New Orleans, LA 70148.

Head Coach: Tom Schwaner. **Assistant Coaches:** *Kenny Bonura, Wally Whitehurst. **Telephone:** (504) 280-7021. ■ **Baseball SID:** Ed Cassiere. **Telephone:** (504) 280-6284. **FAX:** (504) 280-7240.

Home Field: Privateer Park. **Seating Capacity:** 5,225. **Outfield Dimensions:** LF—330, CF—405, RF—330. **Press Box Telephone:** (504) 280-7027.

NEW YORK TECH Bears

Conference: Independent.

Mailing Address: P.O. Box 8000, Old Westbury, NY 11568.

Head Coach: Bob Hirschfield. **Assistant Coaches:** Bill Asermely, Scott Hatten, *Bill Timmes. **Telephone:** (516) 686-7513. ■ **Baseball SID:** Tom Riordan. **Telephone:** (516) 686-7504. **FAX:** (516) 626-0750.

NIAGARA Purple Eagles

Conference: Metro Atlantic (North).

Mailing Address: O'Shea Hall, Niagara University, NY 14109.

Head Coach: Jim Mauro. **Assistant Coaches:** Dan Fontana, Bob Kowalski, Bob Mettler. **Telephone:** (716) 286-8602. ■ **Baseball SID:** David Czarnecki. **Telephone:** (716) 286-8582. **FAX:** (716) 286-8651.

NICHOLLS STATE Colonels

Conference: Southland.

Mailing Address: P.O. Box 2032, Thibodaux, LA 70310.

Head Coach: Jim Pizzolatto. **Assistant Coaches:** Gerald Cassard, Rocke Musgraves. **Telephone:** (504) 448-4808. ■ **Baseball SID:** Jack Duggan. **Telephone:** (504) 448-4282. **FAX:** (504) 448-4924.

NORFOLK STATE Spartans

Conference: Mid-Eastern Athletic (South).

Mailing Adress: 2401 Corprew Ave., Norfolk, VA 23504.

Head Coach: Marty Miller. **Assistant Coach:** Anthony Jones. **Telephone:** (757) 683-9539. ■ **Baseball SID:** Glen Mason. **Telephone:** (757) 683-2628. **FAX:** (757) 683-8199.

NORTH CAROLINA Tar Heels

Conference: Atlantic Coast.

Mailing Address: P.O. Box 2126, Chapel Hill, NC 27515.

Head Coach: Mike Fox. **Assistant Coaches:** *Chad Holbrook, Roger Williams. **Telephone:** (919) 962-2351. ■ **Baseball SID:** Matt Bowers. **Telephone:** (919) 962-7259. **FAX:** (919) 962-0612.

Home Field: Boshamer Stadium. **Seating Capacity:** 3,000. **Outfield Dimensions:** LF—335, CF—400, RF—335. **Press Box Telephone:** (919) 962-3509.

UNC ASHEVILLE Bulldogs

Conference: Big South.

Mailing Address: One University Heights, Asheville, NC 28804.

Head Coach: Bill Hillier. **Assistant Coach:** *Eric Filipek. **Telephone:** (828) 251-6920. ■ **Baseball SID:** Mike Gore. **Telephone:** (828) 251-6923. **FAX:** (828) 251-6386.

UNC CHARLOTTE 49ers

Conference: Conference USA.

Mailing Address: Barnhardt Student Activity Center, 9201 University City Blvd., Charlotte, NC 28223.

Head Coach: Loren Hibbs. **Assistant Coaches:** Greg Brummett, Mike Shildt. **Telephone:** (704) 547-3935. ■ **Baseball SID:** Brent Stastny. **Telephone:** (704) 510-6313. **FAX:** (704) 547-4918.

Home Field: Tom and Lib Phillips Field. **Seating Capacity:** 2,000. **Outfield Dimensions:** LF—335, CF—390, RF—335. **Press Box Telephone:** (704) 547-3148.

UNC GREENSBORO Spartans

Conference: Southern.

Mailing Address: P.O. Box 26168, Greensboro, NC 27402.

Head Coach: Mike Gaski. **Assistant Coaches:** *Neil Avent, Matt Faulkner. **Telephone:** (336) 334-3247. ■ **Baseball SID:** Jeremy Agor. **Telephone:** (336) 334-5615. **FAX:** (336) 334-3182.

UNC WILMINGTON Seahawks

Conference: Colonial Athletic.

Mailing Address: 601 S College Rd., Wilmington, NC 28403.

Head Coach: Mark Scalf. **Assistant Coaches:** Shohn Doty, Rob Flippo. **Telephone:** (910) 962-3570. ■ **Baseball SID:** Joe Browning. **Telephone:** (910) 962-3236. **FAX:** (910) 962-3686.

NORTH CAROLINA A&T Aggies

Conference: Mid-Eastern Athletic (South).

Mailing Address: 1601 E Market St., Moores Gym, Greensboro, NC 27411.

Head Coach: Keith Shumate. **Assistant Coaches:** Ric Chandgie, Larry Farrer. **Telephone:** (336) 334-7371. ■ **Baseball SID:** Larry Barber. **Telephone:** (336) 334-7141. **FAX:** (336) 334-7272.

NORTH CAROLINA STATE Wolfpack

Conference: Atlantic Coast.

Mailing Address: P.O. Box 8501, Raleigh, NC 27695.

Head Coach: Elliott Avent. **Assistant Coaches:** *Billy Best, Mark Fuller, Scott Lawler. **Telephone:** (919) 515-3613. ■ **Baseball SID:** Bruce Winkworth. **Telephone:** (919) 515-1182. **FAX:** (919) 515-2898.

Home Field: Doak Field. **Seating Capacity:** 3,000. **Outfield Dimensions:** LF—340, CF—400, RF—340. **Press Box Telephone:** (919) 515-7643.

NORTHEAST LOUISIANA Indians

Conference: Southland.

Mailing Address: 308 Stadium Dr., Monroe, LA 71209.

Head Coach: Smoke Laval. **Assistant Coaches:** Brad Holland, Everett Russell, Stacey Wilcox. **Telephone:** (318) 342-5395. ■ **Baseball SID:** Troy Mitchell. **Telephone:** (318) 342-5463. **FAX:** (318) 342-5464.

NORTHEASTERN Huskies

Conference: America East.

Mailing Address: 360 Huntington Ave., Boston, MA 02115.

Head Coach: Neil McPhee. **Assistant Coach:** Matt Noone. **Telephone:** (617) 373-3657. ■ **Baseball SID:** Jack Grinold. **Telephone:** (617) 373-2691. **FAX:** (617) 373-3152.

NORTHERN ILLINOIS Huskies

Conference: Mid-American (West).

Mailing Address: 112 Evans Fieldhouse, DeKalb, IL 60115.

Head Coach: Frank Del Medico. **Assistant Coaches:** Trevor Froschauer, Randy Wee, Wally Widelski. **Telephone:** (815) 753-0147. ■ **Baseball SID:** Robert Hester. **Telephone:** (815) 753-1706. **FAX:** (815) 753-9540.

NORTHERN IOWA Panthers

Conference: Missouri Valley.

Mailing Address: 23rd and College, UNI-Dome NW Upper, Cedar Falls, IA 50614.

Head Coach: Dave Schrage. **Assistant Coaches:** Brian Hood, Todd Rima, *Jack Sole. **Telephone:** (319) 273-6323. ■ **Baseball SID:** Robert Anderson. **Telephone:** (319) 273-2932. **FAX:** (319) 273-3602.

NORTHWESTERN Wildcats

Conference: Big Ten.

Mailing Address: 1501 Central St., Evanston, IL 60208.

Head Coach: Paul Stevens. **Assistant Coaches:** Joe Keenan, *Ron Klein, Tim Stoddard. **Telephone:** (847) 491-4652. ■ **Baseball SID:** Joe Stillwell. **Telephone:** (847) 491-7503. **FAX:** (847) 491-8818.

Home Field: Rocky Miller Park. **Seating Capacity:** 1,000. **Outfield Dimensions:** LF—340, CF—400, RF—340. **Press Box Telephone:** (847) 491-4200.

NORTHWESTERN STATE Demons

Conference: Southland.

Mailing Address: 112 Prather Coliseum, 398 S Jefferson, Natchitoches, LA 71497.

Head Coach: John Cohen. **Assistant Coaches:** Robert Hewes, *Sean McCann, Andrew Sawyers, Bill Wright. **Telephone:** (318) 357-4139. ■ **Baseball SID:** Dustin Eubanks. **Telephone:** (318) 357-6467. **FAX:** (318) 357-4515.

NOTRE DAME Fighting Irish

Conference: Big East.

Mailing Address: 112 Joyce Center, Notre Dame, IN 46556.

Head Coach: Paul Mainieri. **Assistant Coaches:** Cory Mee, *Brian O'Connor. **Telephone:** (219) 631-8466. ■ **Baseball SID:** Pete LaFleur. **Telephone:** (219) 631-7516. **FAX:** (219) 631-7941.

Home Field: Frank Eck Stadium. **Seating Capacity:** 2,500. **Outfield Dimensions:** LF—331, CF—401, RF—331. **Press Box Telephone:** (219) 631-9018/9476.

OHIO Bobcats

Conference: Mid-American (East).

Mailing Address: 108 Convocation Center, Richland Ave., Athens, OH 45701.

Head Coach: Joe Carbone. **Assistant Coaches:** Josh Sorge, Bill Toadvine. **Telephone:** (740) 593-1180. ■ **Baseball SID:** Kevin Zerbey. **Telephone:** (740) 593-0054. **FAX:** (740) 593-2420.

Home Field: Bob Wren Stadium. **Seating Capacity:** 3,000. **Outfield Dimensions:** LF—340, CF—405, RF—340. **Press Box Telephone:** (740) 593-0501.

OHIO STATE Buckeyes

Conference: Big Ten.

Mailing Address: 124 St. John Arena, 410 Woody Hayes Dr., Columbus, OH

43210.

Head Coach: Bob Todd. **Assistant Coaches:** Pat Bangston, *Greg Cypret, Brian Mannino. **Telephone:** (614) 292-1075. ■ **Baseball SID:** Greg Aylsworth. **Telephone:** (614) 292-6861. **FAX:** (614) 292-8547.

Home Field: Bill Davis Stadium. **Seating Capacity:** 4,450. **Outfield Dimensions:** LF—330, CF—400, RF—330. **Press Box Telephone:** (614) 292-0021/0024.

OKLAHOMA Sooners

Conference: Big 12.

Mailing Address: 180 W Brooks, Room 235, Norman, OK 73019.

Head Coach: Larry Cochell. **Assistant Coaches:** Brandon Kent, Bill Mosiello, Aric Thomas, Jackson Todd. **Telephone:** (405) 325-8354. ■ **Baseball SID:** Bob Jarvis. **Telephone:** (405) 325-8349. **FAX:** (405) 325-7623.

Home Field: L. Dale Mitchell Park. **Seating Capacity:** 2,700. **Outfield Dimensions:** LF—335, CF—411, RF—335. **Press Box Telephone:** (405) 325-8363.

OKLAHOMA STATE Cowboys

Conference: Big 12.

Mailing Address: 202 Gallagher-Iba Arena, Stillwater, OK 74078.

Head Coach: Tom Holliday. **Assistant Coaches:** John Farrell, Robbie Wine. **Telephone:** (405) 744-5849. ■ **Baseball SID:** Thomas Samuel. **Telephone:** (405) 744-5843. **FAX:** (405) 744-7754.

Home Field: Allie P. Reynolds Stadium. **Seating Capacity:** 3,821. **Outfield Dimensions:** LF—330, CF—400, RF—330. **Press Box Telephone:** (405) 744-5757.

OLD DOMINION Monarchs

Conference: Colonial Athletic.

Mailing Address: Athletic Administration Bldg., Norfolk, VA 23529.

Head Coach: Tony Guzzo. **Assistant Coaches:** Ryan Morris, Dan Nellum, *Juan Ranero. **Telephone:** (757) 683-4230. ■ **Baseball SID:** Carol Hudson. **Telephone:** (757) 683-3372. **FAX:** (757) 683-3119.

Home Field: Bud Metheny Stadium. **Seating Capacity:** 2,500. **Outfield Dimensions:** LF—320, CF—395, RF—320. **Press Box Telephone:** (757) 683-5036.

ORAL ROBERTS Golden Eagles

Conference: Mid-Continent.

Mailing Address: 7777 S Lewis Ave., Tulsa, OK 74171.

Head Coach: Sunny Galloway. **Assistant Coaches:** *Bob Miller, Tim Walton. **Telephone:** (918) 495-7131. ■ **Baseball SID:** Gary Brown. **Telephone:** (918) 495-7094. **FAX:** (918) 495-7123.

OREGON STATE Beavers

Conference: Pacific-10.

Mailing Address: Gill Coliseum, Room 127, Corvallis, OR 97331.

Head Coach: Pat Casey. **Assistant Coaches:** Gary Henderson, *Dan Spencer. **Telephone:** (541) 737-5738. ■ **Baseball SID:** Kip Carlson. **Telephone:** (541) 737-3720. **FAX:** (541) 737-3072.

Home Field: Goss Stadium/Coleman Field. **Seating Capacity:** 2,310. **Outfield Dimensions:** LF—330, CF—400, RF—330. **Press Box Telephone:** (541) 737-7475.

PACE Setters

Conference: Independent.

Mailing Address: 861 Bedford Rd., Pleasantville, NY 10570.

Head Coach: Fred Calaicone. **Assistant Coaches:** Chris Cavanaugh, Tim Kelly. **Telephone:** (914) 773-3413. ■ **Baseball SID:** Nick Renda. **Telephone:** (914) 773-3888. **FAX:** (914) 773-3491.

PACIFIC Tigers

Conference: Big West.

Mailing Address: 3601 Pacific Ave., Stockton, CA 95211.

Head Coach: Quincey Noble. **Assistant Coaches:** Joe Moreno, Jim Yanko. **Telephone:** (209) 946-2709. ■ **Baseball SID:** Mike Dalgety. **Telephone:** (209) 946-2479. **FAX:** (209) 946-2757.

Home Field: Billy Hebert Field. **Seating Capacity:** 3,500. **Outfield Dimensions:** LF—325, CF—390, RF—330. **Press Box Telephone:** (209) 944-5951.

PENNSYLVANIA Quakers

Conference: Ivy League (Gehrig).

Mailing Address: Weightman Hall South, 235 S 33rd St., Philadelphia, PA 19104.

Head Coach: Bob Seddon. **Assistant Coaches:** Bill Wagner, Dan Young. **Telephone:** (215) 898-6282. ■ **Baseball SID:** Carla Shultzberg. **Telephone:** (215) 898-1748. **FAX:** (215) 898-1747.

PENN STATE Nittany Lions

Conference: Big Ten.

Mailing Address: 112 Bryce Jordan Center, University Park, PA 16802.

Head Coach: Joe Hindelang. **Assistant Coaches:** *Randy Ford, Dave Jameson, Jon Ramsey. **Telephone:** (814) 863-0239.

Home Field: Beaver Field. **Seating Capacity:** 1,000. **Outfield Dimensions:** LF—350, CF—400, RF—350. **Press Box Telephone:** None.

PEPPERDINE Waves

Conference: West Coast (Coast).
Mailing Address: 24255 Pacific Coast Hwy., Malibu, CA 90263.
Head Coach: Frank Sanchez. **Assistant Coaches:** *Dave Esquer, David Rhoades. **Telephone:** (310) 456-4199. ■ **Baseball SID:** Al Barba. **Telephone:** (310) 456-4455. **FAX:** (310) 456-4322.
Home Field: Eddy D. Field Stadium. **Seating Capacity:** 2,200. **Outfield Dimensions:** LF—330, CF—400, RF—330. **Press Box Telephone:** (310) 456-4598.

PITTSBURGH Panthers

Conference: Big East.
Mailing Address: P.O. Box 7436, Pittsburgh, PA 15213.
Head Coach: Joe Jordano. **Assistant Coaches:** Joel Dombkowski, Lou Schaper. **Telephone:** (412) 648-8208. ■ **Baseball SID:** Nicole Radu. **Telephone:** (412) 648-8240. **FAX:** (412) 648-8248.
Home Field: Trees Field. **Seating Capacity:** 500. **Outfield Dimensions:** LF—328, CF—380, RF—335. **Press Box Telephone:** None.

PORTLAND Pilots

Conference: West Coast (West).
Mailing Address: 5000 N Willamette Blvd., Portland, OR 97203.
Head Coach: Chris Sperry. **Assistant Coaches:** Ryan Brust, Aaron Vorachek, Billy Winters. **Telephone:** (503) 943-7707. ■ **Baseball SID:** Loren Wohlgemuth. **Telephone:** (503) 943-7439. **FAX:** (503) 943-7242.

PRAIRIE VIEW A&M Panthers

Conference: Southwestern Athletic (West).
Mailing Address: P.O. Box 97, Prairie View, TX 77446.
Head Coach: John Tankersley. **Assistant Coaches:** Matt Berly, Raymond Burgess. **Telephone:** (409) 857-4290. ■ **Baseball SID:** Harlan Robinson. **Telephone:** (409) 857-2114. **FAX:** (409) 857-2408.

PRINCETON Tigers

Conference: Ivy League (Gehrig).
Mailing Address: Jadwin Gym, Princeton, NJ 08544.
Head Coach: Scott Bradley. **Assistant Coach:** Tom Crowley. **Telephone:** (609) 258-5059. ■ **Baseball SID:** Matt Ciciarelli. **Telephone:** (609) 258-3568. **FAX:** (609) 258-2399.

PROVIDENCE Friars

Conference: Big East.
Mailing Address: River Avenue, Providence, RI 02918.
Head Coach: Charlie Hickey. **Assistant Coaches:** *Jonathan Krot, John Navilliat, Sean O'Connor. **Telephone:** (401) 865-2273. ■ **Baseball SID:** Tim Connor. **Telephone:** (401) 865-2272. **FAX:** (401) 865-2583.
Home Field: Hendricken Field. **Seating Capacity:** 1,500. **Outfield Dimensions:** LF—330, CF—402, RF—301. **Press Box Telephone:** None.

PURDUE Boilermakers

Conference: Big Ten.
Mailing Address: 1790 Mackey Arena, West Lafayette, IN 47907.
Head Coach: Doug Schreiber. **Assistant Coaches:** Gary Adcock, *Todd Murphy, Rob Smith. **Telephone:** (765) 494-3217. ■ **Baseball SID:** Brett Swick. **Telephone:** (765) 494-3201. **FAX:** (765) 494-5447.
Home Field: Lambert Field. **Seating Capacity:** 1,100. **Outfield Dimensions:** LF—343, CF—400, RF—342. **Press Box Telephone:** (765) 494-1522.

QUINNIPIAC Braves

Conference: Northeast (North).
Mailing Address: 275 Mount Carmel Ave., Hamden, CT 06518.
Head Coach: Joe Mattei. **Assistant Coaches:** Tim Belcher, Rob Manzo. **Telephone:** (203) 287-3357. ■ **Baseball SID:** Sean Paradis. **Telephone:** (203) 281-8625. **FAX:** (203) 281-8716.

RADFORD Highlanders

Conference: Big South.
Mailing Address: P.O. Box 6913, Radford, VA 24142.
Head Coach: Lew Kent. **Assistant Coaches:** Curtis Brown, *Wayne Smith. **Telephone:** (540) 831-5881. ■ **Baseball SID:** Chris King. **Telephone:** (540) 831-5211. **FAX:** (540) 831-5036.

RHODE ISLAND Rams

Conference: Atlantic-10 (East).
Mailing Address: 3 Keaney Rd., Suite 1, Kingston, RI 02881.
Head Coach: Frank Leoni. **Assistant Coaches:** *John LaRose, Brian Lavoie, Pat Sullivan. **Telephone:** (401) 874-4550. ■ **Baseball SID:** Unavailable. **Telephone:** (401) 874-2409. **FAX:** (401) 874-5354.

RICE Owls

Conference: Western Athletic.
Mailing Address: P.O. Box 1892, MS 548, Houston, TX 77251.

Head Coach: Wayne Graham. Assistant Coaches: Chris Feris, *Jon Prather. Telephone: (713) 527-6022. ■ Baseball SID: Bill Cousins. Telephone: (713) 527-4034, ext. 3. FAX: (713) 527-6019.

Home Field: Cameron Field. Seating Capacity: 2,000. Outfield Dimensions: LF—330, CF—400, RF—330. Press Box Telephone: (713) 527-4931.

RICHMOND Spiders
Conference: Colonial Athletic.
Mailing Address: Robins Center, Richmond, VA 23173.
Head Coach: Ron Atkins. Assistant Coaches: *Mark McQueen, Tag Montague. Telephone: (804) 289-8391. ■ Baseball SID: Phil Stanton. Telephone: (804) 289-8320. FAX: (804) 289-8820.

RIDER Broncs
Conference: Metro Atlantic (South).
Mailing Address: 2083 Lawrenceville Road, Lawrenceville, NJ 08648.
Head Coach: Sonny Pittaro. Assistant Coaches: Tom Petroff, Jeff Plunkett. Telephone: (609) 896-5055. ■ Baseball SID: Bud Focht. Telephone: (609) 896-5138. FAX: (609) 896-0341.

RUTGERS Scarlet Knights
Conference: Big East.
Mailing Address: 83 Rockefeller Rd., Piscataway, NJ 08854.
Head Coach: Fred Hill. Assistant Coaches: Tom Baxter, *Glen Gardner, Rob Vallie. Telephone: (732) 445-3553. ■ Baseball SID: John Wooding. Telephone: (732) 445-4200. FAX: (732) 445-3063.

Home Field: Class of '53 Stadium. Seating Capacity: 1,500. Outfield Dimensions: LF—330, CF—410, RF—320. Press Box Telephone: None.

SACRAMENTO STATE Hornets
Conference: Big West.
Mailing Address: 6000 J St., Sacramento, CA 95819.
Head Coach: John Smith. Assistant Coaches: Jim Barr, *Brian Hewitt, Buck Martinez. Telephone: (916) 278-7225. ■ Baseball SID: Brian Berger. Telephone: (916) 278-6896. FAX: (916) 278-5429.

Home Field: Hornet Field. Seating Capacity: 1,500. Outfield Dimensions: LF—333, CF—400, RF—333. Press Box Telephone: None.

SACRED HEART Pioneers
Conference: Northeast.
Mailing Address: 5151 Park Ave., Fairfield, CT 06432.
Head Coach: Nick Giaquinto. Assistant Coaches: Mark Caron, *Lew DeLuca, Frank Fedak. Telephone: (203) 365-7632. ■ Baseball SID: Matt Bucci. Telephone: (203) 396-8125. FAX: (203) 371-7889.

ST. BONAVENTURE Bonnies
Conference: Atlantic-10 (East).
Mailing Address: Reilly Center, St. Bonaventure, NY 14778.
Head Coach: Larry Sudbrook. Assistant Coach: Ryan Rademacker. Telephone: (716) 375-2641. ■ Baseball SID: Steve Mest. Telephone: (716) 375-2319. FAX: (716) 375-2383.

ST. FRANCIS Terriers
Conference: Northeast (North).
Mailing Address: 180 Remsen St., Brooklyn Heights, NY 11201.
Head Coach: Frank Del George. Assistant Coaches: Tony Barone, *Mike Lopiparo. Telephone: (718) 489-5365. ■ Baseball SID: Jim Hoffman. Telephone: (718) 489-5489. FAX: (718) 797-2140.

ST. JOHN'S Red Storm
Conference: Big East.
Mailing Address: 8000 Utopia Pkwy., Jamaica, NY 11439.
Head Coach: Ed Blankmeyer. Assistant Coaches: Mike Maerten, *Kevin McMullan. Telephone: (718) 990-6148. ■ Baseball SID: Chris DeLorenzo. Telephone: (718) 990-1521. FAX: (718) 969-8468.

Home Field: McCallen Field. Seating Capacity: 1,000. Outfield Dimensions: LF—340, CF—400, RF—340. Press Box Telephone: (718) 990-6053.

ST. JOSEPH'S Hawks
Conference: Atlantic-10 (East).
Mailing Address: 5600 City Ave., Philadelphia, PA 19131.
Head Coach: Jim Ertel. Assistant Coaches: Brian Kenny, Ken Krsolovic, Jack Stanczak. Telephone: (610) 660-1718. ■ Baseball SID: Chris Convery. Telephone: (610) 660-1727. FAX: (610) 660-1724.

SAINT LOUIS Billikens
Conference: Conference USA.
Mailing Address: 221 N Grand Blvd., St. Louis, MO 63103.
Head Coach: Bob Hughes. Assistant Coaches: Mike Barger, *Todd Whaley. Telephone: (314) 977-3172. ■ Baseball SID: Chuck Young. Telephone: (314) 977-3346. FAX: (314) 977-7193.

Home Field: Billiken Sports Center. Seating Capacity: 1,000. Outfield Dimensions: LF—330, CF—395, RF—330. Press Box Telephone: Unavailable.

ST. MARY'S Gaels
Conference: West Coast (West).

Mailing Address: 1928 St. Mary's Rd., Moraga, CA 94575.
Head Coach: John Baptista. **Assistant Coaches:** Joe Millette, Ted Turkington. **Telephone:** (925) 631-4400. ■ **Baseball SID:** Andy McDowell. **Telephone:** (925) 631-4402. **FAX:** (925) 631-4405.

ST. PETER'S Peacocks
Conference: Metro Atlantic (South).
Mailing Address: 2641 Kennedy Blvd., Jersey City, NJ 07306.
Head Coach: Dan Olear. **Assistant Coaches:** Anthony Sciarrillo, Chris Terranova. **Telephone:** (201) 915-9459. ■ **Baseball SID:** Anthony Sciarrillo. **Telephone:** (201) 915-9101. **FAX:** (201) 915-9102.

SAM HOUSTON STATE Bearkats
Conference: Southland.
Mailing Address: P.O. Box 2268, Huntsville, TX 77341.
Head Coach: John Skeeters. **Assistant Coach:** Carlo Gott. **Telephone:** (409) 294-1731. ■ **Baseball SID:** Paul Ridings. **Telephone:** (409) 294-1764. **FAX:** (409) 294-3538.

SAMFORD Bulldogs
Conference: Trans America Athletic.
Mailing Address: 800 Lakeshore Dr., Birmingham, AL 35229.
Head Coach: Tim Parenton. **Assistant Coaches:** Todd Buczek, Gerald Tuck. **Telephone:** (205) 870-2134. ■ **Baseball SID:** Unavailable. **Telephone:** (205) 870-2966. **FAX:** (205) 870-2545.

SAN DIEGO Toreros
Conference: West Coast (Coast).
Mailing Address: 5998 Alcala Park, San Diego, CA 92110.
Head Coach: Rick Hill. **Assistant Coaches:** Chris Cannizzaro, Rick Hirtensteiner, Sean Kenny. **Telephone:** (619) 260-8894. ■ **Baseball SID:** Ryan McCrary. **Telephone:** (619) 260-4745. **FAX:** (619) 292-0388.

SAN DIEGO STATE Aztecs
Conference: Western Athletic.
Mailing Address: Department of Athletics, San Diego, CA 92182.
Head Coach: Jim Dietz. **Assistant Coaches:** *Rusty Filter, Pat Oliverio, Stacy Parker. **Telephone:** (619) 594-6889. ■ **Baseball SID:** Dave Kuhn. **Telephone:** (619) 594-5547. **FAX:** (619) 582-6541.
Home Field: Tony Gwynn Stadium. **Seating Capacity:** 3,000. **Outfield Dimensions:** LF—340, CF—410, RF—340. **Press Box Telephone:** (619) 594-4103.

SAN FRANCISCO Dons
Conference: West Coast (Coast).
Mailing Address: War Memorial Gym, 2130 Fulton St., San Francisco, CA 94117.
Head Coach: Nino Giarratano. **Assistant Coaches:** *Chad Konishi, Troy Nakamura, Nate Rodriguoz. **Telephone:** (415) 422-2934. ■ **Baseball SID:** Kyle McRae. **Telephone:** (415) 422-6162. **FAX:** (415) 422-2929.

SAN JOSE STATE Spartans
Conference: Western Athletic.
Mailing Address: One Washington Square, San Jose, CA 95192.
Head Coach: Sam Piraro. **Assistant Coaches:** Dean Madsen, Doug Thurman. **Telephone:** (408) 924-1255. ■ **Baseball SID:** Hung Tsai. **Telephone:** (408) 924-1217. **FAX:** (408) 924-1291.
Home Field: Municipal Stadium. **Seating Capacity:** 5,200. **Outfield Dimensions:** LF—330, CF—400, RF—330. **Press Box Telephone:** (408) 924-7276.

SANTA CLARA Broncos
Conference: West Coast (West).
Mailing Address: 500 El Camino Real, Santa Clara, CA 95053.
Head Coach: Mike Cummins. **Assistant Coaches:** *Troy Buckley, Greg Gohr, Jeff Hipps. **Telephone:** (408) 554-4882. ■ **Baseball SID:** Jim Young. **Telephone:** (408) 554-4661. **FAX:** (408) 554-6942.
Home Field: Buck Shaw Stadium. **Seating Capacity:** 6,800. **Outfield Dimensions:** LF—350, CF—400, RF—330. **Press Box Telephone:** None.

SETON HALL Pirates
Conference: Big East.
Mailing Address: 400 S Orange Ave., South Orange, NJ 07079.
Head Coach: Mike Sheppard. **Assistant Coaches:** Fred Hopke, Ed Lyons, *Rob Sheppard. **Telephone:** (973) 761-9557. ■ **Baseball SID:** Pat McBride. **Telephone:** (973) 761-9493. **FAX:** (973) 761-9061.
Home Field: Owen T. Carroll Field. **Seating Capacity:** 1,500. **Outfield Dimensions:** LF—335, CF—400, RF—330. **Press Box Telephone:** None.

SIENA Saints
Conference: Metro Atlantic (North).
Mailing Address: 515 Loudon Rd., Loudonville, NY 12211.
Head Coach: Tony Rossi. **Assistant Coaches:** Tony Curro, Paul Thompson, Ira Tilton. **Telephone:** (518) 786-5044. ■ **Baseball SID:** Jason Rich. **Telephone:** (518) 783-2377. **FAX:** (518) 783-2992.

SOUTH ALABAMA Jaguars
Conference: Sun Belt.

Mailing Address: 1151 HPELS Bldg., Mobile, AL 36688.
Head Coach: Steve Kittrell. Assistant Coaches: Ron Pelletier, Ronnie Powell, Scott Southard. Telephone: (334) 460-6876. ■ Baseball SID: Matt Smith. Telephone: (334) 460-7035. FAX: (334) 460-7297.
Home Field: Eddie Stanky Field. Seating Capacity: 3,500. Outfield Dimensions: LF—330, CF—400, RF—330. Press Box Telephone: (334) 460-7126.

SOUTH CAROLINA Gamecocks
Conference: Southeastern (East).
Mailing Address: 1300 Rosewood Dr., Columbia, SC 29208.
Head Coach: Ray Tanner. Assistant Coaches: Stuart Lake, Jerry Meyers, *Jim Toman. Telephone: (803) 777-0116. ■ Baseball SIDs: John Butts, Tom Price. Telephone: (803) 777-5204. FAX: (803) 777-2967.
Home Field: Sarge Frye Field. Seating Capacity: 4,000. Outfield Dimensions: LF—325, CF—390, RF—320. Press Box Telephone: (803) 777-6648.

SOUTH FLORIDA Bulls
Conference: Conference USA.
Mailing Address: 4202 E Fowler Ave., PED 214, Tampa, FL 33620.
Head Coach: Eddie Cardieri. Assistant Coaches: Russ McNickle, Bryan Peters, Tom Reidy. Telephone: (813) 974-2504. ■ Baseball SID: Fred Huff. Telephone: (813) 974-4087. FAX: (813) 974-5328.
Home Field: Red McEwen Field. Seating Capacity: 1,500. Outfield Dimensions: LF—340, CF—400, RF—340. Press Box Telephone: (813) 974-3604.

SOUTHEAST MISSOURI STATE Indians
Conference: Ohio Valley.
Mailing Address: One University Plaza, Cape Girardeau, MO 63701.
Head Coach: Mark Hogan. Assistant Coaches: Greg Goff, Mark Lewis, Brian Schaefer. Telephone: (573) 651-2645. ■ Baseball SID: Marlin Curnutt. Telephone: (573) 651-2937. FAX: (573) 651-2810.

SOUTHEASTERN LOUISIANA Lions
Conference: Southland.
Mailing Address: SLU Station 309, Hammond, LA 70402.
Head Coach: Greg Marten. Assistant Coaches: Johnny Brechtel, Mark Gosnell, Ronnie Kornick. Telephone: (504) 549-2896. ■ Baseball SID: Barry Niemeyer. Telephone: (504) 549-3774. FAX: (504) 549-3495.

SOUTHERN Jaguars
Conference: Southwestern Athletic (West).
Mailing Address: P.O. Box 1085D, Baton Rouge, LA 70813.
Head Coach: Roger Cador. Assistant Coaches: Barret Rey, *Don Thomas. Telephone: (225) 771-2513. ■ Baseball SID: Roderick Moseley. Telephone: (225) 771-2601. FAX: (225) 771-2896.

SOUTHERN CALIFORNIA Trojans
Conference: Pacific-10.
Mailing Address: HER-103, University Park, Los Angeles, CA 90089.
Head Coach: Mike Gillespie. Assistant Coaches: Rob Klein, Andy Nieto, *John Savage. Telephone: (213) 740-5762. ■ Baseball SID: Roger Horne. Telephone: (213) 740-8480. FAX: (213) 740-7584.
Home Field: Dedeaux Field. Seating Capacity: 1,800. Outfield Dimensions: LF—335, CF—395, RF—335. Press Box Telephone: (213) 748-3449.

SOUTHERN ILLINOIS Salukis
Conference: Missouri Valley.
Mailing Address: SIU Arena, Lingle Hall, Room 130D, Carbondale, IL 62901.
Head Coach: Dan Callahan. Assistant Coaches: Dan Davis, *Ken Henderson, Carl Kochan. Telephone: (618) 453-2802. ■ Baseball SID: Gene Green. Telephone: (618) 453-5470. FAX: (618) 536-2152.
Home Field: Abe Martin Field. Seating Capacity: 2,000. Outfield Dimensions: LF—340, CF—390, RF—340. Press Box Telephone: (618) 453-3794.

SOUTHERN MISSISSIPPI Golden Eagles
Conference: Conference USA.
Mailing Address: P.O. Box 5161, Hattiesburg, MS 39406.
Head Coach: Corky Palmer. Assistant Coaches: Lane Burroughs, Michael Federico, *Dan Wagner. Telephone: (601) 266-5017. ■ Baseball SID: Ricky Hazel. Telephone: (601) 266-4503. FAX: (601) 266-4507.
Home Field: Pete Taylor Park. Seating Capacity: 3,678. Outfield Dimensions: LF—365, CF—400, RF—365. Press Box Telephone: (601) 266-5684.

SOUTHERN UTAH Thunderbirds
Conference: Independent.
Mailing Address: 351 W Center St., Cedar City, UT 84720.
Head Coach: DeLynn Corry. Assistant Coaches: Willie Mosher, Kurt Palmer. Telephone: (435) 586-7932. ■ Baseball SID: Steve Johnson. Telephone: (435) 586-7752. FAX: (435) 865-8037.

SOUTHWEST MISSOURI STATE Bears
Conference: Missouri Valley.
Mailing Address: 901 S National Ave., Springfield, MO 65804.

Head Coach: Keith Guttin. **Assistant Coaches:** *Paul Evans, Jamie Sheets, Brent Thomas. **Telephone:** (417) 836-5424. ■ **Baseball SIDs:** Mark Stillwell, Neal Williams. **Telephone:** (417) 836-5402. **FAX:** (417) 836-4868.

SOUTHWEST TEXAS STATE Bobcats
Conference: Southland.
Mailing Address: Jowers Center, Room A-118, San Marcos, TX 78666.
Head Coach: Howard Bushong. **Assistant Coaches:** *Monte Cain, Marcus Hendry. **Telephone:** (512) 245-3586. ■ **Baseball SID:** Blair Cash. **Telephone:** (512) 245-2966. **FAX:** (512) 245-2967.

SOUTHWESTERN LOUISIANA Ragin' Cajuns
Conference: Sun Belt.
Mailing Address: 201 Reinhardt Dr., Lafayette, LA 70506.
Head Coach: Tony Robichaux. **Assistant Coaches:** Anthony Babineaux, Jason Gonzales, *Wade Simoneaux. **Telephone:** (318) 482-6189. ■ **Baseball SID:** Jeff Conrad. **Telephone:** (318) 482-6330. **FAX:** (318) 482-6649.
Home Field: Moore Field. **Seating Capacity:** 3,500. **Outfield Dimensions:** LF—330, CF—400, RF—330. **Press Box Telephone:** (318) 482-6331.

STANFORD Cardinal
Conference: Pacific-10.
Mailing Address: Department of Athletics, Stanford, CA 94305.
Head Coach: Mark Marquess. **Assistant Coaches:** Tom Dunton, Mark O'Brien, *Dean Stotz. **Telephone:** (650) 723-4528. ■ **Baseball SID:** Scott Leykam. **Telephone:** (650) 723-0996. **FAX:** (650) 725-2957.
Home Field: Sunken Diamond. **Seating Capacity:** 4,000. **Outfield Dimensions:** LF—335, CF—400, RF—335. **Press Box Telephone:** (650) 723-4629.

STETSON Hatters
Conference: Trans America Athletic.
Mailing Address: 421 N Woodland Blvd., Unit 8317, DeLand, FL 32720.
Head Coach: Pete Dunn. **Assistant Coaches:** Derek Johnson, Larry Jones, *Tom Riginos. **Telephone:** (904) 822-8120. ■ **Baseball SID:** Cris Belvin. **Telephone:** (904) 822-8131. **FAX:** (904) 822-8132.
Home Field: Melching Field. **Seating Capacity:** 1,200. **Outfield Dimensions:** LF—335, CF—400, RF—335. **Press Box Telephone:** (904) 736-7363.

TEMPLE Owls
Conference: Atlantic-10 (East).
Mailing Address: Vivacqua Hall, 4th Floor, Philadelphia, PA 19122.
Head Coach: Skip Wilson. **Assistant Coaches:** Ed Ross, Steve Young. **Telephone:** (215) 204-7447. ■ **Baseball SID:** Jon Fuller. **Telephone:** (215) 204-4824. **FAX:** (215) 204-7499.

TENNESSEE Volunteers
Conference: Southeastern (East).
Mailing Address: P.O. Box 15016, Knoxville, TN 37901.
Head Coach: Rod Delmonico. **Assistant Coaches:** *Randy Mazey, Larry Simcox. **Telephone:** (423) 974-2057. ■ **Baseball SID:** Jeff Muir. **Telephone:** (423) 974-1212. **FAX:** (423) 974-1269.
Home Field: Lindsey Nelson Stadium. **Seating Capacity:** 4,500. **Outfield Dimensions:** LF—335, CF—404, RF—330. **Press Box Telephone:** (423) 974-3376.

TENNESSEE-MARTIN Skyhawks
Conference: Ohio Valley.
Mailing Address: 40 Skyhawk Fieldhouse, Martin, TN 38238.
Head Coach: Victor "Bubba" Cates. **Assistant Coach:** Michael Spaulding. **Telephone:** (901) 587-7337. ■ **Baseball SID:** Lee Wilmot. **Telephone:** (901) 587-7630. **FAX:** (901) 587-7624.

TENNESSEE TECH Golden Eagles
Conference: Ohio Valley.
Mailing Address: P.O. Box 5057, Cookeville, TN 38505.
Head Coach: Mike Maack. **Assistant Coaches:** *Donley Canary, Brent Chaffin, Pat Portugal. **Telephone:** (931) 372-3925. ■ **Baseball SID:** Rob Schabert. **Telephone:** (931) 372-3088. **FAX:** (931) 372-6139.

TEXAS Longhorns
Conference: Big 12.
Mailing Address: 2101 San Jacinto, Bellmont No. 327, Austin, TX 78705.
Head Coach: Augie Garrido. **Assistant Coaches:** *Tommy Harmon, Burt Hooton. **Telephone:** (512) 471-5732. ■ **Baseball SID:** Mike Forcucci. **Telephone:** (512) 471-6039. **FAX:** (512) 471-6040.
Home Field: Disch-Falk Field. **Seating Capacity:** 6,649. **Outfield Dimensions:** LF—340, CF—400, RF—325. **Press Box Telephone:** (512) 471-1146.

TEXAS-ARLINGTON Mavericks
Conference: Southland.
Mailing Address: P.O. Box 19079, Arlington, TX 76019.
Head Coach: Butch McBroom. **Assistant Coaches:** Clay Gould, Ron Liggett. **Telephone:** (817) 272-2032. ■ **Baseball SID:** Steve Weller. **Telephone:** (817) 272-2239. **FAX:** (817) 272-2254.
Home Field: Allan Saxe Stadium. **Seating Capacity:** 1,200. **Outfield Dimensions:** LF—330, CF—400, RF—330. **Press Box Telephone:** (817) 460-3522.

TEXAS-PAN AMERICAN Broncs

Conference: Independent.
Mailing Address: 1201 W University Dr., Edinburg, TX 78539.
Head Coach: Reggi Tredaway. **Assistant Coaches:** Mike Brown, Mick Tosch, Kiki Trevino. **Telephone:** (956) 381-2235. ■ **Baseball SID:** Jim McKone. **Telephone:** (956) 381-2240. **FAX:** (956) 381-2398.

TEXAS-SAN ANTONIO Roadrunners

Conference: Southland.
Mailing Address: 6900 NW Loop 1604, San Antonio, TX 78249.
Head Coach: Mickey Lashley. **Assistant Coaches:** Chip Durham, Jeremy Tyson. **Telephone:** (210) 458-4805. ■ **Baseball SID:** Rick Nixon. **Telephone:** (210) 458-4551. **FAX:** (210) 458-4569.

TEXAS A&M Aggies

Conference: Big 12.
Mailing Address: P.O. Box 30017, College Station, TX 77842.
Head Coach: Mark Johnson. **Assistant Coaches:** David Coleman, *Jim Lawler. **Telephone:** (409) 845-9534. ■ **Baseball SID:** Alan Cannon. **Telephone:** (409) 845-5725. **FAX:** (409) 845-0564.
Home Field: Olsen Field. **Seating Capacity:** 7,053. **Outfield Dimensions:** LF—330, CF—400, RF—330. **Press Box Telephone:** (409) 845-4810.

TEXAS CHRISTIAN Horned Frogs

Conference: Western Athletic.
Mailing Address: P.O. Box 297600, Fort Worth, TX 76129.
Head Coach: Lance Brown. **Assistant Coaches:** Craig Farmer, Scott Malone, *Donnie Watson. **Telephone:** (817) 257-7985. ■ **Baseball SID:** Trey Carmichael. **Telephone:** (817) 257-7969. **FAX:** (817) 257-7964.
Home Field: TCU Diamond. **Seating Capacity:** 1,500. **Outfield Dimensions:** LF—330, CF—390, RF—320. **Press Box Telephone:** (817) 257-7966.

TEXAS SOUTHERN Tigers

Conference: Southwestern Athletic (West).
Mailing Address: 3100 Cleburne Ave., Houston, TX 77004.
Head Coach: Candy Robinson. **Assistant Coaches:** Arthur Jenkins, Ken Mack, *Brian White. **Telephone:** (713) 313-7993. ■ **Baseball SID:** Gary Abernathy. **Telephone:** (713) 313-7432. **FAX:** (713) 313-7273.

TEXAS TECH Red Raiders

Conference: Big 12.
Mailing Address: Sixth and Red Raider Ave., Box 43021, Lubbock, TX 79409.
Head Coach: Larry Hays. **Assistant Coaches:** *Frank Anderson, Greg Evans, Marty Lamb. **Telephone:** (806) 742-3355. ■ **Baseball SID:** Greg Hotchkiss. **Telephone:** (806) 742-2770. **FAX:** (806) 742-1970.
Home Field: Dan Law Field. **Seating Capacity:** 5,614. **Outfield Dimensions:** LF—330, CF—405, RF—330. **Press Box Telephone:** (806) 742-3688.

TOLEDO Rockets

Conference: Mid-American (West).
Mailing Address: 2801 W Bancroft St., Toledo, OH 43606.
Head Coach: Joe Kruzel. **Assistant Coaches:** Jim Kurbacki, Steve Parrill. **Telephone:** (419) 530-2526. ■ **Baseball SID:** Angela Russo. **Telephone:** (419) 530-3790. **FAX:** (419) 530-3795.

TOWSON STATE Tigers

Conference: America East.
Mailing Address: 8000 York Rd., Towson, MD 21252.
Head Coach: Mike Gottlieb. **Assistant Coaches:** Alan El-Amin, Liam Healy. **Telephone:** (410) 830-3775. ■ **Baseball SID:** Dan O'Connell. **Telephone:** (410) 830-2232. **FAX:** (410) 830-3861.

TROY STATE Trojans

Conference: Trans America Athletic.
Mailing Address: Davis Field House, Troy State University, Troy, AL 36082.
Head Coach: John Mayotte. **Assistant Coaches:** Jerry Martinez, *Rod McWhorter. **Telephone:** (334) 670-3489. ■ **Baseball SID:** Richard Weaver. **Telephone:** (334) 670-3229. **FAX:** (334) 670-3278.

TULANE Green Wave

Conference: Conference USA.
Mailing Address: Wilson Center, Ben Weiner Dr., New Orleans, LA 70118.
Head Coach: Rick Jones. **Assistant Coaches:** Buddy Gouldsmith, Benny Latino, *Jim Schlossnagle. **Telephone:** (504) 862-8239. ■ **Baseball SID:** Krisden Wunsch. **Telephone:** (504) 865-5506. **FAX:** (504) 865-5512.
Home Field: Turchin Stadium. **Seating Capacity:** 5,000. **Outfield Dimensions:** LF—325, CF—400, RF—325. **Press Box Telephone:** (504) 862-8224.

UTAH Utes

Conference: Western Athletic.
Mailing Address: John Huntsman Center, Salt Lake City, UT 84112.
Head Coach: Tim Esmay. **Assistant Coaches:** Todd Delnoce, John Flores, Joe Godri. **Telephone:** (801) 581-3526. ■ **Baseball SID:** Whitney Vernieuw. **Telephone:** (801) 581-3511. **FAX:** (801) 581-4358.
Home Field: Franklin Covey Field. **Seating Capacity:** 12,000. **Outfield

Dimensions: LF—345, CF—420, RF—315. **Press Box Telephone:** (801) 464-6938.

VALPARAISO Crusaders
Conference: Mid-Continent.
Mailing Address: Athletic Recreation Center, Valparaiso, IN 46383.
Head Coach: Paul Twenge. **Assistant Coaches:** Tim Holmes, *John Olson, Ryan Trucke. **Telephone:** (219) 464-5239. ■ **Baseball SID:** Bill Rogers. **Telephone:** (219) 464-5232. **FAX:** (219) 464-5762.

VANDERBILT Commodores
Conference: Southeastern (East).
Mailing Address: 2601 Jess Neely Dr., Nashville, TN 37212.
Head Coach: Roy Mewbourne. **Assistant Coaches:** John Barlowe, *Ross Jones. **Telephone:** (615) 322-4122. ■ **Baseball SID:** Kristi Strang. **Telephone:** (615) 322-4121. **FAX:** (615) 343-7064.
Home Field: McGugin Field. **Seating Capacity:** 1,200. **Outfield Dimensions:** LF—325, CF—380, RF—318. **Press Box Telephone:** (615) 320-0436.

VERMONT Catamounts
Conference: America East.
Mailing Address: 226 Patrick Gym, Burlington, VT 05405.
Head Coach: Bill Currier. **Assistant Coach:** Len Whitehouse. **Telephone:** (802) 656-7701. ■ **Baseball SID:** Bruce Bosley. **Telephone:** (802) 656-1109. **FAX:** (802) 656-8328.

VILLANOVA Wildcats
Conference: Big East.
Mailing Address: 800 Lancaster Ave., Jake Nevin Field House, Villanova, PA 19085.
Head Coach: George Bennett. **Assistant Coaches:** Doc Kennedy, Lou Soscia. **Telephone:** (610) 519-4529. ■ **Baseball SID:** Jonathan Gust. **Telephone:** (610) 519-4120. **FAX:** (610) 519-7323.
Home Field: McGeehan Field. **Seating Capacity:** 2,000. **Outfield Dimensions:** LF—332, CF—402, RF—332. **Press Box Telephone:** None.

VIRGINIA Cavaliers
Conference: Atlantic Coast.
Mailing Address: P.O. Box 3785, Charlottesville, VA 22903.
Head Coach: Dennis Womack. **Assistant Coaches:** Steve Heon, Aaron Weintraub, *Steve Whitmyer. **Telephone:** (804) 982-5775. ■ **Baseball SID:** Larry Little. **Telephone:** (804) 982-5535. **FAX:** (804) 982-5525.
Home Field: Virginia Baseball Field. **Seating Capacity:** 2,300. **Outfield Dimensions:** LF—352, CF—408, RF—352. **Press Box Telephone:** (804) 982-9262.

VIRGINIA COMMONWEALTH Rams
Conference: Colonial Athletic.
Mailing Address: P.O. Box 842003, Richmond, VA 23284.
Head Coach: Paul Keyes. **Assistant Coaches:** Jay Ashcraft., *Chris Finwood, Hank Kraft. **Telephone:** (804) 828-4820. ■ **Baseball SID:** Mike May. **Telephone:** (804) 828-7000. **FAX:** (804) 828-9428.

VIRGINIA MILITARY INSTITUTE Keydets
Conference: Southern.
Mailing Address: Cameron Hall, Lexington, VA 24450.
Head Coach: Scott Gines. **Assistant Coaches:** *Chris Chernisky, Jeff Kinne. **Telephone:** (540) 464-7609. ■ **Baseball SID:** Pete Lefresne. **Telephone:** (540) 464-7253. **FAX:** (540) 464-7583.

VIRGINIA TECH Hokies
Conference: Atlantic-10 (West).
Mailing Address: 364 Jamerson Center, Blacksburg, VA 24061.
Head Coach: Chuck Hartman. **Assistant Coaches:** Jon Hartness, *Jay Phillips. **Telephone:** (540) 231-3671. ■ **Baseball SID:** Dave Smith. **Telephone:** (540) 231-6726. **FAX:** (540) 231-6984.

WAGNER Seahawks
Conference: Northeast (South).
Mailing Address: One Campus Road, Staten Island, NY 10301.
Head Coach: Rich Vitaliano. **Assistant Coaches:** John Crane, Tom Weber. **Telephone:** (718) 390-3154. ■ **Baseball SID:** Bob Balut. **Telephone:** (718) 390-3215. **FAX:** (718) 390-3347.

WAKE FOREST Demon Deacons
Conference: Atlantic Coast.
Mailing Address: P.O. Box 7426, Winston-Salem, NC 27109.
Head Coach: George Greer. **Assistant Coaches:** *Bobby Moranda, Mike Rikard. **Telephone:** (336) 758-5570. ■ **Baseball SID:** Chris Capo. **Telephone:** (336) 758-5640. **FAX:** (336) 758-5140.
Home Field: Hooks Stadium. **Seating Capacity:** 2,500. **Outfield Dimensions:** LF—340, CF—400, RF—315. **Press Box Telephone:** (336) 759-9711.

WASHINGTON Huskies
Conference: Pacific-10.
Mailing Address: Graves Bldg., Box 354070, Seattle, WA 98195.

Head Coach: Ken Knutson. Assistant Coaches: Ed Gustafson, *Joe Ross. Telephone: (206) 543-9365. ■ Baseball SID: Jeff Bechthold. Telephone: (206) 543-2230. FAX: (206) 543-5000.

Home Field: Husky Ballpark. Seating Capacity: 1,500. Outfield Dimensions: LF—327, CF—395, RF—317. Press Box Telephone: (206) 685-1994.

WASHINGTON STATE Cougars

Conference: Pacific-10.

Mailing Address: P.O. Box 641602, Pullman, WA 99164.

Head Coach: Steve Farrington. Assistant Coaches: Russ Swan, *Buzz Verduzco. Telephone: (509) 335-0211. ■ Baseball SID: Jeff Evans. Telephone: (509) 335-2684. FAX: (509) 335-0267.

Home Field: Buck Bailey Field. Seating Capacity: 3,500. Outfield Dimensions: LF—330, CF—400, RF—335. Press Box Telephone: (509) 335-2684.

WEST VIRGINIA Mountaineers

Conference: Big East.

Mailing Address: P.O. Box 0877, Morgantown, WV 26507.

Head Coach: Greg Van Zant. Assistant Coaches: David Brooks, Bruce Cameron, *Doug Little, Ron Moore. Telephone: (304) 293-2308. ■ Baseball SID: John Antonik. Telephone: (304) 293-2821. FAX: (304) 293-4105.

Home Field: Hawley Field. Seating Capacity: 1,500. Outfield Dimensions: LF—325, CF—390, RF—325. Press Box Telephone: (304) 293-5988.

WESTERN CAROLINA Catamounts

Conference: Southern.

Mailing Address: 2517 Ramsey Center, Cullowhee, NC 28723.

Head Coach: Rodney Hennon. Assistant Coaches: Dan Kyslinger, *Mike Tidick. Telephone: (828) 227-7338. ■ Baseball SID: Craig Wells. Telephone: (828) 227-7171. FAX: (828) 227-7688.

Home Field: Childress Field/Hennon Stadium. Seating Capacity: 1,500. Outfield Dimensions: LF—325, CF—390, RF—325. Press Box Telephone: Unavailable.

WESTERN ILLINOIS Leathernecks

Conference: Mid-Continent.

Mailing Address: 213 Western Hall, Macomb, IL 61455.

Head Coach: Kim Johnson. Assistant Coaches: *Deon Dittmar, Dan Duffy, Harry Torgerson. Telephone: (309) 298-1521. ■ Baseball SID: Doug Smiley. Telephone: (309) 298-1133. FAX: (309) 298-3366.

WESTERN KENTUCKY Hilltoppers

Conference: Sun Belt.

Mailing Address: One Big Red Way, Bowling Green, KY 42101.

Head Coach: Joel Murrie. Assistant Coaches: Clyde Keller, Dan Mosier. Telephone: (502) 745-6023. ■ Baseball SID: Michael Finch. Telephone: (502) 745-4298. FAX: (502) 745-3444.

WESTERN MICHIGAN Broncos

Conference: Mid-American (West).

Mailing Address: B-205 Ellsworth Hall, Kalamazoo, MI 49008.

Head Coach: Fred Decker. Assistant Coaches: Scott Demetral, Ken Jones. Telephone: (616) 387-8149. ■ Baseball SID: John Beatty. Telephone: (616) 387-4138. FAX: (616) 387-4139.

Home Field: Hyames Field. Seating Capacity: 4,000. Outfield Dimensions: LF—325, CF—390, RF—340. Press Box Telephone: (616) 387-8630.

WICHITA STATE Shockers

Conference: Missouri Valley.

Mailing Address: 1845 Fairmount St., Campus Box 18, Wichita, KS 67260.

Head Coach: Gene Stephenson. Assistant Coaches: *Brent Kemnitz, Steve Miller, Jim Thomas. Telephone: (316) 978-3636. ■ Baseball SID: Joe McDonald. Telephone: (316) 978-3265. FAX: (316) 978-3336.

Home Field: Tyler Field-Eck Stadium. Seating Capacity: 5,665. Outfield Dimensions: LF—330, CF—390, RF—330. Press Box Telephone: (316) 978-3390.

WILLIAM & MARY Tribe

Conference: Colonial Athletic.

Mailing Address: P.O. Box 399, Williamsburg, VA 23187.

Head Coach: Jim Farr. Assistant Coach: Marlin Ikenberry. Telephone: (757) 221-3399. ■ Baseball SIDs: Dan Booth, Andrew Green. Telephone: (757) 221-3344. FAX: (757) 221-3412.

WINTHROP Eagles

Conference: Big South.

Mailing Address: Winthrop Coliseum, Rock Hill, SC 29733.

Head Coach: Joe Hudak. Assistant Coach: *Mike McGuire. Telephone: (803) 323-2129. ■ Baseball SID: Everett Hutto. Telephone: (803) 323-2129. FAX: (803) 323-2433.

WISCONSIN-MILWAUKEE Panthers

Conference: Midwestern Collegiate.

Mailing Address: P.O. Box 413, Milwaukee, WI 53201.

Head Coach: Jerry Augustine. Assistant Coaches: *Scott Doffek, Todd Frohwirth. Telephone: (414) 229-5670. ■ Baseball SID: Chad Krueger.

Telephone: (414) 229-4593. FAX: (414) 229-6759.

WOFFORD Terriers

Conference: Southern.
Mailing Address: 429 N Church St., Spartanburg, SC 29303.
Head Coach: Ernie May. **Assistant Coaches:** Andy Kiah, Brandon McKillop. **Telephone:** (864) 597-4126. ■ **Baseball SID:** Bill English. **Telephone:** (864) 597-4093. **FAX:** (864) 597-4129.

WRIGHT STATE Raiders

Conference: Midwestern Collegiate.
Mailing Address: 3640 Colonel Glenn Highway, Dayton, OH 45435.
Head Coach: Ron Nischwitz. **Assistant Coaches:** Bo Bilinski, Dan Bassler. **Telephone:** (937) 775-2771. ■ **Baseball SID:** Rob Link. **Telephone:** (937) 775-3666. **FAX:** (937) 775-2818.

XAVIER Musketeers

Conference: Atlantic-10 (West).
Mailing Address: 3800 Victory Pkwy., Cincinnati, OH 45207.
Head Coach: John Morrey. **Assistant Coaches:** Ryan McGinnis, *Joe Regruth. **Telephone:** (513) 745-2890. ■ **Baseball SID:** Ben Fibbe. **Telephone:** (513) 745-3416. **FAX:** (513) 745-2825.

YALE Bulldogs

Conference: Ivy League (Rolfe).
Mailing Address: P.O. Box 208216, New Haven, CT 06520.
Head Coach: John Stuper. **Telephone:** (203) 432-1466. ■ **Baseball SID:** Steve Conn. **Telephone:** (203) 432-1456. **FAX:** (203) 432-1454.

YOUNGSTOWN STATE Penguins

Conference: Mid-Continent.
Mailing Address: One University Plaza, Youngstown, OH 44555.
Head Coach: Mike Florak. **Assistant Coach:** Unavailable. **Telephone:** (330) 742-3485. ■ **Baseball SID:** Rocco Gasparro. **Telephone:** (330) 742-3192. **FAX:** (330) 742-3191.

Amateur Baseball

AMATEURBASEBALL

INTERNATIONAL OLYMPIC COMMITTEE
Mailing Address: Chateau de Vidy, 1007 Lausanne, Switzerland.
Telephone: 41-21-621-61-11. **FAX:** 41-21-621-62-16. **Website:** www.olympic.org.
President: Juan Antonio Samaranch. **Administrative Assistant, Department of International Cooperation/Public Information:** Betty Guignard.

SYDNEY OLYMPIC ORGANIZING COMMITTEE
Street Address: 235 Jones St., Ultimo, New South Wales 2007, Australia. **Mailing Address:** GPO Box 2000, Sydney, New South Wales 2001, Australia. **Telephone:** (61-2) 9297-2000. **FAX:** (61-2) 9297-2020. **Website:** www.sydney.olympic.org.
President: Michael Knight. **Chief Executive Officer:** Sandy Hollway. **General Manager, Sport:** Bob Elphinston.
Games of the XXVIIth Olympiad: Sept. 15-Oct. 1, 2000.

U.S. OLYMPIC COMMITTEE
Mailing Address: One Olympic Plaza, Colorado Springs, CO 80909. **Telephone:** (719) 632-5551. **FAX:** (719) 578-4654.
President: William Hybl. **Executive Director:** Dick Schultz. **Assistant Executive Director, Media/Public Affairs:** Mike Moran.
Olympics, 2000: Sept. 15-Oct. 1, 2000 at Sydney, Australia.

GOODWILL GAMES INC.
Office Address: One CNN Center, South Tower, 12th Floor, Atlanta, GA 30348. **Mailing Address:** P.O. Box 105366, Atlanta, GA 30348. **Telephone:** (404) 827-3400. **FAX:** (404) 827-1539.
President: Mike Plant. **Vice President, Sports:** David Raith.
Goodwill Games, 2001: Summer, Brisbane, Australia.

PAN AMERICAN GAMES SOCIETY, INC.
Mailing Address: 433 Main St., 12th Floor, Winnipeg, Manitoba, R3B 1B3. **Telephone:** (204) 985-1900. **FAX:** (204) 985-4375.
President/Chief Executive Officer: Don MacKenzie. **Vice President, Sports:** Mike Moore. **Manager, Public Relations:** Brian Koshul. **Manager, Media Services:** George Einarson.
Pan American Games, 1999 (baseball competition): Ten teams, July 24-Aug. 2 at Winnipeg (Kenwest Global Park). Qualifier (two teams)/2000 Olympic Games.

INTERNATIONAL BASEBALL ASSOCIATION
Mailing Address: Avenue de Mon-Repos 24, Case Postale 131, 1000 Lausanne 5, Switzerland. **Telephone:** (41-21) 3188240. **FAX:** (41-21) 3188241. **E-Mail Address:** iba@baseball.ch. **Website:** www.baseball.ch.
President: Aldo Notari (Italy). **Secretary General:** John Ostermeyer (Australia). **Executive Director:** Miquel Ortin.

1999 Events
Oceania Championship*	Guam, June 10-20
Pan American Games*	Winnipeg, Manitoba, July 24-Aug. 2
European A Pool Championship*	Emilia Romagna, Italy, July 23-Aug. 3
X World Children's Baseball Fair	Yokohama, Japan, Aug. 1-8
XVIII World Junior Championship	Kaoshiung, Taiwan, Aug. 6-15
All Africa Games*	Johannesburg, South Africa, Sept. 9-18
Asian Championship*	Seoul, South Korea, Sept. 11-19
XIV Intercontinental Cup	Sydney, Australia, Nov. 4-14

*Qualifying tournament for 2000 Olympics

USA BASEBALL
Mailing Address, Corporate Headquarters: Hi Corbett Field, 3400 E Camino Campestre, Tucson, AZ 85716. **Telephone:** (520) 327-9700. **FAX:** (520) 327-9221. **E-Mail Address:** usabasebal@aol.com. **Website:** www.usabaseball.com.
Chairman: Cliff Lothery. **President:** Neil Lantz. **Executive Vice President:** Tom Hicks. **Secretary:** Pam Marshall. **Treasurer:** Gale Montgomery.
Executive Director/Chief Executive Officer: Dan O'Brien Sr. **Director, Marketing/Business Affairs:** Jeff Odenwald. **Director, National Team Baseball Operations:** Paul Seiler. **Director, Junior National Team**

Baseball Operations: Steve Cohen. **Director, Publications:** David Fanucchi. **Assistant, Marketing/Youth Baseball Coordinator:** Ray Darwin. **Senior Advisor to National Teams/Alumni Affairs:** Jerry Kindall. **Director, Merchandise/Apparel Sales:** David Perkins. **Special Events/ Gameday Coordinator:** Tom Lehman.

National Members: Amateur Athletic Union, American Amateur Baseball Congress, American Baseball Coaches Association, American Legion Baseball, Babe Ruth Baseball, Dixie Baseball, Little League Baseball, National Amateur Baseball Federation, National Association of Inter-collegiate Athletics, National Baseball Congress, National Collegiate Athletic Association, National Federation of State High School Athletic Associations, National High School Baseball Coaches Association, National Junior College Athletic Association, Police Athletic League, PONY Baseball, YMCAs of the USA.

1998 Events

COPABE World Junior Qualifier .... Venezuela, April 9-18
Junior Olympic Championships (16 and u.)...... Tucson, AZ, June 19-26
Junior National Team Trials .... Tucson, AZ, July 23-28
XIII Pan American Games .... Winnipeg, Manitoba, July 24-Aug. 2
IBA World Junior Championships (18 and under) ...... Chinese Taipei, Aug. 6-15
USAB Women's National Championships .... Tucson, AZ, Sept.-Oct.
Intercontinental Cup .... Sydney, Australia, Nov. 4-14

BASEBALL CANADA

Mailing Address: 1600 James Naismith Dr., Suite 208, Ottawa, Ontario K1B 5N4. **Telephone:** (613) 748-5606. **FAX:** (613) 748-5767. **E-Mail Address:** info@baseball.ca. **Website:** www.baseball.ca.

Director General: Duncan Grant. **Head Coach:** Greg Hamilton.

Baseball Canada Cup (17 and under): July 15-19, Three Rivers, Quebec.

NATIONAL BASEBALL CONGRESS

Mailing Address: P.O. Box 1420, Wichita, KS 67201. **Telephone:** (316) 267-3372. **FAX:** (316) 267-3382.

Year Founded: 1931.

President: Robert Rich Jr. **Executive Vice President:** Melinda Rich.

Vice President: Steve Shaad. **National Commissioner/Tournament Director:** Larry Davis. **Associate Vice President:** Lance Deckinger. **Director, Administration:** Dian Overaker. **Assistant General Manager:** Mark Chiarucci. **Stadium Manager:** Dave Wellenzohn. **Coordinator, Marketing/Public Relations:** Justin Givens.

1999 NBC World Series (non-professional, ex-professional): Aug. 3-17, Lawrence-Dumont Stadium, Wichita, KS.

INTERNATIONAL BASEBALL FOUNDATION

Mailing Address: 1313 13th St. S, Birmingham, AL 35205. **Telephone:** (205) 558-4235. **FAX:** (205) 918-0800. **E-Mail Address:** ed.ibf5@juno.com.

Executive Director: David Osinski.

INTERNATIONAL SPORTS GROUP

Mailing Address: 142 Shadowood Dr., Pleasant Hill, CA 94523. **Telephone:** (925) 798-4591. **FAX:** (925) 680-1182. **E-Mail Address:** jjones1943 @aol.com.

President: Bill Arce. **Secretary/Treasurer:** Jim Jones.

ATHLETES IN ACTION

Mailing Address: 3802 Ehrlich Rd., Suite 110, Tampa, FL 33624. **Telephone:** (813) 968-7400. **FAX:** (813) 968-7515. **E-Mail Address:** aiatampa@gate.net.

Staff: Jason Lester, Scott Shepherd.

Summer College Leagues

NATIONAL ALLIANCE OF COLLEGIATE SUMMER BASEBALL

Mailing Address: 6 Indian Trail, South Harwich, MA 02661. **Telephone:** (508) 432-1774. **FAX:** (508) 432-9766.

Executive Director: Fred Ebbett. **Assistant Executive Director:** Joel Cooney. **Secretary:** Buzzy Levin.

NCAA Sanctioned Leagues: Atlantic Collegiate League, Cape Cod League, Central Illinois Collegiate League, Great Lakes League, New England Collegiate League, Northeastern League, Northwest Collegiate League, Shenandoah Valley League.

ALASKA BASEBALL LEAGUE

Mailing Address: 601 S Main St., Kenai, AK 99611. **Telephone:** (907) 283-7133. **FAX:** (907) 283-3390.

Year Founded: 1974 (reunited, 1998).

President: Mike Baxter. **Vice President:** Dennis Mattingly. **Publicity**

Director: Dick Lobdell.
   1999 Opening Date: June 9. **Closing Date:** July 27.
   Regular Season: 28 league games.
   Playoff Format: None. Top two teams advance to National Baseball Congress World Series.
   Roster Limit: 22, plus exemption for Alaska residents. **Player Eligibility Rule:** Players with college eligibility, except drafted seniors, and ex-professionals released prior to June 1, 1999.

ALASKA GOLDPANNERS
   Mailing Address: P.O. Box 71154, Fairbanks, AK 99707. **Telephone/ FAX:** (907) 451-0095. **E-Mail Address:** donadennis@juno.com. **Website:** www.goldpanners.com.
   President: Bill Stroecker. **General Manager:** Don Dennis. **Head Coach:** Dan Cowgill (Cal State Northridge).

ANCHORAGE BUCS
   Mailing Address: P.O. Box 240061, Anchorage, AK 99524. **Telephone:** (907) 561-2827. **FAX:** (907) 561-2920.
   President: Eugene Furman. **Executive Director:** Brian Crawford. **General Manager:** Dennis Mattingly. **Head Coach:** Mike Oakland (Cal Poly San Luis Obispo).

ANCHORAGE GLACIER PILOTS
   Mailing Address: P.O. Box 100895, Anchorage, AK 99510. **Telephone:** (907) 274-3627. **FAX:** (907) 274-3628.
   President: Chuck Shelton. **General Manager:** Ron Okerlund. **Head Coach:** Kevin Smallcomb (Mendocino, Calif., CC).

HAWAII ISLAND MOVERS
   Mailing Address: P.O. Box 17865, Honolulu, HI 96817. **Telephone:** (808) 832-4805. **FAX:** (808) 841-2321.
   President/General Manager: Donald Takaki. **Head Coach:** Tom Gushiken (Waipahu, HI, HS).

KENAI PENINSULA OILERS
   Mailing Address: 601 S. Main St. Kenai, AK 99611. **Telephone:** (907) 283-7133. **FAX:** (907) 283-3390. **E-Mail Address:** penoilbb@kenai.net. **Website:** www.kenai.net/penoilbb.
   President: John Lohrke. **General Manager:** Mike Baxter.
   Head Coach: Gary Adcock (Purdue U.).

MAT-SU MINERS
   Mailing Address: P.O. Box 1633, Palmer, AK 99645. **Telephone:** (907) 745-4901. **FAX:** (907) 745-7275.
   President: Bill Bartholomew. **General Manager:** Stan Zaborac. **Head Coach:** Pete Wilk (Georgetown U.).

ALLEGHANY MOUNTAIN COLLEGIATE LEAGUE
   Mailing Address: 151 Beimel Lane, Kersey, PA 15846. **Telephone:** (814) 885-8480. **E-Mail Address:** aaaba@key-net.net.
   Year Founded: 1997.
   President: Roger Beimel. **Chief Executive Officer:** John Kuhn.
   Member Clubs (all teams located in Pennsylvania)**:** Champion Trophies (Brookville), Keystone Baseball Academy (Brockway), Straub Brewers (Kersey), State College.

ATLANTIC COLLEGIATE LEAGUE
   Mailing Address: 401 Timber Dr., Berkeley Heights, NJ 07922. **Telephone/FAX:** (908) 464-8042. **E-Mail Address:** acbl@vs-inc.com. **Website:** www.atlanticcbl.org.
   Year Founded: 1967.
   President: Tom Bonekemper. **Vice President:** Jerry Valonis. **Commissioner:** Robert Pertsas. **Publicity Director:** Ben Smookler.
   Member Clubs: Wolff Division—Delaware Valley Gulls (Philadelphia), Jersey Pilots, Quakertown (Pa.) Blazers, West Deptford Storm (Audubon, NJ). **Kaiser Division**—Jersey City Colonels (Sussex, NJ), Metro New York Cadets, New York Generals, Nassau (N.Y.) Collegians.
   1999 Opening Date: June 1. **Closing Date:** Aug. 15.
   Regular Season: 40 games.
   Playoff Format: Top four teams meet in best-of-3 semifinals. Winners meet in one-game championship.
   Roster Limit: 21 (college-eligible players only).

CALIFORNIA COASTAL COLLEGIATE LEAGUE
   Mailing Address: 4003 Coyote Cir., Clayton, CA 94517. **Telephone/ FAX:** (925) 672-9662. **E-Mail Address:** tsdress@aol.com. **Website:** www.leaguelineup.com/cccl.

Year Founded: 1993.

President/Commissioner: Tony Dress.

Member Clubs (all teams located in California): Fresno Barons, Los Angeles Comets, San Francisco Seals, San Luis Obispo Blues, Santa Barbara Foresters, Santa Maria Stars.

Playoff Format: League champion advances to NBC World Series.

1999 Opening Date: June 1. Closing Date: Aug. 1.

Regular Season: 38 games.

Roster Limit: 33.

CAPE COD LEAGUE

Mailing Address: 7 Nottingham Dr., Yarmouth, MA 02675. Telephone/FAX: (508) 996-5004. E-Mail Address: capecod@gbwebworks.com. Website: www.capecodbaseball.com.

Year Founded: 1885.

Commissioner: Bob Stead. President: Judy Scarafile.

Vice Presidents: Jim Higgins, Bonnie Jacobs, Don Tullie.

Director, Public Relations: Missy Ilg-Alaimo. Electronic Media/Newsletter: Cathie Nichols.

Division Structure: East—Brewster, Chatham, Harwich, Orleans, Yarmouth-Dennis. West—Bourne, Cotuit, Falmouth, Hyannis, Wareham.

1999 Opening Date: June 11. Closing Date: Aug. 15.

Regular Season: 44 games.

All-Star Game: July 24 at Wareham.

Playoff Format: Top two teams in each division meet in best-of-3 semifinals. Winners meet in best-of-3 series for league championship.

Roster Limit: 23 (college-eligible players only).

BOURNE BRAVES

Mailing Address: 25 Washburn, Buzzards Bay, MA 02532. Telephone: (508) 888-5080.

General Manager: Ed Ladetto. Head Coach: Mike Rikard (Wake Forest U.).

BREWSTER WHITECAPS

Mailing Address: P.O. Box 2349, Brewster, MA 02631. Telephone: (781) 784-7409. FAX: (781) 784-2028.

President: Steve Whitehurst. General Managers: Howard Wayne, Sol Yas. Head Coach: Bill Mosiello (U. of Oklahoma).

CHATHAM A'S

Mailing Address: P.O. Box 428, Chatham, MA 02633. Telephone: (508) 945-3841. FAX: (508) 945-9616. E-Mail Address: cthoms@capecod.net.

President: Peter Troy. General Manager: Charles Thoms. Head Coach: John Schiffner (Plainville, Conn., HS).

COTUIT KETTLEERS

Mailing Address: P.O. Box 41, Cotuit, MA 02635. Telephone: (508) 428-3358. FAX: (508) 428-0289. E-Mail Address: bmurpfcape@aol.com. Website: www.capecod.net/kettleers.

President: Ivan Partridge. General Manager: Bruce Murphy. Head Coach: Mike Coutts.

FALMOUTH COMMODORES

Mailing Address: 30 Hancock St., Lexington, MA 02173. Telephone: (781) 862-1762.

General Manager: Ray Warner. Head Coach: Jeff Trundy (The Gunnery School, Conn.).

HARWICH MARINERS

Mailing Address: 3 Coybrook Ln., Harwich Port, MA 02646. Telephone: (508) 432-0662.

General Manager: Jeff Handler. Head Coach: Scott Lawler (North Carolina State U.).

HYANNIS METS

Mailing Address: P.O. Box 852, Hyannis, MA 02601. Telephone: (508) 420-0962. FAX: (508) 790-2684. E-Mail Address: emartin@capecod.net. Website: www.capecodbaseball.com/mets.

President: Everett Martin. General Manager: John Howitt. Head Coach: Tom O'Connell.

ORLEANS CARDINALS

Mailing Address: P.O. Box 504, Orleans, MA 02653. Telephone: (508) 240-5867. FAX: (508) 240-5871. E-Mail Address: djreed@capecod.net.

President: Mark Hossfeld. General Manager: Dave Reed. Head Coach: Don Norris (Georgia College).

WAREHAM GATEMEN

Mailing Address: 71 Towhee Rd., Wareham, MA 02571. Telephone: (508) 295-3956. FAX: (508) 295-8821. E-Mail Address: williams@gatemen.org. **Website:** www.gatemen.org.

President: John Wylde. **General Manager:** Angela Johnson. **Head Coach:** Don Reed.

YARMOUTH-DENNIS RED SOX

Mailing Address: 47 Farm Lane, South Dennis, MA 02660. **Telephone:** (508) 394-9466.

General Manager: Jack Martin. **Head Coach:** Scott Pickler (Cypress, Calif., CC).

CENTRAL ILLINOIS COLLEGIATE LEAGUE

Mailing Address: RR 13, Box 369, Bloomington, IL 61704. **Telephone:** (309) 828-4429. **FAX:** (309) 827-4652. **E-Mail Address:** ciclbb@aol.com. **Website:** www.ciclbaseball.com.

Year Founded: 1963.

President: Duffy Bass. **Commissioner:** Mike Woods. **Vice President:** Claude Kracik.

Member Clubs (all teams located in Illinois): **East**—Danville Dans, Decatur Blues, Twin City Stars. **West**—Bluff City Bombers, Quincy Gems, Springfield Rifles.

1999 Opening Date: June 11. **Closing Date:** Aug. 9.

Regular Season: 48 games.

All-Star Game: July 5 at Quincy.

Playoff Format: Six teams, single-elimination tournament.

Roster Limit: 23 (college-eligible players only).

CLARK GRIFFITH COLLEGIATE LEAGUE

Mailing Address: 4917 N 30th St., Arlington, VA 22207. **Telephone/ FAX:** (703) 536-1729.

Year Founded: 1945.

President/Commissioner: John Depenbrock. **Vice President:** Frank Fannan. **Director, Publicity:** Ben Trittipoe.

Member Clubs: Arlington (Va.) Senators, Bethesda (Md.) Big Train, Herndon (Va.) Optimists, Reston (Va.) Hawks, Southern Maryland Battle-cats, Vienna (Va.) Mustangs.

1999 Opening Date: June 4. **Closing Date:** Aug. 30.

Regular Season: 40 games (split schedule).

Playoff Format: Top four teams meet in best-of-three semifinals. Winners meet in best-of-3 series for league championship.

Roster Limit: 24 (players 20 and under).

COASTAL PLAIN LEAGUE

Mailing Address: 4900 Waters Edge Dr., Suite 201, Raleigh, NC 27606. **Telephone:** (919) 852-1960. **FAX:** (919) 852-1973. **E-Mail Address:** macdonalds@coastalplain.com. **Website:** www.coastalplain.com.

Year Founded: 1997.

Chairman/Chief Executive Officer: Jerry Petitt. **President:** Pete Bock. **Director, Operations:** Mark Cryan. **Director, Media Relations:** Steve MacDonald.

1999 Opening Date: June 4. **Closing Date:** Aug. 7.

Regular Season: 50 games (split schedule).

All-Star Game: July 14 at Wilmington.

Playoff Format: First-half winner meets second-half winner in best-of-3 series for league championship.

Roster Limit: 20 (college-eligible players only).

ASHEBORO

Mailing Address: P.O. Box 4425, Asheboro, NC 27204. **Telephone:** (336) 636-5796. **FAX:** (336) 636-5532.

General Manager: Pat Brown. **Head Coach:** Bill Hillier Jr. (Wake Forest U.).

DURHAM BRAVES

Mailing Address: P.O. Box 126, Durham, NC 27702. **Telephone:** (919) 956-9555. **FAX:** (919) 560-4824.

General Manager: Chad Wood. **Head Coach:** Randy Hood (Campbell U.).

EDENTON STEAMERS

Mailing Address: P.O. Box 86, Edenton, NC 27932. **Telephone/FAX:** (252) 482-4080.

General Manager: Tom Howe. **Head Coach:** Stony Wine (Appalachian State U.).

FLORENCE REDWOLVES

Mailing Address: P.O. Box 809, Florence, SC 29503. **Telephone:** (843) 629-0700. **FAX:** (843) 629-0703.

President: Pete Bock. **General Manager:** David Sandler. **Head Coach:** Bruce Cameron (West Virginia U.).

OUTER BANKS DAREDEVILS

Mailing Address: P.O. Box 1747, Nags Head, NC 27959. **Telephone:** (252) 441-4889. **FAX:** (252) 441-3722.

General Manager: Jeff Brown. **Head Coach:** Chris Finwood (Virginia Commonwealth U.).

THOMASVILLE HI-TOMS

Mailing Address: P.O. Box 3035, Thomasville, NC 27360. **Telephone:** (336) 476-8667.

General Manager: Unavailable. **Head Coach:** Paul Knight (Wingate U.).

WILMINGTON SHARKS

Mailing Address: P.O. Box 15233, Wilmington, NC 28412. **Telephone:** (910) 343-5621. **FAX:** (910) 343-8932. **E-Mail Address:** 9sharks9@wilmington.net.

General Manager: Curt Van Derzee. **Head Coach:** Scott Forbes (U. of North Carolina).

WILSON TOBS

Mailing Address: P.O. Box 633, Wilson, NC 27894. **Telephone:** (252) 291-8627. **FAX:** (252) 291-1224. **E-Mail Address:** tobs@bbnp.com. **Website:** www.tobs.bbnp.com.

President: Brooks Pierce. **General Manager:** Jason Matlock. **Head Coach:** Tom Hager (Michigan State U.).

GREAT LAKES LEAGUE

Office Address: 590 Parkside Dr., Bay Village, OH 44140. **Mailing Address:** P.O. Box 16679, Cleveland, OH 44116. **Telephone:** (440) 892-2692. **FAX:** (440) 871-4221. **E-Mail Address:** ncacoffice@aol.com. **Website:** www.greatlakesbaseball.home.ml.org.

Year Founded: 1986.

President: Barry Ruben. **Commissioner:** Brian Sullivan. **Vice President:** Rob Piscetta.

Member Clubs: East—Columbus (Ohio) All-Americans, Delaware (Ohio) Cows, Northern Ohio Baseball (Strongville, OH), Stark County Terriers (Canton, OH), Youngstown (Ohio) Express. **West**—Grand Lake Mariners (Celina, Ohio), Lima (Ohio) Locos, Michigan Monarchs (Monroe, MI), Michigan Panthers (Livonia, MI), Sandusky (Ohio) Bay Stars.

1999 Opening Date: June 11. **Closing Date:** Aug. 1.

Regular Season: 40 games (split schedule).

All-Star Game: July 25 at Celina, OH.

Playoff Format: First-half champion and second-half champion from each division meet in best-of-3 series. Winners meet in best-of-3 series for league championship.

Roster Limit: 25 (college-eligible players only).

JAYHAWK LEAGUE

Mailing Address: 5 Adams Pl., Halstead, KS 67056. **Telephone:** (316) 835-2589. **FAX:** (316) 755-1285.

Year Founded: 1976.

Commissioner: Bob Considine. **President:** Don Carlile. **Vice President:** Laverne Shumacher. **Director, Public Relations:** Pat Chambers.

1999 Opening Date: June 4. **Closing Date:** July 22.

Regular Season: 40 games.

Playoff Format: League champion advances to NBC World Series.

Roster Limit: 25.

EL DORADO BRONCOS

Mailing Address: 865 Fabrique, Wichita, KS 67218. **Telephone:** (316) 687-2309.

General Manager: J.D. Schneider.

ELKHART DUSTERS

Mailing Address: P.O. Box 793, Elkhart, KS 67950. **Telephone:** (316) 697-2095.

General Manager: Brian Elsen.

HAYS LARKS

Mailing Address: 2706 Thunderbird Dr., Hays, KS 67601. **Telephone:** (785) 625-2137.

General Manager: Laverne Shumacher.

LIBERAL BEEJAYS

Mailing Address: P.O. Box 352, Liberal, KS 67901. **Telephone:** (316) 624-1904. **FAX:** (316) 624-1906.

General Manager: Kim Snell.

NEVADA GRIFFONS

Mailing Address: Box 601, Nevada, MO 64772. **Telephone:** (417) 667-8308.

General Manager: Pat Chambers.

TOPEKA CAPITOLS

Mailing Address: 2005 S West St., Topeka, KS 66604. **Telephone:** (785) 234-5881.

General Manager: Don Carlile.

NEW ENGLAND COLLEGIATE LEAGUE

Mailing Address: P.O. Box 415, Jamestown, RI 02835. **Telephone:** (401) 423-9863, (888) 326-3225. **FAX:** (401) 423-2784. **E-Mail Address:** thutton@ix.netcom.com. **Website:** www.necbl.org.

Year Founded: 1993.

Commissioner: Thomas Hutton. **President:** Fay Vincent. **Publicity Director:** Peter Fontaine.

Member Clubs: Central Mass Collegians (Leominster, MA), Danbury (Conn.) Westerners, Eastern Tides (Willimantic, CT), Keene (N.H.) Swamp Bats, Middletown (Conn.) Giants, Rhode Island Gulls (Cranston, RI), Rhode Island Reds (West Warwick, RI), Torrington (Conn.) Twisters.

1999 Opening Date: June 6. **Closing Date:** Aug. 1.

Regular Season: 42 games.

All-Star Game: July 31 at Keene, NH.

Playoff Format: Top four teams meet in best-of-3 series. Winners meet in best-of-5 series for league championship.

Roster Limit: 23 (college-eligible players only).

NORTHEASTERN COLLEGIATE LEAGUE

Mailing Address: 28 Dunbridge Heights, Fairport, NY 14450. **Telephone:** (716) 223-3528. **E-Mail Address:** vicpines@worldnet.att.net.

Year Founded: 1986.

Commissioner: Dave Chamberlain. **Vice President:** Tom Kenney. **Secretary:** Dick Cuykendall. **Administration Assistant:** Jeff DeLutis.

Member Clubs (all teams located in New York)**: East—** Geneva Knights, Hornell Dodgers, Newark Raptors, Wellsville Nitros. **West—**Cortland Apples, Ithaca Lakers, Rome Indians, Schenectady Mohawks.

1999 Opening Date: June 11. **Closing Date:** Aug. 2.

Regular Season: 40 games.

Playoff Format: Top four teams meet in best-of-3 series. Winners meet in one-game final for league championship.

Roster Limit: 24 (college-eligible players only).

NORTHWEST COLLEGIATE BASEBALL LEAGUE

Mailing Address: 23737 SW Pinecone Ave., Sherwood, OR 97140. **Telephone:** (503) 625-4044. **FAX:** (503) 625-0629. **E-Mail Address:** raineyr@sherwood.or.us.

Year Founded: 1992.

Commissioner: Reed Rainey. **Vice President:** Rob Vance.

Member Clubs (all teams located in Oregon): Bucks, Dukes, Lobos, Ports, Stars, Toros.

1999 Opening Date: June 4. **Closing Date:** Aug. 1.

Regular Season: 32 games (split schedule).

Playoff Format: First-half winner meets second-half winner in best-of-3 series for league championship.

Roster Limit: 20 (college-eligible players only).

NORTHWOODS LEAGUE

Mailing Address: P.O. Box 482, Rochester, MN 55903. **Telephone:** (507) 289-1170. **FAX:** (507) 289-1866. **Website:** www.northwoods-league.com.

Year Founded: 1994.

President: Dick Radatz Jr. **Vice Presidents:** Bill McKee, John Wendel.

Division Structure: North—Brainerd, Grand Forks, St. Cloud, Wausau. **South—**Mankato, Rochester, Southern Minny, Waterloo.

1999 Opening Date: June 4. **Closing Date:** Aug. 8.

Regular Season: 64 games (split schedule).

All-Star Game: July 12 at St. Cloud, MN.

Playoff Format: First-half and second-half division winners meet in best-of-3 series. Winners meet in best-of-3 series for league championship.

Roster Limit: 24 (college-eligible players only).

BRAINERD MIGHTY GULLS

Mailing Address: P.O. Box 122, Brainerd, MN 56401. **Telephone:** (218) 829-3323. **FAX:** (218) 829-9302.

General Manager: Marty Reinertson. **Head Coach:** Eric Coleman (San Jose, Calif., CC).

GRAND FORKS CHANNEL CATS
Mailing Address: P.O. Box 14953, Grand Forks, ND 58208. **Telephone:** (701) 780-9500. **FAX:** (701) 780-9520.
General Manager: Mark Reinhiller. **Head Coach:** Mike Huber (Morton, Ill., JC).

MANKATO MASHERS
Mailing Address: 310 Belle St., Suite L10, Mankato, MN 56001. **Telephone:** (507) 344-8877. **FAX:** (507) 344-0871.
General Manager/Head Coach: Shane Bowyer.

ROCHESTER HONKERS
Mailing Address: P.O. Box 482, Rochester, MN 55903. **Telephone:** (507) 289-1170. **FAX:** (507) 289-1866.
General Manager: Dan Litzinger. **Head Coach:** Tom Fleenor (Rollins, Fla., College).

ST. CLOUD RIVER BATS
Mailing Address: P.O. Box 5059, St. Cloud, MN 56303. **Telephone:** (320) 240-9798. **FAX:** (320) 255-5228.
General Manager: Joe Schwei. **Head Coach:** Pat Shine (U. of California).

SOUTHERN MINNY STARS
Mailing Address: Town Center, 329 N Main St., Austin, MN 55912. **Telephone:** (507) 437-2621. **FAX:** (507) 437-2463.
General Manager: Troy Goergen. **Head Coach:** Brian Reinke (Trinidad State, Colo., JC).

WATERLOO BUCKS
Mailing Address: P.O. Box 4124, Waterloo, IA 50704. **Telephone:** (319) 232-0500. **FAX:** (319) 232-0700.
General Manager: Gary Rima. **Head Coach:** Darrell Handelsman (Centenary College).

WAUSAU WOODCHUCKS
Mailing Address: P.O. Box 2216, Wausau, WI 54403. **Telephone:** (715) 845-5055. **FAX:** (715) 845-5015.
General Manager: Keith Mischlig. **Head Coach:** Keith Chester (Austin Peay State U.).

PACIFIC INTERNATIONAL LEAGUE
Mailing Address: 504 Yale Ave. N, Seattle, WA 98109. **Telephone:** (206) 623-8844. **FAX:** (206) 623-8361.
Year Founded: 1988.
President: Mickie Schmith. **Commissioner:** Seth Dawson.
Member Clubs: Aloha (Ore.) Knights, Bellingham (Wash.) Baseball Club, Coquitlam (B.C.) Athletics, Everett (Wash.) Merchants, Kelowna (B.C.) Grizzlies, Ontario Orchard (Ore.) Meadowlarks, Seattle Performance Radiator Studs, Richmond (B.C.) Budgies, Seattle Cruisers, Yakima (Wash.) Chiefs.
1999 Opening Date: June 1. **Closing Date:** Aug. 1.
Regular Season: 32 games.
Playoff Format: League champion advances to NBC World Series.
Roster Limit: 25.

SHENANDOAH VALLEY LEAGUE
Mailing Address: Route 1, Box 189J, Staunton, VA 24401. **Telephone:** (540) 886-1748. **FAX:** (540) 885-2068. **E-Mail Address:** dmbiery-@cfw.com. **Website:** www.valleybaseball.com.
Year Founded: 1963.
President: David Biery. **Executive Vice President:** Jim Weissenborn. **Secretary:** Charles Geil. **Treasurer:** James Phillips. **Director, Public Relations:** Curt Dudley.
Member Clubs (All teams located in Virginia): Front Royal Cardinals, Harrisonburg Turks, New Market Rebels, Staunton Braves, Waynesboro Generals, Winchester Royals.
1999 Opening Date: June 11. **Closing Date:** Aug. 6.
Regular Season: 40 games.
All-Star Game: July 11 at Front Royal.
Playoff Format: Top four meet in best-of-5 semifinal series. Winners meet in best-of-5 series for league championship.
Roster Limit: 25 (college-eligible players only).

HIGHSCHOOLBASEBALL

NATIONAL FEDERATION
OF STATE HIGH SCHOOL ASSOCIATIONS
Office Address: 11724 NW Plaza Circle, Kansas City, MO 64153. **Mailing Address:** P.O. Box 20626, Kansas City, MO 64195. **Telephone:** (816) 464-5400. **FAX:** (816) 464-5571. **Website:** www.nfhsa.org.
Executive Director: Robert Kanaby. **Associate Director:** Fritz McGinness. **Assistant Director/Baseball Rules Editor:** Brad Rumble. **Director, Publications/Communications:** Bruce Howard.

NATIONAL HIGH SCHOOL
BASEBALL COACHES ASSOCIATION
Mailing Address: P.O. Box 5128, Bella Vista, AR 72714. **Telephone:** (501) 876-2591. **FAX:** (501) 876-2596.
Executive Director: Jerry Miles. **Administrative Assistant:** Elaine Miles. **President:** Herb Kupfer (Omaha, NE).
1999 National Convention: Dec. 3-5 at Tucson, AZ.

NATIONAL TOURNAMENTS

Postseason
SUNBELT BASEBALL CLASSIC SERIES
Mailing Address: 505 North Blvd., Edmond, OK 73034. **Telephone:** (405) 348-3839.
Chairman: Gordon Morgan. **Director:** John Schwartz.
1999 Series: Seminole, Shawnee and Tecumseh, OK, June 22-26 (8 states: Arizona, California, Florida, Georgia, Maryland, Ohio, Oklahoma, Texas).

In-Season
HORIZON NATIONAL INVITATIONAL
Mailing Address: Horizon High School, 5601 E Greenway Rd., Scottsdale, AZ 85254. **Telephone:** (602) 953-4158.
Tournament Director: Eric Kibler.
1999 Tournament: March 29-April 1 (16 teams).

LIONS/BOBBY MORROW INVITATIONAL
Mailing Address: 1200 Billy Mitchell Dr., #A, El Cajon, CA 92020. **Telephone:** (619) 258-2500.
Tournament Organizers: Jim Gordon, Bob Henshaw.
1999 Tournament: March 29-April 1 (80 teams).

NATIONAL CLASSIC
Mailing Address: El Dorado High School, 1651 N. Valencia Ave., Placentia, CA 92870. **Telephone:** (714) 993-5350. **FAX:** (714) 777-8127.
Tournament Director: Iran Novick.
1999 Tournament: April 5-8 in Orange County, CA (16 teams).

SPALDING WEST COAST CLASSIC
Mailing Address: Archbishop Mitty High School, 5000 Mitty Ave., San Jose, CA 95129. **Telephone:** (408) 252-6610.
Tournament Director: Bill Hutton.
1999 Tournament: April 6-8 (16 teams).

STARTER CLASSIC
Mailing Address: Tate High School, Gonzalez, FL 32560. **Telephone:** (850) 968-9522.
Tournament Director: Greg Blackmon.
1999 Tournament: April 5-8 (16 teams).

USA CLASSIC
Mailing Address: 5900 Walnut Grove Rd., Memphis, TN 38120. **Telephone:** (901) 872-8326.
Tournament Organizers: John Daigle, Buster Kelso.
1999 Tournament: March 30-April 2 at USA Baseball Stadium, Millington, TN (20 teams).

WESTMINSTER NATIONAL CLASSIC
Mailing Address: Westminster Academy, 5601 Federal Hwy., Fort Lauderdale, FL 33308. **Telephone:** (954) 771-4615, ext. 526. **FAX:** 954-491-3021.
Tournament Director: Rich Hofman.
1999 Tournament: April 6-9 (16 teams).

SCOUTING SERVICES

PROSPECTS, LLC
(A Division of Baseball America, Inc.)
Mailing Address: P.O. Box 2089, Durham, NC 27702. **Telephone:** (800) 334-8671. **FAX:** (919) 682-2880.
Proprietors: David Rawnsley, Allan Simpson.

SHOWCASEEVENTS

AREA CODE GAMES
Mailing Address: P.O. Box 213, Santa Rosa, CA 95402. **Telephone:** (707) 525-0498. **FAX:** (707) 525-0214.
President, Goodwill Series, Inc.: Bob Williams.
1999 Area Code Games: Aug. 8-14, Long Beach, CA (Blair Field).
World Cup XII: Japan and United States, Aug. 29-Sept. 6, Binghamton, NY; Cooperstown, NY; Long Beach, CA. **Friendship International Series:** Aug. 8-18, Beijing, China. **Goodwill Series VI:** Dec. 17, 1999-Jan. 3, 2000, Adelaide and Brisbane, Australia.

TEAM ONE NATIONAL SHOWCASE
Mailing Address: P.O. Box 8943, Cincinnati, OH 45208. **Telephone/FAX:** (606) 291-4463.
President, Team One Sports: Jeff Spelman.
Assistant Director: Stan Brzezicki. Telephone: (814) 899-8407.
1999 Team One National Showcase: June 18-20, St. Petersburg, FL (Tropicana Field).
Regional Showcases: Florida—June 21-22, St. Petersburg, FL (Tropicana Field); West—July 9-11, Tempe, AZ (Arizona State University); East—July 23-25, Clemson, SC (Clemson University); Midwest—Aug. 13-15, South Bend, IN (U. of Notre Dame).

EASTERN U.S.
PROFESSIONAL BASEBALL SHOWCASE
Mailing Address: 601 S College Rd., Wilmington, NC 28403. **Telephone:** (910) 962-3570.
Facility Director: Mark Scalf.
1999 Showcase: Aug. 4-7, Wilmington, NC (UNC Wilmington).

BASEBALL FACTORY
Office Address: 3290 Pine Orchard Ln., Suite D, Ellicott City, MD 21042. **Telephone:** (800) 641-4487, (410) 418-4904. **FAX:** (410) 418-5434.
President: Steve Sclafani. **Vice President:** Rob Naddelman.

TOP GUNS SHOWCASE
Mailing Address: 7890 N Franklin Rd., Suite 2, Coeur d'Alene, ID 83815. **Telephone/FAX:** (208) 762-1100.
President: Larry Rook. **Commissioners:** Chuck Brayton, Ron Fraser, Gordon Gillespie, Cliff Gustafson, John Scolinos, Gary Ward, John Winkin.
1999 High School National Showcases: High School West, June 21-24, Las Vegas, NV (University of Nevada-Las Vegas); High School East, June 28-July 1, Las Vegas, NV (UNLV). **1999 National Junior College Showcase:** Aug. 16-20, Las Vegas, NV (UNLV).

COLLEGE SELECT BASEBALL SHOWCASE
Mailing Address: 345 Buckland Hills Dr., #9123, Manchester, CT 06040. **Telephone:** (800) 782-3672. **Website:** www.collegeselect.org.
National Director: Tom Rizzi.
1999 Showcase: July 3-5 at Norwich, CT (Thomas Dodd Memorial Stadium).

ALL-AMERICAN BASEBALL
TALENT SHOWCASES
Mailing Address: 6 Bicentennial Ct., Erial, NJ 08081. **Telephone:** (609) 627-5283. **FAX:** (609) 627-5330.
National Director: Joe Barth.

MID-AMERICA
FIVE STAR CAMP
Mailing Address: Champions Baseball Academy, 1819 Taylor Ave., Louisville, KY 40213. **Telephone:** (502) 458-9090.
Owner: John Marshall.
1999 Showcase: July 18-21, Louisville, KY.

YOUTH BASEBALL

NATIONAL ORGANIZATIONS

ALL AMERICAN AMATEUR
BASEBALL ASSOCIATION (AAABA)
Mailing Address: 331 Parkway Dr., Zanesville, OH 43701. **Telephone:** (740) 453-8531. **FAX:** (740) 453-3978.
Year Founded: 1944.
President: John Austin. **Executive Director:** Bob Wolfe.
1999 National Tournament (21 and under): Aug. 8-14 at Johnstown, PA.

AMATEUR ATHLETIC UNION
OF THE UNITED STATES, INC. (AAU)
Mailing Address: P.O. Box 10000, Lake Buena Vista, FL 32803. **Telephone:** (407) 828-3459. **FAX:** (407) 934-7242.
Year Founded: 1982.
Sport Manager/Baseball: Sheldon Walker.

Age Classifications, National Championships

9 and under	*Orlando, FL, July 23-31
10 and under	Kansas City, MO, July 31-Aug. 7
11 and under	*Orlando, FL, July 30-Aug. 7
12 and under	Burnsville, MN, July 30-Aug. 7
13 and under (54/80 foot)	Tulsa, OK, July 30-Aug. 7
13 and under (60/90 foot)	Kingsport, TN, July 30-Aug. 7
14 and under	Chickasha, OK, July 23-31
15 and under	Millington, TN, July 30-Aug. 7
Junior Olympics (16 and under)	Cleveland, OH, July 29-Aug. 7
17 and under	Norman, OK, July 30-Aug. 7
18 and under	*Orlando, FL, July 16-24

National Invitational Championships

10 and under	Sherwood, AR, July 23-31
11 and under	Fort Myers, FL, July 23-31
12 and under	*Orlando, FL, Aug. 6-14
13 and under (54/80 foot)	Knoxville, TN, July 29-Aug. 6
13 and under (60/90 foot)	Site/Dates Unavailable
14 and under	*Orlando, FL, July 23-31
15 and under	*Orlando, FL, July 30-Aug. 7
16 and under	Cocoa, FL, July 30-Aug. 7

Other National Championships: High School Age Group, Brenham, TX, July 15-24. **International Club Baseball** (12 and under), *Orlando, FL, Aug. 21-29.

*Disney's Wide World of Sports Complex, Lake Buena Vista.

AMERICAN AMATEUR
BASEBALL CONGRESS (AABC)
National Headquarters: 118-119 Redfield Plaza, P.O. Box 467, Marshall, MI 49068. **Telephone:** (616) 781-2002. **FAX:** (616) 781-2060.
Year Founded: 1935.
President: Joe Cooper.

Age Classifications, World Series

Roberto Clemente (8 and under)	Wheatridge, CO, July 29-Aug. 1
Willie Mays (10 and under)	Collierville, TN, July 29-Aug. 1
Pee Wee Reese (12 and under)	Toa Baja, PR, Aug. 3-8
Sandy Koufax (14 and under)	Jersey City, NJ, Aug. 4-8
Mickey Mantle (16 and under)	McKinney, TX, Aug. 4-8
Connie Mack (18 and under)	Farmington, NM, Aug. 6-12
Stan Musial (unlimited)	Battle Creek, MI, Aug. 12-16

AMERICAN AMATEUR
YOUTH BASEBALL ALLIANCE
Mailing Address: 12919 Four Winds Farm, St. Louis, MO 63131. **Telephone:** (573) 518-0319. **Website:** www.aayba.com.
Executive Director: Carroll Wood.

Age Classifications, World Series

9 and under	St. Louis, MO, July 31-Aug. 8
10 and under	St. Louis, MO, July 31-Aug. 8
11 and under	St. Louis, MO, July 17-25
12 and under	St. Louis, MO, July 17-25
13 and under	St. Louis, MO, July 17-25
14 and under (54-80 foot)	St. Louis, MO, July 31-Aug. 8
14 and under (60-90 foot)	St. Louis, MO, July 31-Aug. 8
15 and under	St. Louis, MO, July 17-25
16 and under	St. Louis, MO, July 31-Aug. 8
17 and under	St. Louis, MO, July 17-25

18 and under .... St. Louis, MO, July 31-Aug. 8

AMERICAN LEGION BASEBALL

National Headquarters: National Americanism Commission, P.O. Box 1055, Indianapolis, IN 46206. **Telephone:** (317) 630-1213. **FAX:** (317) 630-1369. **Website:** www.legion.org.
    Year Founded: 1925.
    Program Coordinator: Jim Quinlan.
    1999 World Series (19 and under): Aug. 20-24 at Middletown, CT.

BABE RUTH BASEBALL

International Headquarters: 1770 Brunswick Pike, P.O. Box 5000, Trenton, NJ 08638. **Telephone:** (609) 695-1434. **FAX:** (609) 695-2505.
    Year Founded: 1951.
    President/Chief Executive Officer: Ron Tellefsen.
    Executive Vice President/Chief Financial Officer: Rosemary Schoellkopf. **Vice President/Marketing:** Joe Smiegocki. **Commissioners:** Robert Faherty, Debra Horn, Jimmy Stewart.

Age Classifications, World Series

Bambino (11-12)	Mattoon, IL, Aug. 14-21
13-Prep	Tallahassee, FL, Aug. 21-28
14	Clifton Park, NY, Aug. 21-28
13-15	Abbeville, LA, Aug. 21-28
16	Burlington, IA, Aug. 21-28
16-18	Stamford, CT, Aug. 21-28

CONTINENTAL AMATEUR
BASEBALL ASSOCIATION (CABA)

Mailing Address: 82 University St., Westerville, OH 43081. **Telephone/FAX:** (614) 899-2103.
    Year Founded: 1984.
    President: Carl Williams. **Commissioner:** John Mocny. **Franchise Director:** Tanya Wilkinson. **Executive Director:** Roger Tremaine.

Age Classifications, World Series

9 and under	Charles City, IA, July 29-Aug. 9
10 and under	Aurelia, IA, July 29-Aug. 9
11 and under	Tarkio, MO, July 29-Aug. 9
12 and under	Omaha, NE, July 29-Aug. 9
13 and under	Broken Arrow, OK, July 29-Aug. 9
14 and under	Dublin, OH, July 29-Aug. 9
15 and under	Crystal Lake, IL, July 29-Aug. 9
16 and under	Arlington, TX, July 22-Aug. 2
High school age	Cleveland, OH, July 22-Aug. 2
18 and under	Homestead, FL, July 29-Aug. 9
College age	Chicago, IL, July 20-26
Unlimited age	Eau Claire, WI, Aug. 10-16

DIXIE BASEBALL, INC.

Mailing Address: P.O. Box 231536, Montgomery, AL 36123. **Telephone:** (334) 242-8395. **FAX:** (334) 242-0198.
    Year Founded: 1956.
    Executive Director: P.L. Corley.

Age Classifications, World Series

Dixie Youth (12 and under)	Terrell, TX, Aug. 16-21
Dixie 13	Pelham, AL, Aug. 7-12
Dixie Boys (13-14)	Scottsboro, AL, Aug. 7-12
Dixie Pre-Majors (15-16)	Euless, TX, July 31-Aug. 5
Dixie Majors (15-18)	Montgomery, AL, July 31-Aug. 5

DIZZY DEAN BASEBALL, INC.

Mailing Address: P.O. Box 202, Chickamauga, GA 30707.
    Year Founded: 1962.
    Commissioner: Joedy Bates.

Age Classifications, World Series

Minor League (9-10)	Hattiesburg, MS, July 24-29
Freshman (11-12)	Hattiesburg, MS, July 24-29
Sophomore (13-14)	Panama City, FL, July 24-29
Junior (15-16)	Site Unavailable, July 24-29
Senior (17-18)	Baltimore, MD, July 31-Aug. 5

HAP DUMONT YOUTH BASEBALL

Mailing Address: P.O. Box 17455, Wichita, KS 67217. **Telephone:** (316) 721-1779. **FAX:** (316) 721-8054.
    Year Founded: 1974.
    National Chairman: Jerry Crowell. **National Vice Chairman:** Jerold Vogt.

Age Classifications, World Series

10 and under	Fordland, MO, July 30-Aug. 4
11 and under	Russell, KS, July 30-Aug. 4
12 and under	Casper, WY, July 30-Aug. 4
13 and under	Omaha, NE, July 30-Aug. 4
14 and under	Brainerd, MN, July 30-Aug. 4

16 and under .... Harrison, AR, July 30-Aug. 4

LITTLE LEAGUE BASEBALL, INC.

International Headquarters: P.O. Box 3485, Williamsport, PA 17701. **Telephone:** (570) 326-1921. **FAX:** (570) 326-1074.

Year Founded: 1939.

Chairman: James Whittington. **Chairman Elect:** Ted Reich.

President/Chief Executive Officer: Steve Keener. **Director, Communications:** Dennis Sullivan. **Director, Media Relations:** Lance Van Auken. **Director, Special Projects:** Scott Rosenberg.

Age Classifications, World Series

Little League (11-12) .... Williamsport, PA, Aug. 22-28
Junior League (13-14) .... Taylor, MI, Aug. 16-21
Senior League (14-16) .... Kissimmee, FL, Aug. 16-22
Big League (16-18) .... Tucson, AZ, Aug. 8-14

NATIONAL AMATEUR
BASEBALL FEDERATION (NABF)

Mailing Address: P.O. Box 705, Bowie, MD 20715. **Telephone/FAX:** (301) 262-5005. **E-Mail Address:** nabf1914@aol.com. **Website:** www.nabf.com.

Year Founded: 1914.

Executive Director: Charles Blackburn. **Special Events Coordinator, NABF Classics:** Wanda Rutledge.

Age Classifications, World Series

Rookie (10 and under) .... Cincinnati, OH, July 15-18
Freshman (12 and under) .... Sylvania, OH, July 15-18
Sophomore (14 and under) .... Miamisburg, OH, July 22-25
Junior (16 and under) .... Northville, MI, July 29-Aug. 3
High School (17 and under) .... Chillicothe, OH, July 30-Aug. 3
Senior (18 and under) .... Evansville, IN, Aug. 7-11
College (22 and under) .... Baltimore, MD, Aug. 5-9
Major (unlimited) .... Louisville, KY, Aug. 19-23

NABF Classics (Invitational)

13 and under .... Memphis, TN, July 14-18
14 and under .... Memphis, TN, June 30-July 4
16 and under .... Scranton, PA, July 28-31
17 and under .... Fort Myers, FL, July 14-18

NATIONAL ASSOCIATION
OF POLICE ATHLETIC LEAGUES

Mailing Address: 618 N US Highway 1, Suite 201, North Palm Beach, FL 33408. **Telephone:** (561) 844-1823. **FAX:** (561) 863-6120.

Year Founded: 1944.

Executive Director: Joseph Wilson. **Associate Directors:** Brad Hart, Nerilda Lugo.

Age Classifications, World Series

14 and under .... Palm Beach County, FL, Aug. 1-7
16 and under .... Palm Beach County, FL, Aug. 1-7

PONY BASEBALL, INC.

International Headquarters: P.O. Box 225, Washington, PA 15301. **Telephone:** (724) 225-1060. **FAX:** (724) 225-9852. **E-Mail Address:** pony@pulsenet.com. **Website:** www.pony.org.

Year Founded: 1951.

President: Abraham Key. **Director, Baseball Operations:** Don Clawson.

Age Classifications, World Series

Shetland (5-6) ....No National Tournament
Pinto (7-8) ....No National Tournament
Mustang (9-10) ....Irving, TX, Aug. 4-7
Bronco (11-12) ....Monterey, CA, Aug. 5-11
Pony (13-14) ....Washington, PA, Aug. 14-21
Colt (15-16) ....Lafayette, IN, Aug. 10-17
Palomino (17-18) ....Greensboro, NC, Aug. 11-14

REVIVING BASEBALL IN INNER CITIES (RBI)

Mailing Address: 245 Park Ave., New York, NY 10167. **Telephone:** (212) 931-7897. **FAX:** (212) 949-5695.

Year Founded: 1989.

Founder: John Young. **Vice President, Marketing:** Kathleen Francis. **National Manager:** Thomas Brasuell.

Age Classifications, World Series

Junior Boys (13-15) .... *Orlando, FL, Aug. 11-16
Senior Boys (16-18) .... *Orlando, FL, Aug. 11-16
    *Disney's Wide World of Sports Complex, Lake Buena Vista.

T-BALL USA ASSOCIATION, INC.

Office Address: 915 Broadway, Suite 607, New York, NY 10010. **Telephone:** (212) 254-7911, (800) 741-0845. **FAX:** (212) 254-8042. **E-Mail Address:** teeballusa@aol.com. **Website:** www.teeballusa.org.

Year Founded: 1993.

President: Bing Broido. **Executive Vice President:** Lois Richards.

U.S. AMATEUR BASEBALL ASSOCIATION

Mailing Address: 7101 Lake Ballinger Way, Edmonds, WA 98026. **Telephone/FAX:** (425) 776-7130. **Website:** www.usaba.com.
Year Founded: 1969.
Executive Director: Al Rutledge.

Age Classifications, World Series

11 and under	Las Vegas, NV, Aug. 15-21
12 and under	Las Vegas, NV, Aug. 15-21
13 and under	Holbrook, AZ, Aug. 9-14
14 and under	Las Vegas, NV, Aug. 13-20
15 and under	Victoria, BC, Aug. 18-28
16 and under	South Jordan, UT, July 28-Aug. 7
17 and under	Wausau, WI, Aug. 6-14
18 and under	Reno, NV, Aug. 8-14
19 and under	Unavailable

U.S. AMATEUR BASEBALL FEDERATION

Mailing Address: 7355 Peter Pan Ave., San Diego, CA 92114. **Telephone/ FAX:** (619) 527-9205. **E-Mail Address:** halbig@msn.com. **Website:** www.usabf.com.
Year Founded: 1995.
Commissioner: Tim Halbig.

Age Classifications, World Series

12 and under	San Diego, CA, July 22-31
14 and under	San Diego, CA, July 22-31
16 and under	San Diego, CA, July 29-Aug. 7
18 and under	San Diego, CA, Aug. 5-14

UNITED STATES SLO-PITCH
SOFTBALL ASSOCIATION (USSSA)/Baseball

National Headquarters: P.O. Box 1998, Petersburg, VA 23805. **Telephone:** (804) 732-4099. **FAX:** (804) 732-1704. **E-Mail Address:** usssahq@aol.com. **Website:** www.usssa.com.
Assistant Executive Director, Baseball: Jim Swint. **Telephone:** (316) 663-8844.
Year Founded: (1968)/Baseball (1996).

Age Classifications, World Series

9 and under (Major/AAA)	Joplin, MO, July 18-25
10 and under (Major/AAA)	Fort Worth, TX, July 18-25
11 and under (Major/AAA)	Overland Park, KS, July 18-25
12 and under (Major)	Hutchinson, KS, July 18-25
12 and under (AAA)	Baton Rouge, LA, July 18-25
13 and under (Major)	Tulsa, OK, July 18-25
13 and under (AAA)	Canton, OH, July 18-25
14 and under (Major)	Houston, TX, July 18-25
14 and under (AAA)	Sterling Heights, MI, July 18-25
15 and under (Major/AAA)	Winter Haven, FL, July 25-Aug. 1
16 and under (Major/AAA)	Oklahoma City, OK, July 25-Aug. 1
18 and under (Major/AAA)	Cocoa, Fla., July 25-Aug. 1

U.S. JUNIOR OLYMPIC
BASEBALL CHAMPIONSHIP

Mailing Address: 3400 E Camino Campestre, Tucson, AZ 85716. **Telephone:** (520) 327-9700. **FAX:** (520) 327-9221.
Coordinator, Youth Baseball: Ray Darwin.

Age Classifications, Championships

16 and under	Tucson, AZ, June 19-26

YOUTH BASEBALL TOURNAMENT CENTERS

COCOA EXPO SPORTS CENTER

Mailing Address: 500 Friday Rd., Cocoa, FL 32926. **Telephone:** (407) 639-3976. **FAX:** (407) 639-0598. **E-Mail Address:** jbiddle@palmnet.net. **Website:** www.l-n.com/cocoa.expo.
Executive Director: Jeff Biddle.
Activities: Spring training program, instructional camps, team training camps, youth tournaments.
1999 Events/Tournaments (ages 10-18): **First Pitch Invitational,** May 21-23. **Cocoa Expo Internationale,** July 2-8. **Cocoa Expo Summer Classic,** Aug. 9-15. **Cocoa Expo Fall Classic,** Oct. 15-17.

COOPERSTOWN DREAM PARK

Mailing Address: 101 E Fisher St, Salisbury, NC 28144. **Telephone:** (704) 630-0050. **FAX:** (704) 630-0737.
Program Director: Lou Presutti.
Invitational Tournaments: June 19-25 (10 and under); June 26-July 2 (12 and under), July 3-9 (12 and under), July 10-16 (12 and under), July 17-23 (12 and under), July 24-30 (12 and under), July 31-Aug. 6 (12 and under), Aug. 7-13 (12 and under), Aug. 14-20 (12 and under).
National Amateur Tournament of Champions: Aug. 28-Sept. 3 (12 and under).

DISNEY'S WIDE WORLD OF SPORTS

Mailing Address: P.O. Box 10000, Lake Buena Vista, FL 32830. **Telephone:** (407) 938-3802. **FAX:** (407) 363-6601

Baseball Program Manager: Kevin Russell. **Program Coordinator, Baseball:** Michael Krause. **Baseball Specialist:** Pad McMeel.

1999 Events/Tournaments: Sun & Surf Baseball Bash (10 and under, 11, 12, 14, 16), May 28-31. **Salute to Baseball Festival** (10 and under, 11, 12, 14, 16), July 8-14. **Turn Back the Clock Invitational** (10 and under, 11, 12, 14, 16), Sept. 3-6.

INSTRUCTIONAL SCHOOLS/PRIVATE CAMPS

THE BASEBALL ACADEMY

Mailing Address: c/o Bollettieri Sports Academy, 5500 34th St. W, Bradenton, FL 34210. **Telephone:** (800) 872-6425. **FAX:** (941) 756-6891. **Website:** www.bollettieri.com.

Camp Director: Ken Bolek.

CHANDLER BASEBALL CAMP

Office Address: 2000 W Park Rd., Chandler, OK 74834. **Mailing Address:** P.O. Box 395, Chandler, OK 74834. **Telephone:** (405) 258-1720.

Camp Director: Tom Belcher.

BUCKY DENT BASEBALL SCHOOL

Mailing Address: 490 Dotterel Rd., Delray Beach, FL 33444. **Telephone:** (561) 265-0280. **FAX:** (561) 278-6679.

DOYLE BASEBALL SCHOOL

Mailing Address: P.O. Box 9156, Winter Haven, FL 33883. **Telephone:** (941) 439-1000. **FAX:** (941) 439-7086.

President: Denny Doyle. **On-Field Director:** Brian Doyle.

MICKEY OWEN BASEBALL SCHOOL

Mailing Address: P.O. Box 88, Miller, MO 65707. **Telephone:** (800) 999-8369, (417) 882-2799. **FAX:** (417) 889-6978.

PLAYBALL BASEBALL ACADEMY

Mailing Address: P.O. Box 4898, Fort Lauderdale, FL 33338. **Telephone:** (954) 776-6217. **FAX:** (954) 772-4510.

SHO-ME BASEBALL CAMP

Mailing Address: 2080 Creekwood, Harrison, AR 72601. **Telephone:** (870) 743-5450.

Camp Director: Phil Wilson.

TEXAS PRIDE BASEBALL ACADEMY

Mailing Address: Crows Nest, 501 Davis Rd., #208-D, League City, TX 77573. **Telephone:** (281) 332-0994. **FAX:** (713) 871-2024.

Camp Director: Tom Siebert.

SAN DIEGO SCHOOL OF BASEBALL

Mailing Address: P.O. Box 900458. **Telephone:** (619) 491-4000. **FAX:** (619) 469-5572.

COLLEGE CAMPS

Almost all of the elite college baseball programs have summer/holiday instructional camps. Please consult the college section, Pages 299-324, for listings.

AGENTDIRECTORY

ACES, INC.
Sam Levinson, Seth Levinson,
Keith Miller
188 Montague Street
Brooklyn, NY 11201
718-237-2900/Fax: 718-522-3906
email: acesinc1@msn.com

AR APORTS, INC.
Ray Anderson, Ken Landphere
3565 Piedmont Rd, Bldg 3
Suite 720
Atlanta, GA 30305
404-816-3399/Fax: 404-816-8294
email: arsports@aol.com

**BARRY AXELROD, A
PROFESSIONAL
CORPORATION**
Barry Axelrod
2236 Encinitas Blvd, Suite A
Encinitas, CA 92024
760-753-0088/Fax: 760-436-7399

CSMG SPORTS LTD.
Alan Nero, Scott Pucino,
Kennard McGuire, Willie
Sanchez, Hardie Jackson, Melvin
Roman
790 Frontage Road
Northfield, IL 60093
847-441-4315/Fax: 847-441-4145

GLOBAL SPORTS CONSULTANTS
Randell Monaco, Esq.
Reggie Waller
819 Frankfort Ave
Huntington Beach, CA 92648
800-237-6300/Fax: 714-969-2836
email: gsportcn@gte.net

**INTERNATIONAL
MANAGEMENT GROUP**
Casey Close, Brian Peters, Terry
Prince
IMG Center, 1360 E. Ninth
Street, Suite 100
Cleveland, OH 44114

**LAW OFFICE OF JAMES
KAUFMANN**
877 Balboa Lane
Foster City, CA 94404
650-377-0815/Fax: 650-377-0885
email:jrklaw@pacbell.net

PRO AGENTS, INC.
David Pepe, Billy Martin Jr.
90 Woodbridge Center Drive
Woodbridge, NJ 07095
800-795-3454/Fax: 732-855-6117
email: pepeda@wilentz.com

PRO EDGE SPORTS MANAGEMENT
Steve Canter
8871 Wonderland Ave
Los Angeles, CA 90046
323-656-2711

800-716-0504
Fax: 323-656-3711

**PROFESSIONAL SPORTS
MANAGEMENT GROUP**
Alan Meersand
865 Manhattan Beach Blvd, Ste. 205
Manhattan Beach, CA 90266
310-546-3400/Fax: 310-546-4046
email: meersand@aol.com

PRO STAR MANAGEMENT, INC.
Joe Bick
250 East Fifth Street Suite 1500
Cincinnati, OH 45202
513-762-7676/Fax: 513-721-4628
email: prostar@fuse.net

TELLEM & ASSOCIATES
Arn Tellem
11911 San Vicente Blvd., Suite 325
Los Angeles, CA 90049
310-440-2811/Fax: 310-440-2819
email: tellem@aol.com

THE RASMUS FIRM
Sherry Rasmus
500 W. 6th Street, Suite 101
Austin, TX 78701
512-481-0650/Fax: 512-481-0604
email: srasmus@rasmusfirm.com

**SPORTS MANAGEMENT SER-
VICES INTERNATIONAL, INC.**
David Trimble, Warren Hughes,
James Munsey, Jonathon
Grossman, Rich Arena
PO Box 281
Clearwater, FL 35757
1-800-240-2809/Fax: 727-592-9500
email: smsball@earthlink.com

STEINBERG & MOORAD
Leigh Steinberg, Jeff Moorad,
David Dunn, Scott Parker,
Rick Hahn
500 Newport Center Dr., Ste. 800
949-720-8700
Fax: 949-720-1331
Newport Beach, CA 92660
www.steinbergandmoorad.com

**TANZER SPORTS
CONSULTANTS, INC.**
Tommy Tanzer, Steve Alexander,
Jeff Kahn
1567 Aerie Circle
Park City, UT 84068
800-777-7603/Fax: 435-649-6464
email: tanzrball@aol.com

WOOLF ASSOCIATES
Jack Toffey, Gregg Clifton
101 Huntington Ave., Suite 2575
Boston, MA 02199
617-437-1212
email: jtoffey@woolf.arn.com
gclifton@woolf.arn.com

SERVICE DIRECTORY

ACCESSORIES

Adams USA/Neumann Glove
610 South Jefferson Avenue
Cookeville, TN 38503
931-526-2109/931-372-8510
www.adamsusa.comadamsusa@t
naccess.com

American Athletic, Inc.
800-247-3978/Fax: 515-386-4566

American Promotions of Illinois
3455 Vorce Road
Harbor Springs, MI 49740
616-526-0718/616-526-0725
888-426-8054
www.americanpromotions.com
amproil@freeway.net

Life's A Charm
P.O. Box 508
Burton, OH 44021
877-528-1501/440-834-9078

Markwort Sporting Goods
Company
4300 Forest Park Avenue
St. Louis, MO 63108
314-652-3757/314-652-6241
sales@markwort.com
www.markwort.com

McArthur Towels/Playing Field
Products
700 Moore Street
Baraboo, WI 53913
800-356-9168/608-356-7587
sales@mcarthur-towels.com
www.mcarthur-towels.com

R.C. Manufacturing Company
11961 31st Court North
St. Petersburg, FL 33716
888-726-3488/Fax: 813-572-4162

The Ultimate Pitchers Tool
P.O. Box 862
Crane, TX 79731
800-905-8837/915-558-2992

Tuff Toe
726 W. Angus Ave., Suite B
Orange, CA 92868
800-888-0802/Fax: 714-997-9594

ACCOUNTANTS/CONSULTANTS

Resnick Amsterdam Leshner/
Financial, Professional Services
653 Skippack Pike Suite 300
Blue Bell, PA 19422
215-628-8080/215-628-4752
ral@ral-cpa.com
www.ral-cpa.com

AGENTS

Panco Sports Enterprises
800-644-3380/213-876-5984
Fax: 213-876-5076

StrongHold Athletic Management, Inc.
120 E. Parrish Street, Suite 300
Durham, NC 27701
919-688-6335/919-682-8092
Fax: 919-682-5091

AMUSEMENT

Carousels USA
P.O. Box 8087
San Antonio, TX 78208
210-224-8015/210-227-3571
ranger2004@AOL.COM

APPAREL

American Promotions of Illinois
3455 Vorce Road
Harbor Springs, MI 49740
616-526-0718/616-526-0725
888-426-8054
www.americanpromotions.com
amproil@freeway.net

Creative Craze
700 Cimarron Trail
Irving, TX 75063
888-506-0929/972-506-7197

Diamond Pro
1341 West Mockingbird Lane
Dallas, TX 75247
972-647-3393/800-640-6735
diamondpro@txi.com
www.diamondpro.com

Joy Athletic
3555 East 11 Avenue
Hialeah, FL 33013
305-691-7240/305-691-7247
szimmerman@joyathletic.com
www.joyathletic.com

Markwort Sporting Goods Company
4300 Forest Park Avenue
St. Louis, MO 63108
314-652-3757/314-652-6241
sales@markwort.com
www.markwort.com

Minor Leagues, Major Dreams
P.O. Box 6098
Anaheim, CA 92816
714-758-1700/800-345-2421
714-939-0655
mlmd@minorleagues.com
www.minorleagues.com

Rawlings Sporting Goods
1-800-RAWLINGS
www.rawlings.com

Seven Sons
864-574-7660/Fax: 864-574-7611

Star Struck, Inc.
8 F.J. Clarke Circle
Bethel, CT 06801
800-908-4637 Fax: 800-962-8345
www.starstruck.com

Wilson Sporting Goods
773-714-6800/Fax: 800-642-4600

ATHLETIC TOWELS

McArthur Towels/Playing Field Products
700 Moore Street
Baraboo, WI 53913
800-356-9168/608-356-7587
sales@mcarthur-towels.com
www.mcarthur-towels.com

AWARDS/TROPHIES

American Special Promotions
800-501-2257/Fax: 770-271-4006

Barnstable Bat Company
508-362-8046/888-549-8046
Fax: 508-362-3983

Sigma Glass Studio
2318 16th Avenue North
St. Petersburg, FL 33713
813-525-5384/Fax: 813-522-5211

STIX Baseball
800-533-STIX 407-425-3360
Fax: 407-425-3560

BAGS

American Promotions of Illinois
3455 Vorce Road
Harbor Springs, MI 49740
616-526-0718/616-526-0725
888-426-8054
www.americanpromotions.com
amproil@freeway.net

Irwin Sports/Cooper Baseball
800-268-1732/Fax: 800-268-6399

Louisville Slugger / Hillerich & Bradsby
800 West Main Street/P.O. Box 35700
Louisville, KY 40202
502-588-7245/502-585-5226
502-585-1179
www.slugger.com

Markwort Sporting Goods
314-652-3757/Fax: 314-652-6241

Rawlings Sporting Goods
1-800-RAWLINGS
www.rawlings.com

STIX Baseball
1840 South Division Avenue
Orlando, FL 32805
407-425-3360/407-425-3560
www.stixbaseball.com

BASEBALL CARDS

Grandstand Cards
26647 Ventura Bvld. #192
Woodland Hills, CA 91364
818-992-5642/818-348-9122

gscards@aol.com

Minford's Minors
704-733-1145/Fax: 704-733-1145

OSP Sports
Two Hardman Drive
Bloomington, IL 61701
309-663-0325/309-579-2591
800-247-7962/309-579-2324
jkbrooke@originalsmith.com

STB Sports/Minor League Team Sets
310-325-4331/Fax: 310-325-1584

BASEBALLS

American Athletic, Inc.
800-247-3978/Fax: 515-386-4566

American Promotions of Illinois
3455 Vorce Road
Harbor Springs, MI 49740
616-526-0718/616-526-0725
888-426-8054
www.americanpromotions.com
amproil@freeway.net

Jugs Company
11885 S.W. Herman Road
Tualatin, OR 97062
800-547-6843/503-691-1100
info@thejugscompany.com
www.thejugscompany.com

Markwort Sporting Goods Company
4300 Forest Park Avenue
St. Louis, MO 63108
314-652-3757/314-652-6241
sales@markwort.com
www.markwort.com

Master Pitching Machine
4200 NE Birmingham Road
Kansas City, MO 64117
800-878-8228/816-452-7581

National Baseball Congress
P.O. Box 1420
Wichita, KS 67201
316-267-3372/316-267-3382
wranglers@frist.com
www.wichitaeagle.com/nbc

Omni Sports Technologies
P.O. Box 751625
Memphis, TN 38175
800-529-6664/800-816-7227
901-794-1549
ostinc@aol.com
www.omnisportstech.com

Rawlings Sporting Goods
1-800-RAWLINGS
www.rawlings.com

SSK America
800-421-2674/Fax: 310-549-2904

BASES

Adams USA/Neumann Glove
610 South Jefferson Avenue
Cookeville, TN 38503
931-526-2109/931-372-8510
www.adamsusa.comadamsusa@t
naccess.com

Adams USA/Neumann Gloves
931-526-2109/Fax: 931-372-8510

Beacon Ballfields
2222 Evergreen Road
Middleton, WI 53562
608-274-5985/608-836-0724
800-747-5985
beacon@ballfields.com
www.ballfields.com

C & H Baseball
2215 60th Drive East
Bradenton, FL 34203
800-248-5192/941-727-0588
941-748-0012

Markwort Sporting Goods Company
4300 Forest Park Avenue
St. Louis, MO 63108
314-652-3757/314-652-6241
sales@markwort.com
www.markwort.com

BATS

Barnstable Bat Company
P.O. Box 5
Centerville, MA 02632
508-362-8046/508-362-3983
baseball@capecod.net
www.barnstablebat.com

Glomar Enterprises
116 West Walnut Avenue
Fullerton, CA 92832
714-871-5956/714-871-5958
www.glomarbats.com
ross@aol.com

Hoosier Bat Company
4511 Evans Avenue
Valparaiso, IN 46883
219-531-1006/219-465-0877
800-228-3787
baseball@netnitco.net

Irwin Sports/Cooper Baseball
800-268-1732/Fax: 800-268-6399

Louisville Slugger / Hillerich & Bradsby
800 West Main Street, P.O. Box 35700
Louisville, KY 40202
502-588-7245/502-585-5226
502-585-1179
www.slugger.com

Markwort Sporting Goods Company
4300 Forest Park Avenue
St. Louis, MO 63108
314-652-3757/314-652-6241
sales@markwort.com
www.markwort.com

The Original Maple Bat Co.
Maker of SamBat™ & S. Holman Bat
93 Bayswater Avenue
Ottawa, Ontario K1Y 2G2
613-724-2421 Fax: 613-725-3299

Professional Diamond Clubs
Shoaf Street #409-B
Lexington, NC 27292/336-248-8536
336-248-8536

Rawlings Sporting Goods
1-800-RAWLINGS

www.rawlings.com

SSK America
800-421-2674/Fax: 310-549-2904

STIX Baseball
1840 South Division Avenue
Orlando, FL 32805
407-425-3360/407-425-3560
www.stixbaseball.com

TriDiamond Sports
East 9514 Montgomery
Building #25
Spokane, WA 99206
509-891-6435/509-891-4156
Batstdssports@aol.com

Wilson Sporting Goods
773-714-6800/Fax: 800-642-4600

Worth Sports Company
800-423-3714 615-455-0691
Fax: 615-454-9164

Young Bat Company
1449 Eucusta Road
Brevard, NC 28712
828-884-8733/828-862-3842
youngbat@youngbat.com
www.youngbat.com

BATTING CAGES

Batting Cages/Grady Lanier
334-222-9189/Fax: 334-222-9189

Beacon Ballfields
2222 Evergreen Road
Middleton, WI 53562
608-274-5985/608-836-0724
800-747-5985
beacon@ballfields.com
www.ballfields.com

C & H Baseball
2215 60th Drive East
Bradenton, FL 34203
800-248-5192/941-727-0588
941-748-0012

Grady Lanier
206 South Three Notch Street
Andalusia, AL 36420
334-222-9189/334-222-3323
800-716-9189

Jugs Company
11885 S.W. Herman Road
Tualatin, OR 97062
800-547-6843/503-691-1100
info@thejugscompany.com
www.thejugscompany.com

Miller Net Company
1674 Getwell Road
P.O. Box 18787
Memphis, TN 38181
901-744-3804/901-743-6580
miller@mem.net
www.home.mem.net

National Batting Cages
P.O. Box 250
Forest Grove, OR 97116-0250
503-357-6615/800-547-8800

503-357-3727

Omni Sports Technologies
P.O. Box 751625
Memphis, TN 38175
800-529-6664/800-816-7227
901-794-1549
ostinc@aol.com
www.omnisportstech.com

Russell Batting Cages
888-RBC-CAGE
www.groupz.net/RBCCAGE/com

Sterling Net & Twine Co., Inc.
18 Label Street
Montclair, NJ 07042
800-342-0316/Fax: 800-232-6387

BOOKS/VIDEOS

All About Pitching
800-635-2822
www.pitching.com

Global Sports Books
800-350-2665/310-454-6590

MasterPlan Sports
800-282-5254

R. Plapinger Books
Bob Plapinger
P.O. BOX 1062
Ashland, OR 97520
541-488-1200

CAMPS/SCHOOLS

Baseball Fantasy Camps
2100 Constitution Boulevard
Sarasota, FL 34241
941-925-4855/941-925-2394

Cocoa Expo Center
500 Friday Road
Cocoa, FL 32926
407-639-3976/407-639-0598
jbiddle@palmnet.net
www.l-n.com/cocoa.expo

The Baseball Academy
5500 34th Street West
Bradenton, FL 34210
800-872-6425 Fax: 941-756-6891
www.bollettieri.com

Roberto Clemente All-Stars/Headstart
57 Todd Hill Circle
Goldens Bridge, NY 10526
914-232-8100/914-767-0584,
clemente@catch.com
www.catch.com/clemente

Mickey Owen Baseball School
P.O. Box 88
Missouri Highway 96
Miller, MO 65707
417-452-3211
417-452-3209
417-889-6978
417-882-2799
mobs@dialus.com
www.mickeyowen.com

CAPS/HEADWEAR

American Promotions of Illinois
3455 Vorce Road
Harbor Springs, MI 49740
616-526-0718/616-526-0725
888-426-8054
www.americanpromotions.com
amproil@freeway.net

Minor Leagues, Major Dreams
P.O. Box 6098
Anaheim, CA 92816
714-758-1700/800-345-2421
714-939-0655
mlmd@minorleagues.com
www.minorleagues.com

New ERA Cap Co. Inc.
800-989-0445/Fax: 716-549-5424

Outdoor Cap
1200 Melissa Lane
Bentonville, AR 72712
501-273-5870/501-273-2144
sales@outdoorcap.com
www.outdoorcap.com

Star Struck, Inc.
8 F.J. Clarke Circle
Bethel, CT 06801
800-908-4637 Fax: 800-962-8345
www.starstruck.com

Twin City Knitting Company
P.O. Box 1179
Conover, NC 28613
828-464-4830/828-465-3209
fdavis@twave.net
www.twincityknitting.com

CASES

Anvil Cases
15650 Salt Lake Avenue
City of Industry, CA 91745
800-359-2684/Fax: 626-968-1703

CATCHING EQUIPMENT

Rawlings Sporting Goods
1-800-RAWLINGS
www.rawlings.com

SSK America
800-421-2674/Fax: 310-549-2904

Wilson Sporting Goods
312-714-6800/Fax: 800-642-4600

CHAMPIONSHIP RINGS

Balfour Company
300 East Industrial Boulevard
Austin, TX 78745
512-416-3840/512-447-7585
www.balfour.com

CHARTS/CARDS

Allgheny Publishing Company
5346 CastleRockRoad
Roanoke, VA 24018
800-733-0543/540-989-9676
alleghenyl@aol.com

DATABASE SERVICES

Advance Ticket Sales, Inc.
4416 Providence Road, Suite 10
Charlotte, NC 28226
704-365-3274/Fax: 704-365-3749

DIRECT MAIL SERVICES

Advance Ticket Sales, Inc.
4416 Providence Road, Suite 10
Charlotte, NC 28226
704-365-3274/Fax: 704-365-3749

EDUCATION/CONSULTING

Baseball Teaching Ventures, Inc.
888-543-4248/203-661-3012
Fax: 203-869-2629

ENTERTAINMENT

Birdzerk! Zooperstars!
P.O. Box 36061
Louisville, KY 40233
502-458-4020/502-458-0867
wejam@bellsouth.net
www.zooperstars.com

Bleacher Preacher/Jerry Pritikin
150 Maple Street #1307
Chicago, IL 60610
312-664-3231 Fax: 630-543-1215

Carousels USA
P.O. Box 8087
San Antonio, TX 78208
210-224-8015/210-227-3571
ranger2004@AOL.COM

Morganna c/o SRO Events
"Baseball's Kissing Bandit"
3727 E. 31st Street
Tulsa, OK 74135
918-743-8461 Fax: 918-749-6643

Sports Magic Team/Entertainment
807 South Orlando Avenue
Suite N
Winter Park, FL 32789
407-647-1110/407-647-0994
800-646-1110
sportsmagicteam@worldnet.att.net
www.sportsmagicteam.com

The King of Sports/ Mark Out Productions
15183 SW Walker Rd. Suite D
Portland, OR 97006
503-626-1959/503-626-6409
badguyjc@aol.comMarketing, Etc.
www.gameops.com

FIELD CONSTRUCTION/RENOVATION

Alpine Services
5313 Brookeville Road
Gaithersburg MD 20882
301-963-8833/301-963-7901
www.alpineservices.com/asi
asi@alpineservices.com

Beam Clay
Kelsey Park
Great Meadows, NJ 07838-9721
908-637-4191/908-637-8421
partac@accessgate.net

FIELD COVER/TARPS

Beacon Ballfields
2222 Evergreen Road
Middleton, WI 53562
608-274-5985/608-836-0724
800-747-5985
beacon@ballfields.com
www.ballfields.com

C & H Baseball
2215 60th Drive East
Bradenton, FL 34203
800-248-5192/941-727-0588
941-748-0012

Covermaster, Inc
100 Westmore Drive #11-D
Rexdale, Ontario
M9V 5C3 Canada
416-745-1811/416-742-6837,
800-387-5808
info@covermaster.net
www.covermaster.net

FIELD WALL COVERING

Beacon Ballfields
2222 Evergreen Road
Middleton, WI 53562
608-274-5985/608-836-0724
800-747-5985
beacon@ballfields.com
www.ballfields.com

FIELD WALL PADDING

C & H Baseball
2215 60th Drive East
Bradenton, FL 34203
800-248-5192/941-727-0588
941-748-0012

Covermaster, Inc
100 Westmore Drive #11-D
Rexdale, Ontario
M9V 5C3 Canada
416-745-1811/416-742-6837,
800-387-5808
info@covermaster.net
www.covermaster.net

Mancino Manufacturing Company/Field Wall Padding
4732 Stenton Avenue
Philadelphia, PA 19144
800-338-6287/800-949-3595
rpmancino@prodigy.net
www.mancinoinc.com

Promats, Inc./Fence/Padding, Playing Field Equipment, Promotions
P.O. Box 508
Fort Collins, CO 80522
800-678-6287/970-482-7740
promats@aol.com
www.promats.com

FIREWORKS

American Promotions of Illinois
3455 Vorce Road
Harbor Springs, MI 49740
616-526-0718/616-526-0725
888-426-8054
www.americanpromotions.com
amproil@freeway.net

Pyrotecnico
P.O. Box 149
New Castle, PA 16103
800-854-4705/724-652-1288,
info@pyrotecnico.com
www.pyrotecnico.com

FIRST AID

Afassco
PO BOX 1767
CARSON CITY, NV, 89702-1767
702-885-2900/702-885-2997

FLAGS/BANNERS

Olympus Flag & Banner
414-355-2010/Fax: 414-355-1931

FOOD SERVICE

Concession Solutions
16022 26th Avenue NE
Seattle, WA 98155
206-440-9203/206-440-9213
concesssol@aol.com

DiGiovanni's Food Service
888-820-4229/Fax: 941-922-8122

Houston's Peanuts
P.O. Box 160
Dublin, NC28332
910-862-2136/800-334-8383
910-862-8076

Lemon Chill & Moore
2376 Culloden Cover
Memphis, TN 38119
901-761-3414/Fax: 901-761-3997

**Marriott Concessions
and Events Services**
90 S. High Street
Dublin, OH 43017
614-761-2330 Fax: 614-761-9903

Slush Puppie Brands
800-543-0860/Fax: 507-257-3285

Sodexho Marriott Services
90 South High Street
Dublin, OH 43017
614-761-2330/614-761-9903
sbaumgartner@sodexmarriott.com

Volume Services America
201 East Broad Street
Spartanburg, SC 29306
864-598-8600/864-598-8695
vsi@volserv.com

GLOVE CARE/REPAIR

Bat-Away Glove Relacing Co
24370 Tierra De Oro
Moreno Valley, CA 92553
888-238-1052/Fax: 909-924-2243

Henrys BB Club & Glove Repair
719 Moody Street
Waltham, MA 02154-5005
781-891-0621

Louisville Slugger
800-282-2287 502-585-5226
Fax: 502-585-1179

Markwort Sporting Goods Company
4300 Forest Park Avenue
St. Louis, MO 63108
314-652-3757/314-652-6241
sales@markwort.com
www.markwort.com

GLOVES

Adams USA/Neumann Glove
610 South Jefferson Avenue
Cookeville, TN 38503
931-526-2109/931-372-8510
www.adamsusa.comadamsusa@t
naccess.com

**Guerrero Baseball
Gloves/Diamond King Sports**
852 Elmwood Road #269
Lansing, MI 48917
800-826-1464/517-886-8035
517-930-8219

Louisville Slugger / Hillerich & Bradsby
800 West Main Street
P.O. Box 35700
Louisville, KY 40202
502-588-7245/502-585-5226
502-585-1179
www.slugger.com

**Markwort Sporting Goods
Company**
4300 Forest Park Avenue
St. Louis, MO 63108
314-652-3757/314-652-6241,
sales@markwort.com
www.markwort.com

Perez Professional Gloves
P.O. Box 786
Dewitt, MI 48820
517-580-8227/Fax: 517-321-1756

Rawlings Sporting Goods
P.O. Box 22000
St. Louis, MO 63126
1-800-RAWLINGS
www.rawlings.com

STIX Baseball
1840 South Division Avenue
Orlando, FL 32805
407-425-3360/407-425-3560
www.stixbaseball.com

SSK America
21136 S. Wilmington Ave., Ste 220
Long Beach, CA 90810
800-421-2674/Fax: 310-549-2904
gossk@aol.com

Wilson Sporting Goods
773-714-6800/Fax: 800-642-4600

GRAPHIC DESIGN

Low & Inside
P.O. Box 290228
Minneapolis, MN 55429
612-797-0777/612-767-5510
have-a-ball@lowandinside.com
www.lowandinside.com

HITTING MACHINES

Quic Hands
800-295-8851/Fax: 800-295-8851

INTERNET/WORLD WIDE WEB

Mindspring
1430 West Peachtree St, NW/Suite 400
Atlanta, GA 30309
888-MSPRING
www.mindspring.com

Skiltech
635 Corsica Avenue
Bear, DE 19701-2512
302-836-4841/302-836-3314
info@skiltech.com
Internetwww.skiltech.com

INSURANCE

K & K Insurance Group
1712 Magnavox Way
P.O. Box 2338
Fort Wayne, IN 46801
219-459-5662/219-459-5000
219-459-5120
www.kandkinsurance.com

Disability/Life Insurance for Professional Athletes
1-800-655-4340

LOGO DESIGN

OSP Sports
Two Hardman Drive
Bloomington, IL 61701
309-663-0325/309-579-2591
800-247-7962/309-579-2324
jkbrooke@originalsmith.com

Silverman Group, Inc.
700 State Street
New Haven, CT 06511
203-562-6418/Fax: 203-777-9637

MAGNETIC SCHEDULES

Master Marketing International
1749 South Naperville Road Suite 200
Wheaton, IL 60187
800-438-3210
630-653-5125/630-653-5525
mstrmktg@aol.com

MASCOT COSTUMES

Mascot Masters International, LLC
5830 N.W. Expressway, Suite 354
Oklahoma City, OK 73132
405-722-2922/405-810-8644
Fax: 405-810-8480

Olympus Flag & Banner
414-355-2010/Fax: 414-355-1931

MEMORABILIA

B&J Collectibles
800-388-0912
www.b-j.com

Stan's Sports Memorabilia
14 Washburn Place
Caldwell, NJ 07006
201-228-5257/Fax: 201-228-5257

MESSAGE CENTERS

Printing Translux Corporation
110 Richards Avenue
Norwalk, CT 06854
203-853-4321/203-855-8636,
800-243-5544
www.trans-lux.com

Spectrum Scoreboards
10048 Easthaven
Houston, TX 77075
713-944-6200/800-392-5050
713-944-1290
www.specorp.com

MOTION SIGNAGE

Action Graphix
P.O. Box 2337
Jonesboro, AR 72404
870-931-7440/870-931-7528
www.actiongraphix.com-
graphix@actiongraphix.com

MUSIC/SOUND EFFECTS

Sound Creations
2820 Azalea Place
Nashville, TN 37204
615-460-7330/615-460-7331
fran@clickeffects.com
www.clickeffects.com

NATIONAL SHOWCASE EVENTS

Baseball Factory, Inc.
3290 Pine Orchard Lane, Unit D
Ellicott City, MD 21042
800-641-4487/Fax: 410-418-5434

NETTING/POSTS

ATEC
10 Greg Street
Sparks, NV 89431
800-755-5100/Fax: 702-352-2822

C & H Baseball
2215 60th Drive East
Bradenton, FL 34203
800-248-5192/941-727-0588
941-748-0012

Jugs Company
11885 S.W. Herman Road
Tualatin, OR 97062
800-547-6843/503-691-1100
info@thejugscompany.com
www.thejugscompany.com

Master Pitching Machine
4200 NE Birmingham Road
Kansas City, MO 64117
800-878-8228/816-452-7581

Miller Net Company
1674 Getwell Road, P.O. Box 18787
Memphis, TN 38181
901-744-3804/901-743-6580
miller@mem.net
www.home.mem.net

Omni Sports Technologies
P.O. Box 751625
Memphis, TN 38175
800-529-6664/800-816-7227
901-794-1549
ostinc@aol.com
www.omnisportstech.com

Saleen Sportnet
800-382-5399

Sterling Net & Twine Co., Inc.
18 Label Street
Montclair, NJ 07042
800-342-0316/Fax: 800-232-6387

PADDING-FIELD/WALL

Promats, Inc.
P.O. Box 508
Fort Collins, CO 80522
800-678-6287/Fax: 970-482-7740

PHOTOGRAPHY

Wagner Photography
5078 Westminster Drive
Ft. Myers, FL 33919
941-277-3100/941-275-7029
fotoguy22@hotmail.com

PITCHING MACHINES

ATEC
800-755-5100/Fax: 702-352-2822

C & H Baseball
2215 60th Drive East
Bradenton, FL 34203
800-248-5192/941-727-0588
941-748-0012

Jugs Company
11885 S.W. Herman Road
Tualatin, OR 97062
800-547-6843/503-691-1100
info@thejugscompany.com
www.thejugscompany.com

Master Pitching Machine
4200 NE Birmingham Road
Kansas City, MO 64117
800-878-8228/816-452-7581

Omni Sports Technologies
P.O. Box 751625
Memphis, TN 38175
800-529-6664/800-816-7227
901-794-1549
ostinc@aol.com
www.omnisportstech.com

PLAYING FIELD PRODUCTS

Adams USA/Neumann Glove
610 South Jefferson Avenue
Cookeville, TN 38503
931-526-2109/931-372-8510
www.adamsusa.comadamsusa@t
naccess.com

American Athletic, Inc.
800-247-3978/Fax: 515-386-4566

AstroTurf Industries, Inc.
800-233-5714/Fax: 512-259-2952

Beacon Ballfields
2222 Evergreen Road
Middleton, WI 53562
608-274-5985/608-836-0724
800-747-5985
beacon@ballfields.com
www.ballfields.com

C & H Baseball
2215 60th Drive East
Bradenton, FL 34203
800-248-5192/941-727-0588
941-748-0012

Covermaster, Inc
100 Westmore Drive #11-D
Rexdale, Ontario
M9V 5C3 Canada
416-745-1811/416-742-6837,
800-387-5808
info@covermaster.net
www.covermaster.net

Diamond Pro
1341 West Mockingbird Lane
Dallas, TX 75247
972-647-3393/800-640-6735
diamondpro@txi.com
www.diamondpro.com

Midwest Athletic Surfaces
1125 West State Street
Marshfield, WI 54449
715-387-7027/715-387-7027,
www.complusis.net/`wrngtrkt

McArthur Towels, Inc.
800-356-9168/Fax: 608-356-7587

Partac Peat/Beam Clay
Kelsey Park
Great Meadows, NJ 07838
800-247-BEAM/908-637-4191
Fax: 908-637-8421

Promats, Inc.
800-678-6287/Fax: 970-482-7740

Stabilizer Solutions
2218 East Magnolia Street
Phoenix, AZ 85034
800-336-2468/602-225-5902
www.stabilizer-az.coml-
phubbs@stabilizer-az.com

PRINTING

Multi-Ad Services
800-348-6485/Fax: 309-692-5444

OSP Sports
Two Hardman Drive
Bloomington, IL 61701
309-663-0325/309-579-2591
800-247-7962/309-579-2324
jkbrooke@originalsmith.com

Sport Graphics Printing
901 East Mossville Road
Peoria, IL 61615
309-579-2324/309-579-2591
jkbrooke@yahoo.com

TradeMark Printing
345 Shoreway Road
San Carlos, CA 94070
650-592-9103/650-592-2776

PRIZE COVERAGE

SCA Promotions
8300 Douglas Avenue, Suite 625
Dallas, TX 75225
214-860-3712/214-860-3723
hatfield@scapromo.com
www.scapromotions.com

PRODUCT DEVELOPMENT

Baseball Teaching Ventures, Inc.
888-543-4248/203-661-3012
Fax: 203-869-2629

PROFESSIONAL SERVICES

Baseball Opportunities
(Franchise Sales)
602-483-8224

C & H Baseball
2215 60th Drive East
Bradenton, FL 34203
800-248-5192/941-727-0588
941-748-0012

Diamond Pro
1341 West Mockingbird Lane
Dallas, TX 75247
972-647-3393/800-640-6735
diamondpro@txi.com
www.diamondpro.com

**Resnick Amsterdam
Leshner/Financial**
653 Skippack Pike Suite 300
Blue Bell, PA 19422
215-628-8080/215-628-4752
ral@ral-cpa.com
www.ral-cpa.com

PROMOTIONAL ITEMS

American Promotions of Illinois
3455 Vorce Road
Harbor Springs, MI 49740
616-526-0718/616-526-0725
888-426-8054
www.americanpromotions.com
amproil@freeway.net

American Special Promotions
800-501-2257/Fax: 770-271-4006

BallQube
Route 2, Box 190
Cushing, TX 75760
903-863-5600/903-863-5571
sales@ballqube.com
www.ballqube.com

Carousels USA
P.O. Box 8087
San Antonio, TX 78208
210-224-8015/210-227-3571
ranger2004@AOL.COM

Creative Craze
700 Cimarron Trail
Irving, TX 75063
888-506-0929/972-506-7197

Hardball Sports Marketing
2017 Tanners Green Way
Jacksonville, FL 32246
904-220-1295/904-220-1296,
800-292-1628
hardball@leading.net

KR Industries
1200 South 54th Avenue
Cicero, IL 60804-1203
708-863-1200/708-222-1400
brad@krindustries.com

Louisville Slugger
800-282-2287 502-585-5226
Fax: 502-585-1179

Master Marketing International
1749 South Naperville Road, Suite 200
Wheaton, IL 60187
800-438-3210
630-653-5125/630-653-5525
mstrmktg@aol.com

**McArthur Towels/Playing Field
Products**
700 Moore Street
Baraboo, WI 53913
800-356-9168/608-356-7587
sales@mcarthur-towels.com
www.mcarthur-towels.com

STIX Baseball
1840 South Division Avenue
Orlando, FL 32805
407-425-3360/407-425-3560
www.stixbaseball.com

PROMOTIONS

Marketing Etc.
3895 The Highlands, NW

Atlanta, GA 30327
404-842-3824/877-382-8288
404-842-0762,
JAJENNGS@AOL.COM

The Great Gazebo, Inc.
1512 Meadowbrook
East Lansing, MI 48823
800-962-2767/517-337-2011
greatgazebo.com info@greatgazebo.com

SCA Promotions, Inc.
8300 Douglas, Ave., Suite 625
Dallas, TX 75225
214-860-3717/Fax: 214-860-3723

PROTECTIVE FIELD SCREENS

C & H Baseball
2215 60th Drive East
Bradenton, FL 34203
800-248-5192/941-727-0588
941-748-0012

PUBLICATIONS

All About Pitching
800-635-2822

The Baseball Scout Newsletter
508-753-8387/Fax: 508-753-8387

**Braunstein's Met/Yankee
Minor League Reporter**
117 West 74th Street #4C
New York, NY 10023
212-258-0026 Fax: 212-307-9518

Low & Inside
P.O. Box 290228
Minneapolis, MN 55429
612-797-0777 Fax: 612-797-7441
baseball@bitstream.net www.lowandinside.com

PUBLIC RELATIONS/PUBLICITY

Baker Dillon Public Relations
P.O. Box 689
Clovis, CA 93613
404-816-3399/404-816-8294
800-570-1262/209-325-7195,
arsports@aol.com/bakerpr@sirius.com
www.sheldonbaker.com

RADAR EQUIPMENT

ATEC
10 Greg Street
Sparks, NV 83431
800-755-5100/Fax: 702-352-2822

Decatur Electronics, Inc.
715 Bright Street
Decatur, IL 62522
800-428-4315 Fax: 217-428-5302
info@decaturradar.com www.decaturradar.com

Jugs Company
11885 S.W. Herman Road
Tualatin, OR 97062
800-547-6843/503-691-1100
info@thejugscompany.com
www.thejugscompany.com

Omni Sports Technologies
P.O. Box 751625
Memphis, TN 38175
800-529-6664/800-816-7227
901-794-1549
ostinc@aol.com
www.omnisportstech.com

Radar Sales
5640 International Parkway
Minneapolis, MN 55428
612-533-1100 888-782-5537
Fax: 612-533-1400

SAFETY EQUIPMENT

GameFace Sports Safety Mask
800-GAMEFACE/301-682-9770
FAX: 301-682-9780

SOUVENIRS

American Promotions of Illinois
3455 Vorce Road
Harbor Springs, MI 49740
616-526-0718/616-526-0725
888-426-8054
www.americanpromotions.com
amproil@freeway.net

SCOREBOARDS

Fairtron, Division of Trans-Lux
1700 Delaware Avenue
Des Moines, IA 50317
515-265-5305/Fax: 515-265-3364

Nevco Scoreboard Company
301 East Harris Avenue
P.O. Box 609
Greenville, IL 62246-0609
800-851-4040/618-664-0398
618-664-0360
nevco@nevcoscoreboards.com
www.nevcoscoreboards.com

Printing Translux Corporation
110 Richards Avenue
Norwalk, CT 06854
203-853-4321/203-855-8636,
800-243-5544
www.trans-lux.com

Spectrum Scoreboardsz
10048 Easthaven
Houston, TX 77075
713-944-6200/800-392-5050
713-944-1290
www.specorp.com

STADIUM ARCHITECTS

Design Exchange Architects
Polly Drummond Office Park
Building 3, Suite 3205
Newark, DE 19711
302-366-1611/302-366-1657
dexchange@aol.com

Devine deFlon Yaeger Architects
3700 Broadway, Suite 300
Kansas City, MO 64110-2507
816-561-2761/816-561-9222
slondon@ddyarch.com
www.ddyarch.com

DLR Group "Lescher and Mahony"
601 West Swann Avenue
Tampa, FL 33606
813-254-9811 Fax: 813-254-4230
www.dlrgroup.com

Ellerbe Becket
605 West 47th Street, Suite 200
Kansas City, MO 64112
816-561-4443/816-561-2863
www.ellerbebeckett.com

Heery International
999 Peachtree Street NE
Atlanta, GA 30367-5401
404-881-9880/404-875-3273
www.heery.com

HNTB Sports Architecture
1201 Walnut, Suite 700
Kansas City, MO 64106
816-472-1201/816-472-4063
mdinitto@hntb.comHOK Sport
www.hntb.com

HOK Sport Facilities Group
323 West 8th Street
Suite 700
Kansas City, MO 64105
816-329-4277/816-221-1578
www.hok.com/sport

L.D. Astorino & Associates
227 Fort Pitt Blvd.
Pittsburgh, PA 15222
412-765-1700/Fax: 412-765-1711
www.ldastorino.com

STADIUM SEATING

American Seating
616-732-6600/Fax: 616-732-6401

Caddy Products
10501 Florida Avenue South
Minneapolis, MN 55438
800-845-0591/Fax: 612-829-0166

Coasters
415-332-5555/Fax: 415-332-5010

GDS Seating/Interkal, Inc.
616-349-1521/Fax: 616-349-5888

Hussey Seating Company
800-341-0401/Fax: 207-676-2222

Irwin Seating Company
616-784-2621/Fax: 616-784-0269

KR Industries
1200 South 54th Avenue
Cicero, IL 60804-1203
708-863-1200/708-222-1400
brad@krindustries.com

Seating Services
P.O. Box 4
Angola, NY 14006
800-552-9470
716-549-9011/716-549-9003
seatingdcc@msn.com
www.seatingservices.com

Southern Bleacher
715 Fifth Street
P.O. Box One
Graham, TX 76450
940-549-0733/940-549-1365
www.southernbleacher.com

Sturdisteel Company
P.O. Box 2655
Waco, TX 76702-2655
254-666-5155/254-666-4472
roberts@sturdisteel.com
www.sturdisteel.com

TEAM DEALER

All Around Sports
326 Route 22 West
Store 9BB
Green Brook, NJ 08812
732-926-8005/732-926-8007
800-661-0179
www.allaroundsports.net,sales@alla
roundsports.net

TELEMARKETING SERVICES

Advance Ticket Sales, Inc.
4416 Providence Road, Suite 10
Charlotte, NC 28226
704-365-3274/Fax: 704-365-3749

TRAINING SYSTEMS

Arm Strong™/DH Sports, Inc.
934 Prichard Lane
West Chester, PA 19382
888-321-2720/Fax: 610-692-2398

Quic Hands
800-295-8851/Fax: 800-295-8851

Set Pro
800-890-8803

SoloHitter/Sports Lab USA
800-875-3355

True Sport/Rocket Arm
800-32-ROCKET

TICKETS

Easy Computer Systems
P.O. Box 765
Springfield, MO 65615
417-335-3279/Fax: 417-335-5246

National Ticket Company
P.O. Box 547
Shamokin, PA 17872
717-672-2900/800-829-0888
508-695-2410,
ticket@nationalticket.com
www.nationalticket.com

Select Ticketing Systems
344 West Genesee Street
P.O. Box 959
Syracuse, NY 13201
315-479-6663/315-471-2715
info@select-info.com
www.select-info.com

Sport Productions, Inc./Tickets
23775 Commerce Park Road
Cleveland, OH 44122
216-591-2400/216-591-2424

Sports Travel
P.O. Box 50
Hatfield, MA 01038
413-247-7678/413-247-5700
info@4sportstravel.com
www.4sportstravel.com

Ticket Craft
1390 Jerusalem Avenue
Merrick, NY 11566
516-538-6200/516-538-4860
tickets@ticketcraft.com
www.ticketcraft.com

TicketStop
14042 NE 8th Street, Suite 108
Bellevue, WA 98007
800-961-6111/425-641-8151
info@ticketstop.com
www.ticketstop.com

TRAVEL

Broach Baseball Tours
4425 Randolph Road, Suite 315
Charlotte, NC 28211
704-333-9191/704-333-1978
www.broachtours.com

Diamond Travel
1474 East 86th Street
Indianapolis, IN 46240
317-843-3900/317-843-3910
tvldiamond@aol.com

Kensport
110 Paladin Place
Cary, NC 27513
919-380-7476/Fax: 919-380-9265

Sports Travel
P.O. Box 50
Hatfield, MA 01038
413-247-7678/413-247-5700
info@4sportstravel.com
www.4sportstravel.com

Tour With Us
734-528-0583/734-528-9081

World Sport
David Eby
P.O. Box 661624
Los Angeles, CA 90405
800-496-8687/310-314-8870
310-314-8872
wrldsport@aol.com

TROPHIES

BallQube
Route 2, Box 190
Cushing, TX 75760
903-863-5600/903-863-5571
sales@ballqube.com
www.ballqube.com

STIX Baseball
1840 South Division Avenue
Orlando, FL 32805
407-425-3360/407-425-3560
www.stixbaseball.com

TURFMATS-SYNTHETIC

AstroTurf Industries, Inc.
800-233-5714/Fax: 512-259-2952

TURNSTILE ADVERTISING

Entry Media
10151 University Boulevard
Suite 204
Orlando, FL 32817
407-678-4446/407-679-3590,
entremedia@worldnet.att.net

Perey Turnstiles
45 Church Street
Stamford, CT 06906
203-961-8444/203-961-8855
perey@turnstile.com
www.turnstile.com

American Promotions of Illinois
3455 Vorce Road
Harbor Springs, MI 49740
616-526-0718/616-526-0725
888-426-8054
www.americanpromotions.com
amproil@freeway.net

DeLong
515-236-3106/Fax: 515-236-4891

Markwort Sporting Goods Company
4300 Forest Park Avenue
St. Louis, MO 63108
314-652-3757/314-652-6241
sales@markwort.com
www.markwort.com

Rawlings Sporting Goods
P.O. Box 22000
St. Louis, MO 63126
1-800-RAWLINGS
www.rawlings.com

Wilson Sporting Goods
773-714-6800/Fax: 800-642-4600

WIND SCREENING

Promats, Inc./Fence/Padding,
Playing Field Equipment,
Promotions
P.O. Box 508
Fort Collins, CO 80522
800-678-6287/970-482-7740
promats@aol.com
www.promats.com

1999 DIRECTORY INDEX

MAJOR LEAGUE TEAMS

American League

Page	Club	Phone	FAX
28	Anaheim Angels	714-940-2000	714-940-2205
30	Baltimore Orioles	410-685-9800	410-547-6272
32	Boston Red Sox	617-267-9440	617-375-0944
34	Chicago White Sox	312-674-1000	312-674-5116
36	Cleveland Indians	216-420-4200	216-420-4396
38	Detroit Tigers	313-962-4000	313-965-2138
40	Kansas City Royals	816-921-8000	816-921-1366
42	Minnesota Twins	612-375-1366	612-375-7473
44	New York Yankees	718-293-4300	718-293-8431
46	Oakland Athletics	510-638-4900	510-562-1633
48	Seattle Mariners	206-346-4000	206-346-4050
50	Tampa Bay Devil Rays	727-825-3137	727-825-3300
52	Texas Rangers	817-273-5222	817-273-5206
54	Toronto Blue Jays	416-341-1000	416-341-1250

National League

Page	Club	Phone	FAX
58	Arizona Diamondbacks	602-462-6500	602-462-6599
60	Atlanta Braves	404-522-7630	404-614-1391
62	Chicago Cubs	773-404-2827	773-404-4129
64	Cincinnati Reds	513-421-4510	513-421-7342
66	Colorado Rockies	303-292-0200	303-312-2116
68	Florida Marlins	305-626-7400	305-626-7428
70	Houston Astros	713-799-9500	713-799-9794
72	Los Angeles Dodgers	323-224-1500	323-224-1269
74	Milwaukee Brewers	414-933-4114	414-933-3251
76	Montreal Expos	514-253-3434	514-253-8282
78	New York Mets	718-507-6387	718-565-6395
80	Philadelphia Phillies	215-463-6000	215-389-3050
82	Pittsburgh Pirates	412-323-5000	412-323-5024
84	St. Louis Cardinals	314-421-3060	314-425-0640
86	San Diego Padres	619-881-6500	619-497-5454
88	San Francisco Giants	415-468-3700	415-467-0485

MINOR LEAGUE TEAMS

Page	Club	League	Phone	FAX
155	Akron	Eastern	330-253-5151	330-253-3300
145	Albuquerque	PCL	505-243-1791	505-842-0561
155	Altoona	Eastern	814-943-5400	814-943-9050
169	Arkansas	Texas	501-664-1555	501-664-1834
200	Asheville	SAL	828-258-0428	828-258-0320
208	Auburn	NYP	315-255-2489	315-255-2675
200	Augusta	SAL	706-736-7889	706-736-1122
174	Bakersfield	Cal	661-322-1363	661-322-6199
208	Batavia	NYP	716-343-5454	716-343-5620
192	Beloit	Midwest	608-362-2272	608-362-0418
227	Billings	Pioneer	406-252-1241	406-252-2968
156	Binghamton	Eastern	607-723-6387	607-723-7779
163	Birmingham	Southern	205-988-3200	205-988-9698
221	Bluefield	Appy	540-326-1326	540-326-1318
216	Boise	Northwest	208-322-5000	208-322-7432
156	Bowie	Eastern	301-805-6000	301-805-6008
185	Brevard County	FSL	407-633-9200	407-633-9210
221	Bristol	Appy	540-645-7275	540-645-7377
136	Buffalo	IL	716-846-2000	716-852-6530
192	Burlington, IA	Midwest	319-754-5705	319-754-5882
221	Burlington, NC	Appy	336-222-0223	336-226-2498
227	Butte	Pioneer	406-723-8206	406-723-3376
145	Calgary	PCL	403-284-1111	403-284-4343
201	Cape Fear	SAL	910-424-6500	910-424-4325
201	Capital City	SAL	803-256-4110	803-256-4338
163	Carolina	Southern	919-269-2287	919-269-4910
192	Cedar Rapids	Midwest	319-363-3887	319-363-5631
202	Charleston, SC	SAL	843-723-7241	843-723-2641
202	Charleston, WV	SAL	304-344-2287	304-344-0083
185	Charlotte, FL	FSL	941-625-9500	941-624-5158
136	Charlotte, NC	IL	704-357-8071	704-329-2155
164	Chattanooga	Southern	423-267-2208	423-267-4258
185	Clearwater	FSL	727-441-8638	727-447-3924
193	Clinton	Midwest	319-242-0727	319-242-1433
146	Colorado Springs	PCL	719-597-1449	719-597-2491

203	Columbus, GA	SAL	706-571-8866	706-571-9107
137	Columbus, OH	IL	614-462-5250	614-462-3271
222	Danville	Appy	804-791-3346	804-791-3347
186	Daytona	FSL	904-257-3172	904-257-3382
203	Delmarva	SAL	410-219-3112	410-219-9164
186	Dunedin	FSL	727-733-9302	727-734-7661
137	Durham	IL	919-687-6500	919-687-6560
146	Edmonton	PCL	780-414-4450	780-414-4475
222	Elizabethton	Appy	423-547-6440	423-547-6441
169	El Paso	Texas	915-755-2000	915-757-0671
157	Erie	Eastern	814-456-1300	814-456-7520
216	Eugene	Northwest	541-342-5367	541-342-6089
217	Everett	Northwest	425-258-3673	425-258-3675
187	Fort Myers	FSL	941-768-4210	941-768-4211
193	Fort Wayne	Midwest	219-482-6400	219-471-4678
180	Frederick	Carolina	301-662-0013	301-662-0018
147	Fresno	PCL	559-442-1994	559-264-0795
227	Great Falls	Pioneer	406-452-5311	406-454-0811
204	Greensboro	SAL	336-333-2287	336-273-7350
164	Greenville	Southern	864-299-3456	864-277-7369
204	Hagerstown	SAL	301-791-6266	301-791-6066
157	Harrisburg	Eastern	717-231-4444	717-231-4445
228	Helena	Pioneer	406-449-7616	406-449-6979
205	Hickory	SAL	828-322-3000	828-322-6137
174	High Desert	Cal	760-246-6287	760-246-3197
208	Hudson Valley	NYP	914-838-0094	914-838-0014
165	Huntsville	Southern	256-882-2562	256-880-0801
228	Idaho Falls	Pioneer	208-522-8363	208-522-9858
138	Indianapolis	IL	317-269-3542	317-269-3541
147	Iowa	PCL	515-243-6111	515-243-5152
170	Jackson	Texas	601-981-4664	601-981-4669
165	Jacksonville	Southern	904-358-2846	904-358-2845
209	Jamestown	NYP	716-664-0915	716-664-4175
223	Johnson City	Appy	423-461-4866	423-461-4864
187	Jupiter	FSL	561-775-1818	561-691-6886
194	Kane County	Midwest	630-232-8811	630-232-8815
223	Kingsport	Appy	423-378-3744	423-392-8538
180	Kinston	Carolina	252-527-9111	252-527-0498
188	Kissimmee	FSL	407-933-5500	407-847-6237
166	Knoxville	Southern	423-637-9494	423-523-9913
175	Lake Elsinore	Cal	909-245-4487	909-245-0305
188	Lakeland	FSL	941-688-7911	941-688-9589
175	Lancaster	Cal	661-726-5400	661-726-5406
194	Lansing	Midwest	517-485-4500	517-485-4518
148	Las Vegas	PCL	702-386-7200	702-386-7214
139	Louisville	IL	502-367-9121	502-368-5120
209	Lowell	NYP	978-459-2255	978-459-1674
181	Lynchburg	Carolina	804-528-1144	804-846-0768
205	Macon	SAL	912-745-8943	912-743-5559
210	Mahoning Valley	NYP	330-505-0000	330-505-9696
224	Martinsville	Appy	540-666-2000	540-666-2139
229	Medicine Hat	Pioneer	403-526-0404	403-526-4000
148	Memphis	PCL	901-721-6050	901-721-6017
195	Michigan	Midwest	616-660-2287	616-660-2288
170	Midland	Texas	915-683-4251	915-683-0994
229	Missoula	Pioneer	406-543-3300	406-543-9463
166	Mobile	Southern	334-479-2327	334-476-1147
176	Modesto	Cal	209-572-4487	209-572-4490
181	Myrtle Beach	Carolina	843-918-6000	843-946-6273
149	Nashville	PCL	615-242-4371	615-256-5684
158	New Britain	Eastern	860-224-8383	860-225-6267
158	New Haven	Eastern	203-782-1666	203-782-3150
210	New Jersey	NYP	973-579-7500	973-579-7502
149	New Orleans	PCL	504-734-5155	504-734-5118
139	Norfolk	IL	757-622-2222	757-624-9090
159	Norwich	Eastern	860-887-7962	860-886-5996
230	Ogden	Pioneer	801-393-2400	801-393-2473
150	Oklahoma	PCL	405-218-1000	405-218-1001
150	Omaha	PCL	402-734-2550	402-734-7166
211	Oneonta	NYP	607-432-6326	607-432-1965
167	Orlando	Southern	407-649-7297	407-649-1637
140	Ottawa	IL	613-747-5969	613-747-0003
140	Pawtucket	IL	401-724-7300	401-724-2140
195	Peoria	Midwest	309-688-1622	309-686-4516
206	Piedmont	SAL	704-932-3267	704-938-7040
211	Pittsfield	NYP	413-499-6387	413-443-7144
159	Portland, ME	Eastern	207-874-9300	207-780-0317
217	Portland, OR	Northwest	503-223-2837	503-223-2948
182	Potomac	Carolina	703-590-2311	703-590-5716
224	Princeton	Appy	304-487-2000	304-487-8762
225	Pulaski	Appy	540-980-1070	540-994-0847
196	Quad City	Midwest	319-324-2032	319-324-3109

176	Rancho Cuca.	Cal	909-481-5000	909-481-5005
160	Reading	Eastern	610-375-8469	610-373-5868
141	Richmond	IL	804-359-4444	804-359-0731
141	Rochester	IL	716-454-1001	716-454-1056
196	Rockford	Midwest	815-962-2827	815-961-2002
212	St. Catharines	NYP	905-641-5297	905-641-3007
188	St. Lucie	FSL	561-871-2100	561-878-9802
189	St. Petersburg	FSL	727-822-3384	727-895-1556
182	Salem	Carolina	540-389-3333	540-389-9710
218	Salem-Keizer	Northwest	503-390-2225	503-390-2227
151	Salt Lake	PCL	801-485-3800	801-485-6017
171	San Antonio	Texas	210-675-7275	210-670-0001
177	San Bernardino	Cal	909-888-9922	909-888-5251
177	San Jose	Cal	408-297-1435	408-297-1453
189	Sarasota	FSL	941-365-4460	941-365-4217
206	Savannah	SAL	912-351-9150	912-352-9722
142	Scranton/W-B	IL	570-969-2255	570-963-6564
171	Shreveport	Texas	318-636-5555	318-636-5670
197	South Bend	Midwest	219-235-9988	219-235-9950
218	So. Oregon	Northwest	541-770-5364	541-772-4466
219	Spokane	Northwest	509-535-2922	509-534-5368
212	Staten Island	NYP	718-698-9265	718-698-9291
178	Stockton	Cal	209-944-5943	209-463-4937
142	Syracuse	IL	315-474-7833	315-474-2658
151	Tacoma	PCL	253-752-7707	253-752-7135
190	Tampa	FSL	813-875-7753	813-673-3174
143	Toledo	IL	419-893-9483	419-893-5847
160	Trenton	Eastern	609-394-3300	609-394-9666
152	Tucson	PCL	520-434-1021	520-889-2371
172	Tulsa	Texas	918-744-5998	918-747-3267
212	Utica	NYP	315-738-0999	315-738-0992
153	Vancouver	PCL	604-872-5232	604-872-1714
213	Vermont	NYP	802-655-4200	802-655-5660
190	Vero Beach	FSL	561-569-4900	561-567-0819
178	Visalia	Cal	559-625-0480	559-739-7732
197	West Michigan	Midwest	616-784-4131	616-784-4911
167	West Tenn	Southern	901-664-2020	901-988-5246
172	Wichita	Texas	316-267-3372	316-267-3382
213	Williamsport	NYP	570-326-3389	570-326-3494
183	Wilmington	Carolina	302-888-2015	302-888-2032
183	Winston-Salem	Carolina	336-759-2233	336-759-2042
198	Wisconsin	Midwest	920-733-4152	920-733-8032
219	Yakima	Northwest	509-457-5151	509-457-9909

Phone and FAX numbers for minor league offices can be found on pages 122-23.

OTHER ORGANIZATIONS

Page	Organization	Phone	FAX
337	AAABA	740-453-8531	740-453-3978
118	ABC Radio Network Sports	212-456-5185	212-456-5405
117	ABC-TV	212-456-7777	212-456-2877
327	Alaska Baseball League	907-283-7133	907-283-3390
328	Alleghany Mountain Coll. League	814-885-8480	—
337	Amateur Athletic Union	407-828-3459	407-934-7242
337	American Amateur BB Congress	616-781-2002	616-781-2060
291	American BB Coaches Assoc.	517-775-3300	517-775-3600
27	American League	212-931-7600	—
338	American Legion Baseball	317-630-1213	317-630-1369
336	Area Code Games	707-525-0498	707-525-0214
287	Arizona Fall League	602-496-6700	602-496-6384
118	Associated Press	212-621-1630	212-621-1639
127	Assoc. of Prof. BB Players	714-892-9900	714-897-0233
327	Athletes In Action	813-968-7400	813-968-7515
328	Atlantic Collegiate League	908-464-8042	908-464-8042
256	Atlantic League	610-696-8662	610-696-8667
288	Australian Baseball League	61-2-9437-4622	61-2-9437-4155
338	Babe Ruth Baseball	609-695-1434	609-695-2505
125	Babe Ruth Birthplace/Museum	410-727-1539	410-727-1652
127	Baseball Assistance Team	212-931-7822	212-949-5652
327	Baseball Canada	613-748-5606	613-748-5767
127	Baseball Chapel	610-586-4537	610-586-4538
120	Baseball Digest	847-491-6440	847-491-0867
127	Baseball Family	423-692-9291	423-769-4386
127	Baseball Trade Show	727-822-6937	727-821-5819
119	BB Writers Assoc. of America	516-981-7938	516-585-4669
121	Beckett Publications	972-991-6657	972-991-8930
117	CBS-TV	212-975-5230	212-975-4063
117	CNN/SI	404-878-1600	404-588-2057
117	CTV	416-299-2000	416-299-2076
328	California Coastal League	925-672-9662	925-672-9662
291	Calif. CC Comm. on Athletics	916-444-1600	916-444-2616

125	Canadian Baseball Hall of Fame	519-284-1838	519-284-1234
119	Canadian Press	416-507-2154	—
329	Cape Cod League	508-996-5004	508-996-5004
284	Caribbean BB Confederation	809-562-4737	809-565-4654
330	Central Illinois Collegiate League	309-828-4429	309-827-4652
280	Chinese Pro Baseball League	886-22577-6992	886-22577-2606
330	Clark Griffith League	703-536-1729	703-536-1729
330	Coastal Plain League	919-852-1960	919-852-1973
120	Collegiate Baseball	520-623-4530	520-624-5501
121	Coman Publishing	919-688-0218	919-682-1532
338	Continental Amateur BB Assoc.	614-899-2103	614-899-2103
338	Dixie Baseball, Inc.	334-242-8395	334-242-0198
338	Dizzy Dean Baseball	—	
284	Dominican League	809-567-6371	809-567-5720
280	Dominican Summer League	809-532-3619	809-532-3619
116	ESPN/ESPN2-TV	860-766-2000	860-766-2213
120	ESPN Magazine	212-515-1000	212-515-1290
118	ESPN Radio	860-766-2661	860-766-5523
118	ESPN/SportsTicker	201-309-1200	201-860-9742
116	Elias Sports Bureau	212-869-1530	212-354-0980
125	Field of Dreams Movie Site	319-875-8404	319-875-7253
128	Fleer/Skybox	609-231-6200	609-727-9460
117	FOX Sports	310-369-6000	310-969-6192
117	FOX Sports Net	310-444-8123	310-479-8856
257	Frontier League	740-452-7400	740-452-2999
117	FX	310-444-8281	310-479-8856
326	Goodwill Games	404-827-3400	404-827-1539
128	Grandstand Cards	818-992-5642	818-348-9122
331	Great Lakes League	440-892-2692	440-871-4221
338	Hap Dumont Youth Baseball	316-721-1779	316-721-8054
125	Harry Wendelstedt Umpire School	904-672-4879	904-672-3212
116	Howe Sportsdata	617-951-0070	617-737-9960
326	International Baseball Assoc.	41-21-318-8240	41-21-318-8241
327	International Baseball Foundation	205-558-4235	205-918-0800
120	International Baseball Rundown	630-790-3087	630-790-3182
326	International Olympic Committee	41-21-621-6111	41-21-621-6216
327	International Sports Group	925-798-4591	925-680-1182
278	Japan League	03-3502-0022	03-3502-0140
331	Jayhawk League	316-835-2589	316-755-1285
125	Jim Evans Academy of Pro. Ump.	512-335-5959	512-335-5411
122	John Benson's Fantasy Baseball	203-834-1231	—
281	Korea Baseball Organization	822-3461-7887	822-3462-7800
121	Krause Publications	715-445-2214	715-445-4087
339	Little League Baseball, Inc.	570-326-1921	570-326-1074
126	Little League Baseball Museum	570-326-3607	570-326-2267
126	Louisville Slugger Museum	502-588-7228	502-585-1179
25	MLB International	212-931-7500	212-949-5795
126	MLB Players Alumni Association	719-477-1870	719-477-1875
124	MLB Productions	212-931-7900	212-949-5795
124	Major League Players Assoc.	212-826-0808	212-752-4378
124	Major League Scouting Bureau	909-980-1881	909-980-7794
125	Major League Umpires Assoc.	215-979-3200	215-979-3201
289	Maryland Fall League	301-805-6012	301-805-6011
127	Men's Adult Baseball League	516-753-6725	516-753-4031
127	Men's Senior Baseball League	516-753-6725	516-753-4031
276	Mexican League	525-557-1007	525-395-2454
285	Mexican Pacific League	52-642-2-3100	52-642-2-7250
291	NAIA	918-494-8828	918-494-8841
117	NBC-TV	212-664-4444	212-664-3602
291	NCAA	913-339-1906	913-339-0043
291	NJCAA	719-590-9788	719-590-7324
128	National Adult Baseball Assoc.	303-639-9955	303-639-6605
327	Nat'l Alliance of Coll. Summer Ball	508-432-1774	508-432-9766
339	National Amateur Baseball Fed.	301-262-5005	301-262-5005
129	National Association	727-822-6937	727-821-5819
327	National Baseball Congress	316-267-3372	316-267-3382
126	National Baseball Hall of Fame	607-547-7200	607-547-2044
335	Nat'l Classic HS Tournament	714-993-5350	714-777-8127
119	National Collegiate BB Writers	312-553-0483	312-553-0495
335	Nat'l Fed. of State HS Assoc.	816-464-5400	816-464-5571
335	Nat'l HS Baseball Coaches Assoc.	501-876-2591	501-876-2596
57	National League	212-339-7700	
126	Negro Leagues Baseball Museum	816-221-1920	816-221-8424
332	New England Collegiate League	401-423-9863	401-423-2784
332	Northeastern Collegiate League	716-423-3528	
260	Northern League	919-956-8150	919-683-2693
332	Northwest Collegiate League	503-625-4044	503-625-0629
332	Northwoods League	507-289-1170	507-289-1866
25	Office of the Commissioner	212-931-7800	
118	One-on-One Sports Radio Network	847-509-1661	847-509-8149
333	Pacific International League	206-623-8844	602-623-8361
128	Pacific Trading Cards	800-551-2002	—
326	Pan American Games	204-985-1900	204-985-4375

128	Playoff	972-595-1180	972-595-1190
339	Police Athletic Leagues	561-844-1823	561-863-6120
339	PONY Baseball, Inc.	724-225-1060	724-225-9852
125	Pro Baseball Athletic Trainers Soc.	404-875-4000	404-892-8560
127	Pro Baseball Emp. Opportunities	800-842-5618	828-668-4762
125	Pro Baseball Umpire Corp.	727-822-6937	727-821-5819
335	Prospects, LLC	800-334-8671	919-682-2880
285	Puerto Rican League	787-765-6285	787-767-3028
339	RBI	212-931-7897	212-949-5695
128	Roy Hobbs Baseball	888-484-7422	330-923-1967
126	SABR	216-575-0500	216-575-0502
333	Shenandoah Valley League	540-886-1748	540-885-2068
120	Sport Magazine	212-880-3600	212-229-4838
119	The Sporting News	314-997-7111	314-997-0765
118	Sports Byline USA	415-434-8300	415-391-2569
118	Sportsfan Radio Network	800-895-1022	702-740-4171
119	Sports Illustrated	212-522-1212	212-522-4543
118	The Sports Network	416-494-1212	416-490-7010
121	Spring Training BB Yearbook	919-967-2420	919-967-6294
116	STATS, Inc.	847-677-3322	847-470-9160
120	Street and Smith's Baseball	212-880-8698	212-880-4347
326	Sydney Olympic Org. Committee	61-29-297-2000	61-29-297-2020
280	Taiwan Major League	886-22545-9566	886-22514-0802
128	Team Best	770-745-3434	770-745-3433
336	Team One National Showcase	606-291-4463	606-291-4463
264	Texas-Louisiana League	915-673-7364	915-673-5150
336	Top Guns Showcase	208-762-1100	208-762-1100
128	Topps	212-376-0300	212-376-0573
121	Total Baseball	212-319-6611	212-319-3820
121	Ultimate Sports Publishing	206-301-9466	206-301-9420
128	Upper Deck	760-929-6500	760-929-6556
340	US Amateur Baseball Association	425-776-7130	425-776-7130
326	USA Baseball	520-327-9700	520-327-9221
326	US Olympic Committee	719-632-5551	719-578-4654
119	USA Today	703-276-3731	703-558-3988
119	USA Today Baseball Weekly	703-558-5630	703-558-4678
286	Venezuelan League	58-2-761-2750	58-2-761-7661
280	Venezuelan Summer League	58-41-24-0321	58-41-24-0705
266	Western League	530-897-6125	530-897-6124